HIDDEN®
Southwest

"A guide that deals with everything."
—*The Dallas Morning News*

"The book is packed with useful information and is sensibly organized."
—*San Diego Union-Tribune*

"Solid information and touring ideas."
—*Orlando Sentinel*

"The authors manage to find special or unheralded places in such well-trod tourist haunts as Santa Fe and Phoenix."
—*Fresno Bee*

"The book encompasses the scenic treasures of the Southwest: its red rock canyonlands, Native American cliff dwellings, steam trains and opera companies."
—*Arizona Senior World*

HIDDEN®

Southwest

Including Arizona, New Mexico, Southern Utah & Southwest Colorado

EIGHTH EDITION

Ulysses Press®
BERKELEY, CALIFORNIA

Published by:
ULYSSES PRESS
P.O. Box 3440
Berkeley, CA 94703
www.ulyssespress.com

ISSN 1521-9100
ISBN10 1-56975-575-2
ISBN13 978-1-56975-575-4

Printed in Canada by Transcontinental Printing

20 19 18 17 16 15 14 13 12

AUTHORS: Richard Harris, Laura Daily,
    Madeleine Osberger, Steve Cohen
UPDATE AUTHOR: Nicky Leach
MANAGING EDITOR: Claire Chun
PROJECT DIRECTOR: Elyce Petker
COPY EDITOR: Lily Chou
EDITORIAL ASSOCIATES: Ruth Marcus, Stefanie Tamura,
    Kat Brooks, Rebekah Morris, Benjamin Kleiman
TYPESETTERS: Lisa Kester, Matt Orendorff
CARTOGRAPHY: Pease Press
HIDDEN BOOKS DESIGN: Sarah Levin
COVER DESIGN: Leslie Henriques
INDEXER: Sayre Van Young
COVER PHOTOGRAPHY: *main:* horseback ride through the desert
    (James Randklev © Metropolitan Tucson Convention &
    Visitors Bureau); *circle:* Taos Pueblo (© photos.com)
ILLUSTRATOR: Glenn Kim

Distributed by Publishers Group West

Write to us!

If in your travels you discover a spot that captures the spirit of the Southwest, or if you live in the region and have a favorite place to share, or if you just feel like expressing your views, write to us and we'll pass your note along to the author.

We can't guarantee that the author will add your personal find to the next edition, but if the writer does use the suggestion, we'll acknowledge you in the credits and send you a free copy of the new edition.

ULYSSES PRESS
P.O. Box 3440
Berkeley, CA 94703
E-mail: readermail@ulyssespress.com

Acknowledgments

Ulysses Press would like to thank the following readers who took the time to write in with suggestions that were incorporated into this new edition of *Hidden Southwest*: Wayne Hoover of Pittsburgh, PA, and Scott Beeson of Tucson, AZ.

What's Hidden?

At different points throughout this book, you'll find special listings marked with a symbol:

◄ HIDDEN

This means that you have come upon a place off the beaten tourist track, a spot that will carry you a step closer to the local people and natural environment of the Southwest.

The goal of this guide is to lead you beyond the realm of everyday tourist facilities. While we include traditional sightseeing listings and popular attractions, we also offer alternative sights and adventure activities. Instead of filling this guide with reviews of standard hotels and chain restaurants, we concentrate on one-of-a-kind places and locally owned establishments.

Our authors seek out locales that are popular with residents but usually overlooked by visitors. Some are more hidden than others (and are marked accordingly), but all the listings in this book are intended to help you discover the true nature of the Southwest and put you on the path of adventure.

Contents

Maps

OUTDOOR ADVENTURE SYMBOLS

The following symbols accompany national, state and regional park listings, as well as beach descriptions throughout the text.

▲	Camping	➤	Snorkeling or Scuba Diving
🚶	Hiking	🎿	Waterskiing
🚲	Biking	🏄	Windsurfing
🐎	Horseback Riding	🛶	Canoeing or Kayaking
⛷	Downhill Skiing	🚤	Boating
🎿	Cross-country Skiing	🚤	Boat Ramps
🏊	Swimming	🐟	Fishing

ONE

The Southwest

The Southwest is a land unlike any other. It is sheer sandstone cliffs and slickrock mesas, secluded beaches on bright blue lakes, vast deserts alive with giant cacti and unusual animals, high mountain peaks that guard some of the largest wilderness areas in America.

Strange landscapes conceal Indian ruins as old and haunting as Europe's medieval castles. And unlike other parts of the United States, the people who lived in the Southwest when the first white men arrived still live here today. Although it was the first part of the United States where European colonists settled permanently, today it remains, on the whole, one of the least-populated parts of the country.

The Southwest attracts vacationers from around the world at all times of year. It is warm in the winter (some places), cool in the summer (other places) and sunnier than Florida. People come for the climate, the great outdoors, the unique cultural mix and the scenic beauty. Most of all, people come to explore, for the best places in the Southwest are not necessarily marked by big green-and-white signs or entrance gates. In this land of astonishing diversity, you'll find something new around every curve in the road.

Land of contrasts, proudly provincial, the Southwest lives up to its romantic reputation. Lost cities and hidden treasures await your discovery. If curiosity is in your nature, the Southwest is one of the best places on earth to unleash it.

Hidden Southwest is designed to help you explore Arizona, New Mexico, southern Utah and southwestern Colorado. It covers popular, "must-see" places, offering advice on how best to enjoy them. It also tells you about many off-the-beaten-path spots, the kind you would find by talking with folks at the local café or with someone who has lived in the area all his or her life. It describes the region's history, its natural areas and its residents, both human and animal. It suggests places to eat, to lodge, to play, to camp. Taking into account varying interests, budgets and tastes, it provides the information you need whether your vacation style involves backpacking, golf, museum browsing, shopping or all of the above.

This book covers the Southwest in three sections. Arizona, the most recently settled and fastest-growing part, claims among its virtues warm winter weather, famous sunsets and the largest Indian reservation in the country. New Mexico offers antiquity and a unique tricultural heritage that set it apart from anyplace else in America. The land north of the Grand Canyon and Navajo Indian Reservation extending into Utah and Colorado, still largely unpopulated, is best known for its wild canyons and rugged mountains, portions of which are made accessible to the public in no less than six national parks.

The traveling part of the book begins in Chapter Two on the rim of the Grand Canyon. Chapter Three wanders through Indian Country in northeastern Arizona to help you experience the world of the Navajo and Hopi people. Sedona, Jerome, Flagstaff and Prescott are all covered in Chapter Four. Chapter Five travels down the state's western edge from Kingman to Lake Havasu City and the London Bridge. The greater Phoenix area, including nearby Scottsdale, Tempe and Mesa, is revealed in Chapter Six. Chapter Seven ventures east into the mountains and scenic areas from Globe to Pinetop–Lakeside and the Coronado Trail. Chapter Eight moves farther south to Tucson, Tombstone and the Mexican border.

Chapter Nine covers Santa Fe, as well as the Las Vegas and the Los Alamos areas. Chapter Ten focuses on the treasures of Taos and the Enchanted Circle. Chapter Twelve takes a good look at Albuquerque, from the top of a mountain as well as from the city's historic center, then investigates an array of central New Mexico side trips to lakes and volcanic badlands, ruins of abandoned pueblos and Spanish missions. Chapter Thirteen ranges across southern New Mexico from Carlsbad Caverns through Billy the Kid country to the remote canyons of the Gila Wilderness.

The terrain and culture of the Southwest do not stop at the arbitrarily squared-off state lines of Arizona and New Mexico but sprawl untidily over the Four Corners area into neighboring parts of Utah and Colorado. Chapter Fourteen takes you through the geological wonderland of southwestern Utah, including Bryce Canyon, Zion and Capitol Reef national parks. Chapter Fifteen continues into southeastern Utah with visits to Arches and Canyonlands national parks and all the information you need to rent a boat and cruise Lake Powell. Finally, Chapter Sixteen is your guide to the southwestern corner of Colorado, where the top attractions are Mesa Verde National Park and the Durango–Silverton Narrow Gauge Railroad.

What you choose to see and do is up to you. The old cliché that "there is something for everyone" pretty well rings true in the Southwest. In this book, you'll find free campgrounds with hiking trails and fantastic views as well as several playgrounds for the wealthy and well-known. And you can take some of the most spectacular scenic drives anywhere as well as hikes into wild areas that can't be reached by car. Or check into a bed and breakfast that has delightful little galleries and boutiques within walking distance.

There's so much to experience in the Southwest that even most lifelong residents can count on making new discoveries once in a while. First-time vacation visitors are hard-pressed just to make brief stops at the region's best-known highlights, while seasoned travelers often prefer to explore a more limited area in depth and

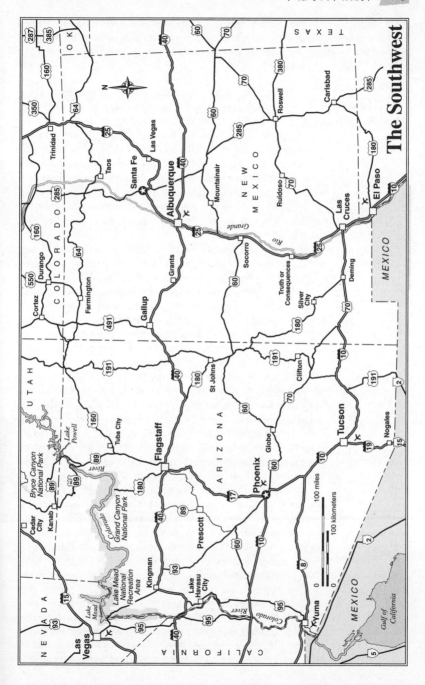

The Southwest

then return on later trips to different spots, perhaps in different seasons. Either way, people generally come back, and often to stay. For the Southwest has so many unique ways—food, landscapes, customs, climate, art, architecture, languages—to create lingering memories.

The Story of the Southwest

GEOLOGY

The walls of the Grand Canyon reveal one billion years in stone. Over countless centuries, geological shifting raised the plateau up to slowly higher elevations as the Colorado River sliced it in half. The dark rocks at river level, which contain no fossils, are some of the oldest matter on the face of the earth. The different layers of color and texture in the layered cliffs attest to times when the area was sea floor, forest and swamp. Tiny fossilized sea creatures from the Paleozoic era, long before dinosaurs, trace the development of some of the first life on the planet up through strata of shale, limestone and sandstone.

The geological features of the Southwest are so varied and spectacular that it is certainly possible to appreciate the landscapes for their beauty without knowing how they formed. But travelers who take a little time to learn about the region's geology in natural history museums or park visitors centers along the way develop a different perspective. They come to see how the many different colors and kinds of surface rock connect in a wonderfully complex formation hundreds of miles across. They learn to explore the panorama in three dimensions, not just two.

For example, Kaibab limestone, the 250,000,000-year-old, 300-foot-thick, grayish-white layer along the top rim of the Grand Canyon, is also visible at Lee's Ferry, a half-day's drive to the east, and at Capitol Reef National Park, a similar distance to the north. The orange Wingate sandstone layer is seen in Capitol Reef as well as in Arches National Park, the Island in the Sky and Newspaper Rock units of Canyonlands National Park, and at Dead Horse Point State Park—all part of the same rock.

The delight of Southwestern geology lies not only in its grand overviews but also in its myriad unique details. Dinosaur tracks. Petrified wood. Huge underground caverns. Pure white gypsum sand dunes. Salt domes, arches, natural bridges, hoodoos and goblins fancifully shaped by water and weather. Huge volcanic boulders pushed great distances by glaciers.

Volcanoes created some of the most dramatic scenery in the Southwest. In some places, like New Mexico's Valley of Fires Recreation Area and El Malpais National Monument, lava has paved the desert floor for many miles into tortured, twisted, surfaces that cannot be crossed, laced with ice caves where water stays frozen even on the hottest summer days. Elsewhere, as in the volcano fields northeast of Flagstaff, Arizona, fields of pumice gravel prevent vegetation from growing but make hiking easy at the foot of picture-perfect volcanic cones.

The Jemez Mountains in northern New Mexico formed from the crumbled remnant of what a number of scientists believe may have been the world's tallest volcano nearly two million years ago. In the canyons of Bandelier National Monument on the slope of the Jemez stand tent rocks, strange spires left behind when steam vents hardened volcanic ash in the distant past. Farther north, near Taos, the massive lava flow from the Jemez volcano forms the walls of deep gorges along the Rio Grande. There are no active volcanoes in the Southwest today, but that could change at any time. Volcanoes have been erupting in the Southwest for millions of years, and the most recent ones exploded less than a thousand years ago. As geologists reckon time, a thousand years is just yesterday.

> One thousand years ago, American Indians of the Southwest had extensive trade contacts, including the Toltecs of central Mexico.

NATIVE PEOPLE Beautifully flaked spear points found near Clovis, New Mexico, in the 1930s yielded evidence that groups of nomadic paleo-hunters were traveling through the Southwest at least 10,000 years ago. They were pursuing mastodons, giant bison, short-faced bear and other big game that lived on the grassy savannah around lakes left behind at the end of the Ice Age. Over the next several thousand years, their successors—the Folsom and Eden cultures—refined their tools and hunting skills, focusing primarily on bison herds, which were now widespread. These hunters lived lightly on the land, only leaving occasional reminders of their presence around campfires in cave shelters that served as tool-making and butchering sites.

HISTORY

Over the next centuries, they learned how to build above-ground masonry dwellings with rooms for storage (the first pueblos) and began incorporating pit houses into the dwellings as ceremonial rooms, or kivas. Ritual leaders skilled in astronomy grew to prominence among the Hohokam farmers of southern Arizona and the Mogollon in southern New Mexico, as well as the ancestors of today's Pueblo people. By A.D. 1000, the Chaco culture had become the most powerful trading culture the Southwest had ever known, but their civilization crashed during a series of droughts and were scattered throughout the Four Corners region by 1150. People concentrated on survival, and when a particularly long drought occurred in the late 13th century, they simply moved down to the more reliable Rio Grande region of New Mexico and the Little Colorado River in Arizona. Here their ancestors—the 19 Pueblos of New Mexico and the Hopi in Arizona—still live today.

While the Pueblos still live today in self-contained adobe dwellings, the people who began joining them in the Southwest at this time were nomadic hunter-gatherers from elsewhere. The Paiute people were among the nomads who began joining the Virgin River Pueblo people in the region north of the Grand Canyon and the Fremont farther north. The Fremont eventually disappeared, possibly folded into the Paiute or other new tribes, but the Paiute remain a presence in southern Utah today. A much larger group of nomads from northwest Canada also gradually wandered into the Four Corners, possibly as early as the 11th century, according to recent evidence. In time, they would break into the Navajo and Apache nations, with the Navajo taking up a pastoral lifestyle in Arizona and New Mexico while the Apache stayed truer to their nomadic lifestyle. Both the Navajo and Apache (and the Utes in Colorado) benefited greatly from the reintroduction to North America of what would become their primary transportation—the horse—by Spaniards in the 16th century.

SPANISH CONQUEST In the year 1540, a Spanish expedition under the command of conquistador Francisco Vasquez de Coronado set out from Mexico City and headed north across the parched, forbidding Chihuahuan Desert in search of the fabled Seven Cities of Cibola. Instead of the gold-paved cities of legend, he found pueblos such as Zuni, occupied by subsistence farmers who drew magical lines of cornmeal in unsuccessful attempts to fend off the Spaniards with their armor, horses and steel swords. Coronado and his followers were the first Europeans to visit the Hopi Mesas, the Rio Grande pueblos or the Grand Canyon. For two years they explored the Southwest, but finding no gold they returned to Mexico City with disappointing reports. After that, exploration of the territory Coronado had visited, which came to be called Nuevo Mexico, was left to Franciscan missionaries for the rest of the 16th century.

BIRTH OF THE NAVAJO NATION

The Pueblo Revolt created the Navajo nation. To persuade their Athabascan neighbors to help chase away the Spanish, Pueblo leaders agreed that the Athabascans could keep the livestock driven off from ranches they attacked. In that way, the tribe came to own sheep and horses, which would profoundly change their culture. When the Spanish colonists returned, many Pueblo people who had participated in the revolt fled to avoid retaliation and went to live with the nomads, bringing with them such advanced technologies as weaving cloth and growing corn. The Athabascan descendants who herded sheep and farmed became known as the Navajo people, while those who held to the old way of life came to be called Apache.

In 1598, a wealthy mine owner from Zacatecas, Mexico, named Don Juan de Oñate mounted an expedition at his own expense to colonize Nuevo Mexico under a grant from the Spanish government. The group consisted of 400 soldiers and settlers, 83 wagons and 7000 head of livestock. Oñate founded the first permanent Spanish settlement near modern-day Española, New Mexico, but the cost of his expeditions bankrupted him and he resigned his position as governor. The new governor, Don Pedro de Peralta, moved the capital to Santa Fe in 1610.

The Spanish colonists grew in number and established villages, farms and ranches up and down the Rio Grande over several generations, but slavery practices and erratic religious policies toward the Indians inspired the Pueblo Revolt of 1680. The people of the Rio Grande pueblos, aided by fierce Athabascan nomads, attacked the Spanish towns and ranches, killing hundreds of settlers and driving the survivors downriver all the way to the site of present-day El Paso, Texas, where they camped for 11 years before soldiers arrived from Mexico City to help them regain Nuevo Mexico.

After the Pueblo Revolt, Nuevo Mexico endured as an outpost of the Spanish empire for another 130 years. During all of that time, the conquerors and colonists were never able to settle the surrounding areas of the Southwest or even establish roads between Nuevo Mexico and other Spanish colonies in California and central Texas. The lands to the north and east were controlled by warrior horsemen of the Comanche tribe, whose raids forced abandonment of Spanish missions such as those at Pecos and Gran Quivira. To the south and west, the Apache and Navajo people used fear to keep Europeans out of the land that is now Arizona.

Nor did the Spanish settlers have any contact with English-speaking American colonists. Near the end of the colonial era, explorers from the United States, such as early U.S. Army explorer Captain Zebulon Pike, who accidentally strayed into Nuevo Mexico were arrested.

TERRITORIAL PERIOD   Starting in 1821, distant events changed the lives of the Spanish inhabitants of the Southwest. Mexico won its independence from Spain, and government policies changed. The border was opened, and trade was established along the Santa Fe Trail, which linked Nuevo Mexico to United States territory. At the same time, all Franciscan monks were exiled from Mexican territory, leaving Nuevo Mexico without spiritual leadership. They were replaced by a lay brotherhood of *penitentes* whose spiritual guidance did much to create a uniquely New Mexican culture and tradition that survives to this day in remote mountain villages around Santa Fe and Taos.

When the Texas republic won its independence from Mexico in 1836, many Texans contended that Nuevo Mexico should be part of their new nation—a sentiment that the people of Nuevo Mexico did not share. Texas troops occupied Nuevo Mexico in 1841, but their authority was not acknowledged. Five years later, when Texas had joined the United States and the Mexican War was underway, federal soldiers took possession of New Mexico. When the war ended in 1848, the peace treaty with Mexico ceded the territories of California and Nuevo Mexico (which included the modern-day states of New Mexico and Arizona) to the United States. To confuse the local people further, 13 years after they had become Americans, the Civil War broke out and Confederate troops from Texas fought numerous battles in New Mexico, briefly capturing Albuquerque, Santa Fe and Mesilla. Before the war ended, New Mexico and its people had been part of five different nations in about 40 years.

The first English-speaking settlers in the Southwest were Mormons, who chose to live free from persecution in the empty desert. Beginning in the 1840s, they established settlements throughout southern Utah and northern Arizona, often in places that are still remote today.

The United States government in the late 19th century was far less tolerant of Indians than the Spanish and Mexicans rulers had been. After the Civil War, the Army set out to make the lands ruled by the Comanches, Apaches, Navajos and Utes safe for homesteaders. The Comanches were annihilated. The Utes, who had roamed from the eastern slope of the Colorado Rockies to the canyonlands of southern Utah, were confined to a narrow reservation south of present-day Durango, Colorado. Kit Carson rounded up the entire Navajo tribe and marched them from their homeland to a reservation in eastern New Mexico, but after explorations revealed nothing of value on the Navajo land, and after thousands of Navajo people had died, he marched the survivors back home to the land where they live today. The longest and most violent army campaign against the Indians was the Apache Wars. Though never numerous, the Apaches were so fierce and elusive that the wars lasted for 19 bloody years, ending in 1884 with the surrender of the rebel leader Geronimo. Only then could settlers from the United States establish the first towns in Arizona.

Law enforcement was unreliable in the territorial era, giving rise to timeless legends of the Wild West. In New Mexico, Billy the Kid and his gang fought against an army of gunmen hired by a ruthless cattle baron in the Lincoln County War. In Utah, Butch Cassidy robbed trains and plundered banks and always eluded capture. In Arizona, Ike Clanton and his boys shot it out with lawman Wyatt Earp and gunman Doc Holliday at Tombstone's O.K. Corral. Out of all the turmoil and gunfire emerged a new multicultural society. In 1912, Arizona and New Mexico became the

47th and 48th states in the union—the last to be admitted until Alaska 50 years later.

MODERN TIMES   The traditional Spanish and Indian cultures of the Southwest remain strong even as waves of visitors and new-comers have swept across the land during the 20th century. Beginning shortly before World War I, artists and writers fleeing Paris's West Bank began to congregate around Taos, New Mexico. Since the 1940s, the Institute of American Indian Arts, the only federal Indian school dedicated to teaching traditional and contemporary art, has established Santa Fe, New Mexico, as the world's leading Indian art market. Exotic locations and reliable sunshine have drawn film production companies to the Southwest ever since 1898 and continue to do so. Today, visual and performing arts form one of the most important industries in many parts of the Southwest.

In World War II, the Southwest became America's center for nuclear research. The nation's best physicists were sent to a top secret base at Los Alamos, New Mexico, deep in a labyrinth of volcanic canyons, to develop the world's first atomic bomb. They tested it in 1945 in the desert near White Sands, New Mexico. After the war ended, nuclear weapons research continued at Los Alamos, as did development of peacetime uses for nuclear energy, bringing a stampede of prospectors and mining companies to the uranium-rich badlands of the Four Corners area. Today, Los Alamos National Laboratory and other federal laboratories in the region also study nuclear fusion, geothermal and solar energy research and genetic studies. The technologies developed at the laboratories have brought private high-tech companies to the major cities of the Southwest. Meanwhile, the nuclear industry

RIDERS OF THE PURPLE SAGE

The allure of Arizona has not gone unnoticed by the publishing and film industry. Zane Grey based many of his western novels on north central Arizona, including *Riders of the Purple Sage* and *West of the Pecos*. Tony Hillerman's contemporary murder mysteries are often set in the Navajo Indian Reservation and Four Corners area and include *A Thief of Time, The Dark Wind* and *Coyote Waits*. *Laughing Boy* by Oliver LaFarge is a Pulitzer Prize–winning novel that describes Navajo life. There have also been many movies filmed in Arizona at Old Tucson Studios, including John Wayne's *Rio Lobo, Rio Bravo* and *El Dorado*; Paul Newman's *The Life and Times of Judge Roy Bean*; Clint Eastwood's *The Outlaw Josey Wales*; and *Gunfight at the O.K. Corral* with Kirk Douglas.

has reached the top of the list of environmental controversies that stir heated debate in the region.

Although population growth since World War II has been phenomenal in the Phoenix, Tucson and Albuquerque areas, most of the Southwest remains sparsely inhabited. Water is the limiting factor. Although a series of huge manmade reservoirs—Lake Powell, Lake Mead, Lake Havasu and others—along the Colorado River runs through the heart of the desert Southwest, the water and electricity from them is used far away in southern California, while the land along the banks of the river remains almost entirely undeveloped.

Well over half of the land in the region covered by this book is owned by the public. Large expanses of grasslands and canyonlands are administered by the federal Bureau of Land Management and leased to ranchers for cattle grazing. Other stretches are military reservations. The region includes 15 national forests, 12 national wildlife refuges and 54 national parks, monuments and recreation areas—more than any other part of the United States.

Tourism is key among the forces that have shaped the modern Southwest. With a relatively small population, few manufacturing industries and limited agriculture, the economy relies heavily on travelers, who support hotels, restaurants and other service businesses. In general, Southwesterners display a friendly, positive attitude toward tourists. Beauty is one of the region's most important natural resources, and there is plenty to share. Besides, as locals like to point out, who would want to live in a place strangers didn't want to visit?

FLORA

Drivers crossing the Southwest at high speed on interstate highways can easily form the mistaken impression that this region is mostly open ranchland so arid that it takes 50 acres to graze a single cow. This is because main highways follow the flattest, most featureless routes. All one has to do is take a detour into the mountains and canyons where the main highways don't go in order to discover that the dry climate and extreme elevation changes create a surprising variety of ecosystems, each with its own unique beauty.

At low altitudes where winter temperatures rarely dip to freezing, cacti and other succulents thrive. Ocatillo, century plants, yuccas and prickly pear, barrel and cholla cacti, as well as mesquite and creosote bushes, are found throughout both the Chihuahuan Desert of southern New Mexico and the Sonoran Desert of southern Arizona. The Sonoran Desert is best known for its magnificent forests of giant saguaro and organ pipe cacti. When spring rains come, which may be once in five years or more, the deserts burst forth for a few weeks in a fantastic display of wildflowers.

Miniature evergreen forests of piñon, juniper and cedar cover the desert hills at higher elevations where winter temperatures fall below freezing. Once every seven years in the fall, piñon trees produce pine nuts, which many consider a delicacy. Cactus and yucca stay small in the high desert.

Mountain forests change with elevation, forming three distinct bands. On the lower slopes of the mountains, ponderosa pine stand 50 feet tall and more. At middle elevations, shimmering stands of aspen trees fill the mountainsides and paint them bright yellow in early October. Douglas fir dominates the higher reaches of the mountains. In some parts of the forest, accessible only by hiking trail and out of reach of timber cutters, fir trees 100 feet tall and bigger around than a man's reach stand spirelike in ancient forests dripping with moss and silence. The San Juan Mountains near Durango, Colorado, contain peaks reaching above timberline, where temperatures always fall below freezing at night and trees will not grow. There is only the alpine tundra, a world of grassy meadows rooted in permafrost where tiny flowers appear for brief moments in midsummer.

The palo verde tree is the Arizona state tree, and the saguaro cactus is the Arizona state flower.

Of all the various ecosystems that characterize the Southwest, the real gems are the riparian woodlands. Since almost all of the Southwestern landscape is dry and can only support the hardiest of plants, plant life flourishes around even the least trickle of year-round running water. Creek and river banks support thick forests of cottonwood trees and tamarisks, along with isolated stands of hardwood trees such as maple and hickory.

FAUNA

Packs of Mexican wolves in Albuquerque's Rio Grande Zoo and the Desert Museum in Carlsbad, New Mexico, are the last of their species, preserved from extinction by a federal captive-breeding program. The Navajo Nation Zoo in Window Rock is also raising Mexican wolves as part of this program.

But other animals of Western legend still roam free in the forests and canyons of the Southwestern back country. Mountain lions, rarely seen because they inhabit remote areas and hunt in the dark, sometimes flash past late-night drivers' headlight beams. Many black bears live deep in the mountains, and in drought summers when food is short they may stray into Albuquerque, Flagstaff or other towns to raid trash cans. Coyotes, the most commonly seen Southwestern predators, abound in all rural areas and frequently surround campgrounds with their high-pitched yipping and howling.

Open rangelands throughout the Southwest support sizable herds of pronghorn antelope alongside grazing cattle. Most visitors to national parks and other protected areas will spot mule deer, and in some parks such as Mesa Verde as well as in the remote canyonlands of southern Utah, wild horses still roam. The elk population in the Southwestern mountains is the largest it has been in this century. Because elk prefer high mountain meadows, only serious hikers are likely to spot one. Herds of mountain sheep live above timberline on the highest mountains of the San Juan and Sangre de Cristo ranges, while their solitary relatives, desert bighorn sheep, live in most desert areas.

The last grizzly bear sighted in the Southwest was in the San Juan Mountains near Silverton, Colorado, in the mid-1970s.

One of the most distinctive regional birds is the magpie, an exotic-looking, long-tailed, iridescent, black-and-white cousin of Asian myna birds. Another is the roadrunner, which is often seen hunting lizards alongside the highway. Large birds often seen by motorists or hikers include turkey vultures, ravens and many different kinds of hawks. Both golden and bald eagles live throughout the Southwest and are occasionally spotted soaring in the distance. Eagles and vultures are about the same size, and the easiest way to tell them apart is to remember that eagles glide with their wings horizontal, while vultures' wings sweep upward in a V-shape.

A thought that preoccupies many visitors to the Southwest is of living hazards like rattlesnakes, gila monsters, scorpions and tarantulas. Poisonous animals live in most parts of the region except for the high mountains. Yet even local residents who spend most weekends hiking say that they rarely encounter one. When outdoors in desert country, walk loudly and never put your hand or foot where you can't see it.

Where to Go

The Southwest is no more one entity than is Europe. Don't try to "see it all" in a single trip or you may find yourself focused so much on covering large distances that you sacrifice quiet opportunities to appreciate the natural beauty you came to see. Deciding what to see and where to go is a tough choice. The good news is, you'll just have to keep coming back and exploring at different times of the year to get to know the "real" Southwest.

To help you with your decisions, we'll entice you with a brief description of each area covered in this book. To get the whole story, read the introduction to each chapter, then the more detailed material on the regions that appeal to you.

The **Grand Canyon**, the largest single geological feature in the Southwest, splits northwestern Arizona between north and south. The "village" on the South Rim of the Grand Canyon, just an hour's drive from interstate Route 40, is developed on a grand scale, complete with an airport. Hikers discover that only a tiny part of either rim of the Grand Canyon is accessible by vehicle, and that a moderate walk can provide total solitude. The North Rim, farther by road from major cities and main routes, is more relaxed and secluded, though still busy enough to make advance lodging or camping reservations essential. Closed during the winter, the North Rim combines perfectly with visits to Lake Powell and the national parks of southwestern Utah, as well as Las Vegas, Nevada.

Northeastern Arizona, also known as Indian Country, includes the vast, sprawling Navajo Indian Reservation, larger than some East Coast states, as well as the remote, ancient mesatop pueblos of the Hopi Indian Reservation, fiercely traditional and independent although completely surrounded by Navajo land. The center of the Navajo world according to legend, Canyon de Chelly is still inhabited by people who herd sheep and live without electricity. Visitors can view their hogans and pastures from high above on the canyon rim but can only enter the labyrinth accompanied by a Navajo guide. Another national park service unit operated by the tribe, Navajo National Monument protects some of the best Ancestral Pueblo ruins in the area. The monument's biggest Indian ruin is only accessible on horseback. The third major park on the reservation is Monument Valley Navajo Tribal Park, a landscape so familiar from the many films, TV shows and advertisements filmed here that visitors may feel like they're driving through a movie as they travel the backcountry road around the valley and visit the hogans of the people who live in this, one of the most remote places in the United States. A tour of Hubbell Trading Post National Historic Site and perhaps a stop at a still-operating trading post will round out your Indian Country experience.

Route 40 through **North Central Arizona** will bring you to Flagstaff, a winter ski resort and college town, sitting on the edge of the dramatic San Francisco Peaks at 7000 feet and blanketed with ponderosa pine trees. Drive south through spectacular Oak Creek Canyon to Sedona, an upscale artist community with a New Age bent and an abundance of shopping. This is also the heart of scenic Red Rock Country, where red sandstone has eroded into dramatic formations of incomparable beauty. Jerome, scenically perched in the Mingus Mountains, is a former mining town that's now home to a small community of artists. Just down the road is Prescott, the original territorial capital of Arizona, which draws visitors with its numerous museums and low-key charm.

Never mind that **Western Arizona** is surrounded by parched desert. The 340-mile-long stretch of the Colorado River that establishes the state's "west coast" border has created an aquatic playground spilling over with unparalleled scenic and recreational opportunities. Kingman is the northern gateway to a succession of lakes, resorts and riverfront coves, as well as to the historic gold and silver mining ghost towns of Oatman and Chloride. The Lake

Mead National Recreation Area extends to include Lake Mohave, where you'll find Bullhead City, Arizona's fastest growing city. Farther south is Lake Havasu City, home to the authentic London Bridge, which was brought over from England and reassembled here. Continue down Route 95 and you'll come to Quartzsite, which attracts more than half a million visitors every January and February to its annual rock and mineral extravaganzas.

Phoenix, the state capital and the largest city in the Southwest, is the focus of **South Central Arizona**. At first, this rectilinear sprawl of suburbs and shopping malls, giant retirement communities, towering office buildings, industrial parks and farmlands full of year-round citrus and cotton crops may seem to offer few charms for the vacationer. But those who take time to explore Phoenix and beyond will soon discover that this city where it is often better to spend daytime hours indoors has more than its share of fine museums. Winter is the time for outdoor adventuring in the Phoenix area, and hiking, horseback riding, boating and fishing opportunities abound. Nearby Scottsdale blends the architecture of the Old West with exclusive shops, galleries, restaurants and night clubs, while other towns within easy day-trip distance of Phoenix, such as Wickenburg, recall grittier and more authentic memories of the rough-and-rowdy mining boomtown era of late-19th-century Arizona.

Towering mountain peaks, sparkling streams and lakes, and dense pine forests surprise many travelers to the high country of **Eastern Arizona**. This forest primeval encompasses the mountain hamlets of Show Low, Pinetop and Lakeside, summer resorts famous for their hiking and fishing, and popular with those trying to escape the scorching temperatures on the desert floor. During winter, skiers flock to the downhill runs and cross-country trails at nearby Sunrise ski resort on the White Mountain Apache Indian Reservation. The forests deepen as you travel east to Alpine, a mountain village just a few miles from the New Mexico border. At the heart of the "Arizona Alps," Alpine is a mecca for nature buffs, who love the profusion of outdoor activities—hiking, camping, hunting and fishing. Alpine is also a northern guidepost along the Coronado Trail, which snakes south through some of the most spectacular scenery in the Southwest to the historic mining town of Clifton. Built along the banks of the San Francisco River, Clifton and its historic Chase Creek Street give a glimpse of what Arizona was like at the turn of the 20th century. Traveling south from Clifton, juniper foothills give way to rolling grasslands and the fertile Gila River Valley, where cotton is king and the town of Safford marks Arizona's eastern anchor of the Old West Highway. This strip of Arizona, stretching 203 miles from Apache Junction to the New Mexico state line, is rich in the frontier history of the

Old West. Tracing a course first charted by Coronado, Geronimo, the Dutchman, Billy the Kid, Johnny Ringo and pioneers looking for a place to call their own, you will pass through cactus-studded valleys, pine-topped mountains, rugged and craggy canyons, lost treasure and historic copper mines. Along the way you can sample the area's history in Globe's plantation-style mansions and antique shops and its pre-history at the Besh-Ba-Gowah archaeological site.

Southern Arizona in the springtime, when the desert flowers bloom, is the closest thing to paradise on earth most of us will find. The secret is well-kept because during the summer tourist season, when most visitors come to the Southwest, Tucson is considerably hotter than paradise—or just about anyplace else. Those who visit at any time other than summer will discover the pleasure of wandering through the forests of giant saguaro cactus that cover the foothills at the edge of town, perhaps learning more at the wonderful Arizona-Sonora Desert Museum and seeing the 18th-century Spanish Mission San Xavier del Bac. For more desert beauty, drive west through the cactus forest of the Tohono O'odham (Papago) Indian Reservation to Organ Pipe Cactus National Monument on the Mexican border. Many people consider the monument to be the most beautiful part of the Southwestern desert. Another great side trip from the Tucson area is Cochise County to the east. National monuments in the rugged, empty mountains preserve the strongholds of Apache warlords and the cavalrymen who fought to subdue them. Old Bisbee, until recently the headquarters for one of the nation's largest open-pit copper mining operations, has been reincarnated as a picturesque, far-from-everything tourist town. Tombstone, meanwhile, milks the tourist appeal of a famous gunfight that occurred more than a century ago to sustain one of the most authentically preserved historic towns of the Old West.

> The cholla cactus prefers to grow in areas that were once stripped of vegetation, such as old Indian ruins.

Visitors to the **Santa Fe Area** find themselves in a magical place where art openings and operas complement rodeos, horse races and wilderness adventures. The sky-high state capital, situated at 7000 feet elevation and backdropped by the spectacular Sangre de Cristo Mountains, is also the oldest colonial city in the United States. Strict guidelines mandate the now well-known Santa Fe–style look of territorial and Spanish Colonial architecture. Thanks to city codes, no highrises block the mountain views or the ever-changing colors at dawn and dusk.

Northwest of Santa Fe is the city of Los Alamos, birthplace to the atomic bomb. Modern in its technology and scientific findings, Los Alamos' laboratories coexist within a stone's throw of ancient ruins and Indian pueblos—in other words, caveman meets the Jetsons. Those who head southeast of Santa Fe will come across the country's original Las Vegas, a charismatic town that may look familiar at first—and second—glance. That's probably because Las Vegas, New Mexico, has been featured in countless silent movies. Perhaps what's most intriguing about the region, however, is the unique population mix, which includes the world's foremost nuclear scientists and major communities of visual artists, performers and writers, plus a colorful and varied cultural melting pot of Anglo, American Indian and Spanish peoples.

Driving north from New Mexico's capital city, you'll pass vast forests and mountain villages centuries old on your way to **Taos and the Enchanted Circle Area.** Taos is a legendary artists' community, a step down in the frenetic category from the hustle-bustle of Santa Fe. It is a casually sophisticated town where galleries and working artists flourish. Surrounding the city are the raging Rio Grande, the Sangre de Cristo Mountains and the Carson National Forest, making recreational pursuits easily accessible for the many sports-minded people who are drawn to Taos' world-class ski slopes. Also in the area is the nation's largest scouting camp and dormant Capulin Volcano.

Northwestern New Mexico is also known for its rich tapestry of experiences. The areas around Grants and Gallup are close enough that they could be glimpsed as day trips out of Albuquerque, but you might consider them as a vacation destination on their own. Here visitors can explore the Indian pueblos of Acoma and Zuni, where American Indians have lived continuously since long before Christopher Columbus sighted land. Grants is situated at the center of an intriguing array of places—the most ancient continuously inhabited pueblos in New Mexico, a vast and forbidding lava bed with ice caves, a landmark where centuries of explorers left their marks and solitary, massive Mt. Taylor, a sacred mountain in Navajo tradition. Gallup, which bills itself as the "Gateway to Indian Country," presents a cultural contrast as striking as any to be found along the Mexican border, as the interstate brings the outside world to the doorstep of the largest Indian na-

WEATHER FOR THE HOT AND COLD BLOODED

In the Southwest, where the high, rugged Rocky Mountains collide with the subtropical Chihuahuan and Sonoran deserts, small changes in elevation can mean big variations in climate. As a rule, climbing 1000 feet in elevation alters the temperature as much as going 300 miles north. For instance, the bottom of the Grand Canyon is always about 20° warmer than the top rim. In Tucson during the winter, some people bask by swimming pools while others ski on the slopes of nearby Mount Lemmon.

tion in the country. Pawn shops, bars and a row of neon motels lend a hard edge to the local ambience, but the annual Inter-Tribal Ceremonial and large concentration of American Indians make it a prime place to view native crafts. In the Four Corners area, you can step out of New Mexico into one of three other states or use every limb to simultaneously be in each of the four—New Mexico, Arizona, Colorado and Utah. It's the only spot in the United States where four states come together. Three rivers also meet at this unique junction, feeding a carpet of desert flora in an area that is often perceived as arid.

Billy the Kid once roamed the area that now encompasses **Albuquerque and Central New Mexico.** Now you can, too. The vast ranchland plains east of the Rocky Mountains haven't changed much since the Kid rode into legend more than a century ago. But Albuquerque is another story. Just another small town on the banks of the Rio Grande downriver from Santa Fe in the heyday of the Wild West, it has been transformed into a bustling metropolis boasting a unique mosaic of lifestyles and cultures. Places, such as the Indian Pueblo Cultural Center, showcase the city's multicultural heritage. But perhaps the best way to gain an understanding of Albuquerque is to walk around the Old Town Plaza, a historic district that preserves the architectural grace of Albuquerque's Spanish Colonial era. Sandia Crest, the massive mountain that flanks the city's Northeast Heights, offers skiing, wilderness hiking, a thrilling tramway ride and cool forests. With a gnarled old forest of cottonwoods along its banks, the Rio Grande has great secluded trails for urban hiking, jogging, bicycling and horseback riding. Traveling east from Albuquerque takes you into the high plains, where the major tourist spots are all lakes. Driving south takes you to Bosque del Apache, where huge flocks of cranes spend the winter months, or to Salinas Missions, a group of national monument units preserving the ruins of Indian pueblos and old Spanish missions. This is the Central New Mexico that beckons the traveler: a mixture of the wild and sublime, the small town and the big city, the past and the present.

Travelers who continue into **Southern New Mexico** face a choice among three different areas, each with its own character. In the east, the premier attraction is Carlsbad Caverns National Park, which draws millions of visitors annually to this remote corner of the state. A visit to Carlsbad Caverns combines easily with a side trip to Ruidoso, a bustling mountain resort town that caters primarily to Texans with its Indian-owned ski slopes and some of the richest horse racing in the country. Nearby, the historic town of Lincoln still remembers the days of Billy the Kid, when it was one of the most lawless places in the Wild West. In south central New Mexico, a series of unique sightseeing highlights—lava fields, Indian petroglyphs, wilderness hiking trails and the vast dunes of

White Sands National Monument—invites vacation travelers to leave the interstate and loop through the Tularosa Valley. The dominant feature in the southwestern sector of New Mexico is the Gila Wilderness, the largest roadless area in the 48 contiguous United States. Gila Cliff Dwellings National Monument is the starting point for hikers entering the wilderness, whether for an afternoon or a month. Visitors with plenty of time to explore the area can drive around the wilderness boundary to see the well-preserved ghost town of Mogollon or walk up a sheer-sided canyon on a series of narrow footbridges known as The Catwalk.

Few people actually live in the wild landscape of hoodoos and slickrock canyons that comprise **Southwestern Utah** and **Southeastern Utah**, but millions of visitors come each year to visit the remarkable string of five national parks, each within a few hours' drive of the next. Each of the five is strikingly different from the others. Arches, Bryce Canyon and Zion national parks all present distinctively shaped stone landscapes, erosion as an art form, en route to the North Rim of the Grand Canyon. Canyonlands, the most challenging to explore thoroughly, is reached by any of three dead-end roads into the park that start a hundred miles apart and do not connect. In Capitol Reef, the least known of Utah's national parks, the remains of an old pioneer community provide a hub for a network of dirt roads and trails through side canyons and among strange rock formations. Canyonlands and the Moab area are favored by backpackers, mountain bikers and river rafters. Besides the national parks, another major destination in southern Utah is Lake Powell, the largest reservoir on the Colorado River. Most of its shoreline is far from any road and only accessible by boat. You can rent anything from a speedboat to a houseboat at one of the marinas and cruise for days, exploring side canyons and isolated desert shorelines.

Southwestern Colorado's top visitor attraction is Mesa Verde National Park, the site of the largest, most impressive and mysterious cliff dwellings in North America. While crowd control to protect archaeological sites means that backcountry hiking opportunities are limited at Mesa Verde, the park roads are ideal for bicycles. Those who prefer to visit Indian ruins in solitude can see less-known ruins at Hovenweep National Monument and sites around nearby Dolores, Colorado. Durango, the area's principal town, has a quaint Old West–Victorian ambience in the central historic district, which is the departure point for the Durango & Silverton Narrow Gauge Railroad. The popular passenger train follows an old rail route to an old mining town in the heart of the San Juan Mountains. Drivers, too, can explore the San Juans and find alpine hiking trails, old mining towns and great campgrounds along the San Juan Skyway, one of the most spectacular scenic routes anywhere.

Many people imagine the Southwest to be a scorching hot place. Part of it—Tucson, Phoenix, southern and western Arizona—lives up to expectations with daytime high temperatures averaging well above the 100° mark through the summer. Even in January, thermometers in this area generally reach the high 60s in the afternoon and rarely fall to freezing at night. The clement winter weather and practically perpetual sunshine have made the Arizona desert a haven for retired persons and migratory human "snowbirds."

When to Go

SEASONS

Yet less than 200 miles away, the North Rim of the Grand Canyon is closed in the winter because heavy snows make the road impassable. Northern Arizona, northern New Mexico and southern Utah and Colorado experience cold, dry winters with temperatures usually rising above freezing during the day but often dropping close to zero at night. The high mountains remain snow-capped all winter and boast several popular ski areas. At lower elevations, lighter snowfalls and plenty of sunshine keep roads clear most of the time.

> The majority of the Southwest's moisture for the entire year falls during monsoon season (July and August), so try to plan outdoor activities in the morning hours.

Springtime in the Southwest is a mixed blessing. Flooding rivers, chilly winds and sandstorms sometimes await visitors in March and early April, but those who take a chance are more likely to experience mild weather and spectacular displays of desert wildflowers. Leaves do not appear on the trees until late April at moderate elevations, late May in the higher mountains.

Throughout the region, June is the hottest month. Even in cool areas such as northern New Mexico, the thermometer frequently hits the 100° mark. In July and August the thunderstorms of what locals refer to as the "monsoon season" usually cool things down quickly on hot afternoons. Although New Mexico and Arizona are pretty much safe from natural disasters like earthquakes, tornadoes and hurricanes, meteorologists have discovered from satellite data that the region has more lightning strikes than anywhere else in the United States.

Autumn is the nicest time of year throughout the Southwest. Locals used to keep this fact to themselves, and until recently tourists in October were about as rare as snowflakes in Phoenix. Nowadays the secret is out, and record numbers of people are visiting during the fall "shoulder season" to experience fall colors and bright Indian summer days.

CALENDAR OF EVENTS

Besides all-American-style annual community celebrations with parades, arts-and-crafts shows, concerts—and, in the Southwest, rodeos—the region has other, less familiar kinds of festivals. Most towns that trace their heritage back to Spanish colonialism observe annual fiestas, normally on the feast day of the town's patron saint. Fiestas tend to mix sacred and secular, with solemn religious processions and dancing in the streets.

JANUARY

Northeastern Arizona   Relive a tradition of the frontier West on the **Hashknife Sheriff Posse's Pony Express Ride** from Holbrook to Scottsdale.

South Central Arizona   Crowds gather in Scottsdale to watch some of the PGA Tour's best golfers at the **Phoenix Open,** one of Arizona's largest spectator events. The **Barrett-Jackson Auction** is a huge classic and collectible car auction in Scottsdale, with over 800 vehicles ranging in price from several thousand to millions of dollars.

FEBRUARY

North Central Arizona   **Gold Rush Days** in Wickenburg features a parade, rodeo, arts-and-crafts show, melodrama, and gold mucking and drilling competitions.

Western Arizona   Quartzsite attracts several hundred thousand rock hounds and gem collectors from around the world for its **Gem and Mineral Show,** held throughout February and in early March.

Eastern Arizona   **Lost Dutchman Days** in Apache Junction near Phoenix is another community celebration full of traditional small-town events—like a Fourth of July in February.

Southern Arizona   The **Tucson Gem and Mineral Show** draws jewelers and collectors worldwide.

MARCH

South Central Arizona   The **Scottsdale Arts Festival** features extensive crafts exhibitions and lots of food.

Southern Arizona   The crowning point of **Tombstone Territorial Days** is a re-enactment of the events leading up to the gunfight at the O.K. Corral.

Southern New Mexico   Each March 9th, Columbus holds a military-style **Columbus Raid Commemoration** to remember the victims of Mexican revolutionist Pancho Villa's 1916 raid.

APRIL

Southern Arizona   Tucson is home to the **International Mariachi Conference,** a weeklong celebration of mariachi music with concerts, workshops, an art exhibit and a golf tournament.

Southern New Mexico Alamogordo's twice-a-year **Trinity Site Tour** (the second is in October) is your chance to see where the first atomic bomb was tested.

Southwestern Utah   The **St. George Art Festival** fills Main Street and the art center with juried art exhibits and continuous musical performances.

North Central Arizona The Sedona Art and Sculpture Walk draws artisans from all over the West to participate in one of the region's major arts-and-crafts fairs.

Southern Arizona Tombstone's **Wyatt Earp Days** celebration fills the Memorial Day weekend with Old West costumes and staged shootouts in the streets and arts and crafts.

Santa Fe Area The **Arts & Crafts Fair** in Los Alamos displays work by over 100 artisans.

Taos and the Enchanted Circle Area The Taos Spring Arts Celebration, continuing over several weekends, features artists' studio tours, performing arts and live entertainment.

Southern New Mexico **Mayfair**, held on Memorial Day weekend, is the big community festival in Cloudcroft.

Santa Fe Area The **Spring Festival and Animal Fair** at El Rancho de las Golondrinas near Santa Fe presents Spanish Colonial craft demonstrations and re-creates 17th-century hacienda life. The **Rodeo de Santa Fe** comes to the state capital with a parade.

Taos and the Enchanted Circle Area The **Taos School of Music Summer Chamber Music Festival** combines concerts by top classical musicians with educational seminars until August.

Albuquerque and Central New Mexico **Madrid Blues Festival** enlivens the old mining town on the Turquoise Trail with live music three Sundays a year (one in May, one in June and one in September) at the local ballfield. **Old Fort Days** in Fort Sumner feature a rodeo, staged bank robbery, melodrama and barbecue. The **New Mexico Arts & Crafts Fair**, held at Albuquerque's State Fairgrounds, is among the state's largest.

Southwestern Utah The **Utah Shakespearean Festival**, from the end of June to October in Cedar City, features plays performed on an outdoor stage along with related seminars, tours and entertainment events.

Southwestern Colorado The **Telluride Bluegrass Festival** packs this little mountain town to overflowing with musicians and fans.

Santa Fe Area Fourth of July begins with a pancake breakfast on the plaza. The **Santa Fe Opera** season opens that week as well and the city's lodging accommodations fill to capacity through August.

Taos and the Enchanted Circle Area The **Fiesta de Taos** fills the streets with a parade and music.

Southern New Mexico The **Ruidoso Arts Festival** is a major juried arts-and-crafts fair with continuous live entertainment.

Southwestern Colorado Durango's four-day **Fiesta Days** offers rodeo events, horse and duck racing and square dancing.

AUGUST   **South Central Arizona**   Payson hosts the **Annual Oldest Continuous Rodeo**, which draws cowboys from all over the Southwest.

Southern New Mexico   Deming hosts the **Great American Duck Race**, where waterfowl race for money and compete in such events as a Best-Dressed Duck Contest and a Duck Queen pageant.

Southwestern Colorado   Telluride hosts its annual **Telluride Jazz Celebration**, one of the biggest in the country. The two-weekend **Chamber Music Festival** featuring outstanding classical music performers happens later in the month.

SEPTEMBER   **Southern Arizona**   **Rendezvous of Gunfighters**, one of several practically identical town festivals held in Tombstone throughout the year, features a parade and a costume party on Labor Day weekend.

Santa Fe Area   The **Santa Fe Fiesta** starts with the ritual burning in effigy of a 35-foot-tall "Old Man Gloom" and continues through a weekend of parades, processions and wild celebration.

Taos and the Enchanted Circle Area   The **Taos Arts Festival,** which runs September to mid-October, presents art exhibits, lectures and an arts-and-crafts fair.

Albuquerque and Central New Mexico   In Albuquerque, the **New Mexico State Fair** has horse racing, top country performers, a rodeo and livestock.

Southern New Mexico   The **16th of September Fiesta** in Mesilla celebrates Mexico's independence with two days of folk dancing, mariachi music and food.

OCTOBER   **Western Arizona**   In Lake Havasu City, **London Bridge Days** commemorates the relocation of the bridge to this improbable site with a parade, live entertainment, costume contests and lots of Olde English fun.

South Central Arizona   The **Arizona State Fair,** held in Phoenix, runs until late October or early November.

Southern Arizona   Tombstone celebrates **Helldorado Days** with music, arts and crafts and gunfight re-enactments.

Santa Fe Area   Costumed volunteers re-create the Spanish Colonial era at **Harvest Festival** at the Rancho de las Golondrinas, a historic hacienda located near Santa Fe.

Albuquerque and Central New Mexico   The **Albuquerque Balloon Fiesta** lasts for a week and a half with races, mass ascensions and other events featuring over 600 hot-air balloons—the world's largest such event.

Southern New Mexico   Ruidoso celebrates fall foliage with a boisterous **Oktoberfest.** In Las Cruces, the **Whole Enchilada Festival** features a parade, live entertainment, races (including a grocery-cart race) and the "World's Largest Enchilada."

South Central Arizona The Four Corner States Bluegrass Festival in Wickenburg presents three days of music as bands compete for thousands of dollars in prize money.

Southern Arizona The largest perimeter bicycling event in the United States, **El Tour de Tucson** is a colorful spectator sport and a charity fundraiser.

Santa Fe Area The artists of secluded Dixon open their homes and workplaces to the public for the **Dixon Studio Tour.**

Albuquerque and Central New Mexico The **Weems Artfest** focuses on visual arts, presenting the works of several hundred artists at the State Fairgrounds in Albuquerque.

Southern New Mexico Nearly 100 exhibitors participate in the **Renaissance Craftfaire**, a juried art show in Las Cruces.

Western Arizona Christmas lights sparkle during Lake Mead Marina's **Parade of Lights**.

South Central Arizona The **Tostitos Fiesta Bowl Parade** in Phoenix has marching bands, equestrian units and floats. Tempe's New Year's Eve **Tostitos Fiesta Bowl Block Party** welcomes the two Fiesta Bowl teams with food, rides, music and fireworks.

Santa Fe Area The Christmas holidays hold particular charm in Santa Fe and Taos, where instead of colored lights, building exteriors glow with thousands of small candles called *farolitos*.

Albuquerque and Central New Mexico **Luminarias** (altar candles) light up the skyline of Albuquerque's Old Town. Between Albuquerque and Santa Fe, the old mining town of Madrid decks itself out with lights and open houses during the first two weeks in December for **Christmas in Madrid**.

Southern New Mexico Las Cruces celebrates the Fiesta of Our Lady of Guadalupe with a **torchlight ascent** of the nearby Tortugas Mountain, musical concerts and other festivities.

CALENDAR OF AMERICAN INDIAN EVENTS

Indian pueblos mark their patron saints' feast days with elaborately costumed ceremonial dances that include a pueblo's entire population, from toddlers to elders. Animal dances are normally held in the winter months and corn dances in the summer. Led by the pueblos' kiva clans, these observances almost certainly evolved from the religious rites of the ancient Ancestral Pueblo people.

Besides Puebloans, a few other tribes welcome outsiders to ceremonial events. In recent years, however, some Indian groups have opted to minimize the presence of non-Indians. In New Mexico, Zuni and Acoma have closed major ceremonies to outsiders, and in Arizona, the Hopi people no longer announce the dates or places of their ceremonial dances in advance. To avoid making yourself and future visitors unwelcome, do not carry a camera during any

Indian ceremony; videocameras and sketch pads are also banned. Do not use alcoholic beverages; possession of alcohol is a crime on Indian lands, and obnoxious drunks are not tolerated. Do accord ancient spiritual traditions the respect they deserve.

In addition to ceremonials, all Indian nations host annual powwows—gatherings of people from many tribes around the country who compete for money in colorful contest dances. There are also a growing number of fairs and markets where Indian artisans display and sell their work—often at a fraction of what you'd pay in Santa Fe or Sedona.

JANUARY **Throughout New Mexico** New Year's Day is celebrated with dances at Taos, Santa Clara, Jemez, Santa Ana, Cochiti and Santo Domingo pueblos. **King's Day** (January 6) is celebrated with animal dances at most pueblos.

Santa Fe Area San Ildefonso Pueblo's **Fiesta de San Ildefonso** features all-day animal dances, including an awe-inspiring dawn procession descending from Black Mesa.

Taos and the Enchanted Circle Taos Pueblo celebrates **New Year's Day** with a turtle dance.

Albuquerque and Central New Mexico New Year's Day is observed at Cochiti Pueblo with dancing.

FEBRUARY **South Central Arizona** Casa Grande is the site of **O'Odham Tash–Casa Grande Indian Days**, including Indian rituals, a rodeo and arts and crafts.

Southern Arizona The **Tohono O'odham Nation Fair** at Sells, west of Tucson on the reservation, features outstanding basketry, pottery, rug and jewelry exhibits as well as a rodeo.

Throughout New Mexico **Candelaria Day** (Candlemas) is observed with ceremonial dances at Picuris and San Felipe pueblos. Later in the month, **deer dances** are held at San Juan Pueblo.

MARCH **Throughout New Mexico** Most pueblos celebrate **Easter**—and the start of the planting season—with basket dances and corn dances. Laguna Pueblo also has dances on the **Fiesta de San José**.

APRIL **Albuquerque and Central New Mexico** At the **Gathering of Nations Powwow** in Albuquerque, more than 3000 costumed dancers from all over the country compete for prize money in one of the biggest Indian events staged anywhere.

MAY **Taos and the Enchanted Circle** Taos Pueblo holds its traditional **Blessing of the Fields and Corn Dance**.

Albuquerque and Central New Mexico The **Fiesta de San Felipe** is observed at the San Felipe Pueblo with a large, spectacular corn dance involving more than 500 dancers. Cochiti Pueblo celebrates the **Fiesta de Santa Cruz** with a corn dance.

Santa Fe Area   San Juan Pueblo observes the **Fiesta de San Juan** with buffalo and Comanche dances.

Albuquerque and Central New Mexico   On Memorial Day weekend, Jemez Pueblo is the site of the **Jemez Red Rocks Arts & Crafts Show.**

North Central Arizona   Traditional arts and crafts can be purchased at the **Annual Hopi Festival of Arts and Culture**, which opens at the Museum of Northern Arizona in Flagstaff.

Santa Fe Area   Nambe Pueblo holds its **Waterfall Ceremonial** on the 4th of July. The **Eight Northern Pueblos Arts and Crafts Fair**, held each year at a different Indian pueblo north of Santa Fe, hosts hundreds of American Indian exhibitors. Picuris Pueblo also hosts its own **Arts & Crafts Fair**. The Jicarilla Apache tribe sponsors the **Little Beaver Roundup and Rodeo**, a weekend-long celebration in Dulce with dances, an Indian rodeo and an arts-and-crafts show.

Taos and the Enchanted Circle   Taos Pueblo holds corn dances on the **Fiesta de Santiago** and the **Fiesta de Santa Ana.**

Albuquerque and Central New Mexico   Corn dances are held at Cochiti Pueblo on the **Fiesta de San Buenaventura** and at Santa Ana and Laguna pueblos on the **Fiesta de Santa Ana.**

Santa Fe Area   Santa Clara Pueblo has corn, buffalo and Comanche dances during the **Fiesta de Santa Clara**. The **Santa Fe Indian Market**, the largest American Indian arts s how and sale anywhere, draws collectors from around the world.

Taos and the Enchanted Circle   A corn dance is held at Picuris Pueblo on **San Lorenzo Feast Day.**

Northwestern New Mexico   At the **Inter-Tribal Indian Ceremonial** held in Red Rock State Park near Gallup, American Indians from more than 50 tribes participate in ritual and contest dances, an arts-and-crafts show, a rodeo and other events. The **Zuni Tribal Fair** includes an arts-and-crafts show, food booths and competition dancing.

Albuquerque and Central New Mexico   As the growing season reaches its peak, the Santo Domingo Pueblo observes the **Fiesta de Santo Domingo** with one of the most spectacular Indian ceremonials in the Southwest—a huge corn dance in the streets and narrow plazas of this ancient village. Corn dances are also held at Jemez Pueblo on the **Fiesta de Nuestra Señora de Los Angeles**, at Acoma Pueblo on the **Fiesta de San Lorenzo**, at Zia and

Laguna pueblos on the **Fiesta de San Antonio** and at Isleta Pueblo on the **Fiesta de San Augustín**. The **Zuni Tribal Fair** includes a rodeo, food booths and competition dancing.

SEPTEMBER **Northeastern Arizona** The **Navajo Nation Fair** in Window Rock has carnival rides, a rodeo, horse races, dance competitions, a pretty-baby contest, and a wonderful arts-and-crafts pavilion.
Santa Fe Area San Ildefonso Pueblo has a corn dance on the **Fiesta de Navidad de Santa María**. The Jicarilla Apache nation joins in social dances, a rodeo and a powwow at the **Stone Lake Fiesta (Go-jii-ya)** in Dulce.
Taos and the Enchanted Circle Taos Pueblo celebrates the **Fiesta de San Geronimo** with buffalo, Comanche and corn dances, a trade fair, foot races and a pole climb.
Albuquerque and Central New Mexico Harvest dances are held at Acoma Pueblo on the **Fiesta de San Estevan**, at Isleta Pueblo on the **Fiesta de San Agustín**, and at Laguna Pueblo on the **Fiesta de Navidad de la Santa María** and the **Fiesta de San José**.
Southwestern Colorado The Southern Ute and Ute Mountain tribes sponsor the **Council Tree Powwow & Cultural Festival** in Delta.

OCTOBER **South Central Arizona** Mesa is the site of the intertribal **Mesa Pow Wow**.
Santa Fe Area A corn or elk dance marks the **Fiesta de San Francisco** at Nambe Pueblo.
Northwestern New Mexico The **Shiprock Navajo Nation Fair**, the oldest of Navajo traditional fairs, features a parade, traditional dances, social song and dance contests, arts and crafts, a carnival, a rodeo and beauty pageants.
Albuquerque and Central New Mexico Laguna Pueblo observes the **Fiesta de Santa Margarita y Santa María** with harvest and social dances. The **Jemez Pueblo Open-Air Market** features food, arts and crafts.

NOVEMBER **Santa Fe Area** Tesuque Pueblo celebrates the **Fiesta de San Diego** with various dances. Jemez Pueblo observes the day with dances and a trade fair.

DECEMBER **Southern Arizona** The Yaqui Indian Reservation on the outskirts of Tucson marks the **Fiesta de Nuestra Señora de Guadalupe** with an 18-hour-long observance that includes masked dancers and processions.
Throughout New Mexico The **Fiesta de Nuestra Señora de Guadalupe** is celebrated at Tesuque, Pojoaque, Santa Clara and Jemez Pueblos with various dances. All New Mexico pueblos hold

tribal **Christmas dances** on the 24th or 25th, often featuring masked Matachines dances that depict the Puebloans' first contact with Europeans.

For free visitor information packets including maps and current details on special events, lodging and camping, contact a visitors center or tourism board. As well as large cities, most small towns have chambers of commerce or visitor information centers. Many of them are listed in *Hidden Southwest* under the appropriate regions. Tourist information centers are usually not open on weekends.

Before You Go

VISITORS CENTERS

Travel information on Arizona is available from the **Arizona Office of Tourism**. ~ 1110 West Washington Street, Suite 155, Phoenix, AZ 85007; 602-364-3700, 866-275-5816; www.arizona guide.com.

For New Mexico, contact the **New Mexico Department of Tourism**. ~ 491 Old Santa Fe Trail, Santa Fe, NM 87503; 800-545-2070, 800-733-6396; www.newmexico.org.

In Utah, you can write or call the **Utah Travel Council**. ~ Council Hall/Capitol Hill, 300 North State Street, Salt Lake City, UT 84114; 801-538-1030, 800-200-1160; www.utah.com.

The **Colorado Tourism Office** provides information on Colorado. ~ 1625 Broadway, Suite 1700, Denver, CO 80202; 800-433-2656; www.colorado.com.

The old adage that you should take along twice as much money and half as much stuff as you think you'll need is sound advice as far as it goes, but bear in mind that in many parts of the Southwest you are unlikely to find a store selling anything more substantial than curios and beef jerky.

PACKING

Southwesterners are casual in their dress and expect the same of visitors. Restaurants with dress codes are few and far between. Even if you attend a fancy $100-a-plate fundraiser or go out for a night at the opera, you'll find that a coat and tie or evening gown and heels instantly brand you as a tourist. Chic apparel in these parts is more likely to mean a Western-cut suit, ostrich hide boots and a bolo tie with a flashy turquoise-and-silver slide, or for women, a fiesta dress with a concho belt, long-fringed moccasins and a squash blossom necklace—all fairly expensive items that you may never have an occasion to wear back home. Relax. Sporty, comfortable clothing will pass practically anywhere in the Southwest.

When packing clothes, plan to dress in layers. Temperatures can turn hot or cold in a flash at any time of year. During the course of a single vacation day, you can expect to start wearing a heavy jacket, a sweater or flannel shirt and a pair of slacks or

Text continued on page 30.

People of the Southwest

The population of the Southwest is often called "tricultural"—Indian, Spanish and Anglo. Each of the three cultures has been an enemy to the others in centuries past, yet all live in harmony as neighbors today. Through centuries of life in close proximity, and despite persistent attempts by both Spanish and Anglos to assimilate the Indian people, each group proudly maintains its cultural identity while respecting the others. The resulting tricultural balance is truly unique to the region.

All three cultural groups share freely in each other's ways. For example, Southwestern cooking blends traditional Pueblo foods—blue corn, beans and squash—with green chile and cooking techniques imported by early Spanish colonists from the Aztecs of central Mexico, and the result is a staple in Anglo kitchens. The distinctive architecture of the desert uses adobe bricks, of Moorish origin and brought to the New World by the Spanish, while the architectural style derives from ancient pueblos and incorporates refinements Anglos brought west by railroad.

An Anglo, in local parlance, is anyone who comes from English-speaking America. Anglos first came to the Southwest less than 150 years ago, after the end of the Mexican War, and are still a minority group in many parts today. Newcomers are often surprised to learn that Americans of Jewish, Japanese and African ancestry, among others, are referred to as Anglos. Many Anglos in the more remote parts of the Southwest, from traditional Mormons in rural Utah to residents of old-fashioned hippie communes and artists' colonies in the mountains of New Mexico, hold to ways of life that are a far cry from modern mainstream America.

The Spanish residents of New Mexico trace their ancestry back to the pioneer era around the year 1600—the time of Don Quixote, of the Spanish Inquisition, of the conquest of the New World by the Spanish Armada. Today, the Spanish remain the dominant political and cultural force in many parts of New Mexico, and travelers can still find isolated mountain villages where many aspects of everyday life remain unchanged since the 17th century. Mexican immigration in the 20th century has created a separate Hispanic subculture in southern New Mexico and Arizona.

Visitors today have little opportunity to experience the uniqueness of such tribes as the Apache, Ute, Paiute and other nomadic tribes for whom confinement to reservations has meant adopting conventional ways of rural life. But among groups such as the Pueblo and Navajo people, who still occupy their traditional homelands, the old ways are still very much alive.

The Pueblo people who live along the Rio Grande in Isleta, Santo Domingo, Cochiti, Tesuque, San Ildefonso, Santa Clara, Taos and other Indian communities are descendants of the Ancestral Pueblo people who built the impressive castlelike compounds at literally thousands of sites such as those we know as Chaco Canyon, Bandelier, Pecos and Salinas. Although they have lived in close contact with Spanish and Anglo neighbors for centuries, the Rio Grande Pueblo people have carefully guarded their own cultural identity. They often have Spanish names and attend services at mission churches, yet they observe Catholic feast days with sacred dances and kiva ceremonies that reach back to pre-Columbian antiquity. While most Pueblo Indians speak English, they converse among themselves in the dialect of their particular pueblo—Tewa, Tiwa, Towa or Keresan.

The more isolated pueblos of western New Mexico and northeastern Arizona retain their own distinctive cultures. The Acoma people, thought to be descendants of the Mesa Verde Ancestral Pueblo people, practice secret rites that are closed to outsiders. The people of Zuni, who speak a language unrelated to any other Indian group and may be the heirs of the Mimbres who lived in southern New Mexico, follow the ancient kachina religion, becoming embodiments of nature's forces in strange, colorful blessing ceremonies. The Hopi people, whose Sinagua ancestors once lived throughout central Arizona from the Grand Canyon to the Verde Valley, have banned non-Indian visitors from many of their religious ceremonies because of their objections to the publication of various books sensationalizing their snake and eagle dances and their ancient tradition of prophecies.

Nowhere is the blending of cultures more evident than among the Navajo, the largest Indian tribe in the United States. The roots of their religious traditions stretch far into the past, and their hogan dwellings originated in the frozen northlands from which they came. Since arriving in the Southwest in the 1400s, they have borrowed from their neighbors to create their own unique culture. They learned to grow corn and weave textiles from the Pueblo people, and to herd sheep and ride horses from the Spanish. Early Anglo traders helped them develop their "traditional" art forms, rugs and silver jewelry. Even the more modern aspects of Navajo life—pickup trucks, satellite dishes, blue jeans—are not so much signs of assimilation into the white man's world as of the continuing evolution of a uniquely Navajo way of life.

jeans, peeling down to a T-shirt and shorts as the day warms up, then putting the extra layers back on soon after the sun goes down.

Other essentials to pack or buy along the way include a good sunscreen and high-quality sunglasses. If you are planning to camp in the mountains during the summer months, you'll be glad you brought mosquito repellent. Umbrellas are considered an oddity in the Southwest. When it rains, as it sometimes does though rarely for long, the approved means of keeping cold water from running down the back of your neck is a cowboy hat.

For outdoor activities, tough-soled hiking boots are more comfortable than running shoes on rocky terrain. Even RV travelers and those who prefer to spend most nights in motels may want to take along a backpacking tent and sleeping bag for irresistible urges to stay out under star-spangled Southwestern skies. A canteen, first-aid kit, flashlight and other routine camping gear are also likely to come in handy. Cycling enthusiasts should bring their own bikes. Especially when it comes to mountain biking, there are a lot more great places to ride than there are towns where you can find bicycles for rent. The same goes for boating, golf and other activities that call for special equipment.

If you're the kind of person who likes to pick up souvenirs for free in the form of unusual stones, pine cones and the like, take along some plastic bags for hauling treasures. A camera, of course, is essential for capturing your travel experience; of equal importance is a good pair of binoculars, which let you explore distant landscapes from scenic overlooks. And don't, for heaven's sake, forget your copy of *Hidden Southwest*.

LODGING   Lodgings in the Southwest run the gamut from tiny one-room mountain cabins to luxurious hotels that blend Indian pueblo architecture with contemporary elegance. Bed and breakfasts can be found not only in chic destinations like Santa Fe and Sedona but also in such unlikely locales as former ghost towns and the outskirts of Indian reservations. They come in all types, sizes and price ranges. Typical of the genre are lovingly restored old mansions comfortably furnished with period decor, usually with under a dozen rooms. Some bed and breakfasts, however, are guest cottages or rooms in nice suburban homes, while others are larger establishments, approaching hotel size, of the type sometimes referred to as country inns.

The abundance of motels in towns along all major highway routes presents a range of choices, from name-brand motor inns to traditional mom-and-pop establishments that have endured for half a century since motels were invented. Older motels along main truck routes, especially interstate Route 40, offer some of the lowest room rates to be found anywhere in the United States today.

At the other end of the price spectrum, the height of self-indulgent vacationing is to be found at upscale resorts in some destinations such as Tucson, Sedona, Ruidoso and Santa Fe. These resorts offer riding stables, golf courses, tennis courts, fine dining, live entertainment and exclusive shops on the premises so that guests can spend their entire holidays without leaving the grounds—a boon for celebrities seeking a few days' rest and relaxation away from the public eye, but a very expensive way to miss out on experiencing the real Southwest.

Other lodgings throughout the region offer a different kind of personality. Many towns—preserved historic districts like Tombstone as well as larger communities like Durango and Flagstaff—have historic hotels dating back before the turn of the 20th century. Some of them have been lavishly restored to far surpass their original Victorian elegance. Others may lack the polished antique decor and sophisticated ambience but make up for it in their authentic feel. These places give visitors a chance to spice up their vacation experience by spending the night where lawman Wyatt Earp or novelist Zane Grey once slept and awakening to look out their window onto a Main Street that has changed surprisingly little since the days of the Old West.

Whatever your preference and budget, you can probably find something to suit your taste with the help of the regional chapters in this book. Remember, rooms can be scarce and prices may rise during the peak season, which is summer throughout most of the region and winter in low-lying desert communities such as Phoenix, Scottsdale and Tucson. Travelers planning to visit a place in peak season should either make advance reservations or arrive early in the day, before the No Vacancy signs start lighting up. Those who plan to stay in Santa Fe, Sedona, Grand Canyon National Park or Mesa Verde National Park at any time of year are wise to make lodging reservations well ahead of time.

Accommodations in this book are organized by region and classified according to price. Rates referred to are high-season rates, so if you are looking for off-season bargains, it's good to inquire. *Budget* lodgings generally run less than $70 per night for

LODGING IN THE NATIONAL PARKS

Both rims of the Grand Canyon, as well as Bryce Canyon and Zion, have classic, rustic-elegant lodges built during the early years of the 20th century. Though considerably more expensive than budget motel rooms, the national park lodges are moderate in price and well worth it in terms of ambience and location. Reservations should be made far in advance.

two people and are satisfactory and clean but modest. *Moderate* hotels range from $70 to $110; what they have to offer in the way of luxury will depend on where they are located, but they generally offer larger rooms and more attractive surroundings. At *deluxe*-priced accommodations, you can expect to spend between $110 and $180 for a homey bed and breakfast or a double in a hotel or resort. In hotels of this price you'll generally find spacious rooms, a fashionable lobby, a restaurant and often a group of shops. *Ultra-deluxe* facilities, priced above $180, are a region's finest, offering all the amenities of a deluxe hotel plus plenty of extras.

Room rates vary as much with locale as with quality. Some of the trendier destinations have no rooms at all in the budget price range. In other communities—especially those along interstate highways where rates are set with truck drivers in mind—every motel falls into the budget category, even though accommodations may range from $19.95 at run-down, spartan places to $45 or so at the classiest motor inn in town. The price categories listed in this book are relative, designed to show you where to get the most out of your travel budget, however large or small it may be.

DINING

Restaurants seem to be one of the main industries in some parts of the Southwest. Santa Fe, New Mexico, for example, has approximately 200 restaurants in a city of just 63,000 people. While the specialty cuisine throughout most of the Southwest consists of variations on Mexican and Indian food, you'll find many restaurants catering to customers whose tastes don't include hot chile peppers.

A number of local restaurants offer "New Southwestern" menus featuring offbeat dishes—green-chile tempura, snow-crab enchiladas—using local ingredients.

Within a particular chapter, restaurants are categorized by region, with each restaurant entry describing the establishment according to price. All serve lunch and dinner unless otherwise noted. Dinner entrées at *budget* restaurants usually cost $8 or less. The ambience is informal, service usually speedy and the crowd often a local one. *Moderately* priced restaurants range between $8 and $16 at dinner; surroundings are casual but pleasant, the menu offers more variety and the pace is usually slower. *Deluxe* establishments tab their entrées from $16 to $24; cuisines may be simple or sophisticated, depending on the location, but the decor is plusher and the service more personalized. *Ultra-deluxe* dining rooms, where entrées begin at $24, are often the gourmet places; here cooking has become a fine art and the service should be impeccable.

Some restaurants change hands often and are occasionally closed in low seasons. Efforts have been made in this book to include places with established reputations for good eating. Breakfast and lunch menus vary less in price from restaurant to restaurant than evening dinners.

The mountains and deserts of the Southwest are clearly the major sightseeing attractions for many visitors. This is a rugged area and there are some important things to remember when driving on the side roads throughout the region. First and foremost, believe it if you see a sign indicating four-wheel drive only. These roads can be very dangerous in a car without high ground clearance and the extra traction afforded by four-wheel drive—and there may be no safe place to turn around if you get stuck. During rainy periods dirt roads may become impassable muck. And in winter, heavy snows necessitate the use of snow tires or chains on main roads, while side roads may or may not be maintained at all.

Some side roads will take you far from civilization so be sure to have a full radiator and tank of gas. Carry spare fuel, water and food. In winter, it is always wise to travel with a shovel and blankets in your car. Should you become stuck, local people are usually quite helpful about offering assistance to stranded vehicles, but in case no one else is around, for extended backcountry driving, a CB radio or a cell phone would not be a bad idea.

Any place that has cowboys and Indians, rocks to climb and limitless room to run is bound to be a hit with youngsters. Plenty of family adventures are available in the Southwest, from manmade attractions to experiences in the wild. A few guidelines will help make travel with children a pleasure.

Book reservations in advance, making sure that the places you stay accept children. Many bed and breakfasts do not. If you need a crib or extra cot, arrange for it ahead of time. A travel agent can be of help here, as well as with most other travel plans.

If you are traveling by air, try to reserve bulkhead seats where there is plenty of room. Take along extras you may need, such as diapers, changes of clothing, snacks and toys or small games. When traveling by car, be sure to take along the extras, too. Make sure you have plenty of water and juices to drink; dehydration can be a subtle but serious problem. Most towns, as well as some national parks, have stores that carry diapers, baby food, snacks and other essentials, though they usually close early. Larger towns often have all-night grocery or convenience stores.

A first-aid kit is a must for any trip. Along with adhesive bandages, antiseptic cream and something to stop itching, include any medicines your pediatrician might recommend to treat allergies, colds, diarrhea or any chronic problems your child may have. Southwestern sunshine is intense. Take extra care for the first few days. Children's skin is usually more tender than adult skin and severe sunburn can happen before you realize it. A hat is a good idea, along with a reliable sunblock.

DRIVING NOTES

TRAVELING WITH CHILDREN

GAY & LESBIAN TRAVELERS

The unique beauty of the Southwest is appealing to many: the wide open spaces stretching for miles and miles invite people who are looking to get away from it all. It's a region that gives people a lot of space, literally, and encourages you to do your own thing, which allows gay or lesbian travelers to feel comfortable here. Whether you're interested in exploring the area's magnificent scenery, sightseeing in the cosmopolitan cities, or just relaxing by the pool, the Southwest has much to offer.

You'll find gay and lesbian communities in a few of the bigger cities such as Santa Fe and Albuquerque, New Mexico. The region also boasts the gay and lesbian hotspot of Phoenix, Arizona, to which this book has dedicated a special "gay-specific" section. Phoenix is home to a large gay and lesbian community and there's a growing number of gay-friendly bars, nightclubs and restaurants.

Gay and lesbian publications providing entertainment listings and happenings are available in some of the larger gay enclaves. *Echo Magazine* is a free biweekly that is distributed in cafés, bookstores and bars. In it you'll find news and entertainment offerings in Phoenix. ~ P.O. Box 16630, Phoenix, AZ 85011; 602-266-0550, 888-324-6624; www.echomag.com. In New Mexico, you can pick up the free monthly *Out! Magazine* (not to be confused with the national magazine called *Out*) at bookstores throughout the state. ~ e-mail mail@outmagazine.com. *Weekly Alibi*, a free, alternative newspaper, offers entertainment listings specifically for the Albuquerque area. You can pick up a copy almost anywhere in Albuquerque—supermarkets, bookstores, city buildings—as well as in Santa Fe, Taos and Rio Rancho. ~ 2118 Central Avenue Southeast, Suite 151, Albuquerque, NM 87106; 505-346-0660; www.alibi.com.

WOMEN TRAVELING ALONE

Traveling solo grants an independence and freedom different from that of traveling with a partner, but single travelers are more vulnerable to crime and should take additional precautions.

It's unwise to hitchhike and probably best to avoid inexpensive accommodations on the outskirts of town; the money saved

WHY IS THE SKY BLUE?

Many national parks and monuments offer special activities designed just for children. Visitors center film presentations and rangers' campfire slide shows can help inform children about the natural history of the Southwest and head off some questions. However, kids tend to find a lot more things to wonder about than adults have answers for. To be as prepared as possible, seize every opportunity to learn more.

does not outweigh the risk. Bed and breakfasts, youth hostels and YWCAs are generally your safest bet for lodging, and they also foster an environment ideal for bonding with fellow travelers.

Keep all valuables well-hidden and hold onto cameras and purses. Avoid late-night treks or strolls through undesirable parts of town, but if you find yourself in this situation, continue walking with a confident air until you reach a safe haven. A fierce scowl never hurts.

These hints should by no means deter you from seeking out adventure. Wherever you go, stay alert, use your common sense and trust your instincts.

If you are hassled or threatened in some way, never be afraid to yell for assistance. It's a good idea to carry change for a phone call and to know the number to call in case of emergency. For more hints, get a copy of *Safety and Security for Women Who Travel* (Travelers Tales, 1998). Most areas have 24-hour hotlines for victims of rape and violent crime. In Tucson, call the **Southern Arizona Center Against Sexual Assault** (SACASA). ~ 1632 North Country Club Road, Tucson, AZ 85716; 520-327-1171, 24-hour hotline 520-327-7273, 800-400-1001. Santa Fe's **Rape Crisis Center** is staffed around the clock. ~ P.O. Box 6484, Santa Fe, NM 87502; 800-721-7273. The **Women's Resource Center** on the University of New Mexico campus offers referrals and counseling. Closed Saturday and Sunday. ~ 1160 Mesa Vista Hall, UNM, Albuquerque, NM 87131; 505-277-3716. Or you can call the **Albuquerque Rape Crisis Center**. ~ 1025 Hermosa Street Southeast, Albuquerque, NM 87108; 505-266-7711.

SENIOR TRAVELERS

The Southwest is a hospitable place for older vacationers, many of whom turn into part-time or full-time residents thanks to the dry, pleasant climate and the friendly senior citizen communities that have developed in southern Arizona and, on a smaller scale, in other parts of the region. The large number of national parks and monuments in the Southwest means that persons age 62 and older can save considerable money with a Golden Age Passport, which allows free admission. Apply for one in person at any national park unit that charges an entrance fee. Many private sightseeing attractions also offer significant discounts for seniors.

The **American Association of Retired Persons** (AARP) offers membership to anyone over 50. AARP's benefits include travel discounts with a number of firms. ~ 601 E Street NW, Washington, DC 20049; 800-424-3410; www.aarp.org.

Elderhostel offers educational courses that are all-inclusive packages at colleges and universities. In the Southwest, Elderhostel courses are available in numerous locations including: in Arizona—Flagstaff, Nogales, Phoenix, Prescott and Tucson; and in New Mexico—Albuquerque, Las Cruces, Santa Fe, Silver City and Taos. Courses are also offered in Durango, Colorado, and Cedar City, Utah. ~ 11 Avenue de Lafayette, Boston, MA 02111; 877-426-8056; www.elderhostel.org.

Be extra careful about health matters. In the changeable climate of the Southwest, seniors are more at risk of suffering hypothermia. High altitudes may present a risk to persons with heart or respiratory conditions; ask your physician for advice when planning your trip. Many tourist destinations in the region are a long way from any hospital or other health care facility.

In addition to the medications you ordinarily use, it's a good idea to bring along the prescriptions for obtaining more. Consider carrying a medical record with you, including your history and current medical status as well as your doctor's name, phone number and address. Make sure that your insurance covers you while you are away from home.

DISABLED TRAVELERS   All of the Southwestern states are striving to make public areas fully accessible to persons with disabilities. Parking spaces and restroom facilities for the handicapped are provided according to both state law and national park regulations. National parks and monuments also post signs that tell which trails are wheelchair-accessible.

There are many organizations offering information for travelers with disabilities, including the **Society for Accessible Travel & Hospitality** (SATH), 347 5th Avenue, Suite 610, New York, NY 10016, 212-447-7284, www.sath.org; and the **Moss Rehab ResourceNet**, MossRehab Hospital, 1200 West Tabor Road, Philadelphia, PA 19141, 215-456-9600, www.mossresourcenet.org.

For general travel advice, contact **Travelin' Talk**, a networking organization. ~ P.O. Box 1796, Wheat Ridge, CO 80034; 303-232-2979; www.travelintalk.net. Its sister company, **Access-Able Travel Source**, provides traveling information on the web: www.access-able.com.

FOREIGN TRAVELERS   **Passports and Visas**   Most foreign visitors need a passport and tourist visa to enter the United States. Contact your nearest U.S. Embassy or Consulate well in advance to obtain a visa and to check on any other entry requirements.

Customs Requirements   Foreign travelers are allowed to carry in the following: 200 cigarettes (1 carton), 50 cigars or 2 kilograms (4.4 pounds) of smoking tobacco; one liter of alcohol for personal use only (you must be 21 years of age to bring in alcohol); and US$100 worth of duty-free gifts that can include an additional quantity of 100 cigars. You may bring in any amount of currency, but must fill out a form if you bring in over US $10,000. Carry any prescription drugs in clearly marked containers. (You may have to produce a written prescription or doctor's statement for the custom's officer.) Meat or meat products, seeds, plants, fruits and narcotics are not allowed to be brought into the United States. Contact the United States Customs Service for further information. ~ 1300 Pennsylvania Avenue NW, Washington, DC 20229; 202-927-1700; www.cus toms.treas.gov.

Legends aren't always as glamorous as they seem: Apparently, before moving to Tombstone, Doc Holliday operated a dental office.

Driving   If you plan to rent a car, an international driver's license should be obtained before arriving in the United States. Some car rental agencies require both a foreign license and an international driver's license. Many also require a lessee to be at least 25 years of age; all require a major credit card. Seat belts are mandatory for the driver and all passengers. Children under the age of five or under 40 pounds should be in the back seat in approved child-safety restraints.

Currency   United States money is based on the dollar. Bills generally come in denominations of $1, $5, $10, $20, $50 and $100. Every dollar is divided into 100 cents. Coins are the penny (1 cent), nickel (5 cents), dime (10 cents) and quarter (25 cents). Half-dollar and dollar coins are rarely used. You may not use foreign currency to purchase goods and services in the United States. Consider buying traveler's checks in dollar amounts. You may also use credit cards affiliated with an American company such as Interbank, Barclay Card, VISA and American Express.

Electricity and Electronics   Electric outlets use currents of 110 volts, 60 cycles. To operate appliances made for other electrical systems, you need a transformer or other adapter. Travelers who use laptop computers for telecommunication should be aware that modem configurations for U.S. telephone systems may be different from their European counterparts. Similarly, the U.S. format for videotapes is different from that in Europe; National Park Service visitors centers and other stores that sell souvenir videos often have them available in European format on request.

Weights and Measures   The United States uses the English system of weights and measures. American units and their metric equivalents are: 1 inch = 2.5 centimeters; 1 foot (12 inches) = 0.3 meter; 1 yard (3 feet) = 0.9 meter; 1 mile (5280 feet) = 1.6 kilometers; 1 ounce = 28 grams; 1 pound (16 ounces) = 0.45 kilogram; 1 quart (liquid) = 0.9 liter.

RV or tent camping is a great way to tour the Southwest. Besides saving substantial sums of money, campers enjoy the freedom to watch sunsets from beautiful places, spend nights under spectacularly starry skies and wake up to find themselves in lovely surroundings that few hotels can match.

Outdoor Adventures

CAMPING

Text continued on page 40.

Desert Survival

ar travel can be risky in some desert areas described in this guidebook simply because they are so remote. Once you venture beyond paved, well-used roads, if your vehicle breaks down it may be days before another human being comes along. In such a situation, a little survival know-how can save your life.

• Most important, carry more drinking water in your vehicle than you can imagine needing. In hot desert conditions, a human being may require two gallons of water per day to stay alive. Dehydration is the major threat to survival.

• When stranded in the desert, do not drink beer or other alcoholic beverages. Alcohol actually makes your body dehydrate more quickly. Taking small amounts of salt with your water will help prevent dehydration.

• Water is often more plentiful in the desert than it appears. Birds, especially doves, visit small waterholes frequently, and you can follow them there. Green vegetation indicates that water lies just below the surface, where you can collect it by digging a hole and straining it. Water from natural sources must be distilled or purified by boiling or by water purification tablets. Not all tablets protect against giardia, the most common organic contaminant in desert areas.

If water does not support green plants or algae, it may contain poisonous alkali and can only be made safe by distillation. You can distill water with a simple solar still made from a sheet of plastic such as the rain fly for a backpacking tent. Dig a hole. Place a can, jar or other empty container in the center of it, and lay the plastic over the top. Put rocks on the plastic around the hole to hold it in place, then place a stone in the center of the plastic, over the container. As the sun heats the air beneath the plastic, water will evaporate from the bottom of the hole. It will condense on the underside of the plastic and run down to the lowest point, where it will drip into the container.

• Juice from the red fruit of the prickly pear cactus can provide lifesaving moisture—and it tastes good. (Be careful of the clusters of tiny spines on the outside of the fruit when cutting it open.) Another storehouse of water is the soft flesh inside a barrel cactus. Damaging cacti on federal land is illegal, however, so resort to chopping open a barrel cactus only in desperate circumstances.

• Stay with your vehicle unless someone in your party needs immediate medical attention and you know that help is nearby. If you must walk out in search of help, leave a note on the windshield telling your travel route and direction and the time you left.

• Stay in the shade during midday heat: inside your vehicle with the windows rolled down, under the vehicle or under a lean-to made with a tarp or blanket. If you hide from the hot sun in the shade of a rock formation, bear in mind that rattlesnakes often have the same idea.

• Use any means possible to attract attention. Lay out bright-colored towels, clothing or camping gear in a giant "X"—the international emergency signal for "stranded"—where it can be seen from aircraft. Use oily rags or green leafy brush to build a smokey signal fire. Watch for the dust plumes of distant vehicles and flash sunlight from a mirror in their direction. Keep the hood of your vehicle up at all times so that anyone who sees you can tell immediately that you're in trouble.

• More and more backroad travelers carry cellular phones in case of emergency. Although these phones don't work in the most remote areas or near the huge power lines that run from dams on the Colorado River, they do work more places than not. A CB radio is rarely helpful.

Most towns have commercial RV parks of some sort, and long-term mobile-home parks often rent spaces to RVers by the night. But unless you absolutely need cable television, none of these places can compete with the wide array of public campgrounds available in national and state parks, monuments and forests. Federal campground sites are typically less developed; only the biggest ones have electrical hookups. National forest campgrounds don't have hookups, while state park campgrounds just about always do. The largest public campgrounds offer tent camping loops separate from RV loops and backcountry camping areas offer the option of spending the night in the primeval Southwest.

With the exception of both rims of the Grand Canyon, where campsite reservations are booked up to 56 days in advance by calling 800-365-2267 (credit cards only), you won't find much in the way of sophisticated reservation systems in the Southwest. The general rule in public campgrounds is still first-come, first-served, even though they fill up practically every night in peak season. To secure a campsite during peak season, travel in the morning to reach your intended campground by early afternoon. Some may find it more convenient to keep a single location for as much as a week and explore surrounding areas on day trips.

For listings of state parks in Arizona with camping facilities and reservation information, contact **Arizona State Parks**. ~ 1300 West Washington Street, Phoenix, AZ 85007; 602-542-4174; www.pr.state.az.us.

The New Mexico State Park and Recreation Division has information on state parks in New Mexico open for camping. ~ P.O. Box 1147, Santa Fe, NM 87504; 888-667-2757; www.nmparks.com.

Fees and regulations for camping in Utah are available from the **Utah Division of Parks and Recreation**. ~ 1594 West North Temple, Salt Lake City, UT 84114; 800-322-3770; www.stateparks.utah.gov.

PARK PASSPORT

Frequent national park visitors should inquire about the interagency **America the Beautiful Pass**, formerly called the Golden Eagle Pass. For just $80, it allows entrance to all of the federally managed units in the United States, replacing other passes such as the National Parks Pass and Golden Eagle Pass. With fees at major parks now in the neighborhood of $20–$25, it's one of the best purchases you'll make during your visit. If you buy it at the entrance station to your favorite park, that facility will financially benefit from the sale. Passes may be also be purchased by calling 888-275-8747 or logging on to http://store.usgs.gov/pass.

To obtain information on camping in Colorado, contact **Colorado State Parks.** ~ 1313 Sherman Street, Suite 618, Denver, CO 80203; 303-866-3437, 800-678-2267; www.parks.state.co.us.

Information on camping in the national forests in New Mexico and Arizona is available from **National Forest Service–Southwestern Region.** ~ 333 Broadway SE, Albuquerque, NM 87102; 505-842-3292; www.fs.fed.us/r3. For national forests in Utah, contact **National Forest Service–Intermountain Region.** ~ 324 25th Street, Ogden, UT 84401; 801-625-5306; www.fs.fed.us/r4. For those in Colorado, contact **National Forest Service–Rocky Mountain Region.** ~ 740 Simms Street, Lakewood, CO 80225; 303-275-5350, 800-280-2267; www.fs.fed.us/r2. Camping and reservation information for parks and monuments is available from the parks and monuments listed in this book or from **National Park Service–Intermountain Support Office.** ~ 1100 Old Santa Fe Trail, Santa Fe, NM 87501; 505-988-6100; www.nps.gov.

Many Indian lands have public campgrounds, which usually don't appear in campground directories. For information, contact: **Navajo Parks and Recreation.** ~ P.O. Box 2520, Window Rock, AZ 86515; 928-871-6647. **Hopi Tribal Headquarters.** ~ P.O. Box 123, Kykotsmovi, AZ 86039; 928-734-2441. **Havasupai Tourist Enterprise.** ~ P.O. Box 160, Supai, AZ 86435; 928-448-2237. The **White Mountain Apache Game and Fish Department.** ~ P.O. Box 220, Whiteriver, AZ 85941; 928-338-4385. The **Mescalero Apache Tribe.** ~ P.O. Box 227, Mescalero, NM 88340; 505-671-4494. **Zuni Pueblo.** ~ P.O. Box 339, Zuni, NM 87327; 505-782-4481.

Also see the "Parks" sections in each chapter to discover where camping is available.

PERMITS

Tent camping is allowed in the backcountry of all national forests here except in a few areas where signs are posted prohibiting it. You may need a permit to hike or camp in national forest wilderness areas, so contact specific forests for more information. Ranger stations provide trail maps and advice on current conditions and fire regulations. In dry seasons, emergency rules may prohibit campfires and sometimes ban cigarette smoking, with stiff enforcement penalties.

For backcountry hiking in national parks and monuments, you must first obtain a permit from the ranger at the front desk in the visitors center. The permit procedure is simple and free. It helps park administrators measure the impact on sensitive ecosystems and distribute use evenly among major trails to prevent overcrowding.

BOATING

Most of the large desert lakes along the Colorado, Rio Grande and other major rivers are administered as National Recreation

Areas and supervised by the U.S. Army Corps of Engineers. Federal boating safety regulations that apply to these lakes may vary slightly from state regulations. Indian reservations have separate rules for boating on tribal lakes. More significant than any differences between federal, state and tribal regulations are the local rules in force for any particular lake. Ask for applicable boating regulations at a local marina or fishing supply store or use the addresses and phone numbers listed in "Parks" or other sections of each chapter in this book to contact the headquarters for lakes you plan to visit.

Boats, from small power boats to houseboats, can be rented for 24 hours or longer at marinas on several of the larger lakes. At most marinas, you can get a boat on short notice if you come on a weekday, since much of their business comes from local weekend recreation. The exception is Lake Powell, where houseboats and other craft are booked far in advance. Take a look at Chapter Fifteen (Southeastern Utah) for details on how to arrange for a Lake Powell boat trip.

River rafting is a very popular sport in several parts of the Southwest, notably on the Chama River and Rio Grande in northern New Mexico, the Green River in southern Utah and the Animas River near Durango, Colorado. The ultimate whitewater rafting experience, of course, is a trip through the Grand Canyon. Independent rafters are welcome, but because of the bulky equipment and specialized knowledge of river hazards involved, most adventurous souls stick with group trips offered by any of the many rafting companies located in Page, Flagstaff, Taos, Santa Fe, Moab and Durango. Rafters, as well as people using canoes, kayaks, windsurfers or inner tubes, are required by state and federal regulations to wear life jackets.

FISHING   In a land as arid as the Southwest, many residents have an irresistible fascination with water. During the warm months, lake shores and readily accessible portions of streams are often packed with anglers, especially on weekends. Vacationers can beat the crowds to some extent by planning their fishing days during the week.

Fish hatcheries in all four states keep busy stocking streams with trout, particularly rainbows, the most popular game fish throughout the West. Catch-and-release fly fishing is the rule in some popular areas such as the upper Pecos River near Santa Fe, allowing more anglers a chance at bigger fish. Be sure to inquire locally about eating the fish you catch, since some seemingly remote streams and rivers have contamination problems from old mines and mills.

The larger reservoirs offer an assortment of sport fish, including crappie, carp, white bass, smallmouth bass, largemouth bass and walleye pike. Striped bass, an ocean import, can run as large as 40 pounds, while catfish in the depths of dammed desert canyons sometimes attain mammoth proportions.

For copies of state fishing regulations, inquire at a local fishing supply store or marina. Information for Arizona is available from the **Arizona Game and Fish Department.** ~ 2221 West Greenway Road, Phoenix, AZ 85023; 602-942-3000; www.gfd.com. The **New Mexico Department of Game and Fish** can give regulations for New Mexico. ~ P.O. Box 25112, Santa Fe, NM 87507; 505-476-8000, 800-862-9310; www.gmfsh.state.nm.us. For rules in Utah, contact the **Utah Division of Wildlife Resources.** ~ 1594 West North Temple, Salt Lake City, UT 84114; 801-538-4700; www.wildlife.utah.com. Colorado's fishing regulation are available from the **Colorado Division of Wildlife.** ~ 6060 Broadway, Denver, CO 80216; 303-291-7533; www.wildlife.state.co.us.

State fishing licenses are required for fishing in national parks and national recreation areas, but not on Indian reservations, where daily permits are sold by the tribal governments. For more information about fishing on Indian lands, contact the tribal agencies listed in "Camping" above.

TWO

The Grand Canyon

Awesome. Magnificent. Breathtaking. It's easy to slip into hyperbole when trying to describe the Grand Canyon, but it's understandable. No matter how many spectacular landscapes you've seen in your lifetime, none can compare with this mighty chasm stretching across the northwest corner of Arizona.

The Grand Canyon comes as a surprise. Whether you approach the South Rim or the North Rim, the landscape gives no hint that the canyon is there until suddenly you find yourself on the rim looking into the chasm ten miles wide from rim to rim and a mile down to the Colorado River, winding silver through the canyon's inner depths. From anywhere along the rim, you can feel the vast, silent emptiness of the canyon and wonder at the sheer mass of the walls, striated into layer upon colorful layer of sandstone, limestone and shale.

More than five million years ago, the Colorado River began carving out this canyon that offers a panoramic look at the geologic history of the Southwest. Sweeping away sandstones and sediments, limestones and fossils, the river cut its way through Paleozoic and Precambrian formations. The layers of rock exposed by erosion on the walls of the Grand Canyon range from 1.7 million to 4.7 million years in age, the oldest exposed rock on Earth. By the time humankind arrived, the canyon extended nearly all the way down to schist, a basement formation.

The Grand Canyon is aptly named—being, perhaps, the grandest geological marvel of them all. It is as long as any mountain range in the Rockies and as deep as the highest of the Rocky Mountains are tall. For centuries, it posed the most formidable of all natural barriers to travel in the West, and to this day no road has ever penetrated the wilderness below the rim. No matter how many photographs you take, paintings you make or postcards you buy, the view from anywhere along the Grand Canyon rim can never be truly captured in two dimensions. Nor can the mind fully comprehend it; no matter how many times you have visited the Grand Canyon before, the view will always inspire the same awe as it did the first time you stood and gazed in wonder at the canyon's immensity and the silent grandeur of its massive cliffs.

The Grand Canyon extends east to west for some 277 miles, from the western boundary of the Navajo Indian Reservation to the vicinity of Lake Mead and the Nevada border. Only the highest section of each rim of the Grand Canyon is accessible by motor vehicle. Most of Grand Canyon National Park, both above and below the rim, is a designated wilderness area that can only be explored on foot or by river raft.

The South Rim and the North Rim are essentially separate destinations, more than 200 miles apart by road. For this reason, we've divided this chapter into five sections covering the developed national park areas on both rims as well as "The Arizona Strip." For the adventuresome, we've also included hiking possibilities in the canyon, as well as two lesser-known areas of the Grand Canyon that are challenging to reach—Toroweap Point in the Arizona Strip on the North Rim and the scenic area below the Indian village of Supai on the South Rim.

With more than 4.5 million visitors a year, the Grand Canyon is one of the most popular national parks in the United States. While many come to enjoy the panoramic vistas, others come to tackle the most challenging hiking trails in the country or to explore the narrow canyons and gorges by pack mule. Whatever reason you choose to visit the Grand Canyon, it will be worth it.

The South Rim

The South Rim is the most accessible area of the Grand Canyon. It's no wonder that you'll find most of the facilities here. The many trailheads leading into the canyon and along the rim make this a good place to start your Grand Canyon tour. *Note:* Many changes are expected in Grand Canyon National Park in the upcoming years. Road maps may become inaccurate so it is advisable to check with the park for updated information. In addition, fees may change.

SIGHTS

If you enter Grand Canyon National Park via the south entrance from Williams or Flagstaff, as most visitors do, you'll drive through **Tusayan**, about a mile south of the park entrance. The IMAX **Theater** in Tusayan shows films about the Grand Canyon on a seven-story, 82-foot-wide wraparound screen with six-track Dolby sound. These films can add an extra dimension to a Grand Canyon visit because they present river-rafting footage, aerial photography and closeup looks at places in the canyon that are hard to reach on foot. Admission. ~ Route 64; 928-638-2203, fax 928-638-2807; www.explorethecanyon.com.

Once inside the park's boundary, the route leads past **Mather Point** lookout and **Yavapai Observation Station**; both offer spectacular views of the canyon. There's a ranger on duty at Yavapai, and from this spot you can see Phantom Ranch, nearly a mile below, the Colorado River and the Suspension Bridge used by hikers of the Kaibab Trail to cross the river.

Grand Canyon Village serves as the commercial hub for the park. It boasts a number of lodges, a bank, a post office, a general store and the Backcountry Information Center. ~ 928-638-7875, 928-638-7644, fax 928-638-2125; www.thecanyon.com.

From the village you can reach **Canyon View Information Plaza**. There's no parking at the plaza, so you'll need to take a shuttle (during slower times of the year it is possible to park at Mather Point and walk to the plaza). Once there, you'll find a comprehensive visitors center where park rangers are on duty to answer questions, and maps and brochures about the park are available. Books about the Grand Canyon, American Indian cultures and related topics are for sale at the nearby Grand Canyon Association Bookstore. You can arrange bike rentals, view an exhibit about the natural and cultural history of the Grand Canyon and find out about ranger programs and audio-visual presentations. If you haven't already received a copy of the park newspaper, *The Grand Canyon Guide*, pick up a copy here. It's full of helpful information, including seasonal events, activities and park services. The plaza is open daily.

The **Rim Trail** is a paved pathway that extends along the edge of the canyon from Yavapai Observation Station, which is three-fourths of a mile east of the visitors center, to Maricopa Point, about three miles west of the center. Beyond Maricopa Point, the Rim Trail continues unpaved to Hermits Rest. Night and day, the Rim Trail is a busy, at times crowded, walkway leading past all the major historical structures on the South Rim. You can sit on a bench and gaze out over the canyon or, at night, gaze up at a blue-black sky glittering with a zillion stars.

Native stone and Oregon pine were the materials used by architect Charles Whittlesey to build the sprawling **El Tovar Hotel** in 1905. Named for an officer in the expedition led by the Spanish explorer Coronado, the rustic lodge was operated by the Fred Harvey Company. It's still considered to be one of the nation's great historic hotels.

Several of the historic buildings set along the canyon rim were built by Mary Colter, an architect hired by the Fred Harvey Company. **Hopi House**, Colter's first effort for Harvey, was built of stone and adobe to resemble a pueblo building. Inside, ceilings are thatched, and there are niches and corner fireplaces, elements that are typical of Hopi pueblo dwellings. Completed on New Year's Day, 1905, Hopi House was originally used as living quarters for Hopi who danced for guests in the evening.

Bright Angel Lodge is another Colter building, dating to 1935. Built on the site of Bright Angel Camp of tents and cabins, the lodge was intended to provide moderately priced accommodations for tourists. Colter incorporated a stone fireplace that represents the rock layers of the canyon. Colter's **Lookout Studio** was completed in 1914. Perched on the edge of the canyon, the studio

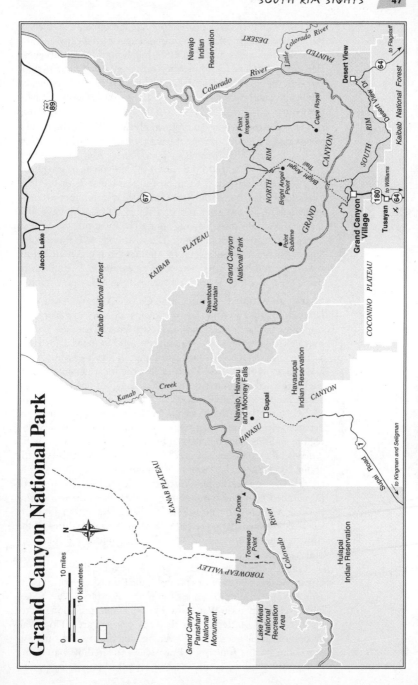

Grand Canyon National Park

was built of native stone profile to make it seem an extension of the canyon wall. It offers exceptional views of the canyon.

Kolb Studio was started in 1904 by photographers Ellsworth L. Kolb and Emery C. Kolb, who took pictures of mule passengers descending Bright Angel Trail. They built their studio at the trailhead. The brothers were the first to film a Grand Canyon river run.

HERMIT ROAD Hermit Road (formerly West Rim Drive) is open to private vehicles only during the winter months. But a free shuttle bus departs from West Rim Interchange, near Bright Angel Lodge. The drive clings to the rim of the canyon as it brings you to a series of overlooks, each more spectacular than the last. **Pima Point** offers one of the best canyon views, and from **Mohave Point** one of longest stretches of river is visible. (Mohave also serves as a good sunset-viewing spot.) The most popular spot to watch the sunset is **Hopi Point**. The road ends at **Hermits Rest**. Shuttle buses run about every 15 minutes from one hour before sunrise to one hour after sunset; it takes about 75 minutes to travel the entire loop if you don't get off the bus.

DESERT VIEW DRIVE From Grand Canyon Village, Desert View Drive (formerly East Rim Drive) extends 25 miles east along the rim to the park's east entrance at **Desert View**. There are several overlooks along the way—**Grandview, Moran** (named for landscape painter Thomas Moran) and **Lipan** (with views of the river and Unkar Rapids). **Yaki Point** (a favorite for watching the sunrise) is reached by shuttle only, which runs from one hour before sunrise to one hour after sunset.

The turnoff for the **Tusayan Museum and Ruins** comes up between Moran and Lipan points. Hopi ancestors inhabited the region, and this ruin, believed to be about 800 years old, is what remains of a hamlet of about 30 people who lived at the site for about 20 years. In the Hopi belief system, the canyon is said to contain the *sipapu*, the hole through which the Earth's first people climbed from the mountaintop of their previous world into this one. Visitors can tour the site by themselves or join a ranger-led walk. Signage along the path explains specific features of the construction and uses of the site. The small museum displays artifacts of ancient life along the rim.

From Desert View, the last stop before exiting the park (or the first if you enter at the east entrance), the Painted Desert is visible as is Navajo Mountain, some 90 miles away. Mary Colter built a multilevel observation **Watchtower** here, her interpretation of prehistoric towers scattered over the Four Corners area. Hopi wall decorations depict ceremonial paintings and designs. An observation room on the fourth level provides an incredible panorama of the surrounding landscape. Visitor information, restrooms and a general store are operated at Desert View, as is a service station (open seasonally).

For the adventuresome, an intriguing Grand Canyon experience that is only accessible by foot is found far downriver near the west end of the canyon. The **Havasu Trail** (10 miles), entirely within the Havasupai Indian Reservation, is reached by leaving the interstate at Seligman (westbound) or Kingman (eastbound) and driving to the Supai turnoff near Peach Springs. From there, the Supai Road (Indian Road 18) goes for 63 miles before it dead-ends and a foot trail descends 2000 feet in eight miles to the Indian village of **Supai,** where about 500 people live. All hikers must check in at the tourist office. From there, the main trail continues for about two more miles into Havasu Canyon, a side canyon from the Grand Canyon, which includes a series of three high waterfalls—75-foot **Navajo Falls,** 100-foot **Havasu Falls** and 200-foot **Mooney Falls**—with large pools that are ideal for swimming. There is a campground between Mooney Falls and Havasu, and from there the trail continues down to the Colorado River in the bottom of the Grand Canyon (day-use only). Whether you plan to stay in the campground or the modern lodge at Supai, advance reservations are essential. ~ For camping: Havasupai Tourist Enterprise, P.O. Box 160, Supai, AZ 86435; 928-448-2121, fax 928-448-2551.

◄ HIDDEN

LODGING

If you're planning a trip to the Grand Canyon it's important to make reservations for lodging early—at least a year in advance! The first thing to do is to write or call for a free Trip Planner offered by the National Park Service. It has information about accommodations, activities, itineraries, and dos and don'ts. ~ Trip Planner, Grand Canyon National Park, P.O. Box 129, Grand Canyon,

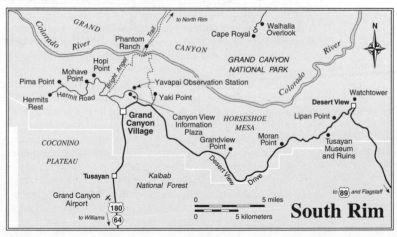

South Rim

AZ 86023; 928-638-7888, fax 928-638-7797; www.nps.gov/grca, e-mail grca_superintendent@nps.gov.

The South Rim offers many lodging choices. For information about South Rim accommodations or same-day reservations, call 928-638-2631. Reservations at any of them can be made up to 13 months in advance by writing to **Xanterra Parks & Resorts, Grand Canyon National Park Lodges.** ~ 14001 East Iliff Avenue, Suite 600, Aurora, CO 80014; 303-338-6000, 888-297-2757, fax 303-297-3175; www.grandcanyonlodges.com.

Top of the line is the **El Tovar Hotel.** Designed after European hunting lodges, El Tovar was built by the Fred Harvey Company in 1905 and some staff members still wear the traditional black-and-white uniforms of the famous "Harvey Girls" of that era. The lobby retains its original backwoods elegance, with a big fireplace, massive wood ceiling beams and dark-stained pine decor throughout. All have full baths, color televisions and telephones. ~ DELUXE TO ULTRA-DELUXE.

More affordable historic lodging is available nearby at **Bright Angel Lodge.** The main log and stone lodge was built in 1935 on the site of Bright Angel Camp, the first tourist facility in the park. Its lobby features Indian motifs and a huge fireplace. Rooms are clean and modest. Some have shared baths, and none have televisions. Besides the rooms in the main building, the lodge also rents several historic cabins, all with televisions and a few with fireplaces. ~ BUDGET TO MODERATE.

On the rim between El Tovar and Bright Angel Lodge are the modern twin stone lodges, **Thunderbird Lodge** and **Kachina Lodge.** Located on the rim trail, these caravansaries are within easy walking distance of the restaurants at the older lodges. All have televisions and phones. ~ MODERATE TO DELUXE.

The largest lodging facility in the park, **Yavapai Lodge** is situated in a wooded setting about a quarter of a mile from the canyon rim, near the general store and about one mile from Grand Canyon Village. The contemporary guest rooms are equivalent in quality to what you would expect for the same price at a national chain motor inn. ~ MODERATE TO DELUXE.

Maswik Lodge is a half mile from the canyon rim at the southwest end of Grand Canyon Village. It presents a variety of motel-style rooms as well as cabins. All the rooms have TVs and phones. ~ MODERATE TO DELUXE.

HIDDEN ▶ No survey of lodgings at the Grand Canyon would be complete without mentioning **Phantom Ranch.** Located at the bottom of the canyon, this 1922 lodge and cabins is at the lower end of the North Kaibab Trail from the North Rim and the Bright Angel and South Kaibab trails from the South Rim. It can only be reached by foot, mule or river raft. Cabins are normally reserved for guests on overnight mule trips, but hikers with plenty of advance notice can also arrange lodging. Bunk beds are available by reservation only in four ten-person dormitories, separated by gender. There is no television at the ranch, and only one pay phone. Food service is provided in the dining room and must be arranged in advance. Do not arrive at Phantom Ranch without reservations! ~ BUDGET.

Located in a remote red-rock canyon on the Havasupai Indian Reservation, the 24 motel-style units at **Havasupai Lodge** is a truly hidden destination. There's a café, swimming in the nearby creek and a convenient barbecue pit. Just two miles away are Navajo, Havasu and Mooney falls. You can also enjoy American Indian–led horseback and hiking tours of this scenic region ($30 entrance fee for reservation). ~ P.O. Box 159, Supai, AZ 86435; 928-448-2111, fax 928-448-2348. MODERATE.

◀ HIDDEN

Mail sent from Phantom Ranch bears the post-mark, "Mailed by Mule from the Bottom of the Canyon."

Just outside the South Rim entrance gate, the community of Tusayan has several hotels and motor inns that are not affiliated with the national park. One of the following might be a good option if you cannot get reservations at one of the national park lodges.

The **Grand Hotel** on the main drag in Tusayan is inspired by the rustic national park lodges of the past. It has a huge lobby, a stone fireplace, American Indian furnishings, a cowboy bar and a restaurant offering Navajo dancing as part of a nightly dinner show. Rooms are basic but comfortable, with Western touches such as wrought-iron fixtures. A quieter unit in the back, overlooking the forest, is available as well. The Grand also boasts the only indoor pool in the area. ~ Two miles from the park entrance on Route 64, Tusayan; 928-638-3333, 888-634-7623, fax 928-638-3131; http://the-grand-hotel-grand-canyon.pacificahost.com. MODERATE.

There are also a number of chain motels to choose from, such as the **Red Feather Lodge**. ~ One and a half miles from the park entrance on Route 64; 928-638-2414, 800-538-2345, fax 928-638-9216; www.redfeatherlodge.com, e-mail info@redfeather lodge.com. MODERATE TO DELUXE. The **Best Western Grand Canyon Squire Inn** is another such establishment. ~ Two miles from park entrance on Route 64; 928-638-2681, 800-622-6966, fax 928-638-2782; www.grandcanyonsquire.com. DELUXE. Or try the **Grand Canyon Quality Inn & Suites**. ~ One mile from park entrance on Route 64; 928-638-2673, 800-221-2222, fax 928-638-9537; www.grandcanyonqualityinn.com. DELUXE TO ULTRA-DELUXE.

For camping information, see page 56.

DINING

The contact information for all South Rim Grand Canyon restaurants is 928-638-2631, fax 928-638-9810.

The most elegant (in fact, the *only* elegant) South Rim restaurant is **El Tovar Dining Room**. Entrées such as filet mignon and

Text continued on page 54.

South Rim
Information

WHEN TO VISIT   The South Rim of Grand Canyon National Park is open all year. Most park visitors go to the South Rim, making it crowded even during the off-season, but the heaviest crowds can be expected during the spring, summer and fall months. Day visitors can expect traffic congestion and even some delays entering the park, especially during the summer. Overnight visitors must plan well in advance. Accommodations within the park are extremely limited and often are booked more than a year in advance. (See "Lodging" listings.)

WEATHER AND ELEVATION   The South Rim of the Grand Canyon is 7000 feet above sea level in a high-desert region. Temperatures during the summer are generally pleasant on the rim, ranging between 50° and 80°. Since the canyon floor lies some 5000 feet below the rim, daytime temperatures there are quite a bit higher, often climbing past 100°. Winter can bring snow, icy roads and clouds that can obscure canyon views. Spring and fall weather can change quickly in the canyon. The park's elevation can affect breathing, and it can take several days to become acclimated.

GETTING TO THE SOUTH RIM   The South Rim of Grand Canyon National Park is about 60 miles north of Williams (via Route 64 from Route 40) and about 80 miles from Flagstaff (via Route 180). Besides the south entrance, through which most visitors enter, the park can be entered from the east near Cameron, off Route 89. **Grand Canyon Railway** operates daily train service from Williams. ~ 928-773-1976, 800-843-8724; www.thetrain.com, e-mail info@thetrain.com. Limited air service is available to Grand Canyon Airport.

ENTRANCE FEES   The tariff for private vehicles is $25; for pedestrians, bicyclists and motorcyclists, it's $12. The fee is nonrefundable, but admission is good for seven consecutive days for both the South and North rims. U.S. seniors over 62 and permanently disabled U.S. citizens may obtain specially priced passes; frequent national-park visitors should inquire about an interagency America the Beautiful annual pass. An annual Grand Canyon passport is also available. Camping reservations can be made online at reservations.nps.gov.

GETTING AROUND THE PARK   A free Village shuttle bus system operates nearly year-round and makes stops within Grand Canyon Village and viewpoints along Hermit Road. The eight-mile-long Hermit Road is closed to private vehicles during the same months. Desert View Drive, however, follows the canyon rim for 25 miles and is open year-round. A hikers shuttle is available to South Kaibab Trail (at Yaki Point). ~ 928-638-3283, fax 928-638-2877. Shuttle transportation between the South and North rims (a four- to five-hour trip) operates seasonally, for a fee. Reservations required. ~ 928-638-2820.

POSTAL, MEDICAL AND OTHER SERVICES　The South Rim has its own post office, located in the shopping center next to Yavapai Lodge. A bank and a general store are also located in the center. Emergency medical service is available 24 hours (dial 911). The South Rim has its own medical clinic (928-638-2551) and dental office (928-638-2395), both operating on limited hours.

SERVICES FOR PERSONS WITH PHYSICAL DISABILITIES　Many buildings in the park are historic and do not meet accessibility standards. However, some structures are accessible with assistance. The *Grand Canyon Accessibility Guide* is available at the visitors center and the Yavapai Observation Station. Free wheelchairs (day-use only) are available at the visitors center, as are special vehicle permits allowing access to Hermit Road during summer months. Wheelchair accessible bus tours are available by prior arrangement (the Village shuttle bus is not wheelchair accessible). ~ 928-638-7888.

PETS　Pets are permitted in the park but must be leashed, and, with the exception of certified service dogs, they're not allowed in lodgings, on park buses or below the rim. There is a kennel on the South Rim. Open daily. ~ 928-638-0534.

BIKES　Bikes are not allowed on most park trails. Mountain bikes are allowed on those roads open to automobile traffic and on 11 miles of prototype trails that have been completed and opened as part of the planned Grand Canyon Greenway. This series of paved, wheelchair-accessible pedestrian and cyclist trails will eventually trace both the north and south rims for a total of 73 miles, with rest areas and several bike-rental and dropoff points along the way.

AND DON'T FORGET　Bring moleskin for potential blisters if you plan to go hiking, and a good pair of binoculars.

salmon tostada are served on fine china by candlelight. Prices are high and the ambience is classy, but casual dress is perfectly acceptable. Three meals are served daily; dinner reservations required. ~ DELUXE TO ULTRA-DELUXE.

More informal surroundings and lower prices are to be found at the **Bright Angel Restaurant** in the Bright Angel Lodge. Menu selections include chicken piccata, grilled rainbow trout and fajitas. Cocktails and wine are available. ~ BUDGET TO MODERATE.

Adjoining the Bright Angel Lodge, the **Arizona Room** specializes in steaks and seafood. The open kitchen lets you watch the chefs cook while you eat. Dinner only. Closed in January and February. ~ MODERATE TO DELUXE.

The South Rim's best snack bar, **Delicatessen at Marketplace**, can be found inside the main grocery store on Market Plaza. On the menu you'll find tasty meat chili in a sourdough bread bowl, fresh-roasted chicken and turkey sandwiches, salads, fruit, yogurt and other fairly healthy choices that will appeal to hikers and those on a budget. ~ Market Plaza, South Rim; 928-638-2262. BUDGET.

In the Yavapai Lodge, the **Canyon Cafe** serves fast food—burgers and fries, pizza and fried chicken—for breakfast, lunch and dinner (open seasonally with varied hours). ~ BUDGET.

There are two other cafeterias in the park. The first is **Maswik Cafeteria** at Maswik Lodge, which serves breakfast, lunch and dinner. ~ Located at the west end of Grand Canyon Village. BUDGET. The **Desert View Trading Post Snack Bar** serves a changing selection of hot meals (seasonal hours). ~ Located 23 miles east of the village along Desert View Drive. BUDGET.

Ice cream, sandwiches and soft drinks are available at the **Hermits Rest Snack Bar** at the end of Hermit Road, as well as at the **Bright Angel Fountain**, near the trailhead for the Bright Angel Trail. Open seasonally. ~ BUDGET.

Outside the park entrance, the town of Tusayan has nearly a dozen eating establishments ranging from McDonald's to Taco Bell and Wendy's.

FRED HARVEY TO THE RESCUE

In 1876, Fred Harvey (with the permission of the railroad) opened a restaurant in the Santa Fe station in Topeka, Kansas, to rescue diners from the rather tasteless food being served on the train. As years went by, a string of Fred "Harvey Houses" (hotels and restaurants) followed the tracks of the Santa Fe line. When the railroad built a spurline to the Grand Canyon in 1901, the Fred Harvey Company was not far behind.

The elk tenderloin with berry reduction at the cavernous **Canyon Star Restaurant** in the Grand Hotel is one of the highlights of a menu that tries hard to cover its Southwest bases in an indifferent dinner-show atmosphere. ~ Two miles from the park entrance on Route 64, Tusayan; 928-638-3333. MODERATE.

Jennifer's Internet Bakery Cafe is a tiny place that offers the best coffee shop atmosphere and food in Tusayan. The breakfast egg dishes, bagels and sandwiches, pies and pastries are all homemade and surprisingly good. For a fee, you can log on to the internet and check your e-mail. ~ Route 64, Tusayan; 928-638-3433. BUDGET.

Other options include the **Coronado Room** located at the Best Western Grand Canyon Squire Inn, which serves prime rib, steaks and daily specials in a Southwestern-style dining room. Dinner only. ~ Route 64; 928-638-2681, 800-622-6966, fax 928-638-0162; www.grandcanyonsquire.com. MODERATE TO DELUXE.

For standard coffee shop fare check out the **Kenyon Room**, also located at the Best Western Grand Canyon Squire Inn, which is open for breakfast and lunch. ~ Route 64; 928-638-2681, 800-622-6966, fax 928-638-0162; www.grandcanyon squire.com. BUDGET.

SHOPPING Of several national park concession tourist stores on the South Rim, the best are **Hopi House**, the large Indian pueblo replica across from El Tovar Hotel, and the adjacent **Verkamp's Curios**. Both have been in continuous operation for almost a century and specialize in authentic American Indian handicrafts, with high standards of quality and some genuinely old pieces.

Other Grand Canyon shops, at least as interesting for their historic architecture as their wares, include the old **Kolb Studio**, originally a 1904 photographic studio and now a bookstore, and the **Lookout Studio**, which has rock specimens and conventional curios. Both are in Grand Canyon Village. Another souvenir shop is the **Hermit's Rest Gift Shop**. ~ End of Hermit Road. The **Desert View Watchtower** has more of the same. ~ Desert View Drive.

NIGHTLIFE Grand Canyon National Park does not have much in the way of hot nightlife. You can take in one of the ranger-produced slideshows presented in the amphitheater, go on a moonlit walk, or simply sit in the dark along the canyon rim and listen to the vast, deep silence. Concerts are sometimes held at the **Shrine of the Ages Auditorium** (the Grand Canyon Chamber Music Concert in September is a must if you're in the area). **Bright Angel Lodge** (303-297-3175) also has weekly live entertainment—usually a folk guitarist. The **Canyon Star Restaurant** hosts a well-done, twice-nightly dance performance by a Navajo troupe. ~ Grand Hotel, two miles from the park entrance on Route 64, Tusayan; 928-638-3333, 888-634-7623.

▼▼▼▼▼▼▼▼▼▼▼▼▼▼
Outdoor Adventures

CAMPING

There are tent/RV sites in Grand Canyon Village at **Mather Campground** ($18 per night, no hookups), first-come, first-served. Reservations may be made up to five months in advance beginning the 5th of each month. ~ 800-365-2267, fax 301-722-1174; reservations.nps.gov. RV sites with full hookups are available at **Grand Canyon Trailer Village** ($24 per night for two people, $2 for each extra person), adjacent to Mather Campground. ~ 303-297-2757. Tent/RV sites are also available on a first-come, first-served basis at **Desert View Campground** ($12 per night, no hookups; closed mid-October to mid-May), 25 miles east of Grand Canyon Village. Outside the park, there's tent and RV camping available on a first-time, first-served basis at the Forest Service's **Ten-X Campground** ($10 per night, no hookups; closed October through April), just south of Tusayan. ~ 928-638-2443.

Camping near Phantom Ranch or anyplace else below the rim requires a backcountry permit, which costs $10 per permit plus $5 per person per night. The number of permits available is limited; to improve your chances of obtaining one, apply four months in advance of your stay. ~ Backcountry Information Center; P.O. Box 129, Grand Canyon, AZ 86023; 928-638-7875, fax 928-638-2125.

RIDING STABLES

At the Grand Canyon, the **Apache Stable** in Tusayan, near the park's south entrance, offers a selection of guided rides to various points within the Kaibab National Forest. One-, two- and occasionally four-hour rides are available. Horseback rides do not go below the canyon rim. Call for reservations. ~ 928-638-2891, fax 928-638-2783; www.apachestables.com.

◆◆

DON'T TRAIL OFF

If you're planning a hiking excursion in the Grand Canyon, remember to stick to the designated trails. Trails are in part designed to drain off water with a minimum of soil erosion; forging your own path may cause future problems. If you do need to venture off the beaten track, make sure the members of your group spread out instead of walking single file. Also, try to avoid meadows and wet areas, which are more likely to be affected by footprints and group travel than more forested and rocky land. When in doubt, remember those words of wisdom from camp counselors of yore: "Take only pictures, leave only footprints." Although in this case, try to avoid even that.

For information on mule trips into the canyon, see "Touring the Grand Canyon" in this chapter.

BIKING

Although trails within the national park are closed to bicycles, Kaibab National Forest surrounding the park on both the North and South Rims offers a wealth of mountain-biking possibilities. The forest areas adjoining Grand Canyon National Park are laced with old logging roads, and the relatively flat terrain makes for low-stress riding.

Located at the South Rim of the Grand Canyon, **Hermit Road** is closed to most private motor vehicles during the summer months but open to bicycles. This fairly level route (eight miles one way) makes for a spectacular cycling tour. Watch out for bus traffic during the summer months. One ride the National Forest Service recommends in the vicinity of the South Rim is the **Coconino Rim Trail** (9.1 miles), a loop trail that starts near Grandview Point and travels southeast through ponderosa forests.

For other suggestions, stop in at the Tusayan Ranger Station just outside the South Rim entrance (928-638-2443) or contact Kaibab National Forest Headquarters. ~ 800 South 6th Street, Williams, AZ 86046; 928-635-8200.

HIKING

The ultimate hiking experience in Grand Canyon National Park—and perhaps in the entire Southwest—is an expedition from either rim to the bottom of the canyon and back. With an elevation change of 4800 feet from the South Rim to the river, or 5800 feet from the North Rim, the hike is as ambitious as an ascent of a major Rocky Mountain peak, except that the greatest effort is required in the last miles of the climb out, when leg muscles may already be sore from the long downhill trek. Strenuous as it may be, hiking the Grand Canyon is an experience sure to stay vivid for a lifetime.

Though some people claim to have done it, hiking roundtrip from the rim to river level and back in a single day is a monumental feat that takes from 16 to 18 hours. Most hikers who plan to go the whole way will want to allow at least two, preferably three, days for the trip. The park service does not recommend attempting to hike from the rim to the canyon bottom during the summer months *unless* starting the trek before 7 a.m. or after 4 p.m. (Though it might be 85° on the rim, it could be 115° at the bottom.) A wilderness permit, required for any overnight trip into the park backcountry, can be obtained free of charge at the backcountry office on either rim. All distances listed for hiking trails are one way unless otherwise noted.

The **Bright Angel Trail** (7.8 miles to the river or 9.3 miles to Phantom Ranch), the most popular trail in the canyon, starts at Grand Canyon Village on the South Rim, near the mule corral. It

Text continued on page 60.

Touring the Grand Canyon

It seems like there are more ways to explore the Grand Canyon than there are routes down its walls. Hikers, mule riders, aviators and even whitewater enthusiasts have all discovered its sporting opportunities.

Of course the most rigorous way to tour the famous chasm is by *hiking*. If you have the time, making your way by foot down to the bottom is an amazing experience. Be forewarned—it is impossible to complete the journey in a day; people are often airlifted out for trying. Rest stops with shade and refreshing cold water are scattered intermittently along the trails. Plan ahead and camp or stay at the Phantom Ranch. (Do not arrive at the Phantom Ranch without reservations!)

For a taste of the Old West, mules are a classic mode of transport. *Mule trips* range from one-day excursions that venture as far as Plateau Point to two- and three-day trips (available November through March) to the bottom of the canyon. The cost is several hundred dollars per person, including meals and accommodations at the Phantom Ranch. Mule trips depart from both the North and South rims. Reservations must be made well ahead of time—as much as a year in advance for weekends, holidays and the summer months. For South Rim departures, contact **Xanterra Parks & Resorts**. ~ 14001 East Iliff Avenue, Suite 600, Aurora, CO 80014; 303-297-2757, fax 303-297-3175; www.grandcanyon lodges.com, e-mail reserve-gcsr@xanterra.com. For North Rim departures, call **Grand Canyon Trail Rides**. Closed mid-October to mid-May. ~ P.O. Box 128, Tropic, UT 84776; 435-679-8665; www.canyon rides.com.

Many "flightseeing" tours offer spectacular eagle-eye views of the Grand Canyon. **Grand Canyon Airlines**' fully narrated tour circles the canyon starting at the South Rim and offers views of the Painted Desert and the confluence of the Colorado and Little Colorado rivers. ~ P.O. Box 3038, Grand Canyon, AZ 86023; 928-638-2407, 800-528-2413; www.grandcanyonairlines.com. With **Air Grand Canyon** you can choose from three different trips ranging from a 50- or 60-minute tour of the Eastern Gorge and the confluence of the Colorado and Little Colorado rivers to a 90-minute flight that visits all the major canyon sights. ~ P.O. Box 3399, Grand Canyon, AZ 86023; 928-638-2686, 800-

247-4726; www.airgrandcanyon.com. Both of these companies operate from Grand Canyon Airport near Tusayan.

Even more thrilling—and more expensive—are *helicopter tours*. Helicopters can fly considerably lower than airplanes, affording an even closer look at the magnificent canyon. Neither helicopters nor planes are allowed to fly beneath the rim, however, keeping the canyon peaceful for hikers and riders. The 45-minute Imperial Flight offered by **Papillon Grand Canyon Helicopters** affords views of the Painted Desert, Marble Canyon and Dragon's Corridor. The shorter North Canyon flight explores the Central Corridor. ~ P.O. Box 455, Grand Canyon, AZ 86023; 928-638-2419, 800-528-2418; www.papillon.com. With **Maverick Helicopters** you can choose the 25- to 30-minute Central Corridor tour, or the 45- to 50-minute tour of both the Central and Eastern Canyon. ~ P.O. Box 3297, Grand Canyon, AZ 86023; 928-638-2622, 888-261-4414; www.maverickhelicopter.com.

If simply looking at the bottom of the canyon isn't enough, water adventurers might consider a *rafting trip* down the Colorado River. Raft trips operate from April through September. Most start at Lee's Ferry, northeast of the national park boundary near Page, Arizona, and just below Glen Canyon Dam. The rafts are motorized, with pontoons, and provide seating for about 14 people.

More exciting are the smaller oar-operated dories that ride closer to the water and occasionally tip over in the rough rapids. Rafting the full length of the canyon, 280 miles from Lee's Ferry to Lake Mead, takes a leisurely eight days, providing plenty of time to hike and explore remote parts of the canyon inaccessible by other means. Many rafting companies also offer shorter trips that involve being picked up or dropped off by helicopter part way through the canyon.

One of the leading raft tour companies is **Grand Canyon Expeditions**, offering eight-day motorized expeditions and fourteen- to sixteen-day rowing trips. Transportation, camping gear and all meals are provided. ~ P.O. Box O, Kanab, UT 84741; 435-644-2691, 800-544-2691. Another good organization is **Arizona River Runners** for multiday motorized or oar-powered trips. Meals and equipment are included. ~ P.O. Box 47788, Phoenix, AZ 85068; 602-867-4866, 800-477-7238; www.raftarizona.com. A complete list of river trip outfitters is available from **Rivers and Oceans**. ~ 928-526-4575, 800-473-4576. Private parties can take the river route through the Grand Canyon. Contact the South Rim visitors center for additional information.

has the most developed facilities, including a resthouse with emergency phones along the upper part of the trail and a ranger station, water and a campground midway down at Indian Garden, where the Havasupai people used to grow crops. The one-day roundtrip hike will take you along a ridgeline to Plateau Point, overlooking the Colorado River from 1300 feet above, just before the final steep descent. Allow about five hours to hike from the rim down to the river and about ten hours to climb back up. It is therefore advisable to camp and make the return trip the following day. Remember, a permit is required for overnight trips. A lot of hikers use this trail, as do daily mule riders—not the route to take if you seek solitude.

Another major trail from the South Rim is the **South Kaibab Trail** (7.3 miles to Phantom Ranch), which starts from the trailhead on Desert View Drive, near Yaki Point. A free shuttle bus takes hikers to the trailhead. The shortest of the main trails into the canyon, it is also the steepest and, due to lack of water and shade along the route, not recommended during the summer months.

Several less-used trails also descend from the South Rim. All of them intersect the **Tonto Trail** (95 miles), which runs along the edge of the inner gorge about 1300 feet above river level. The **Grandview Trail** (3 miles), an old mine access route that starts at Grandview Point on Desert View Drive, goes down to Horseshoe Mesa, where it joins a loop of the Tonto Trail that circles the mesa, passing ruins of an old copper mine. There is a primitive campground without water on the mesa. All camping in the canyon requires a backcountry permit.

The **Hermit Trail** (8.5 miles) begins at Hermits Rest at the end of Hermit Road and descends to join the Tonto Trail. Branching off from the Dripping Springs Trail, which also starts at Hermits Rest, the **Boucher Trail** (11 miles) also goes down to join the Tonto Trail and is considered one of the more difficult hiking trails in the park. Ask for details at the Backcountry Informational Center.

The paved, handicapped-accessible **Rim Trail** (1.5 miles) goes between the Kolb Studio at the west side of Grand Canyon Village and the Yavapai Observation Station. A one-third-mile spur links the Rim Trail with the visitors center. At each end of the designated Rim Trail, the pavement ends but unofficial trails continue for several more miles, ending at Hopi Point near the Powell Memorial on Hermit Road and at Yaki Point, the trailhead for the South Kaibab Trail, on Desert View Drive.

The North Rim

The North Rim of the Grand Canyon receives only about one-tenth of the number of visitors the South Rim gets. Snowbound during the winter because it is 1200 feet higher in elevation, the North Rim is only open from mid-

May through October, while the South Rim is open year-round. The South Rim is more convenient for more travelers since it is much closer to a major interstate highway route and to the large population centers of southern Arizona and California. But if your tour of the Southwest includes destinations such as the Navajo Indian Reservation, Lake Powell, Page, Bryce Canyon and Zion national parks, or even Las Vegas, then your route will take you closer to the North Rim, giving you an opportunity to explore the cooler, quieter side of the canyon.

SIGHTS

Before starting the drive into the park from Jacob Lake, stop at the **Kaibab Plateau Visitors Center**. A small exhibit details information on human habitation and wildlife on the plateau, and a ranger is on duty to answer questions. Closed late October through April. ~ Routes 89 and 67, Jacob Lake; 928-643-7298, fax 928-635-8208; www.fs.fed.us/r3/kai.

The drive across the **Kaibab Plateau** into the park on Route 67 (also called the Kaibab Plateau North Rim Parkway) winds through a forest of ponderosa pine, quaking aspen, blue spruce and Douglas fir, and large open mountain meadows. Mule deer and other wildlife can be seen occasionally in the meadows (early morning and early evening are the best times to spot them graz-

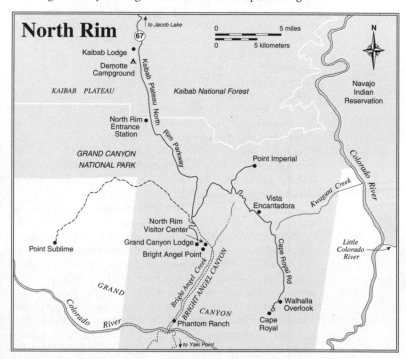

North Rim

to Jacob Lake

67

0   5 miles
0   5 kilometers

N

Kaibab Lodge

Demotte Campground

KAIBAB PLATEAU

Kaibab National Forest

Navajo Indian Reservation

North Rim Entrance Station

GRAND CANYON NATIONAL PARK

Point Imperial

Kaibab Plateau North Rim Parkway

Colorado River

Kwagunt Creek

Vista Encantadora

North Rim Visitor Center

Grand Canyon Lodge

Bright Angel Point

Point Sublime

Bright Angel Creek

BRIGHT ANGEL CANYON

Cape Royal Rd

Little Colorado River

GRAND

Colorado River

CANYON

Phantom Ranch

Cape Royal

Walhalla Overlook

to Yaki Point

ing). In the fall, stands of aspen trees set the landscape ashimmer in a trembling glow of yellow and flame orange.

Several miles into the park, a turnoff at Fuller Canyon Road leads to the scenic drives on **Point Imperial Road** and **Cape Royal Road**. At 8803 feet, **Point Imperial** is the highest point on either rim and commands a stunning view of Mt. Hayden, a huge carved sandstone spire, and the sprawling vistas of the eastern canyon. Cape Royal Road leads to **Vista Encantadora, Painted Desert Overlook** and **Walhalla Overlook**. There's an ancient Anasazi ruin across the road from Walhalla. The drive ends at **Cape Royal**, where you can take a self-guided nature walk and get a look at the Colorado River and the large natural arch called **Angels Window**. Cape Royal is also a popular spot to watch the sun rise or set. (Narrated tours to both Cape Royal and Point Imperial are available. Check at the information desk in the lobby of Grand Canyon Lodge.)

Note that Bright Angel Point's high elevation can make breathing difficult for some people.

Route 67 dead-ends at the **Grand Canyon Lodge**, built of native stone and timber and perched right on the edge of the rim. Verandas on either side of the lodge offer sunny, open spots to view the canyon. At night, the lights of Grand Canyon Village, 11 miles away on the South Rim, are visible.

From the lodge, to the east, a path leads out to **Bright Angel Point**. Though paved, the quarter-mile path clings precipitously to the canyon rim, and rises and falls in some spots. A pamphlet to a self-guided walking tour to Bright Angel Point is available for a quarter. It points out places to look for fossils and where to see **Roaring Springs**, some 3800 feet below and the North Rim's source of water. From Bright Angel Point, which is at an elevation of 8200 feet, there are good views of the South Rim and the San Francisco Peaks near Flagstaff, some 50 miles away. Other viewpoints on the North Rim are reached by foot trails. (See "Hiking" under "Outdoor Adventures.")

HIDDEN ►

On Route 389, nine miles from the Fredonia turnoff and six miles before you reach Pipe Springs, an unpaved road known as the Mount Trumbull Loop turns off to the south. (The other end of the 200-mile "loop" is near St. George, Utah.) This road provides the main access to **Grand Canyon–Parashant National Monument**. Don't forget to fill up the gas tank in Fredonia because you won't find a single gas station or telephone along this route. In fact, you may not even see another vehicle—just wide-open countryside as empty as all of Arizona used to be long ago. The relatively new national monument has no visitor facilities, though future plans call for an interpretive center and camping areas. It spans a vast plateau of sagebrush flats and piñon-juniper forests teeming with mule deer, bighorn sheep and mountain lions. The monument includes **Parashant Canyon**, the largest side canyon of the Grand Canyon, reached via primitive roads in a four-wheel-drive vehicle. It also includes the westernmost part of the Grand Canyon north rim.

The most striking feature of Grand Canyon–Parashant National Monument is **Toroweap Point,** a dramatic vista on the edge of the Grand Canyon. The well-maintained unpaved road to Toroweap Point turns off the Mount Trumbull Loop about 50 miles from the highway; several other dirt roads branch off along the way but if you keep to the road that goes south and looks well used, following the "Toroweap" and "Grand Canyon National Monument" signs wherever you see them, it's hard to get lost. The elevation is 2000 feet lower than at the main North Rim visitor area, so instead of pine forest the vegetation is desert scrub, its roots clinging tenuously to slickrock. Being closer to the river, still nearly 3000 feet below, you can watch the parade of river rafts drifting past and even eavesdrop on passengers' conversations. There is a small, primitive **campground** at Toroweap Point, but no water, restrooms or other facilities. As likely as not, you may find that you have the place all to yourself.

On the North Rim, the only lodging within the park is the **Grand Canyon Lodge,** which consists of a beautiful 1930s-vintage main lodge building overlooking the canyon and a number of cabins— some rustic, others modern, a few with canyon views. Clean and homelike, both rooms and cabins have an old-fashioned feel, though when I visited they seemed a little noisy. North Rim accommodations are in very high demand, so reservations should be made far ahead. They are accepted up to 13 months in advance. Reservations for the lodge are booked through Xanterra, which also handles reservations for the lodges at Bryce Canyon and Zion national parks. The lodge is closed from mid-October to mid-May. ~ Lodge: 928-638-2611, fax 928-638-2554. Reservations: 14001 East Iliff Avenue, Suite 600, Aurora, CO 80014; 303-297-2757, fax 303-297-3175; www.xanterra.com. MODERATE.

LODGING

Just five miles from the entrance to the park, the **Kaibab Lodge** offers basic sleeping accommodations—28 small rooms with private baths in cabin-style buildings set around the main lodge. There are no televisions or phones in the rooms. Three more-developed (and larger) cabins are available, two with microwaves and refrigerators. Reserve well in advance. Closed November through May due to heavy snow. ~ Grand Canyon North Rim Parkway (Route 67); 928-638-2389; www. kaibablodge.com, e-mail info@kaibablodge.com. MODERATE.

Forty-four miles from the North Rim is the **Jacob Lake Inn.** This small, rustic resort complex surrounded by national forest offers motel rooms and cabins, both smoking and nonsmoking, including some two-bedroom units. All cabins have decks and forest views (cabins 28 and 29 front the edge of the forest). Reservations should be made well in advance. ~ Junction of Routes 89 and 67, Jacob Lake; 928-643-7232, fax 928-643-7235; www.jacoblake.com, e-mail jacob@jacoblake.com. MODERATE. For camping information, see below.

DINING

The **Grand Canyon Lodge Dining Room** offers breakfast, lunch and dinner at affordable prices. The food is good, conventional meat-and-potatoes fare and the atmosphere—a spacious, rustic log-beamed dining room with huge picture windows overlooking the canyon—is simply incomparable. Reservations are required for dinner. The lodge also operates a budget-priced snack shop serving breakfast, lunch and dinner in plain, simple surroundings, as well as a saloon offering pizza and sandwiches. Nearby, the camper store sells pizza sandwiches. Closed mid-October to mid-May. ~ 928-638-2611. MODERATE TO DELUXE.

PARKS

KAIBAB NATIONAL FOREST 🏃 🚲 🐎 🏕 This 1,500,000-acre expanse of pine, fir, spruce and aspen forest includes both sides of the Grand Canyon outside the park boundaries. Most recreational facilities are located near the North Rim, where they supplement the park's limited camping facilities. Wildlife in the forest includes mule deer, wild turkeys, elk, several other bird species and even a few bison. There are picnic areas, restrooms and a visitors center. The facilities in the forest close from about October to April. ~ The national forest visitors center is at Jacob Lake, the intersection of Routes 89A and 67; 928-643-7298 (North Rim visitors center), 928-635-4061, fax 928-635-1417 (South Rim); www.fs.fed.us/r3/kai. Jacob Lake Campground is at the same location, while Demotte Campground is 23 miles south on Route 67, about five miles from the national park entrance.

▲ Demotte Campground has about 40 sites, $14 per night, and Jacob Lake Campground has 55 sites, $14 per night. ~ 928-643-8100. RV hookups are available at the privately owned Kaibab Camper Village, $15 for tent sites (two people, $3.50 each additional person), $29 to $31 for motor homes (two people; $3.50 each additional person). Closed mid-October to mid-May. ~ 928-643-7804, 928-526-0924.

▼ ▼ ▼ ▼ ▼ ▼ ▼ ▼ ▼ ▼ ▼ ▼ ▼ ▼

Outdoor Adventures

CAMPING

North Rim Campground ($15 to $20 per night, no hookups) is open year round but requires reservations from mid-May to mid-October. Reservations may be made at 800-365-2267 or online at reservations.nps.gov up to five months in advance beginning the 5th of each month. Rangers at a booth just south of Jacob Lake can advise motorists whether campsites are available within the park and, if not, will direct them to alternate camping in Kaibab

North Rim
Information

WHEN TO VISIT   Although the park remains open for day use until December (or until heavy snow closes the road), visitor facilities on the North Rim of the Grand Canyon are open only from mid-May to mid-October.

WEATHER AND ELEVATION   The North Rim's elevation is 8200 feet. Summers are temperate, with warm days and mild evenings. Winter snow can accumulate to over 12 feet.

GETTING TO THE NORTH RIM   The distance across the canyon from the South Rim to the North Rim is only about ten miles as the crow flies. But the distance in road miles is about 200. Access is on Route 67, from Routes 89 and 89A. From Jacob Lake to the Grand Canyon Lodge, the distance is 45 miles. Page and Lake Powell are about 120 miles to the east. Shuttle transportation between the rims is available daily from mid-May to mid-October for a fee. ~ 928-638-2820.

ENTRANCE FEES   The tariff for private vehicles is $25; for pedestrians, bicyclists and motorcyclists, it's $12. The fee is nonrefundable, but admission is good for seven consecutive days for both the North and South rims. U.S. seniors over 62 and physically disabled U.S. citizens may obtain specially priced passes; frequent national park visitors should inquire about an interagency America the Beautiful annual pass. An annual Grand Canyon passport is also available.

GETTING AROUND THE PARK   The main road into the park deadends at the Grand Canyon Lodge. From there you can walk along a paved but precipitous path to one of the park's most popular overlooks, Bright Angel Point. Before reaching the lodge, a turnoff leads to Cape Royal Scenic Drive, a 20-mile drive to several other lookouts. Van tours are also available; a schedule is posted in the lobby of the lodge.

POSTAL, MEDICAL AND OTHER SERVICES   A general store and a service station are located near the campground. The post office is located in the lodge complex. Dial 911 for emergency medical service. Water is not available along scenic drives or at viewpoints.

SERVICES FOR PERSONS WITH PHYSICAL DISABILITIES   The *Accessibility Guide* is available at the information desk in the lodge lobby. Many of the viewpoints and other facilities are wheelchair-accessible or accessible with assistance.

National Forest, where there are developed campgrounds at **De-motte Park** ($14 per night, no hookups), seven miles north of the canyon rim, and **Jacob Lake** ($14 per night, no hookups). In addition, dispersed primitive camping is allowed beside forest roads within Kaibab National Forest, though not within a quarter mile of the highway.

RIDING STABLES

If the long-haul mule rides down the Bright Angel Trail on the South Rim intimidate you, you may prefer the easier horseback rides on the North Rim. **Grand Canyon Trail Rides** will saddle you up for hour-long, half-day or full-day rides through the forested rim or into the inner canyon. Register in the lobby of the Grand Canyon Lodge. Closed October to May. ~ 435-679-8665; www.canyonrides.com/grandcanyon.html.

BIKING

Although trails within the national park are closed to bicycles, Kaibab National Forest surrounding the park on the North Rim offers a wealth of mountain-biking possibilities. The forest areas adjoining Grand Canyon National Park are laced with old logging roads and the relatively flat terrain makes for low-stress riding.

Toward the west end of the Grand Canyon on its North Rim, visitors to **Toroweap Point** will find endless mountain biking opportunities along the hundreds of miles of remote, unpaved roads in the Arizona Strip.

HIKING

All distances listed for hiking trails are one way unless otherwise noted.

The main trail into the canyon from the North Rim is the **North Kaibab Trail** (14.2 miles). The trail starts from the trailhead two miles north of Grand Canyon Lodge and descends abruptly down Roaring Springs Canyon for almost five miles to Bright Angel Creek. This is the steepest part of the trip. Where the trail reaches the creek, there are several swimming holes, a good destination for a one-day roundtrip. The trail then follows

AUTHOR FAVORITE

Of more than 250 miles of hiking trails in Grand Canyon National Park, my personal favorite is the North Rim's **Widforss Trail** (5 miles), named after artist Gunnar Widforss, who painted landscapes in the national parks during the 1920s. The trail winds along the lip of the plateau through scrubby oak, piñon pines, ponderosa pines and juniper to a remote canyon viewpoint. The viewpoint overlooks a side canyon known as Haunted Canyon.

the creek all the way to Phantom Ranch at the bottom of the canyon. Park rangers recommend that hikers allow a full day to hike from the rim to the ranch and two days to climb back to the rim, stopping overnight at Cottonwood Camp, the midway point. Because of heavy snows on the rim, this trail is not recommended during the winter months.

Without descending below the canyon rim, hikers can choose from a variety of trails ranging from short scenic walks to all-day hikes. The easy, paved, handicapped-accessible **Transept Trail** (2 miles) runs between the campground and the lodge, then continues gradually downward to Bright Angel Point, which affords the best view of the Bright Angel Trail down into the canyon.

The **Uncle Jim Trail** (2.5 miles) starts at the same trailhead as the Roaring Springs Canyon fork of the Bright Angel Trail, two miles north of the lodge. It circles through the ponderosa woods to an overlook, Uncle Jim Point.

The **Ken Patrick Trail** (10 miles) runs from Point Imperial to the Kaibab Trail parking lot.

Visitors to remote Toroweap Point may wish to try the **Lava Falls Route** (1.5 miles), which begins as a jeep road midway between the old ranger station and the point. Although this trail is not long, it is recommended for experienced hikers only, as it is rocky, edgy, very steep, and marked only by cairns, descending 3000 feet to the Colorado River and the "falls"—actually a furious stretch of white water formed when lava spilled into the river. Allow all day for the roundtrip hike and do not attempt it during the hot months.

◄ HIDDEN

Arizona Strip

The rectangular-shaped stretch of Arizona sandwiched between the Colorado River and the borders of Utah and Nevada is referred to as the Arizona Strip. Most of the area is remote, with few paved roads and, aside from Colorado City, Fredonia and Jacob Lake, few towns or settlements for visitors. In January 2000, President Clinton signed an executive order creating Grand Canyon–Parashant National Monument to protect more than a million acres of the Arizona Strip from mining, hunting, off-roading and other environmental abuses.

Along the eastern edge of the Arizona Strip, on the Colorado River, however, the manmade Lake Powell is an increasingly popular resort, especially well-known for houseboat vacations. The nearby town of Page offers ample accommodations and dining options. Page is about 120 miles from the North Rim of the Grand Canyon. Glen Canyon Dam, Lee's Ferry (a prized spot for trophy trout), Marble Canyon and Vermillion Cliffs are along the route to the North Rim from Page.

Text continued on page 70.

Get Your Kicks on Route 66

Williams, a historic mountain town tucked away in the ponderosa pine forest of northern Arizona, is still somewhat undiscovered. But it's only 60 miles southeast from the Grand Canyon and, working hard to get its name on more visitors maps, has adopted (and legally registered) the moniker "Gateway to the Grand Canyon." Founded in 1882, long before it had a savvy chamber of commerce, Williams was known as a tough, bawdy railroad and logging center. Across the street from the railroad yards, brothels and opium dens sprung up to serve the loggers, Chinese laborers, railroad workers and cowboys. At that time, a muddy roadway through town was part of the network of trails known as Old Trails Highway. By the 1920s, the roadway became part of the U.S. highway system and entered cultural lore as Route 66. As the interstate highway system replaced the old Route 66, Williams held out until 1984, when it became the last town along the old route to be bypassed by the interstate.

The first place to stop in Williams is the **Williams Forest Service Visitors Center**, located in the old Santa Fe railroad freight depot, to pick up brochures about attractions or obtain information about lodging, dining or visiting the Grand Canyon. ~ 200 West Railroad Avenue; 928-635-4061, 928-635-4707; www.williamschamber.com.

From the visitors center, a walk around downtown Williams is quite manageable. The historical core extends no more than four blocks in either direction along Route 66 and Railroad avenues. Most of the shops and galleries of interest to visitors are on Route 66, which is only a block from the visitors center. Sidewalks have been brick-paved, and most turn-of-the-20th-century buildings have been restored and now house galleries of Western and American Indian art, jewelry and crafts, collectibles, restaurants and a couple of authentic Route 66 saloons.

The **Grand Canyon Railway** is just across the tracks from the visitors center, in the historic 1908 Williams Depot. Using either turn-of-the-20th-century steam engines (summer months) or 1950s diesel engines (winter), the train leaves Williams in the morning for a two-and-a-quarter-hour trip through Kaibab National Forest to the Grand Canyon, tracing the route that brought early tourists to the park. The return trip to Williams departs from the Grand Canyon in midafternoon. The depot building also houses a small but well-done historical and railroad museum. ~ Williams Depot, Railroad Avenue and Grand Canyon Boulevard; 928-773-1976, 800-843-8724, fax 928-773-1610; www. thetrain.com, e-mail info@thetrain.com.

A drive south about 12 miles on **Perkinsville Road** (referred to locally as the South Road) will bring you to open meadows, where, at dusk, it's not uncommon to spot deer and elk emerging from the forest to graze. Early October, when the aspen trees have turned golden and flame, is an especially lovely time to make the drive during the day to see the fall colors.

LODGING   Williams has several choices for motel accommodations located along historic Route 66, many offering low prices as well as nostalgia. The chamber of commerce can provide a list. ~ 928-635-4061, fax 928-635-1417; www.williamschamber.com.

Visitors looking for a historical connection to Williams' rowdy railroad and mining past might consider booking a room at the **Red Garter Bed and Bakery**. This 1897 Victorian Romanesque building was used as a saloon and a bordello. The original eight cribs on the second floor have been remodeled into four antique-furnished guest rooms. Each room has a private three-quarter bath. Of course, the rooms tend to be smaller than standard hotel or motel rooms, and one of the rooms doesn't have windows, but 12-foot ceilings, over-the-door transoms, skylights and ceiling fans keep things cheerful, bright and airy. Closed December and January. ~ 137 West Railroad Avenue; 928-635-1484, 800-328-1484; www.redgarter.com, e-mail john@redgarter.com. DELUXE.

Savvy travelers interested in a short Grand Canyon trip may want to stay at the **Grand Canyon Railway Hotel**, adjoining the Williams railyard, and enjoy a stress-free return train trip to the South Rim. The attractive historic building has a Western-style lobby featuring the art of Frederic Remington. Rooms are comfy and the restaurant is good. ~ 235 North Grand Canyon Boulevard; 928-635-4010, 800-843-8724; www.thetrain.com, e-mail info@thetrain.com. MODERATE TO DELUXE.

The only hostel on the highway to the Grand Canyon, **Grand Canyon Red Lake Hostel** has a total of 32 beds; private rooms are available. Facilities include a common room (with TV and VCR) and a kitchen area (with microwave, toaster and mini-fridges); showers are coin-operated. ~ 8850 North Route 64, ten miles north of Williams; 928-635-4753, 800-581-4753, fax 928-635-4753. BUDGET.

DINING   This is still cowboy country when it comes to food, and steak and ribs are popular on local menus. Besides platters of steak, barbecued ribs or prime rib, **Miss Kitty's Steakhouse and Saloon** offers up live country music each evening during tourist season. It's a big place, with lots of wood and brick and high beamed ceilings. A balcony rings two sides of the room and a stage and dancefloor occupy one end of the room. It's fast, efficient and fun. ~ In the Mountainside Inn Resort, 642 East Route 66; 928-635-9161. MODERATE TO DELUXE.

Set in a renovated gas station, **Cruiser's Café 66** generates the spirit of Route 66 with antiques and memorabilia galore. Sidle up to gas pumps, neon signs, old photographs and road signs for a closer look at those magical motoring days. Grab a drink at the horseshoe bar before ordering burgers, chicken, steaks or ribs. Seasonal hours. ~ 233 West Route 66; 928-635-2445, fax 928-635-9800. BUDGET TO MODERATE.

SIGHTS Once a remote fortresslike Mormon ranching outpost, **Pipe Spring National Monument** had the only telegraph station in the Arizona Territory north of the Grand Canyon, and was home to the Winsor family and their employees, thus its historical nickname, Winsor Castle. The ranch buildings and equipment are well preserved, and the duck pond provides a cool oasis. Park rangers costumed in period dress re-create the pioneer lifestyle during the summer months. Pipe Spring is jointly managed by the National Park Service and the Kaibab Paiute Indian Reservation, which surrounds the park. Tribal members offer guided hiking at the headquarters across the street. Pipe Spring has the only museum detailing the interesting history of the Paiute people. Admission. ~ Route 389, 13 miles west of Fredonia; 928-643-7105, fax 928-643-7583; www.nps.gov/pisp.

Sprawled over 1.25 million acres in two states, **Lake Powell** boasts 1900 miles of recreational shoreline. Though most of this manmade reservoir lies in Utah, the dam that created Lake Powell —Glen Canyon Dam—was constructed in Page, Arizona.

Page started out as a construction camp for the workers building the Glen Canyon Dam in 1956. The U.S. government had to trade land with the Navajo tribe to acquire the 17-square-mile site, and a road was cut into the remote region from Route 89. The town incorporated in 1975, and today, Page has a population of 8200 residents and an annual visitor count of over three million.

The Page–Lake Powell Tourism Bureau can provide you with information. Closed Sunday. ~ 647 Elm Street, Page; 928-660-3405, 888-261-7243, fax 928-645-6870; www.pagelakepowell chamber.org.

Wedged into a sandstone gorge, **Glen Canyon Dam** took ten years to construct, starting in 1956. Over 400,000 buckets of concrete (a "bucket" holds 24 tons) were poured to build the dam. The dam, which holds back the Colorado River, flooded Glen Canyon and created Lake Powell, the nation's second-largest manmade lake. The powerplant at the toe of the dam produces nearly 1.3 million kilowatts of power, which is sold to municipalities, government agencies and public utilities in seven Western states.

Each year, about a million visitors begin their visit to the dam at the **Carl Hayden Visitor Center**. Exhibits explain the dam's construction and benefits. If you join a free guided tour you'll find yourself descending in a large elevator to a depth of more than 500 feet below the crest of the dam. At one point on the tour, over 100 feet of concrete separates you from the waters of Lake Powell. Expect heightened security at potentially vulnerable federal facilities such as Glen Canyon Dam. You will not be able to take your purse into the visitors center. After parking, pocket some cash before entering the building. ~ Route 89, Page; 928-608-

6404, fax 928-608-6283; www.nps.gov/glca, e-mail glca_chvc@ nps.gov.

By mid-May, Lake Powell's waters are usually warm enough to engage in a variety of water sports. All the marinas except for Dangling Rope rent boats and houseboats in which to explore the area. Contact **Lake Powell Resorts & Marinas** for rentals at Wahweap, Bullfrog and Halls marinas. ~ Lakeshore Drive off Route 89, near Glen Canyon Dam; 928-645-6000, 602-331-5200 (main Phoenix office), 800-528-6154, fax 602-331-5258; www. lakepowell.com.

If you don't want to command your own vessel, you can catch a boat tour or paddle-wheeler cruise at the Wahweap Marina. ~ 928-645-2433, 800-528-6154, fax 928-645-1031; www.lakepow ell.com.

For more extensive history and sightseeing tips on Lake Powell, Stan Jones' *Boating and Exploring Map* is essential to your enjoyment and is available at any Lake Powell shop.

Arizona Strip

0 — 20 miles
0 — 20 kilometers

to Escalante

Grand Staircase–Escalante National Monument

Glen Canyon National Recreation Area

Mt Carmel

Old Paria

Warm Creek

Paria

Lake Powell

San Juan River

Kanab   UTAH

Fredonia   ARIZONA

Rainbow Bridge National Monument

Tower Butte

Navajo Mountain

Navajo Creek

Marble Canyon   Page

VERMILLION CLIFFS

Jacob Lake

Bitter Springs

Navajo National Monument

Kaibab National Forest

Kaibab Lodge

Colorado River

Grand Canyon National Park

NORTH RIM

N

Navajo Indian Reservation

Havasupai Indian Reservation

Grand Canyon Village

SOUTH RIM

Kaibab National Forest

Little Colorado River Gorge

Little Colorado River

Tuba City

Moenkopi

Cameron

POINTS OF INTEREST
Ⓐ Bullfrog Marina
Ⓑ Dangling Rope Marina
Ⓒ Glen Canyon Dam
Ⓓ Hall's Crossing Marina
Ⓔ Lee's Ferry
Ⓕ Navajo Bridge
Ⓖ Wahweap Marina

The name John Wesley Powell pops up everywhere in this area. Major Powell, a Civil War veteran, led two expeditions down the Colorado River through the Grand Canyon, in 1869 and 1871. Powell mapped and kept journals of the 1000-mile journey through the largest uncharted section of the United States. A small museum in Page, the **John Wesley Powell Museum**, chronicles his expeditions and presents a small exhibition of American Indian basketry. Call for schedule. Admission. ~ Lake Powell Boulevard and North Navajo Drive, Page; 928-645-9496, fax 928-645-3412; www.powellmuseum.org, e-mail reservations@powellmuseum.org.

Sunset is a favorite time of day to be on Lake Powell because natural-rock amphitheaters appear to change colors before your very eyes as the late afternoon sun makes its curtain call.

One of the most extraordinary sights of this high-desert region around Page is a **slot canyon**, a narrow passage cut by flash-flood water and wind into the sandstone. The erosion cuts striated patterns into the rock walls, like ripples of water, and as sunlight drifts down from the opening 120 feet above, rock shapes and forms seem to undulate in the light and shadow. Quartz crystals in the rock reflect the light, while magnesium and iron create the dark, reddish colors and calcium and lime give the lighter tones. Photographers love slot canyons. **Carolene Ekis** conducts **photographic and sightseeing tours** to the most impressive and accessible slot canyon in the area. It's located on a Navajo land, so it's not otherwise accessible to the public. ~ 928-660-0739 (mobile), 928-645-9102, fax 928-645-2564; www.antelopecanyon.com.

LODGING   If you've never slept under the stars, being on a **houseboat** on Lake Powell is a great introduction. These floating homes are fully equipped with bunk beds, kitchens, showers and toilets. To make reservations more than a week in advance, contact **Lake Powell Resorts & Marinas.** If preparing less than a week ahead, call Wahweap Marina (928-645-2433) or the marina you're interested in directly. ~ Lakeshore Drive off Route 89, near Glen Canyon Dam; 800-528-6154, fax 602-331-5258; www.lakepowell.com. ULTRA-DELUXE.

Accommodations on the Arizona side of Lake Powell are limited to **Lake Powell Resort,** which is set on the lake's westernmost bay. Rooms are bright and airy; those facing the lake have especially lovely views of the marina, blue waters and rugged lakeshore. Wahweap gets bonus points for its two swimming pools, spa and manicured grounds. ~ 100 Lakeshore Drive; 928-645-2433, 800-528-6154, fax 928-645-1031; www.lakepowell.com. DELUXE.

Courtyard by Marriott occupies a prime spot where the local business loop of Route 89 starts to swing up the mesa into Page.

The property has fine views of Glen Canyon and is surrounded by a golf course. The Southwest adobe-style design fits into the sandstone butte landscape. Each of the 153 rooms are comfortably furnished with two double beds and have a balcony. There is room service, an exercise room, a pool and a spa. ~ 600 Clubhouse Drive, Page; 928-645-5000, 800-321-2211, fax 928-645-5004; www.marriott.com. DELUXE.

Several motels are located along Lake Powell Boulevard, the main drag in Page, including three Best Westerns. The 102-room **Best Western Arizona Inn** has a pool and spa (closed in winter). ~ 716 Rimview Drive; 928-645-2466, 800-826-2718, fax 928-645-2053; www.bestwesternarizonainn.com. MODERATE. Somewhat bigger, the **Best Western Lake Powell**, with 132 rooms offers similar amenities (pool and spa, except in winter). ~ 208 North Lake Powell Boulevard; 928-645-5988, 800-528-1234, fax 928-645-2578; www.bestwestern.com. MODERATE. The smaller, 99-room **Page Travelodge** also has a pool. ~ 207 North Lake Powell Boulevard; 928-645-2451, fax 928-645-9552. MODERATE.

The city of Page has licensed and approved several **bed and breakfast** accommodations; the chamber of commerce will provide a list. ~ 928-645-2741, 888-261-7243, fax 928-645-3181; www.pagelakepowellchamber.org. BUDGET TO MODERATE.

See Chapter Fifteen for accommodations on the Utah side of Lake Powell.

DINING

Aside from having dinner on your rented houseboat or at a campsite along the shore, dining on Lake Powell is limited to the **Rainbow Room** at Wahweap Lodge. Considering the volume of traffic handled in the round, large, two-tiered dining room, the food—prime rib, seafood, chicken, salads and a few American Indian dishes—isn't bad, and it's served in generous proportions. Service is friendly and efficient. Three meals are served. There's also a budget-priced pizza café on the Wahweap launch dock, open May through September. ~ Wahweap Lodge, 100 Lakeshore Drive, Lake Powell; 928-645-2433, fax 928-645-1031; www.lakepowell.com. MODERATE TO DELUXE.

◄ HIDDEN

In Page, the **Dam Bar & Grill** is an unexpected upscale and kind of hip restaurant and bar. The dam theme may be a bit overdone—a "transformer" at the entrance shoots off neon bolts of electricity, one wall of concrete is sculpted like the dam, and heavy wire mesh used to hold back sandstone walls of the gorge becomes decorative partitions between booths. But other touches—a huge etched glass panel separating the bar and the dining room, generous use of wood, linen napkins—and the surprisingly good food show that someone is paying attention. Steak and prime rib are the main events here, but fish also receives excellent attention in the kitchen. Pasta, chicken, sandwiches, burgers and salads round out the menu. No lunch on Sunday. ~ 644 North Navajo Drive, Page; 928-645-2161; www.damplaza.com, e-mail dambar@damplaza.com. BUDGET TO DELUXE.

Even just a slice of pizza (it's huge) at **Strombolli's Restaurant and Pizzeria** is enough to fill you up if you're not too hungry. Otherwise you can order from a menu of traditional Italian dishes, calzones and salads. There's an outdoor covered patio, if the weather's nice, but the view of the commercial strip doesn't offer much to look at. Closed November through February. ~ 711 North Navajo Drive, Page; 928-645-2605. BUDGET TO MODERATE.

For a quick sandwich to eat on the run or for a picnic, try the **Sandwich Place**, where you can also get hot subs and burgers. ~ 662 Elm Street, next to Safeway, Page; 928-645-5267; e-mail dtt@aztrail.com. BUDGET.

See Chapter Fifteen for dining options on the Utah side of Lake Powell.

NIGHTLIFE   Celebrate the night with a sunset dinner cruise aboard the **Canyon Princess**, which departs from the Wahweap Marina. Other types of sunset cruises are also available from Wahweap Marina only. ~ 928-645-2433, 800-528-6154, fax 602-331-5258; www.lakepowell.com.

PARKS   **GLEN CANYON NATIONAL RECREATION AREA** 🏃 🏊 ⛴ 🚣 🛥 🐟 The Colorado River–fed Lake Powell, formed by the Glen Canyon Dam, is the nation's second-largest man-made reservoir. Although all sorts of water sports can be enjoyed at all of its five marinas, the biggest and busiest is the Wahweap Marina, located on the Arizona side. There are hotels, restaurants, two boat ramps, boat rentals, visitors centers,

AUTHOR FAVORITE

I was thrilled to discover that Lake Powell's waters usually warm to a comfortable temperature for swimming by May or early June. During the summer months, when the majority of the three million-plus annual visitors come, the surrounding temperatures can exceed a sizzling 100°. That's my cue to seek cool relief and a relaxing getaway in this stark desert ocean. Even at peak periods like July 4th and Labor Day weekends, when all the rental boats are checked out and hotel rooms booked, Lake Powell still manages to provide ample shoreline for docking and camping and, as always, clear, blue-green water for aquatic pursuits.

picnic areas and restrooms. Day-use fee, $15 for a seven-day pass. ~ Both Routes 98 and 89 lead to Lake Powell. Reach Wahweap Marina via Route 89, six miles north of Page; 928-608-6404, fax 928-608-6283; www.nps.gov/glca, e-mail glca_chvc@nps.gov.

▲ There are campsites and RV hookups available through a private concessionaire, **Wahweap RV Park** (928-645-1009, 800-528-6154), $19 to $30 per night. Free backcountry camping is allowed with a permit. Camping is not allowed within one mile of any developed area.

▼▼▼▼▼▼▼▼

Lee's Ferry

When Europeans began exploring this part of the country in the late 18th century, there were very few places that the Colorado River could be crossed from both sides. Lee's Ferry was one of them. But not since the Anasazi had inhabited the area centuries before had there been any permanent residents. Around 1872, John Doyle Lee and one of his 17 wives, Emma, arrived to set up a ferry across the river. Lee, a Mormon, had been sent by church leaders to establish the ferry as a way to help the Mormons settle in Northern Arizona. Some years before, Lee had been involved in an incident known as Mountain Meadow Massacre, an attack on a wagon train involving Paiute Indians, Lee and other Mormons. Lee was eventually apprehended by authorities and executed. Today, Lee's Ferry is part of the Glen Canyon National Recreation Area.

SIGHTS

There are only seven land crossings of the Colorado River within 750 miles. **Navajo Bridge**, which spans Marble Canyon Gorge, is one of them. There are actually two bridges: a newer structure for vehicles traveling on Route 89A and the older bridge, which pedestrians may walk across to get a look at the 470-foot gorge. Pick up area maps and general books at the visitors center, which also has a permanent exhibit covering geological and historical facts about Lee's Ferry. Closed November to May. ~ Route 89A at the western side of the new bridge; 928-355-2319.

Just to the west of Navajo Bridge, a turnoff to **Lee's Ferry** winds back to the spot where the Colorado and Paria rivers join. At the **ranger station** you can pick up maps and limited information about hiking and fishing in the area. ~ Located five miles north of Marble Canyon, at the top of the hill below the water tower; 928-355-2234, fax 928-645-5409.

A few historical structures still stand at the **old ferry crossing** and at the settlement site known as **Lonely Dell** so called because Emma Lee is reported to have said, "Oh, what a lonely dell" when she first saw the site of her new home. Parking is available at the launch ramp, and from there you can set off on one of several hikes along the river or into the cliffs above. A self-guided walking tour booklet and a hiking map are available at the ranger station.

Back on Route 89A, heading toward Jacob Lake, **Vermillion Cliffs** dominate the landscape to the north. The Navajo sandstone cliffs are clearly reddish even during the bright light of the day but at sunset they take on a more brilliant color. A pullout on the flatlands (about 20 miles east of Jacob Lake) as well as in the foothills (about 11 miles east of Jacob Lake) as the road climbs up the plateau toward Jacob Lake both provide good viewing.

LODGING

Marble Canyon Lodge is located at the turnoff to Lee's Ferry on Route 89A, just west of Navajo Bridge. Motel accommodations are basic but clean. No in-room phones. The lodge also has a restaurant serving breakfast, lunch and dinner, a general store, a gas station and a fly-and-tackle shop. ~ Route 89A at Lee's Ferry turnoff, Marble Canyon; 928-355-2225, 800-726-1789, fax 928-355-2227; www.marblecanyonlodge.com. BUDGET.

About three miles west of Marble Canyon, **Lee's Ferry Lodge** offers quainter (read knotty pine) motel accommodations at the base of the Vermillion Cliffs. The lodge is popular with anglers and has an angler's shop (928-355-2352) offering complete guide services. Reserve ahead of time. ~ Route 89A at Vermillion Cliffs; 928-355-2231, fax 928-355-2371; www.leesferrylodge.com, e-mail info@leesferrylodge.com. BUDGET TO MODERATE.

DINING

In these parts, there's not much to choose from in the way of restaurants. The restaurant at **Marble Canyon Lodge** serves an American-style menu for breakfast, lunch and dinner. ~ Marble Canyon Lodge, Route 89A at Lee's Ferry turnoff, Marble Canyon; 928-355-2225, 800-726-1789, fax 928-355-2227; www.marblecanyonlodge.com. MODERATE TO DELUXE.

About the only other choice is **Vermillion Cliffs Bar & Grill** at Lee's Ferry Lodge, which, happily, serves good food—steaks, chops, burgers and baby back ribs—in a pleasantly rustic and friendly atmosphere. Besides that, it stocks 80 different kinds of beer. Three meals are served. ~ Route 89A at Vermillion Cliffs; 928-355-2231; www.leesferrylodge.com. DELUXE.

PARKS

LEE'S FERRY, GLEN CANYON NATIONAL RECREATION AREA
Halfway along the most direct route between the North Rim and South Rim of the Grand Canyon, this beach area on the river below Glen Canyon Dam makes a good picnic or camping spot. It is situated at the confluence of the Colorado and Paria rivers, which often have distinctly different colors, giving the water a strange two-toned appearance. Today, Lee's Ferry is the departure point for raft trips into the Grand Canyon. Lunch

at one of the shaded picnic tables; restrooms are available. Groceries are 55 miles away in Page; a convenience store located 5 miles away sells snacks and the Arizona license and trout stamp required for fishing. Day-use fee, $15 for a seven-day pass. ~ Located in Marble Canyon about five miles off Route 89A, 85 miles from the North Rim entrance to Grand Canyon National Park and 124 miles from the east entrance to the South Rim; 928-355-2234. To reach Lee's Ferry Campground, take Lee's Ferry Road north about three miles from Marble Canyon. Wahweap Campground and Wahweap RV Park are off Route 89, one mile north of Page. Page Lake Powell Campground is half a mile outside of Page on Route 98.

John Wesley Powell and nine companions charted the Colorado River in 1869 and 1871—by rowboat.

▲ Within Glen Canyon National Recreation Area, **Lee's Ferry Campground** (928-355-2234) has 49 tent/RV sites (no hookups); $10 per night. **Wahweap Campground** (928-645-1059) has over 112 tent/RV sites; $19 per night for tents, $33 per night for RVs. The **Wahweap RV Park** (928-645-1009, 800-528-6154) has 87 sites; $19 to $30 per night. The privately owned **Page Lake Powell Campground** (928-645-3374) has 16 tent sites, $17 per night; and 120 RV sites, $24 to $28 per night.

Transportation

CAR

The Grand Canyon's North Rim is at the end of **Route 67**, which forks off of **Route 89A** at the resort village of Jacob Lake. It is more than 150 miles from the nearest interstate highway—**Route 15**, taking Exit 15 north of St. George, Utah—but is within an easy morning's drive of either Zion National Park or Bryce Canyon National Park or Lake Powell.

Although only 12 miles of straight-line distance separate them, the shortest driving distance between the North Rim and South Rim visitors areas of the Grand Canyon is 216 miles around the eastern end of the canyon via Route 67, Route 89A, **Route 89** and **Route 64**, crossing the Colorado River at Navajo Bridge. The only other alternative for driving from rim to rim is to go by way of Las Vegas, Nevada—a trip of more than 500 miles.

From Route 40, eastbound motorists can reach Grand Canyon Village on the South Rim by exiting at Williams and driving 60 miles north on Route 64. Westbound travelers, leaving the interstate at Flagstaff, have a choice between the more direct way to Grand Canyon Village, 80 miles via Route 180, or the longer way, 105 miles via Route 89 and Route 64, which parallels the canyon rim for 25 miles. These routes combine perfectly into a spectacular loop trip from Flagstaff.

AIR

Flights can be booked from most major cities to **Grand Canyon Airport**, which is located near Tusayan just outside the south entrance to the national park. Airlines that fly there include Air Grand Canyon, Grand Canyon Air, Scenic Airlines and Vision Airlines; Air Vegas and Sunshine Airlines periodically fly in. A shuttle service runs hourly between the airport and Grand Canyon Village. ~ 928-638-2446.

BUS

Trans Canyon Shuttle operates a daily shuttle bus service between the two rims of Grand Canyon National Park. Reservations are required. ~ Tusayan; 928-638-2820.

CAR RENTALS

A car rental agency at the Grand Canyon Airport is **Enterprise Rent A Car**. ~ 520-836-9050, 800-736-8222.

THREE

Northeastern Arizona

East of the Grand Canyon stretches a land of sandstone monuments and steep-walled canyons that turns vermilion by dawn or dusk, a land of foreign languages and ancient traditions, of sculptured mesas and broad rocky plateaus, of pine forests and high deserts. This is the heart of the Southwest's Indian Country.

It is home to the Navajos, the biggest American Indian tribe, and the Hopis, one of the most traditional. To them belongs the top northeastern third of Arizona, 150 miles in length and 200 miles across the state. In addition to this impressive expanse, the Navajo Nation spills into New Mexico, Utah and Colorado.

Here, by horseback or jeep, on foot or in cars, visitors can explore the stark beauty of the land, delve into its uninterrupted centuries of history, then dine on mutton stew and crispy blue-corn piki bread. You can watch dances little changed in centuries or shop for a stunning array of crafts in American Indian homes, galleries and trading posts dating back to the end of the Civil War. And here, in the pit houses, pueblos and cliff dwellings of people who have occupied this land for 12,000 years, are more remnants of prehistoric American Indian life than anywhere else in the United States.

Five generations of archaeologists have sifted through ruins left by the region's dominant prehistoric culture, the Anasazi—Navajo for "ancient enemy." None are more beautiful or haunting than Betatakin and Keet Seel at Navajo National Monument, 45 miles due north of today's Hopi mesas.

Hopi traditions today offer insights about life in those older cities. Traditional and independent, most villages are run by their religious chiefs. Each maintains an ancient, complex, year-long dance cycle tied to the renewal and fertility of the land they regard with reverence. As one Hopi leader put it, the land is "the Hopi's social security." Their multistoried architecture, built on mesa tops, has influenced many 20th-century architects.

Surrounding the Hopis is the Navajo Nation, the largest Indian reservation in the United States. At 29,000 square miles, it is twice the size of Israel. Unlike the village-dwelling Hopis, most of the more than 210,000 Navajos still live in far-flung family compounds—a house, a hogan, a trailer or two, near their corrals and fields. (Some clans still follow their livestock to suitable grazing lands as seasons change.)

This is both an arid, sun-baked desert and verdant forested land, all of it situated on the southeastern quarter of the Colorado Plateau. At elevations of 4500 to 8000 feet above sea level, summer temperatures average in the 80s. July through September is monsoon season, when clear skies suddenly fill with clouds that turn a thunderous lightning-streaked black. These localized, brief, intense summer rains bearing wondrous smells have been courted by Hopi rituals for centuries and are crucial to the survival of their farms.

For the modern adventurer, September and October can be the most alluring months to visit—uncrowded, less expensive, sunny, crisp, with splashes of fall color.

The Colorado Plateau is famous for its rainbow-colored canyons and monuments that have been cut by rivers and eroded by weather. Erosion's jewels here are Monument Valley on the Arizona–Utah border, a stunning pocket of towering red spires, bluffs and sand dunes, and Canyon de Chelly, a trio of red-rock canyons that form the heart of Navajo country.

At the Navajo Nation's southernmost boundary, the world's densest, most colorful petrified logs dot Petrified Forest National Park. They're located amid bare hills that look like they were spray painted by a giant artist and aptly named the Painted Desert.

This mesmerizing geography serves as a backdrop to the region's riveting history. Navajos probably began arriving from the north about four centuries before the Spaniards rode in from the south in the 1540s. The conquistadors brought horses, sheep, peaches, melons, guns and silversmithing—all of which would dramatically change the lives of the indigenous Indians. The Navajos had arrived in small groups, nomadic hunters, primitive compared to their Pueblo neighbors.

Cultural anthropologists now believe the turning point in Navajo history followed the Pueblo Indian Revolt of 1680 when all the village-dwelling Indians of the Southwest united to push the hated Spanish out of what is now New Mexico. When the Spaniards returned a dozen years later, heavily armed and promising slavery for unyielding villagers, many Pueblo people from the Rio Grande fled west to the canyons of Navajo country, intermarrying and living as neighbors for three-quarters of a century.

During that time the Navajos grew in wealth due to their legendary raiding parties—helping themselves to Indian- or Anglo-owned sheep, horses and slaves. By the late 1700s, a much-changed race of part Athabascan and part Pueblo blood—the Dineh, Navajo for "the people"—had emerged. Powerful horsemen, wealthy sheepherders and farmers, they had developed a complex mythology and had surpassed their Pueblo teachers at the craft of weaving.

Navajo "shopping spree" raids continued along the Spanish, Mexican and Anglo frontiers. The United States army built Fort Defiance, near present-day Window Rock, and dispatched Colonel Kit Carson to end the incursions. Carson's tactic was to starve the Navajos out of Canyon de Chelly and neighboring areas by killing their livestock and burning their fields. On March 14, 1864, the first of some 8000 Navajos began what is known as their "long walk"—300 miles at 15 miles a day—to Fort Sumner, New Mexico. Here a 40-square-mile government compound became home to the Navajo for four of their bitterest years. They were plagued by crop failures, hunger, sickness, death and gross government mismanagement. Finally, on June 1, 1868, a treaty was signed, and some 7000 survivors moved back home.

Trading posts became the Indians' new supply source and conduit to the white man's world. While modern shopping centers, crafts galleries and convenience stores have replaced most of them, a few originals remain. The most famous is the rural, creek-side Hubbell Trading Post, a National Historic Site at Ganado. Others worth seeking out include Oljato near Monument Valley and posts at Cameron, Tuba City and Keams Canyon.

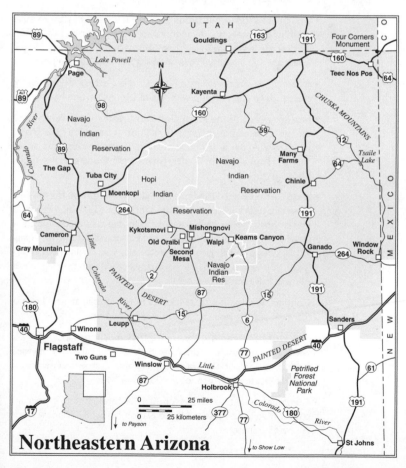

Northeastern Arizona

Text continued on page 84.

Exploring the Navajo and Hopi Nations

This detour from Route 40 offers memorable glimpses of traditional Navajo and Hopi ways of life and a dramatic cross-section of the vast reservations' terrain in just eight hours. It bypasses 124 miles of interstate, including Petrified Forest National Park. All highways on this route are two-lane blacktop unless otherwise indicated.

• Driving eastbound on Route 40, exit on Route 87 just east of Winslow and turn left (north).

• Don't miss **Homolovi Ruins State Park** (page 85), three miles north of the interstate. Abandoned for eight centuries, this archaeological site is striking in its resemblance to the Hopi Mesa villages, which are still inhabited today. Allow a half hour to one hour.

• Continue north on Route 87 for 60 miles across dry, struggling grasslands to the junction with Route 264. Allow one hour.

• Turn left (west) to the **Hopi Cultural Center** (page 96) and visit the museum, where the most traditional tribe in the U.S. tells its own story. Allow a half hour, or more if you plan to shop at the nearby **Hopi Arts & Crafts–Silvercraft Cooperative Guild Shop** (page 100).

• Head east on Route 264 for eight miles to the turnoff for the First Mesa Villages. While ancient villages thrive on top of all three Hopi mesas, those of First Mesa are most accessible for a quick visit. Drive up to the mesa top and the villages of **Hano** and **Sichomovi** (page 98); if time permits, hire a guide to take you on foot to **Walpi** (page 98), where there are no cars, electricity or running water. Allow a half hour to two hours.

• Continue east on Route 264 for 49 miles through an arid basin of marginal grazing land to Ganado. Allow one hour.

• Visit **Hubbell Trading Post** (page 101), more than a century old and still doing business (thanks to the National Park Service), for a fascinating look at the way many Navajos first encountered the outside world's cash economy. Allow one hour.

• Continue east on Route 264 for 30 miles through the junipers and pines of Defiance Mesa in Navajo Nation Forest to Window Rock. Allow 45 minutes.

- Visit the **Navajo Nation Museum Library and Visitors Center** (page 103) for a look at the history, art and culture of the Navajo people. Allow a half hour to one hour—or more if you also take in the neighboring **Navajo Nation Zoological and Botanical Park** (page 103).

- Take Route 264 west back to Ganado. Turn south (left) on Route 191 until it joins Route 40, and head back to Flagstaff through Holbrook and Winslow.

IF YOU HAVE MORE TIME

From Ganado, follow Route 191 north for 30 miles across Ganado Mesa and up Beautiful Valley to **Canyon de Chelly National Monument** (page 106). You can catch worthwhile glimpses of Canyon de Chelly and Canyon del Muerto in a few hours from two scenic rim drives. For a more memorable experience, stay an extra day and take a horse or jeep trip into Canyon de Chelly with a Navajo guide.

During the 20th century the Navajos and the Hopis have moved from a subsistence to a cash economy. The Indian Reorganization Act of 1934 ended overt repressive government policies toward American Indians and launched an era of increased self-government. Since 1961, when oil and coal reserves were found on reservation lands, both tribes have parlayed millions of resulting dollars into paved roads, schools, hospitals, civic centers, low-cost housing, expanded electrical services and running water for more homes. Three mines, three power plants, a 60,000-acre farming project, forest industries and scattered electronic assembly plants are gradually providing jobs for Navajos. But the most widespread employment is the cottage industry—creation of their own arts and crafts.

Today in every village and town you will find the rich and wonderfully evolving legacy of American Indian arts and crafts. From the Navajo—weavings respected worldwide, sand paintings and silver and turquoise jewelry. From the Hopis—some of the finest pottery in the Southwest, superb carvings of wooden kachinas, woven basketry and plaques and masterful incised silver jewelry. You will hear Indian languages and see rich spiritual traditions carried on by new generations. You will experience the history of this Western region, the blend of Indian, Spanish and Anglo cultures. All this in a setting of striking geography.

Southern Navajo Country

Indian Country is a concept that barely does justice to the astonishing diversity of the southern Navajo realm. There is so much to see and do in this region, which also embraces the pastel realm of the Painted Desert, that you may be tempted to extend your stay. Ancient Ancestral Pueblo ruins and colorful badlands are just a few of the highlights.

SIGHTS

On the southwest corner of the Navajo Indian Reservation, during spring runoff—usually March and April—a detour off Route 40 brings you to the thundering, muddy **Grand Falls** of the Little Colorado River—plummeting 185 feet into the canyon of the Little Colorado River. A lava flow from Merriam Crater ten miles to the southwest created the falls about 100,000 years ago. Some years the falls are only a trickle, and even during the best years they dry up by May, resuming again briefly during abundant summer monsoons. It is wise to inquire in Winslow or Flagstaff about the level of the Little Colorado River before making the trip. To get there, turn off Route 40 either at Winona, 17 miles northeast of Flagstaff to Route 15, or at the Leupp Junction (Route 99), ten miles west of Winslow to Route 15. Either way, ask at the turnoff for exact directions. The Winona route is the shortest from the highway—about twenty miles, the last eight unpaved. Note: Do not try to drive on this road after local rainfall.

HIDDEN ▶

Many locals contend the most colorful and dramatic concentration of Painted Desert hills in central Arizona is at **Little Painted Desert County Park**, 15 miles northeast of Winslow. A one-mile hiking trail and picnic tables overlook this vast basin where clay and silt deposited by ancient rivers have eroded into gray, red, purple, ochre and white striped badlands—300 feet to 400 feet tall. Colors are most vivid at dawn and dusk. ~ Route 87, 15 miles north of Winslow; 928-524-4757, fax 928-524-6824.

The scattered broken pottery, rock drawings and crumbling walls speak with quiet eloquence of an ancient past at **Homolovi Ruins State Park** five miles northeast of Winslow. The park contains four major 14th-century pueblos of 40 to 2000 rooms, with over 300 identified archaeological sites, a visitors center and museum where interpretive programs are presented. Nine miles of paved roads and a mile of hiking trails lead to the two largest village ruins, inhabited between A.D. 1150 and A.D. 1450. The park also includes petroglyphs and a pithouse village dating from A.D. 600 to A.D. 900. Hopis believe this was home to their ancestors just before they migrated north to today's mesas. They still consider the ruins—located on both sides of the Little Colorado River—sacred and leave pahos (prayer feathers) for the spirits. Admission. ~ Route 87; 928-289-4106, fax 928-289-2021; e-mail homolovi@ pr.state.az.us.

Winslow, the hub of Northeastern Arizona, is a railroad town and was an early trade center. Its current history goes back to Mormon pioneers who arrived in 1876 and built a small rock fort known as Brigham City, as well as a few other small settlements. The town grew, and soon a water system, stores and an opera house appeared, along with a school, saloons and, that harbinger of all frontier civilizations, sidewalks. The Aztec Land and Cattle Company purchased a million acres of land from the railroad in the late 1800s and thousands of head of cattle were brought in to be handled by local cowboys. The town was incorporated in 1900. For information contact **Winslow Chamber of Commerce**.

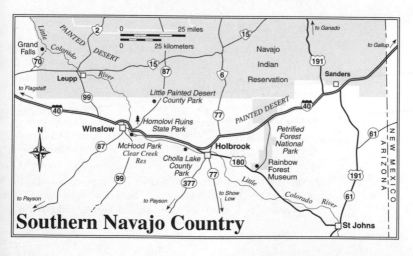

Southern Navajo Country

Closed Sunday. ~ 101 East 2nd Street; 928-289-2434, fax 928-289-5660; www.winslowarizona.org, e-mail winslowchamber@cableone.net.

The **Old Trails Museum** houses changing exhibits related to Winslow's history, including American Indian and pioneering artifacts, and a collection of railroad and Route 66 memorabilia. Closed Sunday. ~ 212 Kinsley Avenue, Winslow; 928-289-5861; e-mail oldtrailsmuseum@yahoo.com.

HIDDEN ►

The **Brigham City Restoration** on the northeastern outskirts of Winslow re-creates one of the earliest settlements in northern Arizona. In 1876, 20 Mormon families and 15 bachelors from Salt Lake City built homes inside the sandstone walls of this fortress, where they manufactured crockery and sponsored meetings of the region's ranchers. Brigham City lasted only five years before crop failures from both flash floods and drought forced its abandonment. ~ North Road, just past the municipal golf course, Winslow.

To the east of Winslow on Route 40 you'll come to **Holbrook**. Headquarters for the Apache Sitgreaves National Forest, Holbrook was named for H. R. Holbrook, first engineer of the Atlantic and Pacific Railroad, forerunner of the Santa Fe Line. It was once a tough cowboy town—the Aztec Land and Cattle Company drove cattle here, a rough-and-tough bunch that shot up everything and earned the name the Hashknife Posse. There are probably more people still wearing ten-gallon hats and cowboy boots here than in any other small town in the West.

Each January, members of the present-day Hashknife Posse carry the mail Pony Express–style from Holbrook to Scottsdale—the only mail run on horseback authorized by the U.S. Postal Service.

The **Historic Navajo Courthouse Museum** is located in the County Courthouse, which flourished from 1898 until 1976. It's now a museum focusing on Holbrook's past, including the town's original one-piece iron jail. The museum is like a musty attic, stuffed with old photos, pioneer utensils and tortoise-shell combs, and even features an old parlor. There's a turn-of-the-20th-century apothecary complete with snake oil and other wonder tonics. It also houses the Holbrook Tourism Information Center, where you can pick up maps and brochures, as well as a historic downtown tour map. Closed weekends from October through May. ~ 100 East Arizona Street, Holbrook; 928-524-6558, fax 928-524-1719; e-mail holbrookchamb@cybertrails.com.

PETRIFIED FOREST NATIONAL PARK   The signs advertising sale of "gems" and "petrified wood" on every other block in Holbrook offer a good clue that **Petrified Forest National Park**

can't be far away. Entrances at the northern and southern gateways to this park are located east of Holbrook—the northern entrance is 24 miles down Route 40, the southern one is 18 miles along Route 180. Visitors centers located at the north and south entrances provide maps, brochures, books and posters, as well as exhibits of the park's geology and history. Either entrance launches you on the 28-mile scenic drive, the best way to see the park. Admission. ~ 928-524-6228, fax 928-524-3567; www.nps.gov/pefo.

The most frequently visited area of the park is the southern section, which holds the greatest concentration of petrified wood. Here, you'll find a wide variety of specimens—from giant logs, to small agatized chunks. Farther north are ancestral Pueblo sites and petroglyphs. The northern end of the park penetrates the **Painted Desert**, an eerie landscape of colorful, heavily eroded mudstone and siltstone that resembles the moon's surface, except for the brightly hued formations.

The scenic drive begins off Route 40 (north) at the **Painted Desert Visitors Center**. Here you'll see a 20-minute film on the mysteries of the making of the forest—silica crystals replacing wood cells—as well as archaeology and problems with petrified wood theft. Adjacent to the visitors center are a cafeteria and gift-shop amenities. ~ 928-524-6228, fax 928-524-3567; www.nps.gov/pefo.

The **Painted Desert Inn National Historic Landmark** is a 1930s pueblo-style building, originally a trading post, restaurant and inn. Detailed hand-carved wood and tin furnishings were made by the Civilian Conservation Corps (CCC). Murals painted by the late Hopi artist Fred Kabotie depict scenes of Hopi life: a winter buffalo dance to ensure return of buffalo each spring, the journey of two Hopis to Zuni lands to gather salt. The inn was entirely restored in 2004 and now boasts the original color scheme by architect Mary Jane Colter. Tours are available; call for details. ~ Two miles north of the visitors center, at Kachina Point on the scenic drive; 928-524-6228, fax 928-524-3567; www.nps.gov/pefo.

South of Route 40 on the scenic drive, the park's midsection contains ancestral sites of ancient American Indian cultures dating from A.D. 300 to A.D. 1400. Scientists have discovered petroglyphs here used as solar calendars. A trail at the **Puerco Pueblo**, the first pullout south of Route 40, leads through the pueblo. Built of stone and masonry walls, the pueblo was home to about 75 people from A.D. 1100 to 1300. The ruin has been partially excavated and restored.

The petrified wood at **Blue Mesa**, where a trail leads through dramatic towering hills, is a favorite of photographers because of its blue, gray and white cone-shaped hills with chunks of agatized wood scattered about. The eroded sandstone formations suggest a mini Grand Canyon. This is also one of the best overlooks of the Painted Desert, whose strange multicolored buttes seem to glow in the distance.

The southern third of the park holds the greatest concentration of petrified logs. **Jasper Forest Overlook** provides a panorama of the area and includes barren hills sprinkled with petrified logs. Notice how the softer claylike soil has eroded from around the heavier petrified wood, creating a mosaic on the desert floor. Some logs are complete with root systems indicating they had grown nearby.

A trail at **Crystal Forest** leads you close to dense pockets of logs, many over 100 feet long and a foot or two in diameter. The large concentration of petrified wood here is mostly chunks scattered about like the remains of an ancient woodpile. Look closely at the logs and you'll see hollows and cracks where early souvenir hunters and gem collectors chipped away clear quartz and amethyst crystals. In fact, fossil destruction and poaching in this area prompted the Arizona Territory to petition Congress to preserve the petrified wood sites.

At the **Rainbow Forest Museum**, photographs, drawings, dioramas and samples tell the story of the area's paleontological history. Outside, the half-mile-long Giant Logs trail leads past enormous rainbow-hued trees. Many of the longest petrified logs (up to 170 feet) are found across the road at the **Long Logs** trail. A side trail leads to **Agate House**, a small eight-room pueblo-style structure built nearly 900 years ago entirely from chunks of petrified wood. Two of the rooms have been partially restored. The scenic drive ends two miles farther south at Route 180. ~ Two miles in from Route 180, near the park's southern entrance; 928-524-6822, fax 928-524-3567; www.nps.gov/pefo.

LODGING

HIDDEN ▶

The last and most elegant of the Southwestern resort hotels built by Fred Harvey's son Henry and the Santa Fe Railway, **La Posada** soon became a favorite haunt of celebrities, tycoons and presidents. The decline of rail travel forced the hotel to close in 1959, and it remained an abandoned shell for nearly 40 years. Reopened in 1998, it is undergoing a room-by-room restoration of its beautiful painted ceilings, stone floors and adobe walls as well as eight acres of gardens. Furniture for the guest rooms is made by hand on the premises. Inspired by 18th-century Mexican haciendas, La Posada has 35 large, lavish rooms and suites, each individually decorated with antiques and historic photos. Some have courtyard views and all have full baths with oversized tubs. The hotel is basically a museum open to the public. ~ 303 East 2nd

Street, Winslow; 928-289-4366, fax 928-289-3873; www.lapo
sada.org, e-mail info@laposada.org. MODERATE TO DELUXE.

The two-story **Comfort Inn** has 72 rooms, each decorated in
typical motel fashion. You'll find a restaurant and an indoor pool
on the premises. A deluxe continental breakfast is included. ~ 1701
North Park Drive, Winslow; 928-289-4638, fax 928-289-5514;
www.bestwestern.com. BUDGET TO MODERATE.

On the western edge of town, the **Lodge at Winslow** has 68
rooms with modern furnishings all on the first floor. There is an
outdoor pool. ~ 1914 West 3rd Street, Winslow; 928-289-4611,
fax 928-289-4428. BUDGET.

For a more conventional resting spot there's the **Adobe Inn**, a
two-story, 54-room Best Western that has typical motel furnishings
and a pool. ~ 615 West Hopi Drive, Holbrook; 928-524-3948, fax
928-524-3612; www.bestwestern.com. BUDGET.

Another Best Western motel is the **Arizonian Inn**, with 70 guest
rooms, contemporary furnishings, a restaurant and a pool. Continental breakfast is included. ~ 2508 East Navajo Boulevard, Holbrook; 928-524-2611, 877-280-7300, fax 928-524-2253; www.
bestwestern.com/arizonianinn. MODERATE.

DINING

◄ HIDDEN

Celebrated by locals and in newspapers from New York to San
Francisco, the **Casa Blanca Cafe** is known for its tacos, chimichangas, cheese crisps and burgers. Choose between booth and
table seating at this ceramic-tiled establishment, which is the oldest Mexican restaurant in the city. The dining room is cooled by

AUTHOR FAVORITE

Fifteen dazzling white stucco wigwams, the sort of kitsch old Route 66 was
famous for, are found in Holbrook. They make up one of the world's most
novel motels, and affordable yet! **Wigwam Motel** "is the funnest place I've
ever slept," insisted our three-year-old neighbor. We couldn't argue. Built
in 1950 by Chester Lewis (six other cities had wigwam motels of similar
design; only one other survives), the wigwams were restored by his children and grandchildren who still operate them. Inside each, matching
red-plaid curtains and bedspreads adorn original handmade hickory furniture. Scenes from the film version of Tony Hillerman's *The Dark Wind*
were filmed here in 1990. There's no extra charge for lulling vibrations
as trains rumble by in the night. ~ 811 West Hopi Drive, Holbrook;
928-524-3048; www.galerie-kokopelli.com/wigwam, e-mail clewis97@
cybertrails.com. BUDGET.

Casablanca fans but, alas, there's no trace of Bogie. ~ 1201 East 2nd Street, Winslow; 928-289-4191. BUDGET TO MODERATE.

In 2000, two years after the restored La Posada Hotel in Winslow roared back to life, chef/owner John Sharpe opened the hotel's upscale **Turquoise Room**. The Southwestern fare highlights regional foods, from locally sourced goat cheese, honey and Hopi piki bread to produce bought at nearby farmers' markets. Roast prime rib, grilled steaks, fresh fish flown in daily, elk and quail are always on the menu, along with homemade gelato and other killer desserts. There's a separate espresso and cocktail bar. Reservations suggested. Open for breakfast, lunch and dinner. ~ 303 East 2nd Street, Winslow; 928-289-2888, fax 928-289-1288; www.theturquoiseroom.net, e-mail dine@theturquoise room.net. MODERATE TO DELUXE.

In Holbrook, the best spot for Mexican cuisine is **Romo's Cafe**, which has been serving tasty south-of-the-border dishes since the 1960s. The decor isn't fancy in this storefront café, but the rear dining room, with its used-brick walls and hanging plants, is a more private setting than the bustling area out front for enjoying green-chile chimichangas or traditional enchilada dinners, as well as American food. In your world travels, don't be surprised to see a Romo sweatshirt—they've turned up as far away as Munich, Germany. Closed Sunday. ~ 121 West Hopi Drive, Holbrook; 928-524-2153. BUDGET.

SHOPPING   Most of the souvenir and gift shops in Holbrook contain a blend of American Indian handiwork and Old Route 66 memorabilia. One of the best is **Julien's Roadrunner** on Old Route 66. The well-stocked shop sells everything from railroad and Route 66 memorabilia to nostalgic signs. The proprietor, Ted Julien, is a long-time resident of Holbrook and a veritable expert on the area's history and attractions. Feel free to ask him anything (even about his competition), but be prepared for thorough and unabbreviated answers. Closed Sunday. ~ 109 West Hopi Drive, Holbrook; 928-524-2388.

Linda's Indian Arts and Crafts is a small shop, but it offers a good selection of American Indian jewelry and Navajo skirts, as well as porcelain dolls and Route 66 memorabilia. Periodically closed weekends. ~ 405 Navajo Boulevard, Holbrook; 928-524-2500.

For the biggest selection of top-of-the-line American Indian arts and crafts, visit **McGee's Beyond Native Tradition**, which sells everything from Hopi jewelry and kachinas to Navajo blankets. ~ 2114 North Navajo Boulevard, Holbrook; 928-524-1977.

Nakai Indian Cultural Trade Center, in business for about three decades, also features top-quality American Indian products as well as jewelry made on the premises. Closed Sunday. ~ 357 Navajo Boulevard, Holbrook; 928-524-2329.

Outside of Petrified Forest National Park, check in at the **Petrified Forest Gift Shop** to pick up sample minerals and geodes (cut on the premises). A variety of natural and polished petrified wood is for sale, from tiny $2 chunks to massive coffee-table slabs costing thousands of dollars. ~ Route 180, 19 miles southeast of Holbrook; 928-524-3470, fax 928-524-6924.

◀ *HIDDEN*

Fred Harvey Painted Desert Gift Shop sells polished and natural petrified wood, from tiny stones to great slabs, plus other gems as well as Southwestern Indian crafts and curios, books, postcards and music. ~ Route 40 entrance to the Petrified Forest National Park; 928-524-3756.

At **R. B. Burnham & Co. Trading Post** is a room lined with naturally dyed yarns. Behind that room is a shrine to Hopi and Navajo crafts. Assembled with much care, and for sale, are gallery-quality Navajo rugs, carved furniture upholstered in Navajo weavings, plus the whole array of American Indian arts and crafts. It's worth a stop even just to look. Closed Sunday. ~ Route 191 at Exit 339 in Sanders; 928-688-2777, fax 928-688-3777.

Silver-and-turquoise Navajo jewelry originated as "wearable wealth" that could be pawned when necessary.

It's pretty quiet out this way. For nightlife activities, the choices are limited.

NIGHTLIFE

PT's boasts live entertainment on some Friday and Saturday nights. Otherwise, there's a nice outdoor patio (with a full bar!) and karaoke machine inside. ~ 1500 East 3rd Street, Winslow; 928-289-0787.

All the action in Holbrook happens at **Young's Corral Bar** where some weekends are filled with the sounds of deejay-spun dance tunes. ~ 865 East Navajo Boulevard, Holbrook; 928-524-1875.

LITTLE PAINTED DESERT COUNTY PARK 🏃 One of the nicest, most colorful chunks of the 40-mile-long Painted Desert is concentrated in this 900-acre park, at 5500-foot elevation near the southern boundary of the Navajo Indian Reservation north of Winslow. In fact, many locals contend that the most colorful and dramatic concentration of Painted Desert hills is located right here. Large 300- to 400-foot-tall fragile mounds of mud slate in grays, reds, purples and yellows tend to change in color intensity throughout the day. Colors are most vivid at dawn and dusk. There's an overlook and two picnic ramadas. ~ Route 87, 15 miles north of Winslow; 928-524-4757, fax 928-524-6824.

PARKS

MCHOOD PARK/CLEAR CREEK RESERVOIR 🛶 🚤 🦆
Once an important water source for Winslow, the deep canyon

five miles from town is now a favorite boating, swimming and picnic area. Fishing is good for trout, bass and catfish. Facilities include a picnic area and restrooms. ~ Take Route 87 south to Route 99, then turn left; 928-289-5714, fax 928-289-3742.

▲ The park's 24 campsites are free; primitive only and park gates remain open at night.

PETRIFIED FOREST NATIONAL PARK 🚶🚴🐎 Straddling Route 40 and abutting the southern boundary of the Navajo Indian Reservation, this 28-mile-long (north to south) park features rolling badlands of the Painted Desert—mainly red-hued hills—north of Route 40. South of Route 40 lies one of the densest concentrations of petrified wood in the world. Each section has a wilderness area. At each entrance is a visitors center with a restaurant, restrooms and a museum. A 28-mile road leads visitors past Painted Desert vistas and short walking trails. Day-use fee, $10. ~ Both park entrances are east of Holbrook: the northernmost is 24 miles along Route 40, the southern one is 18 miles down Route 180; 928-524-6228, fax 928-524-3567; www.nps.gov/pefo.

▲ Backcountry only; a wilderness permit (free at the visitors center) is required.

Western Navajo Country

The Western Navajo Indian Reservation, bordering such wonders as the Grand Canyon National Park and Lake Powell National Recreation Area, is a land of great beauty and ancient sights. President William McKinley signed an order January 8, 1900, deeding these one and a half million acres of land to the Navajos who had migrated westward 32 years earlier after outgrowing their original reserve.

SIGHTS Where Routes 89 and 64 meet, the Navajos operate **Cameron Visitors Center**, offering advice and brochures on tribal attractions. ~ 928-679-2303, fax 928-679-2017.

Follow Route 64 west ten miles to an unpaved spur road and walk a few hundred feet to a dramatic **overlook**. At the bottom of hundreds of feet of sheer canyon walls is a muddy ribbon of the Little Colorado River. Upper limestone cliffs, layered like flapjack stacks, contrast with massive sandstone slabs below, evidence of a shallow sea 250 million years ago. This **Grand Canyon of the Little Colorado Gorge Tribal Park** is owned by the Navajos. A festive air reigns year-round as Indians set up their flag- and banner-bedecked crafts booths in the parking area.

A mile north of the visitors center is **Cameron Trading Post, Motel and Restaurant**, a stone pueblo-style complex established in 1916 by Hopis and Navajos. Long known as an oasis of hospitality, this bustling spot adjoins the Route 89 road bridge over the LCR (as it's known locally), and is a popular stop for travelers. ~ Route 89, Cameron; 928-679-2231, 800-338-7385, fax 928-679-2350; www.camerontradingpost.com, e-mail info@cameron tradingpost.com.

Today this mini-city is a great place to people watch: old Navajo women in traditional velvet blouses, men in tall, black reservation hats and turquoise jewelry accompanied by youngsters in mod T-shirts and tennies. Inside the post, packed with curios and quality crafts, you'll often see a weaver at work.

Next door, don't miss **Cameron Collector's Gallery**, offering antique Indian crafts and outstanding works of contemporary American Indian art—rare chief's blankets, pottery, dolls, weaponry and ceremonial garb. Behind the gallery, **Mrs. Richardson's Terraced Garden** is an oasis of vegetables and flowers.

◄ HIDDEN

> Navajo ceramics are simple, unadorned brown pieces glazed with hot pitch. The pieces look wonderful when made by a master.

North of Cameron, continuing on Route 89 to The Gap, lies the northernmost extension of the **Painted Desert**, an ancient land of silt and volcanic ash hills barren of vegetation. The Painted Desert draws its name from the undulating mounds of multihued sediments that grace the strange landscape. Red sphinx shapes astride crumbling pyramids of eroded solidified sand, these badlands are red and white along some miles; gray and white along others. They're part of the Chinle Formation beloved by geologists for its dinosaur-era fossils.

At **Dinosaur Tracks**, jewelry shacks mark the spot where scientists believe a 20-foot-long carnivorous Dilophosaurus left tracks. For a small fee locals escort you to the several impressions—three-toed footprints twice as big as adult hands. (Look for the reconstructed skeleton of this dinosaur in Window Rock at the Navajo Tribal Museum.) ~ The turnoff is seven miles west of Tuba City on Route 160, then north one-eighth mile along a dirt road.

◄ HIDDEN

Worth a stop in Tuba City, named for a 19th-century Hopi leader, is the hogan-shaped, native stone **Tuba Trading Post**. Built in 1905 during a tourism boom, its door faces east to the rising sun; crafts, groceries and sundries are for sale. Next door, you can enter a built-for-tourists hogan replica. Now administrative and trade center for western Navajos, Tuba City was founded by Mormons in 1877. ~ Main Street and Moenave Avenue, Tuba City; 928-283-5441, fax 928-283-4144.

LODGING

Lodging in Navajo and Hopi country can be summed up in one word: scarce. In an area about the size of Massachusetts, only about 700 guest rooms are available, so it's no wonder reservation motels claim 100 percent occupancy most nights from Memorial Day through Labor Day. If you get stuck, reservation border towns (Holbrook, Winslow and Flagstaff) usually have vacancies, though they too can sell out, especially on weekends of special events.

Padded headboards and brown Santa Fe–style bedspreads and drapes cozy up 112 simple, cement-block rooms in the **Anasazi Inn**, located 42 miles north of Flagstaff. It boasts the Western Navajo Indian Reservation's only swimming pool. ~ Route 89, Gray Mountain; 928-679-2214, 800-678-2214, fax 928-679-2334; www.anasaziinn.com. BUDGET.

Cameron Trading Post and Motel, 40 miles east of the Grand Canyon's east entrance, and 54 miles north of Flagstaff, is a favorite overnight stop in Indian Country. This tiny, self-contained, 112-acre, employee-owned outpost sits on a bluff overlooking the eastern prelude to the Grand Canyon of the Colorado. From 6 a.m. until 10 p.m. or later, the trading post is a beehive of tourists and Navajos mingling to shop, dine or pick up everything from mail and tack to baled hay. It's mainly the tourists who stay overnight in 62 rooms and 4 suites. Established in 1916, the motel rooms are of native stone and wood architecture (variously called Pueblo style or Victorian territorial), as is the rest of the compound. The rooms tend to be a little funkier here than elsewhere on the reservation. ~ Route 89, Cameron; 928-679-2231, 800-338-7385, fax 928-679-2350; www.camerontradingpost.com, e-mail info@camerontradingpost.com. MODERATE.

Off Tuba City's main thoroughfare sits **Dine Inn Motel**, a modern one-story affair with 20 guest rooms. Four of these are furnished with a refrigerator, microwave and couch. ~ Route 160 at Peshlakai Avenue, Tuba City; 928-283-6107. MODERATE.

Students at Tuba City's Greyhills High School are learning the hotel management business by operating the 32-room **Greyhills Inn**. Open year-round to all ages, rooms are comfy and carpeted, with modern interiors. Guests share bathrooms and, for a

AUTHOR FAVORITE

Ambiance is everything at the **Cameron Trading Post Restaurant** on the western Navajo reservation. The food is fine—and you're lucky to find any restaurant at all out here—but for me the hand-carved furniture and view of the Little Colorado make this place very special. After walking through the typically low, open-beam ceiling trading post, you enter a lofty room lined with windows looking out onto the Little Colorado River. Tables and chairs are of carved oak and the ceiling glimmers silver from its patterned pressed tin squares. Thirty breakfast choices include Navajo taco with egg, *huevos rancheros* and hot cakes; for dinner, try the deep-fried fish and chicken or steak entrées. ~ Route 89, Cameron; 928-679-2231, 800-338-7385, fax 928-679-2350; www.camerontradingpost.com/restaurant.html, e-mail info@camerontradingpost.com. BUDGET TO MODERATE.

modest fee, can share meals with Navajo students in their cafeteria during the school year. Peak season is May through October. Closed during school holidays. ~ 160 Warrior Drive, northeast of Bashas off Route 160, near Tuba City; 928-283-6271, fax 928-283-4432. BUDGET TO MODERATE.

If you're not on a cholesterol-free diet, you'll find Indian Country food, as with everything else here, an adventure. Fry bread appears at lunch and dinner with taco trimmings as a Navajo taco, or as bread for a sandwich, or as dessert dripping with honey. Other favorites include mutton stew (usually served with parched corn), chili, Mexican food, burgers and steaks, and for breakfast, biscuits with gravy.

DINING

Anasazi Gray Mountain Restaurant fills its walls with Southwestern kitsch. Entrées (hamburgers, chicken-fried steak, halibut, pepper steak) come with soup or salad, hot rolls, baked potato, cowboy beans or french fries and salsa. They serve breakfast, too. Closed November to February. ~ Route 89, Gray Mountain; 928-679-2203, fax 928-679-2334; www.anasaziinn.com, e-mail info@anasaziinn.com. BUDGET TO MODERATE.

Hogan Restaurant, amid open-beam and wood decor, offers dinners of steak, shrimp and chicken-fried steak, plus the inevitable Navajo taco and a variety of Mexican entrées. Look for the large historic photos of Charles H. Algert, pioneer Indian trader and founder of Tuba Trading Post, shown on horseback in 1898, and an 1872 photo of the Hopi leader Tuba, standing with arms folded. ~ Main Street, Tuba City; 928-283-5260. BUDGET.

The 1916 stone **Cameron Trading Post** is like a department store of Indian crafts, crammed with a good selection of nearly everything—lots of Navajo rugs, cases of jewelry from all Southwestern tribes, kachinas, sand paintings, baskets and pottery. The adjoining Cameron Gallery offers the most expensive crafts including antique Indian weavings, Apache baskets, Plains beadwork, weaponry and ceremonial garb. ~ Route 89, Cameron; 928-679-2231; www.camerontradingpost.com, e-mail info@cameron tradingpost.com.

SHOPPING

Tuba Trading Post emphasizes Navajo rugs, sometimes including small pictorials. Also for sale are kachinas, jewelry and the Pendleton blankets Indians like to give one another for births, graduations and other celebrations. ~ Main Street and Moenave Avenue, Tuba City; 928-283-5441, fax 928-283-4144.

Hopi Indian Country

Three sand-colored mesas stacked and surrounded by a dozen ancient villages form the core of the Hopi Indian Reservation. Completely surrounded by the Navajo Indian Reservation, the villages are strung along 90 miles of Route 264. Home for several centuries to the Hopi, some structures standing today have been used by the same families for 900 years. This fascinating high-desert place (about 4000-foot elevation) is a study in contrasts: it looks stark and poor one minute, then ancient and noble the next.

SIGHTS   Looking for crafts to buy at the homes of Hopi craftsmakers or attending dances are good reasons to visit the villages. **Hopi Indian Dances**, nearly all of them involving prayers for rain for their dry farm plots, occur year-round. Dates are rarely announced more than two weeks in advance. Whether or not you can attend will vary with the dance and the village. Don't miss a chance to attend one. Instructions for visitors will be posted outside most villages. In all cases, leave cameras, tape recorders and sketching pads in the car. Photography is not permitted in the villages or along Hopi roads. To ask for permission to attend, contact the **Hopi Office of Public Relations**. ~ 928-734-3112, fax 928-734-3289; www.hopi. nsn.us, e-mail vcharles@hopi.nsn.us.

> Know your American Indian lingo: a tepee is a conical dwelling, made from buffalo hides and supported by poles; a wigwam is more rounded, made from woven mats or birch bark.

Two miles southeast of Tuba City at **Moenkopi** ("the place of running water"), a village founded in the 1870s by a Hopi chief from Oraibi, note the rich assortment of farm plots. This is the only Hopi village that irrigates its farmland—water comes from a nearby spring. Elsewhere farmers tend small plots in several locations, enhancing their chance of catching random summer thundershowers. The villages of Upper and Lower Moenkopi are the only Hopi villages not situated on or just below one of the three mesas.

It's some 40 miles to the next two villages. **Bacavi**, consisting mostly of prefab homes, was built in 1909 following a political upheaval at Old Oraibi. **Hotevilla**, also a relatively new (built in 1906) village, with its mix of adobe and cinderblock homes at the edge of a mesa, is nonetheless a traditional village known for its dances and crafts. A few miles down the road, on the edge of Third Mesa, **Old Oraibi** is one of the oldest continuously inhabited villages in North America. Hopis lived here as early as 1150. Try the ten-minute walk from the south edge of the village to ruins of a church built in 1901 by H. R. Voth, a Mennonite minister. It was destroyed by lightning. At **Kykotsmovi**, "mound of ruined houses," two miles east, then south one mile on Route 2, the Hopi Office of Public Relations provides visitor information. ~ Route 2; 928-734-3112, fax 928-734-3289; www.hopi.nsn.us, e-mail vcharles@hopi.nsn.us.

Continue east on Route 264 a half dozen miles to **Shungopavi**, Second Mesa's largest village, built at a cliff's edge. It's two more miles to the **Hopi Cultural Center**, the biggest social center for

Indians and visitors. Hopi staffers of this, pueblo-style museum-restaurant-motel-gift shop complex are also pretty knowledgeable about events on the reservation. Admission for museum. ~ At Second Mesa on Route 264; 928-734-2401, fax 928-734-6651; www.hopi.nsn.us.

Just 100 feet west of the complex at the **Hopi Arts & Crafts–Silvercraft Cooperative Guild**, silversmiths work amid the biggest assortment of Hopi-made crafts on the reservation. Closed weekends. ~ 928-734-2463, fax 928-734-6647.

East of the Cultural Center, the two weathered villages of **Sipaulovi** and **Mishongnovi** are strikingly placed above the desert floor on Second Mesa, many of their dwellings carved from stone. It's a steep climb north to both up an unnamed road from Route 264. Founded in the 1680s, both are known for their dances and are worth a visit for the views. Mishongnovi is currently closed, but you can still wander around. Photographs are not allowed. ~ Information: 928-737-2570, fax 928-737-9444.

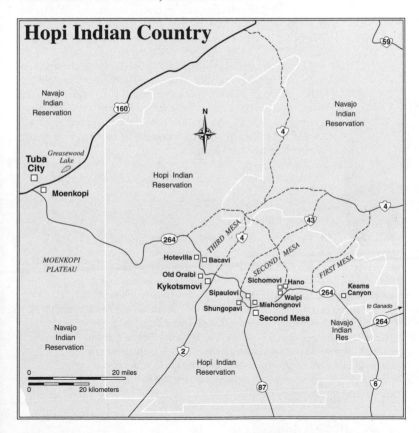

Hopi Indian Country

FIRST MESA   If you have time to make only one stop, visit the trio of villages on First Mesa—**Hano**, **Sichomovi** and **Walpi**. Perched atop the flat oblong mesa, its sides dropping precipitously 300 feet to the desert below, the village locations help you understand why the Hopis believe they live at the center of the universe. Accessible only by a thrilling curvy drive up a narrow road with no guardrails (signs off Route 264 point the way), all three villages seem to grow out of the mesa's beige-colored stone. Vistas are uninterrupted for miles amid an eerie stillness. A guided walking tour (fee) is offered daily. Call ahead, especially February to July during the ceremonial season. ~ Eight miles east of the Secakuku Trading Post; 928-737-2262, fax 928-737-2347.

Most awesome is Walpi. Built some 300 years ago on a promontory with panoramas in all directions, Walpi's houses stack atop one another like children's blocks, connected with wooden ladders. From the parking lot (no cars are permitted in Walpi) the village resembles a great stone ship suspended on a sea of blue sky. Leaders keep the village traditional so that neither electricity nor running water is permitted. Year-round guided **walking tours of Walpi** are offered daily. Sign up at Punsi Hall. ~ 928-737-2262, fax 928-737-2347.

Here, as in the other villages, kivas or ceremonial chambers dug into the earth serve as they have since Hisatsinom days, a refuge where clan dancers fast and observe rituals for days prior to dances. Then on dance days, no longer farmers in denims, the Hopis slowly emerge through ladders on kiva roofs to the hypnotic rhythm of drums and rattles. Transformed in feathers, bells and pine boughs, they appear as sacred beings.

Everyday activities include women baking bread out of doors in beehive ovens or tending clay firings. These are excellent pottery

AUTHOR FAVORITE

I felt a sense of privilege when I witnessed the beauty of a Hopi ceremonial dance, as though I were being let in on a secret ritual. Although some Hopi dances are held in plazas and are open to the public, others are held privately in underground kivas. Many of their dances are appeals for rain or to improve harmony with nature. Starting times are determined by Hopi elders according to the position of the moon, sun and vibrations. The **Powamu Ceremony** or **Bean Dance** in late February is a fertility ritual to help enhance the summer harvest, while the **Snake Dance** is done near the end of August. Live rattlesnakes are used during the ceremony as a form of communication with the Underworld. If you attend a ceremony, remember to respect the proceedings and not take pictures or use tape recorders.

villages. Crude signs in windows invite you into homes of kachina and pottery makers, a wonderful chance to get acquainted with these hospitable people.

Like Walpi, Sichomovi is a medieval-looking little stone town around an ancient ceremonial plaza. Unlike Walpi, you can reach Sichomovi by car (though probably not in a motor home) and wander the narrow, dusty streets without a guide's supervision. There is parking at the Ponsi Hall administrative offices and near the gate that closes off the road to Walpi.

Hano resembles its neighboring Hopi villages, but in language and custom it remains a Tewa settlement of Pueblo Indians who fled Spanish oppression in the Rio Grande region in the late 1690s.

Continuing east on Route 264, Hopi Indian Country ends at Keams Canyon, the federal government administrative center, with tourist facilities (restaurant, Indian art gallery, grocery) clustered around **Keams Canyon Shopping Center**. Well-chosen Hopi and Navajo crafts are for sale. Closed Sunday. ~ Route 264; 928-738-2294, fax 928-738-5250; www.ancientnations.com.

Follow the canyon northeast into the woods. About two miles in, on the left, near a ramada and a small dam, you'll find **Inscription Rock** where Kit Carson signed his name on the tall sandstone wall about the time he was trying to end Navajo raiding parties.

◄ HIDDEN

Designed by Arizona's award-winning architect Benny Gonzales, Second Mesa offers the only tribal-owned tourist complex. Here are 33 rooms of the **Hopi Cultural Center Inn** with their white walls, rosewood furniture, television, desk and vanity. This is a nonsmoking establishment. ~ Route 264 at Second Mesa; 928-734-2401, fax 928-734-6651; www.hopiculturalcenter.com, e-mail info@hopiculturalcenter.com. MODERATE.

LODGING

Hopi's primary meeting place, the **Hopi Cultural Center Restaurant**, with open-beam ceiling and sturdy, wood-carved furniture, offers Hopi options at all meals. Breakfasts include blue-corn pancakes, blue-corn cornflakes with milk and fry bread. For lunch or dinner, nok qui vi—traditional stew with corn and lamb, served with fresh-baked green chiles and fry bread—as well as steak, chicken and shrimp entrées round out the menu. For dessert there is strawberry shortcake. ~ Route 264 at Second Mesa; 928-734-2401 ext. 306, fax 928-734-6651. BUDGET TO MODERATE.

DINING

Murals depicting Hopi mesa life decorate the exterior at **Keams Canyon Cafe**. This simple eatery has such entrées as T-bone steak, roast beef and enchiladas, all served on formica tables. Closed Sunday. ~ Route 264 in Keams Canyon; 928-738-2296. BUDGET TO MODERATE.

Roadside Hopi galleries and shops are abundant. Owned by individual families, by groups of artists or by craftsmakers with na-

SHOPPING

tional reputations, many of these Hopi crafts enterprises are located on or near Route 264. A growing number are in private homes in the mesatop villages, where artisans put out makeshift hand-lettered signs—often propped up by rocks—when they have wares for sale.

Third Mesa's **Monongya Gallery** has large rooms filled with Indian jewelry, some pottery and kachina doll sculptures. ~ Third Mesa; 928-734-2344.

Driving east a half-mile, follow the Old Oraibi signs south to **Old Oraibi Crafts**, specializing in Hopi dawas—wall plaques made of yarn. This tiny shop with a beam ceiling also sells stuffed Hopi clown dolls.

In Second Mesa, west of the Hopi Cultural Center, the pueblo-style **Hopi Arts & Crafts–Silvercraft Cooperative Guild Shop** sells work by more than 350 Hopi craftsmakers, often introducing new artists. You'll see fine, reasonably priced samples of all Hopi crafts—coil baskets, wicker plaques, kachina dolls—from traditional to the contemporary baroque and even the older-style flat dolls, plus silver jewelry, woven sashes and gourd rattles. Prices are good. Staff members are knowledgeable about who the best crafts makers are in any specialty and where to find them. In the shop you'll occasionally see Hopi silversmiths at work. ~ Second Mesa; 928-734-2463, fax 928-734-6647.

HIDDEN ▶ East of the Hopi Cultural Center one and a half miles, on the left, stop at an unassuming-looking **Tsakurshovi** to find the funkiest shop en route, the only place you can buy sweetgrass, bundled sage, cottonwood root, fox skins, elk toes, warrior paint, dance fans, the oldest-style kachina dolls and the largest selection of Hopi baskets on the reservation, amid a delightful hodgepodge of crafts and trade items adored by Hopi dancers. (Owners invented the "Don't Worry, Be Hopi" T-shirts.) ~ Second Mesa; 928-734-2478.

Honani Crafts Gallery, with its stained-glass windows of Hopi dancer designs, sells jewelry made by 16 silversmiths from all three mesas plus kachinas, pottery, books and concho belts. ~ Five and a half miles east of the Hopi Cultural Center, Route 264; 928-737-2238.

It's seven more miles to First Mesa, where Walpi residents welcome you to see pottery and kachinas they've made in Hopi's most picturesque village.

Thirteen miles east, visit **McGee's Indian Art Gallery** at Keams Canyon Shopping Center, distinctive for its Hopi village murals. For sale are a tasteful variety of Hopi and Navajo crafts—concho belts, silver jewelry, wicker plaques, kachinas, sand paintings, moccasins and rugs. Closed Sunday. ~ Route 264, Keams Canyon; 928-738-2295; www.hopiart.com, e-mail sales@hopiart.com.

This is the heart, soul and capital of the Navajo Nation—a strikingly beautiful expanse of canyons, red rocks, forests and mountains where the Navajos have recorded their proudest victories and most bitter defeats. The longer you stay and explore, the more you'll appreciate the ever-evolving culture that is the Navajo Way.

Central Navajo Country

The ruins of ancient cities you'll see also remind us that long before the Navajo arrived this too was homeland to ancestors of the Hopis—the Anasazi.

Forty-five miles east of Keams Canyon, near the small village of Ganado, follow a shaded road a half mile west along a creek to **Hubbell Trading Post National Historic Site**, which still operates as it did when Lorenzo Hubbell, dean of Navajo traders, set up shop here in the 19th century. Now owned by the National Park Service and operated by Western National Parks Associations, Hubbell's remains one of only a few trading posts with the traditional "bullpen" design—shoppers stand outside a wooden arena asking for canned goods, yards of velvet and other household goods. Built in the 1870s, this adobe building looks and smells its age. The floors are uneven from years of wear. Walls are jammed to their open-beam ceilings with baskets, pottery, books, rugs, historical photos, jewelry, postcards, dry goods and grocery items. Tack and tools still dangle from the rafters. ~ Route 264,

SIGHTS

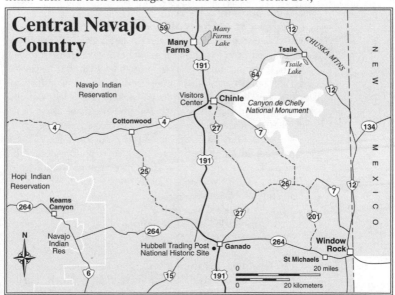

Ganado; 928-755-3254, 928-755-3475 (visitors center), fax 928-755-3405; www.nps.gov/hutr.

Self-guiding tours of the 160-acre complex and exhibits in the **Visitors Center** explain how trading posts once linked the Navajo with the outside world, and how Hubbell was not just a trader but a valued friend of the Indian community until his death in 1930. The Hubbell family continued to operate the post until it was given to the National Park Service in 1967. Also in the Visitors Center is a good selection of Indian-related books. And for a tip, Navajo weavers demonstrating their crafts will pose for photos—but be sure to ask first. (Please obtain consent before snapping pictures on Navajo land.) ~ Ganado; 928-871-7941, fax 928-871-4924.

Forty-five-minute to one-hour-long guided tours (fee) of the **Hubbell House,** with its excellent collection of crafts, give further insights into frontier life and the remarkable trader who lies buried on a knoll nearby.

Navajo-owned ponderosa pine forest lands comprise part of the 30-mile drive to Window Rock, eastward along Route 264. Picnickers may wish to stop a while at **Summit Campground**, where the elevation reaches 7750 feet. ~ Located 20 miles east of Ganado.

Nine miles east of Summit Campground in Window Rock, on your left, before the stateline, stop at the office of **Navajo Nation Tourism**. Here you'll be able to obtain Central Navajo Country maps and tourism information. Closed Saturday and Sunday. ~ 928-871-6436, fax 928-871-7381; www.discovernavajo.com, e-mail info@discovernavajo.com.

Nearby is **St. Michaels Mission Museum** in the white, hand-hewn native stone building that in the late 1890s was the chapel and four-bedroom living quarters for Franciscan friars from Cincinnati. (Sleeping must have been tough on such thin mattresses atop box crates!) Other displays—everything from uncomfortable-looking wooden saddles to vintage typewriters—include old photographs that depict their work and life. You'll see pages of the first phonetic systems they made to help create the written Navajo language. Outside, towering cottonwoods and a friar's three-quarter-acre flower garden create a parklike oasis. Open only from Memorial Day to Labor Day. ~ Three miles west of Window Rock off Route 264, St. Michaels; 928-871-4171, fax 928-871-4186; e-mail stmikesofm@aol.com.

Next door, the **St. Michaels Prayer Chapel** houses a 16-foot wood carving entitled "The Redemption of Humankind," created by German artist Ludwig Schumacher as a gift to American Indians.

East on Route 264 three miles, a rare Indian Country traffic light (at Route 12) marks "downtown" **Window Rock,** a growing, modern Navajo Nation capital. East of the Navajo Nation

Inn, the **Navajo Nation Museum Library and Visitors Center** leads visitors through an overview of historic and contemporary Navajo life and traditions with rotating exhibits. **Navajo Arts & Crafts Enterprise,** located west of the inn, encourages innovation among its members and guarantees the quality of everything it sells. The museum is closed on Sunday. Admission. ~ At the intersection of Route 264 and Loop Road, Window Rock; Navajo Nation Museum: 928-871-7941, fax 928-871-4924; Navajo Arts & Crafts Enterprise: at the intersection of Routes 12 and 264, 928-871-4095, fax 928-871-5180.

The natural setting of **Navajo Nation Zoological and Botanical Park** serves as the stomping ground for domestic and wild animals that figure in Navajo culture and folklore—everything from coyote, wolves, cougars, bears, deer, elk, bobcats, rattlesnakes and prairie dogs. In all, 58 species live here. Displays here include fork-stick and crib-log examples of hogan architecture. A modest botanical garden labels typical high-desert plants: Indian rice grass, Navajo tea, lupine, asters and junipers. Closed Monday and Tuesday. Admission. ~ North of Route 264, Window Rock; 928-871-6573, fax 928-871-6637; www.navajonationparks.org.

> Note that Prohibition is still observed throughout the Hopi and Navajo country. It is illegal to bring or drink alcoholic beverages here.

A row of towering red-sandstone pinnacles that resemble the **Haystacks,** for which they are named, forms the zoo's western boundary.

When you arrive at the street light at the town of Window Rock, follow Route 12 north past Window Rock's shopping center, then drive right a mile to **Tseghahodzani**—"the rock with the hole in it." Here you'll find a sweeping wall, several stories tall, of vermilion-colored sandstone. Almost dead center is an almost perfectly circular "window" 130 feet in diameter eroded in it, offering views to the mountains beyond. John Collier, Commissioner of Indian Affairs in the 1930s, was so stirred by it, he declared it the site for the Navajo administrative center. Visitors can picnic and walk here.

Nearby, stop by the octagonal stone **Council Chambers,** designed as a great ceremonial hogan. Murals painted by the late Gerald Nailor depict tribal history. It is here the 88-member Tribal Council meets four times a year to set policy. You'll hear Navajo and English spoken at all proceedings. Visitors are free to tour the building and watch the meetings. ~ Window Rock; 928-871-6417.

The prettiest route in Indian Country is **Route 12** from Route 40 through Window Rock and on north another 65 miles. The road hugs red-rock bluffs while skirting pine forests, lakes, Navajo homes and hogans surrounded by pasture, orchards and cornfields.

Text continued on page 106.

In the Land of Kachinas

Buying a kachina "doll" is spiritually different from shopping for, say, turquoise jewelry or a Navajo rug, crafts that were developed specifically for sale to non-Indians. Each kachina effigy represents part of a religious tradition that dates back more than a thousand years to the time of the Anasazi and is still vital today among several Pueblo groups, especially the Hopi.

Kachinas are the spirit essence of natural phenomena. Godlike, they live within sacred mountains—particularly the San Francisco Peaks (page 138), also known as the Kachina Peaks. All things in the Hopi world—rain clouds, corn, wild animals, insects, smoke, even death—are represented by their own individual kachinas. Since it is not easy to interact with the kachinas in their spirit form, every Hopi man inherits the duty to represent a single kachina within his village and kiva clan. He does this by dressing in a prescribed costume and participating in day-long dances held frequently between the winter solstice and mid-July. Most important to this impersonation is the kachina mask, believed to give a man the ability to see the world through his kachina's eyes and embody its spirit. Such masks are passed on from one generation to the next and never sold.

At birth, each male Hopi child is given a *tihu* (as kachina "dolls" are called in Hopi), as a reminder of the kachina whose spirit he will adopt upon kiva initiation at age ten. Women are also given *tihu* as a way to bring them the benefits of supernatural allies, since they cannot participate in kiva ceremonies. Once accepted, the kachina effigies are not used as toys but rather displayed in the home, usually hung from a roof beam or wall.

The Hopi have been selling kachina "dolls" to non-Indians since 1857. Most Hopi craftsmen have ethical standards about which *tihu* they will and will not carve for sale. Modern Hopi kachinas are carved in dancers' poses, then painted or dressed in cloth, feathers and bright acrylics. The newer trends feature stylized, intricately detailed figures carved from a single piece of cottonwood root, then stained. In recent years, Navajo craftsmen have begun making commercial "counterfeit" kachinas, against strong objections from Hopi carvers. Some of the most popular dolls made for sale to tourists do not represent authentic kachinas at all. Among these are snake dancers, hoop dancers, Hopi maidens and butterfly girls.

There are sound economic and spiritual reasons to buy your *tihu* directly from a Hopi craftsman. When you visit a village atop one of the three Hopi mesas, watch for handmade signs outside homes announcing kachinas for sale. But first take every opportunity to educate yourself about them. Visit Indian arts museums such as the Hopi Cultural Center (page 96) and the Museum of Northern Arizona (page 128) to see what constitutes a "museum-quality" kachina. Stop at fine-quality Indian arts and crafts galleries and ask plenty of kachina questions.

Keep in mind that when you buy a *tihu*, that kachina's spirit will become a presence in your home. Hopi mythology contains myriad kachinas, not all of them pleasant company. It may be better to share your home with Aholi, who sprouts seed corn and brings the flowers of summer, or Tsil, the running kachina who wears chile peppers on his head, than with someone like Wiharu, the child-eating ogre, or Mastop, the death fly kachina, who sneaks up on women and copulates with them from behind.

Animal kachinas are the friends, advisors, doctors and helpers of the Hopi people. Among the many kachinas whose likenesses you may encounter while traveling in Indian country, the most sacred is Ichivota, the White Buffalo, who symbolizes the unity of all humanity in a oneness of heart, mind and spirit. Other buffalo kachinas serve as advisors in healing rituals. Honan, the badger kachina, another powerful healer, shows people how to find where curative herbs and roots grow. Kweo, the wolf kachina, embodies the hunting spirit, and offerings of cornmeal and prayer feathers are made to him before group hunts.

Other common categories of kachinas include clown kachinas, who act rudely and provide comic relief during ceremonial dances, and bird kachinas, who reprimand the clowns during dances and also carry messages to the supernatural world. The spirits of cloud and thunder kachinas are invoked to bring rain.

HIDDEN ►

Follow signs to the pine-clad Dine College's (formerly the Navajo Community College) **Tsaile Campus** and its tall glass hogan-shaped Ned Hatathli Cultural Center with two floors devoted to the **Hatathli Museum**. From prehistoric times to the present—dioramas, murals, photographs, pottery, weaponry and other artifacts interpret Indian cultures including the Navajo. Wonderfully detailed murals tell the Navajo story of Creation, but you'll need to find someone to interpret it for you as there's little text. Visitors are also welcome in the college's library and dining hall. Closed Saturday and Sunday. ~ Route 12, about 60 miles north of Window Rock; college: 928-724-3311, museum: 928-724-6654, fax 928-724-3327; www.dinecollege.edu.

CANYON DE CHELLY NATIONAL MONUMENT Route 64, to the left off of Route 12, leads to a favorite spot of tourists from around the world, **Canyon de Chelly National Monument** (access is also available three miles east off Route 191 on Route 7, although it's hazardous in winter). By the time the Spanish arrived in the 1540s the Navajos already occupied this trio of slick, towering red-walled canyons that converge in a Y. The canyons and rims are still home to Navajo families, their sheep and horses grazing. Water near the surface moistens corn, squash and melon crops, apple and peach orchards.

It's hard to decide if Canyon de Chelly is most impressive from the rim drives, with their bird's-eye views of the hogan-dotted rural scenes, or astride a horse or an open-air jeep, sloshing (during spring runoff) through Chinle Wash. The best introduction for any adventure is the **Visitors Center**. Chinle, the shopping and administrative center for this part of the reservation, is as plain as its famed canyons are spectacular. ~ Along the main road through Chinle three miles east of Route 101; 928-674-5500, fax 928-674-5507; www.nps.gov/cach.

Be sure to stop at the visitors center **museum**, where exhibits on 2000 years of canyon history plus cultural demonstrations, local artists' exhibits and a ranger-staffed information desk will enlighten you about the area. Next door is a typical Navajo hogan. The center is also the place to hire **Navajo guides**—required if you hike, camp or drive your own four-wheel-drive vehicle into the canyons.

Proud tales of the Navajos' most daring victories are retold daily by guides who also point out bullet holes in the walls from brutal massacres. Thousands of much older ruins leave haunting clues to a people who lived and died here from about A.D. 200 until the late 1300s, when prolonged drought throughout the Four Corners region probably caused them to move to the Rio Grande and other regions of Arizona and New Mexico. Each bend in the canyon reveals ever-taller canyon walls, more pictographs and petroglyphs (historic and prehistoric art drawn on rock walls).

Kit Carson and the Long Walk

The memory of famed frontiersman Kit Carson was tarnished by a military action against the Navajo in 1863, when he was instructed to remove the Indians from their homeland. Carson began his campaign by encouraging the neighboring Ute tribe to raid Navajo bands, destroying their hogans. The Army paid the Utes money for stolen livestock and allowed them to keep Navajo slaves captured in the raids.

As Carson's troops advanced, most of the Navajo took refuge in Canyon de Chelly, where the Army surrounded them, burned their cornfields, and laid siege until the Navajo surrendered. The siege lasted nearly six months, during which time the Indians staved off starvation by butchering and eating stolen Army mules.

The people, numbering about 8000, along with 2000 horses and 10,000 sheep and goats, were driven on a forced march to Fort Sumner in eastern New Mexico, more than 300 miles across arid desert. Many Navajos grew ill from exposure to snowstorms and freezing temperatures as they crossed the windswept high desert. The soldiers gave them white flour and coffee beans, but being unfamiliar with these foods, the Indians mixed the flour with water and drank it, and tried to boil the coffee beans in stew. The combination gave them severe stomach cramps. People who fell by the wayside were shot or left behind to freeze to death. In all, an estimated 3000 people died. The march east is remembered in Navajo lore as the "Long Walk"; along with the subsequent incarceration, it was the biggest factor in galvanizing the Navajo from scattered nomads to a unified tribe.

Moving the Navajo at Fort Sumner proved to be a colossal blunder. Between fuel shortages and crop failures, it cost the U.S. government $1.1 million dollars to intern them for 18 months. Reviewing the situation, General William Sherman reported that it would have cost less to provide them with room and board in a New York hotel. A survey of the Navajo lands revealed nothing of value, and they were eventually marched back to their homeland.

Kit Carson's ruthless campaign against the Navajo was praised by his commanding officer, General James Carleton, as "the crowning act of his long career fighting the savages of the Rocky Mountains." Looking back at the conflict, however, we might draw a different conclusion as to who the real savages were.

Each turn showcases vivid red walls and the yellow-green of leafy cottonwoods thriving along the canyon floor.

North and South Rim drives, each approximately 16 miles one way, take about two hours each to complete. (It's a good idea to bring along brochures that point out geological, botanical and historical sites at each overlook.) **South Rim Drive** follows the Canyon de Chelly, which gives the monument its name. Highlights include **White House Overlook** (located at 5.7 miles; the only nonguided hike into the canyon begins here), to view remains of a multistory masonry village where about 100 persons lived about 800 years ago. On a narrow ledge across the canyon, ancients built retaining walls to try to keep their homes from sliding off the sloping floor into the canyon.

According to the Navajo creation story, Spider Woman wove the world then taught the Navajo to weave.

Spider Rock Overlook (at 16 miles) is a vista of the steepest canyon walls, about a 1000-foot vertical drop. Look right to see Monument Canyon; left to see Canyon de Chelly. The 800-foot-tall spire at their junction is **Spider Rock**, where Spider Woman is said to carry naughty Navajo boys and girls. Those white specks at the top of her rock, Navajo parents say, are the bleached bones of boys and girls who did not listen to mother and father.

North Rim Drive explores the **Canyon del Muerto** ("Canyon of the Dead"), named in 1882 by Smithsonian Institution expedition leader James Stevenson after finding remains of prehistoric Indian burials below Mummy Cave. Highlights include:

Antelope House Overlook (at 8.5 miles), which is named for paintings of antelope, probably made in the 1830s, on the canyon wall left of this four-story, 91-room ruin. Prehistoric residents contributed hand outlines and figures in white paint. Viewers from the overlook will see circular structures (kivas, or ceremonial chambers) and rectangular ones (storage or living quarters). Across the wash in an alcove 50 feet above the canyon floor is where 1920s archaeologists found the well-preserved body of an old man wrapped in a blanket of golden eagle feathers; under it was a white cotton blanket in such good shape it appeared brand new. It is believed he was a neighborhood weaver. Also here, at Navajo Fortress Viewpoint, the isolated high redstone butte across the canyon was once an important Navajo hideout from Spanish, American and perhaps other Indian raiders.

Mummy Cave Overlook (at 15.2 miles) is site of the largest, most beautiful ruins in Canyon del Muerto. The 1880s discovery of two mummies in cists found in the talus slope below the caves inspired this canyon's name.

Massacre Cave Overlook (at 16 miles) is site of the first documented Spanish contact with Canyon de Chelly Navajos. In the winter of 1805 a bloody battle is believed to have occurred at the rock-strewn ledge to your left, under a canyon rim overhang. Hoping to end persistent Navajo raiding on Spanish and Pueblo Indian villages, Antonio de Narbona led an expedition here and claimed his forces killed up to 115 Navajos, another 33 taken captive.

The **Quality Inn Navajo Nation Capitol** bustles with a mix of Navajo politicians and business people in suits and cowboys in black "reservation hats." The 56 rooms are pleasantly decorated with turquoise carpet, Southwest-style wood furniture and matching bedspreads. ~ 48 West Route 264, Window Rock; 928-871-4108, 800-662-6189, fax 928-871-5466; www.explore navajo.com, e-mail info@explorenavajo.com. BUDGET.

LODGING

A parklike scene is the setting for the historic stone and pueblo-style **Thunderbird Lodge**. All 73 adobe-style rooms handsomely blend Navajo and Southwestern architectural traditions. Each features American Indian prints and is an easy walk to the canyon entrance. There's a gift shop and cafeteria. ~ A quarter-mile southeast of Canyon de Chelly National Monument Visitors Center, Chinle; 928-674-5841, 800-679-2473, fax 928-674-5844; www.tbirdlodge.com, e-mail tbirdlodge@frontiernet.net. BUDGET TO MODERATE.

Best Western Canyon de Chelly Motel makes up for its sterile architecture by providing Chinle's only indoor swimming pool (guests only); it has 100 rooms, some for nonsmokers. ~ A block east of Route 191 on Navajo Route 7, Chinle; 928-674-5875, 800-327-0354, fax 928-674-3715; www.canyondechelly.com, e-mail juletsitty@yahoo.com. MODERATE.

Holiday Inn Canyon de Chelly provides more standard lodging in Chinle. It has 108 guest rooms, a seasonal outdoor pool, and an on-site restaurant; guests may arrange canyon tours at the gift shop. ~ Navajo Route 7, Chinle; 928-674-5000, fax 928-674-8264. MODERATE TO DELUXE.

In a modern, spacious room, **Dine at the Quality Inn** is the Navajo capital's biggest restaurant, seating 250 and decorated with Navajo art. The menu includes chicken, steak, Navajo sandwiches, Navajo burgers, beef stew, vegetable stew and a mutton buffet on the first Thursday of the month. Lunch is always busy, the restaurant filled with politicians from nearby tribal headquarters offices. No dinner on weekends. ~ 48 West Route 264, Window Rock; 928-871-4108, fax 928-871-5466. BUDGET TO MODERATE.

DINING

If traditional American Indian food isn't your desire, Window Rock has a few fast-food restaurants (McDonald's, KFC) to tide you over.

Junction Restaurant is one of only two sit-down (nonbuffet) restaurants in Chinle. A mix of peach and blue booths and blonde-wood tables and chairs seat patrons dining on everything from huevos rancheros or biscuits and gravy for breakfast to a crab Louis or hot sandwiches for lunch to American and Navajo specialties for dinner. The carrot cake here is very popular. An adjoining room offers a Navajo Code Talkers exhibit, which details the role the Navajo language played in helping the Allies win World War II. ~ Adjacent to Canyon de Chelly Motel, a block east of Route 191 on Navajo Route 7, Chinle; 928-674-8443, fax 928-674-3715. MODERATE.

Located in the original 1896 trading post built by Samuel Day, **Thunderbird Lodge Restaurant** is little more than a cafeteria, a style of institutional eating that has many fans on the Navajo reservation. Stick with the basics to avoid disappointment. Breakfast and lunch are fine, but you might want to mosey down the road to Chinle for dinner. The restaurant's best selling point is its extraordinary revolving collection of Navajo rugs and other arts and crafts on the walls. ~ Thunderbird Lodge, a quarter-mile southeast of Canyon de Chelly National Monument Visitors Center, Chinle; 928-674-5841; www.tbirdlodge.com/dining.htm, e-mail info@tbirdlodge.com. BUDGET TO MODERATE.

SHOPPING   Be sure to stop at the **Hubbell Trading Post,** whose low stone walls, little changed in 90 years, contain the best Navajo rug selection en route, plus several rooms crammed with jewelry, dolls, books, baskets and historic postcards. ~ Route 264, Ganado; 928-755-3254.

Navajo Arts & Crafts Enterprise sells the work of some 500 Navajo craftsmakers. Selection is excellent and quantity is large—rugs of all styles, Navajo jewelry of all kinds, stuffed Navajo-style

◆◆

JOHN LORENZO HUBBELL—HERO

To American Indians at the turn of the 20th century, John Lorenzo Hubbell was a local hero. He operated a trading post at Ganado, giving the Indians important contact with the outside world. They traded silver work, wool, sheep and rugs for essentials such as flour, coffee, sugar, tobacco and clothing. To smooth the trading process, Hubbell spoke English, Spanish, Navajo and Hopi. He was also a sheriff and a member of the territorial legislature. Hubbell tried improving the lot of American Indians by bringing in a silversmith from Mexico to teach them silver working. But he really gained their respect during a smallpox epidemic. Having had smallpox, he had developed an immunity to it. So he was able to treat the Navajo without getting the disease himself.

dolls. ~ At the intersection of Routes 12 and 264, Window Rock; 928-871-4095.

The **Thunderbird Lodge Gift Shop** provides a good selection of rugs, many of them made in the Chinle area, as well as kachinas, jewelry, baskets and souvenirs. Some of the fine-quality arts and crafts decorating the neighboring cafeteria walls are also for sale. ~ Thunderbird Lodge, a quarter-mile southeast of Canyon de Chelly National Monument Visitors Center, Chinle; 928-674-5841; www.tbirdlodge.com.

LAKE ASAAYI BOWL CANYON RECREATION AREA 🏃 🛶 One of the prettiest of the Navajo fishing lakes, located in the Chuska Mountains known as the "Navajo Alps," Asaayi Lake (el. 7600 feet) is popular for fishing (rainbow trout), picnicking and primitive camping. The 36-acre lake and creek are fishable year-round (ice fishing in winter); fishing permits are available from the Navajo Fish and Wildlife Department (928-871-6451) in Window Rock. You'll find picnic areas, barbecue grills and pit toilets. ~ From Window Rock, take Route 12 to Route 134. Drive northeast four miles then south seven miles on a graded dirt road to the lake; 928-871-6647, fax 928-871-6637; www.navajonationparks.org.

PARKS

▲ Camping is allowed; $15 to $25 depending on the number of campers. Permits are available at the recreation area or at the Navajo Parks and Recreation (928-871-6647, fax 928-871-6637), both in Window Rock.

CANYON DE CHELLY NATIONAL MONUMENT 🏃 🐎 The most famous and popular Navajo Indian Reservation attraction is this 84,000-acre land of piñon and juniper forests cut by a trio of red-walled sandstone canyons. Extending eastward from Chinle to Tsaile, the canyon's rim elevations range from 5500 to 7000 feet while the canyon bottoms drop from 30 feet nearest Chinle to 1000 feet farther east. Cottonwood trees and other vegetation shade farms connected by miles of sandy wash along the canyon bottom. Two major gorges, 27 and 34 miles long, dramatically unveil walls of 250-million-year-old solidified sand dunes in a strata geologists call the Defiance Plateau. Facilities include a motel, restaurant, bookstore, visitors center, museum, crib-log hogan, restrooms, jeep and horse tours, and guided hikes. ~ Located in Chinle, three miles east of Route 191 on Route 7; 928-674-5500, fax 928-674-5507; www.nps.gov/cach. Spider Rock Campground is east of the visitors center on South Rim Canyon Drive.

▲ There are two campgrounds available. Cottonwood Campground has 96 sites (no hookups); no fee. Spider Rock Campground, run by a private concessionaire, offers 47 sites (no hookups); $10 to $15 per night. ~ 928-674-8261; e-mail spiderrock@earthlink.net.

▼▼▼▼▼▼▼▼▼▼▼▼▼▼▼▼▼

Northern Navajo Country

Nature's handiwork in this part of the state exemplifies her unabashed use of warm tones to paint her landscapes, from flame-colored sandstone buttes to red-rock pillars. Traveling here also allows you an experience unachievable in any other part of the United States: being in four states at once, all at the Four Corners Monument. The inevitable Navajo crafts booths offer up necklaces, bracelets, earrings, T-shirts, paintings, sandpaintings, fry bread and lemonade—a splendid way to make something festive out of two intersecting lines on a map.

SIGHTS

To get to Northern Navajo Country from the south, you'll have to pass by **Teec Nos Pos Trading Post**, the usual roadside gallery of Southwest Indian crafts, with an emphasis on area sand paintings and Navajo rugs. ~ Routes 160 and 64; 928-656-3224.

Heading westbound on Route 160, even before travelers reach Kayenta, amazing eroded shapes emerge on the horizon—like the cathedral-sized and -shaped **Church Rock**. Kayenta, originally a small town that grew up around John Wetherill's trading post at 5564-feet elevation, today is both Arizona's gateway to Monument Valley and a coal-mining center.

The 24 miles north to Monument Valley on Route 163 is a prelude to the main event, huge red-rock pillars. **Half Dome** and **Owl Rock** on your left form the eastern edge of the broad Tyende Mesa. On your right rise **Burnt Foot Butte** and **El Capitan**, also called Agathla Peak—roots of ancient volcanoes whose dark rock contrasts with pale-yellow sandstone formations.

MONUMENT VALLEY   A half-mile north of the Utah state line on Route 163 is a crossroads; go left two miles to Gouldings Trading Post and Lodge, or right two miles to **Monument Valley Navajo Tribal Park Headquarters** and Monument Valley Visitors Center. Inside you can see excellent views from a glass-walled observatory. This was the first Navajo Tribal Park, set aside in 1958. Within you'll see more than 40 named and dozens more unnamed red and orange monolithic sandstone buttes and rock skyscrapers jutting hundreds of feet. It is here that you can arrange Navajo-owned jeep tours into the Valley Drive. Admission. ~ P.O. Box 360289, Monument Valley, UT 84536; 435-727-5874.

For a small fee, you can explore the **17-mile Loop Drive** over a dirt road, badly rutted in places, to view a number of famous landmarks with names that describe their shapes, such as **Rain God Mesa, Three Sisters** and **Totem Pole**. At **John Ford's Point**, an Indian on horseback often poses for photographs, then rides out to chat and collect a tip. A 15-minute roundtrip walk from **North Window** rewards you with panoramic views.

The Navajos and this land seem to belong together. A dozen Navajo families still live in the park, and several open their hogans to guided tours. For a small fee, they'll pose for your pictures. A number of today's residents are descendants of Navajos who arrived here in the mid-1860s with Headman Hoskinini, fleeing Kit Carson and his round-up of Navajos in the Canyon de Chelly area. Hoskinini lived here until his death in 1909.

The ultimate cowboy-Indian Western landscape, Monument Valley has been the setting for many movies. Seven John Ford Westerns, including Stagecoach and She Wore a Yellow Ribbon, were filmed in Monument Valley between 1938 and 1963. Other films shot here include How the West Was Won, Billy the Kid and The Trial of Billy Jack.

Gouldings Trading Post, Lodge and Museum, a sleek, watermelon-colored complex on a hillside, blends in with enormous sandstone boulders stacked above it. The original Goulding two-story stone home and trading post, now a museum, includes a room devoted to movies made here. Daily showings can be seen in a small adjacent theater. ~ Two miles west of Route 163, Monument Valley; 435-727-3231, fax 435-727-3344; www.gouldings. com, e-mail gouldings@gouldings.com.

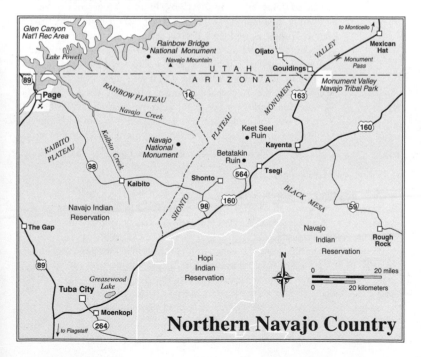

Northern Navajo Country

From Gouldings, it's nearly 11 miles northwest on paved Oljato Road to the single-story stone **Oljato Trading Post**, with Depression-era gas pumps and scabby turquoise door that are visible reminders of its age. The trading post is closed indefinitely but you can peer into the windows and see the dusty shelves that once were filled with goods for sale to local Navajo people.

Back to Kayenta and Route 160, it's a scenic 18-mile drive southwest to the turnoff for the **Navajo National Monument**, which encompasses some of the finest Anasazi ruins. This stunning region showcases the architectural genius of the area's early inhabitants.

To gain an overview of the monument, stop by the **Visitors Center and Museum**, featuring films and exhibits of the treasures tucked away beneath the sandstone cliffs, including a replica of an Anasazi ruin. You'll be impressed by pottery, jewelry, textiles and tools created by the Kayenta Anasazi who lived in these exquisite canyons. There's also a craft gallery selling Zuni, Navajo and Hopi artwork. ~ Route 564, nine and a half miles north of Route 160, or 27 miles west of Kayenta; 928-672-2700, fax 928-672-2703; www.nps.gov/nava.

From the visitors center you can hike an undemanding forest trail to **Betatakin Point Overlook**. Here you'll get an overview of Betatakin Ruin and Tsegi Canyon. One of the ruins here, **Inscription House**, is closed to protect it for posterity. However, it is possible to make the strenuous but rewarding hike to **Betatakin Ruin**, located in a dramatic alcove 700 feet below the canyon's rim. On this trip back in time, you'll see a 135-room ledge house that rivals the best of Mesa Verde. Also well worth a visit is remote **Keet Seel**. Even some of the roofs remain intact at this 160-room, five-kiva ruin. You can only reach this gem with a permit obtained at the visitors center. For more information on the

NATIVE ARCHITECTURE

The first talented architects of Arizona were the local tribes, with their handiwork ranging from cliff dwellings to pit houses. The Anasazi specialized in pueblos on cliff walls in northern Arizona. They mortared together cut stones for walls, while using logs and earth for the ceiling. Considering that rooms were small and without windows, they spent much time on their flat roofs, a perfect surface for chores. The Anasazi also built pit houses, flat-roofed stone houses partially dug into the ground. The Sinagua built pueblos similar to the Anasazi, but they preferred hills rather than canyons. And the Navajo people favored six-sided hogans made of logs and earth.

ranger-led walks to these two well-preserved ruins, see "Hiking" at the end of the chapter.

Back on Route 160, it's about 28 miles southwest to **Elephant Feet**, roadside geologic formations that resemble legs and feet of a gigantic sandstone elephant.

Best Western Wetherill Inn has 54 spacious rooms sporting dark-brown furniture, upholstered chairs, multicolored spreads and matching curtains in Southwest style. Complimentary continental breakfast. ~ Route 163, a mile north of Route 160, Kayenta; 928-697-3231, fax 928-697-3233; e-mail wetherill@gouldings. com. DELUXE.

LODGING

Tour buses full of French, German, Italian and Japanese guests frequent the 162-room **Holiday Inn Monument Valley**. All rooms in the two-story adobe brick buildings offer floral carpets in hallways, whitewashed furniture, upholstered chairs and spacious bathrooms. There's also an outdoor pool. ~ At the junction of Routes 160 and 163, Kayenta; 928-697-3221, 800-465-4329, fax 928-697-3349; www.holidayinnkayenta.com. MODERATE TO DELUXE.

The only lodging right at Monument Valley, **Gouldings Lodge** is nestled at the base of a towering sandstone cliff that provides afternoon shade. The long, low two-story lodge has sliding glass doors leading to balconies for each of the 62 rooms, taking brilliant advantage of the monoliths that dot the landscape. The air-conditioned rooms are decorated in colorful Southwestern motifs. The indoor pool is for guests only. ~ Two miles west of Route 163, Monument Valley; 435-727-3231, 800-874-0902, fax 435-727-3344; www.gouldings.com, e-mail gouldings@gouldings.com. BUDGET TO DELUXE.

Anasazi Inn at Tsegi Canyon, with 57 rooms and a view of the canyon, is the closest lodging to Navajo National Monument. ~ Route 160, ten miles west of Kayenta; 928-697-3793, fax 928-697-8249; www.anasaziinn.com, e-mail anasaziinn@frontiernet. net. BUDGET TO MODERATE.

An American Indian theme prevails at the Holiday Inn's **Wagon Wheel Restaurant**, complete with Anasazi-style walls and sand-painting room dividers. Tables for four and matching chairs are decorated in Southwest style. There's a continental breakfast buffet for diners in a hurry; a salad bar and burgers, sandwiches, Navajo tacos for lunch or dinner; meat and fish entrées for dinner. ~ At the junction of Routes 160 and 163, Kayenta; 928-697-3221, fax 928-697-3349. MODERATE TO DELUXE.

DINING

Chances are you already know what's on the menu at **Burger King**. This one, however, is special because of its "museum"— actually a display case between two seating sections—dedicated to the Navajo Code Talkers. Memorabilia recall the unique way 5000 Navajo men served in World War II, transmitting military radio messages in their native language throughout the Pacific theater of operations. It was the only code the Japanese never succeeded in breaking. The Code Talkers' historical role continues to be a source of great pride among the Navajo people—including the Burger King's owner, whose father was one of them. ~ Route 160, Kayenta; phone/fax 928-697-3534. BUDGET.

HIDDEN ►   Lively, crowded and cheery, **Amigo Cafe** serves fresh (nothing served here comes out of a can) Mexican, American and Navajo entrées. Popular with locals. Closed Sunday. ~ On the east side of Route 163, a mile north of Route 160, Kayenta; 928-697-8448. BUDGET TO MODERATE.

Three levels of dining stairstep a bluff so that the **Stage Coach Dining Room** patrons can enjoy the panoramas of Monument Valley. The light maroon booths and tables of this former cafeteria complement the stunning sandstone bluffs and views outside. The restaurant is known for its Navajo tacos, beef stew and fry bread. There's a salad bar, and nonalcoholic wine and beer are offered. ~ Gouldings Lodge, Monument Valley; 435-727-3231 ext. 404; www.gouldings.com, e-mail gouldings@gouldings.com. MODERATE TO DELUXE.

An all-American menu at **Anasazi Inn Café** offers burgers, steak, chicken and a few Navajo dishes. Open 24 hours during the summer. ~ Route 160, ten miles west of Kayenta; 928-697-3793, fax 928-697-8249; www.anasaziinn.com, e-mail anasaziinn@frontiernet.net. BUDGET TO MODERATE.

SHOPPING   The gift shop at the attractive **Navajo Cultural Center and Museum** carries fine-quality Navajo arts, crafts, literature and

---

NAVAJO CEREMONIAL DANCES

Three popular Navajo dances, which you may be lucky enough to see, are the Corral Dance, the Night-Way Dance and the Enemy-Way Dance. The Corral Dance seeks divine help to avoid dangerous lightning and snake bites; it's so named because part of the ceremony takes place within a corral of branches around a bonfire. The nine-day-long Night-Way Dance supposedly helps people suffering from nervousness or insanity. And the Enemy-Way Dance performed during the summer is a purifying ceremony to help people suffering from nightmares and other "enemies of the mind." Activities are held in a different place for each of the three nights of the ceremony and, at the conclusion, a sheep is slaughtered for breakfast.

music. ~ Next to the Burger King, Route 160, Kayenta; 928-697-3170.

Gouldings Trading Post Gift Shop provides Southwestern tribal crafts and souvenirs for all budgets. ~ Part of Gouldings Trading Post complex, Monument Valley; 435-727-3231.

MONUMENT VALLEY NAVAJO TRIBAL PARK 🏃🚴🏇 Straddling the Arizona–Utah border is the jewel of tribally run Navajo Nation parks. With its 92,000 acres of monoliths, spires, buttes, mesas, canyons and sand dunes—all masterpieces of red-rock erosion—it is a stunning destination. With dozens of families still living here, it is also a sort of Williamsburg of Navajoland. There's a visitors center with shops, showers, restrooms and picnic tables. You must arrange for a guide if you want to explore the park. Admission. ~ On Route 163, 24 miles northeast of Kayenta. The visitors center is east another four miles. The Gouldings complex is west three miles; 435-727-5874; www.navajonationparks.org.

PARKS

▲ Mitten View has 99 sites; $10 per night up to six people in summer; in winter, the restrooms are closed and the fee is $5.

NAVAJO NATIONAL MONUMENT 🏃 Three of the Southwest's most beautiful Anasazi pueblo ruins are protected in the canyons of this 360-acre park, swathed in piñon and juniper forests at a 7300-foot elevation. Inscription House Ruin is so fragile it is closed. Betatakin Ruin, handsomely set in a cave high up a canyon wall, is visible from an overlook. But close looks at Betatakin and the largest site, Keet Seel, require fairly strenuous hikes permitted between Memorial Day and Labor Day. Facilities include a visitors center, a museum, a gift shop, restrooms and picnic areas. ~ Take Route 160 west of Kayenta, turn right at Route 564 and continue nine miles; 928-672-2700.

▲ There are 31 sites in the campground, plus a handful of primitive overflow sites; no hookups, no fee.

▼▼▼▼▼▼▼▼▼▼▼▼▼
Outdoor Adventures

The largest campgrounds on the Navajo reservation are at **Canyon de Chelly** (96 sites, no hookups, free; 47 sites at Spider Rock, no hookups, $10 to $15; Navajo hogans, $25) and **Monument Valley** (99 sites, no hookups, $10 to $25). There are also campgrounds at **Lake Asaayi** (open camping, no hookups, $15 to $25) and **Navajo National Monument** (31 sites, no hookups or water, free). Camping is not permitted on the Hopi Reservation.

CAMPING

There's fishing year-round in Indian Country with a one-day to one-year Navajo tribal license required at all lakes, streams and rivers in the Navajo Nation. No fishing tackle or boats are for rent

FISHING

on the reservation. Boats are permitted on many of the lakes; most require electric motors only.

WESTERN NAVAJO COUNTRY There's trout fishing in the small **Pasture Canyon Lake** just east of Tuba City. Anglers can reach the **Little Colorado River** at Cameron and the Colorado River at Lee's Ferry (see Chapter Two). Although these rivers define most of the reservation's western boundary, sheer rock gorges put them beyond reach in most other places. Get fishing licenses and boating permits from **CSWTA Inc. Environmental Consultant**. Closed Sunday and Monday. ~ Tuba City; 928-283-4323, fax 928-283-4804.

CENTRAL NAVAJO COUNTRY **Whiskey Lake** and **Long Lake** are known for their trophy-size trout, located in the Chuska Mountains, a dozen miles south of Route 134 via logging routes 8000 and 8090. Their season is May 1 through November 30.

All-year lakes stocked with rainbow trout each spring include **Wheatfields Lake** (44 miles north of Window Rock on Route 12) and **Tsaile Lake** (half-mile south of Navajo Community College in Tsaile). Tsaile Lake is also popular for catfish.

Good for largemouth bass and channel catfishing is **Many Farms Lake** (three miles via dirt road east of Route 191 in Many Farms). You can get licenses and permits from **Navajo Fish & Wildlife**. ~ Window Rock; 928-871-6451.

NORTHERN NAVAJO COUNTRY There are no tribal lakes in northern Navajo country, but the reservation boundary follows **Lake Powell** and its tributary, the **San Juan River**. Trout, catfish and bass from Lake Powell take refuge in side-canyon creeks, a few of which can be reached in a four-wheel-drive vehicle. Small boats can put in at **Piute Farms Wash**, north of Oljato and Monument Valley, at one of the most remote parts of Lake Powell.

GOLF The nine-hole **Hidden Cove Golf Course** is carved out of the high desert grasslands and surrounded by scenic mountains and hillsides. Club and cart rentals are available. ~ Exit 283, two

AUTHOR FAVORITE

Every other outdoor experience I've found in Navajo country pales in comparison to a day-long horseback ride into **Canyon de Chelly** with a native guide. **Justin Stables**, located right at the entrance of the reservation, offers two-hour, half-day, all-day and overnight guided tours to White House Ruins (three-hour minimum) and elsewhere in and beyond the canyon. Groups range from 1 to 25 people. ~ 928-674-5678.

miles west of Route 40, Holbrook; 928-524-3097; www.hidden
covegolfcourse.com.

Horses have been an important icon of Navajo culture since the **RIDING**
Spanish introduced them in the mid-16th century. They're a grand **STABLES**
way to connect with a Navajo guide while seeing awesome country through his eyes. Most offer one-hour to overnight or longer options, and there's flexibility on where you go and how long you stay.

NORTHERN NAVAJO COUNTRY Sacred Monument Tours is
the only professionally run Navajo-owned cultural tour company in Monument Valley. They offer hour-long to all-day horseback tours into the valley. ~ Located among the vendors at the
top of the dirt road into the monument. For more information
and reservations, call 435-727-3218, 928-380-4527 (message
phone); e-mail smtours@citilink.net.

Biking is permitted on any paved roads in Navajo Country but **BIKING**
only on the main paved highways on the Hopi Indian Reservation.

SOUTHERN NAVAJO COUNTRY Petrified Forest National Park
routes will often be too hot for daytime summer riding but offer
a splendid way to sightsee in cooler spring and fall seasons.

CENTRAL NAVAJO COUNTRY While you'll find no designated
bike paths or trails within the reservation, bicycles are well suited
to both rim roads at Canyon de Chelly. Cyclists from around the
world are attracted to the uphill challenges of the Chuska Mountain Routes 134 (paved), 68 and 13 (partially paved).

NORTHERN NAVAJO COUNTRY Bicycling is popular along the
paved, pine-clad nine miles of Route 564 into Navajo National
Monument. Mountain bikes are particularly suited to the 17-mile
rutted dirt loop open to visitors in Monument Valley.

Because most of the land covered in this chapter is tribally owned **HIKING**
or in national parks and monuments, hiking trail options are limited. Hopi backcountry is not open to visitors; it is, however, on
the Navajo Indian Reservation. For the mountains, ask for suggestions from area trading posts, or hire an Indian guide by the
hour or overnight or longer. Guides know the way and can share
stories about the area.

A hat, sunglasses and drinking water are recommended for all
hikes; add a raincoat during the July and August monsoon season.
All distances listed for hiking trails are one way unless otherwise
noted.

SOUTHERN NAVAJO COUNTRY Little Painted Desert County
Park has a strenuous one-mile hiking trail descending 500 feet into
some of the most colorful hills in all the Painted Desert. Colors are
most intense early and late in the day.

Petrified Forest National Park's summertime temperatures often soar into the 90s and 100s. Hiking is best early or late in the day. Water is available only at the visitors center at the north and south end of the park, so you're wise to carry extra with you.

A loop that begins and ends at the Crystal Forest stop on the park's 28-mile scenic loop, **Crystal Forest Interpretive Trail** (.5 mile) leads past the park's most concentrated petrified wood stands. You can see how tall these ancient trees were (up to 170 feet), and the variety of colors that formed after crystal replaced wood cells.

An introduction to the Chinle Formation, **Blue Mesa Hike** (1 mile) is a loop interpretive trail that leads past a wonderland of blue, gray and white layered hills. Signs en route explain how the hills formed and are now eroding.

Painted Desert Wilderness Area trailhead begins at Kachina Point at the park's north end. A brief trail descends some 400 feet, then leaves you on your own to explore cross-country some 35,000 acres of red-and-white-banded badlands of mudstone and siltstone, bald of vegetation. The going is sticky when wet. Get free backcountry permits at either visitors center.

CENTRAL NAVAJO COUNTRY Canyon de Chelly's only hike open to visitors without a guide is **White House Ruin Trail** (2.5 miles roundtrip), beginning at the 6.4-mile marker on the South Rim Drive. The trail switchback winds down red sandstone swirls, and crosses a sandy wash (in rainy seasons you will do some wading in Chinle Creek; bring extra socks) to a cottonwood-shaded masonry village with 60 rooms surviving at ground level and an additional ten rooms perched in a cliff's alcove above.

Four-hour, four-and-a-half-mile Navajo-led hikes up the canyon to White House Ruin start at the visitors center at 9 a.m. Navajo guides can be hired at the **Canyon de Chelly National Monument Visitors Center** to take you on short or overnight hikes into the canyon. The maximum group size for private guided hikes is 15 people. ~ 928-674-5500, fax 928-674-5507.

NORTHERN NAVAJO COUNTRY Hiking is not permitted in most of **Monument Valley** without a Navajo guide. Hire one at

RIDE 'EM COWBOY!

Statisticians claim Navajos host more rodeos per year than all other United States tribes combined. Rarely does a summer weekend pass without Navajo cowboys and cowgirls of all ages gathering somewhere on the reservation. To find one when you visit, call *The Navajo Times*, a weekly, in Window Rock (928-871-6641), the Navajo Nation Visitors Center (928-871-6436) or Navajo Radio Station KTNN 660 AM (928-871-2582).

the visitors center (435-727-5874) for an hour, overnight or longer. Fred Cly (ask at the visitors center) is a knowledgeable guide especially good for photo angles and best times of day. Reservations cannot be made in advance of arrival; as soon as you pull into Monument Valley, go to the visitors center parking lot and make tour arrangements for the following day.

Navajo National Monument trails include **Sandal Trail** (.5 mile), a fairly level self-guided trail to Betatakin Ruin overlook; bring binoculars. The ranger-led hike (2.5 miles) to **Betatakin Ruin**, or "ledge house" in Navajo, is strenuous, requiring a return climb up 700 steps. But it's worth the effort for the walk through the floor of Tsegi Canyon. National Park Service guides lead tours on a first-come, first-served basis at the visitors center. The hike to **Keet Seel** (8.5 miles), the biggest Anasazi ruin in Arizona (154 rooms dating from A.D. 950 to 1300) is open to hikers. Much of the trail is sandy, making the trek fairly tiresome, and hikers must wade through cold, shallow water along the way. You can stay only one night; 20 people a day may hike in. A free back-country permit is required, which may be reserved five months in advance. Call 928-672-2700, fax 928-672-2703. Or take your chances and ask about cancellations when you get there.

This is a land of wide-open spaces, but don't despair. Roads have vastly improved in the last decade, easing the way for travelers. Bounded on the south by **Route 40**, two parallel routes farther north lead east and west through Indian Country: the southern **Route 264** travels alongside the three Hopi mesas and Window Rock; the northern **Route 160**, en route to Colorado, is gateway to all the northern reservation attractions. **Route 89**, the main north-to-south artery, connects Flagstaff with Lake Powell, traversing the Western Indian Reservation. Five other good, paved north–south routes connect Route 40 travelers with Indian Country. **Route 99/2** and **Route 87** connect the Winslow area with Hopi villages. **Route 191** leads to Ganado, Canyon de Chelly and Utah. **Route 12**, arguably the prettiest of all, connects Route 264 with Window Rock and the back side of Canyon de Chelly. This is desert driving; be sure to buy gas when it is available.

Transportation

CAR

There is no regularly scheduled commuter air service to Hopi or Navajo lands. The nearest airports are Gallup, New Mexico; Flagstaff, Arizona; and Cortez, Colorado.

AIR

Navajo Transit System offers weekday bus service between Fort Defiance and Window Rock in the east and Tuba City in the west. The system also heads north from Window Rock to Kayenta on weekdays with stops including Navajo Community College at

BUS

Tsaile. ~ Based in Fort Defiance; 928-729-4002, fax 928-729-4454; www.navajotransitsystem.com.

TRAIN   Amtrak's daily "Southwest Chief" connects Los Angeles with Chicago and stops at three Indianland gateway cities: Flagstaff, Winslow and Gallup. ~ 800-872-7245; www.amtrak.com.

JEEP TOURS   Jeeps, either with tops down or with air conditioning on (not all jeeps have air conditioning, so ask operators before you pay money), are a popular way to see Navajo Indian Reservation attractions noted for occasional sand bogs and even quicksand pockets. Navajo guides often live in the region and can share area lore and American Indian humor.

At Canyon de Chelly, **Thunderbird Lodge Canyon Tours** takes visitors on outings in large, noisy, converted all-terrain army vehicles. There are eight-hour trips that cover both Canyon de Chelly and Canyon del Muerto, as well as three-and-a-half-hour trips to either canyon. ~ Thunderbird Lodge, Chinle; 928-674-5841; www.tbirdlodge.com, e-mail tbirdlodge@frontiernet.net.

Monument Valley tour operators all offer half-day and all-day tours of Monument and adjoining Mystery Valley. It's the only way visitors can see the stunning backcountry. Most tours include visits to an inhabited hogan. Some offer lunch or dinner.

Gouldings Monument Valley Tours takes visitors on morning and all-day tours in 20-passenger open-air vehicles. ~ At Gouldings Lodge near Monument Valley; 435-727-3231; www.gouldings.com/tours. Depending on the group's size, **Bill Crawley Monument Valley Tours** uses vehicles ranging from a seven-passenger Suburban to a 30-person bus. ~ Kayenta; 928-697-3463; www.crawleytours.com. **Unimog Tours** does three-hour treks covering 24 miles on the canyon floor (groups of 15 or more only). ~ 928-674-5433; www.canyondechellytours.com.

FOUR

North Central Arizona

When it comes to north central Arizona, visitors soon discover that it's a region of vivid contrasts. The many unusual places to be found in this area vary dramatically in everything from altitude to attitude, from climate to culture. Here, you'll find lege town to artist colony, along with lava cones and red-rock spires, American Indian ruins and vast pine forests, even a meteor crater, all just waiting to be explored.

Set at the edge of a huge volcano field, Flagstaff grew up as a railroad town in the midst of the world's largest ponderosa pine forest. The town was founded in 1882, less than a year before the first steam train clattered through, and thrived first on timber and later on tourism. Today, both freight and passenger trains still pass through Flagstaff (population 53,000). The largest community between Albuquerque and the greater Los Angeles area on Route 40, one of the nation's busiest truck routes, Flagstaff's huge restaurant and lodging industry prospers year-round. In fact, casual visitors detouring from the interstate to fill up the gas tank and buy burgers and fries along the commercial strip that is Flagstaff's Route 40 business loop can easily form the misimpression that the town is one long row of motels and fast-food joints. A closer look will reveal it as a lively college town with considerable historic charm. A short drive outside of town takes you to fascinating ancient Indian ruins as well as Arizona's highest mountains and strange volcanic landscapes.

Less than an hour's drive south of Flagstaff via magnificent Oak Creek Canyon, Sedona is a strange blend of spectacular scenery, chic resorts, Western art in abundance and New Age notions. You can go jeeping or hiking in the incomparable Red Rock Country, play some of the country's most beautiful golf courses, shop for paintings until you run out of wall space or just sit by Oak Creek and feel the vibes. People either love Sedona or hate it. Often both. You'll also have the chance to visit one of the state's best-preserved ghost towns. Jerome, a booming copper town a century ago, was abandoned in the 1950s and then repopulated in the 1960s by artists and hippies to become a tourist favorite today. Prescott is a quiet little town with a healthy regard for its own history. Long before Phoenix, Flagstaff or Sedona came into existence, Prescott was the capital of the Arizona Territory. Today, it is a city of museums, stately 19th-century architecture and century-old saloons. Change seems to happen slowly and cautiously here. As you stroll the streets of town, you may feel that you've slipped back through time into the 1950s, into the sort of all-American community you don't often find anymore.

▼▼▼▼▼▼▼▼▼▼
Flagstaff Area

Flagstaff has been called "The City of Seven Wonders" because of its proximity to the Grand Canyon, Oak Creek Canyon, Walnut Canyon, Wupatki National Monument, Sunset Crater, Meteor Crater and the San Francisco Peaks. Visitors who view Flagstaff from the heights of the San Francisco Peaks to the north will see this community's most striking characteristic: It is an island in an ocean of ponderosa pine forest stretching as far as the eye can see. At an elevation of 7000 feet, Flagstaff has the coolest climate of any city in Arizona. Because of its proximity to slopes on 12,000-foot Agassiz Peak, Flagstaff is the state's leading winter ski resort town. It is also a lively college town, with students accounting for 10 percent of the population.

SIGHTS

A good place to start exploring the area is downtown, toward the west end of Route 66 (the business loop of Route 40). The downtown commercial zone retains its early-20th-century frontier architecture. Neither run-down nor yuppified, this historic district specializes in shops that cater to students from Northern Arizona University, on the other side of the interstate and railroad tracks.

Take time to stroll through the old residential area just north of the downtown business district. Attractive Victorian houses, many of them handmade from volcanic lava rock, give the neighborhood its unique character.

The **Flagstaff Visitors Center** provides ample information on the Flagstaff area. ~ 1 East Route 66, Flagstaff; 928-774-9541, fax 928-556-1308; www.flagstaffarizona.org, e-mail cvb@flagstaff arizona.org.

A sightseeing highlight in the university area is **Riordan Mansion State Historic Park**, a block off Milton Road north of the intersection of Route 40 and Route 17. The biggest Territorial-day mansion in Flagstaff, it was built in 1904 by two brothers who were the region's leading timber barons. Constructed duplex-style with over 40 rooms and 13,000 square feet of living space, the mansion blends rustic log-slab and volcanic rock construction with early-20th-century opulence and plenty of creative imagination. Tour guides escort visitors through the home to see its original furnishings and family mementos. Most of the house is fully accessible. Reservations are suggested. Admission. ~ 409 Riordan

Road, Flagstaff; 928-779-4395, fax 928-556-0253; www.pr.state. az.us, e-mail mdavis@pr.state.az.us.

On a hilltop just a mile west of downtown is **Lowell Observatory**. The observatory was built by wealthy astronomer Percival Lowell in 1894 to take advantage of the exceptional visibility created by Flagstaff's clean air and high altitude. His most famous achievement during the 22 years he spent here was the "discovery" of canals on the planet Mars, which he submitted to the scientific community as "proof" of extraterrestrial life. Building the observatory proved to be a great accomplishment in itself, though. The planet Pluto was discovered by astronomers at Lowell Observatory 14 years after Dr. Lowell's death, and the facility continues to be one of the most important centers for studying the solar system. Take a guided tour of the observatory and see Dr. Lowell's original Victorian-era telescope. The Steele Visitor Center

North Central Arizona

Text continued on page 128.

Two-day Getaway

Exploring North Central Arizona

It's easy to fill a day exploring the unique places that surround Flagstaff. Then take a second day for Route 89A, a two-lane blacktop route 122 miles long that returns you to Route 40 just 47 miles from where you turned off. It's one of Arizona's best scenic drives.

Day 1
- From Flagstaff, take Route 40 a short distance east to Exit 204.

- Visit **Walnut Canyon National Monument** (page 133) and discover the world of the ancient Sinagua cliff dwellers on a short but strenuous hike. Allow one hour.

- Returning to Route 40, head west to Exit 201 and take Route 89 north for ten miles to the turnoff for Sunset Crater and Wupatki national monuments.

- Stop in at the **Sunset Crater Volcano National Monument** (page 132) and take in the beauty of the 1000-foot-tall volcanic cone.

- Follow the 36-mile loop road through the fantastic and varied volcanic landscape of **Sunset Crater** and **Wupatki national monuments** (page 132), stopping at the Wupatki visitors center and ruins. Allow two hours.

- From where the loop road rejoins Route 89, return south to the marked turnoff for Schultz Pass Road.

- Take unpaved **Schultz Pass Road** (page 131) through the pine woods on the slopes of the San Francisco Peaks. Before you know it, you'll be back in Flagstaff. Allow a half hour.

- After a late lunch, take your pick among the various sightseeing possibilities Flagstaff has to offer. You might ride the chairlift at the **Arizona Snowbowl** (page 132), visit the **Museum of Northern Arizona** (page 128) with its excellent Indian and natural history exhibits, or tour **Lowell Observatory** (page 125) for a look at the antique telescope used in the early 1900s to "discover" the nonexistent canals of the Martian civilization.

Day 2 • Leaving Flagstaff, take a leisurely drive down **Oak Creek Canyon** (page 141), stopping for a splash in the chilly mountain stream water at **Slide Rock State Park** (page 142). Allow one hour.

• Arriving in Sedona, take time out to explore a little of Red Rock Country. There are as many possibilities as you have time; for a quick introduction to this unique area, visit **Red Rock State Park** (page 153) and hike the trail along Oak Creek. Allow one hour or more.

• Follow Route 89A west through West Sedona to Clarksdale, a 26-mile drive through pretty Verde Valley.

• Visit the white stone Indian ruins at **Tuzigoot National Monument** (page 153). Allow one hour.

• Continue west on Route 89A for another four miles to Jerome, on a hillside above the Verde Valley. It's a good place to stretch your legs and find lunch. Then drive over the forested hills to the Prescott Valley.

• In Prescott, visit the **Sharlot Hall Museum** (page 157) for a look at 19th-century Arizona. Allow one and a half hours.

• If time permits, also check out the **Phippen Museum of Western Art** (page 158), one of the best Western art museums anywhere. Allow one hour.

• Drive north on Route 89 for 51 miles to rejoin Route 40 at the little crossroads town of Ash Fork.

IF YOU HAVE MORE TIME

If you have extra time in central Arizona, ride the **Verde Canyon Railroad** (page 154), one of the most spectacular scenic train trips anywhere.

presents interactive, hands-on exhibits about astronomers' tools. On most summer evenings, staff holds star talks and help visitors stargaze through one of the center's telescopes. Call for hours. Admission. ~ 1400 West Mars Hill Road, Flagstaff; 928-774-3358, fax 928-774-6296; recorded schedule information, 928-774-3211; www.lowell.edu.

HIDDEN ▶   Overshadowed by Lowell Observatory, the **Northern Arizona University Campus Observatory** actually offers visitors a better chance to look through a larger telescope. Public viewing sessions are held on Friday evenings from 7:30 to 10 p.m. when the sky is clear. (Cardio alert: there's quite a steep climb required to reach this heavenly view.) The observatory is open to the public on Friday night or by special arrangement. ~ Northeast corner of San Francisco Street and University Drive on campus, Flagstaff; 928-523-7170, fax 928-523-1371; www.physics.nau.edu/~naaa.

HIDDEN ▶   The **Arboretum at Flagstaff** is located on 200 acres of meadows and ponderosa forest west of town. There's a passive solar greenhouse; outdoors you'll find constructed wetlands, a 1.2-mile nature trail, shade gardens, butterfly gardens, rare and endangered plant species of the Colorado Plateau, and myriad kinds of herbs. The abundance of native wildflowers (one of the nation's largest collections) during the summer months includes brilliant penstemon, Indian paintbrush, wild rose and scarlet gilia. There's also a tranquil picnic area. Closed October through March. Admission. ~ 4001 South Woody Mountain Road, Flagstaff; 928-774-1442, fax 928-774-1441; www.thearb.org, e-mail leslie.fauset@nau.edu.

The **Arizona Historical Society–Pioneer Museum** presents a program of changing exhibits. Themes are drawn from the history of northern Arizona, including logging, livestock-raising and social life. Highlights include early-day photos of the Grand Canyon. The museum is housed in the historic Coconino County Hospital, also known as the "poor farm." Three annual "living history" festivals are held here: the **Flagstaff Wool Festival**; the **Independence Day Festival**, featuring mountain men, crafts and skills and a Civil War artillery unit; and **Playthings of the Past**, featuring toys, dolls and games. Closed Sunday. Admission. ~ 2340 North Fort Valley Road, Flagstaff; 928-774-6272, fax 928-774-1596; www.arizonahistoricalsociety.org.

The **Museum of Northern Arizona** is known worldwide for its changing exhibits of American Indian artifacts, geology, biology and the fine arts of the Grand Canyon region, as well as a few permanent fixtures like the life-size replica skeleton of a dilophosaurus, a giant carnivorous dinosaur that once roamed the Colorado Plateau. This exhibit in the archaeology gallery charts

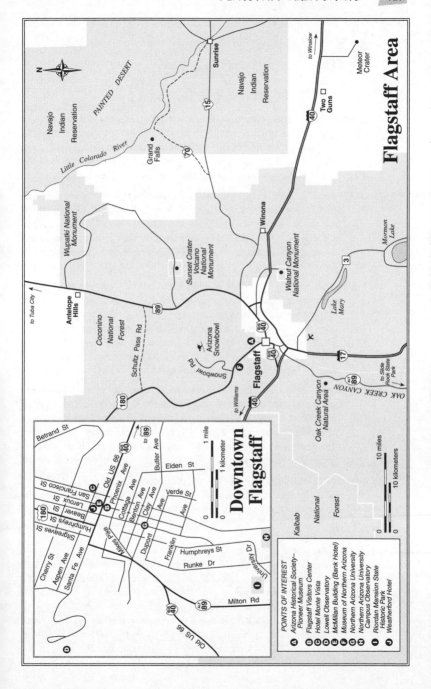

Flagstaff Area

Downtown Flagstaff

POINTS OF INTEREST

- Ⓐ Arizona Historical Society– Pioneer Museum
- Ⓑ Flagstaff Visitors Center
- Ⓒ Hotel Monte Vista
- Ⓓ Lowell Observatory
- Ⓔ McMillan Building (Bank Hotel)
- Ⓕ Museum of Northern Arizona
- Ⓖ Northern Arizona University
- Ⓗ Northern Arizona University Campus Observatory
- Ⓘ Riordan Mansion State Historic Park
- Ⓙ Weatherford Hotel

Historic Flagstaff

Long before motels and restaurants started springing up along old Route 66 in Flagstaff, the town was already a major stopover for travelers seeing the Southwest by train. Not surprisingly, many of the century-old buildings that still stand in Flagstaff were originally built as hotels or saloons. You can glimpse into the town's past on a 20-minute stroll around the compact historic district.

FLAGSTAFF VISITORS CENTER   Start, as old-time visitors did, at the train station near the west end of Historic Route 66, which Amtrak now shares with the Flagstaff Visitors Center (page 124); there's free public parking nearby. Looking directly across the street, you'll see the ornate Italianate facade of the oldest building in town, the Bank Hotel (see below). You can't cross the street here, though.

THE VAIL BUILDING   Walk one block east to the stop light at San Francisco Street and cross Historic Route 66. The Vail Building on the northwest corner is Flagstaff's second-oldest building. After two previous saloons had burned to the ground on this site in two years, the owner rebuilt his saloon of brick in 1888. Today, extensively renovated to give the exterior a pink-and-blue art deco look that seems strangely out of place in Flagstaff, it houses a metaphysical shop. ~ 1 San Francisco Street.

K. J. NACKARD BUILDING   Continuing a half block north on the same side of San Francisco Street will bring you to the K. J. Nackard Building, built by a recent immigrant in 1912. He started Nackard's New York Store here, selling hard-to-get goods that his relatives shipped to him from New York. The building later became Flagstaff's post office and now houses Wolf and Swan Music and Fine Arts. ~ 13 San Francisco Street.

BABBIT BROTHERS BUILDING   Across Aspen Street is the graceful red sandstone Babbit Brothers Building. It was built in 1888 as a mercantile store by the forefathers of Bruce Babbitt, former Arizona governor and

the history and characteristics (such as foodstuffs) of the plateau's human inhabitants since prehistoric times. In the Branigar/Chase Discovery Center, an exhibit of fine arts, part of the museum's collection of five-million-plus objects, now has a regular home. A reception room in this wing has been furnished with Mission-style furniture and a fireplace and is a cozy, comfortable spot to relax. Outside the museum is a half-mile nature trail, which follows along a canyon rim and creek. The gift shop has an excellent collection of American Indian artworks, and there is also a book-

Secretary of the Interior during the Clinton administration. The store is still in operation, though its inventory now leans heavily toward outdoor gear. ~ 101 San Francisco Street.

KINLANI BUILDING   Turn west down Aspen Street for one block to the Kinlani Building on the northwest corner of Aspen and Leroux. It was built in 1925 to house the town's new JC Penney store, but the store vacated the building after less than a year. After decades as an apartment hotel, the Kinlani Building became Flagstaff's first supermarket. It now houses Maloney's Tavern. ~ 31 North Leroux Street.

WEATHERFORD HOTEL   Across Aspen Street, the old Weatherford Hotel ranked among Flagstaff's finest hotels during the railroad era. Western author Zane Grey wrote his classic novel *Riders of the Purple Sage* while staying here. The hotel deteriorated to become a youth hostel and pool hall before being closed down for renovation. The ground floor has been restored to period elegance and houses Charly's Pub and Grill (page 136); the upper floors contain the hotel. ~ 23 North Leroux Street.

RAYMOND BUILDING   Continuing back toward the train station on Leroux Street, you'll pass the Raymond Building, a well-preserved stone building that has massive sandstone block cornices and a decoratively carved archway. R. O. Raymond came to Flagstaff as the doctor for the local logging company but became a rancher and real estate speculator, building this one-story structure in 1911 to serve as his business office. It now houses a gift shop. ~ 13 North Leroux Street.

BANK HOTEL   Leroux Street brings you back to Historic Route 66 at the old Bank Hotel across from the train station. Formally known as the McMillan Building, the oldest building in town was built in 1886 by Flagstaff's first settler, sheep rancher Thomas F. McMillan, and simultaneously housed the town's first hotel and first bank. It later became Flagstaff's opera house. Today it is an arts-and-crafts gallery and offices. ~ 3 North Leroux Street

store. Admission. ~ 3101 North Fort Valley Road, Flagstaff; 928-774-5213, fax 928-779-1527; www.musnaz.org, e-mail info@musnaz.org.

Not far beyond the Museum of Arizona on Route 180 is the turnoff for **Schultz Pass Road**. The unpaved road is rough and dusty, but as a drive it offers glimpses of the spectacular San Francisco Peaks, which tower above Flagstaff. About 14 miles long, the road comes out on Route 89 a short distance south of the turnoff to Sunset Crater National Monument.

◄ *HIDDEN*

The **Arizona Snowbowl,** one of the state's largest ski areas, runs its chairlift as a scenic skyride during the summer months, carrying visitors to timberline at 11,500 feet elevation on the side of Agassiz Peak. From there, spectacular panoramic views stretch out 70 miles and take in the Grand Canyon. Open daily Memorial Day through Labor Day, open Friday through Sunday to mid-October. Admission. ~ Snowbowl Road, seven miles off Route 180; 928-779-1951, fax 928-779-3019; www.arizonasnowbowl.com, e-mail info@arizonasnowbowl.com.

The Apollo astronauts trained at Meteor Crater before their moon landings in the late 1960s.

North of Flagstaff, off Route 89, are Wupatki National Monument and Sunset Crater Volcano National Monument. A paved 36-mile loop road connects both monuments and links up with Route 89 at both ends.

Sunset Crater Volcano National Monument, a bright-colored 1000-foot-tall volcanic cone in the San Francisco Volcano Field, is of recent origin. It first erupted in the winter of 1064–65 and covered the surrounding area in a blanket of black cinder. Admission. ~ Forest Service Road 545; 928-526-0502, fax 928-714-0565; www.nps.gov/sucr.

North of Sunset Crater, **Wupatki National Monument** preserves several pueblo ruins on the fringes of the San Francisco Volcano Field. They were inhabited in the 12th and 13th centuries, at the same time the volcanic activity was at its peak. Repeatedly, fiery (albeit slow-moving) eruptions would drive the American Indians out of the area and volcanic ash would fertilize the land and lure them back. The result was a mixture of many Southwestern cultures including the Anasazi, Cohonina and Sinagua people. A ball court at Wupatki Pueblo suggests that they were also influenced by the more advanced Toltec civilization of central Mexico. Most archaeologists now believe that violence between the tribes was rare and that cultural exchange brought about a renaissance that radiated to other parts of the region. Some Hopi villages today trace their origins to pueblos at Wupatki. Park at the visitors center, where pottery, tools and other artifacts from the various sites are displayed, and take the self-guided walking tour around the Wupatki Pueblo, a remarkably intact 700-year-old stone structure that was one of the largest communities in the area. North of the visitors center, side roads go to two other ruins— Citadel and Lomaki—that are typical of the 2000-plus sites contained within the monument boundaries. To protect such sites, the backcountry is off-limits to visitors. However, rangers guide 16-mile overnight hikes to Crack-in-Rock Ruin in the spring and fall; make reservations at least six months ahead. Admission. ~ Forest Road 545; 928-679-2365, fax 928-679-2349; www.nps.gov/wupa.

Sinagua Indians (the name is Spanish for "without water," referring to a nearby mountain) lived from the Grand Canyon southward throughout central Arizona and are thought to be ancestors of the Hopi people. Small Sinagua cliff dwellings can be found in many canyons near Flagstaff, Sedona and the Verde Valley. One of the most interesting Sinagua sites is at **Walnut Canyon National Monument**. Here, the Indians built more than 80 cliff dwellings containing about 300 rooms in the walls of a 400-foot-deep gorge. The overhanging stone ledges above and sheer cliffs below protected them from the elements and animal predators. A paved one-mile trail takes visitors around an "island in the sky" for a close-up look at the largest concentration of cliff dwellings—about 25 of them—and views of many others. A second trail follows the rim of this beautiful canyon for about three-quarters of a mile. Visitors are not permitted in the national monument backcountry, including the canyon floor. Admission. ~ Take Exit 204 from Route 40 just east of Flagstaff; 928-526-3367; www.nps.gov/waca.

Another fascinating bit of north central Arizona's flamboyant geology is **Meteor Crater**. A shooting star 150 feet in diameter and traveling 30,000 to 40,000 miles per hour struck the earth here 50,000 years ago. The impact blasted a crater 550 feet deep and a mile across. All life within a 100-mile radius was destroyed. Geologist Daniel Barringer theorized a century ago that this was a meteor impact crater. Experts scoffed at the idea, especially since volcanic craters, so common east of Flagstaff, suggested a rational explanation for the phenomenon. He staked a mining claim to search for the huge, valuable mass of iron and nickel that, he was convinced, lay buried beneath the crater. An ambitious drilling operation did not strike a mother lode from outer space but did come up with fragments proving the theory and the geologist's family has been operating the claim as a tourist attraction ever since. The visit is worth the fairly steep admission fee if you take time to go on a guided tour along the main trail. Admission. ~ About 30 miles east of Flagstaff, five miles off Route 40 at Exit 233; 928-289-2362, fax 928-289-2598; www.meteorcrater.com, e-mail info@meteorcrater.com.

LODGING

For a directory of bed and breakfasts throughout Arizona, call or write to the **Arizona Association of Bed & Breakfast Inns**. ~ P.O. Box 36656, Tucson, AZ 85740; 928-527-1912; www.arizonabed-breakfast.com, e-mail info@arizona-bed-breakfast.com.

The large, elegant **Radisson Woodlands Hotel** has spacious and modern guest rooms, with pastel color schemes and king-size beds. Facilities for guests include an indoor whirlpool spa, a steam room, a sauna, a fitness center and a heated swimming pool. Room service and complimentary shuttle service are also among the hotel's amenities. ~ 1175 West Route 66, Flagstaff; 928-773-8888, 800-333-3333, fax 928-773-0597; www.radisson.com. DELUXE.

Flagstaff offers a good selection of bed-and-breakfast accommodations. Among the antique-furnished vintage lodgings available in the downtown area is **The Inn at 410 Bed and Breakfast**, a 1907 home. The nine guest suites are individually decorated in various themes including Victorian, Santa Fe and cowboy. All have fireplaces. Gourmet breakfast is served on the patio during the summer. ~ 410 North Leroux Street, Flagstaff; 928-774-0088, 800-774-2008, fax 928-774-6354; www.inn410.com, e-mail info@inn410.com. DELUXE TO ULTRA-DELUXE.

Theodore Roosevelt and William Randolph Hearst once slept at the **Weatherford Hotel**, now refurbished to show off original fireplaces, balconies and early-20th-century style. See if the door Wyatt Earp shot through still stands in the ballroom, which features an antique bar and stained-glass windows. ~ 23 North Leroux Street, Flagstaff; 928-779-1919, fax 928-773-8951; www.weatherfordhotel.com, e-mail weathotel@weatherfordhotel.com. MODERATE TO DELUXE.

Located in the historic district is the homey **Aspen Inn Bed and Breakfast**, which occupies a restored 1912 home within a five-minute walk from downtown. Three comfortable rooms all include cable TV, DVD players, wireless internet, air conditioning, telephones and stocked mini-refrigerators. Some rooms have fireplaces. Rate includes a full breakfast. ~ 218 North Elden Street, Flagstaff; 928-773-0295, 888-999-4110; www.flagstaffbedandbreakfast.com, e-mail aspeninn@aol.com. MODERATE.

Flagstaff has two hostels. Especially in the summer months, both of these affordable accommodations host backpack travelers of all ages from all parts of the world, and solitary travelers are sure to make instant friends. Try the **Grand Canyon International Hostel**, which has private and dormitory accommodations. It is just one block from the Amtrak station and offers free

AUTHOR FAVORITE

Some folks complain that it's noisy and a little run-down, but I can't resist the old-fashioned feel of Flagstaff's **Hotel Monte Vista**, the only remaining hotel in the heart of the town's historic district. A 1927 hotel now listed on the National Register of Historic Places, the Monte Vista has spacious rooms that feature oak furniture, brass beds and gold-tone bathroom fittings—a touch of old-time elegance. During the hotel's glory days, movie stars used to stay here, and some rooms bear plaques naming the most famous person who ever slept in them: Humphrey Bogart, Jayne Russell, Gary Cooper and John Wayne, to name a few. ~ 100 North San Francisco Street, Flagstaff; 928-779-6971, 800-545-3068, fax 928-779-2904; www.hotelmontevista.com. BUDGET TO MODERATE.

pick-up service from the Greyhound station. Rates include breakfast. ~ 19 South San Francisco Street, Flagstaff; 928-779-9421, 888-442-2696, fax 928-774-6047; www.grandcanyonhostel.com, e-mail info@grandcanyonhostel.com. BUDGET.

Two blocks away, the **DuBeau Route 66 International Hostel** has private and four- to eight-person dormitory rooms. Tours of the Grand Canyon are offered four days a week. Rates include a continental breakfast. Closed early October to early March. ~ 19 West Phoenix Avenue, Flagstaff; 928-774-6731, 928-779-9421 (winter), 800-398-7112; www.grandcanyonhostel.com. e-mail info@grandcanyonhostel.com. BUDGET.

In the pines just five minutes out of town, the **Arizona Mountain Inn** offers B&B rooms in the main inn (rates include a continental breakfast), and one- to five-bedroom cottages with fireplaces and cooking facilities. Amenities include volleyball, horseshoe and basketball areas as well as hiking trails. ~ 4200 Lake Mary Road, Flagstaff; 928-774-8959, 800-239-5236, fax 928-774-8837; www.arizonamountaininn.com, e-mail arizonamountaininn@msn.com. MODERATE.

If the sounds of Flagstaff's many train whistles keep you awake, consider staying in the surrounding Coconino National Forest at the **Arizona Sled Dog Inn**. Located on the edge of rustic Mountainaire, ten minutes south of town via Route 17, this attractive modern lodge has ten peaceful rooms with full baths, log furniture and down comforters, but no distracting phones or TVs. Two large living rooms feature a rock fireplace, a hot tub and a sauna. Full breakfast includes homemade granola. No pets allowed, but the inn is home to a large menagerie of dogs, horses and other friendly furry creatures. ~ 10155 Mountainaire Road, Flagstaff; 928-525-6212, 800-754-0664; www.sleddoginn.com, e-mail info@sleddoginn.com. DELUXE.

DINING

For fine dining, one good bet is the small, homey-feeling **Cottage Place Restaurant**. Specialties include châteaubriand and duet of gorgonzola-encrusted fillet, as well as seafood fettuccini. Reservations are recommended. Dinner only. Closed Monday and Tuesday. ~ 126 West Cottage Avenue, Flagstaff; 928-774-8431, fax 928-774-4071; www.cottageplace.com. DELUXE TO ULTRA-DELUXE.

In the mood for a romantic dinner? Try the **Woodlands Café** at the Radisson Woodlands Hotel. There's booth and table seating at this spacious yet intimate dining room that features atrium windows and forest views. White walls are decorated with photographs of local scenery; the chandelier is crafted from deer racks. You can select from such entrées as pan-seared halibut. You can also order a plain old hamburger. Reservations are recommended. **Sakura,** a popular Japanese restaurant, shares the premises and has the same address and phone number. ~ 1175 West Route 66, Flagstaff; 928-773-9118, fax 928-773-1827. MODERATE TO DELUXE.

A standout among Flagstaff's numerous Chinese restaurants, the **China Star** offers an all-you-can-eat buffet with more than 40 dishes such as Mongolian beef, jalapeño chicken, jalapeño shrimp and beef broccoli. The brightly lit interior is spic-and-span, with hardly a hint of Asian decor. ~ 1802 East Route 66, Flagstaff; 928-774-8880. BUDGET.

One contemporary restaurant in Flagstaff's downtown area emphasizes creative Southwestern dining. Stop in for breakfast, lunch or dinner at **Charly's Pub and Grill**, on the ground floor of the Weatherford Hotel. ~ 23 North Leroux Street, Flagstaff; 928-779-1919, fax 928-773-8951; www.weatherfordhotel.com, e-mail weathotel@weatherfordhotel.com. MODERATE TO DELUXE.

Or you can try **Café Espress**, which specializes in vegetarian, poultry and fish selections. Changing exhibits by local artists adorn the walls. Lunch is served, although dinner is available during special events. ~ 16 North San Francisco Street, Flagstaff; 928-774-0541. BUDGET.

Across from Heritage Square, **Pasto** features atmosphere and food that are pure Old Italy, but service that is the studied elegant graciousness found in higher-end restaurants. The extensive menu has some chef-conceived specialties. Try the lamb osso buco served with parmesan polenta. And whatever else you sample, make sure to save room for tiramisu, a dessert favorite. Reservations are recommended. ~ 19 East Aspen Avenue, Flagstaff; 928-779-1937, fax 928-779-5951; www.pastorestaurant.com. MODERATE TO DELUXE.

For an unusual dining environment, head out of town to the **Mormon Lake Lodge Steak House & Saloon**, which has been in operation since 1924. The restaurant also features ribs, chicken and trout, all cooked over a bed of mountain mesquite embers. The authentic brands from ranches all across Arizona that have

HIDDEN ▶

AUTHOR FAVORITE

Of all the good eateries along the Route 40 corridor, my favorite is **Dara Thai Restaurant**, where a wide assortment of both traditional and innovative Thai entrées are served in an ambience of subdued lighting and rich adornments. Try the house specialty, "evil jungle princess"— strips of chicken stir-fried in coconut milk with lemongrass, straw mushrooms and secret spices. There's also an abundance of vegetarian options including vegetable curries and spicy tofu creations. ~ 14 South San Francisco Street, Flagstaff; 928-774-0047. BUDGET TO MODERATE.

been seared into the wood paneling of the restaurant's walls are said to be the result of one of the wildest branding parties ever. ~ Located 28 miles southeast of Flagstaff on Mormon Lake Road, Mormon Lake Village; 928-354-2227; www.foreverresorts.com/ mormonlakelodge, e-mail scottgoldmll@cybertrails.com. MODER-ATE TO ULTRA-DELUXE.

SHOPPING

Wander around Flagstaff's downtown area and you will find a number of "trading posts." East of downtown is **Jay's Indian Arts**. The store sells jewelry, pottery, kachinas and the like direct from artists on the Navajo, Hopi, Tohono O'odham, Apache and Pueblo reservations. Closed Sunday. ~ 2227 East 7th Avenue, Flagstaff; 928-526-2439; www.jaysindianarts.net, e-mail jaysl flag@aol.com.

Several of Flagstaff's downtown arts-and-crafts galleries host an **Art Walk** with artist receptions on the first Friday of each month. The popular **Artists Gallery**, in the heart of downtown Flagstaff, is an artists' cooperative featuring the work of 40 professional artists specializing in photography, jewelry, painting, stoneware, ceramic art, textile designs, stained glass, metalwork, sculpture and woodwork. Among the highlights are attractive stoneware mugs, plates, bowls and other items featuring mountain scenes created by outdoor enthusiast Mark ("Arne") Arnegard, owner of Flagstaff Pottery. ~ 17 North San Francisco Street, Flagstaff; 928-773-0958; www.theartistsgallery.net.

NIGHTLIFE

Because of the university, Flagstaff boasts both a busy cultural events calendar and a lively nightclub scene. On the cultural side, the performing arts roster includes the **Flagstaff Symphony Orchestra**. The main season runs September through March. ~ 928-774-5107; www.flagstaffsymphony.org. Classical fans may also want to attend a performance of the **Master Chorale of Flagstaff**. ~ 928-714-0300. Also in town is the NAU **Choral Studies Office**; www.nau.edu. ~ 928-523-2642. Most performances are held at the **Northern Arizona College of Fine Arts**. ~ Corner of Riordan Road and Knoles Drive; 928-523-3731; www.nau.edu/spa.

The **Theatrikos Theatre Group** performs at the Flagstaff Playhouse. ~ 11 West Cherry Avenue, Flagstaff; 928-774-1662; www.theatrikos.com. For current performance information, inquire at the Flagstaff Visitors Center or tune in to the university's National Public Radio station, KNAU, at 88.7 on your FM dial. ~ Visitors center: 1 East Route 66; 928-774-9541; www.flagstaff arizona.org.

Charly's Pub and Grill in the Weatherford Hotel has live music Tuesday, Thursday, Friday and Saturday night. Cover. ~ 23 North Leroux Street, Flagstaff; 928-779-1919, fax 928-773-

Text continued on page 140.

In the Land of Volcanos

The raw power of geology presents itself in the Southwest as dramatically as any place on earth. Consider, for instance, Arizona's Grand Canyon, Utah's Bryce Canyon and Colorado's Great Sand Dunes. Yet visitors often drive right past one of the most awe-inspiring of these earth phenomena—the 2000-square-mile San Francisco Volcano Field northeast of Flagstaff.

The **San Francisco Peaks**, Arizona's tallest mountains, were once part of a huge volcano that, according to some geologists, may have approached the elevation of Mt. Everest. But that was back when dinosaurs roamed the earth and the red rocks of Sedona and Canyon de Chelly were mere sand on the sea floor.

Imagine how surprised the Anasazi people who lived at the base of these ancient mountains must have been when, around A.D. 1065, new volcanos began erupting out of their cornfields. They scattered to other areas as their pueblos were buried in red-hot cinders. Volcanic activity continued for 200 years, then died down as quickly as it had started, leaving prime agricultural land fertilized by the deep layer of ash. Rival Indian groups moved in to compete for the rich farmland, which accounts for the variety of architectural styles and fortresslike defenses at the numerous 13th-century pueblo sites of **Wupatki National Monument** (page 128). ~ Forest Service Road 545, visitors center is at 6400 North Route 89; 928-679-2365, fax 928-679-2349; www.nps.gov/wupa.

South of Wupatki, **Sunset Crater Volcano National Monument** (page 128) protects a colorful red-and-black cinder cone 1000 feet tall. A one-mile, self-guided nature trail, which starts one and a half miles away from the visitors center, leads through cinder and lava fields. Hiking is no longer permitted on the slopes of Sunset Crater, since footprints erode and mar the beauty of the perfect cone. Admission. ~ Forest Service Road 545; 928-526-0502, fax 928-714-0565; www.nps.gov/sucr.

Several volcanos in Coconino National Forest, however, can be climbed, including **O'Leary Peak**. One of the most unusual trails in the Flagstaff area is the **Red Mountain Trail**, 33 miles north of Flagstaff off Route 180. A gap in the base of this 1000-foot-high volcanic cone lets you hike from the end of the national forest access road straight into the crater without climbing. Not often visited by tourists, this is a great place to explore with older children.

For a more ambitious adventure, trek the **Strawberry Crater Wilderness**, a roadless area surrounding the volcano cone for which it is named. Among jet-black lava flows that look fresh, bubbly and almost liquid lie the ruins of ancient pueblos and cornfields. There's a hiking trail up the northwest side of the crater to the summit. Of several unofficial paths through the wilderness, the shortest route to the crater starts at Painted Desert Vista, located midway between the Sunset Crater and Wupatki visitors centers.

You can also explore the chilly interior of the mile-long **Lava River Cave**, a subterranean tube of rippled rock dripping with stone icicles. To get there, take Route 180 for nine miles north of Flagstaff, turn west (left) onto Forest Road 245, go three more miles, turn south (left) on Forest Road 171, and go one more mile to the short, marked road to the cave entrance. Bring your own light (and warm clothes).

The San Francisco Volcano Field is close to Flagstaff, which has a wide choice of lodging and restaurants. To maximize the experience, though, why not spend the night at Coconino National Forest's **Bonito Campground** near Sunset Crater Volcano National Monument, where a two-mile hiking trail leads across a lava flow so recent that it almost looks like it's still moving.

8951; www.weatherfordhotel.com, e-mail weathotel@weather
fordhotel.com.

A mixed crowd likes the happy hour at **Granny's Closet**.
Friday is karaoke night. ~ 218 South Milton Road, Flagstaff; 928-
774-8331; www.grannys-closet.com.

Another favorite is the **Mad Italian Public House**, known as
the "Mad I." Diversions such as pool and TV should keep you entertained; if not, there's usually a local band pumping out tunes.
~ 101 South San Francisco Street, Flagstaff; 928-779-1820.

"Take me to the Zoo." That's what locals say when they
want to go to **The Museum Club**, one of the West's best examples of a cowboy roadhouse. Oftentimes rowdy, but always fun,
the Zoo began as a trading post and taxidermy
shop in 1931. It has operated as a nightclub since
1936, and is now listed on the National Register
of Historic Places. The huge log cabin–style building is decorated with an ornate 1880 mahogany bar
and an astonishing number of big-game trophies
mounted on the walls. Legendary country artists who
have performed here include Willie Nelson, Bob Wills
and the Texas Playboys, and Commander Cody and the
Lost Planet Airmen. Cover on weekends. ~ 3404 East
Route 66, Flagstaff; 928-526-9434, fax 928-526-5244; www.
museumclub.com.

The dancefloor of The
Museum Club in Flagstaff
was built around five ponderosa pine tree trunks.
A forked trunk forms
the entryway into the
club.

PARKS

LAKE MARY 🚶 🚴 🛶 ⛵ 🎣 🚤 🛥️ Actually two
long reservoirs, Upper and Lower Lake Mary provide the primary
water supply for Flagstaff. They were created by damming Walnut Creek, which explains why there is no longer any water flowing through Walnut Canyon National Monument. The National
Forest Service operates picnic areas on the wooded lakeshore and
the small Lakeview Campground overlooks the upper lake. Both
lakes are popular places to fish for northern pike, walleye pike and
catfish. The upper lake is also used for powerboating and waterskiing. ~ Located eight miles south of Flagstaff on Lake Mary
Road. From Route 40, take Exit 195-B and follow the signs; 928-
774-1182, fax 928-214-2460; www.coconinoforest.us.

▲ Lakeview Campground has 30 sites; $12 per night. Pine-
grove Campground has 46 sites; $15 per night. Campgrounds are
closed mid-October to mid-April, depending on the weather.

MORMON LAKE 🚶 🚴 🏇 🏕️ The largest natural lake in Arizona, covering over 2000 acres when full, is very shallow, averaging only ten feet in depth and can shrink to practically nothing
during spells of dry weather. As a matter of fact, more often than
not, the lake is dry. Several hiking trails run along the lakeshore
and into the surrounding forest. You'll find a nature trail, lodge,

restaurant and groceries. ~ Lake Mary Road, 26 miles southeast of Flagstaff; 928-774-1182, fax 928-214-2460; www.coconino forest.us.

▲ There are 30 sites at Dairy Springs and 15 sites at Double Springs; $10 per night. Campgrounds are closed October to May, depending on the weather.

Sedona Area

Sedona. The creative and the mystical have always been intrigued by the place. Indians once came here to worship, New Agers to feel the "vibrations," artists to capture the beauty. But no matter the number of its devotees, no one knows exactly why this place has such appeal. Its essence remains elusive. Perhaps part of the seduction is the colors—red-rock mountains that rise from the earth to nestle in brilliant blue sky. The landscape is a dreamy mix of fancifully shaped hoodoos, buttes and spires rising above green piñon and juniper trees, low shrubs and stark patches of reddish rock. Adjacent to Sedona is the spectacular Oak Creek Canyon, named after the creek that formed it by carving into the southern edge of the Colorado Plateau. All of these natural elements are highlighted by an intense sunlight that brings out contrast and color.

The first to discover this special spot were the Indians. About 800 years ago, the Southern Sinagua Indians settled here, leaving behind a 600-room cliff dwelling ruin called Honanki, which is now on the National Register of Historic Places. If you're out hiking, it's worth a side trip to discover these ruins. However, don't be surprised if you are turned away. The ruins are very fragile and are almost disappearing due to impact. They're located on an alcove on the west side of Loy Butte next to Lincoln Canyon.

More settlers came at the turn of the 20th century. At the time, the economic base of the economy was ranching and farming, and apple orchards dotted the area. Writer Zane Grey was also charmed by the area, drawing attention to it in the book *Call of the Canyon* in the 1920s.

With all this attention, it was only a matter of time before tourism became the main attraction. Today about four million people visit the town annually to shop at the numerous art galleries, to nurture their spirits, and to relax amidst a red-rock fantasy.

SIGHTS

Oak Creek Canyon is the most accessible of several magnificent canyons that plunge from the high forests of northern Arizona down toward the low deserts of southern Arizona. A major highway—Route 89A from Flagstaff—runs the length of Oak Creek Canyon, making for a wonderful, though often crowded, scenic drive. After a long, thrilling descent from Flagstaff to the bottom of the canyon, where the creek banks are lined with lush riparian vegetation, the highway passes a number of picnicking, camping and fishing areas sandwiched between clusters of rental cabins and private vacation homes. Unfortunately, these areas are almost always packed to capacity during the summer months, and even finding a place to park so you can dabble your toes in the creek is a problem. Though a hiking trail leads up the less-visited west fork of Oak Creek, no side roads branch off the main highway through the canyon. Adventurous travelers can try Forest Road 535, a good unpaved road that turns off to the west above the beginning of the descent into the canyon. It leads to lush, little-known **Fry Canyon**; another road branches off to a rarely seen vista on the rim of Oak Creek Canyon.

HIDDEN ▶

Midway down the canyon is one of Arizona's most popular state parks, **Slide Rock State Park** (see "Parks" below). At the lower end of the canyon, travelers emerge into the spectacular Red Rock Country, the labyrinth of sandstone buttes and mesas and verdant side canyons surrounding Sedona.

Sedona is a town for shopping, for sports, for luxuriating in spectacular surroundings. It is not the kind of place where you will find tourist attractions in the usual sense. Sedonans refer to the junction of Routes 179 and 89A as "the Y." The commercial district at the Y is known as "uptown Sedona," while the fast-growing, seemingly endless strip of shopping-center development along Route 89A is called "West Sedona."

If you stay on the main roads during your visit, you may wonder what attracts people to Sedona, which at first glance seems to lack the unique personality of other Southwestern towns. To find out what's special about this place, talk to some locals—you'll find them behind the counters of New Age stores and in real estate offices—and follow side roads into the wild red-rock country that surrounds the town. A close-up look at the monumental rock formations and canyons will reveal the amazing complexity of nature in this colorful area balanced midway between cool high-altitude forest and blistering low-altitude desert.

A good place to get your bearings, pick up brochures and have your questions answered is the visitors center at the **Sedona Chamber of Commerce.** ~ Corner of Forest Road at Route 89A, just above the Y; 928-282-7722, 800-288-7336, fax 928-204-1064; www.sedonachamber.com, e-mail info@sedona chamber.com.

Other than Oak Creek Canyon, Sedona's most popular tourist spots are spiritual in nature. The **Chapel of the Holy Cross**, south of town, is a Catholic "sculpture church" built between two towering red sandstone rock formations. It is open to visitors daily from 9 a.m. to 5 p.m. (Sunday from 10 a.m.). Parking

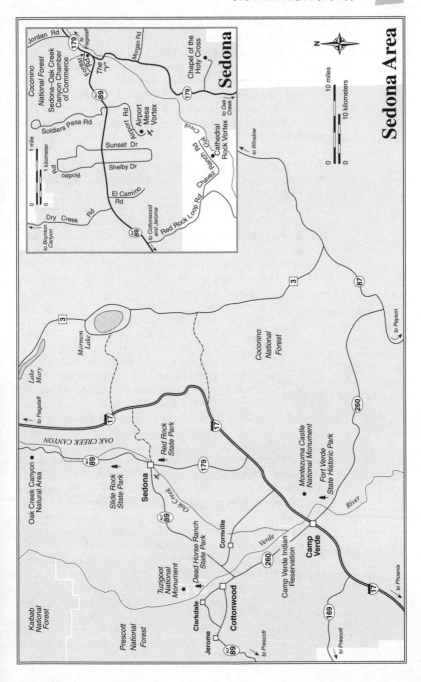

Sedona Area

Inset map — Sedona:

Coconino National Forest

Sedona–Oak Creek Canyon Chamber of Commerce

Jordan Rd

179 to Flagstaff

The "y"

Forest Rd

89

Airport Rd

Soldiers Pass Rd

Airport Mesa Vortex

Sunset Dr

Rodeo Rd

Shelby Dr

El Camino Rd

Dry Creek Rd

to Boynton Canyon

89 to Cottonwood and Jerome

Red Rock Loop Rd

Chavez Ranch Rd

Cathedral Rock Vortex

Oak Creek

to Oak Creek

Morgan Rd

Chapel of the Holy Cross

179

to Winslow

Sedona

1 mile

1 kilometer

Main map:

N

10 miles

10 kilometers

3

87

to Payson

Coconino National Forest

Mormon Lake

3

Lake Mary

to Flagstaff

17

OAK CREEK CANYON

ALT 89

Oak Creek Canyon Natural Area

Slide Rock State Park

Red Rock State Park

17

Sedona

ALT 89

Oak Creek

179

Cornville

Verde

260

Camp Verde Indian Reservation

Montezuma Castle National Monument

Fort Verde State Historic Park

Camp Verde

River

17

to Phoenix

Kaibab National Forest

Prescott National Forest

Tuzigoot National Monument

Dead Horse Ranch State Park

Clarkdale

Jerome

ALT 89

Cottonwood

to Prescott

to Prescott

260

169

17

to Prescott

is very limited. ~ Chapel Road off Route 179, Sedona; 928-282-4069, fax 928-282-3701.

The **Shrine of the Red Rocks**, on Table Top Mesa two miles off Route 89A on Airport Road, features a large wooden cross and a great view of the Red Rock Country.

And then there are Sedona's **"vortexes."** The vortex idea was "channeled" through members of the town's highly visible New Age community several years ago and keeps evolving. For more information, see "In the Land of Vortexes" in this chapter.

Thirty minutes south of Sedona is the **Out of Africa Wildlife Park**, where lions, tigers, bears, wolves and reptiles do their things. There are shows, natural habitat viewing, giraffe-petting and a playground for the kids. There's also a gift shop and restaurant. Closed frequently on Monday and Tuesday; call ahead. Admission. ~ Verde Valley Justice Center Road, Camp Verde; 925-567-2840, fax 925-567-2839; www.outofafricapark.com.

A 45-minute drive south of Sedona via Route 179 and Route 17, **Montezuma Castle National Monument** protects 900-year-old cliff dwellings built by the Sinagua people, ancestors of the Hopi. The ruins got their name from early explorers' mistaken belief that Aztecs fled here and built the structures after the Spanish conquest of Mexico. Though there is no truth to the old theory, archaeologists now know that several centuries before the Spanish arrived, traders used to visit the Southwest, bringing with them architectural methods from central Mexico. The main "castle" is a five-story, 20-room residential structure set high on the cliff. Although visitors cannot climb up to the ruin, the view from the nature trail below will tingle the imagination. The visitors center displays artifacts of the Sinagua and Hohokam cultures. Admission. ~ 2800 Montezuma Castle Highway, Camp Verde; 928-567-3322, fax 928-567-3597; www.nps.gov/moca, e-mail moca_administration@nps.gov.

> The cliffside location of the Montezuma Castle made it a natural fortress. Its inhabitants were somewhat protected by the fact that their "highrise" was accessible only by ladder from above and below.

South of Montezuma's Castle via Route 17, in the small town of Camp Verde, portions of an old cavalry fort from the Apache Wars in the 1870s and early 1880s are preserved as **Fort Verde State Historic Park**. Visitors can walk through the former quarters and officer buildings, and there is also a museum of Arizona military history. The fort formed the start of the **General Crook Trail,** the major patrol and supply route during the Apache Wars, which followed the Mogollon Rim west for more than 100 miles to Fort Apache. Today, the trail is used for hiking and horseback riding. Admission. ~ 125 Hollamon Street, Camp Verde; 928-567-3275, fax 928-567-4036.

For Sedona visitors who wish to explore the surrounding Red Rock Country, there are numerous companies offering jeep tours. They'll usually pick you up at any Sedona lodging. For more information see "Jeep Tours" later in "Outdoor Adventures."

As you drive down Oak Creek Canyon from Flagstaff to Sedona, you will notice several privately owned lodges and cabin complexes in the midst of this spectacular national forest area. You can reserve accommodations at these places and enjoy the canyon in the cool of the evening and early morning, avoiding the midday throngs and traffic of peak season and weekends. Several places are located near Slide Rock State Park.

LODGING

There are simple accommodations at **Don Hoel's Cabins**. Cabins are being remodeled one at a time, so call ahead for availability. Continental breakfast is included. Pet-friendly units available. Closed the weekend after New Year's to the first week of February. ~ 9440 North Route 89A, Sedona; 928-282-3560, 800-292-4635, fax 928-282-3654; www.hoels.com, e-mail cabins@hoels.com. MODERATE TO DELUXE.

Houses, all with fireplaces and fully equipped kitchens, are available at **Forest Houses Resort**. A four-night minimum stay is required from Memorial Day through Labor Day and on major holidays; a two-night minimum applies at all other times. Children and pets are welcome. Closed January to early March. ~ 9275 North Route 89A, Oak Creek Canyon; 928-282-2999, fax 928-282-0663; www.foresthousesresort.com. MODERATE TO DELUXE.

Top of the line **Junipine Resort** offers modern suites and one- and two-bedroom "creekhouses." These individually decorated one- and two-story units are all crafted from wood and stone. Offering mountain, forest or creek views, each 1300- to 1500-square-foot unit comes with a kitchen and redwood deck overlooking the canyon. ~ 8351 North Route 89A, Sedona; 928-282-3375, 800-742-7463, fax 928-282-7402; www.junipine.com, e-mail creekside@junipine.com. DELUXE TO ULTRA-DELUXE.

Garland's Oak Creek Lodge, on the site of one of the original homesteads in Oak Creek Canyon, is the quintessential cabin-in-the-woods experience. It has 16 rustic but well-maintained lodges with air conditioning (no phones or TVs). The food here is the big lure: Huge breakfasts and four-course dinners draw on produce grown in the on-site organic gardens. Dinner, served family style, is open to a very limited number of nonguests. Two-night minimum. Closed mid-November through March. ~ 8067 North Route 89A, Sedona; 928-282-3343; www.garlandslodge.com, e-mail info@garlandslodge.com. DELUXE TO ULTRA-DELUXE.

Canyon Wren Cabins consists of one old-fashioned log cabin and three chalets with loft bedrooms, kitchens, fireplaces, whirl-

Text continued on page 148.

In the Land of Vortexes

Just about every Sedona resident professes to believe in vortexes—power places where energies enter and leave the earth—and can tell you exactly where to find them. The absence of any scientific basis for the notion doesn't seem to bother them. Sedonans share similar experiences at these sites, and this is sufficient confirmation that they are real. They claim that visiting a vortex enhances your psychic powers, emotions and talents, and forces you to face yourself—for better or worse.

Although local visionaries now claim the vortexes were known to ancient Indians, the notion apparently originated in 1987, when more than 10,000 New Agers descended on Sedona to celebrate the Harmonic Convergence, a worldwide weekend of meditation "to awaken and balance the energies of Earth," held simultaneously at sacred sites from Chaco Canyon to Stonehenge. In Sedona, the gathering took place around and on top of Bell Rock. Afterwards, believers coined the term "vortex" to describe the energy they had unleashed, and Sedona has been a metaphysical mecca ever since. Reporting on the Harmonic Convergence, a *Detroit News* reporter quoted Sedona's mayor, Ivan Finley: "As far as I could tell, the earth didn't move—but it was good for the economy."

Before either accepting the vortexes as real or dismissing them, why not go there yourself and see whether you can feel the power that draws many thousands of people to Sedona every year? While some locals identify as many as 13 vortexes in the area, only four are generally recognized:

- The **Airport Mesa Vortex** is a little more than a mile south of Route 89A on Airport Road.

- The **Cathedral Rock Vortex** is near a lovely picnic area alongside Oak Creek, reached from Route 89A in West Sedona via Red Rock Loop Road and Chavez Ranch Road; the rock itself is one of the most photographed places in the area.

- The **Bell Rock Vortex**, a popular spot for UFO watchers, is just off Route 179 south of Sedona near the village of Oak Creek.

- The **Boynton Canyon Vortex**, said to be the most powerful of Sedona's vortexes, is several miles north of West Sedona via Dry Creek Road and Boynton Pass Road. From the well-marked trailhead, a nearly level two-and-a-half-mile hiking trail goes up the canyon through woods and among red-rock formations, passing several small, ancient Sinagua Indian cliff dwellings along the way.

Each vortex reportedly has a radius of ten miles, so you don't need to be standing in one particular spot to feel the force. Many people say they can even sense the power of the vortexes right in the town center of Sedona.

To research the subject of vortexes for yourself, visit one of Sedona's metaphysical book and gift stores such as **Crystal Castle**. ~ 313 Route 179; 928-282-5910. Another good source is **Crystal Magic**. ~ 2978 West Route 89A; 928-282-1622. Both stores have "networking" bulletin boards that let you scan the array of alternative professional services in town—channels, clairvoyants, geomancers and many more. The **Center for the New Age** has vortex information, networking for New Age activities, daily psychic readings and a psychic fair every Saturday. ~ 341 Route 179; 928-282-1949. *Four Corners Magazine* and other free periodicals providing information for and about the local New Age community are widely distributed around town.

Tour companies offering guided trips to the vortexes include **Red Rock Western Jeep Tours** (270 North Route 89A; 928-282-6826, 800-848-7728), and **Earth Wisdom Jeep Tours** (293 North Route 89A; 928-282-4714, 800-482-4714).

To get your mind, body and spirit tuned up for your personal vortex experience, consider staying at the **Healing Center of Arizona**. Reasonably priced amenities include a sauna and a spa. Guests at the center can receive integrated energy therapy, massage and reiki. ~ 25 Wilson Canyon Road; 928-282-7710, 877-723-2811; e-mail johnpaul@sedonahealingcenter.com. MODERATE.

pool tubs and patios, all within walking distance of swimming holes, fishing spots and hiking trails. Rates include continental breakfast. No telephones or televisions; no smoking indoors or out. ~ 6425 North Route 89A, Sedona; 928-282-6900, 800-437-9736, fax 928-282-6978; www.canyonwrencabins.com, e-mail cnynwren@sedona.net. DELUXE.

Farther down the canyon, **Oak Creek Terrace** has resort accommodations ranging from motel-style rooms with queen-size beds and jacuzzis to one- and two-bedroom suites. ~ 4548 North Route 89A, Oak Creek Canyon; 928-282-3562, 800-224-2229, fax 928-282-6061; www.oakcreekterrace.com, e-mail octresor@sedona.net. MODERATE TO ULTRA-DELUXE.

Briar Patch Inn has been a cabin resort since the early 1900s and may be one of the area's most private romantic retreats. Its 18 scattered, rustic, stone-and-wood-panel lodges overlook the creek and have Western-style furnishings and CD players; a few units have decks, fireplaces, TVs and phones. On summer weekends, breakfast is served outside on the terrace accompanied by live classical music. ~ 3190 North Route 89A, Sedona; 928-282-2342, 888-809-3030; www.briarpatchinn.com, e-mail briar patch@sedona.net. DELUXE.

Rising from Sedona's red rock, the stunning **Casa Sedona Bed and Breakfast** echoes its dramatic surroundings. Each of the 16 beautifully decorated units, from the Safari Room to the Cowboy Room, has a fireplace, a private bath and a private deck or balcony complete with postcard-perfect views. A sumptuous breakfast is usually served outside in the courtyard. If you can move after that, you can wander the grounds or make the short trip into town. A two-night minimum stay on weekends may be required. ~ 55 Hozoni Drive, Sedona; 928-282-2938, 800-525-3756, fax 928-282-2259; www.casasedona.com, e-mail casa@sedona.net. DELUXE TO ULTRA-DELUXE.

Located about halfway between Phoenix and the Grand Canyon, Sedona is named after Sedona Schnebly, the wife of the town's first postmaster.

Charming, affordable lodging in Sedona can be found at the **Rose Tree Inn**, which strives for an "English garden environment" and has patios and wireless internet. Some rooms have kitchens and fireplaces. This small inn is close to uptown. ~ 376 Cedar Street, Sedona; 928-282-2065, 888-282-2065; www.rosetreeinn.com, e-mail info@rosetree inn.com. MODERATE TO DELUXE.

Near Uptown Sedona, the **Star Motel** offers standard rooms with telephones, cable TV and refrigerators. There is one deluxe-priced apartment with a fireplace and a kitchen, and a moderate-priced room with a kitchen and balcony. ~ 295 Jordan Road, Sedona; 928-282-3641. BUDGET.

Among the poshest accommodations in town is **Los Abrigados Resort & Spa**. Situated next to the atmospheric Tlaquepaque shopping area, Los Abrigados features fanciful Mexican-inspired modern architecture throughout and elegantly stylish suites with kitchenettes, fireplaces and patios or balconies. Guest facilities include tennis courts, swimming pool, weight room and spa. ~ 160 Portal Lane, Sedona; 928-282-1777, 800-521-3131, fax 928-282-2614; www.ilxresorts.com. ULTRA-DELUXE.

Another top-of-the-line Sedona lodging is **L'Auberge de Sedona.** Individually designed guest rooms and cottages are decorated with furnishings imported from Provence, France, to recreate the atmosphere of a French country inn on 11 acres of creekside grounds within walking distance of uptown Sedona. ~ 301 L'Auberge Lane, Sedona; 928-282-1661, 800-272-6777, fax 928-282-1064; www.lauberge.com, e-mail info@lauberge.com. ULTRA-DELUXE.

Surrounded by spruce, piñon and juniper trees is the aptly named **Apple Orchard Inn**, built on the site of the old Jordan Apple Farm. Despite its wooded location, this bed and breakfast is just a hop, skip and a jump away from uptown. Luxuriate in seven plush, unique rooms, many sporting whirlpool tubs, fireplaces and patios. There's a "cooling pool" with a waterfall on a deck overlooking the mountains. For added pampering, summon the on-call massage therapist for a session. In the morning, drink in majestic mountain views while enjoying breakfast in the cozy dining room. Reservations suggested. ~ 656 Jordan Road, Sedona; 928-282-5328, 800-663-6968, fax 928-204-0044; www.apple orchardbb. com, e-mail info@appleorchardbb.com. DELUXE TO ULTRA-DELUXE.

For basic motel rooms in Sedona, the **White House Inn** in West Sedona, located just before the Dry Creek Road turnoff, provides lodging with phones. ~ 2986 West Route 89A, Sedona; 928-282-6680, fax 928-203-0467; www.whitehouseinn.netfirms.com, e-mail whitehouseinnsedona@yahoo.com. BUDGET.

Visitors seeking to change their lives in Sedona might want to consider staying at the **Healing Center of Arizona**. Amenities, offered for reasonable fees, include a sauna and an outdoor spa. Holistic therapies available to guests at the center include massage, integrated energy therapy and reiki. ~ 25 Wilson Canyon Road, Sedona; 928-282-7710, 877-723-2811; e-mail johnpaul@sedona healingcenter.com. MODERATE.

◄ HIDDEN

L'Auberge de Sedona has an outstanding French restaurant with a view of Oak Creek and memorable prix-fixe dinners. The six-course menu, which changes nightly, typically features pâté, soup, a small baby green salad and entrées such as poached salmon, grilled lamb, venison, quail or chicken. ~ 301 L'Auberge Lane, Sedona; 928-282-1667; www.lauberge.com, e-mail info@lauberge. com. ULTRA-DELUXE.

DINING

An exceptional Continental restaurant in Sedona is **Rene at Tlaquepaque**, which specializes in rack of lamb carved tableside and tableside flambé. The most elaborate French Provincial decor in the Southwest makes this restaurant extra special. Open-air patio dining is available. ~ Route 179 at Tlaquepaque, Sedona; 928-282-9225, fax 928-282-5629. DELUXE TO ULTRA-DELUXE.

El Rincón Restaurante Mexicano is one of those not-too-spicy Mexican restaurants operated with the gringo palate in mind, but whatever it may lack in piquance it makes up for in presentation. A centerpiece of the Tlaquepaque shopping complex's overstated Old Mexico ambience, the restaurant specializes in chimichangas and creative entrées such as shrimp and green chile enchiladas. The menu also features a wide choice of combination plates. ~ Route 179 at The Bridge, Sedona; 928-282-4648, fax 928-282-1429; www.elrinconrestaurant.com, e-mail information@rinconrestaurants.com. MODERATE.

Italian cuisine is featured at the **Hideaway Restaurant**, with tables on balconies over the creek, surrounded by a stand of sycamore trees. ~ Route 179 near Route 89A, Sedona; 928-282-4204. MODERATE.

For health-conscious Thai food, made with all natural, organic ingredients, try **Thai Spices Natural Cuisine of Thailand**, a restaurant located in the White House Inn motel in West Sedona. Closed Sunday. ~ 2986 West Route 89A, Sedona; 928-282-0599, fax 928-282-0553; www.thaispices.com, e-mail info@thaispices.com. BUDGET TO MODERATE.

HIDDEN ► A choice of 101 omelettes is the main attraction at the **Coffee Pot Restaurant**, a local dining spot since the 1950s. Although the brass rails and sautillo tile floors add charm, the brown booths give away the casual atmosphere. On the wall hangs artwork by White Bear, a former Hopi Indian chief. A nice touch is the out-

AUTHOR FAVORITE

Dress up or dress down, it doesn't matter at the **Heartline Café**. The warm, unpretentious courtyard atmosphere and soulfulness of the food shines regardless at this popular brasserie-style restaurant in downtown Sedona. Smoked mozzarella ravioli, rich pecan-encrusted trout, and chicken breast with prickly-pear sauce are just some of the new twists on Continental fare that emerge from chef/owner Charles Kline's well-run kitchen. This is one of Sedona's most beloved restaurants—with good reason. ~ 1610 Route 89A, Sedona; 928-282-0785, fax 928-204-9206; www.heartlinecafe.com, e-mail heartline@heartlinecafe.com. MODERATE TO DELUXE.

door patio. Breakfast and lunch only. ~ 2050 West Route 89A, Sedona; 928-282-6626, fax 928-282-1118. BUDGET.

Another good spot is the **Red Planet Diner**, offering everything from Cajun and Italian food to seafood and steaks in an entertaining "intergalactic" environment. Check out the spaceship fountain and sci-fi scenes. ~ 1655 West Route 89A, Sedona; 928-282-6070, fax 928-282-1840. BUDGET TO MODERATE.

SHOPPING

Sedona's shopping district is one of the three or four best in Arizona. Many of the galleries, boutiques and specialty shops are labors of love, the personal creations of people who spent years past daydreaming about opening a cute little store in Sedona. The town has more than 60 art galleries, most of them specializing in traditional and contemporary American Indian art, "cowboy" art and landscape paintings. Quality is relatively high in this very competitive art market. You can easily spend a whole day shopping your way up and down the main streets of town, leaving your feet sore and your credit cards limp.

Uptown Sedona has an abundance of fine little galleries. One that's easily overlooked but worth checking out is the gallery at the **Sedona Arts Center**. The paintings, ceramics, art glass and jewelry of local artists are featured; quality is high and prices are reasonable. ~ Located at the north end of the uptown commercial core on Route 89A at Art Barn Road, Sedona; 928-282-3809, 888-954-4442, fax 928-282-1516; www.sedonaartscenter.com.

The most relaxing and enjoyable place in Sedona to browse is **Tlaquepaque**, a picturesque complex of two-story Mexican-style buildings that houses specialty shops and restaurants below the "Y" on Route 179. Built with old-looking stone walls, courtyards, tile roofs and flowers in profusion, the Spanish Colonial–style Tlaquepaque looks more like Old Mexico than the real thing. **Environmental Realists** features metal jewelry and handcrafted knives and wood accessories. ~ 928-282-4945. **The Storyteller** carries all sorts of books about Sedona and the Southwest, from cookbooks to history. ~ 928-282-2144.

Sedona has numerous stores for "enlightened" shoppers. The **Golden Word Book Centre** offers New Age literature. ~ 3150 West Route 89A; 928-282-2688. Get your chakras aligned at **Crystal Magic**. ~ 2978 West Route 89A; 928-282-1622. Can't get enough? The **Center for the New Age** has vortex information, networking for in-store New Age activities, daily psychic readings and a "Psychic Faire" every Saturday. ~ 341 Route 179; 928-282-1949; www.sedonanewagecenter.com.

Garland's Navajo Rugs has one of the largest collections of Navajo rugs in the world, with a selection of more than 5000. They hang on rafters, grouped according to subjects ranging from people to storm patterns. There are also kachina dolls in stock. ~ 411 Route 179, Sedona; 928-282-4070; www.garlandsrugs.com.

Shopping enthusiasts will also want to visit **Oak Creek Factory Outlet**, a mall located south of town. This is factory-direct outlet shopping with a difference. The factories represented include Nine West (928-284-1910), Jones of New York (928-284-1919), and Izod/Gant (928-284-9844)—designer goods at discount prices. ~ Route 179, Oak Creek; www.primeretail.com.

NIGHTLIFE Sedona has surprisingly little nightlife. One exception is the **Dahl and DiLuca**, where you can enjoy live music nightly. Weekends offer a jazz band. This is a favorite gathering spot for locals who come here to relax, socialize and enjoy the tasty Italian specialties. ~ 2321 West Route 89A, Sedona; 928-282-5219; e-mail dahlanddiluca@sedona.net.

Other than that, try the lounges in the major resort hotels, or call the **Sedona Arts Center** for its current schedule of theatrical and concert performances. ~ Route 89A at Art Barn Road, Sedona; 928-282-3809; www.sedonaartscenter.com.

PARKS **SLIDE ROCK STATE PARK** 🏃 🏊 Very popular with students from Northern Arizona University, this swimming area midway between Flagstaff and Sedona in the heart of Oak Creek Canyon is almost always packed during warm-weather months. It is a natural water park, with placid pools, fast-moving chutes and a wide, flat shoreline of red sandstone for sunbathing. The state park also includes the Pendley homestead, which is listed on the National Register of Historic Places, and acres of apple orchards. Visitors are not allowed to pick the apples but, during fall, cider made from them is sold at a stand on the trail to the swim area. You'll find a picnic area, restrooms, a volleyball court, a nature trail and a snack bar. Day-use fee, $10 per vehicle. ~ Located

AUTHOR FAVORITE

The best way to discover what's unique about Sedona's culture, as far as I'm concerned, is to browse the bulletin boards at one of the town's largest metaphysical shops, **Crystal Castle**. According to many, the Castle is the New Age capital of the known cosmos. It carries unusual books, incense, jewelry, runes, visionary art and, of course, crystals. In front of the store, a "networking" bulletin board lets you scan the array of alternative professional services in town—channelers, psychic surgeons, clairvoyants, kinesiologists, numerologists and many more. ~ 313 Route 179, Sedona; 928-282-5910; www.crystalcastle.com, e-mail ccastle@sedona.net.

seven miles north of Sedona via Route 89A in Oak Creek Canyon; 928-282-3034, fax 928-282-0245.

RED ROCK STATE PARK 🚶🚴‍♂️ ⛵ Beautiful Oak Creek runs through this 286-acre park situated in the heart of Red Rock Country. Naturalists offer guided walks daily along the six-mile trail system dotted with sycamore and cottonwood trees. The visitors center has natural history exhibits and videos. Fishing is allowed on Oak Creek. There are picnic areas, restrooms and a visitors center. Day-use fee, $6 per vehicle. ~ Drive four miles southwest of Sedona on Route 89A, then turn south on Lower Red Rock Loop Road; the park appears in three miles; 928-282-6907, fax 928-282-5972; e-mail garbeiter@pr.state.az.us.

DEAD HORSE RANCH STATE PARK 🚶🚴‍♂️ ⛵ This 325-acre park, located along the Verde River, has both desert and lush areas that can be enjoyed by walking the extensive hiking trails. Fishing is allowed in the Verde River and the four-acre lagoon, which is stocked with catfish and trout. There are picnic tables, restrooms and showers. Day-use fee, $6 per vehicle. ~ From Cottonwood, take Main Street to 10th Street, then go north for about a mile; 928-634-5283, fax 928-639-0417; e-mail lbovee@pr.state.az.us.

▲ There are 150 sites (some with water and electricity,) $12 per night for no hookups, $19 per night with hookups.

Jerome, located southwest of Sedona on Route 89A, is one of Arizona's most intriguing ghost towns. In the first decades of the 20th century it was a rich silver mining district and, with a population of 15,000, was the fifth-largest city in Arizona. After having been completely abandoned in the 1950s, it was resettled by hippies in the late 1960s and now is a thriving artist's colony with a population of about 500 people.

Verde Valley & Jerome Area

The century-old wooden buildings of Jerome line only the uphill side of the main street, which winds up the steep slope of Cleopatra Hill in a series of switchbacks. The downhill side looks over the roofs of houses and stores on a lower level, offering a spectacular vista of the entire Verde Valley, where the small towns of Cottonwood and Clarkdale, two miles apart, are undergoing a gradual transition from agriculture to a tourism-based economy.

Near the little town of Cottonwood, en route from Sedona to Jerome, is **Tuzigoot National Monument,** an uncharacteristically large Sinagua Indian pueblo ruin. Once home to about 225 people, the fieldstone pueblo stood two stories high and had 110 rooms. Today its white walls still stand on the hilltop and command an expan-

SIGHTS

sive view of the valley. Although the vista is marred by tailings fields from a refinery that used to process Jerome's copper ore, the museum at the national monument offers a good look at the prehistoric culture of the Sinagua people. Admission. ~ Off Route 89A between Cottonwood and Clarkdale; 928-634-5564, fax 928-639-0552; www.nps.gov/tuzi.

One of the most beautiful canyons in the area is remote and rugged **Sycamore Canyon**, which parallels Oak Creek Canyon. Designated wilderness area, this means that no wheeled or motorized vehicles are allowed. The Parsons Trail takes you up the lushly wooded canyon bottom, along Sycamore Creek, for most of its four-mile length, passing several small cliff dwellings resting high above. Camping is not permitted in the lower part of the canyon. For additional information, call the Sedona Rangers Station. ~ Turn off at Tuzigoot National Monument and follow the rough and ready maintained dirt road for about 12 miles to the trailhead at the end of the road; 928-282-4119.

A historic railroad that carries sightseers through some of Arizona's most spectacular country is the **Verde Canyon Railroad**. Revived in November 1990, this train achieved instant popularity as a major tourist attraction. It takes passengers on a 40-mile roundtrip from Clarkdale, just below Jerome. The diesel-powered train winds along sheer cliffs of red rock in curve after curve high above the Verde River, through a long, dark tunnel, over bridges, past gold mines and Sinagua Indian ruins, to the ghost town of Perkinsville and back. Closed Tuesday; check website for train schedule. Admission. ~ 300 North Broadway Street, Clarkdale; 928-639-0010, 800-293-7245, fax 928-639-1653; www.verdecanyonrr.com, e-mail info@verdecanyonrr.com.

Many of Jerome's buildings were constructed of massive blocks of quarried stone to withstand the blasts that frequently shook the ground from the nearby mine. The entire town has been declared a National Historic Landmark.

The hillside town of Jerome is six miles past Clarkdale on Route 89A. The pleasure of Jerome lies in strolling (or climbing) the main street, browsing in the shops along the way and admiring the carefully preserved early-20th-century architecture.

The history of Jerome's mining era is brought to life in three museums. The old Douglas Mansion in **Jerome State Historic Park** at the lower end of town offers an informative 25-minute video called "Ghost Town of Jerome," a three-dimensional model of Jerome showing the underground shafts and tunnels, and a mineral exhibit. Admission. ~ Douglas Road, Jerome; 928-634-5381, fax 928-639-3132.

For a look at mining tools, old photos, and other exhibits about old-time copper mining enter the **Jerome Historical**

Society Mine Museum. Admission. ~ Main Street, Jerome; 928-634-5477; www.jeromehistoricalsociety.org.

The **Gold King Mine Museum** has a re-created assay office, a replica mine shaft and a petting zoo. Admission. ~ Perkinsville Road, Jerome; 928-634-0053; www.goldkingmine.net.

One of the chief delights of visiting Jerome is the chance to stay in a historic landmark, a growing number of which are being converted to bed-and-breakfast inns. Some even claim to be haunted by their colorful past residents.

LODGING

Built for the mining company's chief surgeon in 1916, the **Surgeon's House** is a stately blush stucco, tile-roofed home with colorful terraced gardens facing the Verde Valley. Along with three spacious rooms and suites in the main house, there is a guest cottage decorated with vibrant Guatemalan textiles, stained-glass window hangings, terra-cotta tiles, an old-fashioned upright bathtub painted Chinese red, a secluded patio, and a private deck. Guests have access to the gardens. Complimentary beverages, snacks and a hearty breakfast are included. ~ P.O. Box 998, Jerome, AZ 86331; 928-639-1452, 800-639-1452; www.surgeonshouse.com, e-mail surgeonshouse@surgeonshouse.com. MODERATE TO DELUXE.

An 1898 Victorian bed and breakfast, the **Ghost City Inn** features six rooms with private baths. Visit the Old West in "The Western Room" or soak up the stunning vistas from the "Verde View Room." There's also a jacuzzi to relax in. ~ 541 Main Street, Jerome; 928-634-4678, 888-634-4678; www.ghostcityinn.com. MODERATE TO DELUXE.

For a bit of Arizona history with your meal, visit the **English Kitchen**, the state's oldest continually operating restaurant. Founded by a Chinese immigrant in 1899, the eatery serves standard American comfort food: charbroiled burgers, hot dogs, soups, salads and homemade pies for dessert. Breakfast and lunch only. Closed January and Monday. ~ 119 North Jerome Avenue, Jerome; 928-634-2132. BUDGET.

DINING

Jerome Palace Haunted Hamburger is a meateater's delight, specializing in grilled steaks, chicken and ribs served in a cozy dining room with a fireplace and 90-mile views of the Verde Valley. Both indoor and outdoor seating are available. ~ 410 Clark Street, Jerome; 928-634-0554. MODERATE.

If you're looking for dramatic views of the Verde Valley and food on a par with nearby Sedona, reserve a table at the **Asylum Restaurant**. The eatery, located inside the historic Jerome Grand Hotel atop Cleopatra Hill, gets its name from the old town hospital that was once located here. Dinner entrées include lobster and Gulf shrimp, duck, pork, chicken and pasta, as well as vegetarian specials; the lunch menu tends toward interesting salads and sandwiches. ~ 200 Hill Street, Jerome; 928-639-3197; www.theasylum.biz, e-mail mail@theasylum.biz. MODERATE TO DELUXE.

SHOPPING　Many of Jerome's residents are arts-and-crafts people, and a stroll up and down the town's switchback Main Street will take you past quite a few intriguing shops that offer pottery, jewelry, handmade clothing, stained glass and other such wares.

Designs on You is a two-story shop that sells women's casual and natural-fiber clothing and lingerie. ~ 233 Main Street, Jerome; 928-634-7879.

You can watch jewelers create contemporary designs at Aurum Jewelry. About 40 local artists show their work here, which ranges from a sculptured iron spoon and fork to belt buckles, bolo ties, custom knives and inlaid jewelry. ~ 369 Main Street, Jerome; 928-634-3330; www.aurumjewelry.com.

In the last few years, the heart of the working art movement in town has been centered at the Old Mingus Art Center, which is now filled with studios and galleries carrying everything from paintings to sculpture. The biggest is the Anderson/Mandette Art Studios. One of the largest private art studios in the country, it feels more like a museum as you walk through it. Paintings by Robin Anderson and Margo Mandette hang upstairs. ~ Route 89A, Jerome; 928-634-3438; www.robinjohnanderson.com, e-mail robinj@sedona.net.

NIGHTLIFE　The Old West saloon tradition lives on in Jerome, where the town's most popular club is the Spirit Room in the old Connor Hotel. There is live music on weekend afternoons and evenings and the atmosphere is as authentic as can be. Occasional cover (evenings only). ~ 166 Main Street at Jerome Avenue, Jerome; 928-634-8809, fax 928-649-0981; www.spiritroom.com.

▼▼▼▼▼▼▼▼▼▼
Prescott

Continuing southwest on Route 89A, in the next valley, sits the city of Prescott, the original territorial capital of Arizona from 1864 to 1867. President Abraham Lincoln decided to declare it the capital because the only other community of any size in the Arizona Territory, Tucson, was full of Confederate sympathizers. Until recently, Prescott was a low-key, all-American town that seemed stuck in a 1950s time warp. Within the past few years, however, relatively low real estate prices have spurred explosive suburban development, making Prescott the fastest-growing community in Arizona. Yet its downtown historic district retains a certain quiet charm with few concessions to tourism. Incidentally, Prescott is located at the exact geographic center of the state of Arizona.

Built in 1916, the **Yavapai County Courthouse** sits at the heart of Prescott, surrounded by a green plaza where locals pass the time playing cards and chatting, and tourists rest awhile on park benches. Surrounding the plaza are many of the town's shops, in addition to historic Whiskey Row, where at one time some 20 saloons were open day and night.

The major sightseeing highlight in Prescott is the **Sharlot Hall Museum**, which contains a large collection of antiques from Arizona's territorial period, including several fully furnished houses and an excellent collection of stagecoaches and carriages, as well as a history of the Prescott area in photographs. Sharlot Mabridth Hall was a well-known essayist, poet and traveler who explored the wild areas of the Arizona Territory around the turn of the 20th century. Seeing that Arizona's historic and prehistoric artifacts were rapidly being taken from the state, Ms. Hall began a personal collection that grew quite large over the next three decades and became the nucleus of this large historical museum. The museum's collections are housed in several Territorial-era

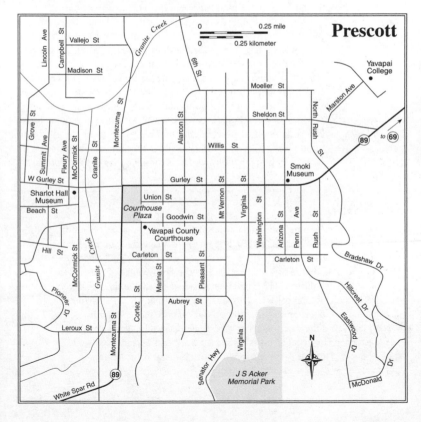

Prescott

buildings brought from around the county, including a home that was built of ponderosa pine logs in 1864 and used as a governor's mansion until 1867. The complex occupies a large park in downtown Prescott. ~ 415 West Gurley Street; 928-445-3122, fax 928-776-9053; www.sharlot.org, e-mail sharlot@sharlot.org.

The **Smoki Museum** houses a large collection of American Indian artifacts from throughout the Southwest. The museum also houses a library and the largest collection of works by Kate Cory, a painter and photographer of Hopi life during the early 20th century. Closed the first two weeks of January. Admission. ~ 147 North Arizona Street; 928-445-1230, fax 928-777-0573; www.smokimuseum.org, e-mail info@smokimuseum.org.

Prescott also has some other noteworthy museums. The **Phippen Museum of Western Art**, six miles north of town, honors cowboy artist George Phippen and presents changing exhibits of art of the American West. It is generally considered one of the best Western art museums in the country. Closed Monday. Admission. ~ 4701 Route 89 North; 928-778-1385; www.phippen artmuseum.org, e-mail phippen@phippenartmuseum.org.

Thirty-four miles east of Prescott you'll find **Arcosanti**, a planned city that will eventually be home to 6000 people. Arcosanti was designed by famed Italian designer Paulo Soleiri, who came to Arizona to study with Frank Lloyd Wright and never left, as a synthesis of architecture and ecology. The complex, which presently houses a gallery, a bakery and café, a foundry, residences and visitor accommodations, a concert stage and more, is pedestrian-oriented. From a distance, its strange skyline looks like some kind of psychedelic theme park, but on closer examination it is a busy construction site where unusual buildings with domes, arches, portholes and protruding cubes expand constantly

◆◆

SHARLOT HALL

One of the most admired women in Arizona history was Sharlot Mabridth Hall, who arrived in Prescott in 1882. She helped manage the family ranch east of Prescott, passing time writing poetry and panning for gold. But in 1909 she became the territorial historian and the first woman in Arizona to hold a political office. In 1924, Hall was asked to go east and represent Arizona in the electoral college. Originally she turned down the offer, not having enough money for suitable clothes. But officials at the United Verde Mine saved the day, buying her a blue silk dress with a fine copper mesh coat. This "copper dress" was a hit back east and gave a free shot of publicity to the Arizona copper industry. Today, you can learn all about her in the Sharlot Hall Museum.

like living organisms, making maximum use of passive solar heat. Although construction has been continuous since 1970, plans for future development extend decades into the future. Tours are offered daily. Continuing construction is financed in part by the sale of handmade souvenir items, particularly bronze-and-ceramic Soleiri wind bells. Other funding comes from the many seminars, conferences, workshops and music events presented each year. ~ Route 17, Exit 262 at Cordes Junction; 928-632-7135; www. arcosanti.org, e-mail arcoinfo@arcosanti.org.

Prescott has several historic downtown hotels. The most elegant of them is the **Hassayampa Inn**, a 1927 hotel listed on the National Register. The lobby and other common areas have been restored to their earlier glory and furnished with antiques. The rooms have been beautifully renovated and all have private baths. Room rates include a complimentary breakfast in the Peacock Dining Room. ~ 122 East Gurley Street; 928-778-9434, 800-322-1927, fax 928-445-8590; www.hassayampainn.com. DELUXE.

LODGING

A smaller hotel on a quiet side street is the **Hotel Vendome**. Rooms in this historic 20-unit 1917 hotel have been nicely restored and decorated in the style of the era. There are four two-room units that feature restored clawfoot tub/showers. ~ 230 South Cortez Street; 928-776-0900, 888-468-3583, fax 928-771-0395; www.vendomehotel.com, e-mail vendomehotel@aol.com. MODERATE TO DELUXE.

For added privacy, try **The Cottages at Prescott Country Inn**. With twelve two-, three- and four-room abodes, this hideaway offers all the comforts of home. Each cottage has its own complete kitchen (with the exception of three) and all are tastefully decorated. Most have a fireplace and patio. The pricing is wonderfully reasonable, too. Continental breakfast served in bed or at your cottage table. ~ 503 South Montezuma Street; 928-445-7991, 888-757-0015, fax 928-717-1215; www.prescottcountry.com. MODERATE TO DELUXE.

A cozy bed and breakfast in a 1934 main house with three guesthouses is the **Prescott Pines Inn**. It has 11 Victorian-style guest accommodations, including a two-story chalet, beautifully decorated in subdued color schemes. Some have fireplaces and others have kitchenettes. Sumptuous full breakfasts are served on rose-patterned china. Reservations are recommended. ~ 901 White Spar Road; 928-445-7270, 800-541-5374, fax 928-778-3665; www.prescottpinesinn.com, e-mail info@prescottpinesinn. com. BUDGET TO MODERATE.

More modest rooms, all with private baths, are available at the **Hotel St. Michael**. The location couldn't be better for those who wish to enjoy the Wild West nightlife of Whiskey Row, on the same block. A full breakfast is included. ~ 205 West Gurley Street;

928-776-1999, 800-678-3757, fax 928-776-7318; www.hotelst michael.net, e-mail hsmevents@cabelone.net. MODERATE.

Prescott also has more than its share of low-priced, basic lodging from which to explore the wild canyons and forests surrounding the city. The prices can't be beat at the Mediterranean-style **American Motel**. Rooms are refurbished in adobe and terra-cotta hues, and some have wonderful old murals on the walls. ~ 1211 East Gurley Street; 928-778-4322, fax 928-778-1324. BUDGET TO MODERATE.

By making reservations well in advance, visitors can stay overnight in **Arcosanti**. Visionary architect Paulo Soleiri's futuristic village has a group of greenhouse guest rooms, each with basic furnishings including two double beds, as well as a Sky Suite with two small bedrooms, a private bath, a kitchenette, a living room and a patio. Room rates are surprisingly low, though late sleepers may find that construction noise is a drawback. ~ Route 17, Exit 262 at Cordes Junction; 928-632-7135, fax 928-632-6229; www.arcosanti.org, e-mail info@arcosanti.org. BUDGET.

DINING

Prescott's finer restaurants include the **Peacock Dining Room** in the Hassayampa Inn. Here you'll find lunch and dinner menus of Continental and American specialties in an elegant old-time atmosphere. An etched-glass peacock lady adorns the front door of this art-deco dining room. Choose between seating at tables or semicircular booths. Tiffany-style lamps add to the quaint atmosphere of this high-ceilinged establishment. Breakfast, lunch and dinner served Monday through Saturday; breakfast and dinner only on Sunday. ~ 122 East Gurley Street; 928-778-9434, 800-322-1927; www.hassayampainn.com. DELUXE TO ULTRA-DELUXE.

A century-old general merchandise store that has been transformed into a popular restaurant, **Murphy's** is a walk through history. A leaded-glass divider separates the bar and restaurant

---

PRESCOTT PUB AND GRUB

With a list of awards as long as my arm, **Prescott Brewing Company** claims to be the town's only brew pub. Regardless, it's a great place to nosh and people-watch simultaneously. In addition to Southwestern-tinged entrées like Angus burgers and Sonoran enchiladas you'll find some vegetarian options: the "Settler's Pot Pie" is a mish-mash of mushrooms, tomatoes, carrots, artichoke hearts, yams and fresh herbs, baked with mozzarella and parmesan cheese and served with—what else?—beer bread. ~ 130 West Gurley Street; 928-771-2795, fax 928-771-1115; www.prescottbrewingcompany.com. BUDGET TO MODERATE.

sections decorated with photos of Prescott's mining heyday. Mahogany bar booths and a burgundy carpet add to the charm of this establishment. You can also enjoy a drink in the lounge offering views of Thumb Butte. Specialties include mesquite-broiled seafood and prime rib of beef along with fresh home-baked bread. ~ 201 North Cortez Street; 928-445-4044, fax 928-778-4844. MODERATE TO DELUXE.

For home-style cooking in Prescott head to the **Dinner Bell Café**. It may not look like much from the outside, but give it a try and you'll find out why this is one of the most popular restaurants in central Arizona. For breakfast try the hubcap-size pancakes or three-egg omelettes. Lunch specials include sandwiches, burgers, salads and hot roast beef. Be sure to sample the homemade salsa. No dinner. ~ 321 West Gurley Street; 928-445-9888. BUDGET.

◄ HIDDEN

Great steaks in a Western setting are the specialties at the **Lone Spur Café**, a local favorite for lunch. Nobody goes away hungry at this downtown joint—breakfast includes generous portions of eggs, biscuits and gravy, cornflake-crusted french toast and pancakes. No dinner. ~ 106 West Gurley Street; 928-445-8202. BUDGET TO MODERATE.

Also good is the **Prescott Pantry** in the Iron Springs Plaza shopping center. This bakery/deli has restaurant seating and offers ever-changing daily specials, hearty sandwiches, espresso drinks and fresh-baked pastries. Closed Sunday. ~ 1201 Iron Springs Road; 928-778-4280. BUDGET.

Because it is old as Arizona towns go, and perhaps because of Sharlot Hall's recognition that it was important to preserve the everyday objects of 19th-century Arizona, Prescott is a good place for antique shopping. As in most antique hunting areas, some items offered for sale do not come from the Prescott area but have been imported from other, less-visited parts of the country. Most, however, are the real thing, and antique buffs will find lots of great shops within walking distance of one another in the downtown area, especially along the two-block strip of Cortez Street between Gurley and Sheldon streets.

SHOPPING

Some of the best places to browse are the indoor mini-malls where select groups of dealers and collectors display, such as the **Merchandise Mart Antique Mall**. ~ 205 North Cortez Street; 928-776-1728. **Prescott Antique & Craft Market** is another such mall. ~ 115 North Cortez Street; 928-445-7156. Nearby is the **Deja Vu Antique Mall**. ~ 134 North Cortez Street; 928-445-6732.

An excellent gallery in town is **Sun West**. Arizona and local artists sell sculpture, pottery, furniture, paintings and jewelry, and there are also rugs woven by the Zapotec people. ~ 152 South Montezuma Street; 928-778-1204.

NIGHTLIFE   Rock-and-roll and blues acts entertain on Friday and Saturday nights, as well as Sunday afternoon at **Piñon Pines Nite Club**. See what the musicians come up with on Wednesday's live jam night. ~ 2701 East Route 89A; 928-445-9935.

Moctezuma's has a deejay on Friday and Saturday. ~ 144 South Montezuma Street; 928-445-1244.

Prescott has its own theater company performing year-round at the **Prescott Fine Arts Theater**. It offers both a main stage and a Family Theater for child-oriented productions. ~ 208 North Marina Street; 928-445-3286; www.pfaa.net.

The Yavapai-Prescott Indian tribe owns **Bucky's Casino** east of Prescott. Besides the usual rows upon rows of slot machines, there is a low-limit poker room featuring seven-card stud, Texas hold-'em and Omaha poker. When you need to refuel for another round of gaming, you can retreat to the **Yavapai Cantina**, a sports bar with snacks and beverages. ~ 1500 Route 69; 800-756-8744 (casino); www.buckyscasino.com.

PARKS   **WATSON LAKE AND PARK** 🚶‍♂️ 🛥 🥾 A labyrinth of granite rock formations along Route 89 just outside of Prescott surrounds pretty little Watson Lake, a manmade reservoir that is locally popular for boating and fishing. The area used to be a stronghold for Apache Indians. More recently, from the 1920s to the 1950s, there was a major resort at Granite Dells and some artifacts survive from that era. Hiking and rock climbing are popular pursuits here. There are restrooms, showers and several picnic areas. Parking fee $2. ~ Route 89, four miles north of Prescott; 928-777-1564, fax 928-771-5845.

▲ There are 42 sites (no hookups); $10 per night. Camping is on a first-come, first-served basis only.

▼ ▼ ▼ ▼ ▼ ▼ ▼ ▼ ▼ ▼ ▼ ▼

Outdoor Adventures

North Central Arizona is a popular region for both downhill and cross-country skiing.

SKIING   **FLAGSTAFF AREA**   Arizona's premier downhill ski area is the **Arizona Snowbowl**, located 14 miles north of Flagstaff on the slopes of the San Francisco Peaks. The ski area has four chairlifts, ranging from the beginners' Hart Prairie Chairlift (3200 feet long with only a 650-foot vertical rise) to the steep Agassiz Chairlift (6450 feet long with a 1981-foot vertical rise to an elevation of 11,500 feet). Skis and boots, as well as snowboards, are available at the rental shop. Snowboarders can use the designated park or share the slopes with skiers. The season runs from mid-December to mid-April. ~ Seven miles off Route 180 on Snowbowl Road; 928-779-1951, 928-779-4577 (snow report), fax 928-779-3019; www.arizonasnowbowl.com, e-mail info@arizonasnowbowl.com.

The small female-owned, family-oriented **Elk Ridge Ski and Recreation Area** is low key, with no lines and no crowds. This tubers-only facility has a day lodge with a deli. Closed Tuesday and Wednesday and from April through December. ~ Four miles south of Williams; 928-635-6587; www.elkskiridge.com, e-mail info@ elkskiridge.com.

For cross-country skiers, the **Flagstaff Nordic Center**, 16 miles north of Flagstaff in Coconino National Forest, maintains an extensive system of trails from mid-November to mid-March, weather permitting. ~ Route 180; 928-779-1951; www.arizonasnowbowl.com, e-mail info@ arizonasnowbowl.com.

> The elevation drop from Flagstaff to Sedona is 2500 feet, and the temperature is often 20° higher in Sedona than in Flagstaff.

For the most spectacular guided tour in town, sightsee from a hot-air balloon.

BALLOON RIDES

SEDONA AREA   Experience the Red Rock Country from the sky with **Red Rock Balloon Adventures**. All rides begin at sunrise and include a champagne picnic. ~ Sedona; 928-284-0040, 800-258-3754; www.redrockballoons.com. Also hovering above is **Northern Light Balloon Expeditions**. Balloon rides last an hour and go over Sedona or along the Mogollon Rim depending on the winds. Each operator launches one trip a day at sunrise and follows it up with a picnic breakfast. ~ P.O. Box 1695, Sedona, AZ 86339; 928-282-2274, 800-230-6222.

For Sedona visitors who wish to explore the surrounding Red Rock Country, the town has an extraordinary number of jeep tour services, offering everything from general sightseeing journeys to spiritual inner journeys. Trips range from one hour to all day, and are fully guided. They'll usually pick you up at any Sedona lodging.

JEEP TOURS

Pink Jeep Tours runs sightseeing trips in—what else—those flashy pink jobs you see darting around town. They provide off-road backcountry tours of the Sedona red rock area, as well as trips to Indian ruins and petroglyphs, which require a little hiking as well as jeeping. The tours focus on American Indian folklore, geology and wildlife appreciation. They also offer tours of the Grand Canyon in custom vans. ~ 204 North Route 89A; 928-282-5000, 800-873-3662, fax 928-282-8818; www.pink jeep.com.

Whether you're looking for a Wild West sightseeing tour that traverses private ranchlands, or a New Age "Vortex Tour" where you can absorb the electromagnetic energy that is said to swirl among select stones in Boynton Canyon, the cowboy-garbed guides at **Red Rock Western Jeep Tours** can provide it; the emphasis on these one-and-a-half to five-hour trips is educational and photographic, so whichever tour you take, you'll doubtless learn as much as you ever wanted to know about the area and take home plenty of pictures. ~ 270 North Route 89A; 928-282-6826, 800-848-7728; www.redrockjeep.com.

Earth Wisdom Jeep Tours runs two- to four-hour trips to the scenic vortex, sacred wheel, remote canyon and rim, ruins and hiking spots. ~ 293 North Route 89A; 928-282-4714, 800-482-4714; www.earthwisdomtours.com, e-mail earthwisdomtours@sedona.net.

GOLF

While you might not be able to golf year-round here, most of the year offers excellent weather for hitting the greens.

FLAGSTAFF AREA   Tee off at the 18-hole, public **Continental Country Club**. There are clubs and golf carts for rent. Closed in winter if there's snow on the ground. ~ 2380 North Oakmont Drive, Flagstaff; 928-526-5125; www.continentalflagstaff.com.

SEDONA AREA   **Sedona Golf Resort**'s 18-hole course designed by Gary Panks is ranked third in the state among public courses. Clubs are available for rent, and the use of a cart is included in the green fee. ~ 35 Ridge Trail Drive; 928-284-9355; www.sedonagolfresort.com. Drive a wedge at the semiprivate, 18-hole, Robert Trent Jones–designed **Oak Creek Country Club**. Carts and clubs can be rented. ~ 690 Bell Rock Boulevard, Sedona; 928-284-1660; www.oakcreekcountryclub.com. Play the greens at the semipublic **Canyon Mesa Country Club**, a nine-hole executive course with red-rock views. Clubs and carts are available for rent. ~ 500 Jacks Canyon Boulevard, Sedona; 928-284-0036. The nine-hole, par-three course at **Radisson Poco Diablo Resort** wends its way among challenging water hazards and a sand trap as well as beautiful stands of willow trees. There are clubs for rent, but no carts; it is a walking course, and metal cleats are prohibited. ~ 1752 South Route 179, Sedona; 928-282-7333, fax 928-282-2090. Go for a hole in one on either (or both) of the two 18-hole courses at the public **Antelope Hills Golf Course**. There are clubs and carts for rent. ~ 1 Perkins Drive, Prescott; 800-972-6818; www.antelopehillsgolf.com.

TENNIS

There is not a lot of tennis in this area, but you should be able to find a few open courts.

FLAGSTAFF AREA   **Thorpe Park** has four lighted public courts. ~ Thorpe Park Road. The public **Bushmaster Park** has two lighted courts. ~ Alta Vista Street. You can call the **Parks and Recreation Department** for more information. ~ 928-779-7690, fax 928-779-7693.

SEDONA AREA   Sedona has no public tennis courts. For a fee, courts are available to the public at **Poco Diablo Resort**, with four courts, two of which are lighted. Hitting assistants are available. ~ 1752 South Route 179; 928-282-7333.

PRESCOTT In Prescott, six tennis courts are open to the public year-round at **Yavapai College.** ~ 1100 East Sheldon Street; 928-445-7300, or 928-778-7071. Public summer courts are also found at **Prescott High School,** which has six courts. ~ 1050 North Ruth Street; 928-445-2322.

The equestrian will find many riding opportunities in this region.

RIDING STABLES

FLAGSTAFF AREA Year-round trips in Coconino National Forest are offered by **Flying Heart Barn,** which also has a horse motel for overnight horsekeeping. ~ 8400 North Route 89, Flagstaff; 928-526-2788.

SEDONA AREA **Red Rock Western Jeep Tours** offers one- or two-hour-long trail rides. ~ 270 North Route 89A; 928-282-6826, 800-848-7728. For one- and two-hour rides through Coconino National Forest, contact **A Day in the West.** ~ 252 North Route 89A; 928-282-4320, 800-973-3662; www.adayinthewest.com.

PRESCOTT **Smokin' Gun Stables** provides guided horse rides into the national forest around Prescott. ~ 1101 Paar Drive; 928-778-9154.

As in the rest of the state, this region is a mecca for biking.

BIKING

FLAGSTAFF AREA Flagstaff has about eight miles of paved trails in its **Urban Trail System and Bikeways System,** linking the Northern Arizona University campus, the downtown area and Lowell Observatory. Maps and information on the trail system are available upon request from the **Parks and Recreation Department.** ~ 211 West Aspen Avenue; 928-779-7690, fax 928-213-4830.

AUTHOR FAVORITE

I must confess a growing distaste for summertime crowds and parking problems. But while every visitor to Flagstaff or Sedona drives through often-crowded Oak Creek Canyon, one of central Arizona's "must-see" spots, few stop to explore the canyon's west fork, a narrow canyon with sheer walls hundreds feet high in places, which is only accessible on foot. You'll need an inexpensive **Sedona Red Rock Pass** to park and hike in the area; they are available from area businesses, at trailheads and from the ranger station. For more information on trails in this area, call the Red Rock Ranger Station, 928-282-4119; www.redrockcountry.org.

Outside Flagstaff, a popular route for all-day bike touring is the 36-mile paved loop road through **Sunset Crater and Wupatki national monuments**, starting at the turnoff from Route 89 about 20 miles northeast of town.

For mountain bikers, several unpaved primitive roads lead deeper into the San Francisco Volcano Field in **Coconino National Forest**. For more information, contact the **Peaks Ranger Station**. ~ 5075 North Route 89; 928-526-0866; www.coconino forest.us.

SEDONA AREA   The same network of unpaved back roads that makes the **Red Rock Country** around Sedona such a popular area for four-wheel-drive touring is also ideal for mountain biking. Get a map from one of the local bike shops and try the dirt roads leading from Soldier Pass Road to the Seven Sacred Pools or the Devil's Kitchen. Or follow the Broken Arrow Jeep Trail east from Route 179 to Submarine Rock. The Schnebly Hill Road climbs all the way north to Flagstaff, paralleling the Oak Creek Canyon Highway. The upper part of the road is steep, winding and very rough, but the lower part, through Bear Wallow Canyon, makes for a beautiful mountain biking excursion.

PRESCOTT AREA   **Thumb Butte Trail** and **Copper Basin** are among the favorite mountain-biking areas around Prescott.

Bike Rentals   In Flagstaff, you can rent mountain bikes and obtain trail information at **Absolute Bikes**. They also offer repair service. ~ 18 North San Francisco Street, Flagstaff; 928-779-5969; www.absolutebikes.net. In Sedona, you'll find trail information, bike rentals and repairs at **Mountain Bike Heaven**. ~ 1695 West Route 89A, Sedona; 928-282-1312; www.mountainbikeheaven. com. **Sedona Sports** also rents bikes. ~ Creekside Plaza, 251 Route 179, Sedona; 928-282-1317; www.sedonasports.com. You can rent a mountain bike by the hour, day or week (complete with helmet, tire pump, repair kit, water bottle, lock and map) at **Ironclad Bicycles**. ~ 710 White Spar Road, Prescott; 928-776-1755; www.ironcladbicycles.com.

ROCK CLIMBING   Many areas in the canyon country of central Arizona are ideal for technical rock climbing. However, safe climbing requires training, practice and proper equipment—all of which are available at the **Vertical Relief Rock Gym** in Flagstaff. Said to be one of the finest indoor climbing facilities in the country, this gym is basically a tall, empty downtown building, its 6000 square feet of windowless interior walls set with stone hand- and footholds. Instructors give daily classes for climbers of all ages and abilities, covering such topics as knots, belaying, rappelling and teamwork. ~ 205 South San Francisco Street, Flagstaff; 928-556-9909; www.verticalrelief. com, e-mail programs@verticalrelief.com.

Lovers of the outdoors will delight in the number and variety of hiking trails this area provides. All distances listed for hiking trails are one way unless otherwise noted.

FLAGSTAFF AREA   Just north of Flagstaff rise the San Francisco Peaks, the highest in Arizona. Numerous trails start from Mount Elden and Schultz Pass roads, which branch off Route 180 to the right a short distance past the Museum of Northern Arizona. Other trailheads are located in Flagstaff at Buffalo Park on Cedar Avenue and near the Peaks Ranger Station on Route 89. Most trails in the Flagstaff area close in winter.

The film version of Zane Grey's *Call of the Canyon* was shot on location in Sedona.

North of the ranger station, off Route 180, the **Elden Lookout Trail** (3 miles) climbs by switchbacks up the east face of 9299-foot Mount Elden, with an elevation gain of 2400 feet and, waiting to reward you at the top, a spectacular view of the city and the volcano fields around Sunset Crater.

The **Fatman's Loop Trail** (2 miles), branching off of Elden Lookout Trail for a shorter hike with a 600-foot elevation gain, also offers a good view of Flagstaff.

From the Buffalo Park trailhead, the **Oldham Trail** (5.5 miles) ascends the west face to the top of Mount Elden. The longest trail on the mountain, this is a gentler climb. The Oldham Trail intersects Mount Elden Road three times, making it possible to take a shorter hike on only the higher part of the trail. **Pipeline Trail** (2.8 miles) links the lower parts of the Oldham and Elden Lookout trails along the northern city limit of Flagstaff, allowing either a short hike on the edge of town or a long, all-day loop trip up one side of the mountain and down the other.

Perhaps the most unusual of many hiking options in the strange volcanic landscape around the base of the San Francisco Peaks is on **Red Mountain**, 33 miles north of Flagstaff off Route 180. A gap in the base of this 1000-foot-high volcanic cone lets you follow the **Red Mountain Trail** (1 mile) from the end of the national forest access road straight into the crater without climbing. Not often visited by tourists, this is a great place to explore with older children.

◄ *HIDDEN*

For maps and detailed hiking information on these and many other trails in Coconino National Forest, contact the **Peaks Ranger Station**. ~ 5075 North Route 89; 520-526-0866; www.fs.fed.us/r3/coconino.

SEDONA AREA   The trailhead for the **West Fork Trail** (14 miles) is in the parking lot (there is a parking fee) of the Call of the Canyon on the west side of Route 89A, ten miles north of Sedona. The first three miles of the trail pass through a protected "research natural area," are heavily used and easy to hike. Farther up, the trail becomes less distinct, requires repeatedly swimming through pools of water while floating your gear and leads into the Red Rock Secret Mountain Wilderness.

A very popular hiking spot in the Red Rock Country is Boynton Canyon, one of Sedona's four "Vortex" areas. According to the New Age community, Boynton Canyon is the most powerful of the vortexes, emanating an electromagnetic psychic energy that can be felt for miles around. Whether you believe or not, it is undeniably beautiful. From the trailhead on Boynton Pass Road—a continuation of Dry Creek Road, which leaves Route 89A in West Sedona—the nearly level **Boynton Canyon Trail** (2.5 miles) goes up the canyon through woods and among red-rock formations. There are several small, ancient Sinagua Indian cliff dwellings in the canyon. If you visit the ruins be aware that the dwellings are very fragile and are disappearing due to impact.

A right turn from Dry Creek Road on the way to Boynton Pass will put you on unpaved Forest Road 152, which is rough enough in spots that drivers of low-clearance vehicles may want to think twice before proceeding. One and a half miles up this road, the **Devil's Bridge Trail** (1 mile) climbs gradually through piñon and juniper country to a long red sandstone arch with a magnificent view of the surrounding canyonlands. You can walk to the top of the arch. Located three miles farther, at the end of Dry Creek Road, is the trailhead for the **Vultee Arch Trail** (1.7 miles), which follows Sterling Canyon to another natural bridge.

PRESCOTT   There are many hiking trails in the national forest around Prescott. One of the most popular is the **Thumb Butte Trail** (1.4 miles), which goes up a saddle west of town, through oak and piñon woods, offering good views of Prescott and Granite Dells. The trail starts from Thumb Butte Park. To get there, go west on Thumb Butte Road, an extension of Gurley Street.

More ambitious hikers may wish to explore the **Granite Mountain Wilderness**. Of its several trails, the one that goes to the summit of the 7125-foot mountain is **Little Granite Mountain Trail** (3.3 miles), a beautiful all-day hike with an elevation gain of 1500 feet. For information on this and other trails in the area, contact the Prescott National Forest—Bradshaw District ranger station. ~ 2230 East Route 69, just east of Prescott; 928-443-8008.

▼ ▼ ▼ ▼ ▼ ▼ ▼ ▼ ▼ ▼
Transportation

CAR

One hundred and thirty eight miles north of Phoenix via Route 17, Flagstaff is located on **Route 40**, the main east–west route across northern Arizona. Grand Canyon–bound travelers leaving the interstate at Flagstaff have a choice between the more direct way to Grand Canyon Village, 79 miles via **Route 180**, or the longer way, 105 miles via **Route 89** and **Route 64**, which parallels the canyon rim for 25 miles.

These routes combine perfectly into a spectacular loop trip from Flagstaff.

Another scenic loop trip from Flagstaff goes south on **Route 89A**, descending through Oak Creek Canyon to Sedona in Red Rock Country, a distance of 26 slow miles. From Sedona, Route 89A continues for 58 more miles through the historic mining town of Jerome, with a steep climb over Cleopatra Hill, to Prescott, the old territorial capital. From there, a 51-mile drive on Route 89 returns travelers to interstate Route 40 at Ash Fork, about 55 miles west of Flagstaff.

AIR

U.S. Airways flies into **Flagstaff Pulliam Airport** (928-556-1234) and **Prescott Municipal Airport** (928-777-1801).

Sedona Sky Treks (928-282-6628) provides on-demand charter service for travelers from the **Sedona Airport** (928-282-4487).

BUS

Greyhound Bus Lines (800-231-2222; www.greyhound.com) stops at the bus terminals in Flagstaff at 399 South Malpais Lane, 928-774-4573; and in Prescott at 820 East Sheldon Street, 928-445-5470.

TRAIN

Amtrak serves Flagstaff daily on its "Southwest Chief" route between Chicago and Los Angeles. The westbound passenger train stops in Flagstaff late in the evening, so arriving passengers will want to make hotel reservations in advance, with a deposit to hold the room late. Amtrak offers a shuttle bus service to the Grand Canyon for its Flagstaff passengers. ~ 1 East Route 66, Flagstaff; 800-872-7245; www.amtrak.com.

CAR RENTALS

Flagstaff has about a dozen car-rental agencies, most of them at the airport. Among the airport concessions are **Avis Rent A Car** (800-831-2847), **Budget Rent A Car** (800-527-0700) and **Hertz Rent A Car** (800-654-3131).

Located downtown, and more convenient for those arriving by train or bus, is **Budget Rent A Car**. ~ 175 West Aspen; 800-527-0700. Also in Flagstaff is an office of **Cruise America**, a nationwide motorhome rental agency. ~ 824 West Route 66; 928-774-4707, 800-327-7799.

At the Sedona Airport, rentals are available from **Arizona Jeep and Car Rentals** (800-879-5337).

For rentals in Prescott try **Hertz Rent A Car** (Prescott Municipal Airport; 928-776-1399, 800-654-3131) or **Budget Rent A Car** (1031 Commerce Drive; 928-778-3806, 800-527-0700).

TAXIS

Flagstaff has more than its share of taxi companies because many public transportation travelers stop there en route to the Grand

Canyon. These cabs will take you anywhere in central Arizona at any time of day or night. Sedona? Phoenix? No problem. Call **A Friendly Cab** (928-774-4444, 928-214-9000) or **Arizona Taxi and Tours** (928-779-1111). Shop and compare—rates vary.

Sedona's local taxi company is **Bob's Sedona Taxi** (928-282-1234). Prescott's taxi company, **Ace City Cab** (928-445-1616), offers discounted rates for senior citizens.

FIVE

Western Arizona

Heading west, the mighty Colorado River pours out of the Grand Canyon, spreads itself into Lake Mead, proceeds through a succession of scenic lakes, resorts and riverfront coves, then rolls south until it reaches the Gulf of California. In its wake, visitors to the region will discover a number of unusual points of interest and unparalleled recreational opportunities—each one surrounded by a distinctive landscape, each one quite different from the others. Here, you'll find broad expanses of sparkling water, summer breezes whipping up whitecaps, waterskiers cutting crystal wakes, colorful sails curled above catamarans, and miles of sandy beaches—all along the Colorado River on Arizona's "West Coast."

Kingman is a good starting point for exploring Arizona's western edge. Set at the crossroads of Routes 93 and 40, the town is strategically placed for excursions to Lake Mead and Hoover Dam, Bullhead City/Laughlin and Lake Mohave, Lake Havasu and its London Bridge, and the Parker Strip and Quartzsite. Along the way, you can explore gold and silver mining ghost towns such as Oatman and Chloride, which cling to a tenuous existence amid scenic surroundings. From Kingman, there's also a steep road that leads to the alpine greenery of Hualapai Mountain Park, where you can picnic and camp.

About 80 miles north of Kingman, on Route 93, is manmade Lake Mead, which is shared by Arizona and Nevada. Created in the 1930s when the Colorado River was backed up by Hoover Dam, Lake Mead is a popular recreation area.

In the forbidding, rocky hills of western Arizona's Mojave Desert, real estate promoters used to sell lots in planned communities sight unseen to gullible people in the East. Most of these would-be towns never even came close to reality, but two "cities" set in the middle of nowhere along desolate stretches of the Colorado River have become the twin hubs of a genuine phenomenon.

Bullhead City, one of the fastest-growing cities in Arizona, is an isolated resort community with an area population of about 40,000 people. Founded as the construction camp for Davis Dam, Bullhead City has no visible reason for its existence except daily sunshine, warm weather year-round, boating and fishing access to the Colorado River—and a booming casino strip across the river in Laughlin, at the extreme southern tip of Nevada.

Even more improbable than Bullhead City is Lake Havasu City, which the *Los Angeles Times* once called "the most successful freestanding new town in the United States." Though it enjoys a great wintertime climate and a fine location on the shore of a 46-mile-long desert lake, there is really no logical explanation for Lake Havasu City—except that, in the 1960s, chainsaw tycoon Bob McCulloch and partner C. V. Wood, Jr., planner and first general manager of Disneyland, decided to build it. Since their planned community had no economic base, they concluded that what it needed was a tourist attraction. They came up with a doozie—the London Bridge. Yes, the *real* London Bridge, bought at auction and moved block by massive granite block across the Atlantic, where it was reassembled over a channel to connect to an island in Lake Havasu. The unprecedented, seemingly absurd plan actually worked, and you can see the result for yourself today.

In addition to London Bridge, Lake Havasu City has an "English Village" to complement it. Nearby, the two sections of Lake Havasu State Park are well-developed recreational areas that take advantage of the lake's 46 miles of shoreline. The Windsor Beach Unit on the upper level of the lake has boat ramps, shaded picnic areas, campsites and more primitive camping areas accessible by boat. The Cattail Cove Unit has similar facilities, plus a marina, restaurant, store and boat rentals.

Near Parker Dam, which impounds Lake Havasu, Buckskin Mountain State Park attracts tube floaters, boaters and waterskiers. Hiking trails into the Buckskin Mountains lead to panoramic vista points and, for some lucky hikers, sightings of desert bighorn sheep.

About halfway down the "coast," the Bill Williams River empties into the Colorado River just above Parker Dam. Upstream is Alamo Lake, a large man-made reservoir created for recreation and flood control. The lake has bass fishing, swimming, boating, canoeing and views of native wildlife, including the bald and golden eagle.

En route to these unusual Arizona communities, you'll have a chance to visit Havasu National Wildlife Refuge. Keep a sharp eye and you may glimpse a bald eagle, peregrine falcon or desert bighorn sheep, along with a wide variety of other fauna.

Downriver from Parker Dam, the town of Parker and the Colorado River Indian Reservation serve as trade centers and jumping-off points for more recreation. Farther south, the town of Quartzsite, which is more a sprawling RV park than a city, attracts several hundred thousand people late January and early February for its annual rock and mineral shows.

▼▼▼▼▼▼▼▼▼▼▼
Kingman Area

At the crossroads of Routes 40 and 93, Kingman has earned a reputation as a comfortable stopover for travelers hurrying between Phoenix and Las Vegas or Los Angeles and Albuquerque. It is also a natural hub for leisurely trips to nearby ghost towns, Hoover Dam, Lake Mead and other recreational resorts along the Colorado River.

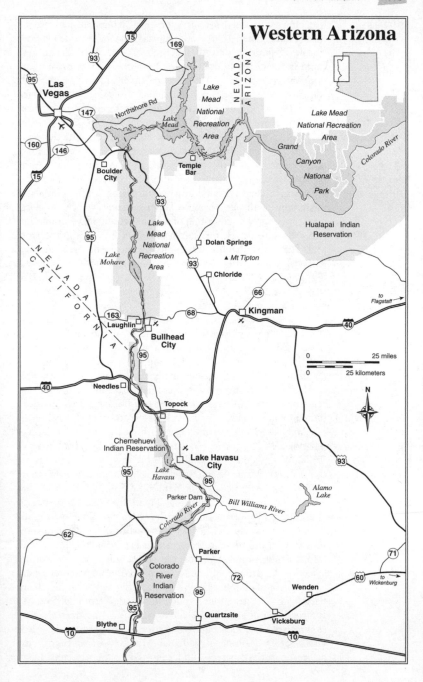

Western Arizona

SIGHTS   **Kingman** was named for surveyor Lewis Kingman, who passed
through the area in 1892 while charting a railroad route between
Needles, California, and Albuquerque, New Mexico. The railroad
camp subsequently built here took his name, but the town didn't
flourish until the early 1900s, when silver and copper deposits
were discovered in the surrounding hills. The mines were depleted
by the 1940s, but the town survived as an important pit stop for
travelers on the Santa Fe railway and old Route 66.

With more than 30 motels and 50 restaurants, modern-day
Kingman continues its tradition as a key provisioning center. Most
of the commercial activity has shifted to Motel Row—East Andy
Devine Avenue—and suburban shopping centers, but there are a
few historical gems around town worth seeing. To find out about
them, stop at the **Powerhouse Visitors Center**, which dispenses
maps, brochures and a listing of the area's annual events and festivals. Be sure to ask for a map of downtown's historic district
tour. The center also houses the Historic Route 66 Association of
Arizona, which offers information on the old transcontinental
highway. ~ 120 West Andy Devine Avenue, Kingman; 928-753-
6106, fax 928-753-6156; www.kingmantourism.org, e-mail tour
info@citilink.net.

An interesting stop is the **Mohave Museum of History and
Arts**, which gives visitors a glimpse of many of the unusual aspects
of northwestern Arizona. A mural and dioramas in the lobby depict the settlement of the region and show how camels used to
be used as beasts of burden in these parts. Kingman is the source
of much of the turquoise mined in the United States, and the museum has a fine collection of carved turquoise objects. American
Indian exhibits include portrayals of the traditional ways of the
Hualapai and Mohave tribes. Other rooms contain a collection of
paintings of U.S. presidents and their first ladies by artist Lawrence
Williams, as well as memorabilia of the town's most famous native son, the late actor Andy Devine. Closed Sunday. Admission.
~ 400 West Beale Street, Kingman; 928-753-3195, fax 928-718-
1562; www.mohavemuseum.org, e-mail mocohist@ctaz.com.

A drive through the older section of Kingman, away from the
chain-store motels and generic coffee shops, reveals a turn-of-
the-20th-century downtown area that is gradually being revitalized. For the time being, you can still admire the architectural
splendor the proud buildings once enjoyed, from Victorian mansions to simple adobe shacks. Some of the sights on the chamber's historic district tour include the Spanish Colonial **Santa Fe
Railroad Depot** at Andy Devine Avenue and 4th Street; the mission revival–style IOOF building at 5th and Beale streets; the classic
Greek-style tufa-stone, glass-domed **Mohave County Courthouse**
at Spring and 4th streets; and, just east of the museum, **Loco-**

Exploring Western Arizona

It's easy to see most of the western Arizona sights that are reachable by car in a single day. (If you had a boat here, of course, you could spend weeks exploring the areas where roads don't go.)

- Start early. From Route 40 Exit 9, a half hour south of Kingman or Bullhead City, drive south on Route 95 for 21 miles to Lake Havasu City. Walk across **London Bridge** (page 192), pondering why this improbable anachronism ranks as Arizona's second-biggest tourist attraction. Allow half an hour, or more if you take a cruise on Lake Havasu. Leave before it gets crowded and hot.

- Return to Route 40. Go west on the interstate to Exit 1, then head north on Route 95 for four miles to Oatman Road. Follow this remnant of old Route 66 to the touristy ex–ghost town of **Oatman** (page 188). In Oatman, pet a "wild" burro. Watch a Wild West shootout. Tour the funky hotel where Gable and Lombard spent a night on their honeymoon. Allow one hour.

- Continue for 27 more miles on Oatman Road, past the ghost town of Goldroad and over Sitgreave Pass, from which you'll get a great view of Kingman (where you'll be in less than half an hour).

- Stop for lunch in Kingman. (See page 176 for dining suggestions.)

- Drive north from Kingman on Route 93 for about eight miles to the marked road that turns off to the east and goes to **Chloride** (page 189). Park your car and spend half an hour strolling the streets (both of them) in this eccentric little ghost town.

- Backtrack to Kingman. Continue through town and follow Hualapai Mountain Park Road for 14 miles to **Hualapai Mountain Park** (page 178), where you'll spend the hottest part of the afternoon walking among the shady pines here. Return to Kingman, Bullhead City or Route 40 before dark.

IF YOU HAVE MORE TIME

Head north to see **Hoover Dam** (page 180) and explore **Lake Mead** (page 178). By the time you get there, you'll be just over the hill from Las Vegas, Nevada—a completely different adventure.

motive Park, where you'll find a 1927 Baldwin steam engine and bright red caboose as the centerpiece.

About an hour's drive east of Kingman are the **Grand Canyon Caverns**, limestone caves with selenite crystals and marine fossils dating back three million years. Guided tours begin with a 21-story elevator ride below ground to the cavern floors for a 45-minute walk along lighted trails equipped with handrails. Above ground are an information center, gift shop and restaurant. Admission. ~ Route 66, 12 miles east of Peach Springs; 928-422-3223, 877-422-4459, fax 928-422-4471; www.gccaverns.com, e-mail info@gccaverns.com.

LODGING   It seems nearly every motel chain is represented in Kingman. Most are located along East Andy Devine Avenue and West Beale Street, and provide dependable lodging. Among the nicer ones, the **Quality Inn** features modern guest rooms, equipped with microwaves and refrigerators. Fitness buffs will like its pool, sauna and workout room. Full breakfast buffet is included. ~ 1400 East Andy Devine Avenue, Kingman; 928-753-4747, 800-869-3252, fax 928-753-5175. BUDGET TO MODERATE.

In the downtown area, the **Arizona Inn** is within walking distance from the historic downtown sights. Comfortable rooms are decorated with dark-wood furniture and cool pastels. ~ 411 West Beale Street, Kingman; 928-753-5521, fax 928-753-6579. BUDGET.

In a town that seems to consist mainly of brand-name motor inns, the historic **Hotel Brunswick** is a refreshing exception. This three-story edifice was the tallest building in western Arizona when it was built in 1909. Abandoned in the 1970s, it has gone through several transformations. Now it's a European-style boutique hotel. The lobby is filled with period antiques, and the guest rooms have eclectic blends of contemporary and old-fashioned furnishings. Rooms vary greatly in size, from economical "cowboy/cowgirl" singles with shared baths to lavish suites with full kitchens. ~ 315 East Andy Devine Avenue, Kingman; 928-718-1800, fax 928-718-1801; www.hotel-brunswick.com, e-mail rsvp@hotel-brunswick.com. BUDGET.

DINING   Dozens of chain restaurants and coffee shops line East Andy Devine Avenue in Kingman, but for some local flavor try **The Kingman Deli**, where the chili is thick and flavorful, and there are over three dozen types of sandwiches. Sample the popular "Sneaky Snake" with ham, turkey, roast beef and swiss cheese, or the "Tumbleweed" with cucumber, avocado, sprouts, tomatoes and swiss cheese. No dinner. Closed Saturday and Sunday. ~ 419 East Beale Street, Kingman; 928-753-4151. BUDGET.

Ask Kingman locals where to find fine dining and they're likely to recommend **Dambar's Steakhouse**, a restaurant equally suited to family-night-out and Friday-night-date clientele. The fare is a selection of beef cuts big and juicy enough to lure the burliest trucker off the interstate. Non-meat eaters can choose a pasta dish or request a special vegetable plate. ~ 1960 East Andy Devine Avenue, Kingman; 928-753-3523, fax 928-718-3500. MODERATE TO DELUXE.

For your Mexican-food fix, visit **El Palacio** of Kingman. In addition to the usual standard items, the menu is peppered with dishes you don't usually find in your typical burrito joint. Try the simmered stew of tripe and hominy, or the *chile relleno* burrito. ~ 401 East Andy Devine Avenue, Kingman; 928-718-0018, fax 928-718-0049. BUDGET TO MODERATE.

A little over an hour east from Kingman, the busy little Route 66 burg of Seligman seems frozen in time, with funky diners like the **OK Saloon and Road Kill Cafe**. The restaurant doesn't really serve road kill; in fact, the babyback ribs are excellent, as are the barbecue sandwiches. This is the kind of joint that has signed dollar bills and a carved naked-lady bar post. ~ 502 West Route 66, Seligman; 928-422-3554. BUDGET TO MODERATE.

SHOPPING

Most of Kingman's commercial activity takes place along Stockton Hill Road and Andy Devine Avenue, two streets that intersect in the downtown area. There's not much before this intersection, but one exception is **Classy Collections**, a quaint little shop featuring Victorian-style antiques and gifts. Closed Sunday. ~ 421 Beale Street, Kingman; 928-753-5002.

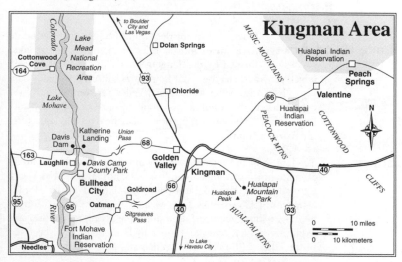

NIGHTLIFE   Locals head to **Mulligan's Bar** at the Hotel Brunswick. Billed as a "businessman's bar," there's an understated tone to the place, and you can find premier beers and cigars. ~ 315 East Andy Devine Avenue, Kingman; 928-718-1800; www.hotel-bruns wick.com.

Or you can catch a flick at **Cinemark**. ~ 4055 Stockton Hill Road, Kingman; 928-757-7985.

PARKS   **HUALAPAI MOUNTAIN PARK** 🏃 This island of forested slopes in the middle of the Mohave Desert is a locally popular picnicking, camping and hiking area. These mountains were once the ancestral home of the Hualapai Indians, until they were forced to relocate by the U.S. military in the 1870s. The Hualapai, whose name translates to "pine-tree folk," now live farther north on a reservation at the west end of the Grand Canyon. Managed by the Mohave County Parks Department, the park offers cool, protected habitat for wildlife including deer, elk, coyotes and occasional mountain lions. There are picnic areas, restrooms, cabins, a softball diamond and hiking trails. Day-use fee, $5. ~ Located 14 miles southeast of Kingman on the paved Hualapai Mountain Park Road; 928-681-5700, fax 928-757-5662; www.hualapai mountainpark.com.

▲ There are 70 tent sites, as well as 11 RV hookups available May to September; $10 per vehicle per night for tent sites, $19 for hookups. Besides tent and RV campgrounds, there are 15 cabins built in the 1930s as part of a Civilian Conservation Corps camp that can be rented for the night ($45 to $85 per night). Reservations are required for cabins: 928-757-0915, 877-757-0915.

▼▼▼▼▼▼▼▼▼▼▼▼
Lake Mead Area

Downriver from the Grand Canyon, the Colorado River turns into a series of manmade desert lakes formed by the dams of the Colorado River Project, which provides: electricity for Southern California, a steady supply of irrigation water for Imperial Valley agriculture, and flood control for all the communities along the once-raging river. With Nevada and California on the other side, the river and lakes form the Arizona state line.

SIGHTS   The largest of the reservoirs is 110-mile-long **Lake Mead**, about 80 miles north of Kingman on Route 93, not far from Las Vegas. Created when the Colorado River was backed up by Hoover Dam from 1935 to 1938, Lake Mead is a popular destination for boating, fishing, windsurfing, waterskiing, lying on the beach or exploring hidden coves and inlets by houseboat. The sheer size of the lake—700 miles of shoreline and nine trillion gallons of

Grand Canyon West

If you're traveling to the Grand Canyon from the west, you may want to take an interesting detour to Grand Canyon West, a growing tourist development on the Hualapai Indian Reservation, east of Hoover Dam. Grand Canyon Resort is on the canyon rim, just two and a half hours away from Las Vegas, Nevada; Kingman; and Peach Springs, off Route 40 on Old Route 66. Small commuter airlines from Flagstaff and Las Vegas offer day trips directly to **Grand Canyon West Airport**, making this one of the quickest and easiest ways of seeing the Big Ditch.

After winning a court battle with the U.S. government to regain a large swath of their ancestral rim-top land, the Hualapai ("People of the Tall Pines") are carefully developing it. A casino has already been built and a large hotel and campgrounds are planned.

SIGHTS   You can reserve a number of sightseeing day tours through Hualapai Lodge's concierge desk (928-769-2219). Scenic helicopter rides are available at the airport. Also popular are native-guided van tours with Hualapai Tours (800-222-6966) into the Grand Canyon. The tour stops at dramatic overlooks such as **Eagle Point**, 4300 feet above the river, and travels **Diamond Creek Road**, the only route into the Grand Canyon. Eagle Point is the site of the **Grand Canyon Skywalk**, an observation desk that juts 75 feet out over the Colorado River, 4000 feet below. The platform is made from four-inch Plexiglass and can withstand earthquakes and winds of up to 100 mph.

LODGING   At present, **Hualapai Lodge** in the small tribal headquarters of Peach Springs is the only lodging available and is the best place to base yourself. Surprisingly attractive and luxurious, the hotel has 60 pleasant rooms, a large lobby and fireplace, and a decent dining room. ~ 900 Route 66, Peach Springs; 702-878-9378, 888-255-9550; www.grandcanyonresort.com, e-mail info@grandcanyonresort.com. MODERATE.

DINING   **Diamond Creek Restaurant** in Hualapai Lodge is the only dining available. It's designed to appeal to river runners with large appetites. You'll find Indian-inspired foods such as Hualapai tacos and stew with Hualapai fry bread, Baja-style Mexican fare and all-American classics such as burgers, ice-cream floats and milk shakes. ~ 900 Route 66, Peach Springs; 888-255-9550; www.grandcanyonresort.com. BUDGET TO MODERATE.

water—and the surrounding jagged canyons and desert sand dunes are reason enough to visit the largest manmade lake in the United States.

The lake is a special favorite of anglers, who take a run at largemouth bass, rainbow, brown and cutthroat trout, catfish and black crappie. Striped bass, which can reach 50 pounds, are the most popular game fish in recent years.

A good way to learn about the lake is to stop at the **Lake Mead Visitors Center**. Located midway between Boulder City and Hoover Dam, the center's botanical garden, exhibits and short movie shown periodically throughout the day describe the area's history and attractions. There are also books for sale that can provide more in-depth information on the area's history, flora and fauna. ~ Route 93 and Lakeshore Road, Boulder City, NV; 702-293-8990, fax 702-293-8029; www.nps.gov/lame, e-mail lame_interpretation@nps.gov.

The easiest way to access Lake Mead from the isolated Arizona shore is at **Temple Bar Marina**. You'll find moderate-priced lodging, a café, gas and provisions here. This is the last outpost for supplies if you plan to boat east of Temple Bar. ~ Reached by a well-marked, paved 28-mile road that turns off Route 93 about 55 miles north of Kingman; 928-767-3211.

Hoover Dam, which impounds Lake Mead, was a tourist attraction in the area even before the first casino was built on the Las Vegas Strip. This huge dam rises 726 feet above the river and generates four billion kilowatt-hours of electricity in a year. Containing over three million cubic yards of concrete, it was completed in 1935. Its Depression-era origins are evident in the art deco motifs that decorate the top of the dam, including two huge Winged Figure of the Republic statues and a terrazzo floor patterned with mystical cosmic symbols.

Discovery Tours allows guests to explore the dam at their own pace. Staff give informal talks every 15 minutes at various stops along the self-guided tour. Purchase tickets at the **Hoover Dam Visitors Center**, which hosts a variety of exhibits and has a stunning overlook. From the center, board an elevator and head into the depths of the dam for further exploration. Admission. ~ 702-494-2517, fax 702-494-2587; www.usbr.gov/lc/hooverdam.

Although more remote, **South Cove/Pearce Ferry** is recommended for its scenic vistas of the lake and craggy peaks of Iceberg Canyon, about 46 miles east of Hoover Dam. Take Route 93 north from Kingman about 40 miles to the Dolan Springs turnoff and drive east. After passing Dolan Springs, you'll enter a massive forest of Joshua trees and the retirement resort of Meadview. Soon, you'll begin to catch glimpses of Lake Mead, from atop Grapevine Mesa. South Cove has only a boat ramp, a picnic area and toilets, but it offers a serene respite, accented by the deep blue waters of Lake Mead and rough-hewn mountains that frame it. The final four-mile stretch of dirt road to Pearce Ferry drops down through steep canyon walls and granite buttes. At the shoreline are primitive campsites, a picnic area, an unpaved boat ramp and plenty of peace and quiet. If the rocky granite corridors remind you of the Grand Canyon, it's because the park's western boundary is just a mile east of here.

There's also a scenic drive that runs along the Nevada side of the lake, where there are more marinas, a campground, a popular public beach and a few small resorts. Take Route 166 from Boulder City through the washes and canyons above the lake until you reach **Northshore Road** (Routes 147 and 167). You can stay on the highway that follows the shoreline all the way to the Valley of Fire State Park, or drop down to the lake at Las Vegas Bay, Callville Bay, Echo Bay or Overton Beach. You'll find food and facilities at all four resorts.

LODGING & DINING

The only lodging on the Arizona shore of Lake Mead is at Temple Bar Marina, where you can rent a room at the modern **Temple Bar Resort,** or one of the older cabins with kitchenettes. You'll also find a restaurant, cocktail lounge, campground, RV park, boat-launching ramp, fuel dock and store. This is the last outpost for supplies if you plan to boat east of Temple Bar. Limited hours

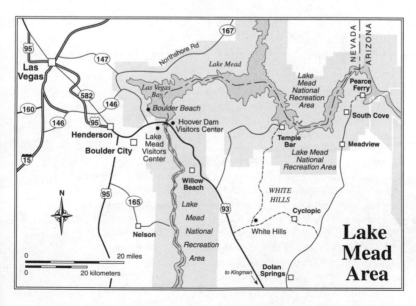

from November through March. ~ 928-767-3211, fax 928-767-4514; www.templebarlakemead.com. BUDGET TO MODERATE.

There's a motel on the Nevada shore of the lake at **Echo Bay Resort and Marina**. Along with a restaurant and lounge, the motel offers modern rooms, an RV village and an airstrip for light aircraft (day-use only). ~ Overton, NV; 702-394-4000, fax 702-394-4182, 800-752-9669; www.sevencrown.com. MODERATE.

Located about a half-mile north of Boulder Beach, **Lake Mead Resort and Marina** has hundreds of boat slips and a popular floating restaurant, coffee shop and cocktail lounge. The marina also operates a lodge (702-293-2074) down the road with 42 budget-priced rooms. Limited menu off-season. ~ 322 Lakeshore Road; 702-293-3484, fax 702-293-3835; www.sevencrown.com, e-mail gmatlmr@aol.com. BUDGET TO MODERATE.

You can also camp or park your RV ($10 for tents, $20 for hookups) at **Callville Bay Resort Marina**, which has a boat launch, store, snack bar and cocktail lounge. The marina rents everything from jet skis to 65-foot houseboats. ~ HCR 30, Box 100, Las Vegas, NV 89124; 702-565-8958, fax 702-565-8498; www.forever resorts.com. BUDGET.

PARKS

BOULDER BEACH 🚶 🚴 ⚓ ⛵ ⚓ 🚣 ⛴ 🛶 The one-mile beach and the clear water of Lake Mead attract year-round beachgoers. There are picnic areas, restrooms and a ranger station. ~ Located two miles north of the Lake Mead Visitors Center; 702-293-8990.

▲ There are over 150 sites; $10 per night for tents and self-contained RVs.

GOOD DAM CRUISE

The most awesome roadside sight on the lower Colorado River is Hoover Dam after dark, when it's floodlit all the way down into the pitch-darkness of Black Canyon. When the full moon sparkles on Lake Mead, it's better than London Bridge! Lake Mead Cruises offers a **Hoover Dam cruise** aboard a three-deck paddleboat, the *Desert Princess*. The 100-foot-long sternwheeler is the largest vessel to ply the waters of the lake, and features a snack bar, two glass-enclosed decks, an open promenade deck, an 80-seat dining room, cocktail lounge and dancefloor. The late afternoon cruise features dinner and stunning views of illuminated Hoover Dam. Cruises leave several times a day from the Lake Mead cruises landing, next to the Las Vegas Boat Harbor, 490-B Horsepower Cove, Boulder City, NV; 702-293-6180, fax 702-293-0343; www.lakemeadcruises.com, e-mail info@lakemeadcruises.com.

Bullhead City/Laughlin Area

Bullhead City, 35 miles west of Kingman via Route 68, owes its prosperity to Laughlin, Nevada, on the far side of the river. The city of Laughlin is a shimmering riverfront resort that has blossomed into Nevada's third-largest gambling center. Because it has few residential and commercial areas of its own, most of the thousands of people who work there live and shop in its Arizona sister, Bullhead City. Laughlin is packed to overflowing every weekend. The rest of the week, the casinos, buffets, lounges and showrooms play host to motorhome nomads who appreciate the opportunity to avoid Las Vegas traffic and avail themselves of Laughlin's vast, free RV parking lots.

But gambling isn't the only attraction in the Bullhead City/Laughlin area. Originally established in 1984 as a retirement town, Bullhead City has matured quickly into a community of more than 40,000—the largest in western Arizona—where residents fall into all age groups and many occupations, from hospitality workers and RV salespeople to telecommuters. The Colorado River and nearby Lake Mohave are major draws, offering year-round water sports such as swimming, boating, fishing and waterskiing. Also within short driving distance are ghost towns, historic mines, and intriguing lost canyons waiting to be explored.

Commercial boat cruises are a popular pastime. Before the bridge across the Colorado River was built in the mid-1980s, visitors used to park on the Arizona side of the river and ride **passenger ferries** across to the casinos on the Nevada shore. Now, on busy weekends when parking lots in Laughlin are full, the ferries still carry people across the river, making for a brief, fun and, best of all, inexpensive cruise. Several companies also offer longer riverboat sightseeing tours down the river from casino docks. One is **Laughlin River Tours**, which runs the *Fiesta Queen* and *Celebration* paddlewheel steamers from the Edgewater Casino dock and the Flamingo Hilton dock. Both are available for on-board weddings. ~ P.O. Box 29279, Laughlin, NV 89028; 702-298-1047, 800-228-9825, fax 702-298-8259; www.laughlinriver tours.com, e-mail steamboatwedding@yahoo.com.

Bullhead City was incorporated in 1984, but it was founded in 1945 when it was the construction camp for Davis Dam, three miles upstream. The town, named for a rock formation now submerged by Lake Mohave, is a collection of lowrise housing tracts, shopping centers and mobile home parks. New housing developments and retirement communities along the Colorado River—Riviera, Fort Mohave and Golden Shores—have extended Bullhead City's outskirts as far south as Topock, at the junction of Route 40.

SIGHTS

The best time to visit Bullhead City/Laughlin is in the winter and spring months, when the daytime temperatures range from 65 to 80°. Temperatures in July and August can reach an astounding 120° or more, making this area the hottest spot in the nation.

There's not much to see or do in Bullhead City, unless pre-fab homes and tilt-up shopping centers are your idea of excitement. So it's no surprise that the most-visited attraction in the area is the strip of casinos across the water on the river's western shore. Unlike their larger cousins on the famed Las Vegas Strip, the Laughlin hotel/casinos are close together and are easily accessible by a concrete strand that follows the river. The best is the **Colorado Belle**, a 600-foot replica of a Mississippi steamboat, complete with three decks and four black smokestacks. In the evening, the paddlewheel "turns" by timed neon light. Inside, the decor is turn-of-the-20th-century New Orleans, with lots of plush red carpeting, glass-globe lamps, brass railings and wrought-iron fixtures. The cluster of shops on the mezzanine level has several restaurants and an old-fashioned candy store. ~ 2100 South Casino Drive, Laughlin; 702-298-4000, 800-477-4837, fax 702-299-0669; www.color adobelle.com, e-mail info@coloradobelle.com.

For a bit of Dodge City by the river try the **Pioneer Hotel and Gambling Hall** next door. The two-story hotel looks like a U-shaped fort, finished with weathered wood panels. The facade of the casino entrance suggests a Wild West boarding house. Swinging doors and a wooden porch lead into a hectic casino. On the river side of the hotel is a waving neon cowboy, River Rick. Laughlin's version of Vegas Vic. The grounds facing the river include a lush flower garden, green grass and shade trees. ~ 2200 South Casino Drive, Laughlin; 702-298-2442, fax 702-298-7462, 800-634-3469; www.pioneerlaughlin.com.

Also worth visiting is the **Don Laughlin's Riverside Resort Hotel & Casino**. Be sure to stop in at the antiques shop just off the casino. The small but interesting collection consists of slot machines, jukeboxes, vintage radios, antique cars and a variety of old neon signs. On display, but not for sale, are antique slots from Don Laughlin's personal collection, including a 1938 vest pocket slot machine and a 1931 slot that paid off in golf balls. The resort also has a 34-lane bowling center. ~ 1650 South Casino Drive, Laughlin; 702-298-2535, 800-227-3849, fax 702-298-2612; www.riversideresort.com.

The **Davis Dam and Powerplant** was built in 1953 to produce hydroelectric power and regulate water delivery to Mexico. The powerplant, downstream from the dam embankment on the Arizona side of the river, is no longer open to the public, but you can walk across the top of the dam for a scenic view of the Colorado River and the Bullhead City–Laughlin area downstream. ~ About three miles north of Bullhead City on Route 68; 928-754-3628, fax 928-754-3620; www.lc.usbr.gov.

Behind the dam lies **Lake Mohave** (part of the Lake Mead National Recreation Area), which extends 67 miles upstream to Hoover Dam. The long, narrow lake (four miles across at its widest point) provides a multitude of recreational opportunities, including fishing, boating, waterskiing and windsurfing. Most of Lake Mohave's shoreline cannot be reached by road because it is flanked by steep cliffs. For boaters, popular destinations include a number of hot springs—including hot waterfalls—along the riverbanks and in side canyons, especially in the Willow Beach area.

Lake Mohave is accessible at only two points in Arizona: Willow Beach, off Route 93 about 60 miles north of Kingman, and Katherine Landing, six miles north of Bullhead City and Laughlin. Canoers can launch below Hoover Dam and paddle down spectacular Black Canyon to Willow Beach, a distance of about 12 miles. (It is not possible to go farther down the lake by canoe because the distance is too great to transport enough drinking water.) **Lake Mohave Resort**, six miles north of Bullhead City, rents houseboats, bass boats and other craft for use on Lake Mohave. ~ Katherine Landing; 928-754-3245, 800-752-9669; www.seven crown.com. **Willow Beach Harbor** also provides 16- and 17-foot-long boat rentals as well as larger deck boats. ~ 928-767-4747; www.willowbeachharbor.com.

On the Nevada shore of Lake Mohave is **Cottonwood Cove Resort**. Facilities include a marina, a motel, boat rentals, a campground and a small RV park. ~ 702-297-1464; www.cotton woodcoveresort.com.

LODGING

On Sunday through Thursday nights, rooms cost significantly less in the casino hotels of Laughlin, Nevada, than they do in Bullhead City on the Arizona side of the Colorado River. In fact, on weeknights, you can rent a spacious, modern room with a king-size bed, remote control television, and designer wallpaper in Laughlin for

RIVER OF THE DAMMED

Davis Dam is one of three dams operating to control flooding and produce hydroelectric power along the Colorado River. Along with the other two—**Hoover Dam** to the north and **Parker Dam**, about 80 miles downstream—they form the Lower Colorado River Dams project. They also divert river water to form three lakes: Lake Mead, Lake Mohave and Lake Havasu. Another six large dams in Colorado, Utah and New Mexico also control the waters of the mighty Colorado.

about the same rate as a plain, somewhat threadbare room in an aging mom-and-pop motel by the interstate in Kingman.

Although there are 10,000 hotel rooms in Laughlin, busy weekends often attract up to 50,000 visitors. You don't need a calculator to figure the result: Reservations are a must.

For most visitors to the Bullhead City/Laughlin area, there is probably not much point to staying on the Arizona side of the river. Most of the motels in Bullhead City are clean and modern but unexceptional, and rates tend to run higher than in the Laughlin casino hotels. Most tend toward weekly or monthly accommodations. They seem to thrive on weekend and peak-season overflows.

For half the year, Bullhead City, AZ, is one hour ahead of Laughlin, NV, which is in another time zone. The rest of the time Nevada switches to daylight-saving time and you won't need to adjust your watch each time you cross the Colorado River.

It's hard to believe that many people averse to gambling would go out of their way to stay in Bullhead City when they could as easily head south to the more family-oriented Lake Havasu City. But if they did, they'd find good noncasino lodging in Bullhead City at the **Bullhead River Lodge**. It is an all-suite motel that rents by the month, ideal for families, with a boat and fishing dock available for use at no charge. ~ 455 Moser Avenue, Bullhead City; 928-754-2250. BUDGET.

Operated by the same folks who run Bullhead River Lodge, **Hilltop Hotel** has 52 rooms and suites. Laundry facilities are available. ~ 2037 Route 95, Bullhead City; 928-758-6620, fax 928-758-6612. BUDGET.

Top of the line, and the closest to the bridge across the river from Bullhead City, is **Don Laughlin's Riverside Resort Hotel & Casino**. The resort's owner conceived the idea of promoting a casino strip here, founded the town that is named after him, and in 1966 converted the old Riverside Bait Shop on this site into Laughlin's first casino. There is also a 26-story hotel tower, swimming pools and a nonsmoking casino. ~ 1650 South Casino Drive, Laughlin; 702-298-2535, 800-227-3849, fax 702-298-2612; www.riversideresort.com. BUDGET TO DELUXE.

It's not quite the Reading, but you can ride the rails on a minipassenger train at the **Ramada Express**. The narrow-gauge railroad shuttles you on a 15-minute ride from the parking lot to the casino, decorated like a Victorian railroad station. Guest rooms in the 1498-room towers behind the casino feature light beige carpets with clean white walls and black furniture. ~ 2121 South Casino Drive, Laughlin; 702-298-4200, 800-243-6846, fax 702-298-6403; www.ramadaexpress.com, e-mail info@ramadaexpress.com. BUDGET TO MODERATE.

Some of the other hotels are famous-name spinoffs from well-known Las Vegas and Reno establishments, such as the **Flamingo**

Laughlin, which is the town's largest with 2000 rooms. ~ 1900 South Casino Drive; 702-298-5111, 800-352-6464, fax 702-298-5177; www.laughlinflamingo.com. MODERATE. Or try the 300-room **Golden Nugget**. ~ 2300 South Casino Drive; 702-298-7111, 800-950-7700, fax 702-298-7279; www.goldennugget.com. Another option is **Harrah's Laughlin**, a very nice hotel over a hill from the others at the south end of Casino Row. ~ 2900 South Casino Drive; 702-298-4600, 800-221-1306, fax 702-298-6802. BUDGET TO DELUXE. The **Colorado Belle**, a showy casino hotel shaped like a giant riverboat midway down the strip, was created by the same company that owns Circus Circus and the Excalibur in Las Vegas. ~ 2100 South Casino Drive; 702-298-4000, 800-477-4837, 702-298-0671; www.coloradobelle.com. BUDGET TO MODERATE.

There is also the 26-story **Edgewater Hotel**, a 1355-unit high-rise. ~ 2020 South Casino Drive; 702-298-2453, 800-677-4837, fax 702-298-8165; www.edgewater-casino.com. MODERATE TO ULTRA-DELUXE.

DINING

Along with a nice view of Lake Mohave, Lake Mohave Resort's restaurant **Tail of the Whale** serves a tasty grilled catfish and other seafood dishes, plus steaks and chops. ~ Katherine Landing just above Davis Dam; 928-754-3245, fax 928-754-1125. MODERATE.

In Laughlin, just about every hotel on Casino Row has an all-you-can-eat buffet featuring 40 or more items, in the budget range for dinner and almost absurdly affordable—no more than you'd spend at a franchise hamburger joint—for breakfast and lunch. To sweeten the deal even more, two-for-one buffet coupons are included in free "fun books" widely distributed in visitors centers and truck stops in Kingman and elsewhere along Route 40. The largest buffet in town is located at the **Edgewater Hotel**. ~ 2020 South Casino Drive; 702-298-2453; www.edgewater-casino.com, e-mail jcarey@mrgmail.com. BUDGET.

Each casino also has a full-service 24-hour coffee shop, many of them featuring $1.99 breakfast specials. Notable among the 24-hour casual places is **Aquarius Diner**, a classic '50s-style diner and coffee shop. ~ 1900 South Casino Drive, Laughlin; 702-298-5111, 800-352-6464, fax 702-298-5177; www.wedoitall vegas.com/aquarius. BUDGET TO MODERATE.

Many, though not all, casinos also have slightly more upscale fine-dining restaurants. **Harrah's Laughlin** offers an intimate atmosphere and a riverside view at the Range Steakhouse. Reservations suggested. Closed Sunday. ~ 2900 South Casino Drive, Laughlin; 702-298-4600, 800-427-7247, fax 702-298-6896. DELUXE.

Another option is the **Prime Rib Room**, where you can supervise the carving at your table. ~ Riverside Resort, 1650 South

Text continued on page 190.

In the Land
of Gold & Ghosts

Western Arizona's ghost towns come in all shapes and sizes. Some have been completely and irrevocably abandoned to the ravages of time; others have risen into new life thanks to tourism. Good examples of both can be found in the barren, rocky hills around Kingman.

Oatman, about 25 miles southwest of Kingman, has gone from rags to riches several times since it was founded in 1900. Its mines produced more than $3 million worth of gold before they played out. After the mines closed, the town survived as a refreshment stop along old Route 66 until 1946, when the highway was rerouted. Almost all Oatman residents moved away, but the town had such a well-preserved Old West look that it was used as a location for many Westerns, including *How the West Was Won*. Oatman's popularity as a tourist destination has made it livelier than ever. With daily staged shootouts on the main street and wild burros that have learned to panhandle food from sightseers, it has become a Disneyesque version of itself.

A resident ghost called Oatie is reputed to haunt the four guest rooms of the former **Oatman Hotel**. The ramshackle two-story adobe building, with an arched facade and corrugated iron walls and ceilings, is on its last legs now. It's most famous for being the spot where Clark Gable and Carole Lombard spent their wedding night after a surprise ceremony in Kingman (Oatman was on the main highway—Route 66—to Hollywood back then). One of Lombard's dresses is displayed in the honeymoon suite. The downstairs museum has old movie posters, rusty mining equipment and period antiques. Thousands of dollar bills are tacked to the walls of the hotel restaurant, which is still in operation. ~ 181 Route 66, Oatman; 928-768-4408.

Just two miles away, near the summit of 3500-foot Sitgreaves Pass, **Gold Road** was founded about the same time as Oatman and grew to about a quarter of the size. Its mine produced more than twice as much gold yet all that remains today are crumbled stone and adobe walls. Why the difference? Landowners in Gold Road destroyed their buildings to reduce their property-tax assessments. Despite their actions, this forlorn ruin of a town is staging a modest comeback as groups of visitors take the **Gold Road Mine Tour** into a shaft that produced 140,000 ounces of pure gold in five years. Admission. ~ 928-768-1600, fax 928-768-9588; www.goldroadmine.com, e-mail goldrd@ctaz.com.

A less touristy example of an Arizona ghost town is **Chloride**, about 23 miles northwest of Kingman via Route 93. Named for the salt deposits in the surrounding hills, this 1860s mining town never quite died because Tiffany's of New York opened a large turquoise mine there after the silver mines closed down. Today, buildings around town have been spruced up by a new wave of residents who seem a little on the eccentric side, judging from the number of homes that display outlandish desert landscaping and exterior decor consisting of road signs and old license plates. There are several cluttered but clearly authentic antique shops, a general store, and an antique gas station. If you want to prolong your ghost-town experience, check into the old gray 12-room **Shep's Miners Inn**, next door to **Shep's Mining Camp Café**. (Look for the "God Bless John Wayne" sign in the café window.) ~ 9827 2nd Street, Chloride; 928-565-4251, 877-565-4251, fax 928-565-3996; www.shepsminersinn.com, e-mail miners4251@aol.com. BUDGET.

Casino Drive, Laughlin; 702-298-2535. BUDGET TO MODERATE.
Yet another choice is the **Alta Villa** for Continental-style cuisine.
~ Flamingo Laughlin, 1900 South Casino Drive, Laughlin; 702-
298-5111. MODERATE TO DELUXE.

In the **Colorado Belle,** you can order a steak, seafood or pasta
in the casually classy Orleans Room. Dinner only. Next door, the
Mississippi Lounge is the only fresh seafood bar in Laughlin. ~
2100 South Casino Drive; 702-298-4000, 800-477-4837, fax 702-
298-0671; www.coloradobelle.com. MODERATE TO ULTRA-DELUXE.

River Palms serves fine American and Continental selections in
The Lodge, designed in a hunting lodge theme with wood-beamed
ceiling and big stone fireplace, all so convincing that you may forget that you're in a casino. Reservations suggested.
Dinner only. ~ 2700 Casino Drive; 702-298-2242;
www.rvrpalm.com, e-mail info@rvrpalm.com.
MODERATE TO ULTRA-DELUXE.

At its widest point, Lake
Mohave is only four miles
from shore to shore.

Country cooking is never out of reach at the
Boarding House Restaurant at the Pioneer Hotel,
where you can feast on a dinner of fried chicken, barbecued ribs or prime rib. The fried chicken and prime rib are
also available during their daily buffet. Save room for
homemade strawberry shortcake. Open 24 hours, but the buffet
closes at 11 p.m. ~ 2200 South Casino Drive, Laughlin; 702-
298-2442. BUDGET TO MODERATE.

SHOPPING   Shoppers will delight in the bargains found at **Preferred Outlets
at Laughlin,** which brings together more than 50 shops offering
everything from clothing, shoes and jewelry to perfumes and lug-
gage. Among them are Gap Outlet, Reebok/Rockport, Maiden-
form, Levi's Outlet and Van Heusen. ~ 1955 South Casino Drive,
Laughlin; 702-298-3650; www.arielpreferred.com.

NIGHTLIFE   Nightlife on the river all happens in Laughlin, where each of the
casinos has at least one, often two, cocktail lounges that don't
charge for watching musical acts that perform here while practic-
ing for Las Vegas. Only one of the casinos has a showroom where
name acts appear: **Don's Celebrity Theatre** has hosted such performers as Roy Clark, the Smothers Brothers, the Oakridge Boys,
Debbie Reynolds and Vicki Lawrence. Cover. ~ Don Laughlin's
Riverside Resort, 1650 South Casino Drive; 702-298-2535, 800-
227-3849, fax 702-298-2612; www.riversideresort.com. The resort also has two danceclubs, as well as six movie theaters.

PARKS   The **Colorado River** and **Lake Mohave** provide a multitude of
recreational activities, including boating, fishing, waterskiing,
scuba diving and windsurfing. Landlubbing hikers will love the
desert and canyons surrounding Bullhead City/Laughlin. Lake

Mohave above Davis Dam actually resembles the river below the dam—the lake stretches for 67 miles through jagged canyons and rocky mountains.

KATHERINE LANDING 🚶 🚲 🛶 🎿 🚤 🐟 ⚓ Located just 640 feet above sea level along Lake Mohave, Katherine Landing's flora and fauna is representative of the surrounding Mojave Desert. Short hikes into the area reveal desert shrubs, cacti and roadrunners, as well as views of the Black and Newberry mountains in the distance. There's striped bass, bluegill and channel catfish for anglers, and there's good swimming at South Telephone Cove. There are restrooms, pay showers, laundry facilities, a picnic area, a full-service marina with boat rentals, fishing tackle and waterski rentals, a motel, a restaurant, a grocery store and a visitors center. ~ Located just north of Bullhead City off Route 68; 928-754-3272, fax 928-754-5614; www.nps.gov/lame.

▲ There are 167 campsites, each with a barbecue grill and a picnic table; the campground has running water; $10 per night.

DAVIS CAMP COUNTY PARK 🛶 🐟 🚤 ⚓ Here at the only public beach on the Colorado River you'll find a stretch of sandy beach where you can swim, fish or launch a jet ski. You can angle here for striped bass, catfish and trout, and there's a marked off swimming area good for children. At the south end of the park is a marsh that's home to variety of birds and other small wildlife. There are restrooms, showers, laundry facilities, barbecue grills and ramadas with picnic tables. Day-use fee, $5. ~ Located about one mile north of Laughlin on the Arizona side of the river; 928-754-7250, fax 928-754-7253; www.mcparks.com, e-mail info@daviscamp.com.

▲ There are 141 sites with full hookups ($19 per night), partial hookups ($16 per night) and an open area for tent camping ($10 per night).

WILLOW BEACH 🐟 🚤 ⚓ Nearby, you can take a self-guided tour of the Willow Beach National Fish Hatchery (928-767-3456) that keeps Lake Mohave stocked. Bait, tackle and fishing licenses are available at the dock; try for trout and striped bass. There are restrooms, picnic grounds, barbecue grills, boat rentals, fuel and a grocery store. ~ On Lake Mohave, about 14 miles south of Hoover Dam off of Route 93; 928-767-4747, fax 928-767-3736.

About 20 miles upstream from Parker Dam, Lake Havasu may be the prettiest dammed lake along the Colorado River. Cool and bright blue in the heart of the desert, this 46-mile-long lake has become a very popular recreation area.

▼▼▼▼▼▼▼▼▼▼▼▼▼

Lake Havasu Area

SIGHTS

Lake Havasu's main claim to fame is **London Bridge** in Lake Havasu City; except for the Grand Canyon, the bridge is the most visited tourist attraction in Arizona. The audacity and monumental pointlessness of the city fathers' moving the bridge here when the city of London decided to replace it draws curiosity seekers in droves. To believe it, you have to see it.

Originally built in 1825 to replace a still older London Bridge that had lasted 625 years, this bridge was sold at auction in 1968. Lake Havasu City's promoters bought it for $2,460,000. The 10,000 tons of granite facing were disassembled into blocks weighing from 1000 to 17,000 pounds each, shipped and trucked 10,000 miles to this site and reconstructed on the shore of Lake Havasu when the city was practically nonexistent. Then a canal was dug to let water flow under the bridge. It is 49 feet wide and 928 feet long, and you can drive or walk across it. Every year, millions do. Is it worth seeing? Absolutely! It's a giant object lesson in the fine line between madness and genius—and one of the strangest sights in Arizona.

For more information about the bridge and the surrounding area head for the **Lake Havasu Chamber of Commerce**. Closed Saturday and Sunday. ~ 314 London Bridge Road; 928-855-4115, fax 928-680-0010; www.havasuchamber.com, e-mail info@havasuchamber.com.

In **Lake Havasu City**, a number of boats offer sightseeing tours from London Bridge, including the large Mississippi riverboat replica *Dixie Belle*. ~ 928-453-6776. **BlueWater Jetboat Tours** runs daily boat excursions from London Bridge to Topock Gorge and the Havasu National Wildlife Refuge from September to May. ~ 928-855-7171, 888-855-7171; e-mail jetboat@earthlink.net.

HIDDEN ►

In the little town of **Topock**, located midway between Bullhead City and Lake Havasu City at the junction of Route 40 and Route 95S, Jerkwater Canoe & Kayak Co. rents canoes and kayaks to explore otherwise inaccessible areas of the **Havasu National Wildlife Refuge**. The company can also provide directions to the beautiful **Topock Gorge**, ancient petroglyph sites and the **Topock Maze**, where Mohave Indians used to go to cleanse their spirits after long journeys. ~ Jerkwater Canoe & Kayak Co.; 928-768-7753, fax 928-768-8162; www.jerkwater.com, e-mail jerkwater@jerkwater.com.

LODGING

The mock Tudor-style **London Bridge Resort & Convention Center**, located adjacent to London Bridge, offers 122 units. These range from studios to one- and two-bedroom suites, all with kitchenettes and cable TV. Along with views of the bridge, the sprawling waterfront resort provides three pools and a spa. ~ 1477 Queens Bay, Lake Havasu City; 928-855-0888, 866-331-

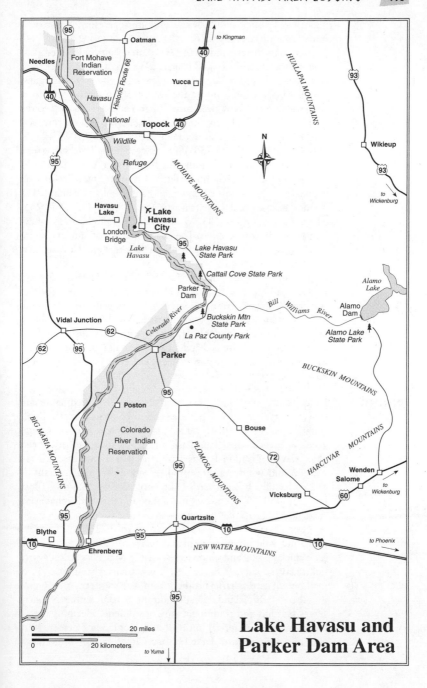

Lake Havasu and Parker Dam Area

9231, fax 928-855-5404; www.londonbridgeresort.com, e-mail info@londonbridgeresort.com. DELUXE TO ULTRA-DELUXE.

Across the bridge and on the island, the **Nautical Inn Resort & Conference Center** has a golf course, as well as a private dock with waterskiing, kayaking, boating and jet-skiing equipment for guest rental. All the rooms are on the waterfront. Each carpeted unit comes with two queen-sized beds, a patio and direct access to the lawn and beach. The suites include refrigerators and microwaves. ~ 1000 McCulloch Boulevard, Lake Havasu City; 928-855-2141, 800-892-2141, fax 928-453-5808; www.nauticalinn.com, e-mail resort@nauticalinn.com. MODERATE TO ULTRA-DELUXE.

Within a half-mile of the bridge, 64 standard motel rooms are available at the **Windsor Inn**, which has a pool and a spa. ~ 451 London Bridge Road, Lake Havasu City; 928-855-4135, 800-245-4135, fax 928-855-3583; www.windsorinnmotel.com, e-mail jkmi@hotmail.com. BUDGET. The **Days Inn** also has similar accommodations, with a pool. ~ 2190 Birch Square, Lake Havasu City; 928-855-4157. BUDGET.

For an economical lodging choice in Lake Havasu City, try **El Aztec All Suites Inn**, located about a mile from the lake and London Bridge. Each of the suites has one bedroom, one bath and a separate living/dining room area, all with plain white walls, as well as a full kitchen with all cooking utensils, dishes and appliances. A queen-size bed and a fold-out sofa make the inn ideal for families. ~ 2078 Swanson Avenue, Lake Havasu City; 928-453-7172, fax 928-855-1685. BUDGET.

DINING

Lake Havasu City, oddly, has virtually no high-priced haute cuisine, but it does have a good selection of pleasant, affordable restaurants. A good place for salads, steaks and seafood is **Shugrue's** in back of the Island Fashion Mall, which has an unbeatable view of London Bridge from the island side through tall wraparound windows. Fresh bakery goods are the specialty. ~ 1425 McCulloch Boulevard, Lake Havasu City; 928-453-1400, fax 928-453-3577; www.shugrues.com, e-mail lakehavasu@shugrues.com. DELUXE TO ULTRA-DELUXE.

Next door to Shugrue's, **Barley Brothers** microbrewery cooks pizzas in a wood-burning oven and also serves salads, pasta, rotisserie chicken, ribs and sandwiches. ~ 1425 McCulloch Boulevard, Lake Havasu City; 928-505-7837; www.barleybrothers.com, e-mail brewmaster@barleybrothers.com. MODERATE.

Also on the island, the **Restaurant & Bar at the Nautical** serves seafood and traditional American menu selections with a lakeside view. ~ Nautical Inn Resort & Conference Center, 1000 McCulloch Boulevard, Lake Havasu City; 928-855-2141. MODERATE TO DELUXE.

Away from the water, a local favorite is **Krystal's**, featuring specialties such as Alaskan king crab legs, lobster tails and mahi-mahi. Dinner only. ~ 460 El Camino Way, Lake Havasu City; 928-453-2999. BUDGET TO MODERATE.

On the mainland side of the bridge, there's the usually busy **Mermaid Inn**, serving fish and chips, clam strips and hamburgers. ~ 401 English Village, Lake Havasu City; 928-855-3234. BUDGET.

SHOPPING

The **Island Fashion Mall** houses a dozen shops selling sportswear, women's fashions and fine jewelry. ~ 1425 McCulloch Boulevard, Lake Havasu City.

NIGHTLIFE

If you're in the mood for something livelier than the cocktail lounges in Lake Havasu City's hotels, try the scene at **Kokomo Havasu**. A deejay spins Top-40 and hip-hop at this multilevel danceclub with a pool. ~ London Bridge Resort, 1477 Queens Bay, Lake Havasu City; 928-855-0888; www.londonbridgeresort.com.

Grab a "desert martini" (a beer with an olive in it) or settle for standard beer and wine at the **Desert Martini**. This pool hall also features darts, shuffleboard and five TVs. ~ 2120 McCulloch Boulevard, Lake Havasu City; 928-855-1818.

PARKS

LAKE HAVASU STATE PARK This shoreline park area in and around Lake Havasu City encompasses most of the Arizona shore of this broad blue lake nestled among stark, rocky desert hills. The park has a campground and rocky swimming beach—Windsor Beach (with boat ramps), north of the center of town. Fish for largemouth bass, striped bass and catfish. There are picnic areas, restrooms, showers and nature trails. Day-use fee, $9. ~ The main automobile-accessible area is at Windsor Beach. Other areas of the park, which includes most of the east shore of Lake Havasu, are only accessible by boat; 928-855-2784, fax 928-855-2647.

▲ The 46 first-come, first-served sites at Windsor Beach (928-855-2784) cost $14 per night. The Aubrey Hills Natural Area, south of Lake Havasu City and operated by the BLM (928-505-1200), has 125 primitive boat-in sites (also first-come, first-served) along the shore. Some have vault toilets, picnic tables and shade structures; $10 per night per boat.

Rent a canoe and glide through the Havasu National Wildlife Refuge—solitary and silent except for abundant birds.

CATTAIL COVE STATE PARK About 15 miles south of Lake Havasu City, Cattail Cove is a 2000-acre lakeside park with ample recreational opportunities. Fishing yields crappie, bluegill and striped and largemouth bass. Nearby, Sandpoint Marina and RV Park (928-855-0549; www.lakehavasu. com/sandpoint) has a restaurant, groceries, laundry facilities and boat rentals. Facilities include picnic areas, restrooms, showers and concessions. Day-use fee, $8. ~ Off Route 95, 15 miles south of Lake Havasu City; 928-855-1223.

▲ There are 173 RV campsites with full hookups; $30 to $38 per night.

HAVASU NATIONAL WILDLIFE REFUGE 🏃 ⛴ 🚤 🛶 Nature buffs will enjoy this wildlife refuge, which straddles the Colorado River from Topock, 20 miles north of Lake Havasu City, to Mesquite Bay, just north of the city. Hikers through the marshy trails are often rewarded with views of a bald eagle, peregrine falcon, or a number of winter visitors: snow and Canada geese and other waterfowl. There are restrooms at Catfish Paradise and Mesquite Bay; showers and laundry facilities are available at 5-Mile Landing. ~ The refuge headquarters is located at 317 Mesquite Avenue, Needles, CA. To get to the park from Lake Havasu, drive north on Route 95 to Route 40, then drive nine miles west to the exit marked Havasu National Wildlife Refuge (Mohave County 227); 760-326-3853, fax 760-326-5745.

▲ There are 74 hookups and 45 dry sites at 5-Mile Landing on Topock Marsh; $7 per night; information, 928-768-2350.

Parker Dam Area

Downstream from Parker Dam, which impounds Lake Havasu, the Colorado River flows through the Colorado River Indian Reservation to Parker, a nondescript trade center about 35 miles south of Lake Havasu City. Just two miles north of Parker, Headgate Rock Dam impedes the Colorado to form Lake Moovalya, an 11-mile stretch of water recreation better known as "The Parker Strip."

SIGHTS

Parker was nothing more than a postal stop until the railroad came through in 1908. Most of the town's development, however, occurred after the river was dammed and tourists began flocking to the lakes upstream. Recreation remains Parker's main reason for existing, along with a moderate climate that attracts several thousand snowbirds, mostly retirees, each winter.

The town itself has little to offer; many of its 3000 citizens live in wall-to-wall RV parks scattered across the scrub-brush hillsides, dotted with an occasional red-tile-roof home. Despite Parker's lackluster appeal, the area is besieged by visitors who enjoy year-round boating, waterskiing and inner-tubing (there's even an annual seven-mile inner-tube race) along the scenic Parker Strip.

The city's main attraction is the **Colorado River Indian Tribes Museum**, a storehouse of prehistoric American Indian artifacts from the Ancestral Pueblo, Hohokam and other tribes, as well as dioramas of pueblos and other dwellings, crafts and folk art of the more modern Mohave, Chemehuevi, Navajo and Hopi people. Visit the gift shop before leaving; it has a good assortment of American Indian publications, baskets, beadwork and other crafts. Closed weekends. ~ 2nd Avenue and Mohave Road, Parker; 928-669-1335.

About 15 miles upstream sits **Parker Dam**, a virtual twin to Davis Dam. One significant difference is that you can see only one-third of Parker Dam; the bedrock foundation is 235 feet below the riverbed. The inner workings of the dam are off-limits to the public; you can, however, walk across the top and enjoy views of the river and reservoir. ~ 760-663-3712, fax 760-663-3212.

If you'd like a change of pace, drive 34 miles south on Route 95 to the town of **Quartzsite**, the site of one of the strangest reunions in Arizona, and possibly the world. Although the dusty scrub-brush town—if you can call it that—consists of just a few motels, restaurants, and RV parks, each winter its population swells from several thousand to about a four million. The reason? The **Quartzsite Gemborees**, shows resembling Bedouin bazaars for rock-swappers and gem collectors. Mostly held in late January and early February, the festivals attract droves of rock and gem aficionados for a metallurgical freakout. In addition to the hundreds of booths, where you can buy everything from healing crystals to 5000-pound slabs of quartz, the festivals feature flea markets, antique and collectibles shows, camel races, country music, an auto show—all choreographed in the tradition of Hunter Thompson. Started in 1964 by a rag-tag group of rock hounds, the original event has grown into a number of shows, becoming Quartzsite's main reason for existence. For further details about the Quartzsite Gemborees, contact Quartzsite Chamber of Commerce; 928-927-5600, fax 928-927-7438; www.quartzsitechamber.org, e-mail info@quartzsitechamber.org.

> If you go gem browsing in Quartzsite, remember that if a stone looks *too* perfect it may not be the real thing.

LODGING

You won't find a bellhop in this part of the country, but there are clean rooms at **El Rancho Motel**, along with a few kitchenettes, microwave ovens, refrigerators, a pool and in-room coffee. ~ 709 California Avenue, Parker; 928-669-2231. BUDGET.

Traveling families will like the **Stardust Motel** because of its oversized rooms and mini-suites, all with refrigerators and microwave ovens, all clean and well-maintained. The motel also has a pool. ~ 700 California Avenue, Parker; 928-669-2278. BUDGET TO MODERATE.

DINING

For home-cooked American dishes, consider the **Paradise Cafe**, a formica-topped, family-run eatery that caters to regular locals who feast on the barbecued chicken, pork ribs, fish and chips, and home-

◄ HIDDEN

made cakes and cobblers. ~ Route 95 at Riverside Drive, Parker; 928-667-2404. BUDGET TO MODERATE.

PARKS

LA PAZ COUNTY PARK 🏖️ 🍴 🚤 🎣 ⛳ You can spread a beach towel or picnic blanket at this grassy recreational area. Located along a one-mile stretch of the Colorado River, the park is perfect for a relaxed family outing. Common catches for anglers are bass, catfish, bluegill, striper, flathead and perch. Swimming is good at the sandy beach. There are covered ramadas, barbecue grills, picnic tables, restrooms, showers, tennis courts, a baseball field and a playground. Day-use fee, $2 per person. ~ Route 95, about eight miles north of Parker; 928-667-2069, fax 928-667-2757.

▲ About a third of the county park is open to tent camping; $14 per night. There are also 35 ramada sites ($16 per night) and 114 RV sites with water and electricity hookups ($20 per night). All camping fees are for two people; there's a $2 charge for each additional person.

BUCKSKIN MOUNTAIN STATE PARK 🚶 🏖️ 🍴 🚤 🎣 ⛳ This state park located near Parker Dam caters to tube floaters, boaters and waterskiers. But you can also hike the nature trails in the mountains that surround the eastern edge of the park. In addition to panoramic vistas of the Colorado River, hikers can sometimes catch a glimpse of desert bighorn sheep that roam the area. Fish for bass, bluegill and catfish. There are restrooms, a picnic ground, a gas dock, inner-tube rentals and a snack bar. Day-use fee, $8. ~ Buckskin Mountain is on Route 95, about 11 miles north of Parker. The River Island unit is another one and a half miles north of Buckskin Mountain; 928-667-3231, fax 928-667-3387.

▲ Buckskin Mountain has 68 sites (water and electric hookups, $20 to $23 per night; cabañas, $22 per night). River Island offers 37 sites (water and electricity hookups; all sites are $23 per night). Restrooms and showers are available at both campgrounds.

ALAMO LAKE STATE PARK 🚶 🐎 🏖️ 🍴 🚤 🎣 ⛳ The main draw at this 5642-acre park is the fishing. The 3000-acre Alamo Lake offers up bass, bluegill, crappie and catfish; get your fishing license from the park concessions stand. Water activities such as waterskiing are other popular pastimes. Facilities include a playground, picnic areas, a concession stand, gasoline, restrooms and showers. Day-use fee, $5 per vehicle. ~ Located about 100 miles from Parker. Take Route 95 from Parker, continue on Route 72 to Route 60. It's about 40 miles from Wenden; 928-669-2088.

▲ There are 250 sites: $19 to $22 per night for hookups; $12 per night for developed sites; $10 per weeknight for undeveloped sites.

This region offers some of Arizona's best fishing. It's open season on all fish year-round at Lake Mead and the abundant Colorado River.

FISHING

LAKE MEAD AREA There's plenty of catfish, bluegill, crappie and striped bass, often tipping the scales at 30 pounds, at **Lake Mead**. Spring and fall are the best seasons. One of the best spots for bass is near the Las Vegas Boat Harbor because of the wastewater nutrients that dump from the Las Vegas Wash. Also worth trying are Calico Basin, Hemenway Harbour the Meadows, Stewarts Point and Meat Hole. For tips on other spots, ask any park ranger or try any of the marinas, which also sell licenses, bait and tackle. For example, **Lake Mead Marina** rents fishing boats and fishing poles and sells bait and other fishing gear at the marina store. ~ 322 Lakeshore Road; 702-293-3484; www.sevencrown.com. Also on the lake is the **Las Vegas Bay Marina**. ~ Lake Mead Drive; 702-565-9111; www.boatinglakemead.com. **Callville Bay Resort & Marina** has licenses, bait and tackle. ~ HCR 30, Box 100, off Northshore Scenic Drive; 702-565-8958; www.callvillebay.com. **Echo Bay Resort and Marina** is a good spot to fulfill your fishing and boating needs. ~ North Shore Road; 702-394-4000; www.sevencrown.com. **Temple Bar Marina** also sells bait. ~ 1 Maine Street; 928-767-3211.

The Overton arm of Lake Mead is one of the best areas for striped bass, whose threadfin shad schools often churn the water in their feeding frenzies.

BULLHEAD CITY/LAUGHLIN AREA Fishing is also excellent along the **Colorado River** near the Bullhead City/Laughlin area. Anglers can fill their creels with striped bass, rainbow trout, bass, catfish, bluegill and crappie. A good spot is the cold water below Davis Dam. There's also good fishing above the dam on **Lake Mohave**, noted for its rainbow trout and bass.

This is one of the wettest parts of the state and opportunities for water sports abound.

BOATING & WATER-SKIING

LAKE MEAD AREA On Arizona's West Coast, you can skip across Lake Mead in a power or ski boat, or simply relax under sail or on the deck of a houseboat. For houseboat and ski boat rentals in the Lake Mead area, try the **Callville Bay Resort & Marina**. ~ HCR 30, Box 100, off Northshore Road; 702-565-8958; www.callvillebay.com. **Lake Mead Marina** has houseboat and ski boat rentals. ~ 322 Lakeshore Road; 702-293-3484; www.sevencrown.com. **Las Vegas Bay Marina** rents pontoons, ski boats, skis and wakeboards. ~ Lake Mead Drive; 702-565-9111; www.boatinglakemead.com. Another place to rent boats at the north end of Lake Mead is **Echo Bay Resort and Marina**. ~ North Shore Road; 702-394-4000; www.sevencrown.com.

BULLHEAD CITY/LAUGHLIN AREA In the Bullhead City/Laughlin area, waterskiing is permitted along the Colorado River from Davis Dam to Needles. The sparsely populated area just below Bullhead City is the best choice. You can also waterski on Lake Mohave north of Davis Dam. For boat rentals and equipment, check out **Lake Mohave Resort**. ~ Katherine Landing; 928-754-3245; www.sevencrown.com.

LAKE HAVASU AREA The lower Colorado River and Lake Havasu are a mecca for watersport enthusiasts, and craft of all kinds are available for rent. **Havasu Springs Resort** rents fishing boats, pontoons and runabouts. ~ 2581 Route 95, Parker; 928-667-3361; www.havasusprings.com. **Bluewater Boat Rentals** has pontoon boats for fishing and waterskiing. They also provide charter boat tours of Topock Gorge. ~ 501 English Village; 928-453-9613, 888-855-7171; www.coloradoriverjetboattours. com. Fifteen miles south of Lake Havasu City, **Sandpoint Marina** rents fishing boats, pontoon boats and houseboats. ~ 928-855-0549; www.sandpointresort.com.

RIVER RUNNING

The 11-mile stretch of Colorado River from Hoover Dam to Willow Beach is open year-round to rafts, canoes and kayaks, but the best time is spring and fall. Expect to see birds and other desert wildlife in this steep-walled wilderness canyon. It's smooth water all the way, with no rapids, and there are hot springs along the river bank. River running requires a permit from the **Hoover Dam Canoe Launch**. Only 30 permits are issued a day; advance reservations are required. ~ 702-293-8204. After securing a permit, find an outfitter with rentals. **Boulder City Outfitters** offers kayaks and canoes. ~ 1631 Industrial Boulevard, Boulder City, NV; 702-293-1190. **Jerkwater Range and Kayaks** has the same. ~ P.O. Box 800, Topock AZ 86436; 928-768-7753.

Whitewater river tours all the way through the Grand Canyon from Lee's Ferry typically take out at Diamond Creek Road, the slackwater before Lake Mead, so you'll see plenty of river runners in this area. A tour company based on the reservation, **The River Runners**, allows you to experience daily flightseeing and river tours by flying you into the canyon by helicopter, then taking you on an eight-passenger pontoon boat on the Colorado. ~ 928-769-2219; www.grandcanyonresort.com.

RIDING STABLES

Hualapai Ranch is a dude ranch aimed squarely at tourists. They offer horseback tours along the rim, wagon rides, cowboy cookouts and mock gunfights in their Western village. You can even get married here. ~ 702-878-9378.

GOLF

KINGMAN AREA Kingman visitors won't be disappointed with the semiprivate 18-hole golf course and driving range at **Valley Vista Country Club**, which boasts some of the best greens in Arizona. Clubs and cart rentals are available. ~ 9686 Concho

Drive; 928-757-8744. The 18-hole **Cerbat Cliffs Golf Course** is a high desert course with a few challenging water hazards and sand traps. Soft spikes are required. You can rent cart and clubs. ~ 1001 East Gates Road; 928-753-6593.

LAKE MEAD AREA   Serving the Lake Mead and Hoover Dam area is the 18-hole **Boulder City Municipal Golf Course**, one of the prettier courses in the greater Las Vegas area, with shade trees and bright green greens. Green fees include a cart, and club rentals are available. ~ 1 Clubhouse Drive, Boulder City, NV; 702-293-9236; www.golfbouldercity.com.

BULLHEAD CITY/LAUGHLIN AREA   In Laughlin, tee off at the 18-hole **Emerald River Golf Course**, a target desert course with narrow fairways and small greens. There are clubs for rent, and the green fee includes the use of a cart. ~ 1155 West Casino Drive, Laughlin; 702-298-0061. In Bullhead City is the nine-hole, semi-private **Chaparral Country Club**. Club and cart rentals are available. ~ 1260 East Mohave Drive; 928-758-3939. The 18-hole **Desert Lakes Golf Course** is about 12 miles south of the Laughlin/Bullhead City bridge. Club rentals are available and carts are included in the green fee. ~ 5835 Desert Lakes Drive, Bullhead City, AZ; 928-768-1000.

LAKE HAVASU AREA   Golfers can choose from two excellent courses around Lake Havasu. The first is the **Bridgewater Links**, a nine-hole, par-three executive course with cart and club rentals. ~ 1477 Queen's Bay Road; 928-855-4777. You'll hope your score is falling down, falling down at the semiprivate **London Bridge Golf Club**. It has two 18-hole desert courses lined with palm trees. There are carts and clubs for rent. ~ 2400 Clubhouse Drive; 928-855-9096. Tee off amid magnificent surroundings at the 18-hole, par-72 championship **Emerald Canyon Golf Course**. A putting green, driving range and pro shop are on the premises. Clubs, carts and lessons are available. ~ 72 Emerald Canyon Drive, Parker; 928-667-3366.

The USGA rates the Emerald River Golf Course the second most-challenging course in Nevada.

TENNIS

Courts are fairly easy to come by if you want to rally away the endlessly sunny days.

BULLHEAD CITY/LAUGHLIN AREA   In Laughlin, guests can use the **Flamingo Laughlin's** three lighted courts. ~ 1900 South Casino Drive, Laughlin; 702-298-5111. The **Riverview RV Resort** has two lighted courts for the exclusive use of campers staying at the resort; no fee. A tennis pro is on call. ~ 2000 East Ramar Road, Bullhead City; 928-763-5800.

LAKE HAVASU AREA   Tennis courts are open to the public for a fee in Lake Havasu City at **London Bridge Racquet and Fitness**

Center. There are six courts, of which four are lighted. The center has a tennis pro. ~ 1407 McCulloch Boulevard; 928-855-6274, fax 928-855-9382.

HIKING

Hikers will be happy with all the forest and canyons this area has to offer. All distances listed for hiking trails are one way unless otherwise noted.

KINGMAN AREA   **Hualapai Mountain Park,** 14 miles southeast of Kingman, has an extensive network of hiking trails through piñon, oak, aspen and ponderosa forest teeming with bird and animal life. Six interconnecting trails totaling six miles, starting from the **Aspen Springs Trail** (1 mile), allow you to custom-design your own hike. Aspen Springs Trail connects with the **Potato Patch Loop** (4-mile loop) and from that trail various spur trails take off—the short and easy **Stonestep Lookout Trail** (.04 mile), and the slightly more ambitious **Aspen Peak Trail** (.7 mile), **Hayden Peak South Trail** (.8 mile) and **Hayden Peak West Trail** (.6 mile).

BULLHEAD CITY/LAUGHLIN AREA   A wonderful, little-known wintertime hike is **Grapevine Canyon** (1 mile). There is no clearly defined trail, but you will have no trouble tracing the tracks of other hikers up the wash along the canyon floor. Some rock scrambling is involved. At the mouth of the canyon are many American Indian petroglyphs dating back 1200 years. Farther up the canyon, a thin waterfall flows year-round. The presence of water in the Grapevine Canyon attracts nocturnal wildlife, and you may see tracks of badgers, skunks, desert bighorn sheep and even mountain lions. The wild grapes that grow here give the canyon its name. Grapevine Canyon is in Nevada, 13 miles west of the Laughlin/Bullhead City bridge on Route 163 and one and a half miles in on the clearly marked, unpaved road to Christmas Tree Pass. There is a parking area near the mouth of the canyon.

HIDDEN ►

LAKE HAVASU AREA   The **Mohave Sunset Walking Trail** in Lake Havasu State Park begins at Windsor Beach and winds for two miles through a variety of terrains from lowlands dense with salt cedar to ridgelines commanding beautiful views of the lake. Signs along the sometimes hilly trail identify common Mojave Desert plant life.

▼▼▼▼▼▼▼▼▼▼▼

Transportation

CAR

On Arizona's "West Coast" along the lower Colorado River, the Bullhead City/Laughlin area is reached by exiting **Route 40** at Kingman and driving 26 miles on **Route 68** through the most starkly stunning scenery in the Mohave Desert, or by exiting Route 40 at Topock, 12 miles east of Needles, California, and driving 35 miles north on **Route 95.** The other major Colorado River resort, Lake Havasu City, is 21 miles south of Route 40 on Route 95. A fascinating backroad route connecting Route 95 with Route 40 at Kingman goes through the historic town of Oatman on its steep climb over Sitgreaves Pass, a drive challenging enough to evoke amazement at the fact that this numberless road used to be part of Old Route 66, the main highway across the Southwest to Los Angeles in the days before the interstate was built.

Allegiant and Sun Country Airlines have charter flights into the **Bullhead City–Laughlin Airport** (928-754-2134). Great Lakes Airlines has regularly scheduled flights to the **Kingman Airport** (928-757-2134). **Lake Havasu City Airport** is serviced by US Airways.

AIR

Greyhound Bus Lines (800-231-2222; www.greyhound.com) stops at the bus terminals in Kingman at 3264 East Andy Devine Avenue, 928-757-8400; and in Lake Havasu City at 1940 Mesquite Avenue.

BUS

Amtrak (800-872-7245; www.amtrak.com) provides service to Kingman (106 4th Street) and Needles, CA (900 Front Street), which is close to Lake Havasu.

TRAIN

Car-rental agencies at the Bullhead City–Laughlin Airport are **Avis Rent A Car** (800-331-1212) and **Hertz Rent A Car** (800-654-3131). Hertz also has rental cars at the Kingman Airport.

CAR RENTALS

SIX

South Central Arizona

If your image of Arizona is cowboys, ranches and hitching posts, think again, partner. For while the flavor of the West is very much evident in the central band of the state, the trappings of the modern age are everywhere—indeed, flourishing and growing apace. Head to its major cities—including Phoenix, Scottsdale, Tempe and Mesa—and you'll find a vibrant arts community, professional sports galore, shopping centers and stores as far as the eye can see, a fine college campus, intriguing architecture, enough golf, tennis and other activities to satisfy anyone and everyone. But if you're hankering for a glimpse of the frontier or a taste of the outdoor life, well, they're here, too: miles of virgin desert, rivers to swim and sail, towns more in the past than the present, trails to roam. So saddle up, friend.

Phoenix takes its name from the legendary phoenix bird, and with good reason: The biggest metropolis between southern Texas and California and the ninth largest in the country, Phoenix is a city taking flight. The population of Phoenix proper is 1,321,000, which balloons to 3,000,000 when you include the 23 satellite towns that blend seamlessly along the valley of the Salt River. Some thousand families a month set up homes in the broad river valley as subdivisions and shopping centers mushroom.

Phoenix today is a far cry from the era of the Hohokam Indians. The Hohokam, meaning "those who vanished," built a network of irrigation ditches to obtain water from the Salt River, part of which is still in use today. Then, as now, irrigation was vital to Phoenix. So much water is piped in to soak fields, groves and little kids' toes that the desert air is actually humid—uncomfortably so through much of the summer. Lettuce, melons, alfalfa, cotton, vegetables, oranges, grapefruit, lemons and olives are grown in abundance in the irrigated fields and groves, lending a touch of green to the otherwise brown landscape. Boating, waterskiing, swimming and even surfing—in a gigantic, mechanically activated pool—are splendid by-products. Did we mention sports? Whatever your game may be, this is sports heaven. In professional competition, Phoenix has baseball (the Arizona Diamondbacks), hockey (the Phoenix Coyotes), football (the Cardinals) and basketball (the Suns). Plus, the Arizona State University Sun Devils play football, basketball and baseball. Still other spectator sports include rodeos and horse racing. For the active set, there are 125 golf courses and hundreds of tennis courts, as well as bike, jogging and horse-riding trails, and opportunities for all kinds of other pursuits.

The action here isn't all on the field. The city has completed a $1.1 billion redevelopment of the downtown that began in 1988. Testimony to the effort are the glitzy Arizona Center, the Mexican-themed Mercado and the 18,000-seat America West Arena next to the Civic Center Plaza.

Metropolitan Phoenix, or the Valley of the Sun, originated in 1850 on the banks of the Salt River and became the capital of the Arizona Territory in 1889. At one time, nearly 25,000 Indians were the exclusive inhabitants of Arizona. The earliest were the Hohokam, who thrived from A.D. 30 until about A.D. 1450. Signs of their settlements remain intact to this day. Two other major tribal groups followed: the Anasazi in the state's northern plateau highlands, and the Mogollon People, in the northeastern and eastern mountain belt. Today there are 23 reservations in Arizona, more than any other state, with an estimated 190,091 Indians from 21 different tribes living in sad testimony to the white settlers' land grabs. Some 150 miles east of Phoenix in the White Mountain region of northern Arizona is the Fort Apache Indian Reservation with a million and a half acres of land. Bordering it, with another two million acres, is the San Carlos Apache Indian Reservation. The largest Indian reservation in North America, the Navajo Nation, home to 210,000 Navajos, begins 76 miles north of Flagstaff and extends into northwestern New Mexico and southeastern Utah. Located almost in the center of the Navajo Indian Reservation is the Hopi Indian Reservation, 11,210 members strong, who have lived on the same site without interruption for more than 1000 years, retaining more of their ancient traditions and cultures than any other Indian group.

In the mid-1500s, the conquistadors arrived, carrying the banner of Spain. They were looking for gold and seeking souls to save. They found more souls than gold and in the process introduced the Indians to cattle, horse raising and new farming methods, augmenting their crops of beans, squash and maize with new grains, fruits and vegetables. The Spanish-Mexican influence is still strongly evident throughout the Southwest. And the gold prospector eventually became the very symbol of the Old West—an old man with a white beard, alone with his trusted burro, looking to strike it rich. You only have to go 30 miles east of Phoenix into the Superstition Mountains to find the lore and the legend and the lure of gold still very much alive today.

Until about the mid-1880s, the Indians accepted the few white miners, traders and farmers who came West, but as the number of settlers grew, friction arose and fighting resulted. The cavalry was called in and one of the most brutal chapters in the history of the Southwest followed. Black troops of the Tenth Cavalry, known as Buffalo Soldiers because of their dark skin and curly black hair, came in large numbers to protect citizens of the Arizona land where Geronimo, Cochise, Mangus, Alchise and other chieftains had dotted the cactus-covered hills and canyons with the graves of thousands of emigrants, settlers and prospectors. Numerous sites throughout the entire state bring those days of conflict into vivid focus—Cochise Stronghold in the Dragoon Mountains south of Willcox, hideout of the notorious

Apache chief; Fort Bowie National Historic Site, an adobe ruin that was a key military outpost during the Indian wars, and nearby Fort Huachuca, an important territorial outpost that's still in operation today as a communications base for the U.S. Army; and Fort Verde State Historic Park, located in Camp Verde on Route 17 between Phoenix and Flagstaff, yet another military base that played a key role in subduing the Apaches in the 1870s.

With the construction of the first railroad in 1887, fast-paced expansion took hold as Phoenix drew settlers from all over the United States. In 1889 it was named the capital of the Arizona Territory, and statehood was declared in 1912.

Once hailed as the agricultural center of Arizona, Phoenix by 1920 was already highly urbanized. Its horse-drawn carriages represented the state's first public transportation. Its population reached 29,053 and the surrounding communities of Tempe, Mesa, Glendale, Chandler and Scottsdale added 8636 to the count.

As farmers and ranchers were slowly being squeezed out, these years of Phoenix's development saw a rugged frontier town trying to emulate as best it could famous cities back East. It had a Boston store, a New York store, three New England–style tea parlors and a number of gourmet shops selling everything from smoked herring to Delaware cream cheese. The region's dry desert air also began to attract scores of "health-seekers." The advent of scheduled airline service and the proliferation of dude ranches, resorts and other tourist attractions changed the character of the city still further.

Today, high-tech industry forms the economic core of Phoenix, while tourism remains the state's number-two job producer. Not surprisingly, construction is the city's third major industry. But Phoenix retains a strong community flavor. Its downtown area isn't saturated with block after block of highrises and apartment houses. The city and all its suburbs form an orderly, 800-square-mile pattern of streets and avenues running north and south and east and west, with periphery access gained by soaring Los Angeles–style freeways. Beyond are the mountains and desert, which offer an escape from city living, with camping, hiking and other recreational facilities.

If the desert isn't your scene, neighboring Scottsdale just might be. Billing itself as "The West's Most Western Town," Scottsdale is about as "Western" as Beverly Hills.

Scottsdale's population of over 200,000 appears to be made up primarily of "snow birds" who came to stay: rich retirees from other parts of the United States who enjoy the sun, the golf courses, the swimming pools, the mountains, the bolo ties and the almost endless selection of handicraft shops, boutiques and over 120 art galleries. Actually, retired persons account for only 20 percent of this fast-growing city, whose median adult age is 41. There are far more yuppies than grandmas.

Scottsdale was only desert land in 1888 when U.S. Army Chaplain Winfield Scott bought a parcel of land located near the Arizona Canal at the base of Camelback Mountain. Before long, much of the cactus and greasewood trees here had been replaced by 80 acres of barley, a 20-acre vineyard and 50 orange trees. Scottsdale remained a small agricultural and ranching community until after World War II. Motorola opened a plant in Scottsdale in 1945, becoming the first of many electronics manufacturing firms to locate in the valley.

Less than a quarter-mile square in size when it was incorporated in 1951, Scottsdale now spreads over 150 square miles. Its unparalleled growth would appear never-ending except that the city is now braced up against the 50,000-acre Salt River Indian Reservation, established in 1879 and home of the Pima and Maricopa people who haven't let their juxtaposition with one of the nation's wealthiest communities go unrewarded. The reservation boasts one of the largest shopping areas in the Southwest, a junior college, thousands of acres of productive farmland and future hotel sites.

The network of satellite communities that surrounds the Phoenix–Scottsdale area, like random pieces of a jigsaw puzzle, is primarily made up of bedroom communities. Tempe to the south is home of Arizona State University. Burgeoning Glendale, to the northwest, was originally founded as a "temperance colony," where the sale of intoxicants was forever forbidden. Mesa, to the east, covering over 100 square miles, is Arizona's third-largest city. Carefree and Cave Creek, to the north, are two communities sheltered by the Sonoran Desert foothills and surrounded by mountains. Carefree was planned for those who enjoy fun-in-the-sun activities like tennis, golf and horseback riding. Cave Creek, a booming ranching and mining center back in 1873, thrives on its strong Western flavor. A bit hokey, but fun. Like

South Central Arizona

fallout from a starburst, these and other neighboring communities all revolve around the tempo, pace and heartbeat of the Phoenix–Scottsdale core.

Beyond the urban centers, you can pull up to a gas station that's the last one from anywhere, visit honky-tonk saloons, skinny-dip in a mountain lake, pan for gold, meet dreamers and drifters. The best way to see the West is to be part of it, to feel the currents of its rivers or the steepness of its hills underfoot. South central Arizona certainly offers ample opportunity.

▼▼▼▼▼▼▼▼▼▼
Phoenix

The history of south central Arizona unravels in smooth, easy chapters through Phoenix's museums and attractions, particularly highlighting its Indian heritage. But this is by no means all you'll find here. The city is also a bustling art mecca, evident from the moment visitors arrive at Sky Harbor Airport, with its array of contemporary and Western artworks on display. The airport's program of changing art exhibits, in conjunction with the Phoenix Art Commission, is a model for similar programs at airports throughout the country. You'll also find art everywhere in the city. Along Piestewa Peak Freeway, a ten-mile stretch that connects downtown Phoenix with the city's northern suburbs, you may think you're seeing things, and you are. The freeway is lined with 35 giant three- and four-foot sculptures—vases, cups, Indian-style pots and other utensils, all part of the city's public arts project "to make people feel more at home with the freeway." Not everyone in Phoenix loves the idea. Detractors have dubbed the freeway art project "Chamber Pots of the Gods."

Surely the last of the rugged Marlboro men can still be seen astride handsome, well-groomed horses in Phoenix, but they're not riding off into the sunset, never to be seen again. Chances are they're heading into the vast expanse of desert land that still surrounds the city proper to recharge their motors. Long considered a scourge of man, arid and untamable, the desert with its raw awesome beauty is now considered by many as the last vestige of America's wilderness. Numerous tour operators offer guided jeep and horseback tours into the desert, but as any Arizonian will tell you, the desert is best appreciated alone. Southwestern Indians have long known the secrets of the desert. Now the settler man comes to turn his face skyward into the pale desert sun.

But whether the city proper or its environs are your scene, trying to take in all the sights and sounds in one trip is a bit like counting the grains of sand in a desert. We suppose it can be done, but who on earth has the time? To help you on your quest, here are some of this city's highlights.

SIGHTS   Phoenix's once lackluster downtown is starting to reap the benefits of some $1.1 billion worth of cultural and architectural enhancements in progress since the late 1980s. A focal point of the **Phoenix Municipal Government Center,** which includes a new city hall, is one of the city's oldest landmarks—the **Orpheum Theatre**, a magnificent 1929 Spanish baroque revival building that was once considered the most luxurious playhouse west of the Mississippi River. The theater gives free public tours of the exterior and is a showcase for performing arts, community and civic events, ballet, children's theater, film festivals and other special events. Tours are conducted on Monday between noon and 1 p.m. if there are no productions then; call ahead. ~ 203 West Adams Street; 602-262-7272.

Spare change? The roof of the Capitol building contains the amount of copper equivalent to 4,800,000 pennies. That's $48,000.

Other improvements are making downtown more pedestrian-friendly, such as the **Margaret T. Hance Park**, a 29-acre greenbelt stretching from 3rd Street to 3rd Avenue, with wooded areas, fountains and a Japanese garden (admission) symbolizing Phoenix's ties to sister city Hemeji, Japan. ~ 602-256-3204, fax 602-534-2635.

The exceptional **Heard Museum**, housed in a lovely old Spanish-style building off Central Avenue, is one of the must-sees in Phoenix—even if you're not a museum buff. Founded in 1929 to house the Heard family collection of American Indian art and artifacts, it underwent huge expansions in 1999, 2004 and 2005. The seven galleries include exhibits on pottery, Indian boarding schools, Arizona's tribes, contemporary art by Indian artists and a display of 250 kachina dolls. There is also an education pavilion, a working artist's studio, an excellent gift shop, a bookstore and a restaurant. Admission. ~ 2301 North Central Avenue; 602-252-8848; www.heard.org.

The neighboring **Phoenix Art Museum** has also undergone an expansion and now takes up an entire block. It has exhibits on Western, Asian, Latin American, European, contemporary and decorative arts and an outstanding fashion design collection that includes accessories and textiles. The museum also presents temporary exhibitions on tour from other major museums. In addition, children can engage in hands-on fun at ArtWorks, an interactive gallery. Call for specific exhibition information. Closed Monday. Admission. ~ 1625 North Central Avenue; 602-257-1222, fax 602-253-8662; www.phxart.org, e-mail info@phxart.org.

The **Arizona Capitol** was built in 1900 to serve as the Territorial Capitol. The building has been restored to the 1912 era when Arizona won statehood. Housed within the building is the **Arizona Capitol Museum**, which provides guided tours of permanent exhibits in the Senate and House Chambers, the Governor's Suite and the Rotunda. A wax figure of the state's first governor, George Hunt, is seated at his partnership desk surrounded by period furnishings. Major artifacts include the original silver service taken from the USS *Arizona* before the battleship was sunk at Pearl Harbor and the roughrider flag carried up Cuba's San Juan Hill during the Spanish-American War, which is brought out for special events. The museum is closed weekends. ~ 1700 West Washington Street; 602-542-4675, fax 602-542-4690; www.lib.az.us/museum/capitol.htm, e-mail capmus@lib.az.us.

Minerals, ores and mining equipment from Arizona and the rest of the world are displayed at the **Arizona Mining and Mineral Museum**, one of the finest of its kind in the Southwest. Closed Sunday. ~ 1502 West Washington Street; 602-255-3791, 800-446-4259, fax 602-255-3777; www.admmr.state.az.us.

Over at the **Arizona's Women Hall of Fame**, you will find a small exhibit dedicated to the women who made Arizona what it is today. Closed weekends. ~ 1101 West Washington Street; 602-255-2110; www.lib.az.us/museum/hof.htm.

Museo Chicano features changing exhibits ranging from local to international focus. Latino culture, arts and history are exhibited, as well as the work of well-known and emerging artists. In addition, the museum offers a popular series of cultural programs and performing-arts events, such as the Mexican Ballet Folklorico with live mariachi bands, and an annual Day of the Dead festival in November. The museum store features Latino fine and folk art, bilingual books and hundreds of posters; it also hosts author readings and book signings. Closed Sunday and Monday. Admission. ~ 147 East Adams Street; 602-257-5536, fax 602-257-5539; e-mail museochicano@juno.com.

Heritage Square is a Southwestern time warp featuring four turn-of-the-20th-century homes: the **Arizona Doll & Toy Museum**; the **Rosson House**, an 1895 Eastlake Victorian that contains an exquisite collection of period furniture; the **Silva House**, a Victorian-style bungalow; and the **Stevens-Haustgen House**. The square also has six other buildings that house eateries, shops and exhibits. There is an admission charge at the Rosson House and the Arizona Doll & Toy Museum. Closed August to Labor Day, and Monday and Tuesday. ~ Heritage Square, 115 North 6th Street; 602-262-5071, fax 602-534-1786; www.rossonhousemuseum.org.

The **Phoenix Museum of History**, located in the Heritage and Science Park next to Heritage Square, focuses on the territorial history of Phoenix from prehistoric to the 1930s and beyond. Many displays are interactive and involve personal stories and historical figures; others include an impressive printing press exhibit and one of the state's oldest mining locomotives. There is a library for research and browsing, as well as a gift shop. Closed Sunday and Monday. Admission. ~ 105 North 5th Street; 602-253-2734, fax 602-253-2348; www.pmoh.org, e-mail info@pmoh.org.

Also next to Heritage Square is the **Arizona Science Center**, which is outfitted with a planetarium, a giant-screen theater and

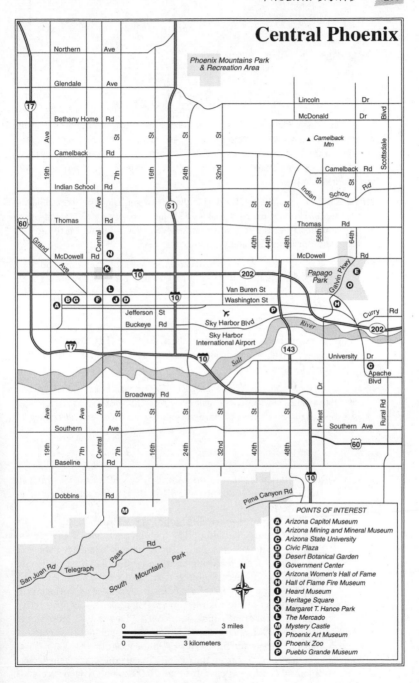

Central Phoenix

POINTS OF INTEREST

- **A** Arizona Capitol Museum
- **B** Arizona Mining and Mineral Museum
- **C** Arizona State University
- **D** Civic Plaza
- **E** Desert Botanical Garden
- **F** Government Center
- **G** Arizona Women's Hall of Fame
- **H** Hall of Flame Fire Museum
- **I** Heard Museum
- **J** Heritage Square
- **K** Margaret T. Hance Park
- **L** The Mercado
- **M** Mystery Castle
- **N** Phoenix Art Museum
- **O** Phoenix Zoo
- **P** Pueblo Grande Museum

0   3 miles

0   3 kilometers

While recent skyscraper construction has replaced most of Phoenix's original downtown buildings, a few—often protected by National Historic Landmark status—remain to show the kaleidoscope of architectural exuberance that characterized the city's early years. These structures can be seen on a two-mile walk from Heritage Square.

FRY BUILDING   The Fry Building is the oldest surviving commercial building in Phoenix, dating back to 1885, just five years after the city was founded. The storefront was remodeled in 1950. ~ Located at the northwest corner of 2nd and Washington streets.

HANNY'S BUILDING   The construction in 1947 of the contemporary-style Hanny's Building inspired a major facelift of the downtown area and the destruction or renovation of most historic architecture. ~ 44 North 1st Street.

PROFESSIONAL BUILDING   The Professional Building gave Phoenix its first centrally located medical offices. Built in 1931, this limestone-sheathed building exemplifies the Art Deco/Moderne style. ~ 137 North Central Avenue.

HOTEL SAN CARLOS   The Hotel San Carlos was built in 1927 in the Renaissance revival style. A gathering place for Hollywood stars, it was one of the first hotels to have steam heat, elevators and air-cooling. It

over 300 hands-on exhibits. Admission. ~ 600 East Washington Street; 602-716-2000, fax 602-716-2099; www.azscience.org, e-mail info@azscience.org.

For a glimpse into the Hohokam culture's past, visit the **Pueblo Grande Museum**. The exhibits include a prehistoric Hohokam ruin, a permanent display on this legendary tribe and a changing gallery featuring Southwestern Indian arts, crafts and archaeology. Of special interest is an outdoor trail that leads visitors to the top of a Hohokam platform mound and through full-sized replicas of Hohokam houses. There is also an interactive exhibit for children. Admission. ~ 4619 East Washington Street; 602-495-0901, fax 602-495-5645; www.pueblogrande.com, e-mail pueblo.grande.museum.pks@phoenix.gov.

Located not far from the central Phoenix museums is the **Desert Botanical Garden**, where more than 50,000 plants from desert lands has recently undergone a multimillion-dollar restoration. ~ 202 North Central Avenue.

SECURITY BUILDING   Also typifying the Renaissance revival style is the Security Building, built down the block from the Hotel San Carlos in 1928. ~ 234 North Central Avenue.

TITLE AND TRUST BUILDING   The Moderne-style Title and Trust Building was the largest office building in Arizona when it was built in 1931. It still has the original travertine and marble floors and etched glass. ~ 114 West Adams Street.

ORPHEUM THEATRE   The 1929 Spanish Baroque revival–style Orpheum Theatre is Phoenix's largest and most architecturally intact theater. A major restoration in 1997 has given it new life as a center for the performing arts. ~ 203 West Adams Street.

WALKER BUILDING   The Walker Building was built entirely of poured concrete in neoclassic revival style in 1920. Originally the location of JC Penney's department store, it later became the headquarters of Central Arizona Light and Power. ~ 302 West Washington Street.

HISTORIC CITY HALL/MARICOPA COUNTY COURTHOUSE   Built in 1928, the Historic City Hall/Maricopa County Courthouse combines elements of most architectural styles that were in vogue in 1920s Phoenix, including Art Deco, Moderne, Spanish Baroque revival and Renaissance revival. ~ 125 West Washington Street. City government moved to the new 20-story City Hall at 200 West Washington Street in 1992.

LUHRS BUILDING AND TOWER   The Luhrs Building (c. 1923), 45 West Jefferson Street, and Luhrs Tower (c. 1929), 13 West Jefferson Street, were each the tallest building in Arizona in the year they were built.

around the world are displayed. You can see this beautiful garden via a self-guided nature walk or a group tour. Featured is a 50-acre showcase of native Sonoran Desert plants, a saguaro forest, a mesquite thicket, a desert stream and an upland chaparral habitat, complete with historic American Indian dwellings. The botanical garden has trail exhibits and interactive displays as well as "islands" of shade that offer relief from the often brutal afternoon sun. Admission. ~ 1201 North Galvin Parkway; 480-941-1225, fax 480-481-8124; www.dbg.org, e-mail media@dbg.org.

Nearby is the **Phoenix Zoo**, which uses natural settings, including a four-acre African Savanna, to showcase over 1300 mammals, birds and reptiles. Phoenix newcomers are frequently startled to find themselves driving along busy Van Buren alongside a family of trumpeting elephants. For a convenient zoo overview take the Safari Train. Popular highlights are the World Herd of Arabian Oryx and the monkey village. Children will especially enjoy the hands-on participatory exhibits. Be sure to visit the one-acre tropical rainforest, home to 15 bird and animal species adopted from around the world. Admission. ~ 455 North Galvin Parkway; 602-273-1341, fax 602-273-7078; www.phoenixzoo. org, e-mail zooqna@thephxzoo.com.

The largest firefighting museum in the world is the **Hall of Flame Fire Museum**. On display are more than 90 restored hand-drawn, horse-drawn and motorized fire engines and hundreds of artifacts. Special games, exhibits and programs, all stressing fire safety, are offered for children. You'll also find a theater where videos are shown. Admission. ~ 6101 East Van Buren Street; 602-275-3473, fax 602-275-0896; www.hallofflame.org, e-mail web master@hallofflame.org.

Tucked away in the foothills of South Mountain Park, the **Mystery Castle** is an 18-room extravaganza fashioned from native stone, sand, cement, water, goat's milk and Stutz Bearcat wire-rim wheels. Warmed by 13 fireplaces, the parapeted castle has a cantilevered stairway, chapel and dozens of nooks and crannies and is furnished with Southwestern antiques. It's known as the "mystery" castle because the builder, Boyce Luther Gulley, thinking he was about to die from tuberculosis, ran away from his Seattle home in a Stutz Bearcat and devoted 15 years to the construction project. It was only after his death in 1945 that the missing builder's family learned of his whereabouts and inherited the castle. Closed Monday through Wednesday from October through June; closed July through September. Admission. ~ End of South 7th Street; 602-268-1581.

Pioneer Arizona Living History Museum re-creates an Old West town using mostly original buildings—a church, schoolhouse, printing shop and blacksmith shop—and featuring costumed interpreters. Living-history exhibitions include cooking, gardening and sewing. At the opera house you'll see melodramas and historic performances all themed to the territorial period, 1858 to 1912. You can also enjoy the picnic area and a restaurant. Closed Monday and Tuesday. Admission. ~ 3901 West Pioneer Road (Pioneer Road exit off of Route 17); 623-465-1052, fax 623-465-0683; www.pioneer-arizona.com.

For a midday break from sightseeing—one the kids will thank you for—stop at **Encanto Park**. The picnic tables and landscaped grounds provide a cool place to lunch or doze, and the on-site Enchanted Island Amusement Park (admission; closed Monday and Tuesday; 602-254-2020) has rides and bumper boats if you can muster the energy. ~ 2606 North 15th Avenue; 602-261-8991.

West of Phoenix, the **Bead Museum** displays a phenomenal collection of beads, jewelry and other adornments from around the world and explains their uses as trade goods, currency, religious items and status symbols. Visitors to this one-of-a-kind nonprofit museum discover that there's more to beads than they ever suspected. ~ 5754 West Glenn Drive, Glendale; 623-931-2737, fax 623-930-8561; www.beadmuseumaz.org.

LODGING

As a major resort and convention center, the Valley of the Sun features some of the most spectacular hotel resorts in the country. It has had the rare distinction of having more *Mobil Travel Guide* Five Star resorts (three of the twelve top-rated resorts nationwide) than any other city in the United States (see "Spoil Yourself" in this chapter). Yet it's not without its share of budget- and moderate-priced hotels and motels, and proliferating bed and breakfasts.

An elegant scene of the past is mirrored in the glossy facade of the present with the rebirth of the **Hotel San Carlos** in the heart of downtown. Built in 1928, the seven-story San Carlos has undergone a multimillion-dollar restoration while keeping its charm intact—a crystal chandelier and period furnishing in the lobby, original bathtubs, basins and furniture in the 109 guest rooms and 12 suites. There's also a rooftop swimming pool. The San Carlos is one of the largest hotels listed in the National Register of Historic Places. ~ 202 North Central Avenue; 602-253-4121, 866-253-4121, fax 602-253-6668; www.hotelsancarlos.com, e-mail info@hotelsancarlos.com. MODERATE TO ULTRA-DELUXE.

The 24-story **Hyatt Regency Phoenix** is across from Civic Plaza downtown. With 712 rooms, it's the city's largest hotel. It has a heated swimming pool, exercise equipment, a café, lounges and a revolving rooftop dining room. Rooms are smallish but tastefully furnished in a light, Southwest style. ~ 122 North 2nd Street; 602-252-1234, 800-233-1234, fax 602-254-9472; www.hyatt.com. DELUXE TO ULTRA-DELUXE.

A find, price-wise, is the **Pyramid Inn**, a two-story brick inn with 30 large rooms and a swimming pool and free airport shuttle

AUTHOR FAVORITE

I'll spend several nights in hostels if it means I can splurge on the luxurious accommodations of **Embassy Suites Biltmore**. Walk through the doors and your first sight is a huge atrium complete with palm trees, tropical plants and waterways shimmering with goldfish. With the price tag comes a complimentary cooked-to-order breakfast. The 232 modern two-room suites each offer a microwave oven, wet bar, refrigerator and dining area. ~ 2630 East Camelback Road; 602-955-3992, 800-362-2779, fax 602-955-6479; www.phoenixbiltmore.embassysuites.com. ULTRA-DELUXE.

service. The neighborhood isn't great, but you can't beat the price. ~ 3307 East Van Buren Street; 602-275-3691, fax 602-267-0448; www.pyramidinn.com, e-mail pyramidinn@att.net. BUDGET.

For those interested in meeting fellow budget travelers, try the **Hostel Metcalf House**. Here's what you get: two dormitory-style rooms (men's and women's) with bunk beds for ten in each. Guests may use the kitchen and community room. Closed during the day and in August. ~ 1026 North 9th Street; 602-254-9803. BUDGET.

The YMCA has 139 rooms in an seven-story downtown building. It's good old Y-style, nothing fancy, but it's clean. For $2 extra, full use of the gym facilities and swimming pool is included. ~ 350 North 1st Avenue; 602-253-6181. BUDGET.

If you want to stay in shape while you're away, try the **Hilton Garden Inn Phoenix/Midtown**, a hotel with 156 rooms, a restaurant and a lounge along with a full-scale athletic club facility including basketball and racquetball courts, sauna and pool. Rooms have contemporary decor, and the workout's great. ~ 4000 North Central Avenue; 602-279-9811, fax 602-285-2932; www. hiltongardeninn.com, e-mail phxmd-salesadm@hilton.com. MODERATE TO DELUXE.

HIDDEN ► The **Maricopa Manor** is a Spanish-style bed and breakfast situated in a garden-like setting of palm trees and flowers in the heart of north central Phoenix. Built in 1928, the inn has seven individually decorated suites, all with private baths. Typical is the Library Suite with its king-size iron bed, private deck entrance, handsome collection of leather-bound books and an antique work desk. The Manor Suite has a double whirlpool tub and a three-sided fireplace. Guests may also use the inn's formal living, dining, music rooms, patio, pool and gazebo spa. Expanded continental breakfast included. ~ 15 West Pasadena Avenue; 602-274-6302, 800-292-6403, fax 602-266-3904; www.maricopamanor.com, e-mail res@maricopamanor.com. DELUXE TO ULTRA-DELUXE.

DINING   Looking for a quick snack? Go to the **Arizona Center**, take the elevator or stairs to the second floor and *voilà!* Here you'll find a whole array of attractive fast-food restaurants all sharing a mutual sit-down dining—**Copper Square Grill, Mi Amigo** and more. ~ Van Buren between 3rd and 5th streets; 602-271-4000, fax 602-271-4417; www.arizonacenter.com. BUDGET.

At **Sam's Cafe** in the Arizona Center, a large patio set amidst fountains is one draw; good Southwestern cuisine is another. Start with *poblano* chicken chowder, then have Hannah's roasted chicken with jalapeño-garlic marinade, or the blackened salmon caesar salad. If the weather is inclement (which it rarely is), indoor dining is also nice, with more fountains and terra-cotta colored walls. ~ 455 North 3rd Street; 602-252-3545, fax 602-252-0334. MODERATE TO DELUXE.

Christo's specializes in Northern Italian cuisine, which means less pasta in favor of meatier fare—chicken *zingarella*, osso buco veal, rack of lamb—and fish dishes such as halibut topped with feta cheese, olive oil, garlic and sliced tomatoes. Sparkling stemware, crisp peach-and-white tablecloths and table flowers add a festive note. No lunch on Saturday. Closed Sunday. ~ 6327 North 7th Street; 602-264-1784, fax 602-230-8953. MODERATE TO DELUXE.

A popular neighborhood restaurant, **Texaz Grill** really looks ◀HIDDEN
like it was transferred over from Dallas with its neon beer signs, glowing jukebox and antique wall memorabilia (old Texas license plates and the like). Steaks come in a variety of sizes, from an 8-ounce filet to an 18-ounce T-bone, but the biggest seller of all is the chicken-fried steak served with heaps of mashed potatoes and buttermilk biscuits, just like in Texas. No lunch on Sunday. ~ 6003 North 16th Street; phone/fax 602-248-7827; www.texaz grill.com, e-mail texaz@texazgrill.com. MODERATE.

What it lacks in decor, **Ham's** makes up for in great cooking. Specials change daily and include beef tips and noodles, fried chicken, barbecued beef and meatloaf, all served with heaps of mashed potatoes, veggies and biscuits. ~ 3302 North 24th Street; 602-954-8775. BUDGET TO MODERATE.

Christopher's Fermier Brasserie ("Farmers' Tavern") features chef-owner Christopher Gross' gourmet fare prepared with fresh local produce. The French-inspired cuisine includes specialties such as truffle-infused smoked sirloin and house-smoked salmon. The menu matches a wine with each entrée and provides a rotating selection of 100 vintages available by the glass. The adjacent wine bar offers cheese and seafood platters and after-meal (or late-night) cigars. Reservations recommended. ~ In Biltmore Fashion Park, 2584 East Camelback Road; 602-522-2344, fax 602-468-0314; www.fermier.com. DELUXE TO ULTRA-DELUXE.

AUTHOR FAVORITE

For a stylish escape from the often awful heat of downtown Phoenix, I pamper myself with high tea at the elegantly Victorian **Spicery**. Located in the Catlin Court Historical District, an area where historic homes have been preserved, this eatery is in a charming 1895 Victorian house. It makes food the way mother used to—homemade soups, salads, chubby sandwiches, fresh-baked bread and pies. The Spicery offers high tea Tuesday through Saturday (by reservation only). Closed Sunday in summer and winter. ~ 7141 North 59th Avenue, Glendale; 623-937-6534; www.thespicery.com. BUDGET.

Wright's is an open, airy dining room at the Arizona Biltmore with a menu featuring New American cuisine. There is raisin and pistachio french toast with warm fruit compote as well as snazzy egg dishes for Sunday brunch. The dinner and Sunday brunch menus are filled with seafood and meat dishes served with intriguing sauces. For dinner, start with an appetizer such as *foie gras* with a currant compote, and then try an entrée such as pan-roasted scallops with Swiss chard or lamb loin with a mushroom ragout. Save room for one of their fabulous desserts. Dinner and Sunday brunch only. Hours vary in summer; call ahead. ~ 2400 East Missouri Avenue; 602-954-2507, fax 602-381-7600; www.arizona biltmore.com, e-mail reservations@arizonabiltmore.com. ULTRA-DELUXE.

> It was the disappearance of the Hohokam Indians that led settlers to select the name "Phoenix" from the symbol of immortality of the ancient Egyptians.

Havana Cafe offers the not-too-spicy cuisine of Latin America, Spain and Cuba in an atmosphere that's more a small, cozy café than in the style of Hemingway's Havana. *Chicharitas*, an appetizer of fried green plantain chips, will get the juices flowing. In addition, you'll find Cuban chicken marinated in orange juice, lime juice and garlic, and paella (for two), the house specialty; sausage; black bean soup; *escabeche*; *picadillo* and more. No lunch on Sunday. ~ 4225 East Camelback Road; 602-952-1991, fax 480-991-0535; www.havanacafe-az.com. MODERATE.

HIDDEN ▶

A spot popular with the downtown office workers eager for a touch of home cooking, **Mrs. White's Golden Rule Cafe** offers pork chops, chicken, cornbread and cobbler. Get there early for a table. No dinner. Closed weekends. ~ 808 East Jefferson Street; 602-262-9256. MODERATE.

SHOPPING   Western wear would seem a natural when hitting the Phoenix shopping scene—and you're right. There's a herd of places selling boots, shirts, buckles and whatever else you might want.

If you're in the market for Western clothes, just to look the part or to get ready for your next rodeo appearance, you might start with **Aztex Hats**, which offers the largest selection of Western hats in Arizona. Closed Sunday. ~ 10658 North 32nd Street; 602-971-9090. **Saba's Western Store**, in business since 1927, included Barry Goldwater among its clientele. There are branches of the store dotted around Arizona. Check their website for locations. ~ 10020 West McDowell Road #104, Avondale; 623-873-0753; www.sabaswesternwear.com. **Sheplers** is part of the world's largest Western-wear chain. ~ 9201 North 29th Avenue; 602-870-8085; www.sheplers.com.

If you like malls and shopping complexes, get ready. Phoenix has them in great abundance. One entertainment complex that has helped revitalize the downtown Phoenix area is the **Arizona Center**, with dozens of restaurants, bars and shops on two levels. People come here to dine, meander through the three-acre garden area, browse in the shops or listen to occasional live entertainment in the evenings. ~ 455 North 3rd Street; 602-271-4000, fax 602-271-4417; www.arizonacenter.com.

You can also shop at old standbys. The **Green Woodpecker** (602-266-7381), a large novelty gift shop, can be found at **Park Central**, which also has several restaurants. ~ 3110 North Central Avenue; 602-264-5575. **Metrocenter** is an enclosed double-deck mall that includes **Dillard's** and **Macy's**. ~ 9617 North Metro Parkway West; 602-997-2641.

For designer merchandise at legendary low prices, head for **Loehmann's**. ~ 3135 East Lincoln Drive; 602-957-8691.

Museum gift shops offer unique finds for selective shoppers. For instance, the **Phoenix Art Museum** carries books, posters, catalogs and art-replica gifts, as well as a special section for kids. Closed Monday. ~ 1625 North Central Avenue; 602-257-2182; www.phxart.org.

The **Desert Botanical Garden** has a gift shop offering foods, spices and jellies made from desert plants, as well as plants, nature books and Southwestern souvenirs and crafts. ~ 1201 North Galvin Parkway; 480-941-1225.

Don't drop just yet. Because after all those malls and other stores, we come to the farmer's markets! Every Thursday from 9 a.m. to 1 p.m., February through April, farmers from around the community sell their freshest produce at decent prices in the courtyard at **Wesley Bolin Park**. ~ 15th and 17th avenues off Washington Street; 623-848-1234.

For a kicker, **Phoenix Park 'N Swap** is the largest open-air flea market in the Southwest, with over 2000 dealers selling or swapping everything from used office furniture and rare antiques to Indian jewelry and rare one-of-a-kind photos of Marilyn Monroe. You can shop to the sounds of live music on weekend mornings. Readers warn there's been an increase of crime at the swap; be sure not to leave anything valuable in your car, and to park as close to the action as possible. Open Wednesday, Friday and weekends. Admission. ~ 3801 East Washington Street; 602-273-1258, fax 602-273-7375; www.americanparknswap.com.

A small town south of Phoenix is the setting for the **Guada-lupe Farmer's Market**. You will find fresh vegetables, exotic fruits and dried chile peppers. ~ 9210 South Avenida del Yaqui, Guadalupe; 480-730-1945. A few blocks north is **Mercado Mexico**, where Mexican pottery and ceramics are sold. ~ 8212 South Avenida del Yaqui, Guadalupe; 480-831-5925.

◄ HIDDEN

Nightlife in south central Arizona is as diverse and far-reaching as the area itself, from twanging guitars of country-and-western bands

NIGHTLIFE

to symphony strings. There are Indian ceremonials and sophisticated jazz as well. To find out what's happening, check the entertainment pages of the *Arizona Republic* and the *Phoenix Gazette*.

The Herberger Theater Center is an ultramodern theater complex housing three separate theaters, including **Center Stage** and **Stage West**, where professional theater performances take place. The Center features the **Actors' Theater**, **Arizona Theater Company** and **Center Dance Ensemble**, which has performed in Phoenix for more than 25 years. ~ 222 East Monroe Street; 602-254-7399, fax 602-258-9521; www.herbergertheater.org, e-mail info@herbergertheater.org.

The **Phoenix Civic Plaza and Symphony Hall** houses the Phoenix Symphony and stages entertainment ranging from opera and ballet to Broadway shows and top-name concert performers. ~ 3rd Street between Monroe and Jefferson streets; 602-262-7272.

PARKS

SOUTH MOUNTAIN PARK 🚶 🚲 🐎 With 16,500 acres, this is the largest municipal park in the world, a vast rugged mountain range that was once American Indian hunting ground. A spectacular view of Phoenix can be seen from Dobbins Lookout, one of four scenic overlooks located 2300 feet above the desert floor. The park offers over 50 miles of well-marked hiking and riding trails. Its steep canyons reveal evidence of ancient American Indian artifacts and petroglyphs. Facilities include picnic areas, restrooms and a sunken concrete stage for park ranger lectures or impromptu sing-alongs. The South Mountain Environmental Education Center (602-534-6324) has displays on the people, history, flora and fauna of the park. Park rangers are also available for questions. ~ 10919 South Central Avenue; 602-495-0222, fax 602-534-6330.

PAPAGO PARK 🚶 🚲 🛶 A part of the Phoenix parks network since 1959, Papago is a neat blend of hilly desert terrain, quiet lagoons and glistening streams. The former American Indian townsite now offers golf, picnic sites, ballfields and fishing. Three lagoons are stocked with bass, catfish, bluegill and trout in winter. (It's free for kids 13 and under but an urban fishing license is required for all others.) Also within its boundaries are the Phoenix Zoo, the Desert Botanical Garden, and the Phoenix Municipal Stadium, where the Oakland A's hold their spring training. You'll also find firepits, restrooms, an archery range, a wheelchair-accessible trail, bike paths and running courses. ~ 625 North Galvin Parkway; 602-262-4837, fax 602-534-5517.

PHOENIX MOUNTAINS PARK & RECREATION AREA 🚶 🚲 One of Phoenix's most familiar landmarks with its craggy, easily identifiable pinnacle, Piestewa Peak is primarily known for its hiking trails. However, the rocky terrain has been moderately developed for other recreational pursuits as well, whether picnicking or curling up in the shade of a towering saguaro with an Edward Abbey tome on the evils of overdevelopment. The picnic ramadas have electricity. Other amenities include drinking water, firepits, tables, benches and restrooms. ~ 2701 East Squaw Peak Drive; 602-262-7901, fax 602-262-7901.

ESTRELLA MOUNTAIN REGIONAL PARK 🚶🚲🐎 With 19,840 acres, Estrella offers abundant vegetation and spectacular mountain views, with peaks within the Sierra Estrella Mountains reaching 3650 feet. The park offers excellent areas for hiking and riding, a rodeo arena and a golf course. Horse and hiking trails abound. There's an amphitheater for lectures and gatherings. Picnic areas and restrooms are located in the park. Day-use fee, $5 per vehicle. ~ Route 10, 16 miles southwest of Phoenix. Take Exit 126 onto Estrella Parkway and follow it five miles south to the park; 623-932-3811, fax 623-932-7718.

> The highest temperature recorded in Phoenix was on June 26, 1990: 122 degrees!

▲ There is "primitive" RV camping (no hookups); $5 per night.

WHITE TANK MOUNTAIN REGIONAL PARK 🚶🚲🐎 Covering 29,572 acres of desert, canyons and mountains, White Tank is the largest park in the Maricopa County Park System. Elevations range from 1402 feet at the entrance to 4083 feet at the park's highest point. White Tank contains an excellent hiking, mountain bike and horse trail system, a seasonal flowing waterfall (reached by a mile-long self-guided hiker's trail) and American Indian petroglyphs scattered throughout. Two wheelchair-accessible trails allow visitors with disabilities to view some of the park's petroglyphs. Facilities include a visitors center, picnic sites, restrooms and showers. Day-use fee, $5 per vehicle. ~ Dunlap Avenue (which turns into Olive Avenue before reaching the park), 15 miles west of Glendale; 623-935-2505, fax 623-535-4291.

▲ There are 36 sites; $10 per night. Backpack camping is $5 per night.

Phoenix Gay Scene

While gay and lesbian activities are found throughout Phoenix, the highest concentration centers around the blocks between Camelback and Indian School roads and between 7th Avenue and 7th Street. This area is home to an array of gay lodging, cafés, bars, shops and nightclubs.

LODGING

You can stay for a week or a month at the gay-owned **Arizona Royal Villa Apartments**. Hotel rooms, junior suites and one-bedroom apartments are available here. All accommodations face the courtyard. The private grounds, located within a walled complex with keyed entry, include a clothing-optional chilled swimming pool, jacuzzi and sunbathing area. Men only. ~ 4312 North 12th Avenue; 602-266-6883, 888-266-6884, fax 602-279-7437; www. royalvilla.com, e-mail rvilla@royalvilla.com. MODERATE.

The men-only **Arizona Sunburst Inn** is an L-shaped ranch house with five large, comfortable rooms furnished in contemporary designs; some rooms have private baths while others share. The outdoor heated pool and jacuzzi are clothing optional. Continental breakfast is served. ~ 6245 North 12th Place; 602-274-1474, 800-974-1474; www.azsunburst.com, e-mail sunbrstinn@aol.com. MODERATE.

DINING

Plaster parrots greet you as you enter **Arriba Mexican Grill** for a festive meal of New Mexican fare generously spiced with Hatch green chile. Dine on delectable shrimp fajitas, *carnitas* flavored with orange and lime, New Mexican enchiladas and fiery Taos tacos amid colorful handpainted murals, a fireplace and a fountain. Wash down your meal, if you're inclined, with some of the 22 brands of tequila. ~ 1812 East Camelback Road; 602-265-9112, fax 602-265-9182; www.arribamexicangrill.com. BUDGET TO MODERATE.

SHOPPING

Unique on Central is a gay-owned shop offering a large selection of cards, gifts, music, videos, travel books and magazines. ~ 4700 North Central Avenue, Suite 105; 602-279-9691; www.uniqueoncentral.com.

NIGHTLIFE

Perhaps the most popular gay bar in the city is **Charlie's**, where you can take two-step and line-dancing lessons two nights a week and dance to good ol' country-and-western music nightly. You can play volleyball outside on Sunday. The scene is mostly men, from 21 to 81 years of age, but all are welcome. ~ 727 West

WEATHER OR NOT? WHILE SOME LIKE IT HOT . . .

All of south central Arizona gets hot, despite the seemingly innocuous average annual temperature of 72°F. Winter is cool and clear, in the 60s; spring is breezy and warm, in the 90s; summer is torrid, often topping 100, and that's when the monsoons come, the swift summer rainstorms that usually arrive late in the day with spectacular flashes of lightning and deep, rolling rumbles of thunder; autumn is marvelously dry and clear, in the 80s. Depending on your weather preference, choose your time to visit accordingly.

Camelback Road; 602-265-0224, fax 602-264-1065; www. charliesphoenix.com.

Join gay and lesbian sports enthusiasts at **Roscoe's on 7th,** a popular sports bar boasting 12 monitors. Daily drink specials include Sunday's do-it-yourself bloody Mary bar. ~ 4531 North 7th Street; 602-285-0833; www.roscoeson7.com.

For a women's sports club that caters mostly to lesbians, head to **Z Girl Club.** A large dancefloor and a lively game room are the attractions. ~ 4301 North 7th Avenue; 602-265-3233.

Once voted the best cruise/leather bar, **The Padlock** is the place to see and be seen for the denim and leather crowd. ~ 998 East Indian School Road; 602-266-5640; www.padlockaz.com.

Club Vibe is a very pink women's bar (although gay men are welcome) with R&B and Top-40 dance music most evenings. Closed Monday through Wednesday. ~ 3031 East Indian School Road; 602-224-9977.

A sports bar with eight large music video screens, plus pool tables, darts, video games, foosball and shuffleboard, **The Locker Room Sports Bar** attracts a mix of lesbians and gay patrons. There's karaoke on Wednesday and Friday nights. ~ 3108 East McDowell Road; 602-267-8707.

The dancing crowd works up a sweat on **Boom Nightclub's** large dancefloor, with state-of-the-art light and sound, Thursday through Saturday nights, when deejays spin high-energy tunes. Cover on Friday and Saturday. ~ 1724 East McDowell Road; 602-254-0231.

Over by the airport stands Phoenix's oldest gay bar, **Nu–Towne Saloon.** Sunday and Tuesday drink specials ensure a convivial bunch at this popular hangout. ~ 5002 East Van Buren Street; 602-267-9959; www.nu-towne.com.

Scottsdale

Like neighboring Phoenix, Scottsdale is proud of its frontier heritage, which can be traced at a number of locations in and near the town. In the Old Scottsdale section, where only 35 years ago Lulu Belle's and the Pink Pony were the only two watering holes for miles around, the buildings all have false fronts, handcrafted signs and hitching posts, and horses still have the right of way. Many restaurants feature waiters and waitresses in period dress. The women have teased hairdos, and the men are all called Slim, Ace, Tex, Shorty and Stretch.

But that's about as Western as it gets. Otherwise, Scottsdale is chic, elegant and expensive. Amid its ties to the past, Scottsdale is a showplace of innovative architecture. The Frank Lloyd Wright Foundation is located here (at Taliesin West), as is the Cosanti Foundation, design headquarters for the controversial prototype town of Arcosanti, some 30 miles from Prescott, where building and nature are being fused.

SIGHTS

Taliesin West/Frank Lloyd Wright Foundation, a National Historic Landmark owned by the Frank Lloyd Wright Foundation, was the architect's Arizona home and studio. Situated on 600 acres of rugged Sonoran Desert, this remarkable set of buildings still astounds architectural critics with its beauty and unusual forms. A variety of guided tours are offered. Closed Tuesday and Wednesday from July through August. Admission. ~ 12621 North Frank Lloyd Wright Boulevard; 480-860-2700, fax 480-451-8989; www.franklloydwright.org, e-mail bevhart@franklloyd wright.org.

The **Scottsdale Museum of Contemporary Art** is housed, appropriately, in an ultramodern concrete-and-steel building complete with understated neon lettering. The collection focuses on the contemporary, with a rotating series of exhibits. An example includes James Turrell's celebrated "skyspaces." It's a good (air-conditioned) place to wander and, if needed, take a break from the more Southwestern-themed art of other local museums. Closed Tuesday in summer, Monday year-round. Admission (free on Thursday). ~ 7374 East 2nd Street; 480-994-2787, fax 480-874-4655; www.smoca.org, e-mail smoca@sccarts.org.

LODGING

The **Mondrian Scottsdale** is located in the heart of "Old Town," close to everything. Its 200 rooms have a colorful and modern motif. You'll find a lounge, a restaurant and a swimming pool. ~ 7353 East Indian School Road; 480-308-1100, 800-697-1791, fax 480-308-1200; www.mondrianscottsdale.com. DELUXE TO ULTRA-DELUXE.

A courtyard—complete with a lagoon, two pools (one with a sand beach and a waterslide) and a jacuzzi—is the center of attention at **SunBurst Resort**. Decked out in contemporary Southwestern decor, the 204 rooms and suites feature French doors and private balconies and are equipped with satellite TV, coffeemakers, minibars and double phone lines. With a restaurant/lounge and a fitness room on-site, you won't have to abandon this modern oasis. ~ 4925 North Scottsdale Road; 480-945-7666, 800-528-7867, fax 480-946-4056; www.sunburstresort.com, e-mail mperdue@sun burstresort.com. DELUXE TO ULTRA-DELUXE.

The **Scottsdale Plaza Resort** is a true find. Set within 40 acres, with 404 rooms, 180 of them suites, the resort features Spanish Mediterranean–style villas throughout, accented with courtyard swimming pools. The rooms are large and styled with Southwestern furnishing and art. Fountains, palm trees, earth-tone tiles, mauve carpeting, acres of fresh-cut flowers and potted greens add cooling touches. There are swimming pools, outdoor spas, tennis courts, indoor racquetball courts, a pro shop, a gym and a putting green. ~ 7200 North Scottsdale Road; 480-948-5000, 800-832-

2025, fax 480-998-5971; www.scottsdaleplaza.com, e-mail info@ scottsdaleplaza.com. DELUXE TO ULTRA-DELUXE.

If you're looking for a gem of a mini-resort, try the 56-room **Best Western Papago Inn & Resort**. Amenities include a heated pool, sauna, lounge and dining room. Guest rooms all overlook a treed and flowered interior courtyard and swimming pool. Environmental "green" rooms—nonsmoking rooms with air and water filter systems—are available for a charge. ~ 7017 East McDowell Road; 480-947-7335, 800-528-1234, fax 480-994-0692; www.papagoinn.com, e-mail papago@interwrx.com. BUDGET TO DELUXE.

Ramada Scottsdale on Fifth Avenue, a secluded retreat in the heart of Scottsdale's premier shopping district, sprawls out around a central courtyard with a large heated swimming pool. Its 92 rooms feature desert colors, king and double queen beds, and separate dressing areas. Rates includes continental breakfast. ~ 6935 5th Avenue; 480-994-9461, 800-553-2666, fax 480-947-1695; www.econolodge.com. DELUXE.

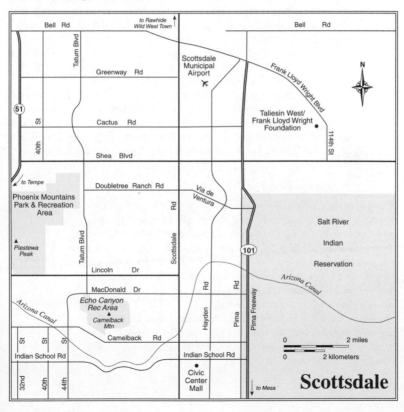

The **Best Western Scottsdale Airport Suites** is a four-story, all-suite hotel designed in a courtyard setting with a heated pool and spa and a restaurant on the premises. Each of the hotel's two-room suites is styled in desert mauve and teals with light Southwestern contemporary furnishings. ~ 7515 East Butherus Drive; 480-951-4000, fax 480-483-9046; www.scottsdalebest western.com. DELUXE.

DINING

Julio G's, established in 1934, somehow manages to combine a '30s art deco, Santa Fe and Mexican truck-stop decor—ceiling fans, black-tile walls and framed vintage-Mexican advertisements—into a trendy contemporary look. The food is much more clearly defined: *pollo magnifico,* beef tacos, bean tostadas, steaming bowls of rice and beans, chili con carne and tortillas. The staff is friendly and attentive. ~ 7633 East Indian School Road; 480-423-0058, fax 480-874-1193. BUDGET TO MODERATE.

Malee's on Main Thai Gourmet is a charming little spot with a bar in one corner, tables inside and a patio, weather permitting, for dining outside. Attractive tableware is set against sandalwood- and eggplant-colored tablecloths. Popular with the art crowd (in Scottsdale that covers a wide swath), the restaurant has an extensive menu that comes in various degrees of spiciness. No lunch on Sunday. ~ 7131 East Main Street; 480-947-6042, fax 480-994-3474; www.maleesonmain.com. MODERATE TO DELUXE.

One of the oldest Mexican restaurants in Scottsdale (also considered the finest by many) is **Los Olivos.** The restaurant was founded in 1945, but the adobe building in which it's located was built in 1928 and is officially listed as one of Scottsdale's historic landmarks. Large and rambling, with viga ceilings, it has several in-

AUTHOR FAVORITE

Plunging down a waterslide might seem like a silly thing for a grown-up to do, but when the temperature tops 100° in the shade, you'll understand why I enjoy it. But why go to a water park when the **Hyatt Regency Scottsdale Resort and Spa at Gainey Ranch** is around? Lounge on the sand beach, take a dip in the jacuzzi beneath a Greek water temple, or swim in the ten pools connected by a network of fountains, waterfalls, and a three-story waterslide. The 490 rooms, suites and *casitas* are modern with Sonoran Desert tones. Amenities here include a health spa, four restaurants, golfing, tennis and an American Indian seed garden and environmental learning center. ~ 7500 East Doubletree Ranch Road; 480-444-1234, 800-554-9288, fax 480-483-5550; www.scotts dale.hyatt.com. ULTRA-DELUXE.

dividual dining rooms inside and patio dining outside. The Mexican cuisine served is primarily Sonoran—enchiladas, seasonal green corn tamales, chimichangas, *chiles rellenos* and steak *picado*. The decor is festive (clay pots, flowers and piñatas) and there's live music and dancing on weekends. Aficionados rate its margaritas among the best in the state. ~ Two locations: 7328 East 2nd Street, 480-946-2256; and 15544 North Pima Road, 480-596-9787; www.azeats.com/losolivos. BUDGET TO MODERATE.

A traditional breakfast spot is **The Original Pancake House**, serving up steaming stacks of golden flapjacks, topped with melted butter, honey, maple syrup, berries or whatever's your pleasure. The restaurant is small—eleven tables and ten booths. The decor is Southwestern with light green and tan colors dominating. Large picture windows in front keep it bright and cheerful. ~ 6840 East Camelback Road; 480-946-4902; www.originalpancakehouse. com, e-mail info@originalpancakehouse.com. BUDGET.

Voltaire is a bastion of French gastronomy, all candlelight and crystal. Chicken provençal, rack of lamb and sweetbreads sautéed in lemon butter and capers highlight the extensive menu. Dinner only. Closed Sunday in July and August. ~ 8340 East McDonald Drive; 480-948-1005. DELUXE.

 Ristorante Sandolo is an Italian café known for its singing gondoliers. The restaurant dishes out Venetian-style entrées, followed by complimentary *sandolo* (similar to gondola) rides on the waterway winding through the Hyatt Regency Scottsdale. Dinner only. ~ 7500 East Doubletree Ranch Road; 480-991-3388, fax 482-443-1278. MODERATE TO DELUXE.

Although chain restaurants are generally frowned on in the travel-writing business, **Roy's of Scottsdale** is an exception. Pacific-Rim influenced, the Asian food is tinged with a touch of the French and a bit of the Hawaiian, and always delicately and deliciously prepared. Dinner only. ~ 7001 North Scottsdale Road; 480-905-1155. DELUXE TO ULTRA-DELUXE.

House of Yang is small, only a few tables and chairs, and it appears to do a large takeout business. But whether you eat in or take out, the House of Yang is a course in Chinese cuisine, serving Szechwan, Hunan, Mandarin and Cantonese. Shrimp with lobster sauce—shrimp, onions and peppers, stir-fried and topped with a black bean sauce—comes with rice, wontons and an egg roll. Mongolian beef is thinly sliced beef served with egg roll, fried rice and wontons. ~ 13802 North Scottsdale Road; 480-443-0188. BUDGET TO MODERATE.

Greasewood Flats is a hot dog, chili and beer kind of place housed in an old graffiti-covered wooden shack in what appears to be a Western junkyard, with discarded school desks, wooden wagons, saddle frames, wagon wheels and egg crates all around

Text continued on page 230.

Spoil Yourself

The American West is big and grand—how inconsistent it would be if its great resort hotels were not just a reach beyond all expectation. And Central Arizona is home to some of the biggest and grandest around.

Inspired by Frank Lloyd Wright and designed by Albert Chase McArthur, the refurbished **Arizona Biltmore** has maintained an aura of ease and luxury since its opening in 1929. From its palm-lined drive, elaborate high portico and immense lobby to its bright, handsomely furnished guest rooms, the 730-room Biltmore is as dramatic and visually exciting as it is comfortable. The "Jewel of the Desert" provides a full range of activities: golf courses, tennis courts, pools, a children's playground, a water slide and a spa, salon and fitness center. ~ 2400 East Missouri Avenue, Phoenix; 602-955-6600, 800-950-0086, fax 602-954-2548; www.arizonabiltmore.com, e-mail azbres@arizonabiltmore.com. ULTRA-DELUXE.

Another ultra-deluxe establishment in Phoenix, to say the least, is **The Phoenician**, the most prestigious and talked-about resort in the Valley of the Sun. Sprawled over 250 acres along the sun-dappled flanks of Camelback Mountain, it's set within a tiered oasis of waterfalls and pools, the largest of which is tiled entirely with mother-of-pearl. Its 654 guest rooms are large and lavish, with most situated in the main hotel. There are also 119 *casita* units with parlor suites that have hand-carved travertine fireplaces. If you really want to make a night of it, there are 4 presidential and 71 luxury suites, and 7 villas. Recreational facilities run the gamut—a 27-hole golf course, lighted tennis courts, tournament croquet and a health and fitness spa. ~ 6000 East Camelback Road, Scottsdale; 480-941-8200, 800-888-8234, fax 480-947-4311; www.the phoenician.com, e-mail info@thephoenician.com. ULTRA-DELUXE.

The Fairmont Scottsdale Princess Resort, an ultra-luxury resort set against the dramatic backdrop of the McDowell Mountains, has 650 rooms. It's one of the Valley's largest hotels. Set on 450 elaborately landscaped acres with a central courtyard, waterfall, five swimming pools and 18th-century Spanish Colonial architecture, the Princess is one of the most visually arresting of its kind. The rooms are large, decorated in Southwestern furnishing, with a hint of Santa Fe. The grounds include seven tennis courts, a fitness center, a spa and two championship golf courses. ~ 7575 East Princess Drive, Scottsdale; 480-585-4848, 800-257-7544, fax 480-585-0086; www.fairmont.com. ULTRA-DELUXE.

With 453 rooms, **Camelback Inn, A JW Marriott Resort & Spa** outside Scottsdale is yet another glorious world-class retreat dramatically nestled in the foothills between the Camelback and Mummy mountains, where landscaped paths wind through gardens of cactus and desert palms. Its Southwestern pueblo architecture and adobe-style *casitas* blend harmoniously into the stunning desert background. For the sportsminded there are championship golf and tennis, swimming, trail rides, a spa, weekly cookouts and fitness facilities. ~ 5402 East Lincoln Drive, Paradise Valley; 480-948-1700, 800-242-2635, fax 480-951-8469; www.camelbackinn.com. ULTRA-DELUXE.

Who says the West is wild? The **Wigwam Golf Resort & Spa** west of Phoenix is an upper-upper-scale resort on 75 acres of what was originally virgin desert. The design is pueblo-style, with 331 desert-brown adobe *casitas* set in a lavish golf and country-club setting—towering palms, green lawns, cascading flowers and fragrant orange trees. Through the use of building materials native to the Southwest, architecture blends with nature. Slate, stone and wood surfaces are accented with Indian themes and desert colors. Championship golf courses, riding, tennis, swimming and other activities keep the body occupied while the mind relaxes. ~ 300 Wigwam Boulevard, Litchfield Park; 623-935-3811, 800-327-0396, fax 623-935-3737; www.wigwam resort.com. ULTRA-DELUXE.

it. But folks line up to get in. Live music Thursday through Sunday. ~ 27000 North Alma School Road; 480-585-9430; www.greasewoodflats.net. BUDGET.

The **Marquesa** is one of the top restaurants in the valley. Even people who normally avoid hotel dining rooms flock to this one in the Fairmont Scottsdale Princess to soak up all of its Old World Spanish ambience and nibble on *tapas* before settling down to more serious pursuits—Marseille bouillabaisse, for instance, or steaming Mediterranean-style paella for two. The Marquesa is also known for its excellent wine list. Dinner Wednesday through Saturday, plus Sunday brunch. ~ 7575 East Princess Drive; 480-585-4848; www.fairmont.com, e-mail scottsdale@fairmont.com. ULTRA-DELUXE.

Don't wear a necktie if you're going to the **Pinnacle Peak Patio** because they'll snip it off and hang it from the rafters. They don't joke about their "no-necktie" policy. In the last 40 years, over a million customers have lost their ties to the butcher knife. That's part of the appeal of this highly informal Western-style steakhouse where 16-ounce mesquite-broiled steaks, with all the beans and fixins, top the menu and the walls reverberate with the sounds of live country bands nightly. No lunch Monday through Saturday. ~ 10426 East Jomax Road; 480-585-1599; www.pinnaclepeakpatio.com, e-mail info@pppatio.com. MODERATE TO ULTRA-DELUXE.

SHOPPING The **Borgata of Scottsdale** may just be a harbinger of a striking new trend in shopping—mini-theme-park shopping malls—this one, a 14th-century-style village with medieval courtyards. International fashions, fine jewelry, unusual gifts and a spate of art galleries await. ~ 6166 North Scottsdale Road; 480-812-0152, fax 480-998-7581; www.westcor.com.

Despite the trendy intrusions, **Scottsdale Fashion Square** remains the city's most fashionable shopping complex. It features top-quality stores like **Neiman Marcus** (480-990-2100) and **Dillard's** (480-949-5869). There's even a shop for the kiddies—**The Disney Store** (480-994-9616). ~ 7014 East Camelback Road; 480-990-7800.

Fifth Avenue Shops comprise the landmark shopping area in the heart of downtown Scottsdale, a sprawl of specialty shops, boutiques, bookstores, galleries, jewelry stores, American Indian crafts shops and restaurants, over 200 in all by latest count. ~ 7121 East 5th Avenue; 480-946-7566. Among them is **Sewell's Indian Arts** with American Indian jewelry, kachinas, Pueblo pottery and Navajo sand paintings. ~ 7087 5th Avenue; 480-945-0962.

Mystery lovers should seek out **The Poisoned Pen**, a mystery bookstore specializing in crime, detective and suspense books from American and British publishers. ~ 4014 North Goldwater Boulevard; 480-947-2974; www.poisonedpen.com.

For you cowpokes, **Porters** is one of the oldest names in Scottsdale cowboy gear and features top-of-the-line name brands. ~ 3944 North Brown Avenue; 480-945-0868.

Arizona West Galleries specializes in Western and Indian War relics and American 19th- and 20th-century Western art, including works by Frederic Remington, Charlie Russell and Maynard Dixon. Closed Sunday. ~ 7149 East Main Street; 480-994-3752.

The **Biltmore Galleries** also has 19th- and 20th-century art, including works by early New Mexico master Nicolai Fechin, Joseph Sharp and Ernest Blumenschein. Closed Sunday. ~ 7113 East Main Street; 480-947-5975.

At **King Galleries of Scottsdale** you'll find a selection of Pueblo pottery with an emphasis on the traditional that never cancels out the innovative. Stone-polished, hand-painted and hand-fired, the pieces are some of the most gorgeous around. Closed Sunday. ~ 7171 Main Street #1; 480-481-0187, 800-394-1843; www.kinggalleries.com.

After New York City and Santa Fe, Scottsdale is the busiest art center in the country, with more than 200 galleries.

Glenn Green Galleries uses the elegant grounds of the posh Phoenician Resort (the gallery is in the hotel's retail corridor) to display the mammoth bronze and stone sculptures of famed Indian artist Allan Houser, as well as sculptors Melanie Yazzie and Eduardo Oropeza. ~ 6000 East Camelback Road; 480-990-9110; www.glenngreengalleries.com, e-mail glenngreengalleries@glenngreengalleries.com.

Simic Contemporary handles wallhangings, sculptures, oils and lithographs from top contemporary artists. Closed Sunday. ~ 7145 East Main Street; 480-946-4911; www.simic.com.

For starters, get an eyeful of the beautiful, Spanish Mediterranean–style **Bar at T. Cook's**. The walls are hand-painted, enhanced by fireplaces and antiques. Daily piano music sets the mood for drinks and conversation. There's also a well-ventilated cigar room. ~ Royal Palms Resort and Spa Inn, 5200 East Camelback Road; 602-840-3610, fax 602-808-3116.

NIGHTLIFE

The **Lobby Bar** features live music—flamenco Wednesday through Saturday and Caribbean steel drums Sunday through Tuesday. ~ Hyatt Regency Scottsdale, 7500 East Doubletree Ranch Road; 480-991-3388.

J. Chew & Company is an intimate, European-style pub with French doors leading to two outdoor patios with fireplaces. During the winter, the schedule varies so call ahead. ~ 7320 Scottsdale Mall; 480-946-2733.

Scottsdale Center for the Performing Arts, located in the beautifully sculptured Scottsdale Mall, hosts a variety of events, including guest performing artists, concerts, lectures, classic cinema and art exhibitions. During the spring, music lovers flock to the concerts held outside on the grassy lawn at the mall's east end. ~ 7380 East 2nd Street. For a schedule, call 480-994-2787; www. scottsdalearts.org, e-mail info@sccarts.org.

Tempe/Mesa Area

Immediately east of Phoenix are the communities of Tempe and Mesa. Continuing out over the desert that stretches on to New Mexico are Apache Junction and Globe. It's as though, heading east, all the big-city sheen dissolves in degrees into the West of the Old West, the pace slows down and you can almost reach up and feel the sky in your hands.

SIGHTS

Bordered by Scottsdale, Mesa, Phoenix and Chandler, **Tempe** was founded in 1872 by Charles Turnbell Hayden, who established the Hayden Flour Mill that year, now the oldest continuously operating business in Arizona. **Old Town Tempe** is where Tempe was originally founded, set up around the old Hayden Flour Mill. Today many of the early homes and buildings have been renovated and serve as restaurants, shops, offices and galleries. ~ North of University Street along Mill Avenue.

Stop by the **Tempe Convention and Visitors Bureau** for maps and information. Closed weekends. ~ 51 West 3rd Street, Suite 105; 480-894-8158, 800-283-6734, fax 480-968-8004; www. tempecvb.com, e-mail info@tempecvb.com.

Forming the character of Tempe is **Arizona State University** (480-965-9011, fax 480-965-2159; www.asu.edu, e-mail askasu@ asu.edu), located in the heart of the city. With its 450-acre main campus, where strikingly modern buildings rise from a setting of palm trees and subtropical plants, Arizona State provides the chiefly residential city with its main industry. A number of outstanding museums dot the campus and are open to the public. **Arizona State University Art Museum** has an extensive collection of American paintings, prints and crafts as well as artworks from Latin America. Closed Sunday and Monday. ~ 480-965-2787; herbergercollege.asu.edu/museum. The **Museum of Anthropology** includes archaeological, physical and sociocultural anthropology exhibits. Closed weekends. ~ 480-965-6224. Highlight exhibits at the **Museum of Geology** focus on rare geologic specimens, seismographs and mammoth bones. Closed weekends. ~ 480-965-7065.

For a trip back in time, visit the outstanding **Tempe Historical Museum**, which covers the history of Tempe from early Indian days to the present. Two changing galleries offer historic exhibits on the area. There are also hands-on displays for children. Closed Friday. ~ 809 East Southern Avenue; 480-350-5100, fax 480-350-5150; www.tempe.gov/museum.

Just east of Tempe, you'll come to the town of **Mesa**. Situated on a plateau, Mesa in Spanish means "table." The town was founded by Mormons in 1883 and was long a farming community. Irrigation canals built by the Hohokam Indians were still used in Mesa until fairly recent times. For information on sights and services in Mesa, stop by the **Mesa Convention and Visitors Bureau**. Closed weekends. ~ 120 North Center Street, Mesa; 480-827-4700, 800-283-6372, fax 480-827-4704; www.visitmesa. com, e-mail info@mesacvb.com.

Mesa Southwest Museum covers the history of the Southwest from the time of the dinosaurs to the settlement of the West, with hands-on exhibits inside. Closed Monday. Admission. ~ 53 North MacDonald Street, Mesa; 480-644-2230; www.mesasouthwest museum.com.

LODGING

Located in the heart of downtown Tempe is the **Tempe Mission Palms Hotel**, with 303 Southwestern-style rooms and a lobby that has a wonderful wooden registration desk with a granite top and intricate millwork. Nice touches in the rooms include paintings of desert palms on the walls, pastel bedspreads, bathrooms with marbleized sinks and a small makeup bureau. Most rooms overlook the lush, palm tree–dotted courtyard with fountains. Other amenities include a restaurant, a sauna, a rooftop swimming pool, whirlpool, exercise room and tennis courts. ~ 60 East 5th Street, Tempe; 480-894-1400, 800-547-8705, fax 480-968-7677; www. missionpalms.com. ULTRA-DELUXE.

The Buttes, A Marriott Resort is a dramatic 353-room, four-story resort built into the mountainsides, with Southwestern styling

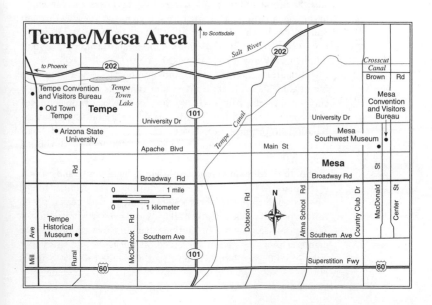

and art throughout. All guest rooms feature a Southwestern decor or rose and earth tones, cactus and wood furnishings. It has two restaurants, a nightclub, pools, tennis courts and all of the modern trim and trappings associated with luxury resort living in the valley, including cascading waterfalls and four romantic mountainside whirlpools. ~ 2000 Westcourt Way, Tempe; 602-225-9000, 888-867-7492, fax 602-438-8622. MODERATE TO ULTRA-DELUXE.

Home of the Fiesta Bowl, Arizona State University has the largest enrollment of any school in the Southwest.

Cornerstone of downtown Mesa, the **Phoenix Marriott Mesa** has 273 rooms, contemporary furnishings, a lounge, a restaurant, a swimming pool and an elegant lobby. ~ 200 North Centennial Way, Mesa; 480-898-8300, 888-236-2427, fax 480-964-9279; www.phoenixmarriottmesa.com, e-mail info@phx marriottmesa.com. ULTRA-DELUXE.

DINING

Casa Reynoso is one of the better Mexican restaurants in town, despite its modest appearance—vinyl booths and wrought iron. Try the *gollo burro* or *chiles rellenos*. Closed Monday. ~ 3138 South Mill Avenue, Tempe; 480-966-0776, fax 480-966-3005. BUDGET.

The Coffee Plantation is a Caribbean-style coffeehouse and retail store in a plantation house. There's indoor and outdoor seating where espresso, cappuccino and specialty coffees are served, along with pastries and desserts. ~ 680 South Mill Avenue, Suite 101, Tempe; 480-829-7878, fax 480-804-1494. BUDGET.

For Italian Continental cuisine, try **John Henry's**. Duck, lamb, steak, seafood and pasta are some of the favorites you can enjoy in this elegant, upscale dining room. Live music Tuesday through Sunday. No lunch. ~ 909 East Elliot Road, Tempe; 480-730-9009, fax 480-831-2487; www.johnhenrysrestaurant.com, e-mail johnhenrys1@qwest.net. MODERATE TO DELUXE.

Though the decor is plain and simple, the food is anything but at **Char's Thai Restaurant**, where an exotic touch of the East comes to Tempe with such offerings as chicken soup with coconut milk, smoked beef salad, curried duck and seafood combinations in peanut sauce. There's also a good selection of Asian beers. ~ 927 East University Drive, Tempe; 480-967-6013. BUDGET TO MODERATE.

South of Mesa in Chandler, **Rawhide Steakhouse and Saloon** is the place to belly up to the bar in an Old West frontier town. There's good things to eat, too—mesquite-grilled steaks, prime rib, barbecued chicken, baby back ribs and even fried rattlesnake. The saloon section has an antique bar and live country music nightly. Dinner nightly; lunch served on weekends and seasonally only. ~ 5700 West North Loop Road, Chandler; 480-502-5600, 800-527-1880; www.rawhide.com, e-mail info@rawhide.com. MODERATE TO DELUXE.

Historic **Old Town Tempe** exudes ambiance with its old-fashioned red-brick sidewalks and planters, tree-lined streets and quaint street lamps. Walk the area and you'll find dozens of shops and restaurants. For clothing, gifts and accessories from around the world, try **Mazar Bazaar**. ~ 520 South Mill Avenue, Suite 201, Tempe; 480-966-9090.

SHOPPING

Those Were the Days! has one of the largest selections of books on antiques and collecting in the Southwest, with more than 13,000 new titles, as well as 50,000 used, out-of-print and rare titles on antiques. As an added bonus, you can buy antiques and kitsch here as folk music constantly plays in the background. ~ 516 South Mill Avenue, Tempe; 480-967-4729; www.twtdbooks. com, e-mail askus@twtdbooks.com.

In addition to the usual mall lineup of anchor stores and chain specialty shops, **Superstition Springs Center** has a full-size carousel for the kids, a soft play area, a desert botanical walk and an amphitheater for free concerts. ~ Intersection of Power Road and the Superstition Freeway, Mesa; 480-396-2570, fax 480-830-7693.

East Side Art in Mesa offers modern paintings, posters and prints, as well as art supplies, classes and framing services. Closed Sunday, except in winter. ~ 9919 East Apache Trail, Mesa; 480-986-5450. **Mesa Contemporary Arts** features contemporary art from around the country. Closed Sunday. ~ 155 North Center Street, Mesa; 480-644-2056.

Grady Gammage Memorial Auditorium, at the Arizona State University campus in Tempe, is a 3000-seat auditorium designed by Frank Lloyd Wright. Its entertainment features range from Broadway productions to symphony orchestra concerts and ballet. Free guided tours of the center are offered on Monday. ~ Tour information: 480-965-4050. Gammage Auditorium box office: corner of Mill Avenue and Apache Street; 480-965-3434; www. asupublicevents.com.

NIGHTLIFE

Serving dinner, drinks and laughs, the **Tempe Improv** is a restaurant/comedy club that has a changing lineup of stand-up comics. No shows Monday through Wednesday. Cover. ~ 930 East University Drive, Tempe; 480-921-9877.

MCDOWELL MOUNTAIN REGIONAL PARK 🚶 🚲 🐎 This 21,099-acre wilderness expanse 15 miles northeast of Scottsdale is one of the region's most scenic parks, with an abundance of vegetation in some areas and majestic mountain views. Elevation ranges from 1550 feet at the southeast corner to 3300 feet along the western boundary. The area is ideal for camping, picnicking, horseback riding, hiking and mountain bike riding. Facilities include picnic areas, restrooms and showers. Day-use fee, $5 per vehicle. ~ Located via McDowell Mountain Road, four miles northeast of Fountain Hills; 480-471-0173, fax 480-471-3523.

PARKS

▲ There are 76 sites (all with RV hookups), first-come, first-served; $18 per night.

North of Phoenix

From cactus flowers to remote mountain lakes, here is a region rich in scenic wonders. Best known for its dude-ranch resorts, mining towns, cool forests and desert playgrounds, this recreational paradise includes the Wild West town of Wickenburg—the Dude Ranch Capital of the World—the three-million-acre Tonto National Forest and some of the Southwest's better ghost towns.

SIGHTS

Established in 1950, **Carefree** is a planned community set in the scenic foothills of the Arizona desert. To the north and east stretches the immense Tonto National Forest. Next door is the old-time town of **Cave Creek**. Once a booming mining camp in the 1880s (gold and silver), Cave Creek wasn't incorporated until a hundred years later. Sheep and cattle were raised here as well. Today Cave Creek leans heavily on its past, boasting a Frontier Town re-creation and annual spring rodeo. For more information contact **Carefree/Cave Creek Chamber of Commerce**. Closed weekends. ~ P.O. Box 734, Carefree, AZ 85377; 480-488-3381, fax 480-488-0328; www.carefree-cavecreek.com, e-mail chamber@carefree-cavecreek.com.

Cave Creek Museum offers exhibits of the desert foothills region, with a restored 1920s tuberculous cabin and a 1950s church, as well as displays of pioneer living, ranching, mining and American Indian artifacts. Closed Monday and Tuesday, and from June through September. ~ 6140 East Skyline Drive, Cave Creek; 480-488-2764, fax 480-595-0838; www.cavecreekmuseum.org, e-mail cavecreekmuseum@juno.com.

To the northwest, on Route 60-89, you will come to the site of the richest gold strike in Arizona. Named after the Austrian settler Henry Wickenburg, who discovered it, **Wickenburg** is primarily known today as a winter resort.

Frontier Street preserves Wickenburg's early-20th-century character with its old-time train depot now housing the **Wickenburg Chamber of Commerce**, and a number of vintage wood and brick buildings. One, the Hassayampa, was once the town's leading hotel. Maps for a self-guided historic walking tour are available at the chamber office. Closed Sunday in August. ~ 216 North Frontier Street, Wickenburg; 928-684-5479, 800-942-5242, fax 928-684-5470; www.wickenburgchamber.com, e-mail info@wickenburgchamber.com.

Before the town jail was built, the nearby **Jail Tree** was used to chain criminals. Friends and relatives brought them picnic lunches. Today the tree is on the property of the Chaparral Ice Cream Parlor, and tykes eat their ice cream cones there now, probably none the wiser. ~ Tegner Street and Wickenburg Way, Wickenburg.

Venture over to the **Desert Caballeros Western Museum**, which covers the history of Wickenburg and the surrounding area with major exhibits divided into various rooms. "Period" rooms include the Hall of History and a Street Scene representing Wickenburg at the turn of the 20th century. Others focus on 19th- and early-20th-century lifestyles. Its art gallery features American Indian art and Western masters of the past and present. There's a special display of cowboy gear. The Museum Park outside offers unique desert landscaping and plants. Admission. ~ 21 North Frontier Street, Wickenburg; 928-684-2272, fax 928-684-5794; www.westernmuseum.org, e-mail info@westernmuseum.org.

Robson's Mining World is an old mining town that supposedly has the world's largest collection of antique mining equipment. Along with seeing the thousands of pieces of equipment, you can stroll through a mineral and gemstone museum, a print shop, a trading post and several other buildings. There is also an ice cream parlor and a moderately priced bed and breakfast on the premises. Closed May through September. Admission. ~ Take Route 60 24 miles west of Wickenburg to Route 71, then go four miles north to Milepost 90; 928-685-2609, fax 928-685-4393; www.robsons miningworld.com.

To the northeast of Phoenix lies **Payson**, district headquarters for the Tonto National Forest. Payson provides a base camp for numerous scenic attractions within the forest primeval. Founded over a century ago as a tiny mining and ranching community, it now thrives on its recreation industry. **Payson Chamber of Com-**

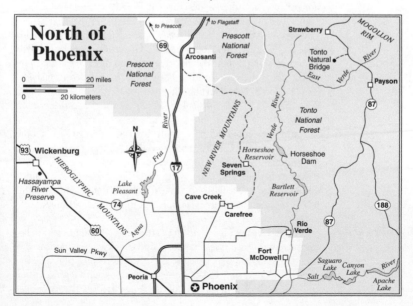

merce offers information on the area. ~ 100 West Main Street, Payson; 928-474-4515, fax 928-474-8812; www.rimcountrycham ber.com.

Prolific writer Zane Grey famously captured the West in his writings about the region. The author had a cabin in Payson, and reportedly enjoyed fishing the local lakes and finding inspiration in his environs. The **Rim Country Museum** will tell you all you want to know about him, as well as the town's history, culture, geology and everything else both fascinating and not. Closed Monday and Tuesday. Admission. ~ 700 Green Valley Parkway, Payson; 928-474-3483; www.rimcountrymuseum.org.

At the peak of the gold rush, Wickenburg had more than 80 mines, with the town growing into what was Arizona's third-largest city at the time.

A state historic monument, **Strawberry School-house** is the oldest standing schoolhouse in Arizona. Built in 1885, its last class was held in 1916. The small mountain village at 6000 feet was named for the many wild strawberries that covered the area when pioneers first arrived. Closed weekdays and October through April. ~ Village of Strawberry; e-mail pinestrawhs@yahoo.com.

LODGING

Located just northeast of Scottsdale, **The Boulders Resort and Golden Door Spa** is built directly against a stunning backdrop of 12-million-year-old granite boulder formations that soar hundreds of feet against the desert sky. Situated on 1300 acres, the resort consists of a main lodge and 160 adobe-style *casitas*, each individually designed to fit the sculptured contours of the desert and the rocks. The hotel is designed in broad architectural sweeps and makes dramatic use of American Indian and regional art and artifacts—Navajo blankets, weavings, pottery, ceramics, paintings, stone sculptures and basketry. Guest rooms feature earth-tone furnishings, hand-hewn, viga ceilings, fireplaces, wet bars, ceiling fans and oversized windows for broad desert vistas. ~ 34631 North Tom Darlington Drive, Carefree; 480-488-9009, 800-553-1717, fax 480-488-4118; www.theboulders.com. ULTRA-DELUXE.

Tumbleweed Hotel is a small downtown Cave Creek hotel made of white slumpstone brick, with 16 rooms in the main building and eight *casita*-style guest suites, all with modern Western-style furnishings and decor. The hotel has a swimming pool. ~ 6333 East Cave Creek Road, Cave Creek; 480-488-3668, fax 480-488-2936; www.tumbleweedhotel.com, e-mail tumblehotel@ aol.com. MODERATE TO DELUXE.

HIDDEN ►

Flying E Ranch is a working cattle ranch—and guest ranch—complete with trail rides, hay rides and chuckwagon cookout dinners on its 20,000-acre spread. There are 17 rooms, plus a heated pool, sauna and spa, and exercise room, along with tennis, volleyball, basketball and shuffleboard. Rates are on the American

Plan—all meals included. Closed May through October. ~ 2801 West Wickenburg Way, Wickenburg; 928-684-2690, 888-684-2650, fax 928-684-5304; www.flyingeranch.com, e-mail vacation@flyingeranch.com. ULTRA-DELUXE.

Another top-notch dude ranch in Wickenburg (this one's listed in the National Historic Register), the **Kay El Bar Ranch** has room for 24 guests in hacienda-style adobe buildings beneath huge salt cedar trees. The living room has a stone fireplace, and outside there's a heated pool for soaking after those long hours in the saddle. There is also a spa here. All meals and horseback riding are included. Closed May to mid-October. ~ Off Rincon Road, Wickenburg; 928-684-7593, 800-684-7583, fax 928-684-4497; www.kayelbar.com, e-mail info@kayelbar.com. ULTRA-DELUXE.

The 76-room **Best Western Rancho Grande Motel** offers guests a pool, whirlpool, playground and restaurant. Rooms are furnished in a contemporary Southwest motif. ~ 293 East Wickenburg Way, Wickenburg; 928-684-5445, 800-854-7235; www.bwranchogrande.com, e-mail info@bwranchogrande.com. MODERATE TO DELUXE.

Best Western Payson Inn is a handsome two-story hotel with Southwestern flavor in the midst of a European-style village of shops and restaurants. Its 99 rooms are well-kept and some have fireplaces. A spa, swimming pool and conference center are on the premises. Rates include a continental breakfast. ~ Route 87, Payson; 928-474-3241, 800-247-9477, fax 928-472-6564; www.bestwesternpaysoninn.com. MODERATE TO DELUXE.

A landmark around these parts for years, **Kohl's Ranch Lodge** sits on the banks of Tonto Creek 17 miles east of Payson. Many of the 66 rooms and cabins overlook the creek and are equipped with outdoor grills and patios. Cabins have stone fireplaces, vaulted ceilings and kitchenettes, and rustic furnishings. Amenities here include a restaurant, lounges, a pool and horseback riding. ~ 202 South Kohl's Ranch Lodge Road, Payson; 520-478-4211, 800-521-3131, fax 520-478-0353; www.ilxresorts.com. MODERATE TO DELUXE.

DINING

Crazy Ed's Satisfied Frog Restaurant and Black Mountain Brewery Beer Garden captures a bit of the Old West with wood tables, sawdust on the floor and weird things on the walls—posters and old farm tools. The house specialty is mesquite-smoked barbecue. The Frog has its own microbrewery and produces seven house brands including Ed's famous chili beer. ~ 6245 East Cave Creek Road, Cave Creek; 480-488-3317; www.satisfiedfrog.com, e-mail info@satisfiedfrog.com. MODERATE TO DELUXE.

Another amphibian-named eatery, **The Horny Toad** is a rustic, informal restaurant with wooden tables and booths, seating about 100 for lunch and dinner. Specialties include fried chicken and barbecued ribs. ~ 6738 East Cave Creek Road, Cave Creek;

480-488-9542; www.thehornytoad.com, e-mail info@thehorny toad.com. MODERATE TO DELUXE.

A Western theme dominates in the Kohl's Ranch Lodge's **Zane Grey Steakhouse**, where painted cowboys cook over a campfire on one wall and a replica of an 1884 hotel, complete with stained-glass windows, covers another wall. Beneath the glow of a wagon-wheel chandelier, diners can enjoy mounds of barbecued ribs, chicken, steaks and seafood. ~ Route 260 East, Payson; 928-478-4211, fax 928-478-0353. MODERATE TO DELUXE.

SHOPPING It's hard to miss **Ben's Saddlery & Shoe Repair**, with a life-sized horse on top of the building. The owner is a roper, and even if you're not in the market for authentic Western gear, it's fun to breathe in the heady smell of leather and saddle soap while walking down aisles stocked with spurs, saddles and boots. Closed Sunday. ~ 174 North Tegner Street, Wickenburg; 928-684-2683, fax 928-684-1328.

Antique lovers have several options in Payson, with the majority of shops off the Beeline Highway. **Payson Antiques** houses dolls, furniture and primitives by a variety of dealers. ~ 1001 South Beeline Highway, Payson; 928-474-8988.

NIGHTLIFE Cozy booths, a pool table and darts draw people to the **Zane Grey Saloon** at Kohl's Ranch Lodge, a rustic log building that has been around for years. On seasonal weekends, dance to live music. ~ Route 260 East, Payson; 928-478-4211.

PARKS **TONTO NATIONAL FOREST** 🧍🚴🐎 🛶 🎣 🏕️ 🚤 Ranging from Sonoran Desert to sprawling forests of ponderosa pine, this national forest covers nearly 2.9 million acres. The Payson and Cave Creek districts are outdoor playgrounds for area residents who can enjoy rafting and fishing on the Verde River. Bartlett and Horseshoe reservoirs serve as watersheds, wildlife habitats and recreational sites for camping, swimming, fishing and boating. **Tonto Natural Bridge State Park** is a popular attraction, as was Zane Grey's cabin until it burned down in 1990. (The Zane Grey Society has plans for its restoration.) Facilities in the national forest include picnic areas, restrooms, showers, a marina, boat rentals, snack stands, a restaurant, and hiking and riding trails. Parking fee, $6. ~ There is access to the forest via Route 87 north from Phoenix to the town of Payson, in the heart of Tonto National Forest. To reach Horseshoe and Bartlett reservoirs take the Cave Creek Road northeast from Carefree to the entrance of the forest. From here Forest Service Road 24 takes you north to Seven Springs Campground. Horseshoe Dam Road continues east seven and a half miles until it forks. Forest Service Road 19 (the right fork) takes you to Bartlett Reservoir; Forest

Service Road 265 (the left fork) takes you to Horseshoe Reservoir. Cave Creek Ranger district: 480-488-3441, fax 480-595-3346. Payson Ranger district: 928-474-7900; www.fs.fed.us/r3/tonto.

▲ The Payson district's Houston-Mesa Campground is conveniently located two miles from Payson. There are 75 tent/RV sites; $15 per night. Seven Springs Campground in the Cave Creek district is on a remote spring and has good access to hiking trails. There are 23 tent/RV sites; $6 parking fee.

HASSAYAMPA RIVER PRESERVE 🏃 A green desert oasis, this riparian area along the Hassayampa River features a cottonwood-willow forest and other vital Sonoran Desert habitats that are being protected by the nonprofit Nature Conservancy. Sit by the banks of spring-fed Palm Lake, a four-acre pond and marsh habitat, and you might spot a great blue heron or snowy egret. Birdwatchers also gather at the preserve to see the more than 280 species of birds that pass through this migration corridor. Naturalists offer guided walks (on the last Saturday of the month) along paths ranging from desert areas with cacti to lusher stretches along the river. Tours start at the visitors center; call ahead for schedule. Facilities here include restrooms and picnic areas. Closed Monday and Tuesday; closed Monday through Thursday in summer. ~ Route 60, three miles southeast of Wickenburg near Mile Marker 114; 928-684-2772, fax 623-544-6843; www.nature.org.

Ten miles north of Payson in the Tonto National Forest is Tonto Natural Bridge, the largest natural travertine bridge in the world.

Out beyond the metropolis, where the bright lights give way to American Indian archaeological sites, you'll find the homeland of the Pima and Maricopa Indians, the site of Arizona's only Civil War battlefield and cotton fields that stretch for miles. Also, mountain peaks, great fishing and, for the born-to-shop crowd, factory-outlet malls. It is an intriguing blend of old and new Arizona.

South of Phoenix

Don't miss **Rawhide Western Town** with its colorful variety of rides and attractions, shops, a steakhouse and a saloon—all mostly located along a rickety Main Street where visitors dodge authentic-looking cowboys and cowgirls on horseback. Western shootouts, fiddlers, a gypsy fortuneteller, stunt shows, a covered-wagon circle and Old West artifacts are all part of the fun. ~ 5700 West North Loop Road, Chandler; 480-502-5600, fax 480-502-1301; www.rawhide.com.

SIGHTS

Gila Indian Center in the Gila River Indian Reservation has an Indian museum (admission), gift shop and restaurant featuring authentic Indian fry bread and Southwestern food. Here, too, is **Gila Heritage Park**, featuring about half a dozen mini Indian villages. There are no tours, but it's interesting just to wander around on your own. ~ Casa Blanca Road, off Route 10 via Route 387, Exit 175; 520-315-3411, fax 520-315-3968; www.gila indiancenter.com.

Farther south is **Casa Grande**, named for the ancient Indian dwellings northeast of town. Casa Grande is known primarily for cotton-growing, industry and a name-brand factory-outlet store that has thrived there in recent years. For additional information, contact **Greater Casa Grande Chamber of Commerce**. Closed weekends mid-May to mid-September. ~ 575 North Marshall Street, Casa Grande; 520-836-2125, 800-916-1515, fax 520-836-6233; www.casagrandechamber.org, e-mail chamber@cgmailbox.com.

> Tom Mix, of cowboy-movie fame, died near Florence in a bizarre car accident: A suitcase flew off the rear shelf of his roadster, crushing his neck.

Casa Grande Ruins National Monument was built by the Hohokam Indians in the early 1300s; the village was abandoned by 1450. Four stories high, and covered by a large protective roof, the main structure is the only one of its size and kind in this area. (The monument grounds contain about 60 prehistoric sites.) The structure is easily viewed via a short path on a self-guided tour. There's a visitors center and museum where ranger talks are presented. Admission, although children under 15 free. ~ State Route 87, about 20 miles east of Casa Grande; 520-723-3172, fax 520-723-7209; www.nps.gov/cagr.

For cowboy fans, the **Tom Mix Monument** honors the silent-movie cowboy star near the spot where he died in an auto wreck in 1940. "In memory of Tom Mix whose spirit left his body on this spot and whose characterizations and portrayals in life served to better fix memories of the Old West in the minds of living men," reads the inscription. For information, call the Florence Chamber of Commerce. ~ Pinal Pioneer Parkway, 18 miles south of Florence; 520-868-9433; www.florenceaz.org, e-mail info@florenceaz.org.

LODGING
The gorgeously over-the-top **Sheraton Wild Horse Pass Resort and Spa** rises like a Las Vegas–style mirage in the Sonoran Desert. This hotel has two enormous wings with a total of 500 luxurious rooms, so be prepared for some walking. Keep your window open and you'll hear coyotes yipping at night and wild horses thundering around just beyond the 36-hole golf course. There is also a two-and-a-half-mile replica of the Gila River that meanders through the grounds, and a riverside pool that has waterfalls cascading from a replica of an ancestral Hohokam ruin. The Maricopa and Pima tribes, which together make up the Gila River Indian Community, own the resort. There are two on-site tribal museums, a Western town and a native-inspired spa. ~ 5594 West Wild Horse Pass Boulevard, Chandler; 602-225-0100, fax 602-225-0300; www.wildhorsepassresort.com, e-mail info@wild horsepassresort.com. DELUXE TO ULTRA-DELUXE.

Francisco Grande Resort and Golf Club is where it's all at in Casa Grande. Originally built by the former owner of the San Francisco Giants, Horace Stoneham, the place has a distinctive baseball theme. The hotel's tower building contains most of its 106 rooms, while other motel-type rooms are located around the courtyard. Furnishings are Southwestern-style throughout, including paintings of cowboys and Western landscapes on the walls. The hotel has a restaurant, lounge (with seasonal entertainment), a swimming pool and wading pool (in the shape of a baseball bat and ball) and golf. ~ 26000 Gila Bend Highway, Casa Grande; 520-836-6444, 800-237-4238, fax 520-381-8222; www.franciscogrande.com. MODERATE TO DELUXE.

Holiday Inn in Casa Grande, a four-story, Spanish-style stucco building, has 176 rooms in contemporary style, an outdoor pool and spa, restaurant and lounge. ~ 777 North Pinal Avenue, Casa Grande; 520-426-3500, 800-858-4499, fax 520-836-4728. MODERATE.

Beautifully set in a 1930s adobe guest ranch surrounded by saguaro cacti, the **Inn at Rancho Sonora** offers six rooms with private baths and entrances plus three fully equipped cottages. Stroll through the enclosed brick courtyard, where a fountain spurts merrily, or take a dip in the outdoor pool and waterfall spa. Continental breakfast included. ~ 9198 North Route 79, Florence; phone/fax 520-868-8000, 800-205-6817; www.ranchosonora.com, e-mail rancho@c2i2.com. MODERATE TO DELUXE.

Located in Chandler's Sheraton Wild Horse Pass Resort on the Gila River Indian Reservation is **Kai** ("seed"), one of the finest restaurants in the south Phoenix area. Executive chef Michael O'Dowd, native chef of cuisine Jack Strong and James Beard–winning consulting chef Janos Wilder are the talents behind the New Western food here, which is about as local as you can get. The menu showcases Gila Reservation–raised produce, shrimp, wild desert foods and seeds, and wild salmon, bison and venison sourced from other Indian reservations. A sunset meal on the balcony facing the Estrella Mountains is about as good as it gets! ~ 5594 West Wild Horse Pass Boulevard, Chandler; 602-225-0100; www.wildhorsepassresort.com, e-mail info@wildhorsepassresort.com. ULTRA-DELUXE.

DINING

Gila River Arts and Crafts Restaurant features Indian fry bread along with burritos, tacos, hamburgers, homemade pies and coffee. No dinner. ~ Gila River Indian Reservation; 520-315-3411. BUDGET.

Mi Amigo Ricardo offers up hot and spicy Mexican specialties —chimichangas, enchiladas, *frijoles*, tamales, *flautas* and *posole*— with beer and wine to soothe the flames. The decor is Mexican, of course, and quite attractive. ~ 821 East Florence Boulevard, Casa Grande; 520-836-3858. BUDGET.

Bedillon's is a restaurant and museum in two separate historic buildings. The museum features Indian artifacts and Western memorabilia. There is also a cactus garden dating from 1917. The menu offers a full range of Southwestern/American cuisine. No lunch on Saturday. Closed Sunday and Monday. ~ 800 North Park Avenue, Casa Grande; 520-836-2045, fax 520-836-6030. MODERATE TO DELUXE.

A small, downtown Casa Grande bakery and café, the **Cook E Jar** serves up breakfast and lunch, as well as take-out bakery goods (even wedding cakes) and sandwiches. Closed Sunday. ~ 100 West 2nd Street, Casa Grande; 520-836-9294. BUDGET.

SHOPPING   **Gila Indian Center** has a shop selling traditional American Indian crafts, silver and turquoise jewelry, sand paintings, kachinas and baskets. ~ Gila River Indian Reservation; 520-315-3411.

Casa Grande, the main town along Route 10 between Phoenix and Tucson, is the site of about 30 factory-owned **outlet stores** in Arizona, mainly located in a sprawling commercial mall off Route 10 (take Exit 198). More than a million shoppers a year come to Casa Grande seeking bargains from such major firms as **Liz Claiborne, Samsonite, Levi's, The Gap** and **Reebok**. For information, call the Outlet at Casa Grande at 520-836-9663, fax 520-836-9580; www.outletsatcasagrande.com.

▼▼▼▼▼▼▼▼▼▼▼▼▼
Outdoor Adventures

Arizona's climate is ideal for recreational pursuits—most of the time. But in the summer, dry heat can be deceiving and you may think it's cooler than it actually is. Keep summer exertion to a minimum and play indoors, where there's air conditioning, if you can.

RIVER RUNNING   Three main rivers in south central Arizona—the Verde, the Salt and the Gila, all east of Phoenix—offer a wealth of recreational activities year-round. A number of companies provide a variety of rafting and tubing expeditions, with pickups, meals and guides included.

SCOTTSDALE   **Cimarron River Co.** has guided two-hour scenic float trips for groups of ten or more on the lower Salt River. The gentle trips, which involve no whitewater, glide through Sonoran Desert landscapes with towering cliffs and stately saguaros. ~ 7902 East Pierce Street; 480-994-1199, fax 480-990-0205. **Desert Voyagers Guided Rafting Tours** offers a variety of half-day trips on the Verde and Salt rivers. ~ P.O. Box 9053, Scottsdale, AZ 85252; 480-998-7238; www.desertvoyagers.com.

TEMPE/MESA AREA   In Mesa, **Salt River Tubing & Recreation** rents large inner tubes and operates a shuttle to carry you up the Salt River so you can tube back down through easy whitewater. They also rent ice chests made especially for tubes, so you can float and picnic. Closed October to May. ~ 1320 North Bush Highway; 480-984-3305; www.saltrivertubing.com.

The Valley's extensive network of canals provides ideal, often shaded tracks.

JOGGING

PHOENIX If you want to jog during the hot summers stick to cooler early-morning hours. Phoenix's **Encanto Park**, three miles north of the Civic Plaza, is an excellent jogging trail.

SCOTTSDALE **Indian Bend Wash Greenbelt** is a dream trail for joggers. It runs north and south for the entire length of Scottsdale, including 13 winding miles of jogging and bike paths within the Greenbelt's scenic system of parks, lakes and golf courses.

Swimming pools are plentiful and popular in south central Arizona; you shouldn't have a problem finding a place for a dip.

SWIMMING

PHOENIX Many public pools are available, about 30 in Phoenix alone. For starters, there's **Cactus Pool**. ~ 3801 West Cactus Road; 602-262-6680. You can also dive into **Grant Pool**.
~ 714 South 2nd Avenue; 602-261-8728. Make a splash at **Starlight Pool**. ~ 7810 West Osborn Road; 602-495-2412. **Washington Pool** will also cool you down. ~ 6655 North 23rd Avenue; 602-262-7198. For additional information and listings, call 602-534-7946. The pools are open only during the summer.

> There are so many swimming pools in south central Arizona, that gathering rain clouds, so it's said, are often colored green from all the chlorine.

    Telephone Pioneer Pool is exclusively for people with disabilities, their families and friends. Closed Friday and Sunday and in December and January. ~ 1946 West Morningside Drive; 602-495-2404.

    The Adobe Dam Recreation Area is home to **Water World Safari** (623-581-1947; www.golfland.com), which features a wave pool, waterslides and a 1100-foot-long Zambezi River complete with little rapids. Open Memorial Day through Labor Day. Admission. ~ Recreation area: Northwest of Adobe Dam, on Pinnacle Peak Road and North 43rd Avenue, Phoenix; 602-506-2930.

TEMPE/MESA AREA In Tempe, **Big Surf Waterpark** includes, among other watercentric attractions, a 300-foot surf slide and raft-riding in a gigantic, mechanically activated fresh-water pool. Open Memorial Day through Labor Day. Admission. ~ 1500 North McClintock Road; 480-947-7873, fax 480-423-9737; www.golfland.com.

For ballooning enthusiasts, the surrounding mountains provide the perfect setting to let it all hang out. Dozens of firms will be happy to take you up, up and away.

BALLOON RIDES & HANG GLIDING

PHOENIX **Hot Air Expeditions** has year-round sunrise and candlelit sunset flights from November through March. ~ 2243 East Rose Garden Loop; 602-788-5555.

For hang gliding, contact the **Sky Masters School of Hang Gliding** for aero-tours and tandem instruction. They also provide equipment rentals, sales and service. ~ Grand Valley Airport; 602-867-6770.

SCOTTSDALE   View desert wildlife and vegetation as you drift through the sky with **Adventures Out West** and **Unicorn Balloon Co.** Sunrise and sunset excursions conclude with champagne and treats. Summer only. ~ P.O. Box 12009-266, Scottsdale, AZ 85267; 800-755-0935.

RIDING STABLES

Dozens of stables, dude ranches and equestrian outfitters are available for saddling up and heading off into desert wilderness for a few hours or a few days under the supervision of a crusty trail boss. If ever there was a place for horsing around, this is it.

SCOTTSDALE   **MacDonald's Ranch** takes riders through their 1300 acres of high desert terrain. ~ 26540 North Scottsdale Road; 480-585-0239.

TEMPE/MESA AREA   **Papago Riding Stables** offers one- and two-hour wrangler-guided trips into the desert foothills of Papago Park, where knolls afford spectacular views of the greater Phoenix area. ~ 400 North Scottsdale Road, Tempe; 480-966-9793.

GOLF

More than half of Arizona's 205 golf courses are located in south central Arizona, making Phoenix and environs the undisputed Golf Capital of the Southwest. Some of the country's finest courses can be found among its resorts, parks and country clubs. Cart and club rentals are generally available.

PHOENIX   One of the most spectacular is the **Wigwam Golf Resort & Spa** in Litchfield Park just west of Phoenix. The club has three separate 18-hole courses with mature landscaping. ~ 451 Old Litchfield Road; 623-935-9414; www.wigwamresort.com.

AUTHOR FAVORITE

Even with my heart in my throat and my stomach somewhere in the region of the floor, I loved floating in a balloon above the desert north of Scottsdale. The **Unicorn Balloon Co.** will take you on flights that ascend to heights of 3000 feet and, at other times, glide just above the treetops to spot deer, javalinas, coyotes and other desert wildlife. The trip finishes with a champagne award ceremony in which passengers receive their "First Flight Certificate." ~ P.O. Box 12009-266, Scottsdale, AZ 85267; 480-991-3666, 800-755-0935; www.unicornballoon.com, e-mail support@unicornballoon.com.

Among Phoenix's top public links is **Encanto Golf Course**, an 18-hole course with club rentals and a golf pro in residence. ~ 2775 North 15th Avenue; 602-253-3963. The 18-hole public **Papago Golf Course** has shade trees and challenging water hazards. There is a pro shop. ~ 5595 East Moreland Street; 602-275-8428. The nine-hole **Palo Verde Golf Course** is a third public course in Phoenix. ~ 6215 North 15th Avenue; 602-249-9930.

SCOTTSDALE Top public courses include the 18-hole **Continental Golf Course**. ~ 7920 East Osborn Road; 480-941-1585. Also open for duffers is the nine-hole public **Coronado Golf Course**, which has a driving range. Eight teaching pros are available. ~ 2829 North Miller Road; 480-947-8364. The **Tournament Players Club of Scottsdale** welcomes the public to its greens. The 18-hole stadium course, built specifically to host the PGA Tour FBR Open, features a unique island green. The club also has two 18-hole desert courses. A pro is available for lessons. ~ 17020 North Hayden Road; 480-585-3600, fax 480-585-3151.

TEMPE/MESA AREA The nine-hole **Pepperwood Golf Course** in Tempe has a golf pro available for lessons. ~ 647 West Baseline Road; 480-831-9457. Or you can bring your clubs to the **Tempe Rolling Hills Golf Course**, where you'll find an 18-hole course in the hilly terrain of the Papago Buttes; there are cart and club rentals, as well as a pro shop, a bar and a restaurant. ~ 1415 North Mill Avenue; 480-350-5275. A "hidden" golfers' option, the **Karsten Golf Course** on the campus of Arizona State University is open to the public. Designed by Pete Dye, the 18-hole championship course has some of the most challenging water hazards and mounds anywhere. It hosts several major tournaments each year. ~ 1125 East Rio Salado Parkway; 480-921-8070.

Almost all of the parks in the valley's vast network have a tennis court; for information, call the **Parks and Recreation Department**. ~ Phoenix: 602-262-6862; Scottsdale: 480-312-2722.

TENNIS

PHOENIX The **Phoenix Tennis Center** is a large facility with 22 lighted public courts. A fee is charged and tennis pros are available. ~ 6330 North 21st Avenue; 602-249-3712. The **Mountain View Tennis Center** is also in the Phoenix area, with 11 lighted public courts. Closed Saturday and Sunday. Fee. ~ 1104 East Grovers Avenue; 602-534-2500.

SCOTTSDALE The city of Scottsdale has no fewer than 40 public courts. Most are hard-surfaced and lighted for evening play. Look for them at **Indian School Park**, where there are 13 courts. ~ 4289 North Hayden Road; 480-312-2740. Or try **Chestnut Park**, 2 courts. ~ 4565 North Granite Reef Road; 480-312-2771. **Mountain View Park**, two courts, is another option. ~ 8625 East Mountain View; 480-312-2584.

TEMPE/MESA AREA Outstanding is the City of Tempe's **Kiwanis Park Recreation Center**. There are 15 "cushioned"-surface, lighted courts available by reservation. ~ 6111 South All-American Way; 480-350-5201.

BIKING

Biking is popular as both recreation and transportation in the valley and outlying areas.

PHOENIX A basic bikeway system was set up for Phoenix in 1987, and since then more than 100 miles of paths have been added. Unfortunately, there's a lot of traffic, so be careful. *The Bikeways Map*, which shows the Phoenix Bikeway System, is available for free at most bike shops, or call the Maricopa Association of Government. ~ 602-254-6300. For special-event biking activities, check out the **Greater Arizona Bicycle Association**. ~ www.bikegaba.org. Phoenix's **South Mountain Park** (10919 South Central Avenue), **Cave Creek** and **Carefree**, located 30 miles northeast of town, offer great biking conditions. Also popular is **Papago Loop Bicycle Path**, which wends through the rolling hills that border the canal edging Papago Park.

SCOTTSDALE Scottsdale's **Indian Bend Wash Greenbelt** has miles of excellent bike paths.

Bike Rentals Need to rent a bike or get one repaired? Try **Try Me Bicycle Shop** for both mountain bikes and road-touring bikes. Closed Sunday. ~ 1514 West Hatcher Road, Phoenix; 602-943-1785. **Arizona Outback Adventures** has just the bike for you, whether you're looking to rent a mountain bike, road bike, hybrid or children's tandem. Repairs are available. ~ 16447 North 91st Street, Suite 101, Scottsdale; 480-945-2881. **Tempe Bicycle Shop** has a variety of bikes to rent. Repairs are also available. ~ 330 West University Drive, Tempe; 480-966-6896.

HIKING

With all that elbow room and knockout scenery, south central Arizona is a hiker's paradise. Visitors, in fact, have been known to park their cars on the highway and impulsively hike up the side of a mountain. *Note:* Be sure to take water with you, and allow plenty of time to get there and back. All distances listed for hiking trails are one way unless otherwise noted.

PHOENIX AREA One of the best park trails in Phoenix's South Mountain Park is the **Mormon Loop/Hidden Valley Loop National Trail** (6 miles) that begins at the Pima Canyon parking lot near 48th Street and Guadalupe Road and ends at the Buena Vista parking area. At the parking lot, a dirt road rambles for a quarter mile to the trailhead where you'll find a sign for Hidden Valley. The trail passes stands of saguaro, but the highlights are The Tunnel—a naturally formed rock tunnel, 50 to 60 feet long, that leads into Hidden Valley—and Fat Man's Pass, a tight squeeze between huge boulders where it is cool year-round. Here children can take turns on Slide Rock, a large, naturally polished, sleek boulder that's as smooth as a playground slide.

The **Phoenix Mountain Preserve** has 50 miles of trails and almost pristine areas virtually in the center of Phoenix. It stretches from Lincoln Drive in Paradise Valley north to Greenway Boulevard, bordered on the west by 19th Avenue and on the east by Tatum Boulevard.

Its most popular trail is the **Piestewa Peak Summit Trail** (1.2 miles) that wraps its way up Piestewa Peak, offering good lookout points along the way, and from its 2608-foot summit, a dramatic view of the city. (The only drawback is the number of fellow hikers you'll meet along the way.)

Camelback Mountain is the valley's best known landmark, and serious hikers truly haven't hiked Arizona until they've conquered it. Part of the Echo Canyon Recreation Area (off McDonald Drive east of Tatum Boulevard; 602-262-4599), Camelback offers sheer red cliffs that in some places rise 200 feet straight up its side. An interpretive ramada near the parking area offers information about the various trails.

Arizona's broad central band stretches across the state in what visiting English author J. B. Priestley once described as "geology by day and astronomy by night."

A relatively easy climb (.8 mile) goes from the ramada to Bobby's Rock, a landmark formation of rocks set aside from the cliff and perfect for rock climbers.

Also beginning at the ramada, the **Camelback Mountain Trail** (1.2 miles) is steep and very rocky, becoming progressively difficult the higher you climb, with a 1300-foot gain in elevation. The view from the top of Camelback Mountain, 2704 feet above sea level, is spectacular, but expect a crowd on weekends.

NORTH OF PHOENIX   A favorite at North Mountain Recreation Area is the **North Mountain National Trail** (1.6 miles), just off 7th Street north of Peoria. The moderate to difficult paved trail climbs from 1490 feet to 2104 feet with scenic views along the way. It ends at the AK-CHIN picnic area.

The historic, 51-mile-long **Highline Trail** in the Tonto National Forest was established in the late 1800s to link various homesteads and ranches under the Mogollon Rim. In 1979, it was designated a National Recreation Trail. With 23 trailheads and spur trails, hikers can explore it in segments and loops. But a word of caution—most of the trails from the highline to the top of the rim are steep, rocky and rugged.

The main trail begins at the Pine Trailhead 15 miles north of Payson off Route 87 and ends at Two-Sixty Trailhead on Route 260. Shorter jaunts include **East Webber Trail** (3 miles), a difficult, little-used stretch that follows Webber Creek before ending at a spring. The most popular is **Horton Creek Trail** (4 miles), which starts at the Upper Tonto Creek Campground.

For the *Highline Trails Guide*, contact the Payson Ranger Station. ~ 1009 East Route 260; 928-474-7900, fax 928-474-7966.

▼▼▼▼▼▼▼▼▼▼▼▼

Transportation

CAR

Visitors driving to Phoenix by car are in for a treat. Arizona's highways are among the best in the country, gas is traditionally cheaper and the scenery in any direction is spectacular—lofty saguaros, magnificent mountains, a cowboy here, a pickup truck there, beer signs blinking faintly in the purple glow of evening. Along the way, small Western towns unfold like storybook pop-ups. **Route 10** traverses the city from the east (El Paso) and west (Los Angeles). From the northwest, **Route 40**, once the legendary Route 66, enters Arizona near Kingman; **Route 93** continues on from there to Phoenix. **Route 17** brings you to Phoenix from the Preston or Flagstaff area.

AIR

Sky Harbor International Airport (602-273-3300; www.phxsky harbor.com) is located four miles from downtown Phoenix and is served by Aeromexico, Alaska Airlines, America West Airlines, American Airlines, American Trans Air, British Airways, Continental Airlines, Delta Airlines, Frontier, Great Lakes Airlines, Hawaiian Airlines, JetBlue Airways, Midwest Sun Country Airlines, Northwest Airlines, Southwest Airlines, United Airlines, US Airways and West Jet.

A variety of ground transportation options are available from Sky Harbor International Airport. **SuperShuttle** offers airport-to-door service 24 hours a day. ~ 602-244-9000, 800-258-3826. **Courier Transportation** also provides transportation to the airport. ~ 602-232-2222. **Arizona Shuttle Service** has service to and from Tucson and Phoenix. ~ 520-795-6771, 800-888-2749; www.arizonashuttle.com.

BUS

Greyhound Bus Lines has service to Phoenix from all around the country. Other stations are found in Mesa and Tempe. ~ 800-229-9424; www.greyhound.com. Phoenix: 2115 East Buckeye Road; 602-389-4200. Mesa: 1423 South Country Club Drive; 480-834-3360. There's a pick-up stop in Tempe at 6th Street and College Avenue.

CAR RENTALS

Rental companies with counters at the airport include **Advantage Rent A Car** (800-777-5500), **Alamo Rent A Car** (800-327-9633), **Avis Rent A Car** (800-831-2847), **Budget Rent A Car** (800-527-0700), **Dollar Rent A Car** (800-800-4000), **E-Z Rent A Car** (800-277-5171), **Fox Rent A Car** (800-225-4369), **Hertz Rent A Car** (800-654-3131), **National Car Rental** (800-227-7368) and **Payless Car Rental** (800-729-5377). Agencies with pick-up service are **Enterprise Leasing and Rent A Car** (800-736-8222) and **Thrifty Car Rental** (800-847-4389).

Valley Metro covers Phoenix and Scottsdale and provides express service to and from other districts within the Valley. It also serves the Phoenix airport. Express buses access Phoenix from Mesa, Tempe and other suburbs. ~ 602-253-5000; www.valleymetro. org. **Ollie the Trolley** offers a free rubber-tire trolley shuttle within the downtown shopping area year-round. ~ 480-970-8130. **Downtown Dash** serves the downtown Phoenix area with free shuttles that depart every six to twelve minutes and loop the downtown area between the ball park, Amercia West Arena, Dodge Theatre, the Arizona Center and Collier Center. ~ 602-262-7242; www.coppersquare.com.

PUBLIC TRANSIT

Taxis are expensive in Phoenix since the city sprawls out in all directions. Going from Point A to Point B, at times, may seem like you're crossing the entire state. Some of the major companies in south central Arizona are **Courier Cab** (602-232-2222), **Discount Cab** (602-266-1110) and **Yellow Cab** (602-252-5252).

TAXIS

SEVEN

Eastern Arizona

Perhaps no other region of the state is as geographically diverse as eastern Arizona. The seemingly endless urban sprawl of Phoenix, Tempe and Mesa quickly gives way to breathtaking scenery in the form of desert gardens, jagged river canyons, rolling grasslands and deep pine forests. Venture here and you will find a wide variety of recreational opportunities, everything from fishing and hunting to hiking and skiing. There's also plenty of history—prehistoric Indian ruins and old mining towns—to be discovered along the way.

The strip of eastern Arizona stretching 203 miles east of Phoenix along Routes 89, 60 and 70 to the New Mexico state line is known as the Old West Highway. Rich in frontier history, it travels a route of the notorious—from Coronado to Geronimo to Billy the Kid.

Anchored on the west by Apache Junction, a growing suburb of the Phoenix metropolitan area and a winter retreat for thousands of snowbirds, the Old West Highway is also the starting point for a scenic detour along the Apache Trail (Route 88). Today's adventurers can wend their way along the trail through the Superstition Mountains, to the reconstructed Goldfield Ghost Town, a series of lakes originating from the Salt River, colorful Tortilla Flat, the Lost Dutchman's Mine and finally Theodore Roosevelt Dam and Lake.

Continue east on the Old West Highway and you'll come to Globe, a quiet town that retains the flavor of the late 1800s. The Old West Highway flattens out east of Globe, and the countryside becomes more arid as you descend into the lower desert. The Mescal Mountains to the south escort you into the Gila River Valley, where the mesas and buttes of the San Carlos Apache Indian Reservation stand out against the sky.

Route 70 branches off Route 60 east of Globe and crosses the southern tip of the 1.8 million-acre San Carlos Apache Indian Reservation, which stretches from the White Mountains to within two miles of Globe, north to the Mogollon Rim and south to Coronado National Forest. An estimated 12,000 Apache live on the reservation, much of it wooded forests that are home to elk, mule deer, wild turkeys, black bear and mountain lions.

On the southern horizon stands Mount Graham, at 10,720 feet one of Arizona's highest peaks. In addition to being a popular fishing, camping and hiking area, the mountain is the site of the Mount Graham International Observatory.

Route 70 continues on to the town of Safford, an important trade center for the Gila River Valley's numerous cotton farmers. From Safford, the Old West Highway cuts through the pastoral Duncan Valley, with its green alfalfa fields, grazing horses and trickling creeks at the eastern edge of Arizona. Duncan, the birthplace of Supreme Court Justice Sandra Day O'Connor, is a fertile source of fire agate, a relatively rare semiprecious stone, which can be picked up right off the ground in designated Bureau of Land Management areas.

North of Duncan on Route 191 is the historic mining town of Clifton, the southern anchor of the Coronado Trail, which climbs through the Apache-Sitgreaves National Forest on its 105-mile journey to Alpine, in the heart of Arizona's Alps.

The Coronado Trail, named for the Spanish explorer who sought the Seven Cities of Gold nearly 500 years ago, practically brushes the Arizona–New Mexico border. The trail runs north–south as Route 191 from St. Johns to Clifton via a winding and twisting paved highway, cutting through rugged mountains and magnificent forests—some of the Southwest's most spectacular scenery.

The White Mountains offer high, cool country dotted with fishing lakes and blanketed in ponderosa pine, spruce, aspen and Douglas fir. At the heart of this area are Pinetop–Lakeside, Show Low and Greer. The main reason folks venture to this part of eastern Arizona is to enjoy the outdoors, whether by fishing, skiing, hiking or simply sitting on a rock with a picnic lunch, breathing in the scent of pine and watching the breeze ripple across a lake. These towns all abound with rustic lodges, inexpensive eateries and plenty of scenic beauty.

Apache Junction Area

At the meeting point of Routes 60, 88 and 89, Apache Junction is in an area of rough lowlands about 30 miles east of Phoenix. Once a sunburned babble of bars, motels and filling stations, it has blossomed into a rustic bedroom community for the Valley of the Sun and a popular snowbird retreat that attracts about 55,000 people each winter, causing local dude ranch operators to complain that there's no range left to ride. A metal impression in the center of the town honors the man believed to have discovered the elusive Lost Dutchman Gold Mine, who died with the secret of its location unspoken. Apache Junction is also the starting point for the 48-mile Apache Trail, Route 88, which slices its way through the Superstition Mountains.

SIGHTS

Apache Junction was unofficially founded in 1922, when a traveling salesman named George Cleveland Curtis put up a tent and sold sandwiches and water to travelers along the highway. A year later he filed a homestead claim and built the Apache Junction Inn.

Others soon followed and by 1950 there were enough residents to form a town. They chose the name Superstition City, but because it was a historical site, the Apache Junction name could not be changed.

Learn about the area's history and sights at the **Apache Junction Chamber of Commerce**, which dispenses maps and brochures. They also operate as a visitors booth, an excellent resource for local information. ~ 567 West Apache Trail, Apache Junction; 480-982-3141, 800-252-3141, fax 480-982-3234; www.apache junctioncoc.com, e-mail info@apachejunctioncoc.com.

For a taste of the Old West, stop at **Goldfield Ghost Town**, which saw its heyday in the 1890s when gold was discovered at the base of the Superstitions. The weathered-wood buildings that house a restaurant, museum and antique shops look original, but they are actually re-creations, constructed in 1988. The old mining and railroad equipment scattered about are authentic, as are the museum's geology and mining exhibits and the underground mine, which you can tour. Other activities available are jeep tours, carriage rides and gold panning. ~ Route 88, four miles north of Apache Junction; 480-983-0333, fax 480-834-7947; www.gold fieldghosttown.com.

Canyon Lake wends its way ten and a half miles upstream through one continuous deep canyon. There are boat facilities, beaches, picnic sites, a snack bar and campsites. Recreational activities include fishing (bass and walleye) and waterskiing. There's also a replica of a double-deck sternwheeler that plies the waters with its cargo of tourists and photographers. ~ Canyon Lake Marina, Route 88; 480-288-9233, www.canyonlakemarina.com, e-mail info@canyonlakemarina.com.

The **Theodore Roosevelt Dam**, completed in 1911 and constructed entirely of quarry stone, is the world's tallest masonry dam. A recent concrete addition, covering the original construction, raised the dam's height to 357 feet. A quarter mile upstream from the dam, a 1000-foot steel arch bridge spans a portion of the reservoir, Roosevelt Lake. ~ Route 88, 45 miles east of Apache Junction (note: half this distance is unpaved).

The **Tonto National Monument** contains the remains of the apartment-style dwellings of the Salado people and is one of the state's better-preserved prehistoric archaeological sites. At the visitors center, you can see Salado crafts and tools and an audio-visual program. A highlight of the park itself is a paved but steep, half-mile self-guiding trail that climbs 350 feet up to the 19-room **Lower Cliff Dwelling**. The 40-room **Upper Cliff Dwelling** is open for tours from November through April (reservations are required). Admission. ~ Route 188, Roosevelt; 928-467-2241.

Back on Route 60, about 25 miles east of Apache Junction near the mining camp of Superior, is the **Boyce Thompson Ar-**

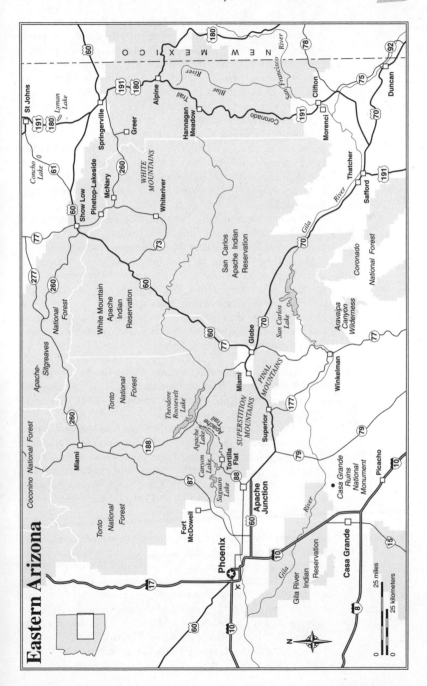

Eastern Arizona

boretum. This Eden-like preserve boasts over 2000 specimens, including cacti, succulents and water-efficient trees and shrubs. Home to over 200 kinds of birds and 40 wildlife species, the arboretum has walking trails that wind through 320 acres of outdoor displays and historic buildings. One long-time resident here, a red gum eucalyptus that rises more than 150 feet and boasts a trunk eight feet in diameter, was planted in 1929 as a six-foot sapling. The interpretive center is located in a 1920s cut-stone house listed on the National Register of Historical Places. In addition, a gift store sells books, cacti and various succulents. The **Clevenger House**, a stone cabin built into a hillside surrounded by an herb garden, is also of interest. Admission. ~ 37615 Route 60; 520-689-2811, fax 520-689-5858; ag.arizona.edu/bta, e-mail btainfo@ag. arizona.edu.

Heading east from the arboretum, Route 60 gradually climbs through Gonzales Pass until the desert gives way to the Tonto National Forest. The two-lane highway cautiously winds through enchanting **Devils Canyon**, an eerie though picturesque region that seems to change its mood as the day's sunlight progresses. Near sundown, when the shadows grow long, the granite rock formations take on the shape of giant trolls and gnomes, and appear to be crouching, as if to pounce on passing motorists. The canyon and highway are narrow, but there are ample pullouts to photograph or simply enjoy the scenery.

LODGING

The small, family-run **Palm Springs Motel** has 12 clean, well-maintained rooms with refrigerators, some with kitchenettes. ~ 950 South Royal Palm Road, Apache Junction; 480-982-7055; e-mail azplmsprmotel@msn.com. BUDGET.

In the Superstition foothills, the **Gold Canyon Golf Resort** features casita-style guest rooms with dark-wood furniture, stone fireplaces, private patios and impressive views of the nearby mountain. Some boast spa tubs. There's also a seasonally heated pool. ~ 6100 South Kings Ranch Road, Gold Canyon; 480-982-9090, 800-624-6445, fax 480-830-5211; www.gcgr.com, e-mail stay@gcgr.com. ULTRA-DELUXE.

DINING

Lake Shore Restaurant is a rustic, casual dining facility on Saguaro Lake with a deck where you can enjoy lunch with a lake view. Shaded by a giant awning, this outdoor eatery is cooled by a mist system and ceiling fans or warmed by outdoor heaters, depending on the season. Start with a strawberry daiquiri and then order from the menu featuring burgers, salads, sandwiches and fried fish (all you can eat on Wednesday and Friday). No dinner on Monday and Tuesday. ~ 14011 North Bush Highway, Tonto National Forest; 480-984-5311, fax 480-986-1210; www.saguarolake.net. BUDGET TO MODERATE.

Down Apache Junction way, **Mining Camp Restaurant and Trading Post** is almost as famous as the Lost Dutchman Gold Mine—and it's easier to find. The long wooden tables, planked floors, tin trays and cups, and family-style, all-you-can-eat dining—chicken, ham and barbecued ribs—make it worth looking for. No lunch Monday through Saturday. Closed Monday through Thursday from June through September. ~ Route 88, Apache Junction; 480-982-3181, fax 480-982-5428; www.miningcamp restaurant.com, e-mail miningcamp@hotmail.com. DELUXE.

There's no shortage of charm at **Tortilla Flat Restaurant**, whose weathered-wood exterior suggests a Wild West saloon. Inside, the natural-wood walls are covered with mining and cowboy artifacts, as well as business cards and currency from around the world. Home-cooked specials include oversized burgers, spicy hot chili and a full Mexican menu. In the saloon section, you can belly up to the solid-wood bar, plant yourself on a barstool topped with a leather saddle and pretend you're in Dodge City. The Judds on the Wurlitzer jukebox will bring you back to reality. Breakfast, lunch and dinner are served. ~ Route 88, 18 miles northeast of Apache Junction; 480-984-1776; www.tortillaflataz.com. BUDGET TO MODERATE.

SHOPPING

If you plan to go looking for the Lost Dutchman Gold Mine, or even if you don't, **Pro Mack South** sells mining equipment, gold pans, lanterns, picks, rope, boots, supplies and just about everything else but the treasure map. Closed Sunday. ~ 1000 West Apache Trail #106, Apache Junction; 480-983-7011, fax 480-983-6765; www.promackminingsupsouth.com, e-mail promack@quik.com.

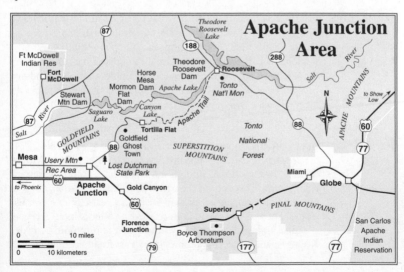

Apache Trail

The **Apache Trail** (Route 88) follows the route originally used by Apache Indians as a shortcut through the Superstition Mountains. It runs about 56 miles one-way from Apache Junction to Theodore Roosevelt Lake, with about 20 unpaved miles above Tortilla Flat. En route are pull-offs for hiking, picnicking or just plain staring at the beautiful scenery.

SUPERSTITION MOUNTAINS   Once past the outskirts of Apache Junction, the road enters the dacite cones of the Superstition Mountains, formed 20 million years ago when cataclysmic earthquakes and widespread volcanic eruptions pushed land masses thousands of feet into the air and left a depression 20 miles wide. Magma from below the earth's surface flowed in and the mountains resulted. The triangular-shaped peak east of the Superstitions is Weaver's Needle, which treasure hunters say is a landmark for the Lost Dutchman Mine.

CANYON LAKE   Continuing north, you'll find a chain of lakes originating out of the Salt River. They include Saguaro, Canyon and Apache lakes. The most accessible is Canyon Lake (page 254). As you proceed upstream, you'll pass geodes embedded in sheer rock walls, deposited by eruptions millions of years ago, on your way to **Tortilla Flat**, which

NIGHTLIFE   From Christmas to Easter, **Tortilla Flat Restaurant** features live bluegrass and country music on an outdoor barbeque patio. ~ Route 88, 18 miles north of Apache Junction; 480-984-1776.

Join the Barleen Family Band at their 500-seat **Barleen's Arizona Opry** for Grand Ole Opry–style entertainment after you indulge in a gut-busting meal. Closed May through October. ~ 2275 Old West Highway, two miles east of Apache Junction; 480-982-7991; www.azopry.com.

PARKS   **USERY MOUNTAIN RECREATION AREA**   This 3324-acre recreational area is just northwest of the Superstition Mountains. It has extensive hiking, mountain biking and horseback riding trails. Throughout the park you will find restrooms, showers and horse-staging areas. Day-use fee, $5 per vehicle. ~ Located east of Phoenix via Apache Boulevard or Superstition Freeway (Route 60). Head east to Ellsworth Road and turn north. At McKellips Road, Ellsworth becomes Usery Pass Road. Continue north to the entrance.

boasts a population of six people. One of the last remnants of the Old West, the town was once a stagecoach stop, complete with a school, general store, restaurant/saloon, hotel and post office, and was home to about 125 people. Today only the general store, post office and restaurant remain.

FISH CREEK HILL & THEODORE ROOSEVELT DAM   About five miles east of Tortilla Flat, the paved road surrenders to dirt and gravel as it climbs to the top of Fish Creek Hill, which provides spectacular views of the canyon below. Descending the hill, the road twists through a narrow chasm along Apache Lake and finally arrives at Theodore Roosevelt Dam (page 254).

TONTO NATIONAL MONUMENT   From Roosevelt Dam you can return to Apache Junction the way you came, but it's almost as fast to return by the 83-mile paved southern route through the old mining camp of Superior. To do this, continue on Route 88 (which becomes paved again at the dam). Soon you will come to Tonto National Monument. After visiting the visitors center and ruins, continue south for about 26 more miles to the intersection with Route 60 near Globe. Turn west (right) and follow Route 60 all the way back to Apache Junction. Along the way, you will come to **Boyce Thompson Arboretum** (page 254), where a stop to enjoy the cacti, birds and wildlife rounds out a perfect daylong adventure.

▲ There are 70 sites, all with RV hookups; $15 per night. Tent sites are also available; $10 per night. ~ 480-984-0032.

LOST DUTCHMAN STATE PARK 🏃 Located in the foothills of the Superstition Mountains, this 292-acre park features eight miles of hiking trails through saguaro, palo verde and other desert flora. Interpretive tours by park rangers are conducted October through April. Facilities include a visitors center, restrooms, showers, picnic tables, drinking water and barbecue grills. Day-use fee, $5 per vehicle. ~ 6109 North Apache Trail, about five miles north of Apache Junction; phone/fax 480-982-4485.

▲ There are 70 sites; $12 per night. There is a dump station.

TONTO NATIONAL FOREST 🏃 🚵 🐎 🏊 ⛵ 🚤
To explore the national forest northeast of Apache Junction, travel the famed Apache Trail (Route 88), which eventually leads to the Salt River chain of lakes—Saguaro, Canyon, Apache and Roosevelt lakes. The lakes have been developed for fishing, boating, picnicking, hiking, biking and camping. Parking fee, $6 per

vehicle ($4 per watercraft) at Butcher Jones Beach on Saguaro Lake. The Salt River itself is a favorite spot for tubing.

There are several privately run marinas in the forest offering a variety of services. The **Saguaro Lake Marina** has boat rentals (weekends only), storage, fuel, tours and a restaurant. There are primitive campsites around the lake, accessible by boat only. ~ Located off Bush Highway; 480-986-5546. The **Apache Lake Marina** offers boat rentals, storage and gas. Three motels, a restaurant, a lounge and a grocery store are also located here. There are RV sites, and tent-camping is allowed all around the lake. ~ Route 88; 928-467-2511. A full-service marina with a restaurant, a gift shop and camping facilities, the **Canyon Lake Marina** is situated 15 miles northeast of Apache Junction. Boat tours are available. ~ Route 88; 602-944-6504.

Throughout the forest you'll find picnic areas, restrooms and hiking and riding trails. ~ The main access road from Apache Junction is Route 88 (Apache Trail). Tortilla Campground is on Route 88 about 11 miles from Apache Junction. Cholla Campground is on Route 188, eight miles north of Roosevelt Dam in Roosevelt. Tonto Basin Ranger District, 928-467-3200, fax 928-467-3239; www.fs.fed.us/r3/tonto.

▲ There are 36 campgrounds; there are no camping fees beyond the daily parking fee ($6 per vehicle, $4 per watercraft). Primitive backcountry camping is also allowed. Reservations are only needed for group sites; call USF Reservations, 800-280-2267. Located near Canyon Lake, Tortilla Campground has 77 tent/RV sites and is open from October through March. Located on the south side of Roosevelt Lake, **Cholla Campground** has 188 tent/RV sites, and **Windy Hill** has 348 tent/RV sites.

▼▼▼▼▼▼▼▼▼▼▼

Globe

East of Devils Canyon, the Pinal Mountains rise to dominate the horizon, until the historic old copper-mining town of Globe wrests control of the horizon. This quiet old copper town, with its many Victorian homes dotting the hillsides, retains the flavor of the late 1800s with an early-20th-century main street, complete with an old-fashioned F. W. Woolworth store. Here, you'll find one of the finest American Indian archaeological sites in the state.

Globe began as a mining town in the 1860s after silver was discovered on the Apache reservation. Located at the eastern end of the Apache Trail, the town was originally called "Besh-Ba-Gowah" by the Apache, meaning "place of metal" or "metal camp." Today, it is named for a spherical silver nugget with markings that resemble the continents. After the silver mines were depleted, copper was discovered, but those mines, too, were shut down by the Great Depression. The town has been dozing in the sun ever since.

The Lost Dutchman Gold Mine

With blunted peaks reaching nearly 6000 feet and razor-edged canyons plunging earthward, the Superstition Mountains comprise an area 40 miles long and 15 miles wide—some of the roughest, rockiest, most treacherous territory in the United States. It was in this rugged territory that Dutchman Jacob Waltz was believed to have discovered the Lost Dutchman Gold Mine.

Waltz supposedly found an old Spanish mine in the Superstitions near what is now Apache Junction. He was vigilant about keeping its whereabouts secret, and died in 1891 without revealing the location. For a while people looked for the mine, then it was forgotten for about 30 years.

In the 1930s, Dr. Adolph Ruth came to the area claiming to have a map of the mine. One hot summer day he went into the area to search, and was never seen again. A few months later his skull was found with what looked like a bullet hole in it. Once again, interest in the mine was sparked and people resumed the search. To this day, the treasure has never been found, but prospectors are still looking. Today in Apache Junction, a statue of Jacob Waltz in the center of the town honors the man believed to have discovered an elusive gold treasure.

To learn more about this local legend, head to the **Superstition Mountain/Lost Dutchman Museum**, which displays historical artifacts pertaining to the story of the Lost Dutchman Gold Mine. You'll also find exhibits of folk art, prehistoric Indian artifacts, Spanish and Mexican crafts and documents, pottery and relics of early cowboys, prospectors and miners. Admission. ~ 4087 North Apache Trail, Apache Junction; 480-983-4888; e-mail smgold@uswest.com.

If you'd like to try your luck in finding the legendary Lost Dutchman Gold Mine, there are a number of companies that offer three- to seven-day—or longer—treks into the Superstitions. With the help of experienced guides, you will lash your gear to packhorses and mount up for a trip where you can pan for gold or simply ride the wilderness trails, camp, cook, bathe in icy streams and sleep out under the stars. For information, try the **O.K. Corral, Inc.** ~ P.O. Box 528, Apache Junction, AZ 85217; 480-982-4040; www.okcorrals.com, e-mail horses@okcorrals.com.

SIGHTS   On your drive into **Globe** (if arriving from the west), you'll notice massive manmade hills of bleached-out dirt, a byproduct of the copper mining operations here. The white mesas, which stretch for a couple of miles, are what's left after the ore has been bleached, crushed and smelted. Attempts to grow vegetation in the miniature moonscape have been all but futile, so the mountains of residue remain, perhaps to be recycled as new mining techniques allow extraction of more copper from them.

For local information, visit the **Globe–Miami Regional Chamber of Commerce and Economic Development Corporation**. Be sure to ask for the walking tour of downtown Globe, and directions to the nearby archaeological sites. Closed on weekends. ~ 1360 North Broad Street; 928-425-4495, 800-804-5623, fax 928-425-3410; www.globemiamichamber.com, e-mail gmr@ cableone.net.

Set among modern homes and paved streets, **Besh-Ba-Gowah Museum and Archaeological Park** is a prehistoric pueblo village built from rounded river cobblestone and mud walls, which surround rooms and plazas. Here, you can climb a rough wooden ladder and examine rooms with pottery and utensils that were used 600 years ago. There's also a pot over a firepit, manos and metates. A nearby museum displays artwork and utensils of the Salado, an advanced band of hunters and gatherers who lived here from A.D. 1100 to 1400. The Salado built a pueblo of more than 200 rooms (146 on the ground floor and 61 second-story rooms) around three central plazas, which housed an estimated 300 to 400 people during its peak. There is also a botanical garden that demonstrates how the Salado utilized the surrounding vegetation. Admission. ~ 1100 Jess Hayes Road, one mile southwest of town at the Globe Community Center; 928-425-0320, fax 928-402-1071; e-mail beshbagowah@cableone.net.

After leaving the archaeological park, you can get an eagle's-eye view of the area by making a right turn on Jess Hayes Road then driving to Ice House Canyon Road and Kellner Canyon, where you will circle up through the beautiful Pinal Mountains for 15 miles. At the 7850-foot level you'll pass through ponderosa pine, ferns and thick foliage. Pull out anywhere and the overlooks will give you sweeping views of Globe and Miami below.

In town, the rip-roaring days of the early miners come to life at the **Gila County Historical Museum** with exhibits of early artifacts, mining equipment and Salado Indian relics dating back to A.D. 1400. The museum is housed in the former Globe–Miami Dominion Mine Rescue and First Aid Station. Closed Sunday. ~ Route 60; 928-425-7385.

The **Old Dominion Mine**, across from the museum on Broad Street, is what's left of what was once the world's richest copper mine. In the 1930s, the depressed price of copper, coupled with increasing water seepage into the mine shafts, forced the closure of the mine. Today the mine belongs to BHP Copper Company and is a valuable source of water, which is vital to the company's other operations in the area.

In downtown Globe stands the **Historic Gila County Courthouse**, built in 1906. This stately stone structure now houses the Cobre Valley Center for the Arts and a small theater. Climb the 26 stone steps and enter the wooden doors to find finished hardwood floors, arched passways, grand rooms with high ceilings and tall windows, and a staircase accented with copper banisters and overhead skylight. ~ 101 North Broad Street; 928-425-0884, fax 928-425-9340; e-mail cvca@theriver.com.

Also worth visiting is the **Globe Elks Lodge**, the world's tallest three-story building, built in 1910. ~ 155 West Mesquite Avenue; 928-425-2161. You can also check out the old **Gila County Jail** (behind the Historic Gila County Courthouse), constructed of reinforced concrete in 1909, with cell blocks transported from the Yuma Territorial Prison. The **Gila Valley Bank and Trust Building**, with its white terra-cotta facade, is an unusual example of the beaux-arts neoclassical style of 1909. The building was the pioneer

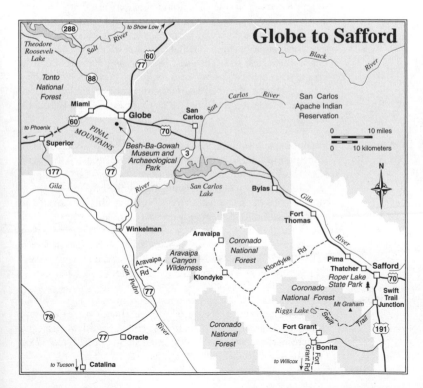

Globe to Safford

branch of the former Valley National Bank. ~ Mesquite Avenue and Broad Street.

The art deco–style **Globe Theater** was built in 1918 and features copper-covered pillars under the movie marquee. ~ 141 North Broad Street.

If you want more history, the city sponsors an **Historic Home and Building Tour and Antique Show** in February. Many of the structures were built by the same stonemasons who worked on nearby Roosevelt Dam. The tour usually consists of six to eight buildings. A recent one included a 1911 home built from dacite stones, a material quarried locally; a church that was hand-built by Episcopalian priests between 1900 and 1908; and a plantation-style mansion built in the late 1800s, complete with upper and lower verandas. For more information call the Globe–Miami Regional Chamber of Commerce and Economic Development Corporation. ~ 928-425-4495, 800-804-5623, fax 928-425-3410; www. globemiamichamber.com, e-mail gmr@cableone.net.

Near the Globe Theater is old Engine No. 1774, one of only seven remaining steam locomotives in existence. Originally, 355 were built between 1899 and 1901. ~ Pine and Oak streets.

Globe is the commercial gateway to the **San Carlos Apache Indian Reservation**, the 1.8-million-acre expanse that's home to nearly 12,000 Apache Indians. Rambling and remote, lush and rustic, the land is a natural habitat for javelina, elk, bear, mountain lions, bighorn sheep, antelope, waterfowl, grouse, quail, rabbits and a variety of freshwater fish. Camping, hunting and fishing are permitted, with licenses. A recreation permit is required for off-road hiking. Tribal lakes offer boating and waterskiing. Contact the Recreation and Wildlife Department. ~ 928-475-2343, fax 928-475-2701.

LODGING

In Globe you'll find the **Super 8**, a 40-unit, two-story motel with contemporary furnishings and a pool. ~ 637 East Ash Street; 928-425-7124. BUDGET.

Globe has a small but growing number of bed-and-breakfast inns. One of the most distinctive is **Noftsger Hill Inn**, located in a former schoolhouse dating from 1907. Six large suites include five of the original classrooms, each with a fireplace, school desk and the original blackboard. No smoking. ~ 425 North Street; 928-425-2260, 877-780-2479, fax 928-402-8235; www.noftsger hillinn.com, e-mail info@noftsgerhillinn.com. MODERATE.

DINING

Most locals agree some of the best food in town is at 24-hour **Jerry's Restaurant**, a fast-paced, coffee shop–style eatery that dishes up hearty portions of steaks, chops, meatloaf, fish and other American standbys. ~ 699 East Ash Street; 928-425-5282, fax 928-425-6703. BUDGET TO MODERATE.

GLOBE PARKS 265

Family-owned and -operated since 1969, **Chalo's Casa Reynoso** is a traditional Mexican restaurant, with entrées ranging from burritos to green chile to *rellenos* to enchiladas. If you've OD'd on spicy foods, they also have your basic hamburger-type offerings. ~ 902 East Ash Street; 928-425-0515; www.chalos.com. BUDGET TO MODERATE.

SHOPPING

The **Cobre Valley Center for the Arts,** located in the Historic Gila County Courthouse, houses arts and crafts produced by local members of the Cobre Valley Fine Arts Guild (*cobre* is Spanish for copper). Media represented include stained glass, ceramics, weaving, painting (oil, acrylic, watercolors), sculpture (stone, metal, wood, plastic), photography, jewelry (silver, stone, beaded) and mixed media. There are also prints, batik silk scarfs, antiques, copper ornaments and gift items. ~ 101 North Broad Street; 928-425-0884; e-mail cvca@theriver.com.

Bacon's Boots and Saddles represents the last of the great saddle makers. The store's owner, Ed Bacon, has been hand-crafting saddles for more than 50 years. A full range of Western wear is also featured. Closed Sunday. ~ 290 North Broad Street; phone/fax 928-425-2681.

West of Globe on Route 60, **Pastime Antiques** is filled with antique furniture, paintings, Western memorabilia, historic photos, old magazines, postcards, posters and other relics and remnants of the past. ~ 150 West Mesquite Street, Miami; 928-425-2220.

NIGHTLIFE

If you prefer an evening nightcap, go to **Under the Palms Cocktails.** ~ 230 North Broad Street; 928-425-2823.

PARKS

TONTO NATIONAL FOREST 🚶🚴🐎⛵ The Globe district, located in the southeast corner of Tonto National Forest, is a popular escape from the desert heat. The Upper Salt River boasts some of the country's best whitewater, as well as fishing and swimming at the calmer stretches. The Pinal Mountains offer endless opportunities for hiking, biking and horseback riding. The forest has picnic areas, restrooms and hiking and riding trails. ~ Main access to the Globe district is Route 60. To reach Upper and Lower Pinal campgrounds from Globe, turn south on Jess Hayes Road and follow signs to the campgrounds. Oak Flat Campground is located right off of Route 60, four miles east of Superior; 928-402-6200, fax 928-402-6292.

▲ There are 86 campgrounds in Tonto National Forest; free to $17 per night. Primitive camping is allowed. Reservations are only needed for group sites in fee areas; call USFS Reservations, 800-280-2267. At a cool 7500 feet, Upper Pinal Campground and Lower Pinal Campground (19 tent sites total; no fee) are popular in the summer. At a lower elevation, Oak Flat Campground (16 tent/RV sites; no fee) is five and a half miles east of Superior.

SAN CARLOS LAKE 🏃 🚤 ⤴ The lake, created by the construction of the Coolidge Dam, has 158 miles of shoreline when full. The fishing is good for catfish, bass and crappie. There's a general store providing bait and other items. The only other facilities are pit toilets. Day-use fee, $7. ~ Located 30 miles east of Globe.

▲ There are 11 RV sites, some with hookups; $10 per night for RVs needing hookups, otherwise wilderness camping is included with a two-day fishing license, but not with the one-day license, which expires at midnight. For fishing licenses, hiking permits, camping and any other information, call the Recreation and Wildlife Department. ~ 928-475-2343, 928-475-2653.

▼▼▼▼▼▼▼▼▼▼
Safford Area

Lying low in the fertile Gila River Valley is Safford, a trade center for the valley's numerous cotton farmers, and jumping-off point for outdoor recreation in the Coronado National Forest. Just west of town are the adjoining communities of Thatcher and Pima. Named to commemorate a Christmas visit by Mormon apostle Moses Thatcher, the town is home to Eastern Arizona College; nearby Pima is the site of the Eastern Arizona Museum.

SIGHTS

Safford's main highway is lined with modern shopping centers, but the downtown district, with its wood-frame and mason buildings, suggests a Midwestern borough. Despite the arid climate, the valley is irrigated by the Gila River and cotton is king here. The **Safford Valley Cotton Growers** have one of a handful of gins in the area that you can tour during season, typically October through January and on Friday afternoons. Call for reservations. ~ Route 191 and 9th Street, Safford; 928-428-0714.

HIDDEN ►

A good first stop is the **Graham County Chamber of Commerce** for brochures and maps. You can also view historical dioramas and exhibits on gems and minerals. Closed Sunday. ~ 1111 Thatcher Boulevard, Safford; 928-428-2511, 888-837-1841, fax 928-428-0744; www.graham-chamber.com, e-mail info@graham-chamber.com.

One of Safford's main landmarks is the **Safford Courthouse**, a neocolonial brick building with white pillars built in 1916. ~ 8th Avenue at Main Street. Nearby, Safford's 1898-vintage city hall was the town's original schoolhouse. ~ 717 Main Street, Safford.

Just outside of town, the quiet residential neighborhoods are dotted with elegant old homes. One of them is the **Olney House**, built in 1890 for George Olney, a former sheriff of Graham County. The two-story home features a plantation-style upper and

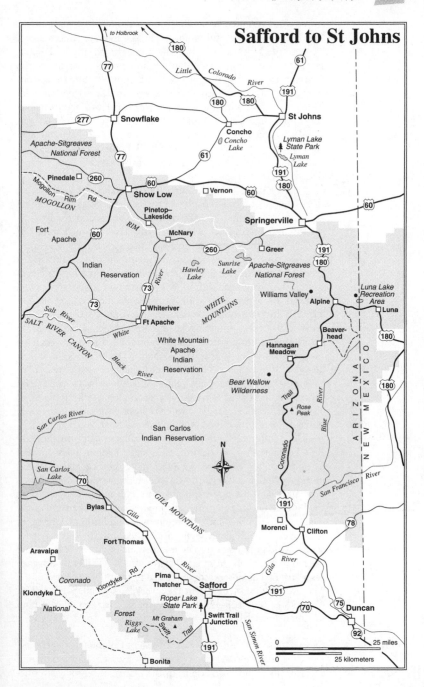

Safford to St Johns

to Holbrook

180

Little   Colorado   River

61

191

277   Snowflake

180   180

St Johns

Apache-Sitgreaves
National Forest

Concho
Concho
Lake

Lyman Lake
State Park
Lyman
Lake

Pinedale   260

Mogollon
Rim   Rd
MOGOLLON

60   Show Low

Vernon   60

191
180

60

Pinetop–
Lakeside

Springerville

191

Fort

Apache   60

RIM

McNary

260   Greer

191
180

Indian

Reservation   River

Hawley
Lake

Sunrise
Lake

Apache-Sitgreaves
National Forest

Luna Lake
Recreation
Area

73

Williams Valley   Alpine   Luna

73

Whiteriver

WHITE

180

Salt   River

SALT RIVER CANYON

Ft Apache

White

MOUNTAINS

Beaverhead

180

White Mountain
Apache
Indian
Reservation

Black   River

Hannagan
Meadow

Bear Wallow
Wilderness

Trail

ARIZONA

180

San Carlos River

San Carlos
Indian
Reservation

Rose
Peak

Coronado

Blue   River

NEW MEXICO

San Carlos
Lake

70

N

San Francisco   River

Bylas

GILA   MOUNTAINS

Gila

Fort Thomas

Aravaipa

Klondyke Rd

Coronado

River

Pima
Thatcher

Morenci   Clifton

78

Klondyke

Safford

191

Gila   River

National

Forest

Roper Lake
State Park

70   75   Duncan

Riggs
Lake

Mt Graham

Swift   Trail

Swift Trail
Junction

San Simon River

92

Bonita   191

0   25 miles

0   25 kilometers

lower front veranda. It is currently a bed-and-breakfast inn (see "Lodging" for more information). ~ 1104 Central Avenue, Safford.

If you feel like getting spaced out in Safford, stop by **Discovery Park**. This complex contains exhibits on the origins of the universe, the history and science of astronomy and radio astronomy, as well as a multimedia room where family activities are held. There is also a 20-inch telescope for daytime and nighttime observations and, perhaps most exciting of all, a full-motion flight simulator. Open to the public Saturday from 4 to 10 p.m. only. Admission. ~ 1651 West Discovery Park Boulevard, Safford; 928-428-6260, fax 928-428-8081; www.discoverypark.com, e-mail discover@discoverypark.com.

Nearby 10,720-foot **Mount Graham** makes for good scenic drives, and its unique ecosphere provides a succession of climate zones, each with its own ecology. The main access road to the mountain is Swift Trail, which at first passes through stands of prickly pear, mesquite, creosote and ocotillo in the lower foothills. As you rise in elevation, the dominant trees are various types of oak, alligator juniper and piñon pine. At a higher elevation (8000 feet) you'll find a profusion of ponderosa pine, Douglas fir, aspen and white fir, some of them dating to A.D. 1200. Botanists say the Douglas firs have survived because the rocky cliffs of the mountains have protected them from the harsh environment. On the drive up the mountain is an apple orchard maintained under a special use permit from the U.S. Forest Service. While the orchard survived the extensive April 1996 fires, 6000 acres on Mount Graham were not as lucky; you'll pass through a number of burned out areas on your trek up the Swift Trail. The first 24 miles of Swift Trail are paved, the last 13 are gravel. The road is closed from mid-November to May.

The **Mount Graham International Observatory** on Emerald Peak outside of Safford features a 1.8-meter Lennon Telescope and a Submillimeter telescope. An 8-millimeter binocular telescope is currently under construction (it will be the world's largest of its type and the most powerful, able to see deeper into space than the Hubble telescope when completed). Further expansion of the facility is continuing and will result in the addition of four other telescopes, including an eight-meter class infrared/optical telescope. All-day tours of the observatory, including a box lunch, are offered to the public from late May to mid-November by advance reservation. The observatory is closed to the public the rest of the year. Admission. ~ 1651 West Discovery Park Road, Safford; 928-428-2730, fax 928-428-8081; mgpc3.as.arizona.edu, e-mail mgi.mail@as.arizona.edu.

LODGING

HIDDEN ▶

Olney House Bed and Breakfast, a Western Colonial Revival home, has three antique-filled guest rooms, all of which share a bath and a parlor. In addition to rooms in the main house, there's a one-bedroom cottage and a circa-1890 studio cottage; both have TVs. Guests start the morning with a full breakfast. Before leaving, be sure to see the pecan tree, which they claim is the tallest in Arizona. ~ 1104 Central Avenue, Safford; phone/fax 928-428-5118, 800-814-5118; www.olneyhouse.com. BUDGET TO MODERATE.

The rest of Safford's lodgings are mostly chain motels. You won't be disappointed with the **Days Inn,** which features rooms with refrigerators and microwaves, a pool and a hot tub. There's a restaurant across the street. ~ 520 East Route 70, Safford; 928-428-5000, 800-329-7466, fax 928-428-7510. BUDGET.

The best restaurant in town is **El Coronado,** a friendly place with blue-vinyl booths, ceiling fans and a deep narrow dining room. The tasty Mexican specialties include green chile chimichangas and quesadillas stuffed with green chile, meat, chicken, chorizo and chopped green chile. American dishes include chicken-fried steak, shrimp and sandwiches. Closed Tuesday. ~ 409 Main Street, Safford; 928-428-7755. BUDGET.

DINING

El Charro Restaurant is a local hangout with formica tables and local artwork on the wall. Mexican specialties include cheese crisps with green chile *con carne*, green or red chile burritos and Sonora enchiladas. Closed Sunday. ~ 601 Main Street, Safford; 928-428-4134. BUDGET TO MODERATE.

The **Branding Iron Restaurant** is a ranch-style building flanked by large trees. They serve Western broiled steaks, chicken, seafood, barbecued ribs in a dining room that overlooks the Gila Valley. Dollar tacos served on Monday. Closed Sunday. ~ 2346 North Branding Iron Lane, Safford; 928-428-7427. BUDGET TO MODERATE.

The small shops on downtown's Main Street are fun to explore. In addition to thrift shops, jewelry stores and Western-wear boutiques, you'll find **Trophies n' Tees,** which has a selection of

SHOPPING

AUTHOR FAVORITE

Across the street from the Quality Inn & Suites, the **Country Manor Restaurant** opens early and stays open late (well, late for this area). Old farm implements hang on the walls and you're likely to see a table of old timers in here shooting the breeze and eating home-cooked meals such as Mexican dishes, homemade soups and pies, chicken-fried steak, liver and onions and meatloaf. ~ 420 East Route 70, Safford; 928-428-7148. MODERATE TO DELUXE.

Arizona souvenirs, caps, sweatshirts and T-shirts. Closed Saturday and Sunday. ~ 513 Main Street, Safford; 928-428-0906.

You can't miss **Pollock's Western Outfitters** with its distressed-wood exterior and horse statue on the roof. Inside, there are the latest Western fashions and accessories. Suppliers include Levi, Rocky Mountain, Justin, Tony Lama, Wrangler, Stetson and Resistol. You'll also find Classic ropes. ~ 610 5th Street, Safford; 928-428-0093, fax 928-348-9102. Behind Pollock's Western Outfitters, **Pollock's Outback Outlet** offers merchandise at discounted prices.

NIGHTLIFE   Locals converge on **Tuttie's American Club.** There's live music once in a blue moon, but the jukebox always cooks! ~ 503 Main Street, Safford; 928-428-2727.

PARKS   **MOUNT GRAHAM** 🚶 🚵 🐎 🚤 ⛵ The highest peak of the Pinaleño Mountains at 10,720 feet is Mount Graham. Drive the 37-mile-long Swift Trail and you'll leave the cactus and mesquites at the base and travel to a forest of ponderosa pine, aspen and white fir, punctuated by charred areas consumed by forest fires in 1996 and 2004. Near the end of the road is 11-acre Riggs Lake, which is stocked with trout (license plus trout stamp required) and also available for boating (electric motors only). The forest's facilities are limited to restrooms and picnic areas. ~ Go south from Safford for seven miles on Route 191 and turn west at the Swift Trail sign. The first 24 miles of the Swift Trail are paved; the last 14 are graded dirt. Swift Trail is closed at the end of the pavement from at least November 15 to April 15. Safford Ranger District: 928-428-4150, fax 928-428-2393.

In late summer and early fall you can purchase fruit at roadside stands around the Mount Graham area.

▲ There are eight developed campgrounds; $10 per night. Primitive camping is allowed free below 9800 feet. (Above 9800 feet is closed to all entry.)

ROPER LAKE STATE PARK 🚤 🎣 🚤 ⛵ In addition to swimming in a 30-acre lake with a beach, you can soak outside in a rock tub filled with water from nearby hot springs. You can fish for catfish, bass, bluegill, trout and crappie from a shady dock. Only boats with trolling motors are allowed. For meals, sit out on the peninsula's grassy picnic area under a grove of shade trees. You'll find restrooms and showers. Day-use fee, $3 per vehicle. ~ Off Route 191, six miles south of Safford; 928-428-6760, fax 928-428-7879.

▲ There are 95 sites, 40 with RV hookups; $12 per night for standard sites and $16 per night for hookups. There are also four cabins; $35 per night.

ARAVAIPA CANYON WILDERNESS 🚶🏇 Aravaipa Creek flows through an 11-mile-long canyon bordered by spectacular cliffs. Lining the creek are large sycamore, ash, cottonwood and willow trees, making it a colorful stop in fall. You may spot javelina, coyotes, coatimundis and desert bighorn sheep, as well as nearly every type of desert songbird and more than 200 other bird species. There are no facilities whatsoever. Permits are required and can be obtained from the Bureau of Land Management's Safford Field Office. ~ To get to the West Trailhead, drive on Route 77 about 11 miles south of Winkelman. Go east on Aravaipa Road; it's 12 miles to the trailhead. For additional routes, check their website. It's advisable to check on road conditions with the Safford Field Office before setting out; high-clearance vehicles are a good idea. 711 14th Avenue, Safford; 928-348-4400, fax 928-348-4450; www.blm.gov/az/sfo.

▲ Primitive camping allowed; $5 per person, per day. The maximum stay is three days/two nights. Closed weekends.

CLUFF RANCH WILDLIFE AREA 🎣 This area contains 788 acres of wildlife sanctuary and recreational areas. Streams from Mount Graham feed four ponds that provide year-round fishing for trout, catfish, largemouth bass and bluegill. Birding is also excellent here. ~ Located about nine miles northwest of Safford; 520-628-5376.

Clifton–Morenci Area

To begin the 44-mile drive from Safford to Clifton, continue east out of Safford on Route 70. The road passes along the edge of Roper Lake State Park and parallels the Gila River for a few miles. Soon after the river parts ways with the road, take a left turn onto 191 North—otherwise, you'll promptly end up in New Mexico. The route is scenic, traveling between the Gila Mountains to the north and the Whitlocks to the south. As you pass the appropriately named Thumb Butte on your right, you'll cross from Graham County into Greenlee County; finally, the road rejoins and crosses over the Gila River, and takes you into Clifton.

The Clifton–Morenci area is a region shaped by its mining past. Today, the continent's second-largest copper mine operates in Morenci, while the copper industry's heyday is preserved along Clifton's historic Chase Creek Street.

SIGHTS

Route 191 follows the San Francisco River, much the way Francisco de Coronado and his conquistadors did, around the bend and into the historic little mining town of **Clifton**, built along the banks of the river.

All around Clifton, the red sandstone cliffs paint a brilliant contrast to the grays and tans of the shale and the tin-and-brick buildings that are reminiscent of the town's golden days at the turn of the 20th century, when copper was king.

The town was founded around 1865, but didn't prosper until copper deposits were discovered in 1872. At first, copper ore had to be shipped to Swansea, Wales, for smelting. Then miners built their own crude adobe smelters along Chase Creek Street and set up a narrow-gauge railroad to transport the ore from the mines on the surrounding hillsides.

At the Greenlee County Historical Museum is the baby chair and doll once belonging to Supreme Court Justice Sandra Day O'Connor, who was born in nearby Duncan.

Many of the remnants of early mining operations remain, along with dozens of old buildings—47 are on the National Register of Historical Places—in early-20th-century architecture. You will find most of them along **Chase Creek Street**, which was once the town's main thoroughfare, lined on both sides with stores, saloons, brothels, churches and even an opera house. Today, the four-block-long street, plus a few narrow alleys, parallels Coronado Boulevard (Route 191), separated by a rudimentary brick wall. But you can still walk among the buildings, many of which have been restored or are in the process of being restored. Most retain their architectural splendor.

For instance, the **Catholic Church**, which was rebuilt in 1917 after being destroyed by flood and fire, has leaded and stained-glass windows, a marble altar and porcelain figures imported from Italy. Down the street is Clifton's first **Town Jail**, which is carved into the side of a granite cliff. Next door is the **Copper Head**, a 19th-century locomotive that once carried ore to the smelters. Across the river, the **Carmichael House** is now headquarters for mine officials. It was built in 1913 for mine president James Carmichael, who once had to flee through the home's storm sewer system to escape a mob of angry strikers. The **Greenlee County Chamber of Commerce**, which has its offices in the old Southern Pacific train depot, dispenses maps and information about the sights and history of the area. Be sure to ask for the walking-tour map of historic Chase Creek. ~ 100 North Coronado Boulevard, Clifton; phone/fax 928-865-3313.

You'll notice a few caves in the mountain above the south side of Chase Creek. These were built by merchants to store valuables such as whiskey, meat and vegetables. They often had rugged steel doors and sometimes were vented with a vertical shaft.

The renovated **Greenlee County Historical Museum** on the west end of Chase Creek has assembled an impressive collection of early Clifton memorabilia, including recollections of Geronimo's birth near the Gila River about four miles from downtown. The photo gallery displays images of the region's history and paintings by Ted De Grazia, one of Arizona's most famous artists and a native of Morenci. Open Tuesday, Thursday and Saturday afternoons. ~ 315 Chase Creek, Clifton; 928-865-3115.

Phelps Dodge Corporation became a major player in Clifton's development at the turn of the 20th century, when it took over most of the local mining operations, about four miles north of town. The original mining camp was called Joy's Camp, but was later renamed **Morenci**, after a town in Michigan. Over the next 50 years, Phelps Dodge, or "PD" as the locals call it (often confused with "Petey"), became one of the largest producers of copper in the world.

Today's Morenci was built by Phelps Dodge in 1969. It consists of a motel/restaurant, a school, a library, two shopping centers, a bowling alley and a supermarket. Phelps Dodge operates the open-pit copper mine here, the second largest in North America.

The **Phelps Dodge Morenci, Inc.** mine is an awesome sight from the viewpoints along Route 191. Most impressive are the earth moving equipment with tires so huge they dwarf a man, the scoop shovels that can unearth 100 cubic tons of ore with one bite, and the futuristic dump trucks with wedge-shaped bays that haul more than 300 tons of material. Reservations required. ~ 4521 Route 191, Morenci; 928-865-4521, fax 928-865-2723.

Continuing north, the highway ascends a series of switchbacks into a high-desert climate zone, with juniper trees seemingly growing from the red-rock formations.

About halfway to Alpine, you can stop at **Rose Peak**, which offers panoramic vistas of the Escudilla Mountains. For even better views, you can hike to the forest lookout tower, about a half-mile off the highway.

LODGING

Each town has its own motel. **Rode Inn Motel** is in the traditional motel style. Rooms are well-kept and offer in-room coffee, microwaves, refrigerators and color cable television. ~ 30 North Coronado Boulevard, Clifton; 928-865-4536, 877-220-6553, fax 928-865-2654; www.rodeinn.com. BUDGET.

The more modern **Morenci Motel** sits on a hill overlooking Clifton and features an adobe brick exterior, wrought-iron fixtures, an adobe-tiled lobby, a restaurant, a lounge and a gift shop. The large rooms are decorated with pastels and Southwestern-style furnishings. ~ Route 191, Morenci; 928-865-4111, fax 928-865-5525. BUDGET.

DINING

PJ's Restaurant, a storefront hole-in-the-wall near the old section of town, is popular with locals who feast on hamburgers or Mexican entrées like chile cheese crisps and green chile plates or red enchiladas. Seating is at the counter or formica dinettes, but the food is tasty and plentiful. ~ 307 South Coronado Boulevard, Clifton; 928-865-3328. BUDGET.

The best place in town to eat is the **Copperoom Restaurant and Sportspage Lounge**, a somewhat plain but cavernous dining room with ceiling fans, wooden tables, captain chairs and a brick fireplace used during the winter. The house specialties include steaks, prime rib, chicken, liver and onions, halibut and several Mexican dishes. No dinner in November or December. ~ Morenci Motel, Route 191, Morenci; 928-865-4111, fax 928-865-5525. BUDGET TO MODERATE.

SHOPPING   There's not much here, but if you run out of toothpaste try **Bascha's**, a grocery store. ~ Morenci Plant Site shopping center, Morenci; 928-865-1820.

NIGHTLIFE   For contemporary surroundings, try the **Copperoom Restaurant and Sportspage Lounge**, a small but surprisingly active bar with a handful of wooden tables and big-screen TVs. ~ Morenci Motel, Route 191, Morenci; 928-865-4111.

▼▼▼▼▼▼▼▼▼▼
Alpine Area

The long and winding road from Clifton up to Alpine is a beautiful one—just make sure you have plenty of gas and supplies before you begin because there are no facilities along the 105-mile stretch. Starting from Clifton, you'll first need to make the 1300-foot climb to Morenci, then bid civilization farewell as you continue the ascent into Apache-Sitgreaves National Forest.

Be aware that this road is subject to closure during winter snow storms. If the road is closed by snow or mudslides, you can drive to Alpine via Routes 78 and 180 through western New Mexico. The detour adds only 20 miles to the trip.

SIGHTS   Twenty-two miles before you reach Alpine is **Hannagan Meadow**, a grassy clearing framed by stately ponderosa pine and blue spruce forests. In addition to excellent hiking trails, there's a rustic mountain lodge and, in winter, cross-country skiing and snowmobiling. ~ Route 191.

The mountain village of **Alpine** is located in the heart of the Apache-Sitgreaves National Forest, or the "Arizona Alps," as it is called locally. The town was founded in 1879 by Mormon settlers who originally named it Frisco, after the San Francisco River. The name was later changed to Alpine because residents thought the area resembled the Alps. The Arizona Alps don't attract the large number of tourists who flock to the Grand Canyon, the Colorado River or other state attractions, but nature buffs will love the region's abundance of outdoor activities—hiking, camping, hunting, fishing and cross-country skiing.

Alpine has no traffic lights or video stores, just a handful of year-round residents and even fewer commercial attractions. Actually it's nothing more than an intersection of Routes 191 and 180, but there are dependable services and lodging. More important, within a 30-mile radius there are 200 miles of trout streams, 11 lakes and numerous campgrounds, plus a country club and golf course.

The region is also a favorite with hunters because it is home to nine of Arizona's ten big-game species, including mule deer, elk, black bear, bighorn sheep and mountain lion. Small-game hunters stalk blue grouse, wild turkey, Gambel's quail and a host of waterfowl.

Your progress through the Blue Range towards Alpine will be marked by the increasing height of the peaks you pass: Mitchell Peak at just under 8000 feet, Rose Peak at almost 8900 feet and Sawed Off Mountain at 9346 feet.

From Alpine, you can strike out in any direction and discover unspoiled forests of tall pines and shimmering aspens, trickling streams, wildflower meadows and clear blue lakes. For detailed maps and descriptions of the area, stop at the **U.S. Forest Service**, where rangers can also advise on current road conditions. The office lobby is now open 24 hours. ~ At the junction of Routes 180 and 191; 928-339-4384, fax 928-339-4323; www.fs.fed.us/r3/asnf.

A picturesque spot is the pristine **Williams Valley**, located seven miles northwest of Alpine via Route 191 and Forest Road 249. Here you can explore 15 miles of hiking trails through wooded forests. Beyond Williams Valley you can drop a line in tiny Lake Sierra Blanca, which is stocked with rainbow and brook trout.

A nice scenic drive from Alpine is the **Blue River–Red Hill Loop**. Drive east three miles from Alpine on Route 180 to Forest Road 281 (the Blue Road turnoff). As you make this turnoff, you will see the western tip of **Luna Lake**, 80 acres of crystal-clear waters surrounded by green meadows and pine forests. Facilities at the lake include a boat dock, campground and small store.

From Route 180, Blue Road winds south through ten miles of rugged hills until it descends past a few horse ranches into Box Canyon, where the road follows the **Blue River**. Continue downstream past jagged Maness Peak nine miles to the junction with Forest Route 567 (Red Hill Road). Along the way are tributaries, such as Centerfire Creek, which are home to small schools of rainbow and brook trout. Drive west on Red Hill Road, which twists and climbs out of the valley, often following ridges with panoramic vistas back to Route 191, about 14 miles south of Alpine.

The wood-paneled **Tal-wi-wi Lodge** offers clean, comfortable rooms featuring rustic furnishings, some with woodburning stoves and spa tubs. The seasonal restaurant serves breakfast and

LODGING

dinner (weekends only). ~ Route 191, four miles north of Alpine; 928-339-4319, 800-476-2695, fax 928-339-1962; www.talwiwi lodge.com, e-mail talwiwi@cybertrails.com. MODERATE.

If you came to the mountains seeking a cozy retreat, try the **Alpine Cabins**, which feature kitchenettes and cable TV. Closed December through March. ~ On Route 180, a half block east of the intersection with Route 191, Alpine; 928-339-4440. BUDGET.

Surrounded by pine forests, the **Coronado Trail Cabins and RV Park** offers a few cozy single-room cabins fully furnished with kitchenettes and bed covers. Barbecue and picnic areas are outside the units. RV sites have full hookups. ~ 25304 Route 191, Alpine; 928-339-4772, fax 928-339-4516; www.coronadotrail cabins.com, e-mail coronadotrail@frontier.net. BUDGET.

A pair of Alpine motels offer clean, well-maintained rooms—some with kitchenettes—at reasonable prices. One is the **Mountain Hi Lodge**. ~ 42698 Route 180; 928-339-4311. BUDGET. Your other choice is the **Sportsman's Lodge**. They have some units with kitchens. ~ 42627 Route 191, Alpine; 928-339-4576, 888-202-1033. BUDGET TO MODERATE.

About 22 miles south of Alpine, **Hannagan Meadow Lodge** rents ten rustic cabins with fireplaces and antique furnishings, and eight rooms in the main lodge, which also has a dining room. One of the oldest inns in the state, the lodge also has a general store. ~ Route 191 at Hannagan Meadow; 928-339-4370, fax 928-428-1012; www.hannaganmeadow.com, e-mail info@hanna ganmeadow.com. MODERATE TO DELUXE.

DINING

You'll find home cooking and a casual, friendly atmosphere at the **Bear Wallow Cafe**. Traditional favorites here include rib-eye steak, top sirloin steak, homemade bread and pies. ~ 42650 Route 180, Alpine; 928-339-4310. MODERATE.

SHOPPING

One-stop shopping is the specialty at **The Tackle Shop**, where you can fill your tank or grab a snack. ~ Routes 180 and 191, Alpine; 928-339-4338.

▼▼▼▼▼▼▼▼▼▼▼▼▼▼
Pinetop–Lakeside Area

Where Route 60 intersects with Route 191 and the Coronado Trail, you'll come to the town of Springerville, where you can make a detour and head west to the recreation and ski area of Pinetop–Lakeside, a winter resort popular with Phoenix residents.

SIGHTS

In the Springerville area, there are two places of interest worth stopping for. Situated on a rim of volcanic rock overlooking the Little Colorado River's Round Valley is **Casa Malpais Pueblo**. Tours originate at the museum in Springerville. Here, you'll learn that the Mogollon people abandoned the pueblo in A.D. 1400, and now the archaeological dig is open to the public. For the best pueblo views, take the guided tour up a steep basalt staircase to the top of the mesa. A tour highlight is the **Great Kiva** made of volcanic rock. Admission. ~ 318 Main Street, Springerville; 928-333-5375, fax 928-333-3512; www.springerville.com/area.html, e-mail sitetour@springerville.com.

Follow a dusty, bumpy road for several miles and the unlikely reward is the **Little House Museum** on the X Diamond Ranch. Inside the two-story building are exhibits relating to the area's history, including ranching and horse show memorabilia. Beside it are two restored cabins more than 100 years old. One contains antique musical instruments ranging from a player piano to a Wurlitzer circus organ. Another building houses the expanding instrument collection as well as an exhibit on John Wayne, who had a ranch next door. Reservations are required and include a substantial tour. Admission. ~ Located just over three miles south of Route 260 on South Fork Road, near Springerville; 928-333-2286, fax 928-333-5009; www.xdiamondranch.com, e-mail info @diamondranch.com.

Apache-Sitgreaves National Forest is habitat for a wide variety of rare and endangered birds, including the Mexican spotted owl, bald eagle and peregrine falcon.

Climbing the steep incline of the Mogollon Rim leads to Show Low, Pinetop and Lakeside, forested hamlets of cabins, motels, resorts and campgrounds in a pine woods setting. Most of the commercial activity takes place in Show Low along Route 60.

The population of **Show Low** swells from about 8500 year-round residents to more than 13,000 during the summer, when the big attractions are excellent trout fishing and big-game hunting in the Mogollon Rim country and White Mountains. Also popular are hiking, horseback riding, golf and scenic drives. Many Arizonans also keep summer homes at the 6400-foot-elevation town to escape the blistering summer temperatures in Phoenix and other "flatlander" communities. During winter, the Sunrise ski resort on the White Mountain Apache Reservation is famous for its downhill runs and cross-country trails.

Southeast of Show Low lie the mountain resort twins of **Pinetop** and **Lakeside**, and beyond, the Indian towns of Whiteriver and Fort Apache. Lakeside is a starting point for hiking, fishing, camping and backpacking in and near the three resort communities, which are connected by a highway lined with motels, restaurants, gas stations and small businesses.

LODGING

A nice alternative to camping out is staying at the **Lake of the Woods Resort**. Thirty-three log cabins are scattered amidst pine trees beside a private lake. All of the cabins have fireplaces, TVs, microwaves, kitchen and dining areas and outdoor barbecues. Although some cabins are geared toward honeymooners, most are more family oriented. Amenities include shuffleboard, horseshoes, spas, a sauna, playground, ping-pong, pool tables and boats for rent. ~ 2244 West White Mountain Boulevard, Pinetop–Lakeside; 928-368-5353; www.privatelake.com. BUDGET TO MODERATE.

Located on Sunrise Lake near the ski resort four miles south of Route 260 is **Sunrise Park Resort**, owned and operated by the White Mountain Apache Tribe. Guests come to fish in summer and ski in winter, staying at one of the 94 modern, nicely furnished hotel rooms. Amenities include a heated indoor pool, indoor and outdoor spas and restaurant and lounge. Closed April to mid-May. ~ Route 273, 20 miles east of McNary; 928-735-7669, 800-772-7669, fax 928-735-7315; www.sunriseskipark.com, e-mail sunrise@cybertrails.com. MODERATE TO DELUXE.

A beautiful setting amidst pine, spruce and aspen trees, rather than luxurious accommodations, are what you pay for at **Hawley Lake Resort**. The resort is remote—12 long, winding miles off Route 260—and situated on a lake in one of the highest points in the White Mountains. In the summer, this area is 40° cooler than the flatlands of Phoenix. The resort has eleven motel rooms and seven cabins overlooking the lake. If you get lucky fishing, the cabins have kitchenettes. The resort is located on the White Mountain Apache Indian Reservation. Amenities include a café, boat rentals, gas and a store. Closed December through April. ~ Route 473, 19 miles east of McNary; 928-335-7511, fax 928-335-7434. MODERATE.

Pastoral is the only word for the setting at **Greer Lodge**, located on the Little Colorado River with a view of meadows and mountains. To many, it is *the* place to stay. Built by hand as a church retreat in 1948 out of ponderosa pine and aspen, it now is a charming getaway with eleven rooms in the main lodge and

AUTHOR FAVORITE

Nicknamed the miniature Grand Canyon, 2000-foot-deep **Salt River Canyon** is a spectacular sight that you can drive right through on Route 60, about 50 miles south of Show Low in the White Mountains. There's a small visitors center at the bottom of the canyon, next to the bridge where Route 60 crosses the Salt River, which carved the canyon millions of years ago. Due to hairpin bends and steep drop-offs on either side of the bridge, drivers should proceed with caution and pay close attention to the road. Rugged unpaved roads leave the main highway and are best attempted by those with four-wheel-drive vehicles and familiarity with remote desert backcountry.

five cabins. The lounge/restaurant area has comfy couches, a huge fireplace, vaulted ceilings and almost floor-to-ceiling windows where guests can look out at the snow falling in winter. Country furnishings warm up the rooms; on-site spa available. There's fly-fishing in stocked ponds in summer. ~ Route 373, Greer; 928-735-7216, 888-475-6343, fax 928-735-7720; www.greerlodge az.com, e-mail information@greerlodgeaz.com. DELUXE TO ULTRA-DELUXE.

Molly Butler Lodge is the oldest lodge in Arizona, established in 1910. Guest rooms are small and very basic, but prices are inexpensive. A nice touch are the plaques on each door with the name and information about a local pioneer. There is a restaurant on the premises. ~ 109 Main Street, Greer; 928-735-7226, 866-288-3167, fax 928-735-7538; www.mollybutlerlodge.com, e-mail itsgreer@cybertrails.com. BUDGET TO MODERATE.

Snowy Mountain Inn is a sprawling resort nestled in the forest near a trout-stocked pond. Accommodations consist of seven separate log cabins, six of which have private spas and all with fireplaces (gas-log) in the living room, housekeeping kitchens and lofts with queen beds and a sitting area. There are also four three-bedroom, two-bath private homes, all with fireplaces and spas. The restaurant/bar has a high vaulted ceiling and a large rock fireplace. Hiking trails can be accessed from the property, which borders on National Forest land. ~ 38721 Route 373, Greer; 928-735-7576, 888-766-9971, fax 928-735-7705; www. snowymountaininn.com, e-mail info@snowymountaininn.com. DELUXE TO ULTRA-DELUXE.

DINING

Charlie Clark's Steak House has been around since 1938. A Western theme predominates, with stuffed deer and wildlife paintings. Prime rib, steak and seafood are the primary offerings. ~ 1701 East White Mountain Boulevard, Pinetop; 928-367-4900, 888-333-0259, fax 928-367-6025; www.charlieclarks.com, e-mail char clks2002@yahoo.com. DELUXE TO ULTRA-DELUXE.

Open year-round despite its name, **The Christmas Tree** serves up elegant versions of comfort food. You can start with fried mozzarella sticks (if cholesterol is not a concern), or opt for the potato skins, dripping with cheese and bacon. Chicken dumplings, a mug of soup, beef stroganoff, lamb chops, fresh fish and lasagna top the entrée list, while the kids will be happy with hot cocoa and chicken nuggets. Closed Monday and Tuesday. ~ 455 North Woodland Road, Pinetop; 928-367-3107; www.christmas treerestaurant.com, e-mail christmastree@cybertrails.com. MODERATE TO DELUXE.

For dining with a sports theme, try the **Scoreboard Restaurant & Sports Bar** at the Snowy Mountain Resort. Cuisine includes "dug out dogs," a "tailgate sausage" sandwich and the real splurge: bread mozzarella triangles. Save room, if humanly possible, for the peanut butter pie. Open Friday and Saturday evenings. ~ 38721 Route 373, Greer; 928-735-7576; www.snowymoun taininn.com, e-mail info@snowymountaininn.com. BUDGET.

SHOPPING   Antiquing is popular in this area. Choices include **The Orchard Antiques** with quality furniture, Nippon china, vintage clothing and primitives; the shop is located in an old house. Closed in winter. ~ 1664 West White Mountain Boulevard, Lakeside; 928-368-6563.

Diamond Creek Jewelry & Antiques has gold and silver estate jewelry, Depression ware, glass and furniture. Closed Sunday. ~ Route 260, Ponderosa Plaza, Pinetop–Lakeside; 928-367-5184.

Primitives, pine and oak furniture, quilts, gifts and gourmet coffee beans are what you'll find at **Country Pine Antiques**. ~ 103 West Yaeger Lane, Pinetop–Lakeside; 928-367-1709.

PARKS   **WOODLAND LAKE PARK** 🏃 🚵 🐴 ⛵ 🚤 🎣 This 580-acre scenic park, located in the middle of Pinetop–Lakeside, offers hiking, equestrian and mountain biking trails, volleyball courts, softball fields, boating and playgrounds. People can fish for trout from the shore and piers, one of which is wheelchair accessible. Tall, thin pine trees surround the lake and a one-mile paved loop trail encircles it. The park is also connected with the White Mountain Trailsystem (see "Hiking" at the end of the chapter). Other facilities in the park are restrooms, picnic tables, barbecues and ramadas. Restrooms are closed in winter. ~ Off Woodland Lake Road, a quarter-mile south of Route 260; 928-368-6700, fax 928-368-8528.

▼▼▼▼▼▼▼▼▼▼▼▼

St. Johns Area

From Show Low, head east on Route 60 and northeast on Route 61 to arrive at St. Johns. Built along the banks of the Little Colorado River, St. Johns, with a population of about 3500, serves as the Apache County seat. The Coronado Trail (Route 180/191), named after the Spanish explorer who first sojourned here, begins innocently enough in the high desert area near St. Johns.

SIGHTS   St. Johns has few sights, except for the **St. Johns Equestrian Center**, which is rapidly becoming one of the premier equestrian facilities in the Southwest, attracting horses and riders from New Mexico, Colorado and Utah, as well as throughout Arizona. Surrounded by rolling hills and juniper-studded deserts, amenities include an 80-acre cross-country course, a rodeo arena, show and dressage rings, a six-furlong race track, stables and RV sites. In spring and summer, the center hosts local and regional events, both Western and English, rodeos and other horse competitions.

~ Adjacent to St. Johns Airport; call St. Johns Parks & Recreation at 928-337-3818.

You can find out about the area's history at the **Apache County Historical Society Museum**, which houses displays that include pioneer memorabilia and a log cabin, as well as a set of prehistoric mammoth tusks and a camel's leg bone, both estimated to be about 24,000 years old. Closed weekends. ~ 180 West Cleveland Avenue, St. Johns; 928-337-4737, fax 928-337-2020.

For more information, contact **St. Johns Regional Chamber of Commerce**. Closed Saturday and Sunday. ~ P.O. Box 929, St. Johns, AZ 85936; 928-337-2000, fax 928-337-2020; www.stjohnschamber.com, e-mail office@stjohnschamber.com.

The northern part of the **Coronado Trail** meanders through a region of juniper-dotted hillsides, alfalfa pastures, grazing cattle and a few sandy-topped buttes about 44 miles southeast of Petrified Forest National Park. The trail then heads south through Apache-Sitgreaves National Forest to Clifton.

> The Coronado Trail is rumored to be the least-traveled federal highway in the U.S. Cars on this road are spaced an average of 19 minutes apart—even during rush hour.

As the Coronado Trail climbs on its journey south, chaparral gives way to pine and aspen, and you pass **Nelson Reservoir**, a 60-acre lake stocked with rainbow, brown and brook trout. If you're ready for a break, there are picnic grounds, restrooms and a boat ramp, but no overnight camping.

South of the reservoir are the rolling **Escudilla Mountains**, a 5000-acre wilderness area with forests of spruce, fir, pine and aspen, and nature trails where hikers are often rewarded with raspberries, elderberries and gooseberries, and glimpses of elk and deer in their natural habitat.

LODGING

St. Johns' lodging scene is unexceptional and almost non-existent, but you'll find well-maintained rooms at **Days Inn**, a trailer-court type of motel with old-fashioned casement windows and adobe-like walls. A lounge adjoins the motel. ~ 125 East Commercial Street, St. Johns; 928-337-4422, fax 928-337-4126. BUDGET.

DINING

For an eclectic menu, stop by the **Rhino's Cafe**, which orchestrates a good rendition of several Italian dishes including lasagna, pizza and calzones. You can also feast on frisbee-sized hamburgers, a slab of barbecue ribs or fresh catfish. Closed Tuesday. ~ 855 West Cleveland Street, St. Johns; 928-337-2223. BUDGET TO MODERATE.

If you're craving something spicier, **El Camino** has a traditional Mexican menu of tacos, enchiladas and tostadas. Closed Sunday. ~ 277 White Mountain Drive, St. Johns; 928-337-4700. BUDGET.

PARKS   **CONCHO LAKE** 🚣 🛥 🚤 ⚓ This lake, stocked with rainbow and brook trout, is a peaceful spot to drop a line. Nonmotorized boating is allowed. Or you may choose to play a round of golf at the neighboring public course. The only facilities in the park are restrooms and a picnic area. ~ Off Route 61, ten miles west of St. Johns.

▲ There's an RV park nearby.

LYMAN LAKE STATE PARK 🏕 🐎 🚣 ⛵ 🎣 🏊 🛥 🚤 ⚓ A 1500-acre lake lures both fishing and boating enthusiasts. In fact, it is the only lake in the White Mountains where powerboating is allowed, so waterskiers and jetskiers flock to Lyman Lake. This is also a good place to swim as there's a cove especially marked off for swimming. Anglers fish offshore for catfish, walleye and largemouth bass. The lake was formed by damming the Little Colorado River and is fed by snowmelt from the slopes of Mount Baldy and Escudilla Mountain. Other attractions include hiking the three trails, which range from a half a mile to one mile in length, and are dotted with Indian petroglyphs. On weekends from May through September, guided tours take hikers to petroglyph sites and a pueblo ruin. This 1200-acre park was the first recreational state park in Arizona and sits at an elevation of 6000 feet. Facilities include restrooms, a store, a gas station and hot showers. Day-use fee, $5 per vehicle. ~ Off Route 180/191, 11 miles south of St. Johns; 928-337-4441, fax 928-337-4649.

▲ There are 61 RV sites with electrical and water hookups and 23 developed sites for tents, complete with picnic tables and barbecue grills; there are also four cabins and four yurts. Beach and wilderness camping are allowed. Fees are $12 per night for tents, $19 per night for RV hookups, $50 per night for cabins, and $35 per night for yurts.

▼▼▼▼▼▼▼▼▼▼▼▼▼
Outdoor Adventures

Eastern Arizona is an angler's paradise with numerous lakes dotting the region around Pinetop–Lakeside and Greer. Anglers will also find plenty of challenge—and game fish—along the Old West Highway.

FISHING

APACHE JUNCTION AREA Saguaro, Canyon, Apache and Roosevelt lakes are popular year-round fishing meccas.

GLOBE San Carlos Lake near Globe is the biggest fishing draw in this area.

SAFFORD AREA Roper Lake in Safford attracts anglers from all over Arizona.

ALPINE AREA In the Alpine area, **Bear Wallow Creek**, a tributary of the Black River, is famous for native Apache trout. Also on the **Black River** at different stops you can try for rainbow trout, while trout and catfish can be found in **Eagle Creek**. East of Alpine and dropping off into the Blue Primitive Area, rainbow trout can be found in **Luna Lake** and the ruggedly remote **Blue River**. North of Alpine you'll find rainbow, brown and brook trout in **Nelson Reservoir**. More casual anglers can seek catfish in the **San Francisco River** near Clifton. You can buy bait, tackle and a license at **The Tackle Shop**. ~ At the intersection of Routes 180 and 191, Alpine; 928-339-4338.

Swimming is ideal at Canyon, Apache and Roosevelt lakes.

PINETOP-LAKESIDE AREA   To fish at the lakes on the White Mountain Apache Indian Reservation, which are stocked with rainbow and brown trout, contact the **Game and Fish Department**. ~ South Route 73, Whiteriver; 928-338-4385. For general fishing information in the White Mountains, stop by the **Arizona Game and Fish Department**. ~ 2878 East White Mountain Boulevard, Pinetop; 928-367-4281.

For private flyfishing, catch and release, try **X Diamond Ranch**. ~ South Fork; 928-333-2286; www.xdiamondranch.com. There are quality waters with rainbow, brown and Apache trout as well as boat rentals and camping May through November at **Hawley Lake**. ~ Route 473, 19 miles from McNary; 928-335-7511. For fishing and camping supplies or a license, check with **Western United Drug**. ~ 105 East Main Street, Springerville; 928-333-4321.

ST. JOHNS AREA   The 60-acre **Concho Lake** is a good spot for rainbow and brook trout (shore fishing only). **Lyman Lake State Park** has a lake stocked with catfish, walleye and largemouth bass. ~ Off Route 180/191, 11 miles south of St. Johns; 928-337-4441.

Eastern Arizona increasingly attracts recreationally minded tourists, and not just in the summer. Locals are somewhat stunned by the growing number of winter visitors here in recent years.

WINTER SPORTS

ALPINE AREA   Cross-country skiing, sledding and snowmobiling are popular at **Hannagan Meadow**, 22 miles south of Alpine on Route 191, where there are over 11 miles of machine-packed trails that are serviced after each storm. The snowmobiles in the area are prohibited from designated ski trails. Another good spot for cross-country skiers is **Williams Valley**, which features twelve miles of groomed ski trails, plus additional miles of marked trails. From Alpine, drive one and a half miles north on Route 191 to the Williams Valley turnoff, Forest Road 249, and continue for five miles.

PINETOP-LAKESIDE AREA   **Sunrise Park Resort** on the White Mountain Apache Reservation has 800 acres of skiable area on three mountains and ten lifts. There's a base elevation of 9200 and a vertical drop of 1800 feet. Facilities include a snowboard park and a kids' ski school, as well as groomed cross-country trails. ~ Located 20 miles east of McNary on Route 273; 928-735-7669,

800-772-7669; www.sunriseskipark.com, e-mail sunrise@cyber trails.com.

GOLF

If you feel the need to tee off in the mountains, greens are scattered throughout the region. Most are nine-hole courses; keep in mind that many are closed in the winter. Cart and club rentals are generally available.

APACHE JUNCTION AREA   In Apache Junction, try one of the two 18-hole courses at the public **Gold Canyon Golf Club**. ~ 6210 South Kings Ranch Road; 480-982-9449.

GLOBE   **Cobre Valley Country Club** has a nine-hole course with lush greens, subtle breaks and slopes, a bar and a pro shop. ~ Route 88 north of Globe; 928-473-2542.

SAFFORD AREA   In the Safford area, the **Mount Graham Country Club** offers an 18-hole course for year-round play, a pro shop and a lounge. ~ Two miles south of Safford at Daley Estates; 928-348-3140.

ALPINE AREA   You can tee off at the semiprivate **Alpine Country Club**, which features an 18-hole course, a restaurant and a lounge. Closed in winter. ~ 58 North County Road 2122; 520-339-4944.

PINETOP–LAKESIDE AREA   The Pinetop–Lakeside area offers **Silver Creek Golf Club**, an 18-hole course with club rentals, a clubhouse and a pro shop. ~ 2051 Silver Lake Boulevard, White Mountain Lake; 928-537-2744. Also in the area is the 18-hole **Pinetop Lakes Golf & Country Club**. Closed in winter. ~ 4643 Bucksprings Road; 928-369-4531. North of Pinetop–Lakeside, the **Bison Golf and Country Club** offers a dramatic contrast between the back nine holes, lined with ponderosa pines, and the front nine in open high-desert terrain. ~ 860 North 36th Drive, Show Low; 928-537-4564.

RIDING STABLES

This is the real Wild West; there's no better place to saddle up and take to the hills. If you're lucky, you may even find the legendary Lost Dutchman Mine and strike it rich—but if you don't, a ride in this beautiful backcountry is its own reward. Giddyup!

APACHE JUNCTION AREA   **Don Donnelly Horseback Vacations & Stables** takes you on two- to three-hour and multiday rides to the foot of the Superstition Mountains and through the Sonoran Desert. ~ 5580 South Kings Ranch Road #3, Gold Canyon; 602-810-7029; www.dondonnelly.com. For trips into the Superstition Mountains, contact **O.K. Corral, Inc.** They offer half-day, full-day (lunch is provided) and longer rides into the wilderness. On longer trips, all gear and food are provided (except for sleeping bags). ~ 2655 East Whiteley Street, Apache Junction; 480-982-4040; www.okcorrals.com, e-mail horses@okcorrals.com.

PINETOP–LAKESIDE AREA   Between Pinetop and Greer at the Sunrise Ski Resort Park on the White Mountain Apache Reservation, you can saddle up at **Blue Sky Stables** for one-hour to half-day trips through the White Mountains, one of the most scenic areas in Arizona. ~ P.O. Box 315, Eagar, AZ 85927; 928-735-7454.

HIKING

If you don't get a chance to go horseback riding, at least take the opportunity to hoof it along some of Eastern Arizona's wilderness trails. Bird and animal enthusiasts should keep an eye peeled for samples of western wildlife; everyone should keep an eye on the panoramic views. All distances listed for hiking trails are one way unless otherwise noted.

APACHE JUNCTION AREA   Usery Mountain Recreation Area offers the well-maintained **Wind Cave Trail** (1.5 mile), which is moderately challenging and popular with local climbers. The moderate-to-difficult **Pass Mountain Trail** (7 miles) takes about four hours to complete.

Blue Sky Stables offers wagon rides in the summer and sleigh rides in the winter.

SAFFORD AREA   **Arcadia Trail** (5.1 miles), located in the Pinaleño Mountains, passes through a forest of Douglas fir, aspen and pine trees, along with wild raspberry vines. As the highest range in southern Arizona, hikers will see a panoramic view of the area.

ALPINE AREA   The 450,000-acre Apache-Sitgreaves National Forest is a hiker's paradise, with terrain ranging from piñon and juniper woodlands to high-elevation forests of spruce and fir, meadows and alpine lakes.

About 14 miles south of Alpine, hikers can explore the **Red Hill Trail No. 56** (9.7 miles), a trek along a dirt road that leads into the Blue Range Primitive Area. From the upper trailhead at the Right Fork of Foote Creek, just off Forest Route 567 a mile east of Route 191, the trail traces the ridges of the Red Hill mountains, then descends along Bush Creek on its way to the Blue River. About seven and a half miles from the upper trailhead, the trail joins the Tutt Creek Trail (#105) for the last two miles of the journey. The lower trailhead is at Tutt Creek near Blue Crossing Campground off Forest Road 567 (Red Hill Road). If you like to do your hiking by horseback, corrals have recently been built at the upper and lower trailheads.

In the **Blue Range Primitive Area**, you'll find spectacular rock formations with steep escarpments, along with thick forests of spruce, fir and ponderosa pine. Keep a sharp watch for black bear, Rocky Mountain elk, bighorn sheep, javelina, mule deer, mountain lions and bobcats. The area is excellent for birdwatching; keep your binoculars trained for the Arizona woodpecker, American peregrine falcon and southern bald eagle.

West of the Coronado Trail (Route 191), the **Bear Wallow Wilderness** contains 11,000 acres including one of the largest stands of virgin ponderosa pine in the Southwest. **Bear Wallow Trail No. 63** (7.6 miles), which begins off of Forest Road 25, traces Bear Wallow Creek downstream from the trailhead (about 31 miles south of Alpine) through jagged canyons of spruce, fir, ponderosa pine and aspen, west to the San Carlos Apache Indian Reservation's eastern boundary. Two shorter trails connect with the main trail and creek from the north: the moderate **Reno Trail No. 62** (1.9 miles) and the very strenuous **Gobbler Point Trail No. 59** (2.7 miles).

There's excellent hiking in the **Escudilla Wilderness Area**, an alpine forest with peaks over 10,000 feet, ten miles north of Alpine. The **Escudilla National Recreation Trail** (3 miles) from Terry Flat takes you to the summit of Escudilla Mountain through aspen groves, pine forests and grassy meadows. The trailhead is along Forest Route 56, four and a half miles east of Route 191. Rangers at the **U.S. Forest Service** (intersection of Routes 191 and 180, Alpine; 928-339-4384) will provide detailed trail maps and advice on current conditions.

There area many guides and outfitters in the Alpine area. Operating out of Alpine is the **Neal Reidhead Alpine Guide Service**. Hikes through Blue River Unit 27 and Unit 1 offer ample opportunities to view bear, elk and bald eagles. ~ P.O. Box 596, Alpine, AZ 85920; 928-339-1936. For a complete list of outfitters, call the **Alpine Ranger District**. ~ 928-339-4384.

PINETOP–LAKESIDE AREA The **White Mountains Trailsystem** contains about 180 miles of trails from Vernon in the east to Pinedale in the west. For a map of trails, stop by the **Lakeside Ranger Station**. ~ 2022 West White Mountain Boulevard (Route 260); 928-368-5111, fax 928-368-6476. The Trailsystem consists of eleven loop trails, with several more short loops and eight connector trails. Some highlights are **Blue Ridge Trail** (8.7 miles roundtrip) in Pinetop–Lakeside, which is easy to moderate. It passes Billy Creek and climbs through tall pines to the top of Blue Ridge with vistas along the way. The **Ghost-of-the-Coyote Trail** (12.5 miles roundtrip) begins near Pinedale. The fairly flat trail winds through juniper and pine forests, parts of which were burned in recent fires.

The **Mogollon Rim Overlook** (1 mile roundtrip) is an easy hike with interpretive placards along the way and beautiful views of the valley below the Mogollon Rim. It's two miles north of Pinetop–Lakeside off Route 260.

ST. JOHNS AREA There are a couple of short trails that pass by ancient petroglyphs in **Lyman Lake State Park**. Along the way, you'll be able to enjoy views of the lake below.

The western anchor of the Old West Highway, Apache Junction, is about 30 miles east of Phoenix via **Route 60**. On its eastern end you can join the Highway at Safford via **Routes 191** from Clifton, or **Route 70**, which crosses to Lordsburg, New Mexico. **Route 180/191** links the Coronado Trail towns of St. Johns, Alpine and Clifton. You can get to the Pinetop–Lakeside area from the west via Route 60, turning onto **Route 260** at Show Low. From the east, Route 260 connects to Route 180 at Springerville.

Transportation

CAR

The closest **Greyhound Bus Lines** (800-231-2222; www.greyhound.com) terminal to Coronado Trail towns is in Willcox about 90 miles southwest of Clifton. ~ 100 North Arizona Street; 520-384-2183.

BUS

Along the Old West Highway, you can get a rental car at **Hatch Brothers Auto Center**. ~ 1623 Thatcher Boulevard, Safford; 928-428-6000.

CAR RENTALS

EIGHT

Southern Arizona

Southern Arizona is a vast region of grasslands and desert punctuated by some of the state's most beautiful mountains. Four ranges have peaks higher than 9000 feet—the Santa Catalinas, Santa Ritas, Huachucas and Chiricahuas. At the heart of the region is Tucson, an urban metropolis rising out of the Sonoran Desert. A rich cultural tradition ranging from the Pima tribe to the Jesuits reflects this community's close ties to neighboring Mexico.

Scattered east of Tucson are portions of the Coronado National Forest. To the southeast, the rolling grasslands and woodland hills around Patagonia are some of the state's best cattle and horse ranchland, while the Elgin area has acres of green vineyards where local wines are produced. Farther east is Sierra Vista, whose claim to fame is Fort Huachuca, a historic military base whose troops defeated Apache leader Geronimo. Some 11,400 soldiers and civilians are still based here. Nearby Tombstone and Bisbee are old mining towns. Tombstone, the town "too tough to die," survives by selling its history. There are museums and exhibits on every corner—each, of course, charging for the pleasure of your company. Visitors flock here to relive the rowdy life of the Old West, from the shootout at O.K. Corral to the gambling at Birdcage Theater. Bisbee has become a quiet artists' colony with a more bohemian flavor. Here, visitors can shop in historic buildings along Main Street, tour old mines and walk along the narrow, hilly streets dotted with Victorian architecture. Up around Willcox are orchards teeming with fruit and vegetables. In autumn, you can pick your own or stop at one of the many roadside stands.

South of Tucson is the most populated portion of southern Arizona. Off Route 19 is Tubac, an artists' community with about 100 studios and galleries. Farther south is the border town of Nogales, where you can bargain for Mexican crafts and sample authentic cuisine. Southwest of Tucson is a large, scarcely populated area containing the Tohono O'odham Indian Reservation, Cabeza Prieta National Wildlife Refuge and Organ Pipe Cactus National Monument. In the westernmost corner of the state is Yuma, a historic town on the Colorado River that attracts residents with its lush, subtropical climate, farmlands fertile with vegetables, citrus trees and groves of date palms.

Although Tucson and southern Arizona abound with history, the real reason people visit is for the natural beauty—for the meditative solitude of a desert that seemingly rolls on endlessly, creating vast spaces for the imagination.

▼▼▼▼▼▼▼▼▼

Tucson

The ultimate insult to a Tucson resident is to say his town is just like Phoenix. Like bickering siblings, the two cities have never gotten along well and each is proud of its unique personality. While Phoenix is a vast, sprawling city that welcomes booming development, Tucson would just as soon stay the same size and keep developers out—especially those who would alter the environment. Phoenix thrives on a fast pace; Tucson is informal, easygoing and in no great rush to get anywhere.

Surrounded by five mountain ranges and sitting in a cactus-roughened desert, Tucson is an arid, starkly beautiful place with wide-open skies and night silences broken only by the howling of coyotes. The highest mountains are powdered with snow in winter; the desert is ablaze with cactus blooms in spring.

Most of Tucson's 12 inches of annual precipitation arrives during the late summer monsoon season when afternoon thunderstorms roll through the desert with high winds and dramatic lightning shows. During summer, the average high temperature hovers around 98°. In winter, average highs are about 65°, making the city a popular spot for winter visitors, who come to golf and relax in the balmy weather.

Basically, Tucson is an affable, unpretentious town that feels comfortable with itself. There's no need to impress anyone here with high fashion—blue jeans are good enough for most places. Nor do wealth and conspicuous consumption have a large following. Most Tucsonians don't come here to make lots of money, but rather to live in a beautiful, natural area that's within driving distance of more of the same.

The cultural heritage of Tucson is a mix of Spanish, Mexican and American Indian. The city is only 60 miles from Nogales and the Mexican border, but you don't have to go that far to find Mexican food, artwork and culture. The red-tiled adobe homes spread across the valley reflect the residents' love of Spanish and American Indian architecture.

The Pima people, who are probably descendants of the Hohokam, were the first in the area. Father Eusebio Francisco Kino, a Jesuit priest, came to work with them and established a chain of missions, including Tucson's famous Mission San Xavier del Bac.

Later, the Spanish flag flew over the city, as did the Mexican, Confederate and United States flags. In 1867, Tucson was the capital of the Arizona Territory. But when the capital moved north, disgruntled Tucson was given the University of Arizona as compensation. This increased the population, and it jumped again just before World War II when nearby Davis-Monthan Air Force Base began training pilots to fly B-17 bombers. Today 503,000 people call Tucson home and live within the metro area's 500 square miles. The university has grown to 35,000 students, and Davis-Monthan is still an active military base with more than 8800 military personnel and civilians.

SIGHTS

Nine miles southwest of Tucson is the **Mission San Xavier del Bac** on the Tohono O'odham Indian Reservation. Known as the White Dove of the Desert, this stunning white adobe church rises from the open desert floor and is picturesquely framed by blue sky and the mountains beyond. Although the Jesuits founded the mission in the 1600s, the present building was built between 1783 and 1797. It is a combination of Spanish, Byzantine and Moorish architecture. Visitors can walk in through weathered mesquite doors, sit on the worn wooden pews, and feast their eyes on the ornate statues, carvings, painted designs and frescoes. In addition to touring the facility, you can attend mass (open to the public), or visit during one of the celebrations. ~ Signs appear as you drive south on Route 19; 520-294-2624, fax 520-294-3438; www.sanxaviermission.org, e-mail info@sanxaviermission.org.

Across the square in the **San Xavier Plaza**, American Indians sell fry bread and crafts.

Drive north to Speedway Boulevard, turn left and you'll reach Gates Pass, where the road begins to twist and you'll have splendid panoramic views of Tucson and the saguaro-dotted landscape of Tucson Mountain Park. This is where you'll find **Old Tucson Studios**, a re-creation of an old Western frontier town. Columbia Pictures created Old Tucson Studios in 1939 as a movie location for the film *Arizona*, and since then more than 300 films and television episodes have been shot here including *Tombstone*, *The Quick and the Dead*, *Gunfight at the O.K. Corral* and *El Dorado*. If a film crew is in town, you can watch them film. Otherwise, ride the narrow-gauge railroad, watch shootouts and stunt shows on the wide dirt streets, enter the adobe and slatboard buildings and listen to dance-hall music, or indulge in shopping. There are concerts held here as well, with headliners such as Pat Benatar and Bo Diddley. Admission. ~ 201 South Kinney Road; 520-883-0100; www.oldtucson.com, e-mail afriend@oldtucson.com.

Just a few minutes down Kinney Road, the **Arizona-Sonora Desert Museum** is part zoo, part natural-history museum and part botanical garden with more than 300 different animals and 1200 plant species indigenous to the Sonoran Desert. Visitors can inspect the aquatic exhibits and the animals in their desert habitats,

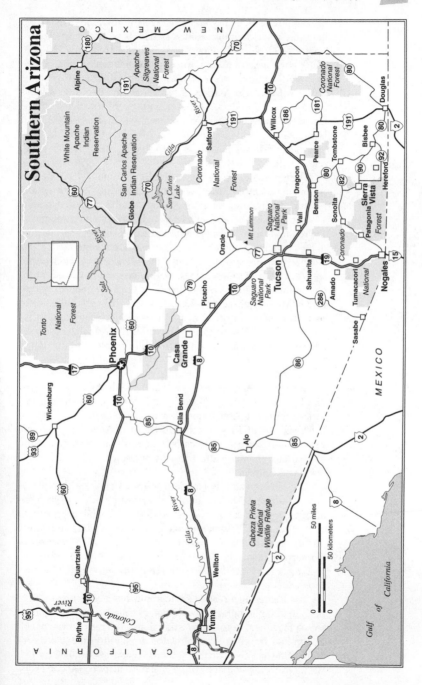

Southern Arizona

or walk inside an aviary and a re-created limestone cave (all exhibits are wheelchair accessible). Definitely worth a visit. Admission. ~ 2021 North Kinney Road; 520-883-1380, fax 520-883-2500; www.desertmuseum.org, e-mail info@desertmuseum.org.

For a panoramic view of Tucson from 3100 feet, drive to the top of **A Mountain**. Settlers of territorial days used it as a lookout for Apache raiders. The latest raiders are students from the University of Arizona, who have been whitewashing the A on it before the first football game of the season since 1915. ~ Take Congress Street exit west off Route 10 to Cuesta Street, then go south onto Sentinel Peak Road.

The El Presidio District's **Historic Block**, running from Church Avenue to Alameda Street, was once part of the Presidio of San Agustin del Tucson, which the Spanish army enclosed with a 12-foot-high adobe wall in 1783. Today, the main attraction in El Presidio is the **Tucson Museum of Art**, a complex specializing in pre-Columbian, modern American and Southwestern art, along with several historic houses and the Plaza of the Pioneers—a showplace for the museum's sculpture collection. Closed Monday. Admission (free on the first Sunday of the month). ~ 140 North Main Avenue; 520-624-2333, fax 520-624-7202; www.tucsonmuseumofart.org, e-mail info@tucsonmuseumofart.org.

Arizona's oldest historical museum, the **Arizona Historical Society Museum** has everything from a full-scale reproduction of an underground mine tunnel to an exhibit on the history of transportation. One special feature is "Life on the Edge: History of Medicine in Arizona." Closed Sunday. Admission. ~ 949 East 2nd Street; 520-628-5774, fax 520-629-8966; www.arizonahistoricalsociety.org, e-mail ahsref@vms.arizona.edu.

A big part of Tucson is the **University of Arizona**, a 352-acre campus dotted with red-brick buildings. If you decide to explore the campus, there are a few worthwhile stops. ~ 520-621-2211; www.arizona.edu.

One definite stop is **Flandrau Science Center**, with a planetarium, a science store, a public observatory with a 16-inch telescope available for public use and science exhibits such as a walk-through model asteroid and night skies exhibit. The facility also houses the state's largest mineral museum. Admission. ~ Corner of University Boulevard and Cherry Avenue; 520-621-7827, fax 520-621-8451; www.flandrau.org, e-mail fsc@u.arizona.edu.

The **Center for Creative Photography** has a collection of more than 50,000 photographs in addition to galleries, a library and research facilities. Photography exhibitions from the permanent collection and traveling exhibitions are displayed in the galleries. ~ 1030 North Olive Road; 520-621-7968, fax 520-621-9444; www.creativephotography.org, e-mail oncenter@ccp.arizona.edu.

The **University of Arizona Museum of Art** has Renaissance and later European and American art, including works by Rembrandt, Dalí, Rothko and O'Keeffe. The collection features more than 3000 paintings, sculptures, drawings and prints. Closed Monday. ~ Southeast corner of Park Avenue and Speedway Boulevard; 520-621-7567, fax 520-621-8770; www.artmuseum.arizona.edu, e-mail azs@u.arizona.edu.

Tucson Botanical Gardens contains a small field of American Indian crops, a cactus and succulent garden, a tropical greenhouse, an herb garden, a sensory garden, a backyard bird garden, a seasonal butterfly display and a xeriscape (arid landscaping) demonstration garden. Perhaps most unusual is the historic garden—lush foliage and flowers that surround and reflect the era of the 1920s Porter House. Admission. ~ 2150 North Alvernon Way; 520-326-9686, fax 520-324-0166; www.tucsonbotanical.org, e-mail info@tucsonbotanical.org.

Fort Lowell Museum is a reconstructed commanding officers' quarters from the days when it was a key military post during the

Apache Indian wars of the 1870s and 1880s. Life on a military post in frontier Arizona is revealed through furnishings, artifacts and displays of military equipment. Closed Sunday through Tuesday. ~ 2900 North Craycroft Road; 520-885-3832.

The late Ted De Grazia gained fame painting impressionistic-style portrayals of the Southwest and its people. Today his home and galleries, the **De Grazia Gallery in the Sun**, are open to the public. Skylights in the adobe structures bathe his paintings in light. Walking through, you pass underneath brick archways and go through landscaped courtyards that he so lovingly tended when he lived here. The unusual architecture, including an iron gate inspired by the historic Yuma Prison, is worth a visit in itself. ~ 6300 North Swan Road; 520-299-9191, 800-545-2185, fax 520-299-1381; www.degrazia.org, e-mail info@degrazia.org.

Pima Air & Space Museum contains one of the largest collections of historic aircraft in the world. Among the 250 aircraft are the Boeing B-29 Superfortress, the type of plane that dropped the first atomic bomb on Japan, and the SR-71 Blackbird, the world's fastest aircraft. Admission. ~ 6000 East Valencia Road; 520-574-0462, fax 520-574-9238; www.pimaair.org.

For a truly unusual experience, stop by the **Biosphere 2 Center**, a controversial three-acre miniature replica of the earth with a tropical rainforest, savannah, marsh and desert. There are small greenhouses where different ecosystems are displayed. Research focus has shifted from sustainable agriculture to global climate changes. On the hourly tours (offered daily), you are taken along paths through the airtight structure and on forays to the living quarters and the command room. You can also see the outside of this high-tech, space-age glass and steel monolith, look through its glass walls and stop by the visitors center. Admission.

TED DE GRAZIA

One of Arizona's most renowned artists was Ted De Grazia, who depicted the Southwest in paintings, prints, bronzes and collector's plates. His distinctive, impressionistic-style works, with their signature bright colors and featureless faces, hang in Tucson's De Grazia Gallery in the Sun. Born in Morenci, Arizona, in 1909, De Grazia spent his life traveling through Mexico and the Southwest, learning the lore of the Apache, Navajo, Yaqui and Papago tribes and collecting three art degrees. One of his most surprising moves came in 1976. To protest the severe taxes on heirs of artists, he burned 100 of his paintings—valued at $1.5 million. He was irate that his wife would have to sell most of these paintings to pay the inheritance tax on their value whenever he died. In 1982, De Grazia died of cancer.

~ 32540 North Biosphere Road (Route 77 Mile Marker 96.5), Oracle; 520-838-6200; www.bio2.com, e-mail sales@bio2.com.

In 2000, then-president Bill Clinton created 129,000-acre **Ironwood Forest National Monument**, which contains more than 200 sites from the prehistoric Hohokam period and remnants of an old mission, among other treasures. Ironwood trees live up to 800 years and attract hawks, owls, bighorn sheep, tortoises and white-winged doves. Of the 600-plus species that thrive here, several are listed as threatened or endangered. The BLM warns visitors to beware of unmarked roads, abandoned mine shafts, poisonous reptiles and insects, extreme heat and flash floods. If this hasn't completely terrified you, it's a beautiful and uncharted landscape to explore. ~ Route 10 at Avra Valley Road, about 25 miles northwest of Tucson; 520-258-7242, fax 520-258-7200; www.az.blm.gov.

LODGING

Although Tucson is known for its upscale, full-service resorts—a haven for those escaping cold winters elsewhere—it also has a number of budget and mid-range accommodations.

Located across the street from the train and bus stations, the **Hotel Congress** is a piece of Tucson's history. This block-long classical brick and marble structure was built in 1919 to serve Southern Pacific railroad passengers, and John Dillinger's gang were among its guests. Geometric Indian designs add character to the lobby, which also provides seating for the Cup Cafe and overflow from the nightclubs. The renovated hotel rooms are decorated with black-and-white-tile bathrooms, black headboards and salmon-colored walls. Of the hotel's 40 rooms, four are hostels with bunk beds and private baths (a hostel card is mandatory; reservations are not accepted for hostel rooms). None of the rooms have televisions, but they have wireless internet and windows that open—a rarity nowadays. Gay-friendly. ~ 311 East Congress Street; 520-622-8848, 800-722-8848, fax 520-792-6366; www.hotelcongress.com, e-mail reservations@hotelcongress.com. BUDGET.

Although it's in the middle of town, the **Arizona Inn**, built in the 1930s, feels like a lush oasis with 14 acres of lawns and gardens thick with orange trees, native cypress and date palms. No two of the resort's 86 rooms are alike, but all are decorated in the manner of the 1930s and some have antiques. The inn also has a swimming pool, tennis courts, a fitness room, a restaurant and a cocktail lounge decorated with 19th-century Audubons. ~ 2200 East Elm Street; 520-325-1541, 800-933-1093, fax 520-881-5830; www.arizonainn.com, e-mail reservations@arizonainn.com. ULTRA-DELUXE.

For quiet lodging amid terraced gardens, stay at **Catalina Park Inn Bed & Breakfast**, a dignified 1927 gem of an inn.

Elegantly decorated, yet steering clear of clutter, the six guest rooms are comfortable and lovely. You're within blocks of the University, although you'd never know it from the peaceful surroundings. Breakfast might include lemon ricotta pancakes or papaya and lime scones. Closed for a month in the summer (usually mid-July to early August). ~ 309 East 1st Street; 520-792-4541, 800-792-4885; www.catalinaparkinn.com, e-mail info@catalina parkinn.com. DELUXE.

Bed and breakfasts are proliferating in Tucson. Built in 1905, the **Peppertrees B&B Inn** is a red-brick Territorial home. There are two Southwest-style two-room guesthouses, a one-bedroom Mexican *casita*, and three main rooms furnished with period pieces from England. French doors lead outside to a beautifully landscaped patio. Full breakfast included. ~ 724 East University Boulevard; 520-622-7167, 800-348-5763; www.peppertreesinn. com, e-mail pepperinn@cox.net. DELUXE.

The Lodge on the Desert is a garden resort hotel with 35 adobe rooms grouped around patios that open to lawns and gardens. Rooms have beamed ceilings, handpainted Mexican tile accents and Monterey furniture, and many have gas-burning beehive fireplaces. Other amenities include a restaurant and a pool with mountain views. ~ 306 North Alvernon Way; 520-325-3366, 800-456-5634, fax 520-327-5834; www.lodgeonthedesert.com, e-mail info@lodgeonthedesert.com. ULTRA-DELUXE.

Comfort Suites/Sabino Canyon, a hacienda-style inn with rooms and suites, overlooks a lush courtyard dotted with Mexican fountains. The 90 guest rooms are clean and comfortable; many have kitchenettes. There is a pool and complimentary breakfast. ~ 7007 East Tanque Verde Road; 520-298-2300, 866-890-1399, fax 520-298-6756; www.comfortsuitestucson.com, e-mail comforttucson@yahoo.com. BUDGET TO DELUXE.

AUTHOR FAVORITE

When I want to stay in the thick of things yet still enjoy peace and quiet, I head for the **Adobe Rose Inn**, located just two blocks from U of A. Built in 1933, the rooms are appointed with '30s-era Southwestern antiques and furnishings; some have kiva fireplaces, mahogany floors, stained-glass windows and skylights that flood the rooms with that legendary Arizona light. The inn's six rooms are split between the main house, a *casita* and a second house. Relax poolside in the courtyard surrounded by desert foliage and encased within thick adobe walls. Free wi-fi. A gourmet breakfast is served. No children under ten. ~ 940 North Olsen Avenue, Tucson; 520-318-4644, 800-328-4122; www.aroseinn.com, e-mail innkeeper@ aroseinn.com. MODERATE TO DELUXE.

The resorts are expensive during winter high season, but most slash prices during the hot summer months. Among the best resorts is the **Westin La Paloma Resort & Spa**. The 487 Southwest-style rooms have private balconies or patios, a sitting area, oversized closet and a stocked fridge. Many of the suites have wood-burning fireplaces and sunken spa tubs. There are three swimming pools (including one with swim-up bar), a Jack Nicklaus golf course, tennis and racquetball courts, a health center, a spa and, for tired parents, day care for the small fry! ~ 3800 East Sunrise Drive; 520-742-6000, 800-677-6338, fax 520-577-5878; www.westinla palomaresort.com. ULTRA-DELUXE.

Spread on 80 acres in the foothills of the Santa Catalina Mountains, the **Westward Look Resort** is a scenic getaway. The 244 rooms here are actually worth spending time in, with their beamed ceilings, couches, refrigerator and wet bar, balconies and Mexican tile trim on the extra-long bathroom sinks. If you ever leave the room, check out the tennis courts, fitness center, pools, spas, two restaurants or lounge. ~ 245 East Ina Road; 520-297-1151, 800-722-2500, fax 520-917-2926; www.westwardlook. com, e-mail reservations@westwardlook.com. ULTRA-DELUXE.

Located in the foothills of the Santa Catalina Mountains, **Loews Ventana Canyon** is a 93-acre, luxury resort. Highlights are an 80-foot waterfall cascading down into a pond, and secluded paths lined with mesquite, squawbush and blue palo verde. Many of the resort's 398 Southwest-style rooms have original artwork, burnished-pine furnishings, private balconies and bathrooms with marble floors. Amenities include five restaurants and lounges, tennis, golf, fitness trails, pools, a health club and shops. ~ 7000 North Resort Drive; 520-299-2020, 800-262-4280, fax 520-299-6832; www.loewshotels.com. MODERATE TO ULTRA-DELUXE.

Looking for a little pampering? Then check out the **Omni Tucson National Golf Resort & Spa**, where you can relax in the European spa with a massage, facial, herbal wrap and other treatments. Located on the northwest edge of town, away from the city's hustle and bustle, the resort offers quiet and mountain views. The 167 suites and rooms have wet bars and private patios overlooking the championship 36-hole golf course or pool; suites also have refrigerators. Other amenities include a gift shop, restaurant, beauty salon, pool, tennis and volleyball. ~ 2727 West Club Drive; 520-297-2271, 800-528-4856, fax 520-297-7544; www.tucsonnational.com. ULTRA-DELUXE.

Located on five acres of Sonoran desert, surrounded by saguaro cacti, is **Casa Tierra Adobe Bed and Breakfast Inn**. With a central courtyard and fountain, it is an elegant hacienda-style inn with vaulted brick ceilings, Mexican-style furnishings and four guest rooms with private patios overlooking the desert. Telescopes offer lovely nighttime viewings of the sky There is a jacuzzi, a workout gym and a large common room with games, stereo, internet access and DVD/VCR. Full gourmet vegetarian breakfast included. Closed in July. ~ 11155 West Calle Pima; 520-578-3058, 866-254-0006, fax 520-578-8445; www.casatierratucson.com, e-mail info@casatierratucson.com. DELUXE TO ULTRA-DELUXE.

For information on bed and breakfasts throughout Arizona, visit **Arizona Association of Bed & Breakfast Inns** online. ~ www.arizona-bed-breakfast.com

DINING

There is an eclectic mix of cuisine in Tucson—Southwest- and Sonoran-style Mexican fare are the specialties.

Mi Nidito is a tiny, tacky, crowded Mexican joint with great food, from enchiladas to *menudo*. Portions are generous and there are always plenty of locals lining up to fatten their waistlines. When Bill Clinton dined here, of course, he did not need to wait in line. Closed Monday and Tuesday. ~ 1813 South 4th Avenue; 520-622-5081. BUDGET TO DELUXE.

Micha's is a larger restaurant owned for many years by the Mariscal family, whose portrait is just inside the door. You won't leave here hungry—even the flour tortillas are about a foot in length. Don't miss the chimichangas, *topopo* salad or grilled shrimp fantasia. No dinner on Monday. ~ 2908 South 4th Avenue; 520-623-5307, fax 520-388-9472; www.michascatering. com. BUDGET TO MODERATE.

Down the street is **Delectables**, decorated with brass chandeliers and turn-of-the-20th-century oak antiques. Inside are wood tables, wood-beamed ceilings and curving tinted windows that look out onto 4th Avenue, while outside are green metal tables covered in floral tablecloths with matching chairs. This eatery offers fresh salmon and roast beef, plus pastas, salads and sandwiches. ~ 533 North 4th Avenue; 520-884-9289, fax 520-628-7948; www.delectables.com, e-mail delectables@delectables. com. MODERATE.

For the innovative in pizza, try **Magpies Gourmet Pizza**. Examples of their fare include The Greek with spinach, basil, garlic, piñon nuts, feta cheese, cheese and sun-dried tomatoes, or Cathy's with garlic, stewed tomatoes, mushrooms, artichokes, roasted red peppers and romano cheese. Located in a small strip center, Magpies has a contemporary look with a black-and-white tile floor, wooden chairs and modern art on the walls. ~ 605 North 4th Avenue; 520-628-1661, fax 520-798-3117; www.mag piespizza.com. BUDGET TO DELUXE.

Cafe Poca Cosa is modern and stylish, with a curved white bar accented with slick black bar stools. The food's focus, however, is home-style Mexican. The menu changes twice daily, and is written on a blackboard that's brought to the table. Specialties include chicken breast in a tasty mango sauce, *pollo en chipotle* (chile) sauce and pork marinated in beer. Customers also rave about the luscious *moles*. Closed Sunday and Monday. ~ 110 East Pennington Street; 520-622-6400; www.cafepocacosainc. com. DELUXE.

At the **Arizona Inn**, you choose the ambience: formal dining room adjoining a courtyard ablaze with tiny lights in the trees, or casual dining in the lounge, on the patio or at the pool. The fare includes Continental, Southwestern, nouvelle and traditional selections. One treat is grilled salmon on saffron orzo with red chili–scallion glaze. Weekly specials will not disappoint. ~ 2200 East Elm Street; 520-325-1541, 800-933-1093; www.arizonainn.com, e-mail reservations@arizonainn.com. ULTRA-DELUXE.

The two boulevards boasting the largest concentration of restaurants in Tucson are Broadway and Speedway.

Tork's is a family-run place with only a handful of tables and delicious Middle Eastern and North African food. The *shawerma* plate with beef, chicken or lamb contains strips of meat cooked with onions and bell peppers. Other choices are the vegetarian falafel plate, hummus dip, tabbouleh and kabobs. Closed Sunday. ~ 3502 East Grant Road; 520-325-3737. BUDGET.

Buddy's Grill is a white-collar hangout. The narrow, blue-and-white room consists mainly of booths. Here, you'll find fajita salads, sandwiches, burgers cooked on a mesquite-wood grill and delicious baked French onion soup. You might also take a peek at the exhibition kitchen. ~ 4821 East Grant Road; 520-795-2226. BUDGET TO DELUXE.

It's hard to miss **Firecracker**: it's the restaurant with the huge flaming torches outside. You probably wouldn't want to miss this one anyway. The reasonably priced Pacific Rim menu might include pan-seared ahi in a spicy ginger cream sauce, or wok-charred salmon with cilantro pesto. The ingredients are always fresh and the exhibition kitchen shows off the talented kitchen staff creating unusual and tasty dishes. ~ Plaza Palomino, 2990 North Swan Road; 520-318-1118, fax 520-318-9886; www.metrorestaurants. com. MODERATE TO DELUXE.

Bentley's House of Coffee & Tea has wooden tables and chairs and the walls display rotating art shows. Food is typical café fare—soups, sandwiches, quiches—while beverages include espresso, gourmet coffee and a wide range of Italian cream sodas. ~ 1730 East Speedway Boulevard; 520-795-0338, fax 520-323-6175. BUDGET.

At the **Blue Willow Restaurant**, you can either dine inside the adobe house with its cozy dining, or opt for the brick, vine-covered courtyard. Either choice is a winner. Although they serve sandwiches and salads at lunch along with full dinners, breakfast is the most popular meal here with 14 omelettes, including one with avocados, jack cheese and green chiles. ~ 2616 North

Campbell Avenue; 520-327-7577, fax 520-327-9585; e-mail blue willowrestaurant@info.net. BUDGET TO MODERATE.

Szechuan Omei Restaurant is a Chinese restaurant where you can choose from more than 135 entrées, including lunch specials. Decor is nothing fancy, just red tablecloths and chairs and the usual Chinese lanterns and paintings. ~ 2601 East Speedway Boulevard; 520-325-7204. BUDGET TO MODERATE.

The Sonoran-style dining room of the **Tanque Verde Guest Ranch** has picture windows facing the desert mountains, a corner fireplace and elegant mahogany tables with carved Mexican chairs. Entrées change, but may include such choices as mesquite-barbecued pork loin ribs with poblano-chile hushpuppies, duckling glazed with prickly pear cactus syrup or broiled salmon with bérnaise sauce. All meals are served. Reservations required. ~ 14301 East Speedway Boulevard; 520-296-6275, fax 520-296-6275; www.tanqueverderanch.com, e-mail dude@tvgr.com. ULTRA-DELUXE.

HIDDEN ▶ **Old Spanish Trail Steak House** specializes in delicious barbecue ribs and chicken, as well as steaks. At night, settle down by the picture window. There's also enclosed patio dining. Closed Monday. ~ 5400 South Old Spanish Trail; 520-885-7782, fax 520-885-7172. MODERATE TO DELUXE.

For Southwestern food, try **Terra Cotta**. The outdoor patio is lit by miniature white lights at night, while the indoor section is decorated in terra-cotta colors and artwork by famous Southwestern names. The huge windows open onto unobstructed views of the mountains. Entrées include large prawns stuffed with herbed goat cheese and Southwestern tomato *coulis*, chipotle/maple–glazed chicken, and pizzas that are cooked in the wood-burning oven and topped with ingredients such as herbed mozzarella, lime and cilantro. No lunch Saturday and Sunday. ~

AUTHOR FAVORITE

It's hard to beat dining at **Anthony's in the Catalinas** with its top-notch views and ambience. The almost-floor-to-ceiling windows look over the city lights in this hacienda-style building. Dinner is served on elegant china with pale pink linens, fresh flowers and classical music playing in the background. Chandeliers hang from the vaulted, beamed ceiling and a large fireplace warms the room in winter. The Continental specialties include veal chop stuffed with prosciutto and fontina cheese, lamb Wellington and châteaubriand. Wash it down with a bottle from the extensive selection of about 1300 wines. Reservations are recommended. ~ 6440 North Campbell Avenue; 520-299-1771. DELUXE TO ULTRA-DELUXE.

3500 East Sunrise Drive; 520-577-8100, fax 520-577-9015; www.dineterracotta.com, e-mail feedback@dineterracotta.com. MODERATE TO DELUXE.

An old-fashioned pancake house with a European feel, **Millie's** ◀ *HIDDEN* **Pancake Haus** is a welcoming spot for breakfast or lunch with its cozy brick and wood interior, tied-back lace curtains, displays of bric-a-brac and pleasant staff. Along with pancake choices, the menu features Russian blintzes, corn cakes, omelets and daily specials. Breakfast and lunch only. Closed Monday. ~ 6530 Tanque Verde Road, 520-298-4250. BUDGET.

For something special, you can't beat **Janos**, which serves French-inspired Southwestern cuisine created by award-winning chef Janos Wilder. Menus are seasonal, but typical entrées are pepito-roasted lamb loin with wild-mushroom spoon bread and ancho-chile sauce, or sesame-crusted ahi with stir-fried Napa cabbage and mango sauce. Dinner only. Closed Sunday. ~ Westin La Paloma Resort & Spa, 3800 East Sunrise Drive; 520-615-6100. ULTRA-DELUXE.

Walk through antique, hacienda-style doors and you're inside **Tohono Chul Park Tea Room**, located in a rustic, 1940s house in ◀ *HIDDEN* the midst of Tohono Chul Park. Unless the weather is bad, opt for outdoor dining in the lush courtyard or on a patio that sits amid a wildflower landscape and offers free entertainment from the birds and other critters that come to nibble. For lunch, innovative sandwiches, soups and salads are served. Other choices are breakfast, Sunday brunch and afternoon tea. No dinner. ~ 7366 North Paseo Del Norte; 520-797-1222; www.tohonochulpark.org. MODERATE.

If you want anything with a Southwestern flair, Tucson is where **SHOPPING** you'll find it. You'll also find shops catering to almost every need, with the majority of the artsy and antique shops downtown and various specialty shopping plazas scattered throughout the town.

Built in 1939, **Broadway Village** was one of the first shopping centers in Arizona. It houses a variety of shops in whitewashed red-brick buildings. ~ Corner of Broadway Boulevard and Country Club Road. The more unusual includes a tiny mystery bookshop called **Clues Unlimited**. Closed Sunday. ~ 123 South East- ◀ *HIDDEN* bourne; 520-326-8533; www.cluesunlimited.com.

In the Broadway Village area there's **Yikes!**, a toy store with unusual gifts, small toys and books. Closed Sunday. ~ 2930 East Broadway; 520-320-5669. Next door, **Picante** sells various imported gift items, T-shirts, ethnic clothing and jewelry. Closed Sunday. ~ 2932 East Broadway; 520-320-5699.

A worthwhile stop in El Presidio District's Historic Block is the **Tucson Museum of Art gift shop,** with contemporary pottery and other artistic gifts. Closed Monday from Memorial Day through

Labor Day. ~ 140 North Main Avenue; 520-624-2333; www.tuc sonarts.com.

Nearby is **4th Avenue** with over 100 shops and restaurants. Shops in this older neighborhood contain vintage clothing, unique fashions, jewelry, books and art. Don't be surprised to find touches such as incense burning in the shops.

Antigone Books specializes in books by and about women as well as gay and lesbian literature. ~ 411 North 4th Avenue; 520-792-3715; www.antigonebooks.com.

Del Sol carries Southwestern clothes and jewelry, and a selection of rugs made by the Zapotecs of Mexico. ~ 435 North 4th Avenue; 520-628-8765; www.delsolstores.com.

On the vintage side, stop by the **Tucson Thrift Shop**, which specializes in costumes and vintage clothing from the 1940s onward. ~ 319 North 4th Avenue; 520-623-8736.

For Mexican imports, check out what is unofficially called the Lost Barrio Warehouse District—a group of shops located in old, red-brick warehouses. **Rustica** sells Southwestern, Peruvian and Mexican furnishings and accessories. Closed Sunday in summer. ~ 200 South Park Avenue; 520-623-4435.

HIDDEN ►

HIDDEN ►

Magellan Trading has wholesale pricing on Mexican glassware as well as handicrafts, artifacts and furniture from Mexico, New Guinea, Indonesia and Africa. ~ 1441 East 17th Street; 520-622-4968; www.magellantraders.com.

Among the many notable downtown galleries is the **Kaibab Courtyard Shops**, which for over 50 years has been a source of collector-quality Hopi kachina dolls, Zuni fetishes, Navajo and Zapotec weavings, Mexican folk art and more. ~ 2837–41 North Campbell Avenue; 520-795-6905.

Saint Philips Plaza is a cluster of Southwest-style shops with red-tile roofs that include art galleries, clothing stores and restaurants. ~ Corner of River Street and Campbell Avenue. Offering a wide choice of contemporary arts and crafts in a variety of media is **Obsidian Gallery**. Closed Sunday from Memorial Day to Labor Day; call ahead. ~ 4320 North Campbell Avenue, Suite 130; 520-577-3598. **Bahti Indian Arts** offers American Indian crafts such as jewelry, rugs, pottery and kachina dolls. ~ 4280 North Campbell Avenue, Suite 100; 520-577-0290.

AUTHOR FAVORITE

As an art buff, I enjoy the art walks that many gallery districts regularly sponsor. Few can compare with the **Tucson Arts District** on the first and third Thursday of the month, when an "Artwalk" is held in the district, making stops at exhibit rooms, galleries and artists' studios. ~ 125 South Arizona Avenue; 520-624-7099, fax 520-886-5155.

El Presidio Gallery Inc., a large fine-arts gallery with original Southwestern art in a variety of media. ~ 3001 East Skyline Drive; 520-299-1414.

North Campbell Avenue has a number of shopping venues. One of the most popular, judging by the ever-crowded parking lot, is Bookman's—*the* place for bibliophiles to browse. The owner claims the largest selection of used books and magazines in the Southwest. Bookman's also has a rare-book room and sells used magazines, records, tapes, video games, computer software and CDs. ~ 1930 East Grant Road; 520-325-5767.

A lovely place to wander and shop is Plaza Palomino, a shopping center without the plastic. Unusual boutiques, galleries, shops and restaurants surround the Spanish-style courtyard, which is lined with shade-giving palm trees and regularly "misted" in the summer heat. Enchanted Earthworks (520-327-7007; www.enchantedearthworks.com) features works by local artists, including jewelry, sculptures, masks and boxes in a variety of media. Maya Palace (closed Sunday; 520-325-6411; www.mayapalacetucson.com) has it all, from comfortable, blouse outfits to swirling Mayan skirts to wedding dresses. They also have a great array of jewelry and gifts. ~ North Swan and Fort Lowell roads; www.plazapalomino.com.

Drive farther down River Road and you'll see River Center, a Southwest-style shopping plaza. The stores surround a brick courtyard with a fountain and waterway. The West (closed Sunday; 520-299-1044) has cookbooks, cards, toys, kids' gifts and needlework supplies, with proceeds going to local women's and children's charities. ~ Corner of River Road and Craycroft Road.

For a fun, unusual children's toy store, stop by Mrs. Tiggy-Winkles. ~ 4811 East Grant Road, Suite 151; 520-326-0188.

Casas Adobes Shopping Center is yet *another* Southwest-style shopping plaza with a variety of specialty shops. ~ 7051 North Oracle Road.

A nearby favorite is Antigua de Mexico, a Latin American import store with Mexican Colonial and Southwestern furniture, folk art, pottery, glassware, tinware and sterling silver from Taxco. ~ 3235 West Orange Grove Road; 520-742-7114.

THE BEST BARS For alternative music—and alternative crowds —peek into Club Congress inside the Hotel Congress. Tucson's unconventional set mixes with the college crowd at this cavernlike place with a red-and-brown-tile floor and dark walls. There's live music Sunday, Wednesday and Friday; a deejay plays tunes the rest of the week. Cover. ~ 311 East Congress Street; 520-622-8848; www.hotelcongress.com.

NIGHTLIFE

Once a blacksmith shop and a country store, today Cushing Street Bar and Restaurant is a popular spot to pass the evening.

Patrons here enjoy drinks at turn-of-the-20th-century tables and chairs amid antiques such as a floor-to-ceiling, 1880s legal bookcase and a circa-1850 cut-glass globe above the bar. There's also an outdoor patio. Enjoy light jazz on the first and third Saturdays of the month. Closed Sunday and Monday. ~ 198 West Cushing Street; 520-622-7984.

Bum Steer is a casual place in a large, barnlike building containing a restaurant, several bars, a video arcade, a volleyball court and three dancefloors (one of which is outside). Inside, everything from cannons to airplanes hang from the vaulted roof (the staff claims over 8000 objects are strung up). There is entertainment on the weekends. Occasional cover. ~ 1910 North Stone Avenue; 520-884-7377.

HIDDEN ►   Graffiti on the tables and walls is the decor at **Bob Dobbs' Bar & Grill**, a local hangout for the college and older crowd. A bright, noisy place, it has indoor and outdoor seating and plenty of televisions for catching the latest sports coverage. ~ 2501 East 6th Street; 520-325-3767.

Trophies is a popular sports bar offering pool, darts, satellite TV and casual fare. ~ Sheraton Tucson, 5151 East Grant Road; 520-323-6262.

Laffs Comedy Club hosts everything from national to local acts. Thursday is college and military ID night. Closed Sunday and Monday. Cover. ~ 2900 East Broadway Boulevard; 520-323-8669; www.laffscomedyclub.com.

Follow the cowboy hats and neon lights and you'll end up at **Cactus Moon Cafe**, a huge place specializing in country music. Western artwork hangs on the walls and rodeos roll on movie screens. A glittering, colored light shines on the dancefloor, which is big enough for two-steppers not to be toe-steppers. Closed Sunday and Monday. Weekend cover. ~ 5470 East Broad-

AUTHOR FAVORITE

My love of people-watching and a good beer drew me to **Gentle Ben's Brewing Co.**, a microbrewery near campus with delicious European-style ales. If you're there at the right time of the day, you can see workers brewing (tours are also available). This two-story building is furnished with recycled tables and chairs, and there's outdoor seating where you can see and be seen. There's deejay music on Tuesday, Thursday and Saturday, and live music on Friday. Closed Sunday in the summer. ~ 865 East University Boulevard; 520-624-4177; www.gentle bens.com, e-mail realbeer@gentlebens.com.

way Boulevard; 520-748-0049; www.cactusmoon.net, e-mail cactusmoontucson@gmail.com.

Berky's Bar is a good place to hear the blues with live music all week long. A mixed crowd hangs out here, ordering drinks from the glass block bar, dancing and shooting pool. Cover Friday and Saturday. ~ 5769 East Speedway Boulevard; 520-296-1981.

The Chicago Bar offers a heady mix of live music. There's R&B on Monday and Tuesday, blues on Wednesday and Sunday, reggae on Thursday and Saturday, and rock or blues on Friday night. Chicago memorabilia covers the walls, from White Sox parking signs to hometown banners. Cover Wednesday through Saturday. ~ 5954 East Speedway Boulevard; 520-748-8169.

Tucson McGraws is a bar and dining room serving steaks and ribs. Step outside, walk down the steps and you'll land on the terrace ramada that looks toward the Santa Rita Mountains and Tucson's beautiful sunsets. ~ 4110 South Houghton Road; 520-885-3088, fax 520-886-1985.

THEATER The **Arizona Theatre Company** has been unofficially called the State Theater of Arizona and performs six or seven varied productions in Phoenix and Tucson from September through May. ~ 330 South Scott Avenue; 520-622-2823 (box office); www.arizonatheatreco.org. Plays by the Arizona Theatre Company and other groups are performed in the restored Spanish Colonial revival **Temple of Music and Art** in Tucson and the **Herberger Theater Center** in Phoenix.

Gaslight Theatre offers corny musical melodramas. Patrons eat free popcorn while hissing at the villain and cheering for the hero or heroine. Many of the comedies are original, written especially for the theater. No productions on Monday. ~ 7010 East Broadway Boulevard; 520-886-9428; www.thegaslighttheatre. com.

Invisible Theatre has classics, musicals and Off-Broadway plays by Arizona playwrights and contemporary dramatists from September through June. ~ 1400 North 1st Avenue; 520-882-9721; www.invisibletheatre.com.

OPERA, SYMPHONY AND DANCE **Ballet Arizona** is the state's professional ballet company. They perform a repertoire of classical and contemporary works including world and national premieres from September through April. ~ 888-322-5538; www. balletaz.org.

Arizona Opera serves both Tucson and Phoenix and produces Grand Opera. The season runs from October through April, and productions have included *Macbeth*, *Othello* and *Madame Butterfly*. ~ 260 South Church Avenue; 520-293-4336; www.az opera.org.

Text continued on page 308.

Calling All City Slickers!

Fueled by romantic images of Western heroes and desert sunsets and indulging in the fantasy of an escape to simpler times, more people than ever are opting to hang their saddles at dude ranches. In Southern Arizona, cowpokes have more than their fair share of choices. Guest ranches here range from resorts where you're more likely to overheat in the jacuzzi than the saddle, to working ranches where wranglers round 'em up and dine on beans and burgers. Whatever the orientation, most have horseback riding, a whole range of outdoor activities, and a casual, secluded atmosphere. Some are closed during the hot summer months, so call ahead.

One of the most luxurious getaways is **Tanque Verde Guest Ranch**, which has been around since the 1860s. It comes complete with indoor and outdoor swimming pools, tennis courts, an exercise room, guided nature walks, a supervised children's program and, of course, horseback riding. Guests stay in one of 70 *casitas* and patio lodges, some with beehive fireplaces, antiques and Indian bedspreads. Sliding glass doors offer stunning desert views. To relax, cozy up in the lobby with a good Western novel by the stone fireplace. ~ 14301 East Speedway Boulevard, Tucson; 520-296-6275, 800-234-3833, fax 520-721-9426; www.tanqueverderanch.com, e-mail dude@tvgr.com. ULTRA-DELUXE.

White Stallion Ranch sprawls across 3000 acres—grazing land for their herd of Longhorn. Guests take breakfast rides, watch rodeos every Saturday afternoon, and pet miniature horses, donkeys, pot-bellied pigs, pygmy goats and a llama at the on-site zoo. Rooms at this ranch have Western decor. Amenities include a fitness center with a sauna, a tennis court, a rec room and a theater. Rates include all meals and activities. Closed June through August. ~ 9251 West Twin Peaks Road, Tucson; 520-297-0252, 888-977-2624, fax 520-744-2786; www.wsranch.com, e-mail info@wsranch.com. ULTRA-DELUXE.

Don't look for TVs or phones inside the 24-room **Lazy K Bar Guest Ranch** because here you're meant to leave the outside world behind. Ranch-style meals are served in a dining room, and Tuesday and Saturday nights are set aside for cookouts beside a waterfall. Afterward, you can relax in the comfortable library with wood paneling and beams, bookshelves, a fireplace and a card table. Rooms are comfortable, carpeted and decorated in a South-western motif. Rates include all meals and activities. Closed June through August. ~ 8401 North Scenic Drive, Tucson; 520-744-3050, 800-321-7018, fax 520-744-7628; www.lazykbar.com, e-mail info@lazykbar.com. ULTRA-DELUXE.

Price Canyon Ranch in the Chiricahua Mountains is a working cattle ranch with a family cabin and one- and two-room bunk houses with baths. Meals are served in the 120-year-old main ranch house, and outdoor barbecues are held in the summer. Visitors can hike or ride horses in the surrounding national forest, or cool off in the swimming pool. Rates include meals, horseback riding and other ranch activities. A three-day minimum stay is required from October through May. ~ Off Route 80 between the 400- and 401-mile markers. Turn onto Price Canyon Road and drive seven miles, Douglas; 520-558-2383, 800-727-0065; www.pricecanyon.com, e-mail pcranch@vtc.net. DELUXE TO ULTRA-DELUXE.

Grapevine Canyon Ranch offers accommodations in guest rooms with country-ranch furnishings and American Indian touches. Visitors also lounge in the sitting room, a cozy place with a wood-beamed ceiling, Indian-design rugs and steer horns over the fireplace. At this working cattle ranch, horseback riding is the main attraction. Three meals are included. ~ Highland Road, Pearce; 520-826-3185, 800-245-9202, fax 520-826-3636; www.arizonaguestranch.com, e-mail info@gcranch.com. DELUXE.

Circle Z Ranch in the foothills of the Santa Rita Mountains is a colorful, unpretentious place built in the mid-1920s. It accommodates no more than 45 people at a time. The ranch's adobe cottages are decorated with brightly painted wicker furniture and Mexican crafts, but don't have TVs or telephones (although a single phone in the lodge is available for use). Instead, recreation centers around horseback riding. There is also a heated pool and a tennis court. The lodge has a massive stone fireplace and bookshelves filled with classics, including Zane Grey titles. Rates include all meals and activities. The ranch has a three-night minimum, and is open from November 1 through May 15. ~ P.O. Box 194, Patagonia, AZ 85624; 520-394-2525, 888-854-2525; www.circlez.com, e-mail info@circlez.com. ULTRA-DELUXE.

Sitting in the foothills of Baboquivari Peak on the Mexican border, **Rancho De La Osa** is a centuries-old Territorial-style ranch. Constructed with handmade adobe block, the 19 guest rooms have fireplaces and Mexican antique furnishings. Activities include horseback riding, biking, hiking and swimming, or sampling cocktails in the Cantina, an old Spanish/Indian mission. The hacienda dining room features gourmet Southwestern cooking. All meals included. ~ 28201 West La Osa Ranch Road, Sasabe; 520-823-4257, 800-872-6240, fax 520-823-4238; www.ranchodelaosa.com, e-mail osagal@aol.com. ULTRA-DELUXE.

Another ranch of note is **Triangle T Guest Ranch**, with 11 cabins, a restaurant, a saloon, nature trails and horseback riding (none during the summer). ~ Route 10, Exit 318, Dragoon Road, Dragoon; phone/fax 520-586-7533, 866-586-7533; www.triangletguestranch.com, e-mail ttgr@earthlink.net. BUDGET TO MODERATE. The 30-room **Rex Resort Ranch** is also worth checking out. Along with horseback riding, biking and hiking, you can enjoy the outdoor spa and junior Olympic–size pool. ~ 131 East Mado Montoso Road, Amado; 520-398-2914, 800-547-2696, fax 520-398-8229; www.rex ranch.com, e-mail info@rexranch.com. DELUXE TO ULTRA-DELUXE.

For classical, pops and chamber concerts there is the **Tucson Symphony Orchestra.** Performances run from September through May. ~ 2175 North 6th Avenue; 520-792-9155, 520-882-8585 (box office); www.tucsonsymphony.org.

Centennial Hall hosts a full lineup on an international scale, from Chinese acrobatics to African dances to Broadway shows. Past performers include Itzhak Perlman, the Prague Symphony Orchestra and George Winston. ~ University of Arizona, 1020 East University Boulevard; 520-621-3341; www.uapresents.org, e-mail uapresents@arizona.edu.

PARKS

GENE C. REID PARK 🏃 🚲 🏊 This 131-acre park is a lush oasis in the desert with grassy expanses dotted with mature trees. There are a wide variety of recreational facilities here, including a recreation center, two golf courses, a swimming pool, a pond, tennis and racquetball courts and a Hi-Corbett field where major league baseball teams come for spring training. Other attractions are Reid Park Zoo and a rose garden with more than 2000 plants. The park has restrooms, picnic tables and ramadas. ~ Located between Broadway Boulevard and 22nd Street, Country Club Road and Alvernon Way; 520-791-3204 ext. 13, fax 520-791-5378.

TUCSON MOUNTAIN PARK 🏃 🚲 🐎 Winding, hilly roads take you through this 20,000-acre, high-desert area brimming with ocotillo, palo verde, mesquite and saguaros and punctuated by mountains with rugged volcanic peaks. A popular spot is the Gates Pass overlook just past Speedway, where you can pull off the road and get a panoramic view of Tucson, Avra Valley and Kitt Peak, and watch Arizona's renowned sunsets. The park includes the Arizona-Sonora Desert Museum and Old Tucson Studios; there is an admission fee to both sites. There are established picnic areas throughout the park, as well as archery and rifle ranges. (Archery hunting is allowed in season with proper permit.) ~ Off Gates Pass Road, about ten miles west of the city limits (no recreational vehicles are allowed on the road). Another entrance is on Kinney Road off Ajo Way; 520-877-6000.

▲ Gilbert Ray Campground has 125 sites, most with electric hookups; $10 per night for tents and $20 per night for RVs; information, 520-883-4200 (December through March), 520-877-6000 (year-round).

FORT LOWELL PARK 🏃 🏊 With its blend of history and recreation, Fort Lowell Park is an ideal family getaway. Fort Lowell was once a major military post and supply depot. Stroll between the trees on Cottonwood Lane and you'll see a number of ruins, including that of the adobe post hospital built in 1875. Farther down is a museum (closed Monday and Tuesday) in the reconstructed officers' quarters. The 59-acre park also has a pond with a fountain and plenty of hungry ducks around the perimeter, and a trail with marked exercise stops along the way. The park also includes tennis and racquetball courts, pool, picnic areas, lighted ball fields and shade ramadas. ~ 2900 North Craycroft Road; 520-791-4873, fax 520-791-4008.

SAGUARO NATIONAL PARK Established to protect the saguaro cactus, found mainly in Arizona, the park is divided into two segments on opposite sides of Tucson. Entrance fee, $10 per vehicle (good for seven days for both districts). For general information, call 520-733-5100; www.nps.gov/sagu.

Rincon Mountain District 🚶 🚴 🐎 A popular segment of Saguaro National Park is the Rincon Mountain District east of town, a 66,621-acre chunk established in 1933. Begin your tour at the visitors center, with dioramas and other exhibits of the geological and botanical history of the park. Then drive along Cactus Forest Drive, a scenic eight-mile-loop showing off tall saguaro cacti with their splayed arms. This district has more than 100 miles of hiking and equestrian trails. You'll also find picnic areas, restrooms and barbecue grills. ~ Drive east on Old Spanish Trail about three miles beyond city limits; visitors center: 520-733-5153.

Tucson Mountain District 🚶 🚴 🐎 The 24,824-acre Tucson Mountain District to the west has a visitors center with orientations to the park, exhibits, maps and books, and features the six-mile-long Bajada Loop Drive that passes dense saguaro forests and American Indian petroglyphs. There are 40 miles of hiking and equestrian trails; biking is limited to the roads. Amenities include picnic areas, restrooms and barbecue grills. ~ Off Kinney Road, two miles north of the Arizona-Sonora Desert Museum; visitors center: 520-733-5158, fax 520-733-5164.

> For the romantically inclined, Sabino Canyon's shuttle has moonlight rides during the full moon from April through June and September through December.

SABINO CANYON RECREATION AREA 🚶 🚴 🐎 One of the most scenic spots in the region is a route that cuts through the Santa Catalina Mountains in the Coronado National Forest. You can either hike, bike or take the shuttle (fee) on a seven-and-a-half-mile roundtrip that climbs a road lined with cottonwoods, sycamores, ash and willow trees. Along the route flows Sabino Creek with its pools and waterfalls that tumble underneath arched stone bridges. The shuttle makes nine stops along the way, so you can jump on or off as you go. It will also take you on the two-and-a-half-mile trip to Bear Canyon Trail, where you then hike two more miles to Seven Falls, which cascade almost 500 feet down the side of a hill. Biking is restricted to before 9 a.m. or after 5 p.m. and is not allowed on Wednesday or Saturday. Facilities in the recreation area are limited to restrooms, picnic areas, a bookstore and a visitors center.

Parking fee, $5 (good at both Sabino Canyon and Mount Lemmon). ~ Located at the north end of Sabino Canyon Road after it intersects with Sunrise Drive; general information, 520-749-8700, fax 520-749-7723; www.fs.fed.us/r3/coronado, or shuttle information, 520-749-2327.

MOUNT LEMMON 🚶 🚴 🐎 🚠 🚣 In the hour's drive from Tucson to the top of Mount Lemmon, you travel from a lower Sonoran Desert zone to a Canadian zone forest, or from cacti to pine forests. For this reason, Tucsonians flock there in summer to escape the heat, and in winter to ski at Mount Lemmon Ski Valley, the southernmost ski area in the United States. If you take Catalina Highway to the top, the steep and winding mountain road will pass Rose Canyon Lake stocked with trout, and the town of Summerhaven, which is rebuilding after the 2003 Aspen fire. Once on Mount Lemmon, you can hike on 150 miles of trails. There are restrooms and picnic areas. Parking fee, $5 (good at both Sabino Canyon and Mount Lemmon). ~ Mount Lemmon is within the Coronado National Forest. Drive east on Tanque Verde Road to Catalina Highway, then head north 25 miles to Summerhaven; 520-749-8700; www.fs.fed.us/r3/coronado.

▲ There are tent and RV sites (no hookups) with toilets and drinking water at Rose Canyon (74 sites, $17 per night) and Spencer Canyon (62 sites, $14 per night). Molina Basin has 37 tent sites; $10 per night. Rose and Spencer canyons are closed in winter; Molina is closed in the summer.

Arizona's state flower, the saguaro cactus, is the largest American cactus. The plant produces white blooms on its tips during May and June.

HIDDEN ► **TOHONO CHUL PARK** Few tourists know about this treasure hidden in northwest Tucson. But walk down the winding paths of the 49-acre park and you'll discover over 1000 species of arid climate plants, many of which are labeled, along with water fountains, grotto pond areas and a greenhouse with plants for sale. In addition, you'll find three exhibit galleries, three museums, gift shops and a tea room, as well as picnic tables, ramadas and restrooms. ~ Off Ina Road at 7366 North Paseo del Norte, about six miles north of the Tucson city limits; 520-742-6455, fax 520-579-1213; www.tohonochulpark.org, e-mail marketing@tohonochulpark.org.

CATALINA STATE PARK 🚶 🚴 🐎 This 5500-acre preserve sits in the Santa Catalina foothills. Highlights include Romero Canyon, a beautiful area with pools shaded by sycamore and oak trees, and adjacent Pusch Ridge Wilderness, home to desert bighorn sheep. The Hohokam once farmed the area, and as you walk through the park you can still see some of the pit houses and ball court ruins. Facilities include restrooms, showers, picnic tables and grills. Day-use fee, $6 per vehicle. ~ Off Route 77, about nine miles north of the city limits at 11570 North Oracle Road; 520-628-5798, fax 520-628-5797.

▲ Catalina State Park Campground has 120 tent/RV sites; $15 per night without hookups, $20 with hookups.

PICACHO PEAK STATE PARK 🏃 The most dramatic part of the park is Picacho Peak, a landmark formation that rises 1500 feet above the desert floor and can be seen for miles around. Believed to be 22 million years old—or four times as old as the Grand Canyon—Picacho Peak was used as a landmark by early explorers. It was the site of the battle of Picacho Pass during the Civil War. The 3500-acre park has seven miles of developed hiking trails that wind past saguaro cacti as well. Facilities include picnic areas, ramadas, showers and restrooms. Day-use fee, $6 per vehicle. ~ Off Route 10 (Exit 219), 40 miles north of Tucson; 520-466-3183, fax 520-466-7442.

▲ There are 85 tent/RV sites; $12 per night without hookups, $20 with electricity hookups.

▼▼▼▼▼▼▼▼▼▼
East of Tucson

The Wild West comes to life in this area of Arizona where murder and lynching were once considered leisure activities, poker was more popular than Sunday church services and whiskey was king. While this region is best known for infamous spots like Boot Hill and the O.K. Corral, it's also the home of historic mining towns like Bisbee, mineral spas and a cowboy hall of fame.

SIGHTS

Get on Route 10 heading east and one of the first attractions you will pass is **Colossal Cave Mountain Park**, one of the largest dry caverns in the world. Set in the Rincon Mountains, it was once home for Indians and outlaws. During 50-minute tours, hidden lights illuminate formations such as the Silent Waterfall and Kingdom of the Elves. On the premises is also a 130- year old working ranch offering trail rides, museums, and wooded picnic areas. Admission. ~ 16721 East Old Spanish Trail, Vail; 520-647-7275, fax 520-647-3299; www.colossalcave.com, e-mail info@colossalcave.com.

◀ *HIDDEN*

Farther east on Route 10 is Benson, where the **Arts & Historical Society** tells the story about how Benson grew along with the arrival of the railroad. Inside are antiques, artifacts and an old grocery store. A gift shop offers local arts and crafts. Closed Sunday and Monday and the month of August. ~ 180 South San Pedro Street, Benson; 520-586-3070.

The spelunkers who discovered **Kartchner Caverns** in 1974 kept their find a secret for 14 years until they had persuaded officials to protect it as a state park. The vast cave opened to the public in 1999 after $28 million in state-of-the-art improvements, which included a wheelchair-accessible paved trail through the caverns, a computerized halogen lighting system and five sets of air-lock doors along the narrow entrance passage to prevent the desert air outside from drying up the "living" cave formations. Visitors to Arizona's largest cave find themselves in a hidden world of subterranean chambers the size of football fields dripping with calcite formations that range from delicate soda-straw stalactites up to 21 feet long and only a quarter-inch in diameter to a 58-foot-tall column that forms the centerpiece of a sound-and-light show. In dramatic contrast to the arid heat of the Chihuahuan Desert above ground, the climate inside the cave is a constant 68° and 99 percent humidity. Reservations are recommended: often tours of the cave are booked solid. Admission. ~ 2980 South Route 90, Benson; 520-586-4100, 520-586-2283 (reservations), fax 602-542-4113.

On your way to the Old West towns of Bisbee and Tombstone, take a detour toward Elgin. You will enter what at first seems an oxymoron—Arizona **wine country**. But there are several wineries out here, and it's a pretty drive through the vineyards.

HIDDEN ▶   In the town of Elgin you'll find **The Chapel of the Blessed Mother, Consoler of the Afflicted**, a small chapel set amid grasslands, vineyards and cottonwood trees. ~ Elgin.

Head south on Route 90 and you can't miss **Fort Huachuca**, a National Historic Landmark founded in 1877 to protect settlers from Apache raiders. The Fort Huachuca soldiers eventually tracked down and defeated Apache leader Geronimo. Today, this 73,000-acre installation is home to the U.S. Army Intelligence Center and School. One highlight is the Fort Huachuca Museum, located in an early 1900s building first used as a bachelor officers' quarters. Inside are military artifacts, dioramas and the history of the fort. The museum annex is across the street, and down the road is the Army Intelligence Museum. For a panoramic view of the fort and town, drive up Reservoir Hill Road. If you'd prefer picnicking, there are plenty of scenic spots amid large, old trees. ~ Sierra Vista; 520-533-5736.

Take Route 92 south and you'll find a place known to birding enthusiasts worldwide. **Ramsey Canyon Preserve** is home to a variety of birds, including 14 species of hummingbirds from mid-April to early September. Also commonly spotted here are white-tailed deer, gray squirrels and coatimundi. The Nature Conservancy owns this 380-acre wooded gorge set in the Huachuca Mountains. No vehicles over 18 feet are allowed. No pets, picnicking or smoking. Admission. ~ Route 92, five miles south of Sierra Vista; 520-378-2785, fax 520-620-1799; www.nature.org.

Hop on Route 90 again for the quick trip to **Bisbee** near the Mexican border. An old mining town and now an artists' enclave, the town is full of Victorian architecture perched on hillsides, along with funky shops and restaurants. For the full history of the town, start at the **Bisbee Mining & Historical Museum**, located in the former General Office Building of the Copper Queen Consolidated Mining Co. This is the first rural museum to become a Smithsonian affiliate. On the front lawn is old mining equipment, while inside the 1897 red-brick building are photo murals, artifacts and walk-in environments that highlight Bisbee's history. The museum also has a large display of rocks and precious minerals once housed at the Smithsonian. Admission. ~ 5 Copper Queen Plaza, Bisbee; 520-432-7071, fax 520-432-7800; www.bisbeemuseum.org, e-mail info@bisbeemuseum.org.

For a first-hand view of mining history, put on a slicker, hard hat and battery-pack light and hop on the underground train at the **Queen Mine Underground Tour**. An ex-miner narrates as he takes you through the Copper Queen Mine, which prospered for more than 60 years before it closed in 1944. The journey is a cool one, so bring a jacket. From here you can also take the **Historic Bisbee & Surface Mine Tour**, a narrated, 13-mile van tour around a 300-acre hole where more than 380 million tons of ore and tailings have been removed. It also travels through the historic section of Bisbee, spotlighting such buildings as the Copper Queen Hotel and the Phythian Castle. Admission. ~ 478 North Dart Road, Bisbee; 520-432-2071, fax 520-432-5191.

Continue your time travel to the Old West at **Slaughter Ranch**, located near the Mexican border. Now a National Historic Land-

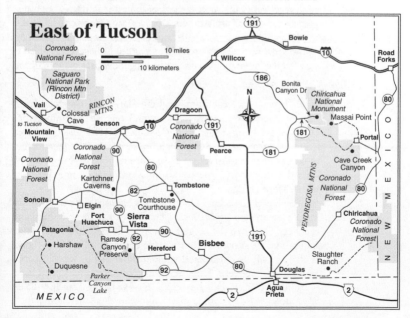

Old Tombstone

Born in 1877 as a silver camp, Tombstone has lived up to its nickname—the town too tough to die. Wild West legends about the Earp brothers, Doc Holliday and Bat Masterson have transformed this National Historic District into southern Arizona's busiest sightseeing destination, and each year the revenues from tourism far surpass the total amount of silver produced by the mine that lies beneath the town streets in Tombstone's heyday.

BIRD CAGE THEATRE Most of Tombstone's early-day historic buildings are along Allen Street. At one end of the main street, the Bird Cage Theatre was built in 1881 as a gambling casino and dance hall; prostitutes plied their trade in its birdcage-like compartments. Never a dull place, the theater was the site of 16 gunfights. If you bother to count you'll find 140 bullet holes riddling the walls and ceilings. The longest poker game in the history of the West reputedly unfolded here . . . it lasted eight years, five months and three days. Admission. ~ 6th and Allen streets; 520-457-3421, fax 520-457-3189; www.tombstoneaz.net, e-mail oldbirdcage@juno.com.

O.K. CORRAL Down Allen Street from the Bird Cage is the O.K. Corral, where legend places the most famous of Tombstone's many shootouts. Life-size figures of the Earp brothers, Doc Holliday and their enemies, the Clantons, stand in the corral as a narrator describes the gunfight. (Actually, the incident did not take place here but in a nearby vacant lot, which is now part of the museum.) An adjacent building showcases old Tombstone

mark, it was once the home of John Slaughter, a former Texas Ranger, sheriff of Cochise County and one of the founders of Douglas. He bought the fertile grassland in 1884 and developed it into a cattle ranch. Slaughter's house and half a dozen other buildings furnished to reflect the era are still on the 140-acre site. Closed Monday and Tuesday. Admission. ~ Geronimo Trail, 15 miles east of Douglas; 520-558-2474, e-mail sranch@vtc.net.

The **Hotel Gadsden** in Douglas is a National Historic Monument that opened in 1907 as a hotel for cattlemen, miners and ranchers. Step into the magnificent lobby to behold a solid white Italian-marble staircase, four marble columns with capitals decorated in 14K gold leaf, and vaulted stained-glass skylights that run its length. Several Hollywood movies have been filmed here. ~ 1046 G Avenue, Douglas; 520-364-4481, fax 520-364-4005; www.hotelgadsden.com, e-mail robin@hotelgadsden.com.

photos and memorabilia. Admission. ~ 308 Allen Street; phone/fax 520-457-3456; www.ok-corral.com, e-mail okcorral@ok-corral.com.

CRYSTAL PALACE AND SILVER NUGGET   Other notorious old houses of booze, gambling and ill repute (now restored and family-friendly) along Allen Street include the Crystal Palace and the Silver Nugget.

ROSE TREE INN MUSEUM   A huge rosebush that spreads across 8600 feet of supports is the main attraction at the Rose Tree Inn Museum, one block off the main street. Planted in 1885, the bush is an awesome sight in April, when it's covered with white blossoms. You can tour the historic adobe home containing local artifacts and period rooms. Admission. ~ 4th and Toughnut streets; 520-457-3326.

TOMBSTONE COURTHOUSE   Now an Arizona state historic park, the Tombstone Courthouse has a restored courtroom and two floors of historic exhibits that reflect the ups and downs of this once-rowdy town. The red-brick building was the town's courthouse from 1882 to 1929. Admission. ~ 3rd and Toughnut streets; 520-457-3311, fax 520-457-2565. Also part of the historic park is the original office of the *Tombstone Epitaph* (as locals say, every Tombstone should have an Epitaph), the second-oldest newspaper in Arizona. The monthly newspaper is still published. ~ 520-457-2211.

BOOTHILL GRAVEYARD   Finally, no visit to Tombstone would be complete without a stop at the Boothill Graveyard, where outlaws and early settlers rest side by side, their graves little more than piles of rocks marked by white metal crosses. This may be the only cemetery around with its own gift shop. ~ Route 80W; 520-457-3300, fax 520-457-9344.

Just west of Route 80, between Douglas and Route 10, is **Cave Creek,** an area of the Chiricahua Mountains. Birdwatchers ◄ *HIDDEN* from all over the world come to try to catch a glimpse of the elegant trogon, a neotropical Mexican summer migrant that breeds here. You'll find a ranger station, a general store and a number of rustic bed-and-breakfasts and self-service cabins in and around the tiny communities of Portal and Paradise, a ghost town five miles to the west.

Southwest of Paradise is **Tombstone.** Prospector Ed Shieffelin staked a silver claim there in 1877 and it became a Wild, Wild West town—and in more recent years the subject of innumerable Western movies. Today the town is extremely touristy, yet almost irresistible. With its rowdy mix of history and cowboy kitsch, Tombstone is the best place in southern Arizona to watch actors stage a gun fight.

After looping off Route 10 to see Sierra Vista, Bisbee and Tombstone, get back to Route 10 and go east to Dragoon, home of the **Amerind Foundation Museum** (an archaeological research facility) and little else. This is a real treasure tucked away amidst the rock formations of Texas Canyon. The research facility and museum have been devoted to American Indian culture and history since they opened in 1937. Visitors walk through the Spanish Colonial revival–style buildings to see exhibits on prehistoric and historic indigenous cultures from both North and South America. The art gallery houses Western artwork, including works by Frederic Remington and William Leigh. Closed Monday and Tuesday. Admission. ~ Dragoon Road, Dragoon; 520-586-3666, fax 520-586-4679; www.amerind.org, e-mail amerind@amerind.org.

More Western history is found farther east on Route 10 in Willcox at the **Chiricahua Regional Museum and Research Center**. There's a bust of Chief Cochise, Indian and mining artifacts, and a mineral and rock collection. Closed Sunday. ~ 127 East Maley Street, Willcox; 520-384-3971, 520-384-4882.

The most famous cowboy of the area was Rex Allen, born in Willcox in 1920. The **Rex Allen Arizona Cowboy Museum** features mementos of Rex Allen's life, from his homesteading and ranch life in Willcox to his movies and television shows. Another section features the pioneer settlers and ranchers of the Willcox area. Admission. ~ 155 North Railroad Avenue, Willcox; 520-384-4583, 877-234-4111; www.rexallenmuseum.org, e-mail info@rexallenmuseum.org.

LODGING

The majority of accommodations in Sierra Vista are along Fry Boulevard—the main commercial thoroughfare through town—and on South Route 92. **Sierra Suites** is a two-story, red-brick hotel that lures guests with complimentary breakfast. The 100 rooms face courtyards, and inside, some have mirrored sliding glass closet doors, glass tables, a chest of drawers, hairdryers, coffeemakers, refrigerators and microwaves. The price includes use of the pool and whirlpool. ~ 391 East Fry Boulevard, Sierra Vista; 520-459-4221, fax 520-459-8449. BUDGET TO MODERATE.

Quality Inn is a two-story, brick building with 103 rooms. Lower-level guest rooms facing the pool have sliding glass doors. Most accommodations have double beds and a desk. ~ 1631 South Route 92, Sierra Vista; phone/fax 520-458-7900, 800-458-0908. BUDGET TO MODERATE.

HIDDEN ►

For a really secluded getaway, venture out to **Ramsey Canyon Inn Bed & Breakfast,** located in the Huachuca Mountains along a winding mountain stream and adjacent to the Nature Conservancy's Ramsey Canyon Preserve and the Coronado National Forest. Accommodations consist of two fully equipped apartments and a six-room bed-and-breakfast inn, with a private bath in each room. Rates include full breakfast and homemade pies in the afternoon. ~ 29 Ramsey Canyon Road, Hereford; phone/fax 520-378-3010; www.ramseycanyoninn.com, e-mail lodging@ramsey canyoninn.com. DELUXE TO ULTRA-DELUXE.

Built in 1917, **Hotel La More/The Bisbee Inn** overlooks Brewery Gulch, once one of the Southwest's wildest streets. Each of the 20 rooms has handmade quilts on the beds, antique dressers with mirrors, and its own sink. Four rooms share bathrooms in the hall. ~ 45 OK Street, Bisbee; 520-432-5131, 888-432-5131, fax 520-432-5343; www.bisbeeinn.com. BUDGET TO DELUXE.

School House Inn Bed and Breakfast is a large, restored, 1918 red-brick schoolhouse just above Garfield Park. The nine themed rooms (reading, writing, arithmetic, etc.) are fairly large, and each has a private bath with a large tub. ~ 818 Tombstone Canyon, Bisbee; phone/fax 520-432-2996, 800-537-4333; www. virtualcities.com/ons/az/b/azb4501.htm. BUDGET TO MODERATE.

The **Bisbee Grand Hotel** is ideally located in the main shopping area in town. The original hotel was built in 1906. There are seven suites with private baths and six rooms. All accommodations reflect the era with period wallpaper, red carpeting, brass beds and antiques. They also have sinks and ceiling fans. Most of the rooms are upstairs, while downstairs is the grand Western Saloon and Billiards Room. Rates include breakfast. ~ 61 Main Street, Bisbee; phone/fax 520-432-5900, 800-421-1909; www.bis beegrandhotel.com, e-mail bisbeegrand@cableone.net. MODERATE TO DELUXE.

The **Jonquil Motel** is a small motor court with seven clean, comfortable rooms. The rooms have televisions but no telephones.

AUTHOR FAVORITE

If I were making a pilgrimage to all the hotels in the Southwest where John Wayne once spent the night, among my favorites (though not the quietest) would be Bisbee's historic **Copper Queen Hotel**. The Copper Queen Mining Co. built the hotel just after the turn of the 20th century when it was a gathering place for politicians, mining officials and travelers, including the young Teddy Roosevelt. A plaque on one door marks the room where John Wayne stayed. The rooms are decorated Victorian style with floral wallpaper and tile bathrooms. The four-story building contains 48 rooms, along with a pool, saloon and dining room. ~ 11 Howell Avenue, Bisbee; 520-432-2216, 800-247-5829, fax 520-432-4298; www.copperqueen.com, e-mail info@copperqueen.com. MODERATE TO DELUXE.

~ 317 Tombstone Canyon, Bisbee; 520-432-7371, fax 520-432-6915; www.thejonquil.com, e-mail mail@thejonquil.com. BUDGET.

The six-room **Tombstone Boarding House** is in two adobe buildings constructed around 1880; all rooms have private entrances and baths. Rooms are tastefully decorated in pastel colors with lacy curtains and Victorian-era furnishings. A full breakfast is served in the Victorian dining room. In the evening, a gourmet dinner is available (at an extra charge). Pet-friendly. ~ 108 North 4th Street, Tombstone; 520-457-3716, 877-225-1319; www.tombstoneboardinghouse.com, e-mail info@tombstone boardinghouse.com. BUDGET TO MODERATE.

DINING

HIDDEN ▶

Horseshoe Cafe is a family-owned restaurant that has been around since 1937. On the walls are Western murals by artist Vern Parker, and the posts in the café display cattle brands of Southern Arizona. A neon horseshoe on the ceiling helps light the room. Entrées include chili, sandwiches, omelettes, burgers, steaks and Mexican specialties. ~ 154 East 4th Street, Benson; phone/fax 520-586-3303. BUDGET TO DELUXE.

Stop by cozy **Grasslands Natural Foods & Café**, which looks like a miniature restaurant plopped in the middle of your kitchen. Salads, pasta salads and quiche provide a light alternative to the typical heavy burritos of the region; baked sandwiches round out the menu. Ingredients are always fresh and organic. If you're reluctant to see the end of your meal, visit their bakery, which sells olive herb sourdough, wheat germ and currant bars and homemade granola. No dinner. Closed Monday and Tuesday and in September. ~ 3119 Route 83, Sonoita; 520-455-4770; www.grasslandsbakery.com, e-mail orders@grasslands bakery.com. BUDGET TO MODERATE.

A sleek art-deco restaurant in a historic 1907 building, **Cafe Roka** offers a wide variety of flavorful pastas and house specialties such as smoked salmon with gorgonzola. Ingredients are fresh and the service charming. Check out the original pressed-tin ceil-

HOT DOG!

If you're in the mood for the biggest hot dog in Cochise County, weighing in at half a pound and measuring a foot long, then saunter over to the **Longhorn Restaurant** and order a Longhorn Dog. If that's not what you crave, they offer other big food options, including a 40-ounce steak. The decor is Western with longhorns hanging over the door and yellowing wanted posters of characters such as Billy the Kid laminated on the tables. ~ 501 East Allen Street, Tombstone; 520-457-3405. BUDGET TO MODERATE.

ings and the marble bar. Live music on Friday and Saturday. Call for summer hours; closed Sunday through Wednesday the rest of the year. ~ 35 Main Street, Bisbee; 520-432-5153; www.caferoka. com. DELUXE.

Rosa's Little Italy is a tiny local eatery that specializes in country-style Italian fare: hearty portions of veal piccata, fettuccini alfredo, antipasto plates and tiramisu for dessert. A good bargain, the portions are large and you get to bring your own chianti—it's BYOB. Dinner only. Closed Monday and Tuesday. ~ 7 Bisbee Road, Bisbee; 520-432-1331. MODERATE.

Enjoy Mexican or American favorites under the watchful eye of Marilyn Monroe at **Grand Cafe Restaurant,** the blonde bombshell appears in paintings, drawings and photographs exhibited throughout the eatery. Burritos, fajitas and flautas are some of the Mexican dishes while T-bone steaks and shrimp scampi are featured on the American menu. Breakfast, lunch and dinner. Closed Sunday. ~ 1119 G Avenue, Douglas; 520-364-2344. BUDGET TO MODERATE.

The **Nellie Cashman Restaurant** is housed in an 1879 building with decor to reflect the era including a stone fireplace, high wood ceilings and photos of bygone years. Although they serve sandwiches and burgers, they're best known for their homemade pies. ~ 117 South 5th Street, Tombstone; 520-457-2212; www. nelliecashman.freeservers.com, e-mail nellcash@hotmail.com. MODERATE TO DELUXE.

Singing Wind Bookshop is in the *really hidden* category. From Route 10, turn north on Ocotillo Road, then go for two and a quarter miles and turn right on West Singing Wind Road. Go half a mile; at the white tank bear left and drive down to the ranch house. Here, there are two huge rooms full of new books about the Southwest, Western Americana and other categories. In addition, there's a room full of children's books. ~ West Singing Wind Road and North Ocotillo Road, two and a quarter miles north of Route 10, Benson; phone/fax 520-586-2425.

SHOPPING

◀ *HIDDEN*

The **Johnson Gallery** carries American Indian arts and crafts and Quezada family pottery. ~ 28 Main Street, Bisbee, 520-432-2126. **The Gold Shop** features innovative, contemporary jewelry created by local and regional artists. ~ 67 Main Street, Bisbee; 520-432-4557.

Allen Street is the heart of shopping in Tombstone, where you will find lots of souvenir shops mixed in with higher-quality jewelry and clothing stores. **Bronco Trading Co.** carries Western wear for cowboys and cowgirls. ~ 410 Allen Street, Tombstone; 520-457-9220; www.broncotrading.com.

Arlene's Southwest Silver & Gold is a large place with American Indian jewelry and artwork including pottery, baskets, kachina dolls and rugs. ~ 404 Allen Street, Tombstone; 520-457-3344.

Spur Western Wear sells Western duds for the whole family. ~ 509 East Allen Street, Tombstone; 520-457-9000.

For Tombstone souvenirs, including hats, books and Western keepsakes such as cow skulls (!), check out **Tombstone Emporium**. ~ 325 Allen Street, Tombstone; 520-457-3854.

The time to travel out to the Willcox area is fall, when farms and roadside stands are selling their produce. The Willcox Chamber of Commerce (800-200-2272) has a brochure listing orchards and mills where you can stop. One is **Stout's Cider Mill**, where you can buy apples, cider, dried fruit, nuts, peaches, apple pies, chile peppers and Arizona desert preserves. ~ 1510 North Circle I Road, Willcox; 520-384-3696; www.cidermill.com.

NIGHTLIFE

HIDDEN ►

Big Boys Arena Bar overlooks the rodeo grounds, where you can watch the scheduled events. Inside, a Western theme dominates. A lasso hangs on the door, cow skulls decorate walls, and you can warm yourself by the big rock fireplace. There are also a pool table and dancefloor, along with outdoor picnic benches. ~ 250 North Prickly Pear Street, Benson; 520-586-9983.

Established in 1902, **St. Elmo Bar** in historic Bisbee is a tradition around here. Memorabilia such as old maps hang on the walls, and seating is mainly stools at the counter. On weekends there's live music and dancing. Entertainment during the week is supplied by the CD jukebox or pool tables. ~ 36 Brewery Avenue, Bisbee; 520-432-5578.

At one time, Tombstone reputedly had saloons and gambling halls making up two of every three buildings.

Adjoining the Copper Queen Hotel, the **Copper Queen Saloon** is a small, dark, intimate place with some early-20th-century furnishings and live music on occasional weekends. ~ 11 Howell Avenue, Bisbee; 520-432-2216.

At the **Stock Exchange Bar**, almost one whole wall is covered with an original board from the Bisbee stock exchange. This historic building has a pressed-tin roof and worn wooden floors. There's a jukebox and occasional live music on the weekend. ~ 15 Brewery Avenue, Bisbee; 520-432-9924.

Walk through swinging doors of **Big Nose Kate's Saloon** and you step back into the Old West. Waitresses dressed as saloon gals serve drinks. Lighted, stained-glass panels depict Tombstone's characters, and old photographs hang on the walls. On Friday you'll find live country-and-western music. Lily Langtry and Wyatt Earp once tipped their glasses here. ~ 417 East Allen Street, Tombstone; 520-457-3107; www.bignosekate.com, e-mail whiskers@bignosekate.com.

The Crystal Palace Saloon has been restored to look like it did when it was built in the 1880s. The long, narrow room has old wood tables and red drapes underneath a copper ceiling. Live music is performed occasionally on Saturday evening and Sunday during the day. ~ 420 East Allen Street, Tombstone; 520-457-3611; www.crystalpalacesaloon.com.

CHIRICAHUA NATIONAL MONUMENT 🏃 The Chiricahua Apaches called this area the Land of the Standing-Up Rocks because throughout the park are huge rock spires, stone columns and massive rocks perched on small pedestals. Geologists believe that these formations were created as a result of explosive volcanic eruptions. For an overview of the park, drive up the winding, eight-mile-long Bonita Canyon Drive. You'll pass pine and oak-juniper forests before reaching Massai Point high in the Chiricahua Mountains where you can see the park, valleys and the peaks of Sugarloaf Mountain and Cochise Head. You can also explore the park on foot via about 20 miles of trails. Other attractions include historic Faraway Ranch and Stafford Cabin. There are picnic tables, restrooms, a visitors center with exhibits, and a bookstore. There are no services inside the park. Day-use fee, $5 per person (seven-day pass). ~ From Willcox, go southeast on Route 186 for 37 miles; 520-824-3560, fax 520-824-3421; www.nps.gov/chir.

▲ There are 22 sites; $12 per night. No backcountry camping is allowed within the monument.

PARKS

Far off the beaten track, southwestern Arizona is home to the world's leading astronomical center, remote ghost towns, wildlife preserves and a sanctuary dedicated to the unusual organ pipe cactus. This is also where civilization disappears and the desert blooms.

South/West of Tucson

Heading south on Route 19, you'll pass the retirement community of Green Valley and arrive at the **Titan Missile Museum**, the only intercontinental ballistic missile complex in the world that's open to the public. Here you'll be taken on a one-hour guided tour into the bowels of the earth, experience a countdown launch of a Titan missile and view a silo. It's an eerie excursion. Reservations are recommended. Admission. ~ 1580 West Duval Mine Road, Sahuarita; 520-625-7736, fax 520-625-9845; e-mail ymorris@titan missilemuseum.org.

SIGHTS

To get away from the high-tech missiles and delve deeper into the area's history, continue farther south on Route 19 to Tubac. Here, the Spanish founded a presidio in 1752 to protect settlers from the Indians. At **Tubac Presidio State Historic Park** visitors can see the remains of the original presidio foundation, the foundation of the Spanish captain's house from the military garrison in 1750, an 1885 schoolhouse, a 1914 community hall and a museum detailing the history of Tubac. Admission. ~ Route 19, Tubac; 520-398-2252.

A few more minutes down Route 19 are the adobe ruins of a Spanish frontier mission church at the **Tumacácori National Historical Park**. Along with the museum, visitors walk through the baroque church, completed in 1822, and the nearby ruins of a circular mortuary chapel and graveyard. Since little has been built in the vicinity, walking across the grounds feels like a walk back in time. Admission. ~ Route 19, Exit 29 on Frontage Road, Tumacácori; 520-398-2341, fax 520-398-9271; www.nps.gov/tuma.

Continuing south, Route 19 hits the Mexican border. **Nogales, Mexico**, is a border town offering bargain shopping, restaurants and some sightseeing. On the other side is Nogales, Arizona. Photographs and artifacts detail the town's history at the **Pimeria Alta Historical Society Museum**, a 1914 mission-style building that once housed the city hall, police and fire departments. Closed Monday through Thursday. ~ 136 North Grand Avenue, Nogales; 520-287-4621.

HIDDEN ▶

Just off of Route 82 you'll pass by some **ghost towns**, including Harshaw and Duquesne. **Duquesne** was a mining center established around the late 1800s with a peak population of 1000 residents, including Westinghouse of Westinghouse Electric. **Harshaw** was settled around 1875 and operated about 100 mines. Today all that's left are ruins and graveyards. Some of the roads en route are extremely bumpy and rugged, so be prepared.

Tucson and the surrounding area is known as the Astronomy Capital of the World with more astronomical observatories than anywhere else. One of the most famous is the **Kitt Peak National Observatory**. Drive up a mountain road and you'll come across the observatory's gleaming white domes and its 24 telescopes. During tours you can step inside some of the telescopes, including the 18-story-high four-meter telescope. There's also a museum with exhibits on the observatory, as well as star-gazing programs. Serious astronomy buffs can spend the night on top for a steep fee. If you're planning on staying awhile, bring food—it's a long haul up the mountain and there's nothing to nibble on at the top. ~ Off Route 386, 56 miles southwest of Tucson; 520-318-8726, fax 520-318-8451; www.noao.edu, e-mail kpno@noao.edu.

Continuing to the west about 100 miles on Route 86, and then heading north on Route 85, you'll come to **Ajo**, a small scenic town whose center is a green plaza surrounded by Spanish Colonial–style buildings. It is also an old copper mining town and as such shows its scars.

The **Ajo Historical Society Museum**, located in what was once St. Catherine's Indian Mission, is a stucco church built in

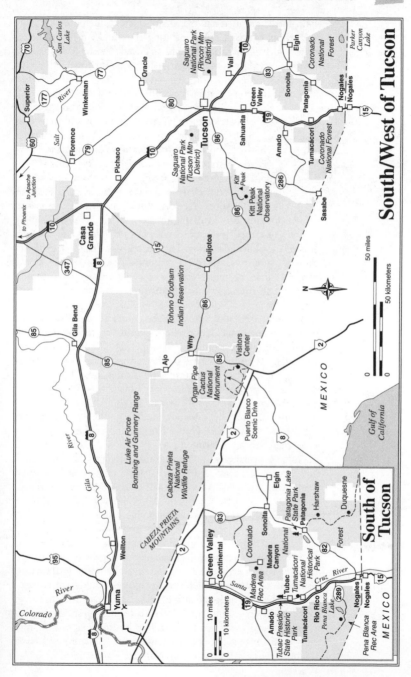

South/West of Tucson

South of Tucson

1942. Inside are artifacts from Ajo's history, including a black-smith shop, dentist's office, printing shop and American Indian artifacts such as old saddles found on graves. Closed May through October, except by appointment. ~ 160 Mission Street, Ajo; 520-387-7105.

Much farther west, near the California border, is **Yuma**. Once a steamboat stop and major crossing on the Colorado River, to-day it's a bustling city that supports farming and basks in a subtropical climate. **Yuma Territorial Prison**, a penitentiary built between 1876 and 1909, is now a state historic park. Despite its infamous rep-utation, written evidence indicates that the prison was humanely administered and was a model institution for its time. Prisoners received regular medical attention and schooling was available to the convicts. Those prisoners who escaped were faced with hostile deserts and the cur-rents of the Colorado River. The prison was closed in 1909 be-cause of overcrowding. Today visitors walk through the gloomy cells and climb the guard tower, where one can see the Colorado River and surrounding area. Admission. ~ 1 Prison Hill Road, Yuma; 928-783-4771, fax 928-783-4772.

The first major construc-tion project in Yuma was the Yuma Territorial Prison.

The military supply hub for the Arizona Territory is now the **Yuma Crossing State Historic Park Quartermaster Depot**, which served the Southwest until it closed in 1883. Several of the orig-inal buildings remain, including the commanding officer's quar-ters and Office of the Quartermaster. Admission. There's a visi-tors center with displays on the park's history. ~ 201 North 4th Avenue, Yuma; 928-329-0471, fax 928-782-7124.

More of Yuma's history comes to light in the **Arizona Histor-ical Society's Sanguinetti House Museum**. Once the home of pi-oneer merchant E. F. Sanguinetti, it now has artifacts, photo-graphs and furnishings of Arizona's territorial period. Just outside are colorful gardens and aviaries with exotic birds. Closed Sunday and Monday. Admission.~ 240 South Madison Avenue, Yuma; 928-782-1841, fax 928-783-0680; www.arizonahistori cal society.org, e-mail azhistyuma@cybertrails.com.

LODGING Located in Madera Canyon, **Santa Rita Lodge Nature Resort** is a perfect birders' getaway. Just outside the large windows in each of the 12 rooms are feeders that attract a number of bird species. Inside the rooms, charts hang with pictures of different types of hummingbirds. The lodge also offers nature programs that meet in the patio area, and staff birders will take guests on birding walks. If (gasp!) you've had enough of birding, extensive nature trails wend through the property. ~ Located 13 miles southeast of Green Valley in the Coronado National Forest; 520-625-8746, fax 520-648-1186; www.santaritalodge.com, e-mail becksted@ aol.com. MODERATE.

Bing Crosby was part-owner of the **Tubac Golf Resort** back in 1959. The 64 rooms and suites are decorated in a Western motif and have tiled bathrooms and patios facing the mountains; some have woodburning fireplaces. The resort has a golf course, tennis court, pool and spa, hiking trails and a full-service restaurant and bar. ~ 1 Avenida de Otero, Tubac; 520-398-2211, 800-848-7893, fax 520-398-9261; www.tubacgolfresort.com, e-mail relaxing@ tubacgolfresort.com. ULTRA-DELUXE.

Esplendor Resort at Rio Rico is a beautiful resort in the San Cayetano Mountain range. All of the rooms have sliding glass doors overlooking the pool or mountains, wood-beamed ceilings, and contemporary Southwestern decor in pastel colors. Amenities include a golf course, tennis courts, horse stables, jacuzzi, exercise room, restaurant and lounge. ~ 1069 Camino Caralampi, Rio Rico; 520-281-1901, 800-288-4746, fax 520-281-7132; www. hhandr.com, e-mail reservations@esplendor-resort.com. DELUXE TO ULTRA-DELUXE.

The **Stage Stop Inn** is a 43-room hotel with a restaurant, a saloon and clean, comfortable rooms (some with kitchenettes) facing the pool in the middle. Movie casts and crew often stay here while filming in the area. The Western lobby showcases an antelope head above the fireplace, cattle brands on the tile floor and Western paintings on the walls. ~ 303 McKeown Avenue, Patagonia; 520-394-2211, 800-923-2211, fax 520-394-2212; www.thestagestopinn.com, e-mail stagestopinn@theriver.com. BUDGET TO MODERATE.

A charming old adobe that was once a boarding house for miners, **Duquesne House Bed and Breakfast** offers four comfortable suites with brick floors and rustic Mexican-style architectural details. All suites have private entrances and private baths. There is also an efficiency apartment without a private entrance. A common room features a woodstove and TV. A pleasant back porch overlooks a garden. Full breakfast. ~ 357 Duquesne Avenue, Patagonia; 520-394-2732; e-mail theduquesnehouse@hotmail.com. MODERATE.

Looking like a miniature dollhouse, **The Guest House Inn** is a charming white house with blue trim and a long front porch dotted with white-cushioned furniture for lazing away the hours. Phelps Dodge once entertained dignitaries at the Guest House Inn, and breakfast is now served on the 20-foot-long walnut dining table where these guests once ate. Inside, the setup is unusual, with a living room in the middle and guest rooms lining either side of the house. Each of the four bedrooms has a private bath and its own decorating scheme. ~ 700 Guest House Road, Ajo;

520-387-6133; www.guesthouseinn.biz, e-mail info@guesthouse inn.biz. MODERATE.

Built during the space races with the Russians, the theme at the **Best Western Space Age Lodge** is obvious. Hand-painted space murals accent the lobby and restaurant. Guest rooms have pictures of rockets blasting off into space and contain whitewashed wood furniture, pastel colors and large, well-lighted mirrors above the counter. There's also a pool, a spa and a restaurant. ~ 401 East Pima Street, Gila Bend; phone/fax 928-683-2273, 866-683-7722; www.bestwesternspaceagelodge.com, e-mail 03004@ hotel.bestwestern.com. BUDGET TO MODERATE.

La Fuente Inn has 96 Southwest-style rooms decorated in pastels. Rooms have VCRs, irons and ironing boards and face the grassy interior courtyard and pool. Prices include a complimentary continental breakfast, happy hour and use of the fitness room. ~ 1513 East 16th Street, Yuma; 928-329-1814, 877-202-3353, fax 928-343-2671; www.lafuenteinn.com, e-mail manager@lafuente inn.com. MODERATE TO DELUXE.

DINING

HIDDEN ►

Even though there's not much in Amado, it's worth a stop to eat at **The Cow Palace**, a local landmark that has been around since the 1920s. While in town to shoot movies, Western stars have frequented the place, and their photos hang on the walls. Decor is rustic Western, with a wagon wheel for a chandelier and red tablecloths, carpet and curtains. Entrées carry on the theme with names such as the Night Rider T-bone steak, Wrangler's stew and Chuck Wagon barbecue beef sandwich. ~ Off Route 19 (Exit 48), 28802 South Nogales Highway, Amado; 520-398-1999; www.cowpalacerestaurant.com. BUDGET TO DELUXE.

Opened in the 1940s as a coffee shop, **Wisdom's Café** is now a restaurant crammed with old photographs, farming tools, velvet paintings, patchwork rugs and other odds and ends. You can spot it on the road by the two gigantic fiberglass chickens in front. If you can get by the chickens, try some of their Mexican food.

AUTHOR FAVORITE

If you've never dined in an 1840s horse stable, stop in at **The Stables** restaurant at the Tubac Golf Resort. Actually, the place is quite nice. Inside are arched windows, cobblestone floors and pottery made by Mexicans and American Indians. Look closely and you might find Apache Indian arrowheads embedded in the restaurant's adobe walls. Dinner focuses on steak, seafood and a lavish Sunday brunch. ~ 1 Otero Road, Tubac; 520-398-2211, 800-848-7893, fax 520-398-9261; www.tubacgolfresort.com, e-mail relaxing@tubacgolfresort.com. DELUXE TO ULTRA-DELUXE.

Closed Sunday. ~ Route 19 frontage road, Tumacacori; 520-398-2397; www.wisdomscafe.com, e-mail celeste@wisdomscafe.com. BUDGET.

San Cayetano Restaurant in the Esplendor Resort at Rio Rico offers Southwestern cuisine as well as a Sunday champagne brunch. Two walls have floor-to-ceiling windows with panoramic views of the mountains. The interior has tables and booths decorated in earth tones to fit a casual Southwestern look. Reservations are recommended. ~ 1069 Camino Caralampi, Rio Rico; 520-281-1901, 800-288-4746; www.hhandr.com, e-mail reservations@esplendor-resort.com. DELUXE.

Patagonia Grill serves standard American fare like burgers and hot and cold sandwiches. Weekend dinner specials branch out with themes such as Italian and Greek. ~ 277 McKeown Avenue, Patagonia; 520-394-0076. BUDGET TO MODERATE.

Located in the Stage Stop Inn is **Home Plate**. The menu includes sandwiches, burgers, steaks, Mexican food and homemade desserts. ~ 303 McKeown Avenue, Patagonia; 520-394-2344. MODERATE.

In 1911, the first plane to land in Arizona did so in Yuma. Almost a century later, you can celebrate this flight of fancy at the **Yuma Landing,** a restaurant rich in aviation history. Menu offerings range from pasta to prime rib to the "Crash Landing" (two beef patties with sautéed mushrooms, bacon and Swiss cheese). Fried everything tops the appetizer list. Try not to board a plane after eating here—it might never get off the ground. Breakfast, lunch and dinner are served. ~ 195 South 4th Avenue, Yuma; 928-782-7427; www.yumalanding.com, e-mail management@yumalanding.com. MODERATE TO DELUXE.

About 80 shops and restaurants make up the town of **Tubac.** Although it's geared to tourists, they've managed to avoid the rubbertomahawk syndrome and you'll find high-quality artwork. All of the shops are within walking distance and are evenly distributed along Tubac Road, Plaza Road and Calle Otero. **SHOPPING**

Tortuga Books, known throughout the Southwest, specializes in philosophy, psychology, children's books, Southwestern literature, greeting cards and CDs. ~ 19 Tubac Road, Tubac; 520-398-2807. **The Pot Shop Gallery and Rodeo June** features signed lithographs by R. C. Gorman, as well as prints, pottery and clay artwork created by Arizona artisans. ~ 16 Tubac Road, Tubac; 520-398-2898. **The Chile Pepper** offers Southwestern gourmet foods, chile food products, chile wreaths, coffees, teas and cookbooks. ~ 22 Tubac Road, Tubac; 520-398-2921. For handcrafted American Indian jewelry, kachinas, sand paintings, baskets and pottery, stop in **Old Presidio Traders.** ~ 27 Tubac Road, Tubac; 520-398-9333.

American Indian–owned and –operated, **Cloud Dancer Jewelry Studio** is a fine-art gallery with one of the largest Hopi kachina collection in Southern Arizona. The gallery also offers custom-designed jewelry with turquoise and precious gems in gold, silver and platinum settings, as well as paintings, pottery and sculpture. ~ 24-1 Tubac Road, Tubac; phone/fax 520-398-2546.

To shop in the older, more historic section of town, go to Calle Iglesia. In this area you'll find **Hugh Cabot Studios & Gallery** housed in a 250-year-old adobe building that used to be a hostelry for Spanish soldiers. This internationally known artist creates Southwestern and general-interest works in several mediums and makes his home in Tubac. Closed Sunday and the last two weeks of July. ~ 10 Calle Iglesia, Tubac; 520-398-2721; www. hughcabot.com.

The **Ajo Art Gallery** has a mixture of contemporary paintings by artists from across the U.S. Closed Sunday and Monday and from May through September. ~ 661 North 2nd Avenue, Ajo; 928-387-7525.

Colorado River Pottery has quite a selection of ceramics made on-site. Closed Sunday. ~ 67 West 2nd Street, Yuma; 928-343-0413, 888-410-2689; www. coloradoriverpottery.com. At **Tomkins Pottery**, George Tomkins creates decorative clay pieces. Closed Sunday and Monday. ~78 West 2nd Street, Yuma; 928-782-1934; www.claystuff.com.

NIGHTLIFE   Scenic mountain views from picture windows draw people to **The Saloon** at the Esplendor Resort at Rio Rico. The contemporary, Southwest-style bar has live Top-40, jazz and dance music on Friday. ~ 1069 Camino Caralampi, Rio Rico; 520-281-1901.

Lutes Casino is one of the oldest continually owned and operated pool and domino parlors in the state. Open since 1920, the place is crammed full of farm implements, paintings and historic memorabilia. ~ 221 Main Street, Yuma; 928-782-2192; www.lutescasino.com, e-mail feedback@lutescasino.com.

For live alternative and rock bands, head on over to **Jimmie Dee's**. Antique signs and assorted knickknacks give this bar an old-timey feel. Closed Sunday. ~ 38 West 2nd Street, Yuma; 928-783-5647.

PARKS   **PATAGONIA LAKE STATE PARK**   The largest recreational lake in Southern Arizona (265 acres) is located in this 645-acre park. Patagonia Lake, nestled amid rolling hills, was created by the damming of Sonoita Creek in 1968. It's stocked with bass, crappie, catfish, bluegill and, in the winter, trout. A small, sandy beach lures swimmers. You can windsurf and waterski here, although waterskiing is not allowed on weekends or holidays from May through October. The park provides picnic areas, restrooms, showers and a marina with boat rentals. Pontoon birding tours (520-287-2791) are offered on Saturday or by request (more often in spring). Day-use fee, $7. ~ Off Route 82, about 12 miles north of Nogales. Follow the signs to the park; 520-287-6965, fax 520-287-5618.

▲ There are 119 sites, including 34 RV hookups and 13 accessible by boat only; hookups are $22 per vehicle, all other sites $15 per vehicle.

PATAGONIA–SONOITA CREEK PRESERVE Nine miles north of Patagonia Lake State Park is a 312-acre sanctuary in a narrow flood plain between the Santa Rita and the Patagonia mountains. The preserve encompasses a one-and-a-half mile stretch of Sonoita Creek lined with large stands of cottonwoods—some a hundred feet tall—as well as Arizona walnut, velvet ash, willows and Texas mulberry. Birdwatchers from all over the world come here because more than 300 species of birds have been seen. It is also home to white-tailed deer, bobcat, javelina, coyote and the most endangered fish in the Southwest, the Gila Topminnow. There are restrooms and water in the preserve. Closed Monday and Tuesday. Day-use fee. ~ From Patagonia, turn northwest off Route 82 onto 4th Avenue, then go left on Pennsylvania Avenue. When the pavement ends, cross the creek and follow the dirt road for one mile. There will be an entrance with the visitors center on your left; 520-394-2400; www.nature.org/arizona.

> Because of its elevation of 3750 feet, Patagonia Lake State Park sometimes has temperatures cooler than Tucson.

CORONADO NATIONAL FOREST The Coronado National Forest (www.fs.fed.us/r3/coronado) in Arizona has 1.7 million acres of public land in 12 sky islands, or mountain ranges that jut above the surrounding desert. Following are three of the highlights:

Madera Canyon 🚶 🚲 🐎 This spot is a great place for birdwatching, with more than 200 species including several varieties of woodpeckers, hawks, wrens and vultures. Driving up through the canyon the desert changes from grassland to forest. Trees on the lower slopes of the Santa Rita Mountains are mesquite, and farther up are live oaks, alligator junipers, cottonwoods and sycamores along Madera Creek. There are more than 70 miles of trails. You'll find restrooms, picnic areas and grills. ~ Located 49 miles south of Tucson. Take Route 19 south from Tucson to Green Valley's Continental Road, then go southeast for 13 miles; 520-281-2296, fax 520-670-4598.

▲ There are 13 sites at Bog Springs Campground; $10 per night per vehicle.

Pena Blanca Lake 🚶 🚤 🚣 Surrounded by oak, cottonwood and mesquite trees and light-colored bluffs, this 39-acre lake is situated at 4000 feet—making it higher and somewhat cooler than Tucson. Fishing is good for bass, bluegill, crappie, catfish and rainbow trout but because of high mercury levels, the Fish and Wildlife Department recommends that you catch and release all but trout. A trail leads around the lake. Also located here are picnic areas, pit toilets and picnic tables. ~ Located five miles north of the Mexican border. Take Route 19 south from Tucson to Ruby Road, then go west for about nine miles; 520-281-2296, fax 520-670-4598; www.fs.fed.us/r3/coronado.

▲ There are 15 sites at White Rock Campground (a quarter-mile from the lake), although there are no lake views; $10 per night per vehicle.

Parker Canyon Lake 🚤 🛥 ↙ Parker Canyon Lake is an 130-acre fishing lake west of the Huachuca Mountains and surrounded by grassy, rolling hills. Bluegill, bass, perch, trout and catfish are the common catches. To assist with the fishing there are boat rentals, bait and a fishing dock. There are also restrooms, picnic areas and a marina store. The marina is closed on Wednesday. ~ From Sonoita, take Route 83 south for 30 miles until it runs into the park; 520-378-0311, fax 520-378-0519.

▲ There are 65 sites in Lakeview Campground; $10 per night. Please note that the campground may be closed depending on funding; call for reservations and closures.

ORGAN PIPE CACTUS NATIONAL MONUMENT 🧍 🚲 This 330,000-acre refuge became a national monument in 1937 to protect the Sonoran desert plants and animals and the unique organ pipe cactus. Start at the visitors center 17 miles south of the northern entrance. Here you can see exhibits and pick up a self-guided tour pamphlet. The only paved road through the park is Route 85. While exploring the monument, you'll pass mountains, plains, canyons, dry washes and a pond surrounded by cottonwood trees. Picnic areas and restrooms are the only facilities in the park. Parking fee, $8 per week. ~ The monument is located 35 miles south of Ajo, and the visitors center is at the 75-mile marker on Route 85; 520-387-6849, fax 520-387-7475; www.nps.gov/orpi.

A good tour at Organ Pipe Cactus National Monument is the Puerto Blanco Scenic Drive, a 53-mile graded dirt loop with numbered stops described on the tour.

▲ There are 208 sites in the main campground; $12 per night. Fresh water is available at the dump station, the visitors center and the campground. Primitive camping ($8 per night) is allowed at four sites in the Alamo campground and anywhere in the backcountry as long as you're a half mile from the road; you can pick up the $5 permits for backcountry camping at the visitors center. No campfires.

CABEZA PRIETA NATIONAL WILDLIFE REFUGE Established in 1939, the 860,000-acre refuge is an arid wilderness rife with cactus and mountains. Passing through the refuge is the 250-mile El Camino del Diablo (Highway of the Devil) that was pioneered by Spanish Conquistador Captain de Anza in 1774—and stretches from Mexico to California. Along the way you pass Cabeza Prieta Mountain with its lava-topped granite peak, and Mohawk Valley with sand dunes and lava flows. Since roads here are rugged and unimproved, four-wheel-drive vehicles are required. Also, beware of the six species of rattlesnakes, and note that Border Patrol activities are high here and visitors should exercise caution. Limited hunting for desert bighorn sheep is allowed in the winter. Refuge and Arizona Game and Fish permits are required. There are no facilities in the refuge; the closest groceries are in Ajo, seven miles east. The refuge roads are sometimes closed for inclement weather; call ahead for conditions. Also, three-quarters of the refuge is closed March 15th through July 15th. ~ You'll need explicit directions, which you can get when you pick up the Refuge Entry Permit at the refuge office in Ajo (1611 North 2nd Avenue). It's advisable to call ahead; 520-387-6483, fax 520-387-5359.

▲ There are three primitive campgrounds with no facilities; no wood fires allowed; no water. Permit required.

Outdoor Adventures

Although water isn't plentiful in Southern Arizona, there are a few lakes where boats are available to rent.

BOATING

EAST OF TUCSON Boat rentals are available at **Parker Canyon Lake**, nestled among the foothills of the Huachuca Mountains. Closed Tuesday and Wednesday. ~ Off Route 83, 30 miles southwest of Sierra Vista; 520-455-5847.

SOUTH/WEST OF TUCSON **Patagonia Lake State Park** offers rowboat, canoe and paddle-boat rentals. ~ Patagonia; 520-287-5545. For an excursion on the Colorado River, try a jetboat tour. **Yuma River Tours** offers boat rides past petroglyphs, homesteads, steamboat landings and mining camps. ~ 1920 Arizona Avenue; 928-783-4400.

SWIMMING

For a retreat from the heat take a plunge at one of Southern Arizona's public pools.

TUCSON **Fort Lowell Park** has an Olympic-size pool. ~ 2900 North Craycroft Road; 520-791-2585. Dive in at **Himmel Park**. Summer only. ~ 1000 North Tucson Boulevard; 520-791-4157. Get wet at **Morris K. Udall Park**. ~ 7200 East Tanque Verde Road; 520-791-4931. **Joaquin Murieta Park** has a public pool. Summer only. ~ 1400 North Silverbell Road; 520-791-4245. Cool yourself down in **Jacobs Park**'s pool. Summer only. ~ 3300 North Fairview Avenue; 520-791-4245. Call **Tucson Parks & Recreation** for more information. ~ 520-791-4873.

BALLOON RIDES

TUCSON A Southern Arizona Balloon Excursion ascends from the Tucson area. Sunrise trips fly high enough for great views of Tucson and the Catalina Mountains and low enough to see wildlife along the Santa Cruz River. ~ 537 West Grant Road, Tucson; 520-624-3599; www.tucsoncomefly.com. Another company hovering above is **Balloon America**, which offers sunrise flights over the Sonoran Desert, the Catalina mountains and the Grand Canyon. Flights operate from October through May. ~ Located near Speedway Boulevard and Houghton Road; 520-299-7744; www.balloonrideusa.com.

SKIING

There's only one place to ski and snowboard in these parts—the **Mount Lemmon Ski Valley**. The southernmost ski-area in North America, Mount Lemmon offers 21 runs, equipment rental, a ski school and a restaurant. ~ 10300 East Ski Run Road, Mount Lemmon; 520-576-1321, 520-576-1400.

RIDING STABLES

If you prefer to let someone else do the walking, there are several horseback riding outfitters in the area.

TUCSON A Western town like Tucson wouldn't be the same without opportunities to go riding. Dudes and dudettes can saddle up at **Walking Winds and El Conquistador Riding Stables**. They offer one- to one-and-a-half-hour rides in the Catalina Mountains. ~ 10000 North Oracle Road; 520-742-4200. Mount a steed at **Pusch Ridge Stables** for one-hour to overnight excursions. All meals and equipment provided. ~ 13700 North Oracle Road; 520-825-1664; www.puschridgestables.com. Saddle up at **Pantano Riding Stables** for a guided trip into Saguaro National Park; rides last one to two hours. ~ 4450 South Houghton Road; 520-298-8980; www.horsingaround.com.

GOLF

Mild winters make this region ideal for golfers, and aficionados can choose between a wide range of private and public courses. All courses listed for the Tucson area have club and cart rentals and golf pros available for lessons.

TUCSON The semiprivate **Omni Tucson National Golf Resort & Spa** has 27 holes—three 9-hole courses that can be played in different combinations. There is a pro shop and a restaurant and bar. ~ 2727 West Club Drive; 520-575-7540; www.tucsonnational.com. Swing your clubs under the sunny skies at **Starr Pass Golf Resort**, an 18-hole mountain course with long fairways, rolling greens and many elevation changes. Carts are mandatory. ~ 3645 West Starr Pass Boulevard; 520-670-0400. Work on your game at **Randolph North Municipal Golf Course**, an 18-hole course with long fairways and water hazards on six holes. The adjacent 36-hole **Del Urich Municipal Golf Course** (Randolph South Municipal Golf Course) has tall trees, lush fairways, straight holes and rolling terrain with elevated tees and greens. Both courses share a pro shop, practice area, driving range and putting green. ~ 600 South Alvernon Way; 520-791-4161; www.tucsoncitygolf.com.

The 18-hole executive **Dorado Golf Course** has a pro shop. ~ 6601 East Speedway Boulevard; 520-885-6751. Go for a hole in one at the public 18-hole **Arthur Pack Desert Golf Course**. ~ 9101 North Thornydale Road; 520-744-3322. ◆◆◆◆◆◆◆◆◆◆◆◆◆◆◆◆◆◆◆◆◆◆◆

The semiprivate **Lodge at Ventana** is a PGA resort course that runs through rocky canyons, arroyos and foothills; a cart is included in the green fee. ~ 6200 North Club House Lane; 520-577-1400. Beware the hazards at the 18-hole **Quail Canyon Golf Course**. ~ 5910 North Oracle Road; 520-887-6161. Tee off at the 18-hole public **El Rio Golf Course**. ~ 1400 West Speedway Boulevard; 520-791-4229; www.elrio countryclub.com. Take aim at the greens on **Fred Enke Golf Course**, an 18-hole desert course with a pro shop. ~ 8251 East Irvington Road; 520-791-2539. Situated on the bank of the Santa Cruz River, the 18-hole **Silverbell Golf Course** sports flat fairways, large greens and nine lakes. There is a pro shop. ~ 3600 North Silverbell Road; 520-791-5235.

> For those without a fear of heights, there's nothing like floating above it all. Ballooning is a great way to escape the heat and get a magnificent view at the same time.

EAST OF TUCSON   A golfing spot east of Tucson is the 18-hole **Turquoise Valley Golf Course**. ~ 1791 West Newell Street, Bisbee; 520-432-3025. In Douglas, the 18-hole **Douglas Municipal Golf Course** has a complete pro shop, a lounge and an adjacent RV park under the same ownership, all in a desert setting surrounded by mountains. Cart rentals only. ~ 1372 East Fairway Drive; 520-364-3722.

SOUTH/WEST OF TUCSON   **Canoa Hills Golf Course** is an 18-hole semiprivate facility. ~ 1401 West Camino Urbano, Green Valley; 520-648-1881. **Pueblo Del Sol Golf Course** is another 18-hole green. ~ 2770 St. Andrews Drive, Sierra Vista; 520-378-6444. At the Resort Rio Rico, the private 18-hole PGA **Rio Rico Golf Course** was designed by Robert Trent Jones, Sr. ~ 1069 Camino Caralampi, Rio Rico; 520-281-1901, 800-288-4746. **Tubac Golf Resort**, an 18-hole course with lots of trees, as well as a restaurant and bar, is the premier spot in Tubac. ~ 1 Otero Road; 520-398-2211. If passing through Safford, check out the 18-hole **Mount Graham Golf Course**. ~ Golf Course Road, Safford; 928-348-3140. In Yuma you can tee off at the 18-hole **Mesa Del Sol Golf Club**. ~ 12213 Calle del Cid; 928-342-1817.

The dry, hot climate provides excellent court conditions all year.   **TENNIS**

TUCSON   When it's not too hot to serve, try the public tennis courts in Tucson. **Fort Lowell Tennis Center** has eight lighted public courts, as well as racquetball courts and a tennis pro; fee. ~ 2900 North Craycroft Road; 520-791-2584. You can swing a racquet at **Himmel Park**, which also has eight lighted courts; fee. ~ 1000 North Tucson Boulevard; 520-791-3276. Or try the **Randolph Tennis Center**, with 25 public courts, all lighted for night play; fee. ~ 50 South Alvernon Way; 520-791-4896. **Pima Community College** has eight lighted courts for public use on a first-come, first-served basis; classes have priority. No fee, no pro. ~ 2202 West Anklam Road; 520-206-6619.

BIKING   If you haven't brought a bike with you, rent one in town and take to the road or trail.

TUCSON   Tucson is a very popular area for bicycling. Some favorite routes include riding on **Oracle Road** north of Ina Road, where cyclists find wide shoulders and beautiful mountain views. On the way back turn into Sun City Vistoso, a large retirement community where the roads are wide and the scenery pretty.

In the mountains or along a river, on asphalt or dirt, through residential areas or among the mighty saguaro, Tucson is bicycle-friendly.

Another popular ride is parallel to the Santa Catalina Mountain foothills along **Sunrise Road** to Sabino Canyon, where you can climb up a challenging, four-mile road through the mountains; just beware of mountain lions in the area. Because of the tour shuttles, Sabino Canyon is only open to bicyclists before 9 a.m. and after 5 p.m., except Wednesday and Saturday when it is closed to bicyclists entirely. For more information, call 520-749-2327.

Starting on North Campbell Avenue and running along the banks of the dry Rillito River is a multi-use **asphalt trail**. Currently it's about four miles long, and more trails are added annually. The **Santa Cruz River Park** has another trail that runs about four miles on both sides of the river.

The **Saguaro National Monument**, both east and west, also offers a number of good trails, both for mountain and road bikes, as does the hilly **Tucson Mountain Park**. Both are in scenic areas studded with cactus and mountains. Another enjoyable route is along the **Old Spanish Trail** from Broadway Boulevard to Colossal Cave.

For more information and maps on bicycling in the area, contact the **City of Tucson bicycling coordinator** at 520-791-4213.

EAST OF TUCSON   Good areas for bicycling can also be found outside of Tucson. Bikeable roads east of the city are **Route 90**, which you can take to Sierra Vista and then on to Bisbee, and **Route 80** through Tombstone.

SOUTH/WEST OF TUCSON   A good ride is to take **Route 83** from Colossal Cave, past Sonoita and Patagonia to Nogales. This road has little traffic and wide shoulders.

Bike Rentals   You can also rent a mountain bike and buy a trail map at **Broadway Bicycles.** ~ 140 South Sarnoff Drive, Tucson; 520-296-7819. Equipment and rentals are available at **Tucson Bicycles,** where they also organize group rides. Closed Sunday. ~ 4743 East Sunrise Drive, Tucson; 520-577-7374.

With trails lacing its many national monuments, recreation areas and state parks, Southern Arizona is built for hiking. You can view old adobe ruins, lime kilns, ancient petroglyphs and geological marvels, or scale one of the many peaks, for a stellar view of your surroundings. All distances listed for hiking trails are one way unless otherwise noted.

HIKING

TUCSON   In the Rincon Mountain District in Saguaro National Park is the **Freeman Homestead Nature Trail** (1 mile), a loop that starts off the spur road to the Javelina picnic area and descends from a saguaro forest to a small wash filled with mesquite trees. Along the way you pass the ruins of an adobe house built in the 1920s.

The **Cactus Forest Trail** (7 miles) takes you though a saguaro forest between Broadway Boulevard and Old Spanish Trail. You also pass the remains of the first ranger station built in the park, and two kilns used to process lime around the turn of the 20th century.

For a trek on **Mount Lemmon,** follow the **Wilderness of Rocks Trail** (4 miles). The trailhead is a mile and a half past Ski Valley. On the way are pools along Lemmon Creek and thousands of eroded and balanced rocks.

Pima Canyon Trail (7.6 miles) in the Santa Catalina Mountains is a difficult trail that climbs from 2900 to 7255 feet through a bighorn-sheep management area. Along the way you'll pass Pima Canyon Spring and good views of Tucson and A Mountain. Beyond the spring, the trail becomes steeper and harder to follow. At the top you'll find good views of Cathedral and Window rocks. To get there, follow Christie Drive north until it dead-ends at Magee Road. Go right and park. Carry lots of water.

In the **Tucson Mountain District** the **King Canyon Trail** (3.5 miles) begins off of Kinney Road across from the Arizona-Sonora Desert Museum, then climbs up to a picnic area and beyond to the top of Wasson Peak (elevation 4687), the highest point in the area.

The short **Signal Hill Petroglyphs Trail** (.13 mile) goes up a winding path along a small hill off Golden Gate Road. At the top are rocks with ancient Indian petroglyphs on them.

The **Valley View Overlook Trail** (.75 mile) on the Bajada Loop Drive descends into two washes and ends on a scenic ridge overlooking most of Avra Valley.

Hunter Trail (2 miles) in Picacho Peak State Park offers scenic views as it climbs from 2000 to 3374 feet in elevation.

EAST OF TUCSON To find **Lutz Canyon Trail** (2.9 miles), drive 12 miles south of Sierra Vista on Route 92 to Ash Canyon Road. Hikers walk past old mine workings in a narrow, deep canyon with oak, juniper and Douglas fir. The trail is extremely steep. ~ Sierra Vista Ranger District: 520-378-0311.

The moderately strenuous **Crest Trail** (5.5 miles) in the **Coronado National Memorial** runs along the crest of the Huachuca Mountains, which afford a great view of northern Mexico on clear days. ~ 520-366-5515.

Picacho Peak State Park's Hunter Trail was named for Captain Sherod Hunter, a Confederate officer who placed lookouts at Picacho pass and was involved in the battle that occurred here in 1862.

Within the **Chiricahua National Monument** you'll find **Massai Point Nature Trail** (.5 mile), which starts at the geology exhibit at Massai Point and takes you past a large balanced rock, a board with a description of the park's geologic story and views across Rhyolite Canyon.

The **Sugarloaf Trail** (.9 mile) takes you to a fire lookout at the top of Sugarloaf Mountain, the highest point within the monument.

Natural Bridge Trail (2.5 miles) begins at the Bonita Canyon scenic drive, then passes a natural rock bridge and climbs through oak and juniper woodlands to a pine forest.

Heart of Rocks Loop Trail (8-mile loop) winds through pine and fir forests and some of the park's most impressive rock formations, including Big Balanced Rock, Punch and Judy and Totem Pole.

Built as a supply artery for fire fighters stationed in the high Chiricahuas, **Greenhouse Trail** (3.5 miles) ascends 1500 feet. You'll pass Cima Cabin, the fire fighters' headquarters, and Winn Falls, which flows during the summer. To get there, go north off Cave Creek Spur Road onto Greenhouse Road and drive half a mile.

The **Coronado National Forest** offers the **South Fork Trail** (6.8 miles). Beginning off Cave Creek Road at the road end in South Fork Forest Camp three and a half miles above Portal, Arizona, it passes South Fork Cave Creek, one of the most famous bird-watching canyons in the Chiricahua Mountains and a 70-foot-tall finger of red rhyolite called Pinnacle Rock. It starts in a forest of sycamores, cypress and black walnut trees and leads to huge Douglas fir trees and the small bluffs above the South Fork Cave Creek. ~ Douglas Ranger District: 520-364-3468.

SOUTH/WEST OF TUCSON Kent Springs–Bog Springs Trail Loop (4.3 miles) within the Santa Rita Mountains climbs from 4820 feet to 6620 feet. Along the way are three seasonal springs, which create an unusually lush area with large sycamore, silver leaf oak, Arizona bamboo and walnut trees alive with birds. Exit off of Route 19 at Madera Canyon and park near the Bog Springs campground.

Transportation

From Tucson, **Route 10** runs north toward Phoenix, then crosses **Route 8**, which heads west toward Gila Bend and Yuma. **Route 85** from Gila Bend goes south, turns into **Route 86**, cuts through the Papago Indian Reservation and goes to Tucson. South of Tucson is **Route 19** to Nogales, while the main thoroughfare east from Tucson is Route 10 toward New Mexico. Jutting south off Route 10 are **Route 83** to Sonoita, **Route 90** to Sierra Vista, **Route 191** to Douglas, and **Route 186** to Chiricahua National Monument.

CAR

AIR

Aerolitoral, Alaska Airlines, American Airlines, Continental, Delta Air Lines, Frontier, JetBlue Airways, KLM, Northwest Airlines, Skywest, Southwest, United Airlines and US Airways fly into **Tucson International Airport.** ~ 520-573-8100; www.tucsonairport.org.

   Yuma International Airport (928-726-5882; www.yumaininternationalairport.com) is served by United Express and US Airways, while **Sierra Vista Municipal Airport** (800-554-5111) is served by Great Lakes Airlines.

TRAIN

Amtrak (800-872-7245; www.amtrak.com) services the area with the "Texas Eagle" and the "Sunset Limited," stopping in Tucson at 400 North Toole Avenue (520-623-4442), in Benson at 4th and Patagonia streets, and in Yuma at 281 Gila Street.

BUS

Greyhound Bus Lines (800-231-2222; www.greyhound.com) services Tucson from around the country. ~ 471 West Congress Street; 520-792-3475. Other stations in Southern Arizona include Nogales at 35 North Terrace Avenue, 520-287-5628, and Yuma at 170 East 17th Place, 928-783-4403; in Benson at 680 West 4th Street, 520-586-3388; and in Willcox at 100 South Arizona Avenue; 520-384-2183.

CAR RENTALS

At Tucson International Airport are **Avis Rent A Car** (800-331-1212), **Dollar Rent A Car** (800-800-4000), **Hertz Rent A Car** (800-654-3131) and **National Car Rental** (800-227-7368).

   Car-rental agencies at the Yuma International Airport are **Avis Rent A Car** (800-331-1212), **Budget Rent A Car** (800-404-8033), and **Hertz Rent A Car** (800-654-3131).

Enterprise Rent A Car serves the Sierra Vista Municipal Airport. ~ 800-325-8007.

PUBLIC TRANSIT   For extensive bus service throughout Tucson, call **Sun Tran.** ~ 520-792-9222; www.suntran.com. Local bus service in Nogales is **Dabdoub Bus Service.** ~ 520-287-7810.

TAXIS   Leading cab companies in Tucson include **Allstate Cab Co.** (520-888-2999), **Checker Cab Co.** (520-623-1133) and **Yellow Cab Co.** (520-624-6611).

NINE

Santa Fe Area

Native cultures scoff at the notion that Christopher Columbus discovered this continent. Even as the Europeans endured the Dark Ages, the ancestors of today's Pueblo Indians had expanded from living in pit houses around the time of Christ to multistory stone villages. The extended clans who lived in these villages grew corn, beans and squash, made pottery, traded across the United States and Mexico, and engaged in elaborate agricultural ceremonies marked by the solstices. The apotheosis of their culture flowered, but then eventually withered amid the great houses and towns of remote Chaco Canyon, which was linked to the rest of the 25,000-square-mile San Juan Basin in northwestern New Mexico by a sophisticated road system. The Chaco phenomenon that had swept through the Southwest and beyond by A.D. 950 fell apart dramatically by 1150, probably due to extended drought, diminishing natural resources, and political disarray, scattering thousands of villagers throughout the region. By A.D. 1300, many former Chacoans and later Mesa Verde people had moved south to the Rio Grande and were building pueblos in and around what is now Santa Fe.

The first Spanish settlers claimed this aptly named "Kingdom of New Mexico" in 1540 and the Spanish made Santa Fe a provincial capital in 1610. Over the next seven decades, Spanish soldiers and Franciscan missionaries sought to convert the Pueblo Indians of the region. Tribespeople numbered nearly 100,000, calling an estimated 70 burnt-orange adobe pueblos (or towns) home.

In 1680 the Pueblo Indians revolted, killing 400 of the 2500 Spanish colonists and driving the rest back to Mexico. The Pueblos sacked Santa Fe and burned most of the structures (save the Palace of the Governors), remaining in Santa Fe until Don Diego de Vargas reconquered the region 12 years later.

When Mexico gained independence from Spain in 1821, so too did New Mexico. But it wasn't until the Mexican-American War that an American flag flew over the territory. In 1848 Mexico ceded New Mexico to the United States and by 1912 New Mexico was a full-fledged state.

Why have people always flocked to this land of rugged beauty? The absolute isolation provided by the fortresslike hills in Los Alamos appealed first to the American Indians, later to scientists. The natural barriers surrounding sky-high Santa Fe, coupled with its obvious beauty, have always made it a desirable city and deserving capital, located at the crossroads of north and south.

Some maintain the lands around Santa Fe are sacred. Each year there's a pilgrimage to the modest Santuario de Chimayo church, said to be constructed on sacred and healing ground. The American Indians, who successfully rejected the white man's attempts to force-feed them organized religion, have blessed grounds and rituals that remain secret to all outsiders. The spirituality takes many forms. For example, semifrequent supernatural occurrences are reported as straight news.

There's also the magic light and intense colors that artist Georgia O'Keeffe captured so accurately on canvas. The high-altitude sun beaming on the earth tones helps to create shadows and vibrancies not to be believed, from subtle morning hues to bold and majestic evenings. Watching a sunset unfold over the Sangre de Cristo and Jemez mountains can be a spiritual experience as oranges, pinks and violets, chalk-colored pastels and lightning-bolt streaks of yellow weave together a picture story with no plot. (Sangre de Cristo is Spanish for "Blood of Christ," a reference to the red hue that can color the mountains at sunset, especially when they are covered with snow.) Color even emerges in everyday life, as blood-red chile *ristras* line highway stands against a big blue sky.

In fact, many of Santa Fe's earliest Anglo residents were painters, sculptors, musicians, novelists and poets. They came to Santa Fe for the same reason Gauguin went to Tahiti and Hemingway to Paris: to immerse themselves in exotic surroundings in hopes of finding new artistic dimensions. Today Santa Fe continues to grow as a regional arts center of international repute, boasting some 200 art galleries, 30 publishers, 17 performance stages and 13 major museums.

Many newcomers, like the region's tourists, are here because of the climate. These high, dry mountain towns are pleasingly warm during spring and fall. Summer can bring intense heat and the winters are cold enough to make Santa Fe and nearby Taos viable ski areas. Summer and fall are particularly popular among vacationers. Santa Fe averages 14 inches of rainfall a year, and 30 to 34 inches of snow.

Others come for the Santa Fe area's cultural mix, which is as colorful and varied as the weather. Anglo, Indian and Spanish peoples coexist, each group more accepting of the others' beliefs yet holding on strong to their own time-honored traditions. New generations living on the pueblos seem less apt to follow the old ways and more interested in the outside world. Whether this is prompted by materialism, survival of the race or both remains to be seen. Still, where other regions have been homogenized by prosperity, in no way are the pueblo peoples tossing aside their proud heritage.

The same goes for the physical remains in the centuries-old cities. Rigorous zoning laws maintain Santa Fe's image by restricting architecture to either the adobe brick or Territorial styles. Fortunately, ordinances make it difficult for developers to raid and tear down. Las Vegas (New Mexico, not the glittering gambling mecca in Nevada) has nine historic districts, with architecture ranging from adobe to Italianate.

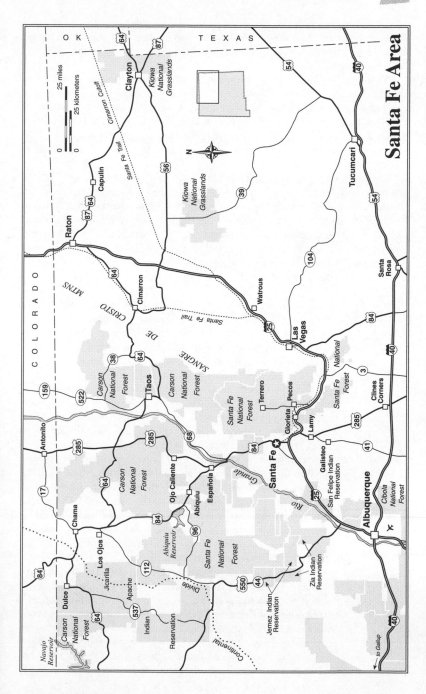

Santa Fe Area

The city of Los Alamos, birthplace of the atomic bomb, remains an interesting contrast to the old and new. Modern in its technology and scientific findings, Los Alamos' laboratories coexist within a stone's throw of ancient ruins and Indian pueblos.

Tradition also blends well with modern culinary influences as evidenced in Santa Fe's original cuisine. New styles of cooking in many of the exciting restaurants of the region rely upon old recipes, with a twist. Piquant food is distinctive and uses home-grown chiles and family recipes, blue-corn tortillas and Navajo bread. Rejection of Anglo-izing has made the area unique. Whether it's in the names, lifestyles or biting scents of sage and piñon, in the Santa Fe area, everything has an accent to it.

Above all, however, this is still a land of "mañana," where a majority lives by the philosophy that "if it doesn't get done today, there's always tomorrow." On Sundays, life moves markedly slower than in the rest of the country. This can translate into a frustrating experience as the laissez-faire attitude carries over onto roads that seemingly change numerals in midstream. (The truth is that roads here follow ditches and arroyos and other natural land features.) But if you find yourself lost or learn that your laundry wasn't done on time, just remember: In the Santa Fe area, there's always tomorrow . . . and tomorrow.

Santa Fe

A trivia game asks what's the oldest state capital in the United States. The answer of Santa Fe, which has been home to a government seat since 1610, is always a stumper. Not only does the "City Different" defy the government center stereotype (a domed capitol building and proper tree-lined streets), but unlike most state capitals, it's not easy to get to.

You can't take a commercial jet or even a train into Santa Fe. Albuquerque, an hour's drive south, is the closest large airport, and the city of Lamy, about 17 miles south, is the nearest Amtrak stop. But the independent Santa Feans seem to like it this way. And once you arrive, you'll find it's well worth the trouble.

Strict guidelines mandate the Territorial and Spanish Colonial architecture that characterizes the well-known Santa Fe style. Thanks to city codes, there are no highrises blocking the mountain views or the ever-changing colors at dawn and dusk. This attractive capital, situated at 7000 feet elevation and backdropped by the spectacular Sangre de Cristo Mountains, is becoming desirable to more and more people who are fleeing their urban homes for Santa Fe's natural beauty and culture.

Those rushing to relocate here either part or full time have driven housing prices to outer-space levels. Fledgling artists aren't being represented in galleries, as owners can only afford to stock their high-rent shops with proven names. Chain stores have been sneaking into the commercial core around the Plaza looking for the all-too-important tourist dollar. The invasion of brand names such as Starbuck's and Banana Republic has sparked local opposition and a clamor to ban chain stores downtown.

By digging a little deeper, it's still possible to find a soul amid Santa Fe's slickening veneer. Avoiding summer holiday weekends, such as Memorial Day or Labor Day, will find favorite tourist spots less crowded and Santa Feans more willing to have a chat. The city is quite beautiful in the fall, when the leaves are changing and the days are still balmy.

SIGHTS

There is plenty to see in Santa Fe, from palaces of worship to galleries to the Indian Market, but save time for the **State Capitol**, one of the only round capitol buildings in the United States. Built in the shape of the Pueblo Indian Zia, the three-story structure, with a red-brick roofline and whitewashed trim, symbolizes the circle of life: four winds, four seasons, four directions and four sacred obligations. It also resembles a much larger version of a Pueblo Indian ceremonial kiva. The roundhouse was built in 1966 to replace an older capitol building (now known as the Bataan Building) down the block. Display cases around the capital rotunda tell the Indian and Spanish history of the state, and you'll find locally made art scattered throughout (the walls are literally covered with artwork). The governor's office has its own gallery, which is open to the public for a viewing reception early in the month. Guided tours of the capitol are available (reservations required) during summer months. Open weekdays yearround; open Saturday from Memorial Day through the last Saturday of August. ~ Paseo de Peralta and Old Santa Fe Trail; 505-986-4589; www.legis.state.nm.us.

> Constructed by the Spanish in 1609–1610, the Palace of the Governors served as capital of Nuevo Mexico, Spain's northernmost colony in the New World, before the Pilgrims landed at Plymouth Rock.

The Tlaxcalan people from Mexico built the **San Miguel Mission** in 1598, making it the oldest continuously used church in the U.S. But this was probably considered sacred ground before that, as there is evidence of human occupation dating back to A.D. 1300. San Miguel is an amazing archive of everything from pyrographic paintings on buffalo hides and deer skin to a bell from Spain that dates back to 1856! Admission. ~ 401 Old Santa Fe Trail; 505-983-3974.

Not surprisingly, the oldest church is located near the **Oldest House in U.S.**, an earthen structure believed to have been built in 1250. Admission. ~ 215 East De Vargas Street.

Meander up the **Old Santa Fe Trail** through the parklike setting and over the mountain runoff–fed Santa Fe River. Pass by traditional irrigation ditches called *acequias*, which carry moisture from the hills found throughout the city.

Those who believe in miracles must make a point of stopping by the tiny **Loretto Chapel**, patterned after France's Saint Chappelle, which holds the beautiful "miraculous staircase." When the chapel was built, craftsmen failed to install any way to reach the choir loft. Short on funds, the nuns prayed to Saint Joseph, patron of carpenters, for a solution to the problem. The story goes that a man came armed with only a saw, hammer and hot water to shape the wooden staircase. He worked for months and built a staircase that makes two 360-degree turns but has no visible means of support. When it came time for payment, the man mysteriously disappeared. Admission. ~ 207 Old Santa Fe Trail; 505-982-0092, fax 505-984-7921; www.lorettochapel.com, e-mail information@lorettochapel.com.

Continue up the Santa Fe Trail to the **Plaza**, built in 1610 by Don Pedro de Peralta as an end to the Santa Fe Trail. (A marker in the Plaza commemorates its completion.) There's always plenty of excitement revolving around this town square. American Indians roll out their blankets and hawk their wares to tourists on the sidewalks surrounding the Plaza. Their prices have been adjusted to meet Santa Fe's ever-increasing popularity. If you're lucky, there will be live music and dancing.

America's oldest governmental building, the **Palace of the Governors** may be more historically significant than the artifacts it houses. Once held by Pueblo Indians, the 1610 adobe fortress has been used as governmental headquarters for Spain, Mexico, the Confederacy and the territorial United States. Today the Palace houses exhibits of fascinating regional history. There's also a photograph archive, history library and gift shop. Closed Monday from Labor Day through Memorial Day. Admission. ~ 105 West Palace Avenue, on the Plaza; 505-476-5100, fax 505-476-5104; www.palaceofthegovernors.org.

Situated west of the Palace of Governors, the **Museum of Fine Arts** is a prototype of the architectural revival style called New Old Santa Fe or Pueblo Revival. The building is a reproduction of New Mexico's "Cathedral of the Desert" exhibit at the 1915 Panama-California Exposition in San Diego. Completed in 1917, it embodies aspects of the Spanish mission churches in the region. Notice the ceilings of split cedar *latillas* and hand-hewn vigas. Housing more than 20,000 pieces of art, the museum is a repository for works of early Santa Fe and Taos masters as well as contemporary artists. Closed Monday. Admission. ~ 107 West Palace Avenue, on the Plaza; 505-476-5072, fax 505-476-5076; www.mfasantafe.org, e-mail ellen.zieselman@state.nm.us.

The **Georgia O'Keeffe Museum** occupies three moderately historic buildings connected by hallways in a formerly nondescript part of downtown now known as "the O'K District." You'll find it behind the Eldorado Hotel, three blocks west of the Museum of Fine Arts. Grouped in stark exhibit spaces with otherwise bare white walls and sandstone floors are more than 1100

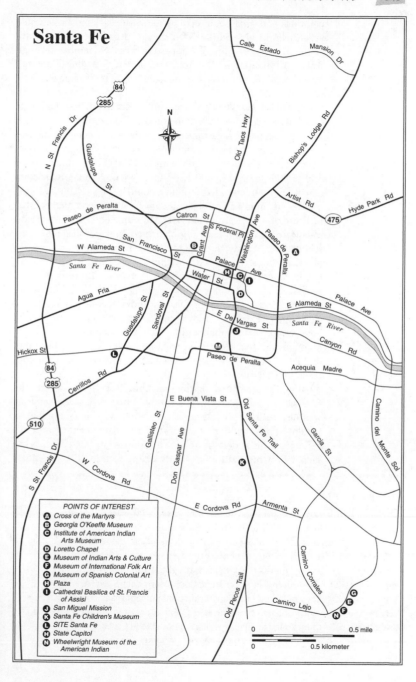

Santa Fe

N

POINTS OF INTEREST

- **A** Cross of the Martyrs
- **B** Georgia O'Keeffe Museum
- **C** Institute of American Indian Arts Museum
- **D** Loretto Chapel
- **E** Museum of Indian Arts & Culture
- **F** Museum of International Folk Art
- **G** Museum of Spanish Colonial Art
- **H** Plaza
- **I** Cathedral Basilica of St. Francis of Assisi
- **J** San Miguel Mission
- **K** Santa Fe Children's Museum
- **L** SITE Santa Fe
- **M** State Capitol
- **N** Wheelwright Museum of the American Indian

0   0.5 mile
0   0.5 kilometer

paintings and small sculptures by New Mexico's most celebrated artist, who lived in Santa Fe for the last decade before her death at the age of 90. Closed Wednesday from November through April. Admission. ~ 217 Johnson Street; 505-995-0785, fax 505-995-0786; www.okeeffemuseum.org, e-mail main@okeeffe museum.org.

Before leaving the Plaza area, you'll want to pop into **La Fonda Hotel**, which calls itself the "inn at the end of the trail," for a drink in the popular bar or a meal in its impressive dining room. You can glean as much information here about what's going on in town as you can at the chamber of commerce. ~ 100 East San Francisco Street; 505-982-5511, 800-523-5002; www.lafondasantafe.com, e-mail reservations@lafondasantafe.com.

One of Santa Fe's most significant sightseeing highlights is the **Institute of American Indian Arts Museum**. This downtown museum is part of the federally chartered Indian college-level art school (one of only three in the U.S.). Exhibits are arranged to place contemporary artwork within a context of tribal tradition. For instance, located just beyond the main entrance is the welcoming circle, a circular space symbolic of the cycles of nature and the continuity of the American Indian people. Here, before viewing the exhibits, visitors can gather their thoughts in the quiet, contemplative manner in which American Indians have traditionally approached art appreciation. Admission. ~ 108 Cathedral Place; 505-983-1777; www.iaiamuseum.org, e-mail museum receptionist@iaia.org.

If you're interested in attending church services, consider the **Cathedral Basilica of St. Francis of Assisi**, whose cornerstone was laid in 1869 by Archbishop Lamy. With its stained-glass windows, bronze door panels and smaller Sacrament Chapel, it's certainly the grandest church in the Southwest. In a corner is the sacred La Conquistadora ("Lady of the Conquest"), the oldest

PUEBLO PRIDE

While Pueblo Indians have lived in the Santa Fe area for at least 800 years, the pueblos within Santa Fe County nowadays are quite small, totaling only a few hundred residents. Many of Santa Fe's American Indian residents are drawn from other parts of the country by the Santa Fe Indian School, a college prep school for youths from tribes throughout the Southwest, and the Institute of American Indian Arts, the nation's only college-level art school for indigenous people. Artists and craftspeople from many tribes rely on the abundance of Santa Fe galleries that exhibit contemporary and traditional American Indian art, as well as special events such as the huge annual Indian Market, for most of their income.

representation of the Madonna in the United States. Devotion to the woodcarved statue has been maintained for more than 300 years. In the early morning light, La Conquistadora appears positively heavenly. ~ 131 Cathedral Place; 505-982-5619, fax 505-989-1952.

If you're traveling with kids consider a stop at the **Santa Fe Children's Museum**. Budding architects can design and build a room from a variety of materials; young musicians can compose original tunes on an assortment of xylophones; and future physicists can marvel at the echoing sound dishes. Earthworks, an educational, one-acre garden, harbors a greenhouse, wetlands and hummingbird and butterfly gardens. There's also a rock-climbing wall. Closed Monday and Tuesday. Admission. ~ 1050 Old Pecos Trail; 505-989-8359, fax 505-989-7506; www.santafechildrens museum.org, e-mail children@santafechildrensmuseum.org.

A recent addition to the city's roster of museums, SITE **Santa Fe** is a private nonprofit "artspace" designed to accommodate traveling art exhibits. Free from the strictures of government-run museums, SITE Santa Fe often presents more daring and progressive shows than can be found elsewhere in town. The vast freeform space—it used to be a warehouse—is flexible enough to fit all kinds of visual-arts exhibits and also hosts nationally known poets and performance artists. Closed Monday and Tuesday. Admission. ~ 1606 Paseo de Peralta; 505-989-1199, fax 505-989-1188; www.sitesantafe.org, e-mail info@sitesantafe.org.

SITE Santa Fe is located in Santa Fe's newest city park, the **Historic Railyard**, on the train tracks just west of Guadalupe Street. After a long, drawn-out planning process, the new park is starting to become the most vibrant place in Santa Fe. The historic Santa Fe Railway, which runs scenic train rides to Lamy, is headquartered here (a new light rail between Santa Fe and Albuquerque will have its main hub in the railyard). Scheduled to be built in 2007 are a farmers' market building, a plaza, an underground parking lot, shops, live-work spaces, a movie theater, and a building for the popular youth-arts center Warehouse 21. **El Museo Cultural** (505-827-7750; www.elmuseocultural.org), opposite SITE Santa Fe, aims to interpret and preserve Hispanic culture, not just in New Mexico but throughout the world. It has exhibits, classes, plays and markets in a warehouse setting, next to the **Railyard Performance Center**, a great place to take a yoga class, learn African dancing, or free dance. ~ Paseo de Peralta; 505-982-3373, fax 505-982-3126; www.sfrailyardcc.org.

Impressive is a good way to describe the privately owned **Wheelwright Museum of the American Indian**, which presents ever-changing exhibits of traditional and contemporary American Indian artwork, including Navajo weavings, textiles and jewelry. Closed Sunday. ~ 704 Camino Lejo; 505-982-4636, 800-607-4636, fax 505-989-7386; www.wheelwright.org, e-mail info@wheelwright.org.

The nearby **Museum of International Folk Art** houses the world's largest collection of folk art—130,000 artifacts from all around the globe. Toys, miniatures, textiles and religious art are colorfully displayed in the Girard Wing. The Hispanic Heritage Wing highlights four centuries of New Mexico's Latino folk culture. Costumes, textiles and quilts number among the exhibits in the Neutrogena Wing and Lloyd's Treasure Chest. The museum plaza, café and parking lot also afford a spectacular view of the Jemez Mountains, southwest of Santa Fe, and the Sangre de Cristos to the north. Closed Monday from early September to late May. Admission. ~ 706 Camino Lejo; 505-476-1200, fax 505-476-1300; www.moifa.org.

Southwestern American Indians are the focus of the **Museum of Indian Arts & Culture**, with exhibits drawn from extensive collections of the museum's Laboratory of Anthropology. A permanent display of ancient and contemporary pottery is featured in the Buchsbaum Gallery; exhibits tell the history of American Indians in the Southwest; and a sculpture garden showcases American Indian artists. The library and archives contain countless records, photographs and manuscripts. Docent tours are available. Closed Monday. Admission. ~ 710 Camino Lejo; 505-476-1250, fax 505-476-1330; www.miaclab.org, e-mail info@miaclab.org.

Inaugurated in 2002, the **Museum of Spanish Colonial Art** boasts a varied collection of more than 3000 pieces that spans five continents and four centuries. Specializing in Spanish Colonial pieces, its rotating and permanent exhibition consists of furniture, paintings, metal work, weaving and pottery, displayed in a historic 1930 adobe designed by John Gaw Meem. There's also creations by 20th-century Hispanic artists on view. Closed Monday from Memorial Day to Labor Day. Admission. ~ 750 Camino Lejo; 505-982-2226; www.spanishcolonial.org, e-mail info@spanishcolonial.org.

Wandering up to **Canyon Road** (see "Art Everywhere You Look" and "Shopping" below), you'll pass by historic haciendas and witness firsthand the center of Santa Fe's burgeoning arts community. This shopping district is where the founders of Santa Fe's artist community resided, and in 1935 the first gallery was established (it's no longer there). Early in the 20th century the narrow old river road ran through a low-rent district with secluded compounds of small residences and studios. Now it's home to literally hundreds of galleries, and an important landmark for artists everywhere. Yet Canyon Road does not flaunt its history, focusing instead on the business at hand: buying and selling art.

If you continue up Canyon Road beyond the galleries and shops and the broad, green neighborhood park, you'll come to **Cristo Rey Church**. Don't be deceived by the historic look of this adobe church. It was actually built in 1940 in the style of Spanish Colonial mission churches (such as those in Chimayo, Las Trampas and Truchas on the High Road to Taos) to house a stone altarpiece dating back to 1760. This treasure, one of the finest works of early New Mexican religious sculpture, depicts God and a number of saints. ~ At the corner of Cristo Rey Street and Canyon Road; 505-983-8528, fax 505-992-6836; www.cristorey santefe.parishesonline.com, e-mail cristorey@qwest.net.

Randall Davey Audubon Center is named for a painter known for his horse-racing themes. When he died, Davey's family left his 135-acre estate to the National Audubon Society in 1983. As you stroll the easy walking trails that circle the oak and piñon terrain, you may encounter a wide variety of animal life, including rabbits, skunks, raccoons and deer. Birdwatchers are likely to spot magpies, piñon jays, ravens and dozens of songbird species. A visitors center includes a bookstore with an excellent selection on the natural history of New Mexico. The home, including Davey's studio and an exhibition of his works, opens for tours on Monday. ~ 1800 Upper Canyon Road; 505-983-4609, fax 505-983-2355; www.nm.audubon.org.

In the 1700s, some people used red chile as a meat preservative, while others rubbed it on their gums for toothaches.

To take in the whole picture of Santa Fe, hoof it up to the **Cross of the Martyrs**, located in the city's Marcy Park section. There are stairs by Paseo de Peralta and Washington Avenue that you have to climb to earn the bird's-eye view of the city.

Settle into a private hot tub overlooking the mountains under the starlit sky at **Ten Thousand Waves**, located just a few minutes from downtown Santa Fe. This authentic Japanese health spa also offers a variety of full-body massages, facials and herbal wraps. They're open late, so after a long day of sightseeing, come in for pampering. Fee. ~ 3451 Hyde Park Road; 505-982-9304, fax 505-989-5077; www.tenthousandwaves.com, e-mail info@ tenthousandwaves.com.

About 15 miles southwest of Santa Fe is **Rancho de las Golondrinas**, a restored Spanish hacienda dating back to 1710. It was once the last *paraje* (inn) before Santa Fe on the grueling journey along El Camino Real, the "Royal Highway," which brought traders and settlers from Mexico City to Northern New Mexico. The 200-acre grounds still operate as a working ranch, growing traditional crops and raising sheep. Coming here is like stepping back in time. Call for theme weekends. Closed Monday and Tuesday from June through September; closed November through March. In April, May and October, open for guided tours only. Admission. ~ Route 25, Exit 276, go to 334 Los Piños Road; 505-471-2261, fax 505-471-5623; www.golondrinas.org, e-mail mail@golondrinas.org.

LODGING   Adjacent to the Loretto Chapel, the striking Pueblo-style **Inn and Spa at Loretto** features interior wall murals and Southwest decor that reflect the heritage of New Mexico. Some of the 135 rooms and suites have kiva fireplaces and private balconies. Those looking for mind/body rejuvenation will enjoy the services of the on-site spa. Other amenities include a restaurant with an outdoor terrace. ~ 211 Old Santa Fe Trail; 505-988-5531, 800-727-5531, fax 505-984-7968; www.innatloretto.com, e-mail reservations@hotelloretto.com. ULTRA-DELUXE.

Red-brick coping and windows trimmed in white signal the traditional Territorial-style architecture of the **Hotel Plaza Real**. Situated around a central courtyard, the hotel's 56 rooms feature massive wood beams and Southwest-style furniture. Nearly all units have a fireplace and most have a patio or balcony. But a word to the wise: Some rooms are small and second-floor units feature steep, narrow staircases. The restaurant serves dinner. Underground hotel parking is $12. ~ 125 Washington Avenue; 505-988-4900, 800-279-7325, fax 505-983-9322; www.hotel plazareal.com. ULTRA-DELUXE.

Considering the amount of noise on the street it fronts, guest rooms at the **Inn on the Alameda** are surprisingly quiet. Everything emphasizes sunny and clean—from the pristine adobe walls to the beautiful slate tiles and the modern artwork. Many guest rooms are pleasantly decorated in Southwest style, with wicker and wood-cane furniture; all come with fluffy robes for guest use. Breakfast is included. There's also complimentary wine and cheese in the afternoon. ~ 303 East Alameda Street; 505-984-2121, 800-289-2122, fax 505-986-8325; www.innontheala meda.com, e-mail info@inn-alameda.com. ULTRA-DELUXE.

Literally the "inn at the end of the Santa Fe Trail," **La Fonda Hotel** is a Santa Fe institution. Though the original adobe hotel from the 1700s is gone, the latest incarnation still caters to weary travelers in search of pleasant lodging and fine food. Each room is unique, with hand-painted wooden furniture and room accents; many feature balconies and fireplaces. A central meeting spot for area sightseeing tours and recreational activities, La Fonda hums with excitement. A newsstand, an art gallery, shops, a restaurant and a cantina all add to the bustle. ~ 100 East San Francisco Street; 505-982-5511, 800-523-5002, fax 505-988-2952; www.lafondasantafe.com, e-mail reservations@lafonda santafe.com. ULTRA-DELUXE.

Guests and staff alike often report sightings of Santa Fe's most notorious phantom, the ghost of Julia Staab, on the grand staircase that ascends from the lobby of **La Posada de Santa Fe**. The sprawling downtown resort has been expanded over the years to completely surround the mansion of a 19th-century local banker, and while the old house remains Victorian in character, the rest of the hotel blends classic and contemporary Southwestern styles. Luxurious rooms and suites, many with kiva fireplaces, fill not only the main inn but also casitas clustered throughout six acres of beautifully landscaped grounds. There's a large spa facility that includes steam rooms, whirlpools, exercise facilities and a heated outdoor pool. ~ 330 East Palace Avenue; 505-986-0000, 800-727-5276, fax 505-982-6850; www.rockresorts.com. ULTRA-DELUXE.

If you find bigger is always better, then be sure to book a room at the looming, yet lovely, 219-room **Eldorado Hotel**. Lovers of classic Santa Fe architecture just about choked when this monolith was constructed. Yet few who venture inside find fault with the brass-and-chrome-fixtured lobby bar, heated rooftop pool, two cocktail lounges and adjacent shops. Double rooms are done in a very Southwestern style. ~ 309 West San Francisco Street; 505-988-4455, 800-955-4455, fax 505-995-4555; www.eldorado hotel.com, e-mail rez@eldoradohotel.com. ULTRA-DELUXE.

Bed-and-breakfasts don't come more elegant than the **Madeleine Inn**, a pale-yellow Victorian "belle dame" on a quiet street in the historic downtown. All seven rooms have luxurious furnishings; several have four-poster beds, private baths or showers, cable TV and air conditioning. The baked goods here are to die for, and win raves from returning guests. Little known even to Santa Feans, nonguests can now enjoy the incredible scones and tea cakes accompanied by specially blended teas in the polished-wood living room. A top-rated, full-service Indonesian-style spa is in an adjoining building (massages are available in-room). The

AUTHOR FAVORITE

I love the **Inn of the Anasazi**'s personal touch, from the homemade juice and introduction letter at check-in to the escorted tour of the hotel by a bellman, and thoughtful turn-down service and dimming of bedroom lights. Its understated elegance has made the Anasazi a favorite among well-heeled visitors. Decor throughout the small inn is decidedly low key— neutral tones prevail. The 57 guest rooms are charmingly bedecked with four-poster beds, viga ceilings, kiva fireplaces, cast-iron furniture, angelic figurines and handknitted cotton blankets. Instead of "do not disturb" signs, hotel attendants place leather-tied blocks over doorknobs. ~ 113 Washington Avenue; 505-988-3030, 800-688-8100, fax 505-988-3277; www.innoftheanasazi.com, e-mail anasazi@rosewoodhotels.com. ULTRA-DELUXE.

inn books quickly, so reserve well ahead. ~ 106 Faithway Street; 505-982-3465, 888-877-7622; www.madeleineinn.com, e-mail info@madeleineinn.com. DELUXE TO ULTRA-DELUXE.

Afternoon tea attracts a high-tone crowd to the **Hotel St. Francis**, one of the prettiest properties in town. Each of the 82 rooms and suites is unique with high ceilings, casement windows, brass and iron beds and antique furniture. Original hexagonal tile and porcelain pedestal sinks give the bathrooms a lush yet historic feel. A spacious lobby hosts the famous afternoon tea, complete with finger sandwiches and scones. ~ 210 Don Gaspar Avenue; 505-983-5700, 800-529-5700, fax 505-989-7690; www. hotelstfrancis.com, e-mail reservations@hotelstfrancis.net. MODERATE TO ULTRA-DELUXE.

HIDDEN ▶

The scent of piñon wood pervades the polished and contemporary **Hotel Santa Fe**, on the edge of Santa Fe's historic Guadalupe district. Large rooms, many of which have a separate sitting area, are handsomely decorated in those oh-so-familiar Southwestern colors and hand-carved furniture. The first off-site Indian project in the state, the hotel is more than half-owned by the Picuris Indian Pueblo. The Picuris and other American Indians work keep the hotel running. ~ 1501 Paseo de Peralta; 505-982-1200, 800-825-9876, fax 505-984-2211; www.hotelsantafe.com, e-mail hotelsantafe@newmexico.com. DELUXE.

> Typically, the farther you move away from Santa Fe's Plaza, the more hotel prices drop. But beware of a few of the 1950s-style hotels lining Cerrillos Road— some are dives!

Not to be confused with the neighboring Hotel Santa Fe, the **Santa Fe Motel & Inn** has bungalow-style dwellings and standard lodge rooms, some with kitchenettes. Given its prime location, within walking distance of the Plaza, the Santa Fe Motel & Inn is probably the best value for the money. A hot breakfast is included. ~ 510 Cerrillos Road; 505-982-1039, 800-930-5002, fax 505-986-1275; www.santafe motel.com, e-mail info@santafemotel.com. MODERATE.

The **El Rey Inn**, with its lush garden property filled with fountains and patios, stands tall against neighboring hotels. Decor varies between Indian pueblo, Victorian and Spanish. Some rooms have oriental rugs; others feature brick floors. Omnipresent in all the units is a keen attention to detail and cleanliness. ~ 1862 Cerrillos Road; 505-982-1931, 800-521-1349, fax 505-989-9249; www.elreyinnsantafe.com. MODERATE TO DELUXE.

HIDDEN ▶

The **Inn of the Turquoise Bear** is located in a secluded southside adobe mansion that originally belonged to poet/philanthropist Witter Bynner, a leader of Santa Fe's literary community for four decades beginning in the Roaring Twenties. Among the many luminaries who stayed here as Bynner's houseguests were composer Igor Stravinsky, poet Robert Frost, actors Errol Flynn and Rita Hayworth, and playwright Thornton Wilder. Each of the ten guest rooms has traditional Santa Fe–style decor and modern amenities from VCRs to terry-cloth robes and fresh, fragrant flowers. The inn is pleasantly shaded by lofty ponderosa pines on an acre of grounds with terraced gardens, old stone benches and flagstone footpaths. Gay-friendly. ~ 342 East Buena Vista Street; 505-983-0798, 800-396-4104, fax 505-988-4225; www.turquoisebear.com, e-mail bluebear@newmexico.com. MODERATE TO ULTRA-DELUXE.

DINING

Homemade granola and goat's milk yogurt start the day at the **Inn of the Anasazi**. The innovative kitchen creates indescribable cuisine that blends many elements, flavors, exotic grains and organic ingredients. Homemade breads, seafoods and wild game feature prominently in the menu. The inn's beautiful 92-seat dining room alone is worth a visit. Sunday brunch also served ~ 113 Washington Avenue; 505-988-3236, 800-688-8100; www.inn oftheanasazi.com, e-mail reservations@innoftheanasazi.com. DELUXE TO ULTRA-DELUXE.

Like the regulars on TV's *Cheers*, "sometimes you want to go where everybody knows your name." At the always-lively **Santa Fe Baking Company**, owner Eric Struck and his brothers really do know everybody's names (and learn yours the moment you walk in). Try the delicious and generously portioned breakfast burritos, huevos rancheros, *chilaquiles* and other egg dishes, as well as great homemade pastries like Pueblo Pie, a Southwest take on spiced apple pie. There are two soups daily, oversized sandwiches and salads, including the warm salmon fillet served over greens with soy-vinaigrette dressing. Live music at weekend brunch. Free wi-fi. ~ 504 West Cordova Road; 988-4292; www. santafebakingcompanycafe.com. BUDGET.

Caffe latte never tasted so good as in the Bohemian atmosphere of the **Aztec Café**, where you'll find lively conversation, tasty bagels and sandwiches, and art worthy of discussion. Closed at dusk. ~ 317 Aztec Street; 505-820-0025; www.aztec cafe.com. BUDGET.

Modern American cuisine in a hip setting with good people-watching makes **Zia Diner** a fun place to come on your own. Sit at the counter or come with pals and the kids and grab a big table. There's food here for everyone, like meatloaf, burgers, pizza and a Mount Everest–size pile of fries. Breakfast is also served. Zia moves a good crowd through. The Zia bar in the rear hops, too. ~ 326 South Guadalupe Street; 505-988-7008, fax 505-820-7677; www ziadiner.com. BUDGET TO MODERATE.

In the old railroad station is **Tomasita's**, which on the surface looks like a tourist trap. But the food—Tomasita's wins raves for its green chile and *chiles rellenos*—and the margaritas wipe away any disparaging thoughts. Closed Sunday. ~ 500 South Guadalupe Street; 505-983-5721, fax 505-983-0780. BUDGET.

Southwestern cuisine and Continental-style entrées with a tangy Creole snap dominate the menu at **Pink Adobe**, where the favorite entrée is steak served with green chiles and mushrooms. No lunch on weekends. ~ 406 Old Santa Fe Trail; 505-983-7712, fax 505-984-0691; www.thepinkadobe.com, e-mail enchantjoe@earthlink.net. MODERATE TO DELUXE.

If you're hankering for prime beef, the **Bull Ring** is an upscale steak house with white linen tablecloths and an extensive wine list. No lunch on Saturday and Sunday. ~ 150 Washington Avenue; 505-983-3328, fax 505-982-8254; e-mail bullrest@aol.com. ULTRA-DELUXE.

Of the four Japanese restaurants in Santa Fe, **Shohko Café** has the freshest seafood and best sushi bar. *Sake* and tempura ice cream are very viable accompaniments. No lunch on Saturday. Closed Sunday. ~ 321 Johnson Street; phone/fax 505-982-9708. MODERATE TO DELUXE.

The Coyote Café made a big splash when it first opened and was soon ranked among the top 100 restaurants in the country. The ever-evolving menu typically includes pan-roasted chicken breast and green-chile polenta with black-bean sauce. Some locals feel the Coyote is overrated, but it remains a favorite among the visiting crowd. ~ 132 West Water Street; 505-983-1615, fax 505-989-9026; www.coyote-cafe.com, e-mail reservations@coyote-cafe.com. ULTRA-DELUXE.

A bright, cheerful second-story restaurant in the downtown Plaza Mercado, **Blue Corn Café** is another favorite. The New Mexican menu covers all the basics (enchiladas, tacos and tamales). ~ 133 West Water Street; 505-984-1800, fax 505-984-2104. BUDGET TO MODERATE. They also operate a brew pub. ~ 4056 Cerrillos Road; 505-438-1800.

Designed by architect Alexander Girard, who is best known for the amazing collection he donated to the Museum of International Folk Art, **The Compound Restaurant** is where you'll

AUTHOR FAVORITE

My stomach rumbles at the thought of the **Santacafé**, where herbs are exalted and only the freshest of foods find their way to the table. The combination of flavors never disappoints, from the starter (shiitake and cactus spring rolls, for instance) to the grand finale (warm chocolate upside-down cake, anyone?). What's best about Santacafé is it doesn't try too hard when delivering its New American cuisine. Then again, it doesn't have to. No lunch on Sunday, except for Sunday brunch in summer. ~ 231 Washington Avenue; 505-984-1788, fax 505-986-0110; www.santacafe.com, e-mail santacafe@aol.com. DELUXE TO ULTRA-DELUXE.

probably want to go for a very special evening. Foie gras, lamb, caviar and fresh fish are attentively served in this restored hacienda. The impressive wine cellar has some rare vintages. No lunch on Saturday and Sunday. ~ 653 Canyon Road; 505-982-4353, fax 505-982-4868; www.compoundrestaurant.com. ULTRA-DELUXE.

El Farol has an ambience as good as its food. Hot and cold Spanish *tapas* and entrées are its forte. Try one of the house specialties—paella, cold curry chicken or shrimp sautéed in garlic, lime and sherry—for a filling meal. ~ 808 Canyon Road; 505-983-9912, fax 505-988-3823; www.elfarolsf.com. ULTRA-DELUXE.

Considered one of Santa Fe's finest restaurants, **La Casa Sena** boasts both a main dining room and a smaller cantina. The restaurant, part of a restored 1860 adobe casa, covers its walls with paintings by early Santa Fe masters. Fine, fresh ingredients are used (even the water is from their own well), resulting in fabulous dining adventures. Entrées take regional favorites and give them a creative twist like grilled chorizo-stuffed pork chop, and trout baked in adobe and served with sun-dried-tomato-saffron risotto. Outrageous! ~ 125 East Palace Avenue, Sena Plaza; 505-988-9232, fax 505-820-2909; www.lacasasena.com, e-mail info@casasena.com. DELUXE TO ULTRA-DELUXE.

La Casa Sena Cantina is a bustling crowded space, and everything from food to song is artistically presented. In fact, nowhere else in Santa Fe does the green-chile chicken enchilada come with a rousing rendition of "Phantom of the Opera" (or whatever the server's in the mood for).The limited seasonal menu includes such specialties as grilled chicken and jack cheese quesadillas with roasted zucchini, red and yellow peppers, pine nuts and habañero salsa. Waiters and waitresses perform excerpts from popular musicals, then follow with a sampling of show tunes. Patrons come and go between sets, making their way among the tiny butcher-block tables and baby grand piano. ~ 125 East Palace Avenue, Sena Plaza; 505-988-9232, fax 505-820-2909; www.lacasasena.com, e-mail info@lacasasenacom. MODERATE TO ULTRA-DELUXE.

If a huge old Mexico–style lunch followed by a siesta is what you're after, then seek out **The Shed**, where wise eaters come before noon to avoid the lines. Blue-corn tortillas wrapped around cheese and onion specialties are served on sizzling plates with *posole* on the side. Consider starting your meal with some fresh mushroom soup and ending it with lemon soufflé. Dinner reservations recommended. Closed Sunday. ~ 113½ East Palace Avenue; 505-982-9030, fax 505-982-0902; www.sfshed.com, e-mail info@sfshed.com. BUDGET TO MODERATE.

Cafe Pasqual's, in the heart of downtown, seats just 50 and is festooned from floor to ceiling with brightly painted items from

Mexico. Chef Katherine Kagel offers an eclectic menu that reflects the best of Mexican and Asian cuisines. At breakfast, try *huevos motuleños*, a classic egg dish from the Yucatán, or a breakfast trout, served grilled or as hash. At dinner, go for something exotic, such as Asian-style tamales. A plus here: Almost all the ingredients are sustainably sourced and include free-range meats and eggs, wild-caught fish, and organic fruits and vegetables. Breakfast is first-come, first-served, and the line is usually long. ~ 121 Don Gaspar Avenue; 505-983-9340, 800-722-7672; www.pasquals. com, e-mail info@pasquals.com. MODERATE TO DELUXE.

The four-star **Geronimo**, on artsy Lower Canyon Road, lives up to its billing. Housed in a cozy white-walled historic adobe, this is just the place to push the boat out during your stay. Delicious elk tenderloin is a perennial favorite, as are potato-crusted sea scallops with tatsoi salad and caviar sauce. Appetizers include a perfectly cooked lobster tail served over angelhair pasta, while desserts tend toward the decadent, such as sweet mango napoleon with Swiss chocolate and cassis coulis. One insider tip: The elk and several other specialties can also be found on the lunch menu, at a much reduced price, so if you're on a budget, plan on eating here earlier in the day. ~ 724 Canyon Road; 505-982-1500. DELUXE TO ULTRA-DELUXE.

When you gotta have a pizza fix, head for **Il Primo Pizza** for some cheesy, Windy City–style deep dish. ~ 234 North Guadalupe Street; 505-988-2007. BUDGET TO MODERATE.

Breakfast lovers head to the homey little **Tecolote Cafe**, which whips up heart-healthy breakfast burritos in addition to omelettes bursting with gooey filling, and baskets of biscuits and muffins. Singles sit at a community table, ideal for meeting local folks. For lunch, the burgers, enchiladas and burritos are popular. No dinner. Closed Monday. ~ 1203 Cerrillos Road; 505-988-1362. BUDGET.

GLOBAL SHOPPING

The past decade has seen Santa Fe emerge as a collectors market for ethnic art from all over the world. Following is a sampling of Santa Fe's international diversity. **Project Tibet** works with Santa Fe's Tibetan community to aid refugees internationally. The gallery here carries *thankas* (sacred paintings), Buddhist religious objects, clothing and books. ~ 403 Canyon Road; 505-982-3002. **Fourth World Cottage Industries** carries imported handicrafts, textiles and the like from around the world. ~ 102 West San Francisco Street, upstairs; 505-982-4388. **Origins** is a chic boutique with traditional and designer clothing for women from all over the world. ~ 135 West San Francisco Street; 505-988-2323.

In a city known for its history and architecture, what everyone remembers about Santa Fe is . . . the shopping. Myriad arts-and-crafts shops plus oodles of galleries crowd the Plaza and nearby Canyon Road, a two-mile street lined with fine art stores.

SHOPPING

For silver jewelry, pottery and handwoven blankets of exquisite detail, look no further than beneath the portal of the Palace of Governors on the Plaza where Indian artisans gather to market their wares.

Always-exciting images by well-known 19th- and 20th-century shooters can be viewed at **Andrew Smith Gallery**. ~ 203 West San Francisco Street; 505-984-1234; www.andrewsmith gallery.com, e-mail info@andrewsmithgallery.com.

◄ *HIDDEN*

Well-priced casual clothing makes **Chico's** a good place to purchase wearable souvenirs. ~ 328 South Guadalupe Street, 505-984-1132; and 122 West San Francisco Street, 505-984-3134.

Operated by Joseph Sisneros, great-grandson of the Jaramillo pioneer family, **Rancho de Chimayo Collection** features works of Spanish-Colonial and American Indian masters. The collection includes 19th- and 20th-century santero art, Pueblo pottery and contemporary gold and silver, American Indian jewelry, painting and sculpture. ~ Sena Plaza, 127 East Palace Avenue; 505-988-4526; www.ranchochimayo.com, e-mail gallery@ranchochimayo.com.

Bodhi Bazaar, in the Sambusco Center, has women's contemporary casual and dressy clothing. ~ 500 Montezuma Street; 505-982-3880.

An unusual bookstore, **The Ark** is found well off the beaten track in a hideaway hacienda. Books on healing, astrology and UFOs, crystals and incense fill this New Age haven. ~ 133 Romero Street; 505-988-3709; www.arkbooks.com.

Find gold jewelry and brilliant earth stones like sugilite at **Spirit of the Earth**. ~ 108 Don Gaspar Street; 505-988-9558. **LewAllen and LewAllen Jewelry** has branched out from designer Ross LewAllen's original ear cuffs into pendants, safari bracelets, beading and wildlife-theme wearables. ~ 105 East Palace Avenue; 505-983-2657, 800-988-5112; www.lewallenjewelry.com, e-mail contactus@lewallenjewelry.com.

Cotton garments and accessories for women and children fill the shelves at **Pinkoyote**. ~ 220 Shelby Street; 505-983-3030; www.pinkoyote.com.

For outrageous greeting and postcards, try the **Marcy Street Card Shop**. Closed occasionally on Sunday. ~ 75 West Marcy Street; 505-982-5160. **The Chile Shop** has pottery, *ristras*, chile powders and cookbooks. ~ 109 East Water Street; 505-983-6080; www.thechileshop.com.

Silver and gold buckles shake hands with leather and skin belts as well as custom-made Western boots at **Tom Taylor Co.**

◄ *HIDDEN*

Text continued on page 360.

Art Everywhere
You Look

During the early days of Santa Fe's art colony, painters shipped their works by rail to be sold back East. Today, though, some 200 art galleries are within walking distance of the Plaza, and the world comes to Santa Fe for art.

The place to start a gallery tour is midway between the Plaza and Canyon Road, at the **Gerald Peters Gallery**, the largest private art gallery west of the Mississippi River. Its rooms are full of museum-quality 19th- and 20th-century American works by such notables as Frederic Remington and Georgia O'Keeffe. There's also a magical gallery of wildlife art. Closed Sunday. ~ 1011 Paseo de Peralta; 505-954-5700, fax 505-954-5754; www.gpgallery.com. Next door, **Nedra Matteucci Galleries** also ranks among the finest in town. Here you'll find works by artists such as early Western landscapists Albert Bierstadt and Thomas Moran as well as paintings by legendary Santa Fe and Taos painters of the 1920s and a secluded one-acre sculpture garden. Closed Sunday. ~ 1075 Paseo de Peralta; 505-982-4631. The **Wyeth Hurd Gallery** represents N. C. Wyeth, Peter Hurd, Andrew Wyeth, and a dozen other members of this four-generation dynasty of American artists. Closed Sunday. ~ 206 East Palace Avenue; 505-989-8380; www.wyethhurd.com.

Among the myriad galleries on the streets surrounding the Plaza, a fascinating place that often goes unnoticed is **Andrew Smith Gallery**. This shop is stacked with limited-edition prints by Ansel Adams, Elliott Porter and many others, including photo portraits of Ernest Hemingway and Albert Einstein. Closed Sunday. ~ 203 West San Francisco Street; 505-984-1234; www.andrewsmithgallery.com. Important American Modernists, Regionalists and contemporary painters are shown at **Cline Fine Art**. Closed Sunday. ~ 131 West San Francisco Street; 505-982-5328; www.clinefineart.com. **Owings-Dewey Fine Art** carries works by classic Santa Fe artists and serves as estate representative for two of the city's leading early painters, William Penhallow Henderson and Will Shuster. Closed Sunday. ~ 76 East San Francisco Street; 505-982-6244; www.owingsdewey.com.

There is a cluster of galleries along West Palace Avenue between the Plaza and the Georgia O'Keeffe Museum. The **LewAllen Contemporary** is modern, hooked into "the scene" and always worth your time. ~ 129 West Palace Avenue; 505-988-8997; www.lewallen contemporary.com. Directly across the street, the **Wadle Galleries** exhibit the finest in representational art. Closed Sunday. ~ 128 West Palace Avenue; 505-983-9219; www.wadlegalleries.com.

The greatest concentration of galleries can be found along Canyon Road, which runs east (uphill) from Paseo de Peralta. The center of Santa Fe's original art colony, Canyon Road is now a rather exclusive enclave given over to retail galleries instead of back-room studios. Lovers of bronze sculpture should check out **Meyer Gallery** and its huge selection of impressionist paintings by well-known artists. ~ 225 Canyon Road; 505-983-1434; www.meyergalleries.com. In the same compound is one of the country's oldest galleries (in business since 1860), **Munson Gallery**, featuring paintings and sculpture. ~ 225 Canyon Road; 505-983-1657; www.munsongallery.com. Situated in an 1850s historic adobe home, the **Waxlander Gallery** displays the work of 22 painters and exhibits large sculptures in an outdoor garden amid colorful flowers. ~ 622 Canyon Road; 505-984-2202, 800-342-2202; www.waxlandergallery. com, e-mail art@waxlander.com.

Galleries open new exhibits by hosting receptions, with snacks, wine and an opportunity to meet the artist, on Friday evenings between 5 and 7 p.m. year-round. Listings of the week's receptions are found in the weekly *Santa Fe Reporter* and in the Friday *Pasatiempo* supplement to the *Santa Fe New Mexican*. During the summer months, Canyon Road gallery owners band together to sponsor **Canyon Road Art Walks** with refreshments and music during the Friday 5-to-7 time slot.

~ La Fonda Hotel, 108 East San Francisco Street; 505-984-2231; www.tomtaylorbuckles.com, e-mail ttbuckles@aol.com.

For tribal arts there are numerous choices, including **La Fonda Indian Shop**. ~ La Fonda Hotel, 100 East San Francisco Street; 505-988-2488. You can also try **Tin-Nee-Ann** for Southwestern arts and crafts. Closed Sunday. ~ 923 Cerrillos Road; 505-9881630.

NIGHTLIFE   **La Cantina** has singing waiters and waitresses and one heck of a wine list. ~ 125 East Palace Avenue, Sena Plaza; 505-988-9232; www.lacasasena.com.

For a nightcap, try the gracious Victorian bar in **La Posada de Santa Fe** with its chandeliers and leather chairs and cushy couch by the fireplace. If the weather's nice, take a sip on the outdoor patio. ~ 330 East Palace Avenue; 505-986-0000, 866-331-7625; www.laposada.rockresorts.com.

A mix of politicians, tourists and plain old working folks can be found at the **Pink Adobe**, a handsome watering hole located around the corner from the State Capitol. ~ 406 Old Santa Fe Trail; 505-983-7712.

Before New Mexico adopted the moniker of Land of Enchantment, it was known as the Sunshine State.

El Farol is a cantina where locals love to hang out and drink. With a spirit all of its own, El Farol attracts real people (including loads of tourists who have discovered its just-like-real-Santa-Fe ambience). You can hear live music here every night, including flamenco, R&B and jazz. Cover for flamenco shows. ~ 808 Canyon Road; 505-983-9912, fax 505-988-3823; www.el farolsf.com.

Even more down home is the mucho macho **Evangelo's**, where the beer is cheap, cheap, cheap. Live music, mostly rock-and-roll, jazz and blues almost every night. Occasional cover. ~ 200 West San Francisco Street; 505-982-9014.

The lounge in **La Fonda Hotel** during happy hour gurgles with the energy of locals and visitors. Hot hors d'oeuvres and music are fine accompaniments to the loaded margaritas. ~ 100 East San Francisco Street; 505-982-5511, fax 505-988-2952; www. lafondasantafe.com.

For a relaxed atmosphere right on the Plaza, go to the **Ore House**. Live music, including blues, folk and country, on Friday and Saturday. ~ 50 Lincoln Avenue; 505-983-8687; www.ore houseontheplaza.com.

Vanessie of Santa Fe is *the* place to see and be seen. Pianist Doug Montgomery, who performs at this upscale piano bar Sunday through Tuesday, is a local celebrity. The rest of the week other entertainers step in and keep the Baldwin concert. Gay-friendly. ~ 434 West San Francisco Street; 505-982-9966, fax 505-982-1507; www.vanessiesantafe.com.

For live Norteño (traditional northern Mexican) dance music and a local crowd, drop into **Tiny's Lounge** on Friday and Saturday nights. It's hidden toward the back of a small shopping center near the intersection of St. Francis Drive and Cerrillos Road southwest of downtown. ~ 1015 Pen Road; 505-983-9817. ◀ HIDDEN

OPERA, THEATER, SYMPHONY AND DANCE   Music and moonlight fill the **Santa Fe Opera**, one of the country's most famous (and finest) summer opera companies. Blending seasoned classics with exciting premieres, the Opera usually runs from late June through August in the open-air auditorium. Though all of the seats are sheltered, the sides are open and warm clothing and raingear are suggested, since evenings can be cold and/or wet. ~ Route 84/285; 505-986-5900, 800-280-4654, fax 505-995-3030; www.santafeopera.org.

Community theater of the highest order is found at **Santa Fe Playhouse**, the oldest continuously running theater company west of the Mississippi. It offers year-round theatrical entertainment with musicals, comedies, dramas and dance. ~ 142 East De Vargas Street; 505-988-4262; www.santafeplayhouse.org.

The beautiful Paolo Soleri Outdoor Theater of the Santa Fe Indian School campus serves as home to the **Santa Fe Summer Concert Series**, which brings big-name acts to town May through September. ~ On the campus of the Santa Fe Indian School, 1501 Cerrillos Road; 505-989-6300.

The **Santa Fe Symphony** performs both traditional and contemporary classical works at Lensic Performing Arts Center from October through May. ~ 211 West San Francisco Street; box office: 505-983-1414, 800-480-1319; www.santafesymphony.org.

Founded in 1980, the **Santa Fe Pro Musica** performs from September through May at Lensic Performing Arts Center (211 West San Francisco Street) and the Loretto Chapel (211 Old Santa Fe Trail). ~ 505-988-4640, 800-960-6680, fax 505-984-2501; www.santafepromusica.com.

The **Santa Fe Chamber Music Festival** (505-983-2075) performs at both the Saint Francis Auditorium (inside the Museum of Fine Arts) and Lensic Performing Arts Center, where the **Santa Fe Concert Association** (505-984-8759) performs as well.

The sizzling **Teatro Flamenco** returns to Santa Fe each summer (late June through August) for a series of flamenco dance concerts and workshops under the direction of Maria Benitez. Performances are held at the Lodge at Santa Fe (750 North St. Francis Drive). ~ 505-955-8562, 888-435-2636; www.maria benitez.com, e-mail flamenco@mariabenitez.com.

GAY SCENE   Santa Fe has long been known as a safe haven for large numbers of gay men and women. There is not much of a gay cruising scene, however, and gay-oriented clubs come and go at whim. The martini bar **Swig** was founded by Santa Fe's most high-profile gay partnership, Cliff Skoglund and Robert Hall, owners of the phenomenally successful Geronimo restaurant. Swig is now under new ownership, but it remains in a class of its own. It's about the only place in Santa Fe where you can live out your Nick and Nora fantasies and dress to the nines while sampling Asian tapas and elegant cocktails in low-lit, exotically themed rooms. ~ 135 West Palace Avenue; 505-955-0400.

PARKS   **HYDE MEMORIAL STATE PARK** 🏃 🏠 A small park (350 acres) in the mountains high above Santa Fe, Hyde Park's woodsy and sheltered feeling gives visitors the impression they're light years away from the city. This park is a good base for cross-country skiing or hiking in the Santa Fe National Forest. There are picnic areas, restrooms and a sledding hill. Day-use fee, $5 per vehicle. ~ Route 475, about seven miles northeast of Santa Fe; 505-983-7175, fax 505-983-2783.

▲ There are 43 tent sites, $10 per night; and 7 RV sites with electric hookups, $14 per night. Reservations (mid-May to Memorial Day only): 877-664-7787.

▼▼▼▼▼▼▼▼▼▼▼▼
Road to Taos

Route 68, the main highway from Santa Fe to Taos, parallels the Rio Grande, where early summer motorists can see whitewater rafters and kayakers by the hundreds—and plenty of traffic. Taos makes for an inviting day trip from Santa Fe (or vice-versa), traveling one way by the slower High Road to Taos and returning via the main highway. If this is your plan, avoid Española, midway between Santa Fe and Taos, on weekend evenings, when slow-cruising lowriders can paralyze highway traffic.

As you leave the Santa Fe area en route to Taos, take a detour through Tesuque, home to a number of film and TV celebrities and perhaps Santa Fe's most beautiful suburb.

SIGHTS   En route, if you can keep from being intrusive, visit Archbishop Lamy's private chapel at the **Bishop's Lodge**. Small, private and very holy are words that characterize this sanctuary along the Little Tesuque Stream. *Vigas* have replaced the former rafters in this intimate chapel, but the archbishop's cloak, hat and crucifix remain. Guided tours are available. It's quite possible a visit here will inspire you to read Willa Cather's classic, *Death Comes for the Archbishop*. ~ Bishop's Lodge Road, Santa Fe; 505-983-6377; www.bishopslodge.com, e-mail bishopslodge@bishopslodge.com.

Across Route 285 from the village of Tesuque is **Tesuque Pueblo**. Considered one of the most traditional of the pueblos, Tesuque continues to have a strong agricultural emphasis, which results in organic food products for sale. Bright designs characterize their pottery. The pueblo also operates Camel Rock Casino, where the main highway crosses tribal land. No cameras. Call for hours. ~ Route 84/285, Tesuque; 505-983-2667, fax 505-982-2331.

Pojoaque Pueblo, one of the smallest of the northern Rio Grande Indian pueblos, hosts special fiesta days and has a visitors center where handcrafted items are sold. The pueblo's **Poeh Cultural Center** (505-455-3334) includes a museum. The tribe has converted its old elementary school building into the glitzy neon Cities of Gold Casino. ~ Route 84/285; 505-455-3460, fax 505-455-7151 (visitors center).

Go left on Route 502 to **San Ildefonso Pueblo,** where you'll see beautiful burnished black matte pottery in the tradition of the late Maria Martinez. Current potters here continue to create artistic

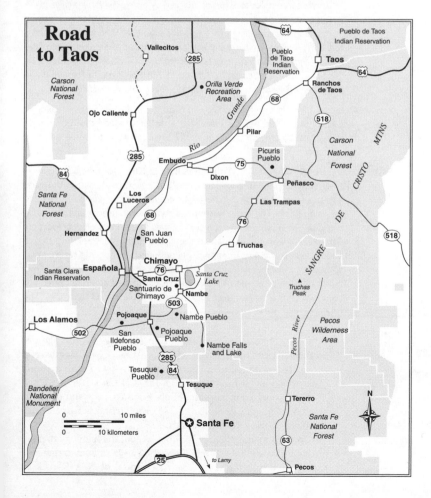

The High Road to Taos

This paved backroad route takes you through a series of traditional villages along the foothills of the Sangre de Cristo Range, where ways of life have not changed much since territorial times. Although it is only slightly longer than the main highway route—52 miles versus 45 miles—it takes about twice as long thanks to winding roads, village speed zones and irresistible photo opportunities.

NAMBE PUEBLO Drive through Pojoaque to County Road 503; turn right and drive three miles to a turnoff marked by a sign to Nambe Lake. Make a right onto the paved highway and wind past the cottonwoods to Nambe Pueblo and the sparkling Nambe Falls picnic site. This area was once a Spanish province where early settlers developed their communal land grants. Many Nambe residents are descendants of those early settlers. The falls are closed late September to mid-March. Photography fee; admission to the falls. ~ Route 1, Nambe; 505-455-2036, fax 505-455-2038.

CHIMAYO Turn left on Route 520 and head through the Chimayo Valley to Chimayo. Located between the Sangre de Cristos and the Rio Grande Valley, the Chimayo Valley is a fertile area at the confluence of three streams.

SANTUARIO DE CHIMAYO Within the village of Chimayo is the Santuario de Chimayo, the place of countless miracles. Legend has it that in the early 1800s a man who saw a shining light coming from the ground dug and found a crucifix. The cross was moved to a church nearby and placed on the altar. The next morning the crucifix was found in its original location. The crucifix was moved back to the church, but again disappeared and ended up in its original location. This continued until people realized that someone or something wanted it to remain at this site. So, a church was built in Chimayo between 1814 and 1816. This is probably one of the reasons why people believe the Santuario's dirt is blessed. El Santuario, "The

wonders. There's also a museum (closed weekends) on site displaying jewelry, costumes and religious artifacts. Visitors must register at the visitors center. Photography is allowed with a permit (fee). Admission. ~ Route 502; 505-455-3549, fax 505-455-7351.

If you opt not to take the High Road to Taos and continue north out of Santa Fe on Route 285, you'll come across the jolly sandstone **Camel Rock Monolith**.

Continuing north past Española, where the highway divides, drive a little farther on Route 68 to the San Juan Pueblo sign. **San Juan Pueblo** was the site of the first capital of New Mexico in

Shrine," remains a magic place where people with ailments come to feel God's healing touch. There's an annual pilgrimage to the church beginning on Good Friday. Testaments to its healing powers are everywhere, as discarded crutches, braces and *retablos* (paintings of saints done on wood) fill the church's side rooms. ~ County Road 94; 505-351-4889.

TRUCHAS   After visiting Chimayo, head north on Route 76 to the town of Truchas with its little weaving and woodcutting shops. It is a burgeoning arts center whose people are undoubtedly inspired by the splendid scenery of the Sangre de Cristos and New Mexico's second-highest mountain, 13,102-foot Truchas Peak.

LAS TRAMPAS   Continue north on Route 76 to Las Trampas. Once a walled adobe village—to protect it from "wild" Indians—Las Trampas is home to the 18th-century **Church of San Jose**, an oft-photographed mission church with mud plastering and early paintings. ~ Route 76, Las Trampas.

PICURIS PUEBLO   After passing through Las Trampas you'll come to Peñasco. Turn on Route 75 through the Picuris Pueblo to see the native pottery, weaving, silversmithing, beadwork and remains of a pueblo from the 13th century. Picuris, with its standing roundhouse, remains one of New Mexico's smallest pueblos. Admission. ~ Route 75, Peñasco; 505-587-2519, fax 505-587-1071.

SAN FRANCISCO DE ASIS   From Picuris, rejoin Route 75 for a few miles until you connect with Route 518 and pass over the landmark U.S. Hill Vista, an early, tortuous trading route. After driving over hill and dale, when Route 518 meets with Route 68, head straight to the Ranchos de Taos. There you'll find San Francisco de Asis, a Spanish Colonial adobe church that was the favorite of photographers Eliot Porter and Ansel Adams and painter Georgia O'Keeffe. It's home to Henri Ault's amazing *The Shadow of the Cross*, which some say is miraculous. Ault's painting depicts Christ carrying a cross when observed from one angle. In different lighting, however, the cross cannot be seen. Closed Saturday and Sunday. Admission to *The Shadow of the Cross*. ~ Route 68, Ranchos de Taos; 505-758-2754, fax 505-751-3923.

1598. Geometric designs and luster define the red-incised pottery. Woodcarvings and weavings are also for sale on site. ~ 505-852-4400, fax 505-852-4820.

Near San Juan Pueblo, on the east side of the highway, stands the controversial **Don Juan Oñate Monument**. This controversial $4 million bronze statue, a larger-than-life mounted figure of the first conquistador to attempt to colonize New Mexico, is considered by some to be a political boondoggle and an affront to the Indians of the Española Valley. Latinos, however, view it as a tribute to their proud cultural heritage. Notice where one of

Oñate's boots has been welded back on; parties unknown once sawed it off in protest because Oñate cut the left legs off Acoma Pueblo warriors following an uprising in 1608.

HIDDEN ▶   Continuing north on Route 68, the unpaved **River Road** parallels the highway and Río Grande. The oldest road in the valley, it serves several old haciendas that date back to colonial times. To explore it, follow any of the marked roads that turn west off the highway and intersect it. Of particular interest is Los Luceros, a hacienda that grew into a village and served as the county seat from 1821 to 1860.

Another 15 miles or so north on Route 68 takes you to the turnoff to the verdant town of **Dixon**, where artists hold studio visits the first weekend in November. ~ Route 75; information on studio visits: 505-579-9179; www.dixonarts.org.

In this fragrant valley is the **La Chiripada Winery**, which has a tour (by appointment only) and tasting room (tasting fee). ~ Route 75, Dixon; 505-579-4437, 800-528-7801; www.lachiripada.com, e-mail chiripa@cybermesa.com.

From there it's just a couple more miles on the "river road" to Pilar and the **Orilla Verde Recreation Area**, a nice rest stop on the river's edge. (See Chapter Ten for more information.)

If you return to Route 68 to travel north toward Taos, you'll discover that the highway was built by the U.S. Army and first called Camino Militar. Completion of this road helped end centuries' worth of isolation in Taos.

LODGING   On the northern edge of town are two rather rural alternatives to the city lodging experience. The **Bishop's Lodge Resort & Spa** is the better of the two primarily because of its rich history. The property along the Little Tesuque Stream was once the private retreat of Archbishop Jean Baptiste Lamy. The bishop's sacred, private chapel still stands behind the main lodge and guided tours are available. Since 1918, the 450-acre ranch has hosted guests who choose from horseback riding, swimming, meditative hikes and tennis. Well-kept guest rooms are decorated in ranch motif, while a spa and wellness center is also available. ~ Bishop's Lodge Road, off Route 84/285, Santa Fe; 505-983-6377, 800-419-0492; www.bishopslodge.com, e-mail bishopslodge@bishopslodge.com. DELUXE TO ULTRA-DELUXE.

Rooms at **Casa Escondida** are beautifully furnished with antiques and woodwork. The eight rooms run the gamut from a one-bedroom adobe suite to cozier single rooms with queen beds. A full hot breakfast is served in the sunny dining room. Put your feet up while lounging under their charming covered porch or slip into their outdoor hot tub. Things are quiet and peaceful here—there are no TVs at the inn. ~ P.O. Box 142, Chimayo, NM 87522; 505-351-4805, 800-643-7201, fax 505-351-2575; www.

casaescondida.com, e-mail info@casaescondida.com. MODERATE TO DELUXE.

Located on the famed high road to Taos, **Hacienda Rancho de Chimayo** is a splendid seven-room retreat. Antique beds made of mahogany and iron, as well as traditional Chimayo handwoven draperies and rugs, give the rooms a homey feel. All rooms adjoin a beautiful courtyard and have fireplaces crafted from adobe as well as pine floors and *vigas*. The inn itself is adjacent to a popular New Mexican restaurant. This place is a real gem. ~ County Road 98, Chimayo; phone/fax 505-351-2222, 888-270-2320; www.ranchodechimayo.com, e-mail rdc@espanola nm.com. MODERATE.

◀ HIDDEN

Before it gets any trendier, check out the **Tesuque Village Market** and its casually chic atmosphere. The Tesuque chile-cheeseburger, stir-fry veggie plate and salads are highly recommended, as are the breakfast burritos. There's a full wine cellar and good choices by the glass. ~ Route 591 and Bishop's Lodge Road, Tesuque; 505-988-8848, fax 505-986-0921. BUDGET TO MODERATE.

DINING

◀ HIDDEN

Tucked into the mountains about 40 minutes north of Santa Fe, **Restaurante Rancho de Chimayo** serves authentic New Mexican meals in an adobe house. Bill of fare includes tamales, enchiladas, tacos and flautas plus specialties like steak, trout, marinated pork cutlets served in a red-chile sauce and chicken breasts topped with chile sauce and melted cheese. Leave room for the homemade *sopaipillas* and honey. During summer months, ask for the outdoor patio seating. Closed Monday from November through April. ~ County Road 98, Chimayo; 505-351-4444, fax 505-351-4375; www.ranchochimayo.com. MODERATE.

When you're writing a guidebook about New Mexico, it's hard to decide whether the **Tesuque Pueblo Flea Market** belongs in the shopping or sightseeing section. Just as every flea market reflects its surrounding community, this northern New Mexico gather-

SHOPPING

◀ HIDDEN

AUTHOR FAVORITE

As far as art galleries go, none is quite like the **Shidoni Foundry**, where bronze pourings take place on Saturdays. The art foundry, gardens and contemporary gallery are world-renowned among purveyors of fine art. You can experience Shidoni's charm with a stroll through the foundry's two large, peaceful parks, where dozens of metal sculptures—many of them monumental in size and price—await corporate buyers. Closed Sunday. ~ Bishop's Lodge Road, Tesuque; 505-988-8001, fax 505-984-8115; www.shidoni.com, e-mail shidoni@shidoni.com.

ing place contains Spanish, Anglo and American Indian traders alike. Pull over to the side of the road, shuffle through the dust and you'll find everything from pinto beans to auto parts to fine turquoise jewelry. The flea market is open every Friday, Saturday and Sunday. ~ To get there head seven miles north from Santa Fe on Route 84/285, turn left after the opera house; www.tesuque pueblofleamarket.com.

For eight generations the Ortega family has been weaving brilliant sashes, vests, purses and jackets as well as world-famous rugs and blankets at their wonderful little shop, **Ortega's Weaving**. Closed Sunday. ~ At the corner of County Road 98 and State Road 76, Chimayo; 505-351-4215; www.ortegasweaving.com.

Next door, the **Galeria Ortega** is a good place to check for Southwestern gifts (pottery, kachinas, paintings, candles) and books on regional topics. Closed Sunday, except in the summer. ~ County Road 98 and Route 76, Chimayo; 505-351-2288; www.galeria ortega.com.

For a sampling of local talent in Truchas, stop by the **Hand Artes Gallery**, featuring folk and contemporary fine art. Closed Sunday. ~ Route 76 and County Road 75, Truchas; 505-689-2443, 800-689-2441, fax 505-689-2443; www.collectors guide.com/handartes.

Also in Truchas is the **Cardona-Hine Gallery**, featuring the contemporary paintings of Alvaro Cardona-Hine and Barbara McCauley. ~ Off Route 76, on County Road 75, Truchas; 505-689-2253, 866-692-5070, fax 505-689-2903; www.cardonahine gallery.com.

PARKS   **NAMBE FALLS AND LAKE** 🏃 🛶 A double-drop waterfall tumbles down from Nambe Lake to a small picnic and camping area among the cottonwoods that line the Río Nambe. The lake is generously stocked with trout, and since it is on tribal land a New Mexico fishing license is not required. Instead, anglers pay a daily fee to the pueblo; these fees are the primary source of income for this small tribe. The falls are closed October to mid-March. Day-use fee, $8 (without fishing fee), $10 (including fishing fee). ~ To get there, turn east at Pojoaque onto Route 503 and continue for six miles, past the pueblo turnoff, to the lake entrance; 505-455-2034, fax 505-455-2038; www.nambepueblo.com.

▲ The Nambe Falls campground has 7 shelter rentals and 25 tent/RV sites with water and hookups; $20 to $30 per night.

▼▼▼▼▼▼▼▼▼▼
Las Vegas Area

The slow-paced town of Las Vegas, with its refreshingly real central plaza, is the county seat of three-million-acre San Miguel County. A practically undiscovered gem, it reflects the heritage of northern New Mexico. The surrounding region takes in the Pecos River, rushing from the high peaks of the

Pecos Wilderness down a deep canyon and past ancient Indian ruins, as well as the magnificent mountain country around Hermit's Peak. To the north lies the strangely silent land around Mora, one of a small cluster of traditional villages that are slowly turning into ghost towns. Few travelers take the time to explore the Las Vegas area, just an hour's drive from Santa Fe; for those who do, a wealth of history and natural beauty awaits.

SIGHTS

You can follow the route of the old Santa Fe Trail through Las Vegas all the way to Raton by driving Route 25 as it skirts the southern Sangre de Cristo Mountains and getting off at historic sites along the way. About 15 minutes east of Santa Fe (north on Route 25) is the turnoff for **Glorieta,** a tiny hamlet best known for its large Baptist convention and retreat center, and for being the site of the **Glorieta Battlefield,** the westernmost skirmish in the Civil War. After turning off, drive east toward

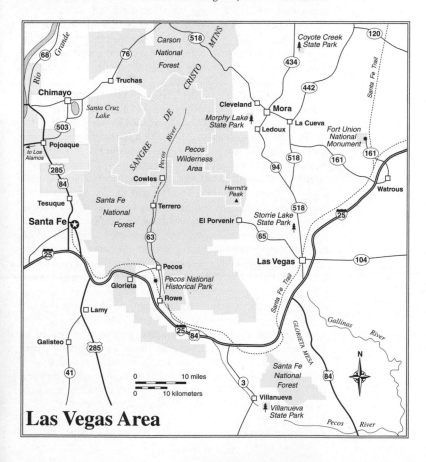

Las Vegas Area

the tiny community of Pecos. You'll pass a brown National Park Service sign commemorating the 1862 Battle of Glorieta Pass. Considered one of the most significant but least-known battles in the West, the battle was fought between Union troops and Confederates from Texas who had already taken southern New Mexico and were now trying to capture Santa Fe as a base from which to seize control of the Colorado and California gold-fields. By audaciously sneaking up behind the Confederates and stealing the supply wagons, the Union Army won a major victory at Glorieta Pass.

Pecos (population 1500) is a tiny town that consists of two gas stations, two general stores, two excellent small restaurants, a U.S. Forest Service ranger station serving the nearby Santa Fe National Forest and spectacular Pecos Wilderness, and two places typical of every New Mexican village: a Catholic mission church and a bar. Much of the predominantly Spanish-speaking population ekes out a living in the surrounding national forest, cutting *vigas*, *latillas* and firewood or grazing small herds of cattle, horses and goats. Unpaved roads (many of them passable by passenger car—check at the ranger station for suggestions) lead into the forest in all directions from the village; it's a beautiful area, full of spotted, rolling hills.

When the late actress Greer Garson and her husband donated 365 acres to preserve a postclassic pueblo civilization, they made possible the creation of **Pecos National Historical Park**. Walk among ruins dating back to A.D. 1200, a pueblo thought to have stood four to five stories back in 1451 when it had a population of 2000 (more than live in the Pecos area today). By the 17th century the Franciscan monks had taken over the pueblo and built a pair of mission churches. You can still see the remains of the huge church, *convento* and garden walls alongside the ancient pueblo ruins. Rampant disease and famine coupled with Comanche Indian raids in the mid-1800s led to the pueblo's abandonment, but survivors moved to Jemez Pueblo, where even today they form a separate clan and speak a dialect distinct from other Indians at the pueblo. When visiting, be careful to respect the privacy of the spirits that may haunt this incredible site. The ancient pueblo people were quite leery of strangers, forbidding them to set foot on pueblo land even when Pecos Pueblo was a center for trade with the Plains people. Trading parties actually had to camp outside the city wall. Tours of the Glorieta Battlefield and the historic Forked Lightning Ranch are also available with reservations. Admission. ~ Route 63, two miles south of Pecos; 505-757-6414 ext. 240, fax 505-757-8460; www.nps.gov/peco, e-mail peco_visitor_information@nps.gov.

Going west from the park and Pecos village, the road winds along a scenic river canyon painted with scrub oak. Along the way you'll pass a lake where the locals fish for dinner, a trout hatchery, a monastery and clusters of summer cabins. The upper Pecos River is renowned for its catch-and-release fly fishing, and on summer weekends you'll find the riverbanks lined with fishermen.

North of Pecos on Route 63 is the settlement of **Terrero**, the site of a long-abandoned refinery that used to process gold and other ores from the surrounding mountains. The pavement ends about four miles north of Terrero, and the unpaved road, steep and rough in spots, continues to a series of trailheads and large, well-developed campgrounds at the south portal of the Pecos Wilderness.

About 50 miles from Pecos is the country's original **Las Vegas**. The area's modern-day roots go back to the railroad's heyday, when Las Vegas was an important mercantile center. Las Vegas' destiny to become a major port of entry for supply wagons on the Santa Fe Trail began in 1835, when the Mexican government gave land grants to 29 individuals. By 1879, railroad tracks were laid east of the Gallinas River in "New Town"; not surprisingly, Railroad Avenue and the neighborhood boomed. But by 1905, railroad traffic was diverted south and the once-expanding city, whose population in the late 1800s rivaled Denver's, dwindled.

The diverse origins of people who came during Las Vegas' prime left an architectural legacy of everything from Territorial and Italianate styles to Victorian designs. In fact, Las Vegas has nine historic districts and more than 900 historically designated buildings. Movie buffs may recognize the distinctive-looking town as the setting of numerous silent films.

As you enter the city, you'll want to first head to the historic **Plaza**, the center of Old Town. The Plaza dates back to the 1600s with the Spaniards, although archaeological digs in Las Vegas show that the Paleo Indians lived here as early as 8000 B.C.

◆◆◆

DAY TRIP TO LA CUEVA

La Cueva National Historic Site, part of the Mora land grant of 1835, is an exceptionally beautiful sight in the springtime. Built around a hacienda completed in 1863, La Cueva was a major agricultural center and the home of an adobe mill that ground flour for generations. Electricity was generated here until 1949. You can visit the old mill and the Mercantile Building, now the **Salman Ranch Store**, a peaked-roof adobe that sells locally produced jams, syrups and the like, along with dried flowers and wildflower seeds. Closed Tuesday and Wednesday from January to mid-May. Northeast of the store is **San Rafael Mission Church**, a building graced with handsome French Gothic windows. ~ Route 442, off of Route 518, 25 miles north of Las Vegas; 505-387-2900.

Afterward, stop by the **Las Vegas–San Miguel Chamber of Commerce** for maps of walking tours, hiking trails and information on Las Vegas' history. Closed weekends. ~ 513 6th Street, Las Vegas; 505-425-8631, 800-832-5947; www.lasvegasnew mexico.com, e-mail chamber@worldplaces.com.

Next to the municipal courts is **The City of Las Vegas Museum & Rough Rider Memorial Collection**, which has mementos of the Spanish-American War donated by Rough Riders. It also exhibits artifacts and other historical items from northeastern New Mexico, starting with the Santa Fe Trail. Closed Monday from May through September, and Monday and Sunday from October through April. ~ 727 Grand Avenue, Las Vegas; 505-454-1401, fax 505-425-7335; www.lasvegasmuseum.org, e-mail museum@desertgate.com.

Pretty buildings line the street of **New Mexico Highlands University**, which was established in 1893, bridging the rivaling Old and New Towns. The school is well known for its fine arts, performing arts and technical programs. ~ 901 University Avenue, Las Vegas; 505-425-7511, 877-850-9064, fax 505-454-3599; www.nmhu.edu.

Yet the pride of the area is the **United World College**, a beautiful red-slate structure that looks like a castle, complete with turrets. The school's unique setting and approach to learning draw students from around the world. To find the college, drive up the campus's pretty **Hot Springs Canyon** past painted barns, a picturesque little church and a couple of colorful wall murals. ~ Near the former spa of Montezuma, Las Vegas; 505-454-4200, fax 505-454-4274; www.uwc-usa.org.

Well-marked natural hot springs baths, located right off the highway in view of the United World College, are offered in varying temperatures.

For a splendid drive, continue on Route 65 through Gallinas Canyon into the heart of the Sangre de Cristos and on up to the hiker's paradise of 10,263-foot **Hermit's Peak**.

Backtracking to Las Vegas and then north on Route 518 takes you to the boardsailing-haven of **Storrie Lake State Park**. A short drive farther north on scenic Route 518 puts you in **Mora**, known as the breadbasket of the area during the heyday of the Santa Fe Trail when it grew wheat.

In the nearby town of **Cleveland** is the **Cleveland Roller Mill Museum**, a 1900s flour mill that operated until 1947. The building, which is on the National Register of Historic Places, has original mill equipment and also covers local and regional history. The outside of the mill is open year-round; open weekends from Memorial Day through Labor Day. Admission. ~ Off Route 518, Cleveland; 505-387-2645; www.angelfire.com/folk/roller_mill, e-mail dancas@nnmt.net.

Northeast of Las Vegas via Interstate 25 is **Fort Union National Monument,** which beginning in 1851 and through 1891 was the largest military post in the region and headquarters for soldiers who protected Santa Fe Trail travelers from raids. A self-guided trail and visitors center explains its rich history. Admission. ~ Route 161, Watrous; 505-425-8025, fax 505-454-1155; www.nps.gov/foun, e-mail foun_administration@nps.gov.

Victoriana is alive in the center of Las Vegas at the historic **Plaza Hotel.** Originally built in 1882 in the Italianate bracketed style, the Plaza was the first major inn constructed after the railroad's arrival. A century later, original features such as tin ceilings and window bracketing were uncovered. Rooms are decorated in period furniture, antiques and floral accents typical of late-19th-century buildings in the West. There's an on-site restaurant and lounge. ~ 230 Plaza, Las Vegas; 505-425-3591, 800-328-1882, fax 505-425-9659; www.plazahotel-nm.com, e-mail lodging@plaza hotel-nm.com. MODERATE TO DELUXE.

LODGING

Or drive just a few miles to the "new" section of town and the hacienda-style **Inn on the Santa Fe Trail** for the best rooms for the price in the area. The property is handsomely decorated in oak and whitewashed pine furniture crafted by a Las Vegas artisan. Southwestern paintings cover pink walls. Fiberglass tubs are found in the bathrooms. ~ 1133 Grand Avenue, Las Vegas; 505-425-6791, 888-448-8438, fax 505-425-0417; www.innonthesantafe trail.com, e-mail davidfenzi@yahoo.com. BUDGET TO MODERATE.

The stars are the main draw at the aptly named **Star Hill Inn** set on 200 wooded acres in Sapello, 10 miles north of Las Vegas. Eight attractive one- and two-bedroom log cabins with stocked kitchens and handcrafted furniture are scattered around Star Hill and are a popular retreat for lazing, birding and hiking during the daytime. There is a meditation garden as well as a labyrinth. Nightly star tours are offered by owner/astronomer Phil Mahon, or you can rent your own telescope from the inn. There's a two-night minimum; detailed directions will be sent upon reservation confirmations. ~ P.O. Box 707, Sapello, NM 87745; 505-429-9998; www.starhillinn.com, e-mail stay@starhillinn.com. DELUXE TO ULTRA-DELUXE.

The **Landmark Grill,** the most elegant restaurant in Las Vegas, has an English look highlighted by Corinthian columns and tablecloths. Indulge in the linguine alfredo with shrimp, the charcoal-broiled steak or the alligator (when available). The intimate setting has been known to whet appetites of all kinds. ~ Plaza Hotel, 230 Plaza, Las Vegas; 505-425-3591; www.plazahotel-nm.com. MODERATE TO DELUXE.

DINING

HIDDEN ▶   Located between a used-car lot and a hair salon, the **Mexican Kitchen** is the kind of place you'd normally pass right by. But we took a seat at one of the formica tables and noticed signed autographs from *General Hospital* soap opera stars who stopped by this redecorated drive-in while shooting an episode nearby. Perhaps the word-of-mouth reviews had already started. For excellent burritos, tacos and enchiladas at inexpensive prices, we wouldn't hesitate to return. Breakfast, lunch and dinner are served. Closed Tuesday and Wednesday. ~ 717 Grand Avenue, Las Vegas; 505-454-1769. BUDGET TO MODERATE.

Don't be deterred by the shabby exterior of **Estella's Café**. Thoughtfully prepared American and Mexican cuisine dominate the menu. The green chile comes highly recommended. Open Monday through Wednesday for lunch, Thursday through Saturday for lunch and dinner. Closed Sunday. ~ 148 Bridge Street, Las Vegas; 505-454-0048. BUDGET TO MODERATE.

A reader's suggestion brought us to **El Rialto Restaurant & the Rye Lounge**, where you can down a few Mexican beers amid models of old trains and cars before stepping into the dining room. Fare such as fajitas, steak and enchiladas are prepared Southwest/New Mexican style; steaks and lobster have deluxe to ultra-deluxe price tags. Closed Sunday. ~ 141 Bridge Street, Las Vegas; 505-454-0037. BUDGET TO ULTRA-DELUXE.

SHOPPING   Readers will find books of every description in **Tome on the Range**, Las Vegas's independent bookstore. ~ 116 Bridge Street, Las Vegas; 505-454-9944; www.tomeontherange.com. **Second Tome Around**, their used bookstore across the street, is a great place to while away an afternoon. The café here serves soups, quiches, pastries and coffee. There's also free wi-fi. ~ 131 Bridge Street, Las Vegas; 505-454-8511.

NIGHTLIFE In Las Vegas, a bumping jukebox, cold beer and a late last call make **La Cantina Lounge** a lively nightspot. ~ 603 East Lincoln Street, Las Vegas; 505-425-9883.

PARKS   **STORRIE LAKE STATE PARK** 🏊 ⛵ 🏕 🚤 🐟 🎣 A pretty mountain lake that's favored by gung-ho windsurfers who like the consistent breezes, and families who enjoy the jewel of a setting and the swimming. There is a visitors center, picnic area, toilets and showers. Entrance closes at sunset year-round. Day-use fee, $5 per vehicle. ~ Route 518, four miles north of Las Vegas; 505-425-7278, fax 505-425-0446.

▲ There are 46 developed sites (25 with RV hookups); tent sites are $10 per night and hookups are $14 per night. Primitive camping is allowed along the lake's shore; $8 per night.

MORPHY LAKE STATE PARK 🏕 🚤 🎣 A scenic mountain lake and park that's a popular fishing spot for everyone. Unspoiled barely does justice to this little jewel. There are pit toilets, tables and grills. No motorboats are allowed. Closed November through March. Day-use fee, $5 per vehicle. ~ Route 94, four miles west of Ledoux; 505-387-2328, fax 505-387-5628.

▲ There are 20 developed sites ($10 per night).

COYOTE CREEK STATE PARK 🏃 ↙ Fishing and camping are the main attractions in this compact 80-acre park, but there are also hiking trails, picnic sites and a playground as well as a visitors center. Amenities include restrooms and showers. Day-use fee, $5 per vehicle. ~ Route 434, 17 miles north of Mora; 505-387-2328, fax 505-387-5628.

▲ There are 67 sites including 17 with electric hookups and 20 primitive sites. Fees per night are $8 for primitive sites, $10 for standard sites and $14 for hookups. Reservations (mid-May to September): 877-664-7787.

The Pajarito Plateau, a broad, pine-forested shelf of lava and ash, spans the eastern slope of the Jemez Mountains. This unusual mountain range is circular because some 200,000 years ago it was the base of a single volcano larger than any active volcano on earth today. The elements have carved the plateau into canyons with sheer orange-and-white walls where ancient cliff-dwellers made their homes.

▼▼▼▼▼▼▼▼▼▼▼▼
Los Alamos Area

This geological labyrinth made the plateau a perfect place for the government to hide its top-secret A-bomb laboratory during World War II. Throughout the Cold War, as the brains behind the bomb continued to move into the area, Los Alamos boomed to become the wealthiest town in the state. Today, the future of this community surrounded by wilderness is uncertain as it slips into post–Cold War history.

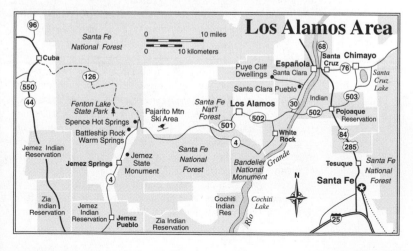

In fact, history is an ever-present reality throughout the land between Santa Fe and Taos. It can be captured in such places as Bandelier National Monument, with its ruins of Indian pueblos and cliff dwellings from the 13th century, as well as still-inhabited Indian pueblos and Spanish mountain villages, where the ways of life from centuries past still endure.

SIGHTS   Los Alamos was developed in the early 1940s by the U.S. government for scientists working on the highly secretive Manhattan Project. The isolated town in the high-altitude Jemez Mountains boasted a spectacular setting, with scenery of dense forest and Indian pueblos; an extinct volcano formed a natural barrier on the other side. About the only thing here was the private Los Alamos Ranch School for Boys, but it was easily closed and the Manhattan Project, an experiment that would change the course of history, was underway.

> The first atomic bombs bore the nicknames "Fat Man" and "Little Boy."

Bright young minds were imported to create the first atomic bombs that eventually helped end World War II. But, alas, the inventors and their families were forced to live behind a wall of secrecy, where mail was subject to a censor's pen and passes were needed for leaves.

It was physicist Robert Oppenheimer, architect of the atomic bomb, who once said: "The notion of disappearing into the New Mexico desert for an indefinite period disturbed a good many scientists."

Los Alamos National Laboratory remains the major presence in the city and accounts for the lion's share of local jobs. The Department of Energy still owns the laboratory that employs more than 7000 for national security studies, metallurgy, genetics information and geothermal and solar research. Los Alamos, obviously, still attracts the intelligentsia.

Los Alamos is warming (no pun intended) to visitors after decades as an ultra-insular community. The bomb was invented under a veil of secrecy; people in Santa Fe (only about 35 miles away) didn't even know what was going on "up there."

No matter how you feel about the atomic age, a visit to the **Bradbury Science Museum** is a must. Three dozen exhibits are interspersed with photographs, a timeline, films and letters, including one from Albert Einstein to President Roosevelt; the Robert Oppenheimer story is detailed. The museum is alternatingly frightening and enlightening. There is a tech lab/classroom; a recent exhibit discussed laboratory research to protect the environment. ~ 15th and Central streets, Los Alamos; 505-667-4444, fax 505-665-6932; www.bsm.lanl.gov, e-mail museum@lanl.gov.

To understand a little more about this unique town, be sure to stop at the **Los Alamos Historical Museum**, which covers pre-bomb history dating back to the Pleistocene era, artifacts from the now-closed boy's school and items from the World War II era. There is a small pre-Columbian Indian pueblo ruin in the park behind the museum. ~ 1921 Juniper Street, Los Alamos; 505-662-4493, fax 505-662-6312; www.losalamoshistory.org, e-mail historicalsociety@losalamos.com.

Adjacent to the historical museum is a 1928 log building, home of the **Art Center at Fuller Lodge**. This national landmark, once a recreation hall for ranch school students, hosts exhibits by native and visiting artists. Closed Sunday. ~ 2132 Central Avenue, Los Alamos; 505-662-9331, fax 505-662-9334; www.artfulnm.org, e-mail artful@losalamos.com.

Nearby is the gleaming **Larry R. Walkup Aquatic Center**, the highest-altitude Olympic-size indoor pool in the United States, serving athletes and recreational swimmers who enjoy a splash. Admission. ~ 2760 Canyon Road, Los Alamos; 505-662-8170, fax 505-662-8034; www.losalamos.nm.us/rec, e-mail lacrec@losalamos.nm.us.

The earth is hot around Los Alamos less because of radioactivity than its volcanic history, and hot springs bubble forth to the delight of those who enjoy a refreshing and relaxing dip. In their natural state are the **Spence Hot Springs** (Route 4, about seven miles north of Jemez Springs) and **Battleship Rock Warm Springs** (Route 4, about five miles north of Jemez Springs). Short, well-trod foot paths take off from the respective parking areas.

At the more developed **Jemez Springs Bathhouse**, private indoor tubs are available, as well as an assortment of wraps and massages. Admission. ~ Route 4 near the town of Jemez Springs; 505-829-3303, 866-204-8303; www.jemezspringsbathhouse.com.

One mile north of the city of Jemez Springs is the **Jemez State Monument**. The monument, officially recognized in 1935, honors pre-Columbian Indian ruins, including the ruins of a pueblo and the remains of a Spanish mission, the Church of San Jose de los Jemez, which was built in 1621–22. A tiny museum offers exhibits that explain some of the Jemez history. Closed Tuesday from November through April. Admission. ~ Route 4; phone/fax 505-829-3530; www.nmculture.org.

Valle Grande was created about a million years ago when a volcano's summit seemingly crumbled and spewed ash as far east as Texas. It left a broad basin called a caldera (thought to be the largest of its kind) that stretches about 15 miles in diameter. The Valle Grande is also home to one of the largest elk herds in the United States. It was nominated for national park status three times between 1926 and 1990, but the move was repeatedly blocked for political reasons. Finally, in 1999, Congress approved the acquisition of the Valle Grande by the Valles Caldera

Trust. Now called the **Valles Caldera National Preserve**, this experiment in land management allows you a more solitary experience than you might get in other wilderness areas. Winter and summer activities include fishing, hiking, van and horse-drawn wagon tours and more. To preserve the integrity of the wilderness area's solitude, only a limited number of visitors are allowed to enter at any time. Reservations required for most activities. Generally closed mid-week so, call ahead. Check their website for details. Fee for certain activities. ~ Route 4, 14 miles west of Los Alamos; 505-661-3333, 877-851-8946, fax 505-661-0400; www.vallescaldera.gov.

HIDDEN ▶

Along Route 4 on the way to Bandelier, take a two-mile detour in the town of White Rock and follow signs to the **Overlook**. Sitting on this volcanic peninsula you can gaze down to the Rio Grande, which curves in a broad sweep far below. Sedimentary cliffs and a tableau of distant mountains complete the panorama.

Bandelier National Monument encompasses 32,737 acres of scenic wilderness. The Pueblo people, who settled in this part of the Jemez Mountains in the 1100s, farmed this comparatively lush area in Frijoles Canyon until the mid-1500s. The canyon walls bear their symbols. Most of Bandelier, named for archaeologist Adolph Bandelier, is wild backcountry, with several riparian oases. Strenuous climbs up steep cliffs are required to explore much of the backcountry, although there are shorter trails that are wheelchair accessible. Admission. ~ Route 4, ten miles south of Los Alamos; 505-672-3861 ext. 517, fax 505-672-9607; www.nps.gov/band.

Roughly 7000 archaeological sites are said to surround the Los Alamos area.

Start your perusal of the park at the visitors center with a ten-minute slide show of "The Bandelier Story." The short, self-guided Main Loop Trail takes off from the visitors center near the Frijoles Creek and passes **Tyuonyi** ("Meeting Place"), a circular village believed to have once stood three stories high. Its single entrance has led to speculation that this large and impressive structure was used for defending the village.

Behind Tyuonyi is **Talus House**, which has been completely reconstructed to give visitors an idea of what the homes along the cliff would have looked like. The trail continues to the longest structure at Bandelier, aptly named **Long House Ruin**, nestled under a cliff. It's full of ancient pictographs and petroglyphs.

You can continue on the trail for a half mile and scramble up several somewhat scary ladders to the **Alcove House**, which affords a great overall view of the canyon. Backtracking to the visitors center, hike down Frijoles Canyon across the creek to the

Upper Falls and then view yet another waterfall about a half-mile down the path.

If your appetite is whet for ruins, then drive a few dozen miles northwest to the **Puye Cliff Dwellings**, a fascinating little ancient city. Inhabited by up to 1500 people between the years of 1250 to 1577, Puye is currently operated by the neighboring Santa Clara Pueblo, whose occupants are probably descendants of the original settlers. The excavated ruins of the ancient apartment-like complexes are evident from miles away as you approach the site. Upon arrival, choose either the Cliff Trail or the Mesa Top Trail for exploring. Admission. The dwelling is currently closed due to fire damage. Call for more information. ~ Located 11 miles off Route 30, west of Española; 505-753-7330.

After exploring the cliff dwellings, drive six miles west to gorgeous **Santa Clara Canyon**, a nice place for a picnic lunch or fishing stop.

LODGING

A two-story bungalow with a wooden deck that spans the upper floor, the **North Road Inn** is home to 14 comfy rooms. All are decorated with hints of the Southwest and boast refrigerators, microwaves (a few with full kitchens), high-speed internet and cable TV. Pancakes, eggs and the like are made to order every morning and a scrumptious breakfast buffet with fresh fruit and baked goods is served on the weekends. This is a pleasant alternative to Los Alamos' larger motels. ~ 2127 North Road, Los Alamos; 505-662-3678, fax 505-662-3678; www.thenorthroad inn.com, e-mail northroad@losalamos.com. MODERATE.

The 85 rooms at the **Quality Inn & Suites Los Alamos**, located in a wooded area of town, are bright and pleasant with a Southwestern flair. Complimentary high-speed internet and a continental breakfast are provided. ~ 2175 Trinity Drive, Los Alamos; 505-662-7211, 877-424-8432, fax 505-661-7714; www.qualityinn losalamos.com, e-mail info@qualityinnlosalamos.com. MODERATE.

A similar dwelling is the **Best Western Hilltop House Hotel**, which caters to businesspeople with mini-suites and executive suites. Amenities include a sauna, an indoor heated pool and a deli. ~ Trinity Drive and Central Street, Los Alamos; 505-662-2441, 800-462-0936, fax 505-662-5913; www.bestwesternlos alamos.com. MODERATE.

DINING

If you need bagels and cream cheese and lots of hot coffee to start your day, head to **Ruby K's Bagel Café**, a great place to hang out, check e-mail on your laptop and watch the world go by. Soups, sandwiches, paninis and salads, along with fruit smoothies, are available at lunch. ~ 1789 Central Avenue, Suite 2, Los Alamos;

505-662-9866; www.rubykbagel.com, e-mail yum@rubykbagel. com. BUDGET.

The **Blue Window Bistro** got its name from the New Mexican tradition of painting windows blue to keep away evil. It remains one of Los Alamos's most reliable restaurants, serving fresh, light food in an attractive airy setting. At lunch, there are homemade soups, salads, crêpes, wraps and sandwiches. Dinner is a feast for foodies, with entrées such as Prince Edward Island mussels and linguini, chicken marsala, and fresh Atlantic salmon prepared differently each evening. A popular brunch is available on Saturday only and includes eggs benedict. ~ Mari Mac Village, 813 Central Avenue, Los Alamos; 505-662-6305. BUDGET TO DELUXE.

Gyros, moussaka and other Mediterranean and North African treats are on the menu at the **Pyramid Café**, an offshoot of the popular Santa Fe eatery. There's a falafel all-you-can-eat lunch buffet and belly dancing on Friday nights. Cheap and cheerful ethnic eating. Closed weekends. ~ 751 Central Avenue, Los Alamos; 505-661-1717. BUDGET.

Lemongrass & Lime specializes in fresh-tasting Vietnamese and Thai food made from recipes and supplies imported directly from Bangkok. The friendly owners make this a local favorite. ~ 160 Central Park Square, Los Alamos; 505-661-4221. BUDGET.

Old-fashioned homestyle cooking is what packs them in at the **Hill Diner**. At this fun eatery, you'll find great burgers, chicken-fried steak and other retro specials (Friday is ribs night). Save room for a piece of pie with your cup of joe. ~ 1315 Trinity Drive, Los Alamos; 505-662-9745; www.hilldiner.com, e-mail diner@lane.bz. BUDGET.

NIGHTLIFE   Every Friday night in the summer, the **Los Alamos Concert Series** offers free Americana, blues and country music shows. Most concerts take place in Ashley Park. ~ 109 Central Park Square, Los Alamos; 505-661-4891; www.gordonsconcerts.com, e-mail info@gordonsconcerts.com.

PARKS   **BANDELIER NATIONAL MONUMENT** 🏃 Nestled in the Jemez Mountains are cave and cliff dwellings and village sites that were once home to the ancestors of the present Pueblo people. Hiking trails lead the curious visitor around sheer-walled canyons and mesas. There's a visitors center to get you started. Food service is available in the park. No pets allowed. A fee of $12 per private vehicle is good for seven days. ~ Route 4, about ten miles south of Los Alamos; 505-672-3861 ext. 517, fax 505-672-9607; www.nps.gov/band.

▲ There are 95 sites during the summer, about 30 sites during the off-season; $12 per night for individual sites, $35 per

Taking a Chance

Nothing in recent years has changed the look of New Mexico's major highways as much as the rise of Indian gaming. Advertised by glittering billboards and bright computerized displays, the state's Pueblo and Apache tribes operate 11 gambling casinos throughout the state, including four between Santa Fe and Taos. Although gaming is largely unrestricted, most casinos offer blackjack, craps, roulette, poker, Caribbean stud, pai gow poker, video poker, slot machines and bingo. Most also have budget-priced all-you-can-eat buffets.

Indian gaming has been a highly controversial topic in New Mexico since it first appeared in 1997. Opponents assert that it encourages compulsive gambling, ruins lives and drains the local economy. There can be no doubt, though, that casinos have improved the finances of Indian tribes. Visitors to Tesuque Pueblo, for instance, can see how beautifully the once-crumbling center of the pueblo has been restored, and gaming proceeds have financed the development of other businesses such as Tesuque Natural Farms, a tribal enterprise that raises llamas and grows amaranth, a traditional Aztec grain. Casinos provide employment for about 2000 people in northern New Mexico.

The closest casino to Santa Fe, Tesuque Pueblo's **Camel Rock Casino** is known for its Las Vegas–style showroom concerts, which run the gamut from country and Norteño bands to oldies-but-goodies rock groups. ~ nine miles north of Santa Fe Route 84/285; 505-984-8414; www.camelrockcasino.com.

New Mexico's largest casino, **Cities of Gold** at Pojoaque operates over 700 slot machines in a building that used to be the local high school. It is also the first Indian casino in the state to build adjacent lodging accommodations. ~ Route 84/285, 16 miles north of Santa Fe; 505-455-3313; www.citiesofgold.com.

Santa Clara Pueblo has not yet opened a casino but has entered into a compact for a large planned gaming resort in Española, where much of the town is on Indian land. Meanwhile, Española residents risk their money at San Juan Pueblo's **OhKay Casino**. ~ One mile north of Española; 800-752-9286; www.ohkaycasino.com.

Taos Pueblo has the state's smallest gaming facility, **Taos Mountain Casino**, located near the turnoff from the highway to the pueblo. ~ Two miles north of Taos; 505-737-0777; www.taosmountaincasino.com.

night at group sites (reservations required). Call 505-672-3861 ext. 534 for group campsite reservations.

HIDDEN ▶   **FENTON LAKE STATE PARK** 🚴 🏕 🚤 🚣 🎣 Sheltered in a ponderosa pine forest below 1000-foot red cliffs, the park surrounds a 37-acre trout lake that allows no motorboats or swimming. (But rowboats are allowed and there is access.) In winter, cross-country skiers appreciate the two miles of groomed trails and enjoy gliding around the frozen lake through deep snow. Campsites fill early in the summer, in spite of the fact that Fenton Lake's 7800-foot elevation makes for cool, cool nights. There are picnic areas and restrooms throughout the park and accessible fishing areas as well. Day-use fee, $5 per vehicle. ~ Take Route 4 until you reach Route 126, 45 miles west of Los Alamos; 505-829-3630, fax 505-829-3412.

▲ There are 37 developed tent sites, $10 per vehicle; and 5 sites with electricity and water, $14 per vehicle.

▼▼▼▼▼▼▼▼▼
Chama Area

Heading north on Route 84 from Santa Fe will eventually lead to Chama, a forgotten town near where a little-used backcountry highway crossed the Colorado state line— until the railroad returned. Now thousands of visitors each summer come to Chama to ride the narrow-gauge steam train into the aspen forests of the Colorado mountains and back. Along the way you'll pass through Georgia O'Keeffe country with its bluebird skies, yucca plants and red-brushed hills in the high desert. The muddy, red-tinged Rio Chama sidles along the highway.

SIGHTS   Traveling from the Los Alamos area, driving north on Route 84 you pass through **Española**. Founded in the 1880s as a railroad stop (although it was discovered by the Europeans as early as 1598), you'll notice the community remains true to its Hispanic heritage in everything from culture to churches. Although it has evolved into a bedroom community for Santa Fe, Española's claim to fame has always been as the "Low-rider Capital" of the world. Cruise Main Street on a Saturday night to see spiffed-up vehicles and macho young men.

Turning west on Route 84 at Española takes the traveler through the ink spot of a town called Hernandez. Stop at **Romero's Fruit Stand** to pick up authentic *ristras* (strings of chiles), local honey and raspberry and cherry cider before continuing your trip north. ~ Route 84/Chama Highway, Hernandez; 505-753-4189.

The scenery of sage-filled hills and open vistas will probably start to look more and more familiar as you continue north on Route 84. This is the region that inspired artist Georgia O'Keeffe to create her magic on canvas. The small town of **Abiquiu**, which was settled in the 1700s on an American Indian ruin at the river's bend, was O'Keeffe's home for many years. The **Georgia O'Keeffe House**, the celebrated artist's winter home for 35 years, is where she painted some of her most famous pictures. O'Keeffe's home is open for public tours by reservation only. Plan ahead! The tours, which run Tuesday, Thursday and Friday from mid-March through November, are booked up one to two months in advance. Admission. ~ P.O. Box 40, Abiquiu, NM 87510; 505-685-4539, fax 505-685-4551; www.okeeffemuseum.org.

Ghost Ranch, originally a dude ranch frequented by East Coast luminaries in the 1930s and '40s, is now operated by the Presbyterian Church as one of the most popular conference centers in the state, thanks partly to its spectacular setting among bright-colored cliffs and spires of sandstone, limestone, gypsum and shale. The ranch is also a paleontologist's dream. Dinosaur skeletons found on the grounds include the crocodile-like *Phytosaur*, the rare armored *Typothorax*, and lots of examples of the ten-foot-long,

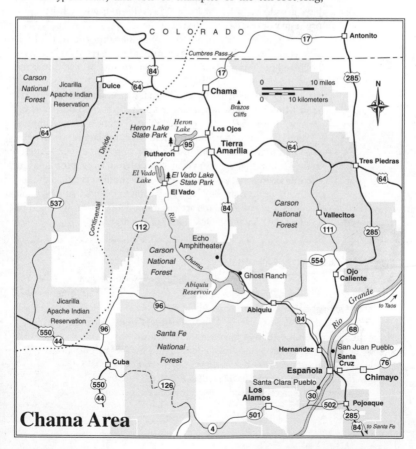

Chama Area

flesh-eating *Coelophysis*, New Mexico's official state fossil. You can see them on display in the **Ruth Hall Museum of Paleontology and Anthropology** on the conference center grounds. Museum is closed Sunday and Monday in winter. ~ Route 84, Abiquiu; 505-685-4333, fax 505-685-4519; www.ghostranch.org.

HIDDEN ►

About a mile north of Ghost Ranch, an unpaved road turns off Route 84 to the west and follows the Chama River for 13 rough miles to the **Monastery of Christ in the Desert**. The modernistic, freeform adobe complex was founded by three Benedictine monks in 1964. Today's 30 resident monks make a living by selling handcrafts such as soap, lip balm and lotion, and renting out a dormitory-style guesthouse where visitors can experience the monastic way of life for a few days or weeks. Dedicated to maintaining the time-honored Benedicting rituals, much of the music sung in the daily masses is largely derived from the tradition of Gregorian chant. There are no phones, though the monks *do* have a website. ~ Forest Road 151, Abiquiu; www.christdesert.org, e-mail porter@christdesert.org.

HIDDEN ►

A few miles north again on Route 84 takes you to the trails and natural wonder of **Echo Amphitheater**. Years of erosion have hollowed out this gargantuan sandstone theater. A picnic area and campground are available.

At an altitude of 8000 feet, **Chama**, located in the southern San Juan Mountains just nine miles from the Colorado border, is becoming more and more popular as a recreation area. Although Chama has only about 1000 residents, it is the largest town in this wild mountain area where most of the population lives scattered in tiny, traditional Spanish villages or down narrow dirt roads into the solitary reaches of the Apache lands. Summer is still high time, but with more than 300 miles of trails in the Carson National Forest, snowmobile safaris are common in the little town that bills itself as the "Snowmobile Capital of the Southwest."

AUTHOR FAVORITE

When I've been sitting in the car all day, my neck tends to stiffen and my shoulders develop knots—I know it's time for a soak in some mineral hot springs and maybe a massage. About a half-hour drive north from Española is the no-frills spa called **Ojo Caliente Mineral Springs**, one of the oldest health resorts in the country. Soak in the springs, or perhaps take an herbal wrap or indulge in a massage. Five minerals—iron, soda, lithia, sodium and arsenic—bubble up from the ground. Admission. ~ Route 285, Ojo Caliente; 505-583-2233, 800-222-9162, fax 505-583-9198; www.ojocalientespa.com, e-mail waters@ojocalientespa.com.

Tourism, ranching and lumbering are the lifeblood of Chama, which experienced its first population explosion in the early 1880s with the building of the railroad. The train served mining camps that were digging into this rich region. Records show those were wild times, as bustling saloons and rowdy gambling halls lined the main drag.

Like most Wild West towns, Chama had its bust, too. But in 1974 the governments of Colorado and New Mexico purchased 64 miles of rail and restored the coal-fired steam train as a historic tourist attraction. The "double-header" (twin-engine narrow-gauge) **Cumbres and Toltec Scenic Railroad** leaves Chama every ◄ *HIDDEN* day between Memorial Day weekend and mid-October to chug over hill and dale, through meadows and past groves of piñon, oak, aspen and juniper. Admission. ~ Route 17, Chama; 505-756-2151, 888-286-2737, fax 505-756-2694; www.cumbresand toltec.com, e-mail rrinfo@cumbresandtoltec.com.

Nestling against the river's edge, fording a trestle and hugging high passes, the train makes a 64-mile one-way trip to Antonito, Colorado (you ride a van back), or shorter roundtrips to Osier, Colorado. It travels through the valley of Los Piños River, which bursts with iris, sunflower and Indian paintbrush. The steam train moves along up the four percent grade of 10,015-foot Cumbres Pass and burrows through two tunnels to the Toltec Gorge. Autumn is a nice time to see the aspen trees alight the forest. No matter what the season, the ride may be chilly and snow always a possibility. It's not a ride for anyone in a hurry. The trip takes six and a half hours.

Ten miles south of Chama on Route 84 is **Los Ojos**, a town that was founded around 1860. Plenty of Los Ojos' original houses remain standing. The architecture mixes traditional adobe construction with turn-of-the-20th-century pitched roofs, Victorian influences and gingerbread trim. Here you can visit **Tierra Wools**, where artisans keep centuries-old native weaving traditions alive. Closed Sunday from November through May. ~ Route 84, Los Ojos; 505-588-7231, 888-709-0979, fax 505-588-7044; www. handweavers.com, e-mail tierrawools@zianet.com.

The **Brazos Cliffs** abut the skyline south of Chama, and for about three weeks each spring a waterfall of snow runoff cascades off 11,289-foot Brazos Peak. ~ Route 512, seven miles east of Route 84.

The tribal members residing on the unspoiled **Jicarilla Apache Indian Reservation** (505-759-3242, fax 505-759-3005; www.jica rillaonline.com) open up their lands for hunting, fishing and camping on the mountain lakes. In the Jicarilla's commercial center of **Dulce**, on Route 64, 25 miles west of Chama, you'll find a tribal arts-and-crafts shop and a small museum.

LODGING

Aside from the Monastery of Christ in the Desert, there are only two places to spend the night in the Abiquiu area. One is the **Abiquiu Inn**. This 19-room inn has contemporary guest rooms decorated in earth tones, outfitted with the conventional amenities. In addition, there are five casitas, three with private verandas and hammocks. The inn's greatest appeal is location: It is hard to imagine where one might sleep further from city lights or closer to starry skies than in Abiquiu. ~ Route 84, Abiquiu; 505-685-4378, 888-735-2902, fax 505-685-4931; www.abiquiuinn.com, e-mail info@abiquiuinn.com. MODERATE TO DELUXE.

HIDDEN ►

Unbeknownst to many, **Ghost Ranch Abiquiu** offers basic rooms for a reasonable price in a retreat center atmosphere. Call for reservations; it's often booked up by conferences. ~ 401 Old Taos Highway, Abiquiu; 800-821-5145, fax 505-986-1917; www. ghostranch.org. MODERATE.

If the rugged outdoors call you, along with elegance and a hot tub, try **The Lodge at Chama**, an interesting combination of the deluxe and the down home. The 22 Southwestern-style rooms are clean and spacious and the spa facility is the epitome of luxury. Room packages aren't cheap, but some may include various combinations of recreational activities on the 36,000-acre ranch such as hiking, hunting and fishing, as well as upper-end meals in the lodge's fine restaurant. There is also a complimentary bar. ~ P.O. Box 127, Chama, NM 87520; 505-756-2133, fax 505-756-2519; www.lodgeatchama.com, e-mail reservations@lodgeatchama.com. ULTRA-DELUXE.

DINING

El Parasol is a legend around these parts. Nothing more than a busy, fast-food taco stand, it turns out surprisingly tasty, authentic Mexican favorites. So authentic in fact, that you'd be hard-pressed to find an English-speaking employee. The *carne adovada* burritos and crispy chicken tacos doused in green or red salsa are crowd pleasers. ~ 602 Santa Cruz Road, Española; 505-753-8852. BUDGET.

The **Abiquiu Inn Café** specializes in Middle Eastern, Southwest and Italian food. Breakfast, lunch and dinner are served. ~ Route 84, Abiquiu; 505-685-4378, 800-447-5261; www.abiquiuinn. com, e-mail abiquiuinn@zianet.com. MODERATE.

Let your nose lead you: The spicy, peppery smell of native cuisine hails from **Vera's Mexican Kitchen**, where *rellenos*, burritos and enchiladas await. Closed Wednesday. ~ Route 84, Chama; 505-756-2557. BUDGET.

SHOPPING

The **Narrow Gauge Gift Shop** sells train-related souvenirs such as engineers caps (naturally!) and T-shirts at fair prices. Closed November through April. ~ Route 17, Chama; 505-756-2963.

The timeless art of weaving is revitalized by the wool artisans and growers of **Tierra Wools**, who gladly offer their wares through a cooperative showroom. Closed Sunday from October through April. ~ Route 84, Los Ojos; 505-588-7231.

Foster's Hotel, Restaurant and Saloon, a historic hotel where you will want to stop for a drink, has been in business since 1881. ~ 4th and Terrace streets, Chama; 505-756-2296.

NIGHTLIFE

ABIQUIU RESERVOIR 🐾 ⛵ 🛶 🚤 ⛵ All water sports are permitted in this 4000-acre reservoir, an Army Corps of Engineering project, which was created by damming the Rio Chama. The colors of the day, especially sunsets, are splendid in the wonderfully pastel-colored country that artist Georgia O'Keeffe loved so much. Fishing yields channel catfish, salmon, smallmouth bass and a variety of trout. Facilities include picnic areas, bathrooms and showers. Boat launch fee, $3 per day. ~ Route 84, seven miles northwest of Abiquiu; 505-685-4371, fax 505-685-4647; www.spa.usace.army.mil/abiquiu.

PARKS

> A large state trout hatchery along Pecos River keeps Monastery Lake jumping, and many Pecos residents depend on it as a year-round food source.

▲ Riana Campground (505-685-4561) has 54 sites. Fees are $5 per night for walk-in sites, $10 for vehicle-accessible sites and $14 for hookups. Free from late October to mid-April, when all water and electricity are shut off. Reservations are recommended: 877-444-6777.

EL VADO LAKE STATE PARK 🐾 ⛵ 🚣 🚤 ⛵ This is a beautiful mountain lake for waterskiing and fishing (the latter of which is popular year-round). In the winter, ice anglers head for the frozen waters. There are picnic areas and playgrounds. Day-use fee, $4 per vehicle. ~ Route 112, 14 miles southwest of Tierra Amarilla; information through State Parks Department, phone/fax 505-588-7247.

▲ There are 80 developed sites, $10 per night; unlimited primitive sites, $8 per night; and 19 RV sites, $14 per night. Reservations: 877-664-7787.

Use bait or fly, but don't head home without taking back some tall fish tales from your trip to the Enchanted Circle. Pack your pole and perambulate over to the Pecos River or one of the area's lakes.

Outdoor Adventures

FISHING

SANTA FE In the Santa Fe area, the fish are probably biting at the **Pecos River**. In the upper reaches of the canyon, all fishing is catch-and-release. If you want to eat the trout you catch, head for **Monastery Lake**, on the river just north of Pecos and downstream from the state trout hatchery. Try **High Desert Angler** for fishing tackle rental and flyfishing guide service. ~ 451 Cerrillos Road; 505-988-7688. Bait is available at **Adelo's Town and Country Store** in Pecos. ~ 505-757-8565.

ROAD TO TAOS   **Nambe Lake**, on the Nambe Pueblo reservation, is well stocked with rainbow trout; a state fishing license is not required, but a day-use fee is charged.

LAS VEGAS AREA   Serious anglers head for the **Upper Pecos River**, a designated catch-and-release area that boasts trout of formidable size, midway between Santa Fe and Las Vegas. If you want to keep your catch and cook it, the place to go is **Monastery Lake** on the north edge of the village of Pecos. **Adelo's Town and Country Store** (505-757-8565) at the main road intersection in Pecos (on Route 63) carries fishing supplies and sells licenses. Near Las Vegas, **Morphy Lake State Park** and **Storrie Lake** are stocked with trout.

> The Santa Fe Ski Basin is the most heavily traveled trailhead for access to the vast, rugged expanse of the Pecos Wilderness.

LOS ALAMOS AREA   A truly hidden local fishing hole is **Los Alamos Lake**. The former town reservoir is now used exclusively by the few anglers who find their way to it along the rough two-mile forest road that starts from *under* the big bridge near the Los Alamos National Laboratories administration building at the west end of town.

BOATING & WIND-SURFING

Some prefer playing on the water when it's not rushing over large rocks. If you don't have your own windsurfing or boating equipment, you can hunt down one of the Storrie Lake sailboard-rental outfits, or go with a boat rental on scenic Heron Lake, a "no-wake" lake.

In the Chama area, hire an 18-foot pontoon boat or 17-foot V-hull and boat from **Stone House Lodge**. ~ 95 Heron Lake Road, Los Ojos; 505-588-7274.

RIVER RUNNING

Shooting the rapids is an increasingly popular activity in the Santa Fe area, so get your feet wet on a tame or tumultuous guided tour of the Rio Grande or the Rio Chama. Many outfitters are ready and willing to help immerse you in the fun of wave riding.

SANTA FE   Although the Santa Fe River rarely flows, several Santa Fe–based rafting companies shuttle the adventurous northward to get their feet wet on tumultuous guided tours of the Rio Grande near Taos or tamer ones on the Rio Chama near Abiquiu. Many outfitters are ready and willing to help immerse you in the fun of wave riding. Rafting season is late spring through early summer, when the rivers are swollen by runoff from the melting mountain snow pack. Weekend releases of water from El Vado Lake near Chama keep the river flowing all summer. **New Wave Rafting Co.** runs daily tours from Santa Fe in rafting season, including full-day trips on the Rio Grande and three-day runs on Rio Chama. Food and gear are provided. ~ Route 5, 70 CR 84B; 505-984-1444, 800-984-1444; www.newwaverafting.com. Another outfitter for the region is **Santa Fe Rafting**, which offers half-day, full-day and overnight trips on the Rio Grande and the Chama. ~ 1000 Cerrillos Road; 505-988-4914, 800-467-7238; www.santaferafting.com. **Kokopelli Rafting Adventures** embarks on half- and full-day whitewater excursions on the Rio Grande and the Rio Chama (class I to class IV rapids). They also have inflatable kayak trips on the river and sea kayaks on some of the local lakes. Food is provided on full- and multi-day trips. ~ 551 West Cordova Road #540; 505-983-3734, 800-879-9035; www. kokopelliraft.com.

Don't be fooled by the seemingly dry New Mexico landscape: The mountains are situated in a moisture belt that in an average year receives more snow than the Colorado Rockies. When storm clouds part, be prepared for warm, sunny days in the high desert. The ski season runs from Thanksgiving through April, weather permitting, but may vary from resort to resort.

SKIING

SANTA FE How many capital cities have a full-service ski area within a 30-minute drive? **Ski Santa Fe**, located up the winding, twisting Hyde Park/Ski Basin Road, 17 miles northeast of the Plaza, has six lifts and 45 trails—20 percent beginner, 40 percent intermediate and 40 percent advanced—covering 460 skiable acres with a vertical drop of 1703 feet. There are no limits on snowboarding. Ski and snowboard rentals and lessons for children and adults are available. ~ Route 475; 505-982-4429, fax 505-986-0645; www.skisantafe.com, e-mail info@skisantafe.com.

LOS ALAMOS AREA **Pajarito Mountain Ski Area**, located five miles west of Los Alamos up a startlingly steep paved road, is one of the state's least-known large ski areas, with 37 trails and a 1400-foot vertical drop. Across the road a free, groomed ten-kilometer course takes cross-country skiers into the high meadows of the Jemez Mountains. The cross-country trails are open whenever there is snow. The resort operates Friday through Sunday from mid-December to mid-March. ~ Camp May Road; 505-662-5725; www.skipajarito.com, e-mail ski@skipajarito.com. **Bandelier National Monument** has limited ungroomed trails. ~ Route 4; 505-672-3861, fax 505-672-9607; www.nps.gov/band.

CHAMA AREA In Chama, the community-trail system maintains nearly four miles of groomed cross-country tracks in the **Rio Grande National Forest**.

Ski Rentals For Nordic and alpine skis, snowboards and snowshoes, try **Alpine Sports**. Sometimes closed Sunday from April to November. ~ 121 Sandoval Street, Santa Fe; 505-983-5155. Tele-

mark, cross-country ski and snowshoe rentals, backcountry supplies and repairs, and maps of the Cumbres Pass are available
through **Chama Ski Service**. Closed mid-April through November, and on weekends or by appointment only. ~ 1551 Alamo
Drive, Chama; 505-756-2492.

GOLF

Believe it or not, the New Mexico desert harbors great golfing.
Lush courses provide a cool respite from summer heat and primo
playing conditions even in the dead of winter. (And there's no
charge for the fabulous scenery.) Most courses have club and cart
rentals as well as a resident pro.

SANTA FE   Practice your swing on the 18-hole semiprivate course
or driving range at the **Santa Fe Country Club**. ~ 1000 Country
Club Drive; 505-471-0601. The public **Marty Sanchez Links de
Santa Fe** has both an 18-hole championship course and a par-3, 9-
hole course offering mountain views. A driving range, putting
green and pro shop are additional features. ~ 205 Caja del Rio;
505-955-4400.

LAS VEGAS AREA   In Las Vegas, tee off at **New Mexico Highlands University Golf Course**, a nine-hole course that is open to
the public. They also have a driving range. ~ 200 Mills Avenue and
Country Club Drive; 505-425-7711.

LOS ALAMOS AREA   Duffers in Los Alamos play at the **Los Alamos Golf Club**, one of the first 18-hole golf courses in New Mexico. ~ 4250 Diamond Drive; 505-662-8139.

TENNIS

There's plenty of space to serve and volley in the Enchanted Circle.
Hit one of the area sports stores and head for the parks.

SANTA FE   Santa Fe vacationers can take a swing at any of several municipal courts—**Atalaya Park** (717 Camino Cabra; two
courts), the **Fort Marcy Complex** (Old Taos Highway and Morales
Road; two courts) and **Larragoite Park** (Agua Fria Street and
Avenida Cristobal Colon; two courts). All have hard-surface pub-

AUTHOR FAVORITE

Bandelier National Monument has miles of maintained hiking trails in a
wilderness area known as **Tsankawi**, which is located in a separate section
of the monument. Tsankawi is accessible by a 1.5-mile loop trail that winds
through lush piñon-juniper woodland, past petroglyphs to a high mesa and
the unexcavated Tsankawi Ruins, a condo-style site and nearby cliff
dwellings. The trail provides spectacular views of the Española Valley. ~
The trailhead is near the intersection of Routes 4 and 502.

lic courts for daylight use only, first-come, first-served. **Alto Park** (1121 Alto Street), **Herb Martínez/La Resolana Park** (2240 Camino Carlos Rey) and **Salvador Pérez Park** (610 Alta Vista Street) have four lighted courts each. Court information is available at 505-955-2100.

LOS ALAMOS AREA   In Los Alamos, there are four hard-surface lighted courts at **Urban Park** (48th and Urban streets) and two unlit courts at **Canyon Road Tennis Courts** (Canyon Road and 15th Street) and three unlit courts at **Barranca Park** (Barranca Road and Loma de Escolar). ~ 505-662-8170.

Wondering how to acquire that true Western swagger? Hop in the saddle and ride the range—or just take a lesson—with one of the several outfitters in the area.

RIDING STABLES

SANTA FE   For a unique riding experience, the **Broken Saddle Riding Company** offers one- to three-hour small group tours of the Cerrillos Hills, site of historic turquoise and silver mines, on well-trained Tennessee Walkers and Missouri Fox Trotters. ~ Cerrillos; 505-424-7774; www.brokensaddle.com.

You can saddle up at **Bishop's Lodge Stable and Wrangler's Store**, part of the historic Bishop's Lodge Resort on 500 acres of piñon-juniper woodland in the Big Tesuque Creek drainage, three miles north of Santa Fe on Bishop's Lodge Road. Miles of trails along Big Tesuque Creek take you into the foothills of the Sangre de Cristo Mountains with seasoned wranglers. Private one- to two-hour horseback rides are available daily and are open to nonguests. No riders younger than eight years old are permitted. ~ North Bishop's Lodge Road, Santa Fe; 505-983-6377 ext. 4013, 800-732-2240 ext. 4013.

If you haven't noticed the high altitude yet, why not get in touch with your environment by going for a two-wheeled spin? You'll be amply rewarded for your huffing and puffing with breathtaking views.

BIKING

SANTA FE   From the Santa Fe Plaza, pedal to **Ski Basin Road**, which takes cyclists up a windy and at times steep 17-mile two-lane road through heavily wooded national forest land to the Ski Santa Fe area. To enjoy a shorter trip at a more forgiving altitude (the ski area is at 10,400 feet), just ride the eight miles to Hyde State Park.

A killer ten-mile ride for mountain bikers starts north of the Picacho Hotel on St. Francis Drive, crosses Dead Man's Gulch and Camino La Tierra before heading into the foothills of **La Tierra**. Circle back to the hotel via Buckman Road.

The most spectacular mountain-bike trip in the Santa Fe area starts at **Aspen Vista**, on Ski Basin Road midway between Hyde Park and the ski area. A six-mile access road for the broadcast towers on top of 12,010-foot Tesuque Peak is off-limits to motor vehicles but open to cyclists. It offers a long climb through a shimmering aspen forest, ending with a panoramic view of the Pecos Wilderness from a perch at the edge of a sheer cliff that drops 2000 feet to inaccessible Santa Fe Lake. Coasting back down is a mountain bikers' thrill of a lifetime.

LOS ALAMOS AREA Sweeping curves and roller-coaster hills make **Route 4**, a two-lane highway through White Rock to Bandelier National Monument, the most popular paved-road cycle tour in the state. In fact, cyclists often outnumber cars.

Bike Rentals In Santa Fe, **Mellow Velo Bikes**, located in El Centro, offers mountain-bike rentals, plus beginning to expert road- and mountain-bike tours. Grab a latte from their espresso bar while suiting up. ~ 102 East Water Street; 505-982-8986; www.mellowbike.com.

HIKING   When it comes time to travel without wheels, rest assured that the hiking trails in this region offer plenty of incentive for lacing up your boots. Just outside the city limits of Santa Fe, national forest land beckons and the hiker can disappear almost immediately into the dozens of trails that dip around peaks and to mountain lakes. All distances listed are one way unless otherwise noted.

The **Winsor Trail** (9 to 14 miles) meanders from 7000 to 11,000 feet, sidling along Big Tesuque Creek. Start at the top of Ski Basin Road and traipse through stands of aspen and evergreen and, finally, above timberline to 12,000-foot-plus Santa Fe Baldy. If you prefer a longer hike, begin in Tesuque along the creek. The gentle Borrego Trail branches off of Winsor.

LAS VEGAS AREA A trail to **Hermit's Peak** (4 miles) gains nearly 3000 vertical feet after starting at 7500 feet. A narrow and rocky path, the view is spectacular. Find it by following Route 65 to the parking lot at El Porvenir, 15 miles northwest of Las Vegas.

LOS ALAMOS AREA The majority of Bandelier National Monument is considered undisturbed backcountry. Several forest fires have scorched areas of the plateau within the monument boundary. A large forest fire in 1996 burned a vast expanse of forest west of **Painted Cave** near the southwestern boundary, a 12-mile backpacking expedition that takes all day one way. The tough six-mile trail to the ancient **Yapashi pueblo site** passes near a 1997 forest fire area in Lummis Canyon, then scales down one side and up the other of 600-foot-deep Alamo Canyon.

Plenty of gratification without a whole lot of effort is found on the **Main Loop Trail** (1 mile roundtrip) in Frijoles Canyon at Bandelier National Monument. Start from the visitors center and walk past the big kiva and the condominium-style dwelling (known as Long House) built into the canyon wall.

Trail to the Falls, an entirely downhill 400-foot hike, (1.5 miles) crosses Rio de los Frijoles, follows the creek and passes some impressive cliffs and tent rocks before arriving at the falls.

Transportation

Route 25 is the favored north–south road through New Mexico, accessing Las Vegas and Santa Fe. Route 68 heads south from Taos to Santa Fe, while Route 285/ 84 heads north from Santa Fe through Española all the way to Chama and the New Mexico/Colorado border.

Route 64 skirts across the northern edge of New Mexico passing through the Four Corners Area and across to Chama. For New Mexico road conditions, call 800-432-4269.

CAR

AIR

Santa Fe does have a municipal airport, but the last commercial service there was discontinued in 2005 because flying directly to or from Santa Fe was much more expensive but not much faster than using Albuquerque International Sunport, now the only major commercial passenger terminal in the state. See "Transportation" in Chapter Twelve for more information.

Taxis and hotel courtesy vans wait for passengers in front of the airport terminal in Albuquerque. Santa Fe Shuttle (505-243-2300, 888-833-2300) and Sandia Shuttle (505-474-5696, 888-775-5696; www.sandiashuttle.com) provide transportation between Albuquerque and Santa Fe.

BUS

TNM&O Coaches services Santa Fe and Las Vegas. ~ 858 St. Michaels Drive, Santa Fe; 505-471-0008.

TRAIN

Amtrak serves Santa Fe via the village of Lamy, 17 miles from town. ~ 800-872-7245; www.amtrak.com.

CAR RENTALS

Avis Rent A Car (800-831-2847) has an office at the Santa Fe airport and in town. Hertz Rent A Car (800-654-3131) has an office at the airport. Enterprise Rent A Car (800-736-8222) offers free shuttle service from the airport. Budget Rent A Car (800-527-0700) has an office in town.

PUBLIC TRANSIT

With their chic tan and turquoise paint jobs designed by local artist Sally Blakemore, the natural gas–propelled Santa Fe Trails buses are an excellent way to navigate Santa Fe. Route M takes you from the downtown area to the Indian Arts, Folk Art and Wheelwright museums as well as to St. John's College. Route #2 serves the crop of motels along Cerrillos Road and continues to the Villa Linda Mall, located on the far west side of town. This bus also makes it possible to avoid nasty downtown parking problems by leaving your vehicle at the De Vargas Mall (Guadalupe Street at Paseo de Peralta) and taking a five-minute bus ride downtown. Buses run every half hour from 6:30 a.m. to 10 p.m. weekdays; Saturday schedules vary for each route. ~ 505-955-2003, 505-955-2001.

In Los Alamos, the **Los Alamos Bus System** provides regularly scheduled bus service on a variety of routes. No weekend service. ~ 505-662-2080.

TAXIS

Santa Fe's only taxi service is **Capital City Cab Co.** ~ 505-438-0000.

WALKING TOURS

Perhaps the most down-to-earth method of touring cities like Santa Fe is via a walking tour. Local guides provide rich historical and personal insight to their communities as you stroll ancient streets and narrow lanes. Most tours last about two to three hours and may include visits inside area museums. For information on tours, contact **Aboot About Santa Fe**. Fee. ~ El Dorado Hotel & Spa lobby, 309 West San Francisco Street, or Hotel St. Francis lobby, 210 Don Gaspar Avenue; 505-988-2774; www.accesssantafe.com.

Afoot in Santa Fe conducts two-hour morning jaunts. Fee includes admission to the Loretto Chapel. ~ Inn at Loretto, 211 Old Santa Fe Trail; 505-983-3701.

TEN

Taos and the Enchanted Circle

Painters Ernest Blumenschein and Bert Phillips were on their way to Mexico in 1898 when their wagon broke an axle and they found themselves stranded in Taos. In the end, however, it mattered very little. For in the people, the landscape and the crisp mountain light they found subject matter so compelling that their paintings inspired a generation of artists from the East and Europe to follow in their talented footsteps.

The Sangre de Cristo Mountains ("Blood of Christ") abut the town of Taos, which sits at an altitude of nearly 8000 feet above sea level on the east, and the Rio Grande River forms the city's western boundary. The Enchanted Circle is the name commonly given to an 80-mile loop route from Taos that crosses the crest of the Sangre de Cristos and circles all four sides of Wheeler Peak (elevation 13,161 feet), the highest mountain in New Mexico. The drive along the Enchanted Circle affords incomparable vistas of the heart of the high country, perspectives that could hardly help but inspire great works of art.

By the 1920s, Taos enjoyed a reputation as one of the greatest artists' colonies in America, thanks in large part to the sponsorship of local grand dame Mabel Dodge Luhan, a flamboyant New York heiress who married a man from Taos Pueblo and invited guests such as D. H. Lawrence, Georgia O'Keeffe, Ansel Adams, Willa Cather and Aldous Huxley to visit. (Her house is now a bed-and-breakfast inn.)

In the late 1960s, Taos gained brief notoriety for its hippie communes, where young people from the city joined in attempts to return to the Pueblo Indian way of life. Clearing the land and building communal homes of adobe, they sought to create a simple lifestyle in tune with nature. Simple it wasn't. Besides the hard physical labor they experienced, these freewheeling pioneers had to cultivate their own food, debate communal politics and wrestle with the problems and possibilities of their newfound sexual freedom. Life became a grand experiment. The old-time communes were revealed to the outside world in former Taos filmmaker Dennis Hopper's '60s epic *Easy Rider*. Soon over 3000 hippies set up house in the Taos area. Although the days of drugs and free love have long since vanished, the pursuit of spiritual enlightenment remains a strong force here.

But the fact that artists and idealists have taken to this part of New Mexico has hardly disrupted the deep cultural traditions that have characterized this area for thousands of years. Powwows, for instance, began in the days when Taos was one of the most distant outposts of the Rio Grande Pueblo Indians. These intertribal gatherings provided opportunities for trade, dancing and politics between the Pueblo Indians and the nomadic Arapahoe and Ute people who roamed the plains and mountains to the north. Today, powwows at Taos Pueblo attract participants from as far away as Canada. The pueblo itself draws throngs of non-Indian travelers from around the world each year to see this tiny, five-story town where the residents continue to live without electricity or running water in accordance with ancient custom.

After the first Spanish settlers came, Taos served as a marketplace for trade between the colonists and the Indians. In the 1820s, it became the outpost where mountain men emerged from the southern Colorado Rockies to trade for supplies. (At least one legendary frontiersman, Kit Carson, settled down in Taos, where he lived out his later years as one of the few Anglos in the Spanish and Indian community.) Today, tourism is the town's main industry. It seems that Taos residents (native Pueblo people, descendants of Spanish settlers and contemporary artists and sculptors alike) still support themselves in the same time-honored traditions— trading with visitors from the outside world.

Taos Area

Just as Santa Fe is a unique city, with all the social and economic complexity that term implies, Taos (population 6200) is a unique small town, not exactly easy to understand but certainly direct in its unconventionality. Painters and writers form the backbone of this peaceful yet eccentric frontier outpost, where American Indians, graying hippies and Spanish villagers alike walk in extraordinary beauty. The hodgepodge of architectural styles—Victorian-era frame houses, now stuccoed over in hues of tan, clustered with adobe haciendas from the Spanish Colonial period and Indian houses stacked like honeycombs—only serves to enhance the town's compelling landscape.

SIGHTS

Surrounded by mesas, canyons and mountain peaks, **Taos** has plenty of outdoor recreation year-round. The Taos Box, a wilderness canyon through which the Rio Grande tumbles and roars, offers plenty of whitewater rafting in early summer. Visitors who rent horses from the stables at Taos Pueblo can ride into the reservation's forested mountain highlands, which are otherwise off-limits to non-Indians. Hikers and backpackers find an alpine wonderland among the 13,000-foot summits of the Wheeler Peak area. For those who prefer more conventional sports, the biggest challenge to playing any of the area's golf courses and tennis courts is focusing on the ball instead of the stunning mountain scenery.

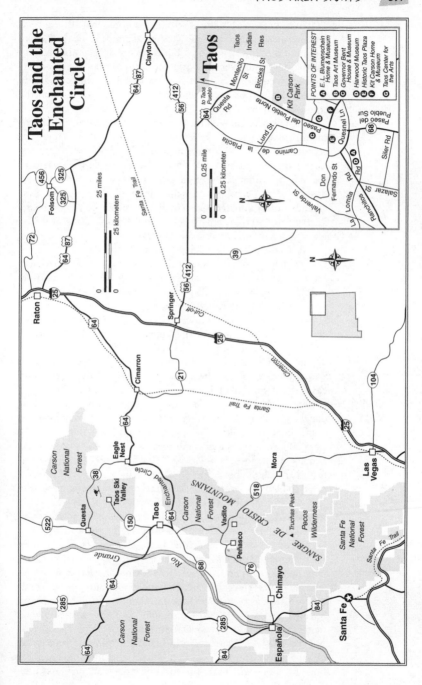

Taos and the Enchanted Circle

Taos

POINTS OF INTEREST

- **A** E. L. Blumenschein Home & Museum
- **B** Taos Art Museum
- **C** Governor Bent House & Museum
- **D** Harwood Museum
- **E** Historic Taos Plaza
- **F** Kit Carson Home & Museum
- **G** Taos Center for the Arts

Taos Indian Res

Montecito St

Brooks St

Kit Carson Park

to Taos Pueblo

Questa Rd

Paseo del Pueblo Norte

Paseo del Pueblo Sur

Quesnel Ln

Lund St

Camino de la Placita

Don Fernando St

La Lomita Rd

Ranchitos Rd

Salazar St

Siler Rd

Valverde St

0   0.25 mile
0   0.25 kilometer

N

25 miles
25 kilometers
0
0

Clayton

64 87

64 87

412

56

412

39

Folsom

456 325

325

72

64

Raton

25

64

Springer

56 412

Cut-off

25

Cimarron

21

Santa Fe Trail

Santa Fe Trail

104

25

Las Vegas

Cimarron

Carson National Forest

Eagle Nest

38

Taos Ski Valley

Enchanted Circle

522

Questa

150

Taos

64

Carson National Forest

Vadito

518

Mora

SANGRE DE CRISTO MOUNTAINS

Truchas Peak

Pecos Wilderness

Peñasco

76

Santa Fe National Forest

Rio Grande

64

285

Carson National Forest

64

285

66

Chimayo

84

Santa Fe

Santa Fe Trail

Española

285

84

64

N

Given the superb natural setting, it's ironic that stifling gridlock and auto pollution plague Taos' main artery, Paseo del Pueblo, in all but the slowest seasons. But there's really no other way to get to Taos, and given the large local opposition to airport expansion, it could remain this way for a while. So be ecologically minded, leave your car at your residence and walk around the compact commercial core.

The **Historic Taos Plaza**, as is true in so many Southwestern towns, is its lifeblood. The Plaza has for centuries remained the commercial center for tourism and throughout the centuries, three flags—Spanish, American and Mexican—have flown over the stucco buildings. Plaza galleries and shops merit at least a day's visit. You can pick up sightseeing information at the **Taos Chamber of Commerce**. Open daily in summer. ~ 1139 Paseo del Pueblo Sur; 505-758-3873, 800-732-8267, fax 505-758-3872; www.taoschamber.com, e-mail info@taoschamber.com.

Kit Carson Park is a 25-acre verdant park in the center of town that houses the grave of frontiersman Kit Carson. There are picnic areas, a playground and restrooms. ~ 211 Paseo del Pueblo Norte, Taos; 505-758-8234, fax 505-758-2493; www.taos gov.com, e-mail dmartinez@taosgov.com.

The following five museums can be visited with one discounted ticket (available at all locations) that's both transferable and good for one year:

Blending the sophistication of European charm with a classic Taos adobe, the **E. L. Blumenschein Home and Museum** showcases the paintings of Blumenschein (a co-founder of the Taos Society of Artists); his wife, Mary Greene Blumenschein; their daughter, Helen; and many other Taos artists. The fully restored home, built in the late 1700s, is filled with furnishings from the early 20th century, as well as European antiques. Admission. ~ 222 Ledoux Street, Taos; 505-758-0505, fax 505-758-0330; www.taos historicmuseums.com.

Two blocks southwest of the Plaza, at the west end of historic Ledoux Street, is the **Harwood Museum of Art**, New Mexico's second-oldest museum. A Pueblo Revival–style adobe compound, the Harwood showcases the brilliant work of the Taos Society of Artists, core of the local artists' colony. It also includes the octagonal Agnes Martin Gallery, featuring work by the internationally acclaimed artist and Taos resident. The museum's collection of 19th-century *retablos* (religious paintings on wood) will also fascinate. Closed Monday. Admission. ~ 238 Ledoux Street, Taos; 505-758-9826, fax 505-758-1475; www.harwood museum.org, e-mail harwood@unm.edu.

The **Taos Art Museum/Fechin House** features portrait paintings by Russian artist Nicolai Fechin, who also designed the building, along with over 300 works by more than 50 Taos artists.

Closed Monday. Admission. ~ 227 Paseo del Pueblo Norte, Taos; 505-758-2690, fax 505-758-7320; www.taosmuseums.org.

American Indian and Hispanic art fill the **Millicent Rogers Museum,** a memorial to the late Standard Oil heiress. Within the 15 galleries are rare examples of jewelry, textiles, basketry, paintings and pottery, as well as some exhibits by contemporary artists. Closed Monday from November through March. Admission. ~ Off Route 64, four miles north of Taos Plaza; 505-758-2462, fax 505-758-5751; www.millicentrogers.org, e-mail mrm@millicent rogers.org.

South of Taos at the **Martinez Hacienda,** you might discover craftsmen chinking the dark wooden walls of a sheep barn to ward off winter's cold. One of the only fully restored Spanish Colonial adobe haciendas in New Mexico, the fortresslike home is constantly being replastered to maintain its structural integrity. Inside, area artisans who perpetuate century-old skills through a living-history program demonstrate weaving, quilting, wood carving and other folk arts. Open daily in summer, open sporadically from

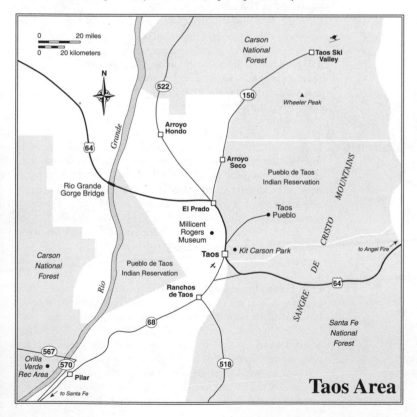

Taos Area

November through April; call ahead. Admission. ~ Ranchitos Road, Route 240; 505-758-1000, fax 505-758-0330; www.taos historicmuseums.com, e-mail thm@taoshistoricmuseums.com.

Governor Bent House and Museum has American Indian artifacts and war-era memorabilia from the first governor of New Mexico. It's worth about 15 minutes of your time. Admission. ~ 117 Bent Street, Taos; 505-758-2376.

Three miles north of the city, the distant past endures at the **Taos Pueblo**, the northernmost of all pueblos. These original adobe buildings appear much as they did when Spanish explorers first viewed them in 1540. This village is a First Living World Heritage Site and follows traditional ways, with no electricity or running water for the remaining families living in the pueblo buildings. Food is sometimes cooked in an outdoor *horno* (oven) and water is drawn from the river that breeches the heart of the pueblo. Local artisans sell mica-flecked pottery, silver jewelry, moccasins, boots and drums here. Since the pueblo closes occasionally for ceremonial purposes, call ahead. The pueblo closes for ten weeks in late winter to early spring. Admission; camera and artist sketching fees. ~ Route 64; 505-758-1028, fax 505-758-4604; www.taospueblo.com, e-mail tourism@taospueblo.com.

Just north of the turnoff to the pueblo turn right on Route 150 for a trip to the **Taos Ski Valley**. The road rises and rolls past churches and tiny hotels through the sleepy towns of Arroyo Seco and Valdez. Making the 12-mile trip at dusk, when the light reflects from the aspen trees in ever-changing hues, can be a magical experience.

LODGING   Located south of the historic district, the **Sagebrush Inn** looks just like any other Pueblo-style hotel from the outside. But open the hefty front door and it's a totally different world. Rooms are dark and romantic, usually decorated with Navajo rugs and pottery and equipped with fireplaces. A pool and hot tubs are nice amenities. Breakfast is included. ~ 1508 Paseo del Pueblo Sur, Taos; 505-758-2254, 800-428-3626, fax 505-758-5077; www. sagebrushinn.com, e-mail sagebrush@newmex.com. MODERATE TO DELUXE.

Distinctive Pueblo-style architecture marks the **Holiday Inn Don Fernando de Taos**. Rooms are designed around central courtyards and connected by walkways that meander through landscaped grounds. Standard rooms are oversized, while suites have living rooms, fireplaces and hospitality bars. All feature Southwestern styles, including hand-carved New Mexican furniture. A large heated pool, a hot tub, a tennis court and an on-site restaurant and lounge add to the friendly ambience. Complimentary shuttle service within a five-mile radius is offered. ~ 1005 Paseo del Pueblo Sur, Taos; 505-758-4444, 800-759-2736, fax 505-758-0055; www.holiday-taos.com, e-mail holiday@new mex.com. DELUXE.

The most economical lodging in Taos is the **Indian Hills Inn–Taos Plaza**, a vintage pueblo-style hotel that dates back to the early 1900s with an annex of rooms added in 1997. Located just two blocks from the plaza, within walking distance of dozens of galleries and restaurants, the inn has 55 rooms, most facing a peaceful interior patio and one-acre yard with shade trees and picnic tables. Standard rooms have two queen-size beds and typical motel amenities, while upgrade rooms have a king-size bed, Southwestern-style furniture and fireplaces. A pool and all-new room furnishings were added in 2006. ~ 233 Paseo del Pueblo Sur, Taos; phone/fax 505-758-4293, 800-444-2346; www.newmex. com/indianhillsinn, e-mail indianhills@newmex.com. MODERATE.

Taos bed and breakfasts are extraordinary and becoming ever more popular. Hidden on a lovely lane about three blocks south of the Plaza is **Casa de las Chimeneas**, a guesthouse for those who love being pampered. The largest of the eight units has a living room with a collection of books and magazines. The rooms have custom pieces by local furniture makers, tiled bathrooms and views of the Southwestern-style gardens and fountains. There's a hot tub on site and a large common area, as well as an exercise room, a spa, a sauna and laundry facilities. Breakfast and a buffet dinner are included in the rates. ~ 405 Cordoba Road, Taos; 505-758-4777, 877-758-4777, fax 505-758-3976; www.visit taos.com, e-mail casa@newmex.com. DELUXE TO ULTRA-DELUXE.

One of the area's original bed and breakfasts, **La Posada de Taos** provides a homey atmosphere in its huge book-filled living room and open, sunny dining room. The 100-year-old house has

AUTHOR FAVORITE

The **Laughing Horse Inn** is a century-old hacienda transformed into a European-style pension. As the name implies, it helps to have a sense of humor when staying here: one guest room has chile pepper–motif lights and the inn's floor varies between old wood and varnished dirt. What it may lack in luxury, it more than makes up for in personality with its low *viga* ceilings, a traditional adobe mud floor, and memorabilia from the early New Mexico literary-magazine publisher who had his printing press here. The communal kitchen offers light snacks for next-to-nothing prices. Breakfast is included. ~ 729 Paseo del Pueblo Norte, Taos; 505-758-8350, 800-776-0161, fax 505-751-1123; www.laughinghorseinn. com, e-mail laughinghorse@laughinghorseinn.com. BUDGET TO DELUXE.

been lovingly remodeled with six guest units, each with tiled baths and antique furnishings. Five of the units are inside the inn itself, the sixth is a honeymoon cottage across the adobe-walled courtyard. All but the Taos Room sport private patios and kiva fireplaces; some have jacuzzi tubs. ~ 309 Juanita Lane, Taos; 505-758-8164, 800-645-4803, fax 505-751-4696; www.laposa dadetaos.com, e-mail laposada@laposadadetaos.com. DELUXE.

La Doña Luz Inn is a remarkable inn with 15 units, each a treat in itself. Built around a patio overflowing with flowers, all but two rooms feature an American Indian fireplace and American Indian and Spanish Colonial artifacts; some include jacuzzi tubs and mountain views. The Rainbow Room has a rooftop sundeck with private hot tub, while the Kit Carson Room has a log bed, a sitting room with a cast-iron wood-burning stove and a clawfoot tub in the bathroom. This inn includes a wheelchair-accessible unit. ~ 114 Kit Carson Road, Taos; 505-758-4874, 800-758-9187, fax 505-758-4541; www.ladonaluz.com, e-mail info@ladonaluz.com. MODERATE TO ULTRA-DELUXE.

HIDDEN ► Every room at **Casa Benavides Bed & Breakfast Inn** is unique, but they share a common quality—luxury. Several meticulously restored buildings, including an old trading post and an artist's studio, make up the 35-room complex. This crème de la crème property is elegantly furnished with tile floors, handmade furniture, kiva fireplaces, down comforters and a bevy of unusual antiques. The cost of a room includes a sumptuous breakfast served in a bright, airy dining room, and afternoon tea. The inn also has lavish gardens and two hot tubs, as well as a lovely art collection. ~ 137 Kit Carson Road, Taos; 505-758-1772, 800-552-1772, fax 505-758-5738; www.taos-casabenavides.com, e-mail casabena@ newmex.com. MODERATE TO ULTRA-DELUXE.

Proving that good things often come in small packages, the exotic eco-resort of **El Monte Sagrado**, three blocks from downtown Taos, has just 36 sumptuous, oversized suites and casitas decorated in American Indian and international themes. The suites overlook a healing circle in the center of the property, and the casitas, which sleep two to eight, are in renovated historic adobe buildings nearby. This boutique hotel is a showcase of sustainable design and includes buildings made from recycled materials and an elaborate water-purification system. The resort has a full-service spa and healing workshops. ~ 317 Kit Carson Road, Taos; 505-758-3502, 800-828-8267; www.elmonte sagrado.com, e-mail info@elmontesagrado.com. ULTRA-DELUXE.

Mabel Dodge, Georgia O'Keeffe, Ansel Adams, D. H. Lawrence and Dennis Hopper were but a few of the inventive minds that spent quality time at the historic, pueblo-style **Mabel Dodge Luhan House**. Located on a secluded street off

Taos Counterculture Lives On

Back in the 1960s, young people from all over the country abandoned city life and migrated to the mountains of New Mexico. Soon, over 3000 hippies set up house in the Taos area. Hoping to settle into a simple life in tune with nature, they built communal adobe homes and harvested their own food. This lifestyle, however, was far from simple and required hard physical labor, not to mention, debates over how the community would operate and under which rules they would agree to live. With so many new elements and an awakening sexual freedom, life offered an array of possibilities for them to explore.

In the forefront of this back-to-the-land movement, the New Buffalo Commune in Arroyo Hondo north of Taos was featured in *Look* and *Life* magazines, as well as *Playboy*, *Newsweek* and *Esquire*. Actor-filmmaker Dennis Hopper chose it as the location for an idyllic segment of the movie *Easy Rider*. Craft industries and spiritual connections thrived here—but it was the nudity, rock-and-roll and drugs that made the headlines. By the 1980s, the commune had collapsed, and in 1989 it was converted into the New Buffalo Bed & Breakfast.

Not far away, the commune of Lama was founded by a utopian sect under the leadership of psychologist-turned-guru Baba Ram Dass. Formerly known as Dr. Richard Alpert, he had taught at—and been fired from—Harvard alongside Timothy Leary. But while Leary became an outspoken LSD advocate, Ram Dass took a different path, retreating to the New Mexico mountains to teach Hindu meditation to a select group of followers. Lama grew into a villagelike, family-oriented spiritual community that endured a 1996 forest fire, which destroyed everything except the central dome housing the library, a meditation kiva and a ceremonial area.

After the fire, New Buffalo threw open its guest rooms to the homeless residents of Lama. In doing so, the owners forfeited their summer tourist trade, and the B&B went out of business. While it did reopen for a year, it is now **New Buffalo Center**, which accommodates a very limited number of guests, so call far in advance. It is in a solar-powered traditional-style adobe compound with two greenhouses and loads of charm and culture. ~ 108 Lower Arroyo Hondo Road, Arroyo Hondo, NM 87513; 505-776-2015; www.newbuffalocenter.com, e-mail bobfies@zianet.com. MODERATE TO DELUXE.

Although the days of drugs and free love have long since vanished, the pursuit of spiritual enlightenment remains a strong force in the Taos area. Baba Ram Dass worked tirelessly raising funds to rebuild Lama until he suffered a disabling stroke in 1997. Today the foundation offers indoor and outdoor lodging accommodations, as well as a music room and a historic library. ~ 505-586-1269; www.lamafoundation.org, e-mail lama@lamafoundation.org.

Kit Carson Road, its nine rooms, a two-bedroom cottage and an adjacent eight-room guesthouse are charmingly decorated and offer ample opportunity to relax amid cottonwood and willow trees after a hard day of sightseeing. Reserve the glass-enclosed solarium for views of the Sacred Mountains; light up the kiva fireplace before curling up with a book on the hand-carved bed in Mabel's room. Full breakfast included. ~ 240 Morada Lane, Taos; 505-751-9686, 800-846-2235, fax 505-737-0365; www.mabeldodgeluhan.com, e-mail mabel@mabel dodgeluhan.com. MODERATE TO ULTRA-DELUXE.

Epicenter of Taos activity is the enormously popular **Historic Taos Inn**. A National Historic Landmark, the inn comprises several separate houses from the 1800s. Forty-four rooms are decorated in a Southwestern motif with Mexican tile, locally designed furniture and hand-loomed Indian bedspreads; most have kiva fireplaces. If the inn is booked, which it may very well be (it has won *Wine Spectator* magazine's "Best Of" Award of Excellence 18 years in a row) set aside an evening to enjoy a drink and the free wireless internet in the lobby, which is as comfortable as any living room. A favorite hangout for locals, also known as "Taoseños." ~ 125 Paseo del Pueblo Norte, Taos; 505-758-2233, 800-826-7466, fax 505-758-5776; www.taosinn.com, e-mail reser vations@taosinn.com. DELUXE TO ULTRA-DELUXE.

Visit the **Dreamcatcher Bed and Breakfast**. Choose from a room with a sunken bedroom or one with traditional Southwestern furniture. Saltillo tile floors, kiva fireplaces, and private entrances also characterize some of the seven quiet rooms. A full breakfast is included with a night's stay. ~ 416 La Lomita Road, Taos; 505-758-0613, 888-758-0613, fax 505-751-0115; www.dreambb.com, e-mail dream@taosnm.com. MODERATE TO DELUXE.

It's hard not to get lost while walking around the compound known as the **Quail Ridge Inn**. Low-slung buildings containing fully equipped apartment-size rooms dot the landscape. A casual, country-club variety of clientele clogs the pool and tennis courts. The self-contained resort offers so many on-site amenities and diversions that you need not ever leave the complex, which would be a crying shame considering all there is to see in Taos. Rates sometimes include breakfast. ~ 88 Taos Ski Valley Road, Taos; 505-776-2211, 800-624-4448, fax 505-776-2949. DELUXE.

Skiers, hikers and other adventuresome spirits looking for an ultra-cheap experience should seek out the **Hostelling International—Taos**, also known as the **Abominable Snowmansion**. The hostel has seven dorm rooms (four can be converted into private family rooms) with large closets, dressing areas, bathrooms and showers. A piano, a pool table, a fireplace, a conversation area, vegetable gardens and high-speed internet are also available to guests. There are Indian tepees or a bunkhouse for additional sleeping arrangements. Camping is also allowed. Showers and use of the kitchen are included in the price. ~ Taos Ski Valley Road, Arroyo Seco; 505-776-8298, fax 505-776-2107; www.snow mansion.com, e-mail snowman@newmex.com. BUDGET.

Close to the Taos Ski Area, with outrageous views of the Sangre de Cristo Mountains, is luxurious **Salsa del Salto**. Goose-down comforters warm the king-size beds. Leather couches in the common area are placed in front of the two-story stone fireplace—a good place for getting horizontal after a long day on Taos' tough slopes. The pool, tennis and badminton courts, croquet course and hot tub help take the edge off as well. Tea and sweets are served daily, and guests rave about the omelettes. ~ Route 150, one mile north of Arroyo Seco; 505-776-2422, 800-530-3097, fax 505-776-5734; www.bandbtaos.com, e-mail salsa@taosnm. com. MODERATE TO DELUXE.

If long days of skiing and multicourse meals are enough to satisfy you, consider a stay in the Taos Ski Valley at one of several European-flavored lodges like the simple but comfortable **Hotel St. Bernard**. Location, location, location and a family atmosphere prevail at this 28-room chalet-style dwelling. Reservations are made by the week only; all meals, lift tickets and ski school are included in the price. High-speed internet available throughout the hotel. Closed early April to mid-December. ~ Taos Ski Valley Road, Taos; 505-776-2251, fax 505-776-5790; www.stbernardtaos.com, e-mail stbhotel@newmex.com. ULTRA-DELUXE.

> At least one legendary frontiersman, Kit Carson, settled down in Taos, where he lived out his later years as one of the few Anglos in the Spanish and Indian community.

Located about one and a half miles from the ski area is the **Austing Haus B&B**, the largest timber-frame building in North America. As the name implies, this charming 24-unit bed and breakfast has an Austrian ambience. The glass dining room (open in winter only) is truly elegant. Closed mid-April to mid-May. ~ Taos Ski Valley Road, Taos; 505-776-2649, 800-748-2932, fax 505-776-8751; www.austinghaus.net, e-mail manager@austing haus.net. DELUXE.

DINING

Lamb entrées top the list of house specialties at **Lambert's of Taos**. Established in 1989 by the former chef at Doc Martin's, Lambert's serves imaginative presentations of mahimahi, salmon, swordfish and other fresh seafood in the parlor rooms of a refurbished Territorial-era house that exudes an atmosphere of gracious frontier living. The menu also includes beef, wild game and poultry selections. Dinner only. ~ 309 Paseo del Pueblo Sur, Taos; 505-758-1009; www.lambertsoftaos.com. DELUXE TO ULTRA-DELUXE.

Pizza Emergency has great New York–style pizza and a name you won't quickly forget. Also on the menu are baked pastas, hot submarine sandwiches and salads. They have free delivery in the

Taos area, but only until 9 p.m.—well before the pizza bug typically strikes. ~ 316 Paseo del Pueblo Sur, Taos; 505-751-0911. BUDGET TO MODERATE.

Housed in an old adobe building, **Roberto's** offers Northern New Mexican cuisine. The menu features tacos, enchiladas, homemade tamales and *chiles rellenos*. Dinner only. Closed Tuesday in summer; closed every day but weekends and holidays November and December. ~ 122-B Kit Carson Road, Taos; 505-758-2434. MODERATE.

Caffe Tazza, a newsstand café, makes for a wonderful stop in the middle of the day. ~ 122 Kit Carson Road, Taos; 505-758-8706. BUDGET.

You could eat three meals a day in the award-winning **Doc Martin's** (a Taos favorite for 70 years), and never get bored. Blue-corn and blueberry hotcakes at breakfast make the mouth water, as does Doc's famous *chile relleno* platter for lunch. But it's at dinnertime when the kitchen really shines. Savor the grilled pork tenderloin with green-chile mustard and spaghetti squash, specials like the blue corn–dusted boneless trout, and try to save room for dessert. Sunday brunch is served. ~ 125 Paseo del Pueblo Norte, Taos; 505-758-1977, fax 505-758-5776, 888-519-8267; www.taosinn.com. DELUXE TO ULTRA-DELUXE.

The funky sign on local institution **Michael's Kitchen** might grab you, but the sweets' cabinet could lock you into a stranglehold. Spill-off-your-plate-size breakfasts pack 'em in on ski mornings; diner-type meals are served the rest of the day. Closed November. ~ 304-C Paseo del Pueblo Norte, Taos; 505-758-4178; www.michaelskitchen.com, e-mail ninneman@michaels kitchen.com. MODERATE.

Tucked into an arty old house right off the main drag, the **Dragonfly Café** is a homey place with small wooden tables where you'll feel comfortable dining alone or with a friend. Home-baked breads accompany hearty and filling omelettes, Swedish pancakes and other tasty breakfast goodies. At lunch, you'll find

AUTHOR FAVORITE

Fine dining is one of my passions, and in my subjective opinion the finest in Taos is at **Joseph's Table**. Candlelight and frescoed walls set the stage for outstanding cuisine at this chef-owned restaurant. The menu, which changes daily, emphasizes organic ingredients. A typical dinner might be an appetizer of New Mexico squash blossoms stuffed with crab and buffalo mozzarella, followed by an entrée of apricot rosemary–glazed salmon. No lunch on weekends. ~ 108-A South Taos Plaza, La Fonda Hotel, Taos; 505-751-4512; www.josephstable.com. DELUXE TO ULTRA-DELUXE.

Vietnamese chicken salad, panini sandwiches and other light fare. Sit inside or outside on the shady patio. ~ 402 Paseo del Pueblo Norte, Taos; 505-737-5859; www.dragonflytaos.com, e-mail info@dragonflytaos.com. BUDGET TO MODERATE.

The emphasis is on fresh at the **Apple Tree,** a charming house converted into a restaurant. The Apple Tree offers innovative interpretations of standard poultry, fish and meat dishes. Killer desserts top off the menu. Sunday brunch is available. ~ 123 Bent Street, Taos; 505-758-1900; e-mail appletree@newmex.com. MODERATE TO ULTRA-DELUXE.

Just north of Taos, **Orlando's New Mexican Café** is a tiny, family-owned eatery that manages to stand out in a sea of restaurants also offering New Mexican cuisine. Its simple, home-cooked meals, prepared with local ingredients, are just like grandma's. Classic offerings include enchiladas and burritos; also try their fish and chicken tacos, vegetarian *posole* and the unusual avocado pie, a silky Mexican take on an American favorite. ~ 1114 Don Juan Valdez Lane, El Prado; 505-751-1450. BUDGET TO MODERATE.

For outstanding margaritas, *chiles rellenos*, blue-corn tortillas and other regional food plus Caribbean seafood specialties and fish tacos, try the **Old Blinking Light Restaurant.** And did I mention the margaritas? Dinner only. ~ Mile Marker 1, Taos Ski Valley Road, four miles north of Taos; 505-776-8787; e-mail mike@theoldblinkinglight.com. MODERATE TO ULTRA-DELUXE.

Sate après-ski hunger by moseying on down the hill to **Tim's Stray Dog Cantina.** Quaff multiple varieties of margaritas served in pitchers while chowing down on the *piri-piri* shrimp, homemade green-chile stew and mud pie that will push your cholesterol count right off the Richter scale. Closed early April to Memorial Day. ~ Cottam's Alpine Village, Taos Ski Area; 505-776-2894, fax 505-776-1350; e-mail straydog@newmex.com. BUDGET TO MODERATE.

The Taos "mystique" has always lured artists and craftsmen, so expect to find lots of shops and galleries around the Plaza and surrounding streets.

SHOPPING

For a deal on moccasins, stop by the **Taos Moccasin Company.** ~ 216-B Paseo del Pueblo Sur; 505-751-0032. **Old Taos Traders** is a traditional favorite for Mexican imports. ~ 127 North Plaza, Taos; 505-758-1133.

Antiques and beautiful oriental rugs fill the front and back yards of **Patrick Dunbar Colonial Antiques,** which is interesting to visit even if you can't afford a single thing. Closed Sunday in winter. ~ 222 Paseo del Pueblo Norte, Taos; 505-758-2511.

Touristy, yes, but wonderful too, is R. C. Gorman's **Navajo Gallery,** which specializes in Gorman's paintings and sculpture of Navajo women. ~ 210 Ledoux Street, Taos; 505-758-3250; www.rcgormangallery.com.

There are many great bookstores in Taos. A favorite is **Moby Dickens Bookshop**, which has plenty of places to sit and read. A cat named Ruby guards the door. ~ 124-A Bent Street; 505-758-3050; www.mobydickens.com.

Brodsky Bookshop has lots of new and used American Indian and Southwestern titles as well as poetry and literature. Closed Sunday. ~ 226-A Paseo del Pueblo Norte, Taos; 505-758-9468.

> The Taos economy in the late 16th century included slavery—Navajo warriors traded Hopi and Zuni captives for livestock.

Taos Artisans Gallery is an impressive cooperative of iron sculpture, jewelry, pottery and woven clothing. ~ 107-A Bent Street; 505-758-1558. Another gem of an art cooperative is **Open Space Gallery**, where more than a dozen local artists show their work. ~ 103-B East Plaza, Taos; 505-758-1217.

La Lana Wools uses fine natural fibers to make sweaters, coats, yarns and jackets. Native plants are used to dye the fiber. ~ 136 Paseo del Pueblo Norte, Taos; 505-758-9631; www.lalanawools. com. **Taos Mountain Outfitters** sells outdoor garb and equipment for trekking into the high country. ~ 114 South Plaza, Taos; 505-758-9292; www.taosmountainoutfitters.com.

NIGHTLIFE For a taste of local flavor, swing by the **Taos Inn's Adobe Bar**. Jazz, flamenco and American Indian flute can be enjoyed several nights a week. ~ 125 Paseo del Pueblo Norte, Taos; 505-758-2233; www.taosinn.com, e-mail reservations@taosinn.com.

Hot times are had at the **Sagebrush Inn Bar**, with nightly live music and country-and-western dancing. No music Sunday through Wednesday. ~ 1508 Paseo del Pueblo Sur, Taos; 505-758-2254.

You'll find live entertainment in El Monte Sagrado's **Anaconda Bar** Monday through Saturday. ~ 317 Kit Carson Road, Taos; 505-758-3502, 800-828-8267; www.elmontesagrado.com.

Taos' best sports bar, complete with brewpub and a boisterous crowd, is the **Old Blinking Light**, which occasionally features live music. Don't leave without trying a margarita. ~ Mile Marker 1, Ski Valley Road, Taos; 505-776-8787.

For a drink in the Taos Ski Valley, check out the margaritas at **Tim's Stray Dog Cantina**. ~ 105 Sutton Place, Taos Ski Area; 505-776-2894.

PARKS **CARSON NATIONAL FOREST** 🏃 🚴 🐎 🦌 🎣 The challenge of scaling Wheeler Peak, whose 13,161-foot summit is the highest point in New Mexico, brings mountaineers from all over the country. The lower, gentler mountains southeast of Taos, which local villagers have been using communally as a source of firewood and summer pasturage for centuries, contain hundreds of miles of rough forest roads, many of which are ideal for mountain-bike and four-wheel-drive adventures in the summer and cross-country skiing in the winter. Farther south, the 13,102-foot Truchas Peak crowns the roadless immensity of the Pecos Wilderness. Roads and amenities are closed January through April. ~ Accessed by Route 150 (Taos Ski Valley Road) and by Routes 518, 75 and 76 (collectively called the High Road to Taos); 505-758-6200, fax 505-758-6213; www.fs.fed.us/r3/carson.

▲ Capulin and La Sombra Campgrounds, located one half mile apart on Route 64 about seven miles east of Taos, have a total of 24 tent and RV sites (no hookups); $8 to $15 per night. Farther west, off of Route 518 near Tres Ritos, Agua Piedra and Duran Canyon Campgrounds have a total of 56 campsites (no hookups); $8 to $15 per night. These campgrounds are closed October through April.

ORILLA VERDE RECREATION AREA
Situated on the banks of an ultrascenic stretch of the Rio Grande, the park is renowned for its trout fishing but equally popular for day outings, like whitewater rafting, and weekend camping. The only facilities are picnic areas, showers and restrooms. Closed weekdays from December through April. The Rio Grande Gorge Visitor Center (505-751-4899) is their homebase and has the best information. Day-use fee, $3. ~ Route 570, two miles north of Pilar; 505-758-8851, fax 505-758-1620.

▲ There are 23 campsites (no hookups); $7 per night. No water in winter.

Enchanted Circle Area

The Enchanted Circle is the name given to the 84-mile loop formed by Routes 522, 38 and 64. From Taos, the paved route winds through subalpine evergreen forests around the base of Wheeler Peak, the highest mountain in New Mexico (elevation 13,161 feet). Along the way you'll find ski resorts, a recreational lake in a basin surrounded by mountain peaks, and a moving tribute to the men and women who served in the Vietnam War.

SIGHTS

On a hillside overlooking Eagle Nest Reservoir, midway through the Enchanted Circle tour (see "Driving Tour" in this chapter), the Vietnam Veterans Memorial State Park pays tribute to soldiers who fought in Vietnam. Set against the backdrop of the Sangre de Cristo Mountains, this 24-acre monument is one of the largest in the country. It includes a visitors center with extensive exhibits dedicated to the memory of those who lost their lives as well as access to computerized archives of KIA (killed in action) and MIA (missing in action) soldiers. There's also an interdenominational chapel on the premises. ~ Route 64, Angel Fire; 505-377-6900, fax 505-377-3223; e-mail nmparks@state.nm.us.

Just 11 miles southwest of Questa, where the Enchanted Circle tour rejoins the main highway, is the **Wild Rivers Recreation Area**, the ideal place to see the Rio Grande and Red River in their natural state. The Art Zimmerman Visitors Center features geologic exhibits, interpretive displays and rangers who will help you make the most of this scenic area. Most visitors flock to La Junta Point overlooking the junction of these free-flowing rivers. Self-guiding nature trails show you how the Rio Grande Gorge was etched out over the centuries by wind and water. The numerous hiking trails in this area include several steep climbs leading down to the water. Proceed with caution. Admission. ~ Route 378; 505-770-1600, 505-758-8851, fax 505-751-1620; www.nm.blm.gov.

Thirteen miles south of Questa is the **D. H. Lawrence Ranch**, a memorial to the British writer built by his widow, Frieda. When Mabel Dodge Luhan gave the land that is now the D. H. Lawrence Ranch to the writer's wife, Frieda returned the favor with a gift: the original manuscript to *Sons and Lovers*. Now a field center for the University of New Mexico, it can be readily visited during the daytime hours. ~ Off Route 522, 20 miles north of Taos; 505-776-2245, fax 505-776-2408.

Another 13 miles south is the junction of Routes 522 and 64. Go west on Route 64 until you reach the **Rio Grande Gorge Bridge**. You may want to hold your breath while crossing this suspension bridge, 650 feet over the Rio Grande.

LODGING Bring the family to the full-service **Angel Fire Resort Hotel**, where ultraspacious guest rooms, bedecked in pastel colors and Southwestern styles, offer plenty of closet space and can easily accommodate rollaway beds. ~ North Angel Fire Road, Angel Fire; 505-377-6401, 800-633-7463, fax 505-377-4200; www.angel fireresort.com, e-mail reservations@angelfireresort.com. DELUXE TO ULTRA-DELUXE.

Also in Angel Fire, the **Wildflower Bed & Breakfast** is a traditionally designed contemporary home with a wide front porch and sunny back deck area, both looking out on meadows that are full of colorful native flowers in the warm months. Second-floor dormers contain the five guest bedrooms, three with private baths. Perhaps the best part of a stay at this B&B is the gourmet breakfast, featuring such items as banana french toast, Swedish oatmeal pancakes and sourdough biscuits with eggs. There's a two-night minimum stay in winter. Closed in April. ~ P.O. Box 575 (40 Halo Pines Terrace), Angel Fire, NM 87710; 505-377-6869; www.angelfirenm.com/wildflower, e-mail wildflower@afweb.com. MODERATE TO DELUXE.

The guest accommodations at **Cottonwood Lodge** are situated above the Enchanted Circle area's most unique gift store (items featured are chainsaw-carved). Each of the three units opens onto a conversation area, and each has a TV with VCR and a full kitchen with microwave and dishwasher; the rooms are furnished with antiques. The shore of Eagle Nest Reservoir is just a short walk away. ~ 124 East Therma Street, Eagle Nest; 505-377-3382, 800-377-3955, fax 505-377-2446; www.angelfirenm.com/cottonwood, e-mail cottonwood@angelfirenm.com. MODERATE.

Prices drop at the **Laguna Vista Lodge**, just 12 miles north of Angel Fire on the pretty road to Eagle Nest. Motel rooms and suites are available. ~ Route 64, Eagle Nest; 505-377-6522, 800-821-2093, fax 505-377-6626; www.lagunavistalodge.com, e-mail laguna@newmex.com. MODERATE TO DELUXE.

For a laidback vacation complete with rustic cabins, a small private fishing lake and easy access to the Red River, head for **Rio Colorado Lodge**. Paneled with tongue-and-groove knotty pine, the 21 one- to three-bedroom units come with full kitchens or kitchenettes. Many offer fireplaces. Families especially appreciate the large picnic areas (with barbecue pits) and playground for the kids. ~ 515 East Main Street, Red River; 505-754-2212, 800-654-6516, fax 505-754-3063; www.redrivernm.com/riocolorado, e-mail riocoloradolodge@msn.com. MODERATE TO DELUXE.

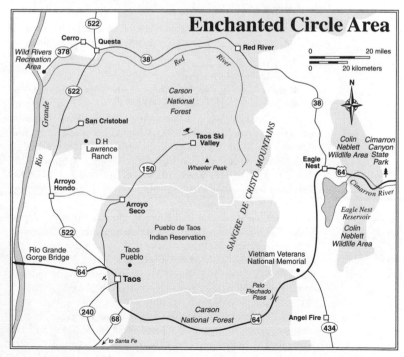

DRIVING TOUR
The Enchanted Circle

The Enchanted Circle is the name given to the 84-mile loop formed by Routes 522, 38 and 64.

PALO FLECHADO PASS   Drive south of downtown Taos to Route 64 and cruise over scenic Palo Flechado Pass, which was used by American Indians and Spaniards who came from the plains via the Cimarron River. Along the way are several places to pull over for a picnic or snapshot.

ANGEL FIRE   Upon reaching the intersection of Route 434, turn south for a quick visit to the resort town of Angel Fire. In winter it's a favorite destination for intermediate skiers, while in summer, golfers, hikers and lovers of chamber music flock to Angel Fire.

WHEELER PEAK   Back on Route 64 you'll soon come to **Eagle Nest Reservoir**, a fine sailing, windsurfing and fishing lake that affords a spectacular lookout. Be sure to get a good look at Wheeler Peak, the state's highest peak at 13,161 feet above sea level.

EAGLE NEST   At the lake's north shore is the village of Eagle Nest, with a handful of restaurants and shops. From there it's 24 windy miles to

A short walk to the ski slopes, **Lifts West Condominium Resort Hotel** features contemporary, two-story units, all with fireplaces and wall-to-wall carpeting. Many have complete kitchens and balconies or decks. A heated pool, restaurant and shopping mall are on the premises. Summer rates are budget while winter rates skyrocket to the ultra-deluxe category. ~ 201 West Main Street, Red River; 505-754-2778, 800-221-1859, fax 505-754-6617; www.liftswest.com, e-mail lifts@redriver.org. MODERATE TO ULTRA-DELUXE.

On the banks of the Red River by the ski lifts is the **Alpine Lodge**. Rooms and apartments are well-maintained, all with porch or balcony. Nearby ski rentals make the Alpine a convenient spot for skiers. ~ 417 West Main Street, Red River; 505-754-2952, 800-252-2333, fax 505-754-6421; www.thealpinelodgeredriver. com, e-mail info@thealpinelodgeredriver.com. MODERATE TO ULTRA-DELUXE.

The 26 rooms at **The Lodge at Red River** are rustic, but the central location is appealing. Closed April to mid-May and late September to mid-November. ~ 400 East Main Street, Red River;

Cimarron through the Cimarron Range (one of the easternmost ranges of the Sangre de Cristo Mountains), the Colin Neblett Wildlife Area and Cimarron Canyon.

CIMARRON CANYON STATE PARK   Three miles east of Eagle Nest are the towering walls of Cimarron Canyon State Park. Be sure to watch your speed, and after dark be on the lookout for deer as you travel through the narrow canyon. ~ Route 64; 505-377-6271.

RED RIVER   Return to Eagle Nest; just north of the town (where Route 64 becomes Route 38) is an open and pretty valley ringed with high mountains. Drop down Bobcat Pass into Red River, yet another Wild West village. Though touristy, this early-20th-century goldmining town retains a certain charm from its rip-roaring gambling, brawling and red-light district days. A ski area rises out of its center and national forest land surrounds it completely.

QUESTA   Continuing east on the Enchanted Circle, which hugs Red River, you'll drive past plenty of forest and camping spots until you reach the honey-producing town of Questa. From Questa, 22 miles south on Route 522 will bring you back to Taos. Along the way, you may wish to stop and visit the D. H. Lawrence Ranch, the Rio Grande Gorge Bridge or the Millicent Rogers Museum.

505-754-6280, 800-915-6343, fax 505-754-6304; www.redriver nm.com/lodgeatrr, e-mail lodge@newmex.org. MODERATE.

DINING

Eager to trade fast-food for a table set with real silver? Then take a seat in the dining room at **The Lodge at Red River**. Specialties like rainbow trout, charbroiled pork chops and fish tacos will make up for all the cheeseburgers you've suffered. Entrées come with salad or soup and vegetables. The bar is a pleasant après-ski stop. Breakfast, lunch and dinner are served. Closed April to mid-May and late October to mid-November. ~ 400 East Main Street, Red River; 505-754-6280, 800-915-6343; www.redrivernm.com/ lodgeatrr, e-mail lodge@redrivernm.com. MODERATE TO DELUXE.

Capo's Corner is an Italian chain restaurant that serves reliable pasta with homemade sauces, piping hot pizza, sandwiches, and meat and fish entrées in a large room with two fireplaces. Just the ticket after spending all day on the slopes. ~ 110 Pioneer Road, Red River; 505-754-6297. BUDGET TO MODERATE.

Corny as it may sound, you won't waddle away hungry from **Texas Red's Steakhouse**, which specializes in slabs of beef, big hamburgers and other hearty Western-style meals. Dinner only. Limited hours in April and November. ~ 111 Main Street, Red River; 505-754-2964, fax 505-754-2309; www.texasreds.com. MODERATE TO DELUXE.

NIGHTLIFE   Music from Angel Fire is a great place to rub elbows with New Mexico's patrons of the arts. Since 1983, the organization has hosted a variety of rotating artists whose music will soothe the most savage of beasts. There is a chamber music festival in the summer. ~ P.O. Box 502, Angel Fire, NM 87110; 505-377-3233, 888-377-3300, fax 505-989-4773; www.musicfromangelfire.org, e-mail info@musicfromangelfire.org.

Over the mountain in Red River, stop in at **Bull o' the Woods Saloon**, where a deejay plays country music and classic rock, and there's live music on weekends during the summer. Closed in April. ~ 401 Main Street; 505-754-2593. A bar with live country-and-western on weekend nights is the **Motherlode** at The Lodge at Red River. Closed April and May. Cover. ~ 400 East Main Street, Red River; 505-754-6280.

PARKS   **CARSON NATIONAL FOREST** 🏃 🚲 🐎 🛶 ⛺ Like the Santa Fe National Forest, which adjoins it on the south, Carson National Forest is split by the Rio Grande Valley into two separate units. The western part extends from the spectacular red, white and yellow cliffs around Abiquiu northward to the Colorado state line, encompassing the gently rolling pine forests of the San Pedro and Canjilon Mountains. The portion of the Rio Chama above Abiquiu Lake has been designated a National Wild and Scenic River by the U.S. Congress and is a popular rafting area. The Canjilon Lakes and a number of other remote lakes reached by forest roads in the north are favorites with local anglers. ~ Accessed by numerous forest roads off Route 84 between Española and Chama; 505-684-2486, fax 505-684-2486; www.fs.fed.us/r3/carson.

▲ The lakeside campground at Canjilon Lakes has 40 sites (no hookups); $5 per night. Closed September through May.

CIMARRON CANYON STATE PARK 🏃 🚲 🐎 🛶 Granite formations tower above a sparkling stream where brown and rainbow trout crowd the waters and wildlife congregates. There are some hiking trails, but fishing is the most popular park activity. Facilities are limited to picnic areas and restrooms. Day-use fee, $5 per vehicle. ~ Route 64, 14 miles west of Cimarron; 505-377-6271, fax 505-377-2259.

▲ There are 88 developed sites (no hookups); $10 per vehicle per night. No water from mid-September to early May. Reservations: 888-664-7787.

Known as *Los Llanos*, "the plains," the wide-open country spills from the edge of the mountains across the empty northeastern corner of New Mexico and on into Oklahoma and the Texas Panhandle. Those who take the time to visit Capulin Volcano can stand at the top of this extinct, solitary cone that rises out of the prairie and appreciate the vastness of this land. Most travelers, however, hurry through the area on the interstate without realizing that the two-lane highway from Raton through Cimarron and through the Sangre de Cristo Mountains is a beautiful shortcut to both Taos and Santa Fe. Both Cimarron and Raton preserve their frontier heritage in historic buildings and small museums full of Old Western artifacts.

East of Cimarron

The settlement of **Cimarron,** where plain and pasture meet rugged mountains, was founded in 1848 with entrepreneur Lucien Maxwell's land grant. Life was cheap at this outpost on the mountain branch of the Santa Fe Trail; death from a gunfight was not uncommon. Cimarron the town and Cimarron the river lived up to the Spanish translation of their name—wild and untamed. While that may have described Cimarron a century ago, these days it's just a mellow small town. The rambling river waters too have been calmed by the establishment of Eagle Nest Reservoir.

SIGHTS

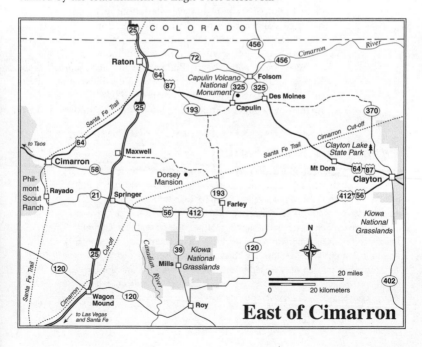

East of Cimarron

A trip to Cimarron wouldn't be complete without a peek inside the historic **St. James Hotel,** with its partly renovated interior and completely authentic funkiness. Built in 1873 by one of Abraham Lincoln's chefs, some say the St. James is haunted by outlaw ghosts of the past. ~ Route 21, Cimarron; 505-376-2664.

Originally built as a grist mill, the **Old Mill Museum** now offers a panoramic view of local history from chuckwagons to regional paintings. And while the collection does include sleighs and American Indian pottery shards, it focuses on ranching, mining and homesteading in the Cimarron area. You'll be surrounded by treasures of the past. This exhibit is not to be missed. Closed Thursday and October through April, weekends only in May and September. Admission. For information about the museum call the Cimarron Chamber of Commerce. ~ Off Route 21, Cimarron; phone/fax 505-376-2417; www.cimarronnm.com, e-mail chamber@springercoop.com.

More down to earth is the **Philmont Scout Ranch,** the nation's largest scouting camp. In 1922, the Tulsa oil baron Waite Phillips bought a 300,000-acre ranch south of Cimarron. In 1941, he donated a total of 127,000 acres to the Boy Scouts of America. Today, a small museum features local artifacts and works of Ernest Thompson-Seton, one of the founders of the Boy Scouts. Also here is **Villa Philmonte,** the former home of Waite Phillips. There are guided tours of the mansion every half hour in summer and once or twice daily off-season. Call ahead for hours. ~ Route 21, about four miles south of Cimarron, Philmont; 505-376-2281, fax 505-376-2636; www.scouting.org/philmont.

Seven miles south of the Philmont Scout headquarters is the **Kit Carson Museum,** a living-history exhibit illustrating the life of 1850s-era settlers like Kit Carson (who lived here). Operated by the Boy Scouts of America, this old adobe compound is a ter-

sights

AUTHOR FAVORITE

Dorsey Mansion may be a long way from anywhere, but it's definitely worth the excursion. The stone and log mansion was once the heart of a ranch rumored to extend 60 miles in length. Now it's a landmark—listed on the National Register of Historic Places—adorned with an Italian marble fireplace and a number of intriguing gargoyles. Carved snakes and bobcats lunge from the intricate stone fountain. Don't try to visit in inclement weather; the clay roads are exceptionally slick when wet. Tours are offered daily. Reservations recommended. Admission. ~ From Springer, drive 24 miles east on Route 56, then 12 miles north on a dirt road; 505-375-2222; www.dorseymansion.com, e-mail shenning@dorseymansion.com.

rific place to learn pioneer arts and crafts; the place even boasts a hardworking blacksmith and candlemakers. Closed late August through May, except by appointment. ~ Route 21, Rayado; 505-376-4621 (summer), 505-376-2281 ext. 256 (winter).

Continuing another 38 miles northeast of Cimarron on Routes 64 and 25, you'll come to **Raton** (elevation 6666 feet), a small New Mexican city located on the original Santa Fe Trail. Raton, with its scenic mesas, sits at the foot of Raton Pass and was first founded as a railroad outpost.

Visits to Raton should begin with a walking tour of the **Raton Downtown Historic District**, one of New Mexico's most distinguished Main Street districts. Some of the buildings have been completely restored, others are in the midst of rehabilitation and a few cry out for love and care. This is an opportunity to see an array of styles and period pieces from the late 19th to the early 20th centuries—truly an architectural timeline. This area is on the National Register of Historic Places. Pick up the walking-tour brochure at the **Raton Chamber and Economic Development Council**. ~ 100 Clayton Road, Raton; 505-445-3689, 800-638-6161, fax 505-445-3680; www.raton.info, e-mail ratonchamber@bacavalley.com.

The most worthwhile area attraction is the **Capulin Volcano National Monument**. Now extinct, the mile-wide cone of the volcano rises more than 1200 feet above the flat plains. The volcano is believed to be 56,000 to 62,000 years old. A visitors center and small museum provide information on the natural wonder. ~ Route 64/87, Capulin, 30 miles east of Raton; 505-278-2201, fax 505-278-2211; www.nps.gov/cavo, e-mail cavo_administration@nps.gov.

Route 325 leads north from here to the town of **Folsom**. This short (seven miles) and beautiful trip is backcountry New Mexico driving at its best. Winding through picturesque valleys you'll descend to this little hamlet, worth visiting if only to see the impressive turn-of-the-20th-century native stone Catholic church and the 1888 Folsom Hotel. There are also a number of intriguing old adobe houses.

Hop on Route 325 until you reach the junction with Route 64 at Des Moines. Forty-five miles east on Route 64 will bring you to the town of Clayton. Rich in dinosaur history, this area of northeastern New Mexico has plenty of giant tracks to prove it. If you yearn to play amateur paleontologist, visit the **Clayton–Union County Chamber of Commerce**, where they make dinosaurs their business. Closed Saturday and Sunday from Labor Day through Memorial Day. ~ 1103 South 1st Street, Clayton; 505-374-9253, 800-390-7858; www.claytonnewmexico.org, e-mail cuchamber@plateautel.net.

The kind folks at the COC will no doubt direct you to **Clayton Lake State Park**, where you can see 500 dinosaur tracks from over 100 million years ago. First found in 1982 after a flood removed a layer of silt, the tracks here are etched in Dakota mudstone. Admission. ~ Route 370, 12 miles north of Clayton; 505-374-8808, fax 505-374-2461; www.claytonlakestatepark.com, e-mail charles.jordan@state.nm.us.

LODGING

Best bet by far in Cimarron is the spooky **St. James Hotel**, where famous residents such as Buffalo Bill Cody and Annie Oakley hung their Wild West duds. Built in 1880 and then lovingly restored and reopened a century later, this landmark has rooms with original period furniture. Each unit is unique and ghosts haunt the hallways, so you may ask to inspect your room before renting. Phones and TVs are available in an adjoining motel annex but not in the rooms of the historic hotel. ~ Route 21, Cimarron; 503-376-2664, 866-472-5019, fax 503-376-2623; e-mail stjames@springercoop.com. MODERATE TO DELUXE.

Built in 1912 on 225 acres in the foothills six miles south of Cimarron, **Casa del Gavilan** is a sprawling Pueblo Revival–style adobe ranch that was originally built as a family home for industrialist Jack Nairn and his wife Gertrude. The couple entertained many artists here; today the home is filled with works by Western artists such as Frederick Remington and Charles Russell. The four guest rooms have a plush, old-fashioned feel from a bygone era but are comfortably furnished. There is also a separate guesthouse with two bedrooms. All have private baths. A full breakfast is served in the dining room or on the patio. ~ P.O. Box 518, Cimarron, NM 87714; 505-376-2246, 800-428-4526; www.casadelgavilan.com, e-mail info@casadel gavilan.com. MODERATE.

DINING

Heck's Hungry Traveler is an unpretentious coffee shop where you'll enjoy tripledecker club sandwiches, half-pound burgers and cheese enchiladas. Booth and table seating are available. Be sure to try the homemade soups and pies. Breakfast and lunch served year-round; dinner also served mid-April to mid-November. ~ Route 64, Cimarron; 505-376-2574. BUDGET TO MODERATE.

The bullet holes in the ceiling are the last reminders of the **Carson Maxwell Room's** days as a saloon and gambling hall. Today, the chandeliers, upholstered chairs and candles set the mood for elegant dining. Crab, stuffed prawns, filet mignon, tenderloin, bison, pot roast, and vegetarian pasta primavera might be a few of the selections from the diverse menu. Dinner only. ~ St. James Hotel, Route 21, Cimarron; 505-376-2664, fax 505-376-2623. DELUXE.

The more casual **Vera's Coffee Shop** offers budget-priced fare such as burgers and salads. Open for breakfast, lunch and din-

In the Land of Three Cultures

No other place reflects the tricultural heritage of northern New Mexico as much as Taos does. Here, at the northern gateway to the Pueblo lands, the native people met and traded with nomadic outlanders such as the Utes, Apaches and Comanches for many centuries before the first Spanish conquistadores set foot in New Mexico. Here, too, as in few other places around the region, Spanish settlers built a town within easy walking distance of a large Indian pueblo. And here, at the dawn of the 20th century, artists and writers came from such faraway places as New York, Great Britain, France and Russia to establish a colony dedicated to capturing the traditions of the local people.

Multiculturalism has not always translated into tolerance or brotherly love, though. In the early days of Spanish colonialism, Puebloans from Taos south to the Albuquerque area revolted and killed the majority of the settlers, driving the survivors out of New Mexico. Taos Plaza is also reputed to have been the site of a market where Navajo raiders brought people kidnapped from Zuni and other western pueblos and sold them to the Spanish as slaves. And when New Mexico became United States territory in the 1840s, newly appointed governor Charles Bent, whose house is now a museum (page 394), was assassinated by the locals after serving less than a year in office. Cultural conflicts have plagued Taos as recently as the late 1960s and early '70s, when the town became a mecca for hippies, whose philosophy of psychedelics and free love offended the conservative, mostly Catholic populace.

On the whole, however, the three cultures have maintained a surprisingly peaceful balance over the centuries. Indian fighter Kit Carson retired to Taos with his Hispanic wife and became an ally of the local Puebloans. New York heiress Mabel Dodge married Tony Luhan, an Indian from Taos Pueblo, and became the artist colony's leading patron. Some hippie communes from the 1960s grew into spiritual centers, while others became bed and breakfasts. When the nearby Buddhist spiritual community of Lama was destroyed by a forest fire in 1996, the entire town and Pueblo of Taos rallied together to provide food and shelter for the homeless Lama residents.

Today, more than any other community in northern New Mexico, Taos is dedicated almost entirely to tourism. This town with a population of only about 5000 plays host to approximately three million visitors a year. Viewed in historical perspective, the tourist trade is a continuation of Taos' centuries-old role as the place where New Mexico meets the rest of the world.

ner. ~ St. James Hotel, Route 21, Cimarron; 505-376-2664, fax 505-376-2623. BUDGET TO MODERATE.

For morning coffee and hot-out-of-the-oven donuts, go to **Grace's Bakery**. They also serve omelettes and breakfast burritos; sandwiches are available at lunch. Breakfast and lunch only. Closed Sunday. ~ 134 North 2nd Street, Raton; 505-445-3781. BUDGET.

Founded by Jim Pappas and Gus Petritsis in 1923, **Pappas' Sweet Shop Restaurant** was such a popular candy store and soda fountain that the owners added a full-fledged restaurant. Run today by Jim's son, Mike, the Territorial-style establishment overflows with memorabilia: historic photos, train sets and classic car models. The eclectic menu ranges from lobster tail and prime rib to stuffed jalapeños. Toasted coconut pie and fried ice cream are just a few of the choices for dessert. Also on the premises are a coffee shop and gift shop. Closed Sunday. ~ 1201 South 2nd Street, Raton; 505-445-9811, fax 505-445-3080; e-mail papcfy@ aol.com. MODERATE TO ULTRA-DELUXE.

Restaurant options are few and far between in eastern New Mexico, but there's one thing you can count on. Out here, where cattle ranching is the only industry, the food at steak houses is a big, juicy cut above what you'll find at freeway-exit fast-food eateries.

If it's atmosphere you are looking for, it's hard to beat the velvet-cushioned banquettes at the **Eklund Hotel Dining Room and Saloon**. Built in 1892, this three-story rock-walled landmark is a real find. Mounted game oversee the hand-carved bar, one of the most beautiful in the state. Appointed with gold floral wallpaper, a marble fireplace and historic photographs, the dining room may tempt you to take out your camera. The menu emphasizes New Mexican specialties, though it also offers surf and turf and prime rib. ~ 15 Main Street, Clayton; 505-374-2551, fax 505-374-2500; www.theeklund.com. BUDGET TO DELUXE.

Knotty pine paneling, *vigas* and handcrafted furniture make **Hi Ho Café** an inviting place to try American and Mexican specialties. Steaks and burgers are always popular here, but you can opt for the soup and salad bar. Sandwiches and child's plates are also available. Breakfast, lunch and dinner are served. ~ 1201 South 1st Street, Clayton; 505-374-9515. BUDGET.

SHOPPING Cowboys and cowgirls (and Western wanna-bes) will find all the proper accessories at **Solano's Boot & Western Wear**, one of the largest shops of its kind in northern New Mexico. Saunter on in and "git" yourself a custom-made hat or an embroidered shirt. A wide selection of jackets and belt buckles completes the inventory. ~ 101 South 2nd Street, Raton; 505-445-2632; www.solanos westernwear.com.

As you could no doubt guess from the name, the **Heirloom Shop** carries antiques and collectibles, including advertising signs. This shop also boasts an excellent array of quilts, Depression glass and china. ~ 132 South 1st Street, Raton; 505-445-8876.

One way to beat Santa Fe's high prices for American Indian artifacts and collectibles is to head for **Santa Fe Trail Traders.** The Navajo, Hopi and Zuni artwork, from jewelry, fetishes and sand-paintings to kachinas and blankets, is well priced for such high-quality merchandise. Closed Sunday in winter. ~ 100 South 2nd Street, Raton; 505-445-2888; www.santafetrailtraders.com.

If you're planning to fish, camp, hike or golf in beautiful north-eastern New Mexico, head over to **Knott's Sportsman Supply.** Just about everything you could possibly need for life in the outback is on sale here, including maps, regional guides and athletic equipment. Anglers are certain to appreciate the complete selection of fishing rods, lures and flies. Closed Sunday. ~ 1015 South 1st Street, Clayton; 505-374-8361.

NIGHTLIFE

The **Raton Arts and Humanities Council** presents an impressive year-round calendar of adult and children's drama, musical solo-ists, symphony orchestras and touring dance companies. Most of the events are staged in the rococo Shuler Theater (131 North 2nd Street), opened to the public in 1915 and restored in the early 1970s. Original show curtains are in use today and the lobby mu-rals are a must-see. Their offices are located in a gallery with ex-hibits. ~ 145 South 1st Street, Raton; phone/fax 505-445-2052; www.ratonarts.com.

PARKS

CLAYTON LAKE STATE PARK 🚶 🛶 🚤 🎣 This prairie lake is a good spot for birding. Not only do Canada geese and several species of ducks winter here, bald eagles are also a common sight. Anglers also find that the lake offers excellent trout, cat-fish and bass fishing, and four state-record walleyed pikes have been caught here. Perhaps the most unusual feature of the park is its dinosaur trackway. Along the lake's spillway, more than 500

AUTHOR FAVORITE

For a special treat, I pay a visit to the **Cimarron Art Gallery**. Sculpture, paintings, jewelry and earrings are found here. And it is probably the only gallery in the Southwest with a working 1937 soda fountain—yes, they do serve ice cream in the gallery, and no, I generally can't resist indulging myself. Closed Sunday in the off-season. ~ 337 9th Street, Cimarron; 505-376-2614; www.cimarronartgallery.com, e-mail wdbd gers@springercoop.com.

dinosaur footprints have been preserved and identified. Interpretive markers identify the prints of several different types of herbivorous and carnivorous dinosaurs and ancient crocodiles. Day-use fee, $5. ~ Off Route 370, 12 miles northwest of Clayton; 505-374-8808, fax 505-374-2461.

▲ There are 30 developed sites ($10 per night), and an additional 7 with electric and water hookups ($14 per night). The campground has restrooms with showers.

▼▼▼▼▼▼▼▼▼▼▼▼▼

Outdoor Adventures

FISHING

Anglers find the fishing grand in these parts. Near Taos, head for the Rio Grande. Roads run to the river at Orilla Verde and Wild Rivers Recreation Areas. More adventuresome anglers can hike down the steep volcanic cliffs of the Rio Grande Gorge to remote stretches of the river in search of trophy-size rainbow and brown trout.

TAOS AREA   Los Rios Anglers sells and rents flyfishing tackle and guides half- and full-day fishing trips along the Rio Grande and its tributaries. ~ 126 West Plaza Drive, Taos; 505-758-2798. In the summer, tackle is available at **Cottam's Skiing and Outdoor Shop.** ~ 207-A Paseo del Pueblo Sur; 505-758-2822; www.cottams skishops.com.

ENCHANTED CIRCLE AREA   Dos Amigos Anglers Co. provides bait and tackle in Eagle Nest. They also offer instruction, half-day and full-day flyfishing trips. ~ 247 Therma Drive; 505-377-6226.

RIVER RUNNING

West of Taos, the Rio Grande flows through a spectacular 400-foot-deep gorge nicknamed the Taos Box. Both the Rio Grande and the Chama River, which flows into the Rio Grande between Taos and Santa Fe, have been designated by the United States government as Wild and Scenic Rivers, with environmental protection similar to federal wilderness areas. Both are full of river rafts and kayaks during the late spring and early summer when the rivers are swollen with runoff from snow-melt in the nearby mountains.

TAOS AREA   There are several rafting guide services in the Taos area. **Los Rios River Runners** takes half-day, full-day and overnight trips on the Class I, III and V rapids of the Rio Grande—including the worldfamous Taos Box—and the smooth current of the Rio Chama. If you really want to go all out, they'll arrange for an astronomer, a Celtic musician, a yoga teacher or a wine expert to accompany you. All meals, tents and camping gear are provided. ~ P.O. Box 2734, Taos, NM 87571; 505-776-8854, 800-544-1181; www.losriosriverrunners.com, e-mail whitewater@newmex.com.

Native Sons Adventures also guides whitewater raft trips through the Class II to IV Taos Box and the Class II and III Lower Gorge (a good starting trip for beginners). ~ 1033 Paseo

Green Chile,
Blue Corn & Piñon Nuts

New Mexico's distinctive cuisine has strong roots in the Pueblo Indian culture as adapted by Spanish settlers. It is set apart from Tex-Mex and Mexican food by three ingredients that are unique to the state.

Green chile, which is ubiquitous in New Mexican restaurants and kitchens, is the same hot pepper that is crushed into chili powder—in fact, New Mexico produces virtually all of the chili powder in the United States—but locals prefer to harvest it before it turns red and eat it as an ultra-spicy vegetable. Grown mainly in the small communities of Hatch and Chimayo, it is sold by the bushel during the late August to mid-September harvest season. The seller roasts the chiles, making the inedible outer skin easy to remove, and the buyer divides them into bags and freezes them to last the rest of the year. Green chile is almost never served outside New Mexico. If the plant is grown elsewhere, the green chile pods lose their flavor, as they do when dried or canned. Enjoy it while you can. If you want to take the taste of New Mexico home as a souvenir, your best bet is green chile preserves, sold in many Santa Fe and Taos curio shops.

Blue corn, a variety of Indian maize, has been cultivated by the Pueblo people for at least 1200 years. They hold it sacred because it is the color of the sky and of turquoise, the most precious of stones among Southwestern Indians. Spanish settlers grew blue corn obtained from the Indians, and it accounts for much of the corn grown in New Mexico today. The corn kernels have tough outer shells and so cannot be eaten directly off the cob. Instead, they are traditionally crushed into meal, mixed with water and made into tortillas or ground into a fine powder and boiled in water to make a souplike beverage called *atole*, which Indian shamans and Spanish *curanderos* claim has healing powers.

Piñon nuts form inside the cones of the piñon trees that dot the hills and mesas of northern New Mexico. All the trees in a particular area produce nuts at the same time, but only once every seven years. Local villagers harvest them by placing a sheet around the bottom of a tree, then lassoing the treetop with a rope and shaking it vigorously until the nuts fall out. The nuts are then sold by the roadside or wholesaled to local supermarkets. It is a common practice in northern New Mexico to mix piñon nuts, shell and all, with whole-bean coffee and grind them together, giving the coffee a rich, chocolatelike flavor. Coffee with piñon is sold in many supermarkets and makes an unusual souvenir or gift.

del Pueblo Sur; 505-758-9342, 800-753-7559; www.nativesons adventures.com.

Far Flung Adventures operates from El Prado and runs the Taos Box and the Rio Chama. They offer half-day, full-day and overnight trips. Meals and tents are provided. ~ P.O. Box 707, El Prado, NM 87529; 505-758-2628, 800-359-2627; www.farflung.com.

SKIING

This area boasts New Mexico's best alpine skiing. In fact, Taos Ski Area is so popular that Taos has become the only town in New Mexico where winter, not summer, is the peak tourist season. The ski season runs roughly from Thanksgiving through March, but may begin earlier or end later depending on weather conditions. Ski rentals and instruction are available at all the resorts listed here.

TAOS AREA　Granddaddy of New Mexico's alpine ski resorts is **Taos Ski Valley**, with a summit elevation of nearly 12,000 feet above sea level and a vertical drop of 2612 feet. Taos boasts more than 1200 acres of bowls and chutes served by ten chairs and two surface lifts. Taos has a reputation as one of the most challenging ski areas in the Rocky Mountains, with about half of the trails designated as expert. Snow conditions at Taos Ski Valley are available 24 hours a day by calling 505-776-2916. ~ Route 150/Taos Ski Valley Road; 505-776-2291; www.skitaos. org, e-mail tsv@skitaos.org.

ENCHANTED CIRCLE AREA　Forty-five minutes away from Taos, **Red River Ski Area** is an increasingly popular family ski area with a 1600-foot vertical drop. Seven lifts serve 290 acres of trails, rated 32 percent beginner, 38 percent intermediate and 30 percent expert. Snowboarding is allowed. Snow conditions at Red River are available 24 hours a day by calling 505-754-2220. ~ Route 38, Red River; 505-754-2223; www.redriverskiarea. com, e-mail info@redriverskiarea.com.

An even gentler ski area is **Angel Fire**, where five lifts carry skiers up to 10,677 feet elevation for a vertical descent of 2077 feet on 26 percent beginner, 50 percent intermediate and 24 percent expert trails. Snowboarding is allowed on all runs as well as in the

BLACK JACK KETCHUM'S FINAL DAYS

The notorious bandit Black Jack Ketchum committed his last crime near Twin Mountain, just four miles away from Folsom. He was apprehended and brought to Folsom after wounding himself during a train robbery. Following his conviction a year later, Ketchum was convicted and hung in Clayton on April 25, 1901. His last words were: "Let her rip."

terrain parks. ~ Route 434; 505-377-6401, 800-633-7463; www.
angelfireresort.com.

Sipapu Ski Area—the oldest ski slope in northern New Mex-   ◄ HIDDEN
ico, built in 1952—is especially popular with snowboarders
thanks to its two terrain parks. The small ski area covers only 65
acres, with a peak elevation of just over 9000 feet and a 1055-foot
vertical drop. Four lifts serve 31 trails. ~ Route 518, Vadito; 505-
587-2240, 800-587-2240; www.sipapunm.com, e-mail customer
service@sipapunm.com.

Cross-country skiers who prefer the peaceful sounds of nature will enjoy gliding through the **Enchanted Forest**, which has
no services save for a warming hut. ~ Route 38, Red River.

Ski Rentals   To rent your sticks in Taos, visit **Cottam's Skiing
and Outdoor Shop**, where they will set you up with downhill and
cross-country skis, snowboards and snowshoes. ~ 207-A Paseo
del Pueblo Sur; 505-758-2822; www.cottamsskishops.com.

Angel Fire Resort Rental Shop at the mountain base rents
snowboards, snowshoes, skis and downhill and Nordic equipment. They also offer repairs and tunings. ~ Angel Fire; 800-469-
9327; www.angelfireresort.com. **SkiTech Discount Ski Rentals**,
convenient to Angel Fire, rents downhill and cross-country skis,
snowboards and snowblades. ~ North Angel Fire Road, Village
Center; 505-377-3213, 800-531-7547. For cross-country ski or
snowshoe rentals, lessons or a moonlight ski tour, check in at
Millers Crossing, a shop that runs the Nordic ski area at Enchanted Forest. ~ 417 West Main Street, Red River; 505-754-
2374, 800-966-9381; www.enchantedforestxc.com.

Beautiful terrain and varied trails make this a great area to see   **RIDING**
on horseback. Several ranches in the region outfit trips, including   **STABLES**
one run by a local tribe that leads trips on reservation land.

TAOS AREA   Ride with the American Indians on the Great Spirit's
property at the **Taos Indian Horse Ranch**, where tribal guides
lead groups of one to twenty riders on two-hour and longer tours
through parts of Taos Pueblo's mountainous 100,000-acre reservation. Children's rides are also available. Reservations needed.
~ 1 Miller Road, Taos Pueblo; phone/fax 505-758-3212.

ENCHANTED CIRCLE AREA   East of Taos, one-hour to half-day
trail rides are offered by **Roadrunner Tours, Ltd.** You can also take
an overnight camping trip on horseback. ~ Route 434, Angel
Fire; 505-377-6416, 800-377-6416.

The scenic mountain roads are perfect for bicycle rides of all   **BIKING**
lengths and levels.

TAOS AREA   A relatively difficult five-mile loop trail called **De-
visadero** allows for a good view of the town of Taos. Start across

from the El Nogal picnic area on Route 64 and get ready to climb 1300 vertical feet of elevation.

ENCHANTED CIRCLE AREA   La Jara Canyon (Route 64, on the horseshoe between Taos and Angel Fire) is a meandering two-mile climb to an alpine meadow that appeals especially to those new in the (bike) saddle.

Wait until late afternoon to take the three-mile **Cebolla Mesa Trail** (Route 522, about 18 miles north of Taos) for the splendid sunsets. Pedal near the rim of the 800-foot Rio Grande Gorge at Cebolla Mesa. Start the trip at the intersection of Cebolla Mesa Road and Route 522 and ride to the campground.

Bike Rentals & Tours   Gearing Up Bicycle Shop rents mountain and road bikes, sells new bicycles and accessories and has a repair shop on the premises. Shuttle services are also available to trails around the area. ~ 129 Paseo de Pueblo Sur, Taos; 505-751-0365; www.gearingupbikes.com. Along with mountain-bike rentals, **Native Sons Adventures** offers half- and full-day bike tours. The Pedal to Paddle excursion combines biking and river rafting in the Rio Grande Gorge. ~ 1033-A Paseo de Pueblo Sur; 505-758-9342, 800-753-7559; www.nativesonsadventures.com.

HIKING   From a gentle trail following a creek to a challenging ascent of New Mexico's highest mountain, 13,161-foot Wheeler Peak, the Enchanted Circle is filled with hiking possibilities.

TAOS AREA   Most hiking trails in the Taos area start from the Ski Valley. The ultimate hike is the seven-mile trail to the summit of **Wheeler Peak**. Though not particularly steep, the rocky trail is for conditioned hikers only because of the high altitude.

The **Carson National Forest** near Taos has more than 20 marked trails of varying difficulty that wind in and around some of the state's more magnificent scenic spots.

Yerba Canyon Trail (4 miles) begins in the aspens and willows, but snakes through fir and spruce trees as you approach the ridge. As its name would suggest, the trail follows Yerba Canyon for most of its length and makes a difficult 3600-foot climb before reaching Lobo Peak. The trailhead is on Taos Ski Valley Road, a mile up the hill from Upper Cuchilla Campground.

From roughly the same access point as the Yerba Canyon Trail is the **Gavilan Trail** (2.4 miles), a colorful though difficult hike that primarily follows alongside Gavilan Creek. Steep in its early section, the trip flattens out as it opens into meadows near the ridge.

In the Red River area you'll find the trail to **Middlefork Lake** (2 miles), which climbs 1200 vertical feet to a glacier lake.

Another way to the summit of Wheeler Peak, longer and more difficult than the route from the Taos Ski Valley, the **East Fork Trail** (10 miles) starts from a trailhead near the end of

Route 578, the road that serves the vacation cabin area south of Red River.

ENCHANTED CIRCLE AREA   Perhaps the most spectacular high-mountain hike in the Sangre de Cristos is the **Truchas Peak Trail** (11 miles), which starts at the Pecos Wilderness portal at Santa Barbara Campground off the High Road to Taos. The long, gradual ascent leads to the long ridgeline connecting the triple peaks of this 13,102-foot mountain where mountain sheep are often seen grazing on the alpine slopes.

Transportation

CAR

From Santa Fe, head north on **Route 285/84**. Near Española, **Route 68** leads north to Taos. **Route 64** weaves across the northern area of the state, passing through Taos and Cimarron. Note: Parts of the highway that cross high through Carson National Forest are closed during the winter. For New Mexico road conditions, call 800-432-4269.

AIR

Most visitors to the Taos area usually fly into **Albuquerque International Sunport** (see "Transportation" in Chapter Twelve). Both **Faust's Transportation** (505-758-3410, 888-830-3410) and **Twin Hearts Express** (505-751-1201, 800-654-9456) provide shuttle service to Taos from the Albuquerque airport.

Air charters to Taos are available; contact the **Taos Regional Airport**'s aviation services to make arrangements. ~ 505-737-9790; www.taosaviation.com.

BUS

TNM&O Coaches provides service to Taos from Albuquerque via Santa Fe. The line continues northeast to 1386 Paseo del Pueblo Sur in Taos and then to Raton. ~ 505-758-1144; www.tnmo.com.

CAR RENTALS

If you'd like to rent a car in Taos, try **Enterprise Rent A Car**. ~ 334 Paseo del Pueblo Sur; 505-737-0514, 800-325-8007. **United Chevrolet and Toyota** rents cars in Raton. ~ 505-445-3644.

PUBLIC TRANSIT

You need a car in this region because public transportation is nearly nonexistent. Most visitors flying into Albuquerque will rent a vehicle there. There is a bus system, **The Chili Line**, which provides limited service in Taos only. ~ 505-751-4459.

WALKING TOURS

Call **Taos Historical Walking Tours** if you'd like to stroll about the ancient streets of Taos with a local guide. Tours leave at 10:30 a.m. from the Mable Dodge Luhan House at 240 Morada Lane. Available Monday to Saturday from June through September. They also offer guide services for bus tours (fee). ~ Phone/fax 505-758-4020.

ELEVEN

Northwestern New Mexico

Half-wild horses gallop across the sagebrush desert around Chaco Canyon in northwestern New Mexico, a land of timeless mystery and profound loneliness. These beautiful creatures are owned, in a loose way, by Navajo herders, none of whom are seen. Traditional Navajo people choose to live in isolation, building their homes out of sight of main roads and other houses. The only signs of human habitation are the strange, scarecrowlike effigies marking the turnoffs to hidden dwellings.

Although deserted now, the San Juan Basin was the site of one of the great capital cities of the Americas over a thousand years ago. An Ancestral Pueblo city stood at the center of this trade empire that spanned the Southwest, linked by an impressive network of ancient "highways." Travelers who venture on dusty washboard roads across the Indian lands to Chaco Canyon will discover mysterious ruins, all that is left of this enigmatic ancient site. Chaco Canyon's fame has spread in recent years, enough to draw hundreds of visitors in a single day, but why the Ancestral Pueblo people chose to build in this desolate place remains a mystery (and why they abandoned it likewise a puzzle). A visit still provides an experience best described as mystical.

The Navajo nation, the largest and fastest-growing Indian tribe in the United States, controls most of the northwestern quadrant of New Mexico. Royalties from coal mining on the reservation provided the means of purchasing vast sprawls of arid rangeland east and south of the official reservation boundary. And while overpopulation, air pollution and economic depression characterize this part of the state, it also boasts colorful people, an incomprehensible language and fascinating folk ways. In short, the Navajo Nation is a true Third World country within the borders of the wealthiest nation on earth.

Other tribes inhabit the region, as well. The Jicarilla Apache Indian Reservation lies to the east of the Navajo lands, and farther south are a string of pueblos that have been occupied since the very first Spaniard, a shipwrecked accountant named Cabeza de Vaca ("Cow's Head"), stumbled upon them after trekking clear across Texas in 1527. Among the pueblos are Acoma, with its fairytale setting overlooking an enchanted landscape of strange rock formations from the top of a steep, isolated mesa, and ancient Zuni, where the people speak a language utterly unlike any other on earth. The American Indians have been here so long that their legends, passed on by spoken word from each generation to the next, contain eyewitness accounts of the volcanic eruptions that created the huge malpais, or lava badlands, on the outskirts of the town of Grants.

Nowhere is the memory of the Spanish soldiers who explored this region in the mid-1500s as vivid as in the mesas south of Route 40 between Grants and Gallup. Here, in the poor and remote villages of the Zuni Indian Reservation, lies the reality behind the "golden cities of Cibola" legend that lured the first explorers northward from Mexico City. Here, too, stand the cliffs of El Morro, where Indians, Spanish explorers and Anglo settlers alike carved messages in stone to create a "guest register" spanning 800 years.

The town of Grants, formerly the center of the uranium boom that swept northwestern New Mexico in the 1950s and died in the 1970s, is now little more than an inexpensive place for interstate truckers to spend the night. Yet its location, sandwiched between the lava badlands and the forested slopes of Mt. Taylor, is ideal for taking advantage of the wonders of the surrounding lands.

Near the western boundary of New Mexico, Gallup is the largest border town adjoining the Navajo Indian Reservation. It presents a cultural contrast as striking as any to be found along the Mexican border, as the interstate highway brings the outside world to the doorstep of the largest Indian nation in the United States.

Just over an hour's drive west of Albuquerque on Route 40, Grants is situated at the center of an intriguing array of places—the most ancient continuously inhabited pueblos in New Mexico, a vast and forbidding lava bed with ice caves that bear the marks of centuries of explorers, and a mountain held sacred in Navajo tradition.

Grants Area

The main reason to stop in Grants is to visit the easy-to-overlook interagency **Northwestern New Mexico Visitor Center** south of Exit 85 off Route 40. Occupying a 13,000-square-foot building with huge picture windows looking out to the quiet volcanic beauty of El Malpais and the Zuni Mountains, rangers here can help you plan your trip. There's an excellent bookstore, and the award-winning film *Remembered Earth* plays in the 60-seat auditorium. ~ 1900 East Santa Fe Avenue, Grants; 505-876-2783.

SIGHTS

More than 7000 native people reside in **Laguna Pueblo**, a pueblo that dates back to the turn of the 17th century. Old Laguna is situated on a hillside overlooking the interstate midway between Albuquerque and Grants; the centerpiece is **San Jose de Laguna Church**, a mission church in use since the pueblo's founding. Most Laguna residents live in modern villages scattered across the reservation. ~ 505-552-6654, fax 505-552-6941.

Travelers in no particular hurry and tired of dodging trucks on the interstate can catch a remnant of **Old Route 66** at Laguna.

The road parallels Route 40 and plays peekaboo with it all the way to the Acoma reservation.

Acoma Pueblo (Sky City) has a beautiful new cultural center at the base of Acoma Mesa. Opened in 2006, the stone building is the pride of the tribe and has a history museum, revolving exhibits about pottery and art, and an excellent restaurant serving Native-inspired foods. ~ 505-552-7860; www.skycity.com.

The village has been inhabited continuously since it was built on a solitary mesa top above a valley of stone pillars in the 12th century—earlier than the pueblos at Salinas, Bandelier or Pecos. New houses are still being built on the roofs of houses centuries old. There is no school bus service, electricity or running water on the mesa, so today only 15 families live in Sky City year-round. Most work as potters or pottery painters. More than 400 well-maintained homes in the old pueblo are used as spiritual retreats and summer houses by their owners, who live in modern reservation towns near the interstate. Shuttle buses carry visitors up the steep road, built by a motion-picture crew in 1969, for an hour-long guided tour of the pueblo. Those who choose to can hike back down on the short, steep trail used by Acoma residents for at least 800 years before the road was built. For schedule information, call the **Acoma Visitors Center**. Fee for photographing. Admission. ~ Located 15 miles east of Grants on Route 40, take Exit 89 and drive another 15 miles south on Indian Road 38; 800-747-0181, fax 505-552-7883; www.skycity.com.

Grants got its start as a railroad stop back when the region's major industry was carrot farming. In 1950 a Navajo sheepherder discovered a strange yellow rock that turned out to be radioactive, and Grants suddenly became the center of a uranium mining boom. Today, despite its prime location amid many of western New Mexico's best sightseeing highlights, Grants is a low-key highwayside town with few of the trappings of a tourist mecca.

Those who wish to learn more about the uranium era can do so at the **New Mexico Mining Museum**, where visitors ride an elevator down from the museum's main floor to explore an underground mine replica. The Grants Chamber of Commerce shares the same building. Closed Sunday. Admission. ~ 100 North Iron Street, Grants; 505-287-4802, 800-748-2142, fax 505-287-8224; www.grants.org, e-mail discover@grants.org.

Route 53, a quiet secondary highway, leads south and west of Grants to two national monuments—the first ever established in the United States and one of the newest. The highway continues across the Ramah Navajo and Zuni Indian reservations. Near the pueblo of Zuni, Route 602 goes north and returns to Route 40 at Gallup.

Malpais is Spanish for "badland," and the 114,277-acre **El Malpais National Monument** protects one of the largest lava

beds in New Mexico. The highways that border the lava flow—
Route 53 on the west and Route 117 on the east—are connected
by County Road 42, a rugged dirt road that runs along the west
and south perimeters; these roads should only be attempted in
a high-clearance vehicle. Though there are no developed campgrounds, primitive camping is allowed (free backcountry permits
are available at the monument's Information Center). Hiking opportunities in the national monument are discussed in the
"Hiking" section at the end of the chapter.

For a spectacular panoramic view of El Malpais, stop at
Sandstone Bluffs, an overlook 200 feet above the monument.
From here you'll spy Mt. Taylor to the north, the chain of craters
to the west and the lava bed–filled valley. ~ Route 117, ten miles
south of Route 40.

Stock up on maps and information at **El Malpais Information Center**, located on Route 53, 23 miles south of the Route

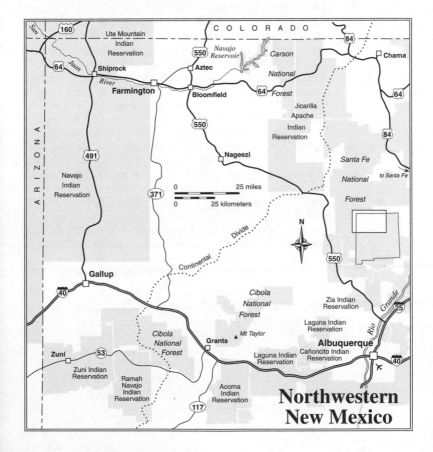

Northwestern
New Mexico

40 turnoff. A hiking trail, part of the Continental Divide National Scenic Trail, and geological exhibits are the center's highlights. Backcountry tent camping is allowed with a permit. ~ On Route 53 between mile markers 63 and 64; phone/fax 505-783-4774; www.nps.gov/elma.

At **El Morro National Monument**, a 15-minute drive west on Route 53 from Bandera Crater, a white-sandstone bluff marks the location of a 200,000-gallon waterhole. Atop the high bluff are the ruins of Atsinna, a 13th-century pueblo where about 1500 people lived. The Indians carved petroglyphs along the trail near the waterhole, starting a tradition that would last 800 years. When conquistador Don Juan de Oñate camped by the pool in 1605, returning after his trip to the Gulf of California, he scratched an inscription in the sandstone to memorialize his passing. Spanish explorers added their often-lengthy messages to the rock face until 1774. The absence of inscriptions for 75 years bears mute witness to the social turmoil surrounding the Mexican Revolution and the Mexican War. The first English inscription appeared in 1849, and soldiers, surveyors and pioneers continued to carve their names in the cliff. In 1906, President Theodore Roosevelt declared El Morro the nation's second national monument, and defacing the rock with its historical graffiti has been prohibited ever since. Admission. ~ HC 61 Box 43, Ramah; 505-783-4226, fax 505-783-4689; www.nps.gov/elmo.

LODGING

There are more than ten motels in town. The more modern franchise motels, located near the easternmost Grants exit from Route 40, include the **Best Western Inn and Suites**, with large rooms as well as amenities like an indoor swimming pool and a sauna. Breakfast is included in the rates. ~ 1501 East Santa Fe Avenue, Grants; 505-287-7901, 800-528-1234, fax 505-285-5751. BUDGET.

Farther west along Santa Fe Avenue are a number of independent motels, all budget. Several of them formerly belonged to

AUTHOR FAVORITE

A rewarding stop on a quick visit to El Malpais is **Bandera Crater and Ice Cave**, a privately owned tourist concession that might eventually be acquired as part of the monument. Separate easy trails take visitors to the crater of one of the volcanoes that made the lava field and to a subterranean ice cave, a lava tube where the temperature stays below freezing even on the hottest summer days. Admission. ~ Route 53, 25 miles south of Route 40; 505-783-4303, 888-423-2283, fax 505-783-4304; www.icecaves.com, e-mail icecaves@cia-g.com.

national chains, still recognizable under fresh coats of paint. The 24-room **Sands Motel** is a block off the main route and offers a little more peace and quiet. There are refrigerators in every room and a complimentary continental breakfast is served. ~ 112 McArthur Street, Grants; 505-287-2996, 800-424-7679, fax 505-287-2107. BUDGET.

A genuinely different bed-and-breakfast inn near Grants is the **Cimarron Rose Bed & Breakfast,** a ranchlike compound among the ponderosa pines at 7700 feet elevation on the Continental Divide. The location is secluded and ideal for hiking, mountain biking, cross-country skiing, birdwatching and honeymooning. Accommodations are in modern, comfortable rooms and suites with full kitchens. A continental breakfast featuring homemade muffins and other goodies is served. ~ 689 Oso Ridge Route, 30 miles southwest of Grants; 505-783-4770, 800-856-5776; www. cimarronrose.com. MODERATE TO DELUXE.

◀ HIDDEN

Along Grant's main drag is **El Cafecito,** a moderately sized joint. Patrons love the stuffed *sopaipillas* and big combo plates. Closed Sunday. ~ 820 West Santa Fe Avenue, Grants; 505-285-6229.

DINING

The **Mission Gallery Coffee House and Guest House,** located in a former church, is an unexpected and very welcome find in rather drab downtown Grants, better known as a uranium mining center than as a tourist haven. The artist-owners are recent transplants; there's plenty of art to browse in the café while you sip excellent coffee and pastries and chat with the friendly locals. The renovated guesthouse in the back is available for rent, if you decide to stay the night. ~ 422 West Santa Fe Avenue, Grants; 505-285-4632. BUDGET.

Fancier, but still inexpensive, is **El Jardin,** featuring more sophisticated Southwestern cuisine such as chimichangas, flautas, fajitas and *machaca* burritos. ~ 319 West Santa Fe Avenue, Grants; 505-285-5231. BUDGET.

For a more upscale night out in Grants, **La Ventana** is it. Dark and intimate, the one-room restaurant is decorated in a typical Southwestern motif, with kachinas on the walls and Indian rugs underfoot; there's a sunken bar upon entering. The food varies from steak and seafood to prime rib. Sandwiches at lunch might include turkey and guacamole on seven-grain bread. Closed Sunday. ~ 110½ Geis Street, Grants; 505-287-9393, fax 505-287-7490. MODERATE TO ULTRA-DELUXE.

BLUEWATER LAKE STATE PARK 🏃 🎣 🚤 🛥 🚣 Secluded in a valley halfway between Grants and Gallup, this picturesque reservoir dates back to the 1920s. The lake is stocked with trout, catfish and tiger musky. A variety of watersports is allowed; swim at your own risk. One of the several hiking trails here be-

PARKS

gins near the campground and leads down to a lush side canyon. Facilities include picnic tables, restrooms and showers. Day-use fee, $5. ~ Route 412, seven miles south of Exit 63 from Route 40, which is 19 miles west of Grants; 505-876-2391, fax 505-876-2307.

▲ There are 120 sites (14 with RV hookups); primitive camping is allowed near the lake. Fees per night are $10 for primitive sites, $10 for developed sites and $14 for hookups. Reservations: 877-664-7787 (available mid-May to mid-September).

RAMAH LAKE 🚣 ⛴ Mormon settlers created this small lake (pronounced "ray-mah") in the 1880s for irrigation. It operated for generations as a private fishing lake and has been open to the public since 1987. Fishing is good for trout; there are also a few bass, bluegill and even catfish. Facilities are limited to restrooms and a small boat dock. ~ Route 53 in Ramah. Ramah is near the eastern boundary of the Zuni Indian Reservation, 50 miles southwest of Grants. Information about the lake can be found at the Lewis Trade Center, which also issues fishing licenses; 505-783-4368, fax 505-783-4372.

▼▼▼▼▼▼▼▼▼▼
Gallup Area

Gallup is the largest town on the boundary of the Navajo Indian Reservation, which sprawls across vast tracts of New Mexico, Arizona and Utah. Most of the 200,000 Navajo people live scattered across the land, no home within view of another, on a reservation larger than the states of Connecticut, Vermont and Massachusetts put together. The Navajo people come to Gallup to shop and sell their jewelry, rugs and other handicrafts to traders. Today, as savvy collectors are visiting Gallup in search of good bargains on high-quality work by Navajo and Zuni artisans, the previously decrepit downtown area is being gentrified and occupied by fine art galleries and shops.

SIGHTS   The main feature at **Red Rock State Park** is its rodeo grounds nestled in a sheer-walled canyon. A small museum exhibits ancient, historic and contemporary American Indian arts and crafts, by artists from various tribes in the region. The park also contains archaeological sites dating back over a thousand years. Closed weekends. ~ Off Route 40, just east of Gallup; 505-722-3839, fax 505-726-1277; e-mail rrsp@ci.gallup.nm.us.

Gallup rests astride old Route 66 (called Historic 66 in Gallup) just 22 miles from the Arizona border. Located near both the Navajo and Zuni Indian reservations, this historic town of 20,000 bills itself as the "Gateway to Indian Country." Pawn shops, bars and a row of neon motels lend a hard edge to the local ambience, but the annual Inter-Tribal Ceremonial and large concentration of American Indians make it a prime place to view native crafts.

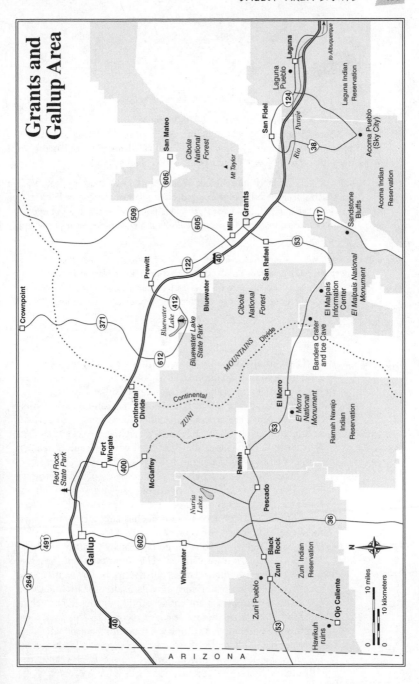

Grants and Gallup Area

ARIZONA

SCENIC DRIVE
Zuni Country

You can drive form Grants to Gallup—a distance of 65 miles—in less than an hour on Route 25 and see very little of interest. But if you're willing to turn this leg of your journey into an all-day trip, the paved two-lane route outlined here will show you some of New Mexico's best "hidden" sights.

EL MALPAIS   Taking Route 40 Exit 82 at Grants, head south on Route 53, which skirts the edge of the jagged, black lava flow known as El Malpais ("the badland"). Continue for 26 miles until you enter the ponderosa forest. Stop a minute at Sandstone Bluff for a panoramic view of the lava flow.

BANDERA CRATER AND ICE CAVE   Visit Bandera Crater and Ice Cave (page 432), a private concession within El Malpais National Monument. Take a hot hike up a gentle lava slope to the interior of the volcanic crater, then cool off in the ice cave. Allow one and a half hours.

HIDDEN ►   The **Gallup-McKinley County Chamber of Commerce** is a good place to pick up information on the area. While you're here, take a moment to visit the **Navajo Code Talkers Room**, which showcases these World War II heroes. Awards and photos chronicle the wartime experiences of the 200 code talkers, with particular attention paid to the first 29 inductees. Closed weekends. ~ 103 West Historic 66, Gallup; 505-722-2228; www.thegallupchamber. com, e-mail hwy66@cia-g.com.

Situated on Route 53 about 30 miles west of El Morro and 40 miles south of Gallup is **Zuni Pueblo**, the largest pueblo (population approximately 10,000) in New Mexico. The modern town of Zuni has evolved from a pueblo called Halona, which had been established for centuries when Coronado arrived in 1540, believing it to be one of the fabulously wealthy, mythical "Seven Golden Cities of Cibola." The town does not look like anything special at first glance, but the more you wander the back streets, the more antiquity reveals itself. Stone foundations 800 years old support many modern buildings in Zuni Pueblo, and crumbling stone storage sheds in people's yards may have been built long before Christopher Columbus first set sail. Keep your ears perked here, for the Zuni people speak a language unlike any other known American Indian dialect. Photography fee. ~ Route 53; 505-782-7283, fax 505-782-7002.

EL MORRO NATIONAL MONUMENT   Continue for 16 more miles on Route 53 to the turnoff for El Morro. Visit El Morro National Monument (page 432). Many tourists are content with a look at the inscriptions around the spring at the base of the cliff left by early Spanish and Anglo exploration parties, but take time to climb the petroglyph-lined trail up the back side of the rock and be surprised by the spectacular setting of the ancient Indian ruins on top. Allow one and a half hours.

ZUNI PUEBLO   Continue on Route 53 for 32 more miles to Zuni Pueblo, where it's best to park near the highway and see the pueblo on foot. Take a walk through the back streets of Zuni Pueblo (page 436), where modern construction materials blend seamlessly with stone walls that were ancient when conquistador Coronado saw them 460 years ago and mistook the pueblo for a legendary city of gold. Don't miss the tribal museum. Allow one hour.

HAWIKUH   If you have extra time, take the 12-mile unpaved road from Zuni south to the ruins of Hawikuh, an ancestral pueblo of the Zuni people. From Zuni, backtrack six miles on Route 53 and turn north on Route 602. A 25-mile drive through beautiful pink and white hills will bring you back to Route 40 at Gallup.

LODGING

Gallup has more motels comparable in quality and price to those in Grants. It also has one unique historic hotel that is both rustic and elegant. The **El Rancho Hotel** was built in 1937 by the brother of film producer D. W. Griffith. This is where movie stars stayed while shooting Westerns in the surrounding red-rock canyon country. Ronald Reagan (surely you remember him before he was president) checked in here in the 1940s. Other illustrious guests included John Wayne, Humphrey Bogart, Spencer Tracy, Katharine Hepburn, Alan Ladd and Kirk Douglas. Rich, dark wood polished to a gleam predominates in the larger-than-life two-story lobby. There are accommodations in both the old hotel and the modern annex next door. There's also an outdoor pool. ~ 1000 East Historic 66, Gallup; 505-863-9311, 800-543-6351, fax 505-722-5917; www.historicelranchohotel.com, e-mail el rancho@cnetco.com. BUDGET TO MODERATE.

◄ *HIDDEN*

The only lodging on the Zuni Reservation is the **Inn At Halona**, situated close enough to the pre-Columbian pueblo that guests feel like a part of the timeless village life. The eight-room inn looks like a family home, with a laundry room, private baths in six of the rooms, wireless internet and local Indian art on the walls. The owners enjoy sharing their knowledge of Zuni traditions, and each guest is given a small Zuni-produced craft as a memento of their stay. ~ 23-B Pia Mesa Road, Zuni; 505-782-4547, 800-752-3278,

fax 505-782-2155; www.halona.com, e-mail halona@nm.net.
MODERATE.

DINING Take a break for superb espresso and coffee drinks, baked goods and revolving art exhibits at **The Coffee House**, a much-needed respite from truckstop fare along Route 40. Salads and sandwiches are served at lunch and dinner, along with New Mexican favorites such as *posole*. ~ 203 West Coal Avenue, Gallup; 505-726-0291. BUDGET.

New Mexican food is served up at **Genaro's**, a well-hidden café specializing in stuffed *sopaipillas*. Closed Sunday and Monday, two weeks at the end of June and two weeks at the end of December. ~ 600 West Hill Avenue, Gallup; 505-863-6761. BUDGET.

New Mexican beef dishes such as *carne adovada* and green-chile steak appear on the menu at **Panz Alegra**. They also serve Italian fare and seafood at dinner. Closed Sunday. ~ 1201 East Historic 66, Gallup; 505-722-7229. MODERATE TO DELUXE.

SHOPPING Prices for American Indian wares are normally lower in Gallup than in Santa Fe or Albuquerque, but quality varies. State law protects American Indians and collectors alike from fraud in the sale of American Indian–made goods, but it can still require a discerning eye to distinguish handmade crafts from those made in factories that employ American Indians or determine which items are genuinely old as opposed to "antiqued." Still, the region has been a major American Indian arts-and-crafts trading center for more than a century, and it is possible to find valuable turn-of-the-20th-century Germantown blankets and forgotten pieces of "old pawn" turquoise and silver jewelry.

The largest concentration of American Indian traders is found along Historic 66 between 2nd and 3rd streets. The oldest shop on the block is **Richardson's**, where the modest facade gives little hint of the treasures in several large rooms inside. This is one of several downtown pawn shops that serve as "banks" for the Navajo people, continuing the tradition whereby the American

JEWELRY CENTRAL

American Indian jewelry is said to be the leading industry in Gallup. The number of wholesalers, galleries and pawn shops specializing in jewelry (and rugs) supports this claim, as does the presence of buyers and collectors from all over the world. As the biggest town on the edge of the Navajo Indian Reservation and the nearest town to Zuni (the largest of New Mexico's Indian pueblos), Gallup is the natural location for trading companies dealing directly with American Indian artists and craftsworkers.

Indians store their individual wealth in the form of handmade jewelry, using it as needed for collateral and redeeming it for ceremonials. Closed Sunday. ~ 222 West Historic 66, Gallup; 505-722-4762, fax 505-722-9424.

Those interested in the materials and techniques of making American Indian jewelry can learn about them on a visit to **Thunderbird Jewelry Supply**. Closed Sunday. ~ 1907 West Historic 66, Gallup; 505-722-4323.

Recently, galleries have been appearing along Coal Street, Gallup's main drag situated a block south of Historic 66. Several of them emphasize contemporary American Indian and Southwestern arts. For jewelry along Coal Street, try **Indian Jewelers Supply Co.** Closed Sunday. ~ 601 East Coal Street; 505-722-4451.

Zuni Pueblo has several well-stocked American Indian galleries, particularly **Turquoise Village**. Closed Sunday. ~ Route 53; 505-782-5522, 800-748-2405.

There's not much in terms of nightlife in Gallup, but there are a few bars and sports clubs mostly within local chain hotels around town. The **City Lights Lounge and Sports Bar** is located in the Holiday Inn. Closed Sunday. ~ 2915 West Historic 66; 505-722-2201. Another is **Rookies Sports Bar** at the Best Western Inn & Suites. ~ 3009 West Historic 66; 505-722-2221.

NIGHTLIFE

ZUNI LAKES The Zuni tribe operates several fishing lakes in the hills of the reservation. (A permit must be obtained from tribal headquarters on Route 53 in Zuni, Mustang in Zuni Lewis Trading Post in Ramah or Wal-Mart or Lowes in Gallup.) Boating is allowed at three of the lakes (Blackrock, Pescado and Nutria Lakes, although Nutria Lakes numbers one through three have been dry for over a decade), though gasoline motors are prohibited. Blackrock Lake has picnic facilities and a playground. Boating fee, $2. ~ Blackrock Lake is three miles east of Zuni off Route 53. Eustace Lake is within Zuni village limits. Nutria Lakes are seven to eleven miles north of Route 53 going toward Ramah. Ojo Caliente is 17 miles south of the Zuni village on Route 2. Pescado Lake is 17 miles east of Zuni off Route 53; 505-782-5851, fax 505-782-2726; www.ashiwi.org.
▲ There are primitive sites at Blackrock Lake, Ojo Caliente, Nutria Lakes, No. 4 and Eustace Lake. Campgrounds at six of the lakes are open all year; $10 per night and $5 each additional night.

PARKS

RED ROCK STATE PARK Named for the red sandstone cliffs that lend an austere beauty to the surrounding area, the 640-acre park's main feature is its rodeo grounds, which can be found clinging to the side of the canyon. There are also picnic tables, restrooms, showers, a museum and trails. The park is the site of several important Indian events, concerts and community activities, including the annual Inter-Tribal Ceremonial, the largest powwow in the United States. Closed weekends. ~ Located just off Route 40 east of Gallup; 505-722-3839, fax 505-726-1277; e-mail rrsp@ci.gallup.nm.us.

▲ There are 150 sites with hookups; $18 per night.

Four Corners Area

Farmington is the natural base camp for sightseeing in the Four Corners area, the sole hub in the continental United States where four states— New Mexico, Arizona, Colorado and Utah—meet. Three rivers, the San Juan, Animas and LaPlata also converge here, dispelling the notion that this is dry, dusty desert country. In fact, Farmington was founded on farming, hence its name, although the easygoing town now has industry and mining at its financial base.

The true highlight of the region, however, is its rich American Indian history. The area abounds in Pueblo ruins and offers numerous museums that provide a glimpse into the religious and cultural lives of the ancient Navajo, Chaco and Anasazi tribes.

SIGHTS   Start your sightseeing tour of the region on Route 491, about 30 miles southwest of Farmington at **Shiprock Peak**. Solidified lava and igneous rock comprise this neck of a volcano, which can be seen by air from more than 100 miles away. The towering Ship Rock rises from a great stretch of nothing but sand and rock. (American Indians called it a "rock with wings.") The site has no services. ~ Off Route 491.

When you're done admiring the natural beauty at Shiprock pinnacle, head north on Route 491 until you reach the town of Shiprock. From here, it's another 30 miles east on Route 64 to the laidback town of Farmington.

Take your brochures and maps to **Orchard Park**, in the center of downtown, where you can peruse your options. ~ Main and Orchard streets, Farmington.

For an overview of the area's cultural and outdoor offerings, check in at the **Farmington Museum and Visitors Center at Gateway Park** (505-599-1174, fax 505-326-7572). There's an oil and gas exhibit, a children's gallery, a reconstruction of a 1930s trading post and an exhibit of the geologic history of the San Juan Basin, as well as traveling exhibits. Also here is the **Farmington Convention and Visitors Bureau**, where you can get your fill of town literature. Closed Sunday. ~ 3041 East Main Street, Farmington; 505-326-7602, 800-448-1240; www.farmingtonnm.org, e-mail fmncvb@earthlink.net.

Next you'll find **Salmon Ruin**, which has remains from an 11th-century pueblo, including a large kiva, built by the Chaco people. You can take a virtual tour of remote outlying Chaco villages in the visitors center. Ongoing stabilization of the site's exposed structures continues to this day. Admission. ~ 6131 Route 64, Bloomfield; 505-632-2013, fax 505-632-8633; www.salmon ruins.com, e-mail sreducation@sisna.com.

At Salmon Ruin is **Heritage Park**, a re-creation of habitation units, from sand dune campgrounds to tepees and hogans, representing man's occupation in the San Juan Valley. The on-site museum houses regional artifacts, too.

Driving from Farmington northeast on Route 550 brings you to the charming town of **Aztec**, which boasts ancient Indian ruins and turn-of-the-20th-century buildings. Aztec's modern-day renaissance, which took place in the 1890s, still shows its Victorian influence in the downtown area. For more information, call the **Aztec Chamber of Commerce & Visitors Center**. Closed Sunday. ~ 110 Ash Street, Aztec; 505-334-9551, 800-334-9551, fax 505-334-7648; www.aztecchamber.com, e-mail aztec@digii.net.

Your first stop on a whirlwind tour of Aztec should begin at the old City Hall, where the **Aztec Museum** displays all kinds of bric-a-brac, like minerals and rocks, Victorian fashions, sleighs and buggies, tools used by the early settlers, an oilfield exhibit and a pioneer village with an authentically furnished post office, general store, bank and log cabin. Closed Sunday. Admission. ~ 125 North Main Street, Aztec; 505-334-9829.

Strolling along Aztec's Main Street, you'll see many turn-of-the-20th-century buildings, including the **Odd Fellows Hall** (107 South Main Street) and **Miss Gail's Inn** (300 South Main Street).

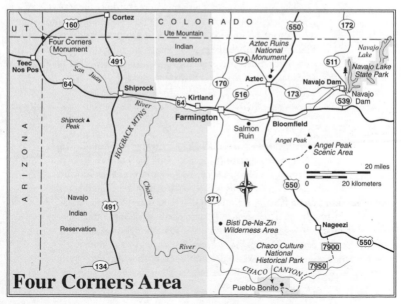

Four Corners Area

On a side street is the **Presbyterian Church** (201 North Church Street), which was built of adobe brick in 1889.

Another building worth a look-see is the **Denver & Rio Grande Western Railway Depot**. No tracks remain on the site of this commercial building turned residence, but the 1915 structure is a classic reminder of the railway's heyday. ~ 408 North Rio Grande, Aztec.

Aztec's buildings seem perfectly modern in comparison to the ancient **Aztec Ruins National Monument**, a major prehistoric settlement chock full of 12th-century pueblo ruins, including a restored kiva. (Despite its misleading name, no Aztec Indians ever inhabited this area.) Both the Chaco civilization to the south and the Mesa Verde settlement to the north probably influenced Aztec's development. Admission. ~ Ruins Road, Aztec; 505-334-6174; www.nps.gov/azru, e-mail azru-interpretation@nps.gov.

A visit to the ruins is a must, for its sheer accessibility as much as for its wonders. First take the self-guided trail that begins just outside the visitors center. You'll come upon the **West Ruin** and the magnificently restored **Great Kiva**. West Ruin could be compared to a present-day apartment building because as many as 300 people may have lived there at a single time; most unusual is a line of green sandstone on one outer wall. The kiva, an underground chamber that's traditionally used for religious ceremonies, was carefully constructed of sandstone blocks from materials that were hand-carried from quarries miles away. The kiva was excavated in 1921 and reconstructed about 12 years later.

The open plaza area was the center of daily life in Aztec. Wandering north out of the main ruins takes you to the **Hubbard Site**, a kiva that's unique in that it has three concentric circular walls. Presumably this building was used for religious ceremonies (it's now back-filled for protection). Another tri-walled kiva, largely unexcavated, exists in a nearby mound.

FOUR CORNERS MONUMENT

There's something both silly and irresistible about driving to **Four Corners** to stick each foot in a different state (Colorado and Utah) and each hand in still two others (Arizona and New Mexico) while someone takes your picture from a scaffolding. But then, this is the only place in the United States where you can simultaneously "be" in four different states. The inevitable Navajo crafts booths offer up jewelry, T-shirts, paintings, sandpaintings, fry bread and lemonade—a splendid way to make something festive out of two intersecting lines on a map. Fee. ~ From Farmington, head west on Route 64 until you cross the Arizona/New Mexico border. At Teec Nos Pos, Arizona, head north on Route 160 for about ten miles.

Off the beaten path is the **East Ruin** and its annex, thought to be the second and later civilization at Aztec. Both are largely un-excavated and must be viewed from a distance. Adjacent to the Aztec ruins is a tree-lined picnic area, a nice shady place for a snack or repose after wandering through the ancient cultural center.

To return to ruin sightings like desolate Angel Peak, you must backtrack to Aztec or take Route 550 south through Bloomfield toward Albuquerque.

Angel Peak, a multimillion-year-old geologic formation, is a sacred dwelling place to the Navajos. A five-mile unpaved, dirt road along the rim offers great views of the pastel-hued mesas and buttes. Camping and picnicking are allowed, though no water is available. After Angel Peak, continue on to Chaco Canyon, the epicenter of Anasazi life.

Reflecting the simplicity of lifestyle and slower pace of the region's people, the lodging choices in and around Four Corners are characterized by their cleanliness and efficiency.

LODGING

Cast-iron sculptures honoring the "ancient ones" decorate the walls of the peach-hued rooms at the **Anasazi Inn**. Handsome quilt prints in a Southwestern scheme and spotless bathrooms are reason enough to try this centrally located lodge. ~ 903 West Main Street, Farmington; 505-325-4564, fax 505-326-0732. BUDGET.

If bigger is better, then **Best Western Inn and Suites** has something over its chain competitors on the same street. Extra-large rooms are great for families and help give the inn a leg up. A sizable indoor pool in a tropical setting may make you forget you're in desert country. There's also a fitness center and a game room for children. ~ 700 Scott Avenue, Farmington; 505-327-5221, 800-600-5221, fax 505-327-1565; www.newmexico-innand suites.com, e-mail lenore@swibestwestern.com. MODERATE.

With just 36 rooms, the **Farmington Lodge** falls into the small, no-frills category. Most of the well-maintained rooms have refrigerators. ~ 1510 West Main Street, Farmington; 505-325-0233, fax 505-325-6574. BUDGET.

Kokopelli's Inn may be the most "hidden" accommodation in this guidebook. The owner, a consulting geologist, originally built the cave-cum-B&B as his office—but clients worried about transporting their maps and gear down the trail, which follows the cliff's edge. In fact, the single-unit bed and breakfast is in a cave beneath 70 feet of rock, with its entrance in a sheer sandstone cliff outside of town. The luxury guest apartment is complete with some custom furniture, Indian rugs, VCR, DVD player, CD stereo system, microwave oven with stove and washer/dryer, as well as a stone jacuzzi under a waterfall shower. Make reservations well in advance. Closed end of November through February. ~ 3204 Crestridge Drive, Farmington; 505-326-2461, fax 505-325-9671;

◀ HIDDEN

www.bbonline.com/nm/kokopelli, e-mail kokoscave@hotmail.com.
ULTRA-DELUXE.

The charming **Casa Blanca Inn**, set high on the bluff above
the San Juan River, is a slice of unexpected luxury in down-to-
earth Farmington. There are four hacienda-style rooms and two
casitas off a peaceful courtyard. All feature fine linens, refrigerators, coffeemakers and coffee grinders, cable TV, phones and
wireless internet. A full Southwestern breakfast is served. There's
an onsite gift shop that sells Navajo rugs and other local arts and
crafts. ~ 505 East La Plata Street, Farmington; 505-327-6503,
800-550-6503, fax 505-326-5680; www.casablancanm.com, e-
mail info@casablancanm.com. MODERATE.

Its location on a busy highway is definitely a drawback, but
you can shut out most of the world's noise in the 20 tidy rooms
of the **Enchantment Lodge**. ~ 1800 West Aztec Boulevard, Aztec;
505-334-6143, 800-847-2194, fax 505-334-9234. BUDGET.

Most people come to Aztec for the mysterious ruins. But a
visit to its historic Main Street is well worth your time. Smack in
the middle of the main drag is **Miss Gail's Inn**, a 1905 palace of
antiques. The Country Victorian rooms—some with partial
kitchens—are large enough for multiday living. Weekly rates available fall and winter are a bargain. It's a good place to hang your
hat if you plan on thoroughly exploring the Four Corners area.
Breakfast included. ~ 300 South Main Street, Aztec; 505-334-
3452, 888-534-3452, fax 505-334-9664. BUDGET TO MODERATE.

DINING

Spinach-and-feta-cheese croissants served piping hot out of the
oven, spicy green chili chicken enchiladas, and cornbread are only
a few of the healthy, homemade delectables at **Something Special
Bakery & Tea Room**. It's open for breakfast and lunch. Vegetarian entrées available. Closed Saturday and Sunday. Call ahead. ~
116 North Auburn Avenue, Farmington; 505-325-8183, fax 505-
327-2859. BUDGET.

Among the many eateries offering wholesome "American cuisine" in downtown Farmington, **TJ's Downtown Diner** is just a
tad better. Along with homemade soups and pies, TJ's also features
daily Mexican specials. Breakfast and lunch only. Closed Sunday.
~ 119 East Main Street, Farmington; 505-327-5027. BUDGET.

How hot do you like your green chile? For authentic Mexican
cuisine, try the **El Charro Cafe**. ~ 737 West Main Street, Farmington; 505-327-2464. BUDGET. Its primary competition is the **Los
Rios Café**, which serves New Mexican cuisine as well as burgers
and fries. Closed Sunday. ~ 915 Farmington Avenue, Farmington;
505-325-5699. BUDGET.

Nestled in Farmington's downtown, **3 Rivers Eatery and
Brewhouse** is a local favorite with an extensive menu and vibrant

ambience. Down an on-site brewed beer and grab a steak, burger or pasta dish. With high tin ceilings, beer coasters on the wall and friendly chatter in the air, 3 Rivers is a great place to get some grub and gab. ~ 101 East Main Street, Farmington; 505-324-2187, fax 505-327-1963; www.threeriversbrewery.com, e-mail john@threeriversbrewery.com. MODERATE TO DELUXE.

SHOPPING

Try the **Foutz Trading Co.** for splendid Navajo crafts such as silver jewelry and intricately beaded barrettes. Closed Sunday. ~ Route 64, Shiprock; 505-368-5790; www.foutztrade.com.

If you've been on the road for awhile and could use some "herbal fitness," stop in at **Herbal Alternatives** and pick up natural remedies for all that ails you. Closed Sunday. ~ 6510 East Main Street, Farmington; 505-327-3205.

NIGHTLIFE

Farmington is not exactly a late-night town, but it does boast a few nightclubs with live music. Check out the **Top Deck Bar** for live country on Wednesday, Friday and Saturday, karaoke on Tuesday, and rock-and-roll on Thursday. Cover charge Wednesday, Friday and Saturday. ~ 515 East Main Street, Farmington; 505-327-7385.

Lively and colorful dramas, including *Black River Traders*, are performed mid-June to mid-August at the **Lions Wilderness Park Amphitheater**. ~ College Boulevard, Farmington; 505-326-7602, 877-599-3331 (tickets).

NAVAJO LAKE STATE PARK   **PARKS**

This idyllic spot offers boating, fishing, swimming and even scuba diving at three recreation areas—Pine River, Sims Mesa and the San Juan River. Navajo Lake's sparkling waters and nearly 200 miles of shoreline is chock full of cold and warm water species of game fish, including trophy trout, catfish, pike, Kokanee salmon and bass. The park features a visitors center, marinas, picnic sites and restrooms. Day-use fee, $5. ~ Take Route 173 to Route 511, 23 miles east of Aztec; 505-632-2278, fax 505-632-8159.

> Navajo Lake remains New Mexico's second-largest lake.

▲ There are 157 sites at Pine (54 with electricity and 9 with full hookups), 46 at Sims Mesa (24 with hookups) and 47 (23 with hookups) at Cottonwood Campground on the San Juan River. Fees are $10 per night for standard sites, $14 for electricity and $18 per night for full hookups. Reservations: 877-664-7787.

ANGEL PEAK SCENIC AREA   A heavenly looking 40-million-year-old geologic formation appears to be suspended within a lovely colored canyon. The five-mile-long road around the canyon rim offers fine vistas of the buttes and badlands in this land of the

Text continued on page 448.

In the Land
of Ancient Ones

An intricate highway system, irrigation ditches and 13 great house ruins have led archaeologists to speculate that Chaco was once a center for the Ancestral Pueblo civilization. The canyon has remained in a comparatively pristine state largely because access is difficult on rutted dirt roads. A debate continues on whether the road should be upgraded, but those who believe Chaco remains in better shape because of its inaccessibility have prevailed so far. Unless you're driving an expensive sports car or the road is slippery from rain, it's worth the bumpy ride to view 13 major ruins and the remains of a culture suspected to have begun in Chaco around A.D 900. Note: Services are virtually nonexistent, so come fully prepared with food, water and gas.

The fascinating civilization of 1000 years ago has left in its wake traces of advanced art forms like pottery and weaving. The Chaco Ancestral Pueblo people were farmers who probably fled the drought-stricken area in the 13th century. Chaco is considered to be the center of Ancestral Pueblo culture (the developed road network tells us that) and religious ceremony (as all the kivas left behind indicate). Site excavation began in the late 1890s and continues today through the University of New Mexico's Chaco Research Institute.

Park rangers conduct guided walks through the cultural sites in Chaco Canyon, or you can grab a trail guide from the visitors center and chart your own path through this eerily silent land. Self-guided trails are found at Pueblo Bonito, Chetro Ketl and Casa Rinconada. Admission. ~ Located 54 miles south of Bloomfield via Route 550 and County Roads 7900 and 7950; 505-786-7014 ext. 221, fax 505-786-7061; www.nps.gov/chcu.

Closest to the visitors center is the partially excavated **Una Vida** ruin, with its five kivas and 150 rooms. Because it was built on a mound, Una Vida appears higher than it actually is. Petroglyphs and remains from hogans huddle in the surrounding rock. From the paved park road is the **Hungo Pavi** ruin, an easy trek from the car. Down the road is **Chetro Ketl**, with its estimated 500 rooms and

16 kivas one of the largest Chacoan villages. Chetro Ketl's expansive plaza section is thought to be typical of great houses of that time.

A short jaunt in the other direction from the same trailhead brings you to the amazing **Pueblo Bonito**, which was probably the heart and soul of Chaco. While there were probably less than a thousand permanent residents, those who lived here are thought to have been elite priestly leaders who were skilled in astronomical tracking and determining the dates of ceremonies that would bring people from the whole San Juan Basin. The four-story stone masonry complex is obviously the product of painstaking craftsmanship.

Pueblo del Arroyo, a high-standing D-shaped house, with its 280 rooms and 20 kivas, is found nearby along the paved road. **Kin Kletso**, which was built in two stages, had 100 rooms and five kivas. It may have risen as high as three stories. Take the trail that begins here to the prehistoric **Jackson Stairs**, one of the more impressive stairways in the Anasazi world, and try to figure out the farming terraces of the Anasazi.

Past Kin Kletso is Casa Chiquita, where the hike from the central canyon to the unexcavated great house of **Peñasco Blanco** is well worth the effort. On the south side of the paved park road is **Casa Rinconada**, one of the largest kivas in the Southwest. A trail that begins here winds to the South Mesa and the great house of **Tsin Kletsin**, a structure seven rooms strong.

The more adventurous and archaeology-minded can wander in search of "outlier" sites of Chaco Canyon, like Pueblo Pintado and Kin Ya-ah. Free backcountry permits (required before setting out) and directions are available from the visitors center. Camping is also permitted here, but you should be well prepared: Campers in Chaco Canyon must come equipped with plenty of provisions, although water is available. The closest groceries and gas are 21 miles away, most of them on dirt roads, near the County Road 7900 turnoff on Route 550. Gallo Campground is located about one mile east of the visitors center. There are 49 sites, including 5 RV sites (no hookups); $10 per night.

"sacred ones." The only facilities are picnic tables, fire rings and restrooms. ~ Take Route 550 to the Angel Peak turnoff, about 17 miles southeast of Bloomfield; 505-599-8900, fax 505-599-8998.

▲ There are nine primitive sites, no water; no fee.

BISTI DE-NA-ZIN WILDERNESS AREA   🚶🐎   Nearly 45,000 acres of eroded shale, clay and sandstone spires, mesas and sculpted rock that defy description were naturally sculpted in this former inland sea. Large reptiles and mammals were thought to walk these lands about 70 million years ago; fossils and petrified wood are all that remain in this desolate area of badlands. No developed trails, facilities or signs mar this protected wilderness, pronounced "bis-tye." No bicycles allowed. ~ Route 371, 36 miles south of Farmington; 505-599-8900, fax 505-599-8998.

▲ Primitive camping allowed, no water; no fee.

▼▼▼▼▼▼▼▼▼▼▼▼
Outdoor Adventures

FISHING

A variety of catches are found in the lakes of the Four Corners area, so try your luck with the plentiful trout or one of the other fish often caught here. Equipment is available at some sites; others are more remote.

FOUR CORNERS AREA   The San Juan River at the base of the Navajo Dam in **Navajo Lake State Park** is the site of quality waters teeming with trout. One of the largest lakes in New Mexico, Navajo provides angling opportunities for bluegill, bass, trout, pike and catfish. Try **Born-n-Raised on the San Juan River** for flyfishing equipment and guide services. ~ 1791 Route 173, Navajo Dam; 505-632-2194. **Rizuto's Fly Shop** rents flyfishing gear and also offers half- and full-day fishing float trips on the San Juan River. ~ 1796 Route 173, Navajo Dam; 505-632-3893.

Morgan Lake produces trophy largemouth bass, and is also great for catfish. ~ Four miles south of Kirtland, next to Four Corners Power Plant.

SKIING

Who needs a resort? Excellent cross-country skiing can be found on county and national forest roads—minus the crowds and lift lines.

GRANTS AREA   Primitive roads on **Mt. Taylor** are used for cross-country skiing in winter. For information on routes and conditions, contact the Cibola National Forest–Mt. Taylor District Ranger Station in Grants. Closed weekends. ~ 1800 Lobo Canyon Road; 505-287-8833, fax 505-287-4924.

BIKING

Opportunities for mountain biking abound in a region with beautiful scenery and many unpaved roads.

GRANTS AREA   Mountain biking is allowed on trails and roads throughout the **Cibola National Forest**. Many bikers recently have been testing their skills on the **Mt. Taylor summit trail** and the **McGaffey region**. Trails in the BLM **Conservation Area** on Route 117 near El Malpais National Monument are also open to bikers.

FOUR CORNERS AREA There's only one trail in Chaco Canyon where you can ride nonmotorized bikes, and that's the mile-and-a-half **Wijiji Trail**.

Northwestern New Mexico boasts several national forests and monuments with trails for hiking. From 11,000-foot peaks to fascinating archaeological sites to rugged, trailless wilderness areas, there's something for everyone to explore. All distances are one way unless otherwise noted.

HIKING

GRANTS AREA Unpaved roads lead through **Cibola National Forest** to within a mile of the summit of **Mt. Taylor**, the 11,301-foot mountain that dominates the skyline north of Grants. A trail that starts near the junction of Forest Roads 193 and 501 climbs more than 2000 feet up the southwest side of the peak to the mountain-top in three miles. Another, the Gooseberry Trail, begins near La Mosca Peak Overlook and ascends the north ridge to reach the summit of Mt. Taylor in a mile.

Though there are no defined trails at **Sandstone Bluffs** you can descend to the bluffs' base for a trek alongside the lava beds.

Other trails into El Malpais start along unpaved County Road 42, which skirts the western and southern edges of the monument. The road requires a high-clearance vehicle. The **Big Tubes Area Route** (2-mile loop) leads to Big Skylight Cave, which then branches off to Caterpillar Collapse, Seven Bridges and Four Window Cave; Big Skylight and Four Window are both entrances to the same immense lava tube, part of a system that is 17 miles long. For more information, call 505-783-4774, fax 505-285-5661.

AUTHOR FAVORITE

In the spring and fall months, El Malpais National Monument south of Grants presents some unusual hiking possibilities. One of my memorable adventures in the lava lands was hiking the **Acoma-Zuni Trail** (7.5 miles), which crosses the lava fields between routes 53 and 117. Said to be part of a trade route that linked the Zuni and Acoma pueblos in ancient times, the trail is level, but the lava is so rough and uneven that even a short walk from either trailhead will prove quite strenuous. If you decide to do the entire seven and a half miles, plan for a full day of hiking or arrange a two-vehicle shuttle.

Transpsortation

CAR

To the west of Albuquerque on **Route 40**, it is a two-hour drive to Grants and another hour to Gallup. From Gallup, head north on **Route 491**, which meets with Route 64 near Shiprock. **Route 64** skirts across the northern edge of New Mexico, passing through the Four Corners area and across to Chama. For New Mexico road conditions, call 800-432-4269.

AIR

Most visitors will fly into **Albuquerque International Sunport**; see Chapter Twelve for more information.

Charter service to **Four Corners Regional Airport** (505-599-1395) in Farmington is provided by Mesa Airlines, Great Lake Airlines, United Express and America West Express.

BUS

Greyhound Bus Lines (800-231-2222; www.greyhound.com) provides service to Grants at McDonald's, 1700 West Santa Fe Avenue; and in Gallup, 827 East Montoya Boulevard, 505-863-3761.

TNM&O Coaches provides service from Albuquerque to Farmington. ~ 101 East Animas Street, Farmington; 505-325-1009.

TRAIN

Amtrak's "Southwest Chief" stops in Gallup. ~ 210 East Historic 66, Gallup; 800-872-7245; www.amtrak.com.

CAR RENTALS

A car is essential to touring this area. If you are flying in and out of Albuquerque, rent a car there (see Chapter Twelve for information). For rental cars in northwestern New Mexico, try **Enterprise Rent A Car**. Closed Sunday. ~ 2111 West Historic 66, Gallup; 505-722-5820, 800-736-8227.

For rentals at the Four Corners Regional Airport in Farmington, try **Avis Rent A Car** (800-331-1212), **Budget Rent A Car** (800-527-0700) or **Hertz Rent A Car** (800-654-3131).

TWELVE

Albuquerque and Central New Mexico

Billy the Kid once roamed this area. Now you can, too. The vast ranchland plains east of the Rocky Mountains haven't changed much since the Kid rode into legend more than a century ago. But Albuquerque is another story. Just another small town on the banks of the Rio Grande downriver from Santa Fe in the heyday of the Wild West, it has been transformed into a bustling metropolis boasting a unique mosaic of lifestyles and cultures. This is the central New Mexico that intrigues the traveler: a mixture of the wild and the sublime, the cowboy and the Indian, the small town and the big city, the past and the present.

History is part of the enchantment of Albuquerque and its environs; geography is another. In fact, the setting is one thing the residents love most about their home. Sandia Peak towers a mile above the eastern city limit. Rural farmland follows the Rio Grande south. And to the west is a wide and beautiful emptiness. Visitors are often surprised by the abruptness with which the city gives way to wilderness at Albuquerque's edge. Route 40 plunges into a parched, overgrazed, alkaline high-desert wasteland that gradually reveals its stark beauty in twisting arroyos and jagged black-lava fields with fortresslike rock mesas and solitary mountains rising like islands from an arid sea.

Central New Mexico is a compelling combination of the high, cool forests of the Rocky Mountains to the north and the rocky, sunbaked Chihuahuan Desert stretching a thousand miles to the south. If you don't like the weather, you can just move on. In June, the hottest month of the year, when air conditioning becomes essential in Albuquerque, a short drive into the mountains offers shade, cool streams and occasional patches of unmelted snow. In January, skiers can enjoy nearby slopes and then return to lower elevations where snowfalls are infrequent and light.

The mix of mountain coolness, desert dryness and southern latitude produces evening temperatures that drop to about 50° even in mid-summer and daytime highs above freezing in the dead of winter. In autumn, people watch the month-long procession of bright-gold foliage gracefully descending from the mountain heights to the cottonwood bosquet along the rivers. In springtime, new greenery spreads slowly up the slopes toward the sky.

If you're headed toward Santa Fe from Albuquerque, consider taking the Turquoise Trail (Route 14), a more relaxed and less congested route that crosses the rugged San Pedro Mountains and offers a handful of interesting sights, including a restored old mission church and an old mining town.

Cultural contrasts are just as dramatic. This is a melting pot of Navajo and Pueblo Indians whose lifestyles were upset by the Spanish exploration that began in the 1500s. Also mixed in are Norteño descendants of Spanish and Mexican colonists (New Mexico was a province of Mexico from 1821 until the 1848 treaty that ended the Mexican War with the United States) and Anglos who began settling here in the early 1800s. All these cultures come together in modern-day Albuquerque, a polyglot of a city where ancient ceremonies and futuristic technological research, fiestas and hot-air balloon races, and cowboys and entrepreneurs exist side by side.

Equally fascinating sights await beyond Albuquerque's city limits. The eastern plains, where most travelers stop only to exit the interstate for gasoline and a bite to eat, offer beaches and water sports on several large, manmade lakes along the Pecos and Canadian rivers. You'll find the grave of Billy-boy himself in the town of Fort Sumner, along with sites long abandoned to wind, weather and wildflowers (but just aching to be discovered).

Near the small town of Mountainair at the foot of the Manzano Mountains, sightseers can explore Spanish and Indian ruins from centuries past, one-time American Indian trade centers and headquarters for missionary efforts during the colonial era. Outside Socorro, located just off the interstate, nature lovers visiting between November and March can witness the spectacular congregation of tens of thousands of snow geese, Canada geese and sandhill cranes.

Faint remnants of conquest can be found throughout the area, left by Spanish soldiers who explored central New Mexico in the first half of the 16th century. These reminders of the past include the site of Coronado's bridge near Santa Rosa and the ruins of the massacred pueblo of Kuaua at Coronado State Monument near Albuquerque.

This sounds like a lot to see and do, and it is. But the astonishing news is that every place described in this chapter is within three hours' drive of Albuquerque. What more incentive do you need?

Albuquerque

▼ ▼ ▼ ▼ ▼ ▼ ▼ ▼ ▼   If you plan to explore central New Mexico, make Albuquerque your starting point. You'll find that much of the sightseeing here is rooted in the past, but the city also offers a fine collection of art museums and nightspots. Many scenic wonders of nature are within the city limits or nearby. And when the day is done, there are plenty of places in which to eat and sleep.

SIGHTS   Perhaps the best place to begin is **Old Town**, the original center of Albuquerque during the Spanish colonial and Mexican eras. West of the modern downtown area, this lowrise district can be reached by taking Central Avenue west from Route 25 or Rio

Exploring Albuquerque

The commercial hub of New Mexico, Albuquerque is not the tourist mecca that Santa Fe or Taos is, but it does have sights worth seeing. Since it's one of the few cities in this guidebook with a major airport, it's the first place that many visitors to the Southwest see. Here's how to see the best of the city in a day.

• Visit **Petroglyph National Monument** (page 458) on the city's western edge for a look at the ancient Puebloan shamanic art. Allow one and a half hours, including driving time.

• Take your pick among the city's museums and nature parks. My suggestions: if you have kids along, go to either the **Rio Grande Zoo** (page 456) or the **New Mexico Museum of Natural History and Science** (page 454). Allow one and a half hours for either place. If not, your time might be better spent at the cool, calm **Albuquerque Aquarium** (page 456) and neighboring **Rio Grande Botanic Garden** (page 456), both included on the same ticket. Allow one and a half hours.

• Have lunch at the **Indian Pueblo Cultural Center** (page 456).

• Driving to the east side of the city, ride the **Sandia Peak Tramway** (page 459) to the summit of Sandia Crest. At the top there is a long, easy hiking trail with the best view in New Mexico, so plan to spend the afternoon.

• Late in the day, after descending from the mountaintop, head over to **Old Town** (page 452), a good place to stroll and dine.

Grande Boulevard south from Route 40. Situated around an attractive central plaza with a bandstand, many buildings in Old Town date as early as 1780. After 1880, when the railroad reached Albuquerque and the station was constructed a distance from the plaza, businesses migrated to the present downtown and Old Town was practically abandoned for half a century.

Revitalization came when artists, attracted by bargain rents, established studios in Old Town. Galleries followed, as did gift shops, boutiques and restaurants. Today, it's easy to while away half a day exploring the restored adobe (and more recent "pueblo-ized" stucco) structures, hidden patios, brick paths, gardens and balconies of Old Town, mulling over the handmade jewelry and pottery offered by American Indian vendors or just people-watching from a park bench.

Home of the largest public exhibition of rattlesnakes in the world, Old Town's **American International Rattlesnake Museum** could surprise you with some interesting facts about what may be the world's most misunderstood reptile. Bet you didn't know that our founding fathers almost elected the timber rattlesnake instead of the bald eagle as the national symbol. And while it may not have any hands-on exhibits, this museum overflows with rattlesnake artifacts and artwork. Admission. ~ 202 San Felipe Street Northwest; phone/fax 505-242-6569; www.rattlesnakes.com.

Two of the city's best museums lie on opposite sides of Mountain Road, about a block from Old Town Plaza. The **Albuquerque Museum of Art & History** contains art and history exhibits, including the permanent "Four Centuries: A History of Albuquerque" display that features the largest collection of Spanish colonial artifacts in the United States. See maps, armor and weapons that belonged to the conquistadors, medieval religious items brought by early missionaries and ordinary household items that evoke the lifestyle of early settlers along the Rio Grande. The museum underwent a major expansion in 2005 and now boasts a new exhibitions gallery, special events hall, gallery store and museum café. Closed Monday. Admission. ~ 2000 Mountain Road Northwest; 505-243-7255, fax 505-764-6546; www.cabq.gov/museum, e-mail lvenzuela@cabq.gov.

Nearby, the **New Mexico Museum of Natural History and Science** features unique and imaginative exhibits that let visitors walk through time, explore an Ice Age cave, stand inside an erupting volcano and see the world's largest dinosaur. A planetarium and a five-story movie screen are also here. The museum is closed on non-holiday Mondays in January and September. Admission. ~ 1801 Mountain Road Northwest; 505-841-2800, 866-663-4667, fax 505-841-2866; www.nmnaturalhistory.org.

Also in the area is Albuquerque's scariest tourist attraction, the **National Atomic Museum**. Exhibits here trace the development

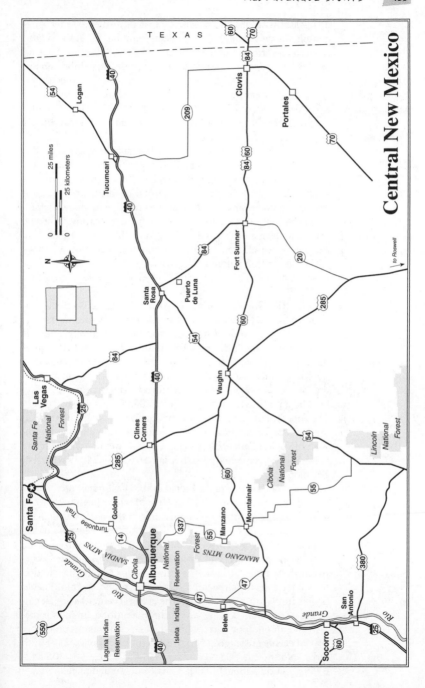

Central New Mexico

of nuclear weapons, from Albert Einstein's original letter (suggesting the possibility) to President Franklin D. Roosevelt to replicas of various atomic bombs from the 1940s and '50s and videos of nuclear tests. There are exhibits on nu-

The Mexican name for the Rio Grande is "Rio Bravo."

clear medicine, radiation in the environment, nuclear power and Madame Curie. Admission. ~ 1905 Mountain Road Northwest; 505-245-2137; fax 505-242-4537; www.atomicmuseum.com, e-mail info@atomicmuseum.com.

Enclosures at the clean, imaginatively designed **Rio Grande Zoo** are designed to resemble the animals' natural habitats as much as possible. Of the more than 250 species that live there, the most unusual residents are a pack of Mexican lobos, a small wolf subspecies that is extinct in the wild. Of the two dozen lobos that survive in a federal captive-breeding program, the majority has been bred at the Rio Grande Zoo. The Adventure Africa area features 17 exhibits, including warthogs and Cape Griffon vultures. Admission. ~ 903 10th Street Southwest; 505-764-6200, fax 505-764-6249; www.cabq.gov/bio park/zoo.

The **Rio Grande Botanic Garden** fills ten acres of the Rio Grande bosque west of Old Town with formal, walled theme gardens and a glass conservatory in which Mediterranean and desert environments are re-created. The 45,000-square-foot **Albuquerque Aquarium** traces the varied aquatic environments found along the Rio Grande as it makes its way from the Rocky Mountains to the Gulf of Mexico. There's a coral reef exhibit and an eel cave, but the aquarium's centerpiece is its 285,000-gallon shark tank. The zoo, the botanic garden and the aquarium, along with the fishing lakes at Tingley Beach, are collectively known as the **Northwest Biological Park**. Admission. ~ Central Avenue Southwest and New York Street; 505-764-6200, fax 505-764-6249; www.cabq. gov/biopark.

North of downtown, the **Indian Pueblo Cultural Center**, jointly owned and operated by all 19 of New Mexico's pueblos, has one of the finest American Indian museums in the state. Through artifacts and displays, it traces the history of New Mexico's native population over a span of 20,000 years. Exhibits of traditional pottery and other arts and crafts show the stylistic differences between the various pueblos. The museum also features a collection of photographs from the Smithsonian Institution taken of Pueblo people in the late 19th century. The cultural center has retail galleries, a restaurant serving American Indian food, an indoor theater and an outdoor plaza where dance performances and other special events are staged every weekend. Admission. ~ 2401 12th Street Northwest; 505-843-7270, 866-855-7902, fax 505-842-6959; www.indianpueblo.org, e-mail info@indianpueblo.org.

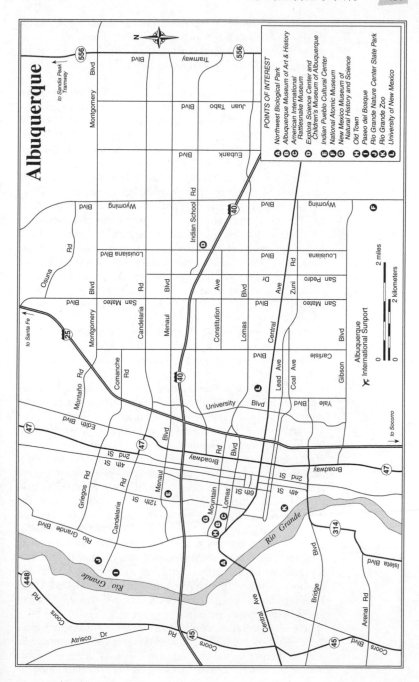

Albuquerque

N

to Sandia Peak
Tramway

556

Montgomery Blvd

Tramway

556

Juan Tabo Blvd

Eubank Blvd

Wyoming Blvd

Indian School Rd

40

Blvd

Wyoming

F

Osuna Rd

Louisiana Blvd

Louisiana Rd

D

San Pedro Dr

Zuni Ave

San Mateo Blvd

San Mateo

to Santa Fe

25

Montgomery

Candelaria Rd

Menaul Blvd

Constitution Ave

Lomas Blvd

Central Blvd

Comanche Rd

Montaño Rd

40

Carlisle Blvd

Lead Ave

Coal Ave

Gibson Blvd

Yale Blvd

C

Albuquerque
International Sunport

0   2 miles

0   2 kilometers

Edith Blvd

47

University Blvd

to Socorro

Griegos Rd

2nd St

4th St

47

Menaul Blvd

Broadway

Rio Grande Rd

Blvd

12th St

6th St

2nd St

4th St

Broadway

47

Candelaria Rd

Rio Grande Blvd

Mountain

Lomas

E

G
B
C
H

X

Rio Grande

314

Bridge Blvd

Isleta Blvd

448

Coors Rd

Rio Grande

I

A

Central Ave

Arenal Rd

Atrisco Dr

45

Coors Rd

45

Coors Blvd

POINTS OF INTEREST

- **A** Northwest Biological Park
- **B** Albuquerque Museum of Art & History
- **C** American International
  Rattlesnake Museum
- **D** Explora Science Center and
  Children's Museum of Albuquerque
- **E** Indian Pueblo Cultural Center
- **F** National Atomic Museum
- **G** New Mexico Museum of
  Natural History and Science
- **H** Old Town
- **I** Paseo del Bosque
- **J** Rio Grande Nature Center State Park
- **K** Rio Grande Zoo
- **X** University of New Mexico

East of downtown, the **University of New Mexico** offers a varied choice of on-campus museums and cultural events. ~ The campus is bordered by Central Avenue, Girard Boulevard, University Boulevard and Indian School Road; 505-277-0111, fax 505-277-2987; www.unm.edu.

The **Maxwell Museum of Anthropology** displays selections from the university's huge international collection of artifacts. Its "People of the Southwest" exhibit simulates an archaeological dig in progress. Closed Sunday and Monday. ~ University Boulevard, between Central Avenue and Lomas Boulevard on campus; 505-277-4404, fax 505-277-1547; www.unm.edu/~maxwell.

The **University Art Museum** holds the largest collection of fine art in New Mexico, numbering over 30,000 pieces. Closed Saturday and Monday. ~ Center for the Arts; 505-277-4001, fax 505-277-7315; unmartmuseum.unm.edu, e-mail mcerto@unm.edu.

The university has a separate art museum, the **Jonson Gallery**, which displays selections from a 2000-piece collection of the works of early-20th-century New Mexico artist Raymond Jonson, as well as works from contemporary New Mexico artists. Closed Saturday through Monday. ~ 1909 Las Lomas Boulevard Northeast; 505-277-4967, fax 505-277-3188; www.unm.edu/~jonsong, e-mail jonsong@unm.edu.

Northrop Hall (505-277-4204), the geology building, has a **Geology Museum** and a **Meteorite Museum**, and next door in Castetter Hall is the university's **Museum of Southwestern Biology** (505-277-1360).

Along the dark volcanic escarpment on Albuquerque's western perimeter, visitors can find perhaps the largest assemblage of petroglyphs in the Southwest—more than 20,000 specimens at 350 archaeological sites within the 11-square-mile **Petroglyph National Monument**. The drawings were chipped into the patina of rock surfaces 800 to 1000 years ago. Some are representational pictures of animal, human and supernatural figures, and others are abstract symbols, the meanings of which have provided generations of archaeologists with a fertile topic for speculation. In the Boca Negra Canyon (parking fee), there are several self-guided trails, including the Mesa Point Trail, that lead you past petroglyphs. To reach the visitors center, take the Unser exit from Route 40, then drive north for three miles to the intersection of Unser Boulevard and Western Trail. Boca Negra Canyon is an additional two miles north of the visitors center, off Unser. ~ 4735 Unser Boulevard Northwest; 505-899-0205, fax 505-899-0207; www.nps.gov/petr, e-mail petr@nps.gov.

For many travelers, the ultimate experience is a trip up **Sandia Peak** (elevation 10,378 feet) east of Albuquerque. The mountain rises so sharply on the city's eastern boundary that from either bottom or top it looks as if a rock falling from the cliffs along the ridgeline would land in someone's yard in the fashionable Northeast Heights neighborhood a mile below. On a typically clear day, you can see almost half the state from the summit.

While the summit can be reached by car (see "Turquoise Trail" Driving Tour on page 476) or on foot (see "Hiking" at the end of the chapter), the most spectacular way to climb this mountain is via the **Sandia Peak Tramway**. It takes just 15 minutes to ascend the 2.7-mile cable, and all the while you'll enjoy eagle's-eye views of rugged canyons in the Sandia Wilderness Area; you may even catch a glimpse of Rocky Mountain mule deer grazing on a distant promontory. At the peak are observation decks, a deluxe-priced restaurant, the Four Seasons Visitors Center with breathtaking views in every direction, plus a gift shop at the lower terminal. The tram closes twice a year (once in April, once in October) for regular maintenance. Admission. ~ 10 Tramway Loop Northeast; 505-856-7325; www.sandiapeak.com, e-mail info@sandiapeak.com.

The Sandia Peak Tramway is the world's longest aerial tramway.

LODGING

As New Mexico's largest city, Albuquerque has lodgings for every taste. One downtown grand hotel that predates World War II has been restored to the height of luxury. The emerging bed-and-breakfast scene features small, homey places that range from Victorian mansions to contemporary suburban guesthouses. Rates for Albuquerque accommodations are much lower than the cost of comparable lodging in Santa Fe or Taos. *Note:* Reservations are advised for all bed and breakfasts.

Conrad Hilton's second hostelry, built in 1939, has been lovingly restored as the city's showpiece downtown historic hotel, **La Posada de Albuquerque**. The lobby, with its vaulted ceiling and Indian murals, sets the tone—a blend of old-fashioned elegance and unique New Mexican style. Handmade traditional New Mexico furniture graces the modern guest rooms. Closed for renovations until 2008. ~ 125 2nd Street Northwest; 505-242-9090, 800-777-5732, fax 505-242-8664; www.laposada-abq.com, e-mail info@laposada-abq.com. MODERATE TO DELUXE.

Located within walking distance of Old Town, Route 66 and downtown Albuquerque, the **Brittania & W. E. Mauger Estate B&B** is a historic Queen Anne home with high ceilings and hardwood floors. The estate has eight bedrooms, each with a private bath and refrigerator, and two townhouses. It offers full breakfast, as well as wine and hors d'oeuvres in the afternoon. ~ 701 Roma Street Northwest; 505-242-8755, 800-719-9189, fax 505-842-8835; www.maugerbb.com, e-mail maugerbb@aol.com. MODERATE TO ULTRA-DELUXE.

The **Old Town Bed and Breakfast** is actually east of Old Town in a quiet residential neighborhood within easy walking distance of restaurants, shops, the New Mexico Museum of Natural History and the Albuquerque Museum. It features pueblo-style adobe architecture, a patio and two guest quarters. The bottom two-room suite has a separate sitting area and a kiva fireplace. ~ 707 17th Street Northwest; 505-764-9144, 888-900-9144; www.inn-new-mexico.com, e-mail nancyhoffman@earthlink.net. MODERATE TO DELUXE.

Closer to the plaza, the **Böttger Mansion of Old Town** is in a 1912 Victorian home listed on the National Register of Historic Landmarks. The eight guest rooms are individually decorated with Victorian furnishings; one includes a jacuzzi. ~ 110 San Felipe Street Northwest; 505-243-3639, 800-758-3639; www.bottger. com, e-mail info@bottger.com. DELUXE.

Strolling among the Territorial-style lowrises of Old Town, it would be easy to imagine yourself in an earlier century were it not for the towering presence of the 11-story **Hotel Albuquerque at Old Town** a block away. The grounds at this Heritage hotel preserve natural desert landscaping, while the large lobby bursts with Southwestern designs and colors. Views from the upper floors are arguably the most spectacular in town. ~ 800 Rio Grande Boulevard Northwest; 505-843-6300, 800-237-2133, fax 505-842-8426; www.hotelabq.com. DELUXE TO ULTRA-DELUXE.

Families traveling together who appreciate the extra space and amenities of a suite can find weekend bargain rates at several of Albuquerque's all-suite hotels. For example, the **Best Western Barcelona Suites** off Route 40 has suites with separate bedrooms and kitchen facilities that include refrigerators and microwaves. Rates include full breakfast. ~ 900 Louisiana Boulevard Northeast; 505-255-5566, fax 505-266-6644. MODERATE.

The **Marriott Pyramid North** is easy to spot; just look for its stepped pyramid shape along Route 25 in the commercial zone north of the city. Inside you'll find an atrium with a rock water-

AUTHOR FAVORITE

Bed and breakfasts abound in Albuquerque these days, and for my money the most interesting is **Casas de Sueños**, three blocks from Old Town Plaza. The 21 small houses and duplexes surrounding courtyard gardens began as an artists' colony in the 1940s. Each living unit is individually designed and furnished; many have kitchen facilities, some have fireplaces or hot tubs. A full American breakfast, sure to start your day on a delightful note, is included with your stay. ~ 310 Rio Grande Boulevard Southwest; 505-247-4560, 800-665-7002, fax 505-242-2162; www.casasdesuenos. com, e-mail info@casasdesuenos.com. MODERATE TO DELUXE.

fall, two glass elevators and Santa Fe/Southwestern motifs. The 310 guest rooms feature such amenities as coffeemakers, hair dryers, full-size vanity mirrors, ironing boards and high-speed internet. ~ 5151 San Francisco Road Northeast; 505-821-3333, 800-262-2043, fax 505-822-8115; www.marriott.com/abqmc, e-mail abqsales@jqh.com. DELUXE.

Also on the city's north side off Route 25, and catering to a business clientele, the **Wyndham Albuquerque Airport** offers some classy touches, from the sunny atrium lobby to the bright, contemporary Southwest-style guest rooms, not to mention the indoor-outdoor swim-through pool. ~ 2910 Yale Boulevard Southeast; 505-843-7000, 800-996-3426, fax 505-843-6307; www.wyndham.com. MODERATE TO DELUXE.

Near the eastern bank of the Rio Grande in Los Ranchos de Albuquerque, **Sarabande Bed and Breakfast** is a six-room inn with Southwestern–style accoutrements and *latilla* ceilings. Entered through a lovely courtyard, this adobe-style home also offers fountains and private patios. The owners prepare extravagant breakfasts in their country kitchen and then serve them outside. Bicyclers will find this a great location because of its proximity to a number of scenic routes near the Rio Grande, and after a day of pedaling visitors can look forward to soaking in the hot tub. There's also a swimming pool. ~ 5637 Rio Grande Boulevard Northwest; 505-345-4923, 888-506-4923, fax 505-345-9130; www.sarabandebb.com, e-mail janie@sarabandebb.com. MODERATE TO DELUXE.

Built in the 1930s by famed architect John Gaw Meem (widely known as the father of Santa Fe style), **Los Poblanos Inn** offers cozy indoor spaces that open onto beautiful courtyards, spectacular mountain views and 25 acres of lush gardens. Hand-carved doors, traditional tile fixtures and wood-burning fireplaces are found in each of the inn's lovingly furnished guest rooms. ~ 4803 Rio Grande Boulevard Northwest; 505-344-9297, fax 505-342-1302; www.lospoblanos.com, e-mail info@lospoblanos.com. DELUXE TO ULTRA-DELUXE.

Step back into Southwest history by taking a room at the **Hacienda Antigua**. The 1790 adobe hacienda was built in the Spanish colonial era and still retains its 19th-century ambience. The eight guest rooms are individually decorated with antiques including iron beds, kiva fireplaces and a century-old clawfoot bordello tub. There are plenty of opportunities to relax, whether you choose to take a dip in the pool, a soak in the outdoor hot tub or a turn in the orchard. The gourmet breakfast is a special treat. Gay-friendly. ~ 6708 Tierra Drive Northwest; 505-345-5399, 800-201-2986, fax 505-345-3855; www.haciendantigua.com, e-mail info@haciendantigua.com. DELUXE TO ULTRA-DELUXE.

Visitors looking for budget accommodations should take Central Avenue east beyond the University of New Mexico campus. Central used to be Route 66, the main east–west highway through Albuquerque before the interstates were built. Although the old two-lane highway has become a wide commercial thoroughfare, several tourist courts dating back to that earlier era still survive along Central between Carlisle and San Mateo boulevards.

On the east edge of town, near the Central Avenue/Tramway Boulevard exit from Route 40, is another concentration of franchise lodgings. Although this area is a long way from central destinations like Old Town and the university, it is a convenient location from which to ride the tramway or drive up Sandia Peak.

One option is **American Motor Inn Best Western.** ~ 12999 Central Avenue Northeast; 505-298-7426, 800-366-3252, fax 505-298-0212. Another hostelry is **Econo Lodge.** ~ 13211 Central Avenue Northeast; 505-292-7600, 800-553-2666, fax 505-298-4536. MODERATE.

Contemporary in style, the **Hilton Albuquerque** is the finest of several major hotels that cluster northeast of the Route 25 and Route 40 interchange. It's also where native New Mexican Conrad Hilton started his hotel chain. ~ 1901 University Boulevard Northeast; 505-884-2500, 800-445-8667, fax 505-889-9118. MODERATE TO DELUXE.

The first bed and breakfast to open in Albuquerque, **Casita Chamisa B&B** has three units with a private bath, entrance and fireplace in a 19th-century adobe home. The shady, forested acreage that is the Casita Chamisa's setting is also an archaeological site, and the innkeeper is happy to show a video that explains all about it. Children are welcome, and pets also, by prior arrangement. There's an indoor heated pool and hot tub. A hearty breakfast, is included with the room. You won't find a nicer host. ~ 850 Chamisal Road Northwest; 505-897-4644; www.casitachamisa.com, e-mail info@casitachamisa.com. MODERATE TO DELUXE.

Several first-rate, suburban bed and breakfasts are located in the Paseo del Norte area of Albuquerque and on the other side of the Rio Grande. **Adobe and Roses** rents a two-unit adobe guesthouse and a suite. The traditional New Mexico architecture features brick floors, Mexican tiles and *vigas*. All units have fireplaces as well as private entrances and kitchenettes. Full breakfast is included (10 percent discount for longer stays and no breakfast). ~ 1011 Ortega Road Northwest; 505-898-0654. MODERATE.

DINING

La Placita Dining Rooms, in an adobe hacienda on the Old Town Plaza, features hand-carved wooden doorways and a garden patio. Replenish your strength after shopping in historic Albuquerque with *carne adovada* or an *enchilada ranchera*. The *sopaipillas*, drenched in honey, are excellent as a dessert. Salads, burgers and sandwiches will satisfy less adventurous eaters. ~ 208 San Felipe Street Northwest; 505-247-2204, fax 505-842-9686. BUDGET TO MODERATE.

A popular Mexican restaurant is **La Hacienda**. The Spanish colonial atmosphere, with *ristras* and lots of Southwestern art on the walls, fits right in with the Old Town experience. The menu includes steak and seafood dishes and local cuisine such as fajitas. ~ 302 San Felipe Street Northwest; 505-243-3131, fax 505-243-0090. MODERATE.

In one of Old Town's oldest buildings, circa 1785, **High Noon** serves enchiladas and burritos as well as steaks, seafood and pasta to the strains of live flamenco guitar music. A house specialty is the pepper steak served with a pepper and cream cognac sauce. ~ 425 San Felipe Street Northwest; 505-765-1455, fax 505-255-4505; e-mail hnrsaloon@qwest.net. MODERATE TO ULTRA-DELUXE.

While the decor of **The Original Garcia's Kitchen** raises a lot of questions (like what's that huge diamondback rattlesnake skin doing over the entry way to the dining room, and who decided to put all the family trophies in the window?), no one ever second-guesses the kitchen. Take a booth or counter seat and feast on the blue-corn enchilada plate, green-chili stew or *chicharrones* and beans. It's packed during the breakfast hour, when *huevos a la Mexicana* (scrambled eggs, jalapeños, tomatoes and onion) and *huevos locos* (eggs with shredded beef or ham) are among the entrées. Gringo breakfasts like french toast are also served. Breakfast and lunch only. There are six other Garcia's Kitchen locations around Albuquerque. ~ 1113 4th Street Northwest; 505-247-9149, fax 505-765-1675; www.garciaskitchen.com. BUDGET.

The menu at **McGrath's**, the restaurant at the Hyatt Regency Albuquerque, features pork, beef, lamb and chicken prepared in a

AUTHOR FAVORITE

When in Albuquerque, I make a point of eating at the **Frontier Restaurant**, across the street from the main entrance to the University of New Mexico. It may not be fancy, but it's certainly cheap. I go there because they serve the best green chile stew anywhere, not to mention the biggest cinnamon rolls. The lively student environment blends intellectual conversation, a varied art collection and general rowdiness. Food choices include burgers and *huevos rancheros* (served all day). Open 24 hours. ~ 2400 Central Avenue Southeast; 505-266-0550, fax 505-266-4574; www.frontierrestaurant.com. BUDGET.

variety of ways. ~ 330 Tijeras Avenue Northwest; 505-766-6700, fax 505-843-2710. DELUXE TO ULTRA-DELUXE.

A different kind of local cuisine can be found at the **Pueblo Harvest Café** in the Indian Pueblo Cultural Center. Open for breakfast and lunch, this restaurant serves traditional Pueblo Indian dishes such as fry bread, Indian tacos and *posole*. Hamburgers and other mainstream fare are also served. Breakfast and lunch only. ~ 2401 12th Street Northwest; 505-843-7270, 866-855-7902, fax 505-842-6959; www.indianpueblo.org, e-mail info@indian pueblo.com. BUDGET.

It's hard to top the New Mexican fare at **El Patio**, a charming brick bungalow renowned for its inexpensive *chiles rellenos* and beef fajitas. Dine out on the patio if it's nice out. ~ 142 Harvard Drive Southeast; 505-268-4245. BUDGET.

A favorite Albuquerque restaurant for unusual food is the **Artichoke Cafe**. Here the menu changes frequently to take advantage of fresh, seasonal ingredients. Choices are wide ranging, including all of your basic meats, pastas and salads. As one might expect, the first item on the menu is an artichoke—steamed and served with three dipping sauces. Paintings by local artists brighten the walls. No lunch on Saturday and Sunday. ~ 424 Central Avenue Southeast; 505-243-0200; www.artichokecafe.com, e-mail contact@artichokecafe.com. MODERATE.

Farther out on Central Avenue, you can get a green-chile cheese dog, a rich, thick chocolate shake and a big dose of nostalgia at the **66 Diner**, a 1950s-style roadside diner designed with Historic Route 66 buffs in mind. Breakfast on weekends only. ~ 1405 Central Avenue Northeast; 505-247-1421, fax 505-247-0882; www.66diner.com. BUDGET.

A place where the green chile will knock (or maybe burn) your socks off is **Sadie's Dining Room**. This establishment is as local as it gets, and is next door to a bowling alley. ~ 6230 4th Street Northwest; 505-345-5339, fax 505-345-9440. BUDGET TO MODERATE.

MADAME MCGRATH'S

McGrath's, the restaurant at the Hyatt Regency Albuquerque, is named after the madame of Vine Cottage, one of the most prosperous women in town at the turn of the 20th century. Always one step ahead of the authorities, Lizzie McGrath came up with a unique strategy for defeating the intent of an ordinance outlawing parlor houses in the vicinity of local churches. Rather than relocate her own house of ill repute, she bought the neighboring Lutheran Church and had it moved. (Her thriving business was allowed to stay put.)

New Southwestern cuisine is the specialty at **Casa Chaco**. A full-scale restaurant located within the Hilton Albuquerque, it features such delicacies as grilled Rocky Mountain lamb stuffed with spinach and pine nuts, roasted pork porterhouse grilled with prickly pear sauce and apples and mesquite-smoked prime rib. Breakfast, lunch and dinner. ~ 1901 University Boulevard Northeast; 505-884-2500, fax 505-889-9118. DELUXE.

Firehouses seem to be a popular theme for Albuquerque restaurants. The **Gruet Steakhouse** is located in what was once a real fire station and today stands as one of the city's finest surviving examples of the "Pueblo Deco" architecture that sprang up along Old Route 66 in the 1930s. The fare at this restaurant is highly imaginative. A typical dinner might include crackling pork shank with melted cabbage and leeks, house-made applesauce or ahi tuna Wellington. Dinner only. ~ 3201 Central Avenue Northeast; 505-255-2424; www.gruetsteakhouse.com, e-mail gruetsteaks@yahoo.com. DELUXE TO ULTRA-DELUXE.

One of the most attractive restaurants on Nob Hill, **Scalo** is a contemporary split-level dining room with white tablecloths and an open kitchen. Small plates like wood-oven roasted quail, medium ones like corn risotto with chile-garlic shrimp, and large dishes like veal scallopine with fennel orange salad let diners mix, match and share meals. It's a great place for variety that's also tasty. Dinner only; lunch sometimes served, call ahead. ~ 3500 Central Avenue Southeast; 505-255-8781, fax 505-265-7850; www.scalonobhill.com, e-mail info@scalonobhill.com. MODERATE TO DELUXE.

Albuquerque's young and oh-so-cool crowd converges at **Gold Street Cafe** for morning lattes and breakfast burritos. Sit outside or dine indoors in a very modern and very trendy setting. Breakfast offers chile-glazed bacon, buttermilk pancakes and green-chile cheese biscuits. They also do lunch and dinner. ~ 218 Gold Street Southwest; 925-765-1633. MODERATE.

Neon cacti and painted *vigas* complement the Southwestern cuisine at **Papa Felipe's**. Booths and table seating are available, but the prices (and the food) are what satisfy customers at this adobe-style establishment, complete with whitewashed bricks and a saltillo tile floor. Specialties include *carne adovada* and chicken fajitas. ~ 9800 Menaul Boulevard Northeast; 505-292-8877, fax 505-292-8802; www.papafelipes.com. BUDGET TO MODERATE.

Located in the heart of the Nob Hill district, the original **Flying Star Cafe** is a popular hangout for anyone who wants to see and be seen. Grab a seat inside or at a table on the sidewalk anytime from 6 a.m. to almost midnight and anyone from university students to military personnel to neighborhood gay residents will be your neighbor. Famous for the goodies produced at their on-site bakery and for their coffee, which is roasted in-house daily, Flying Star also has a café menu with delicious homemade items. On the weekend there is an extended brunch menu. There are several locations. ~ 3416 Central Avenue Southeast, 4501 Juan Tabo Northeast, 8001 Menaul Boulevard Northeast and 4026 Rio Grande Boulevard Northwest; 505-255-6633, fax 505-232-8432; www.flyingstarcafe.com, e-mail info@flyingstarcafe.com. BUDGET.

One of the city's better Asian eateries, **ABC Chinese Restaurant** is entered through a lacquered dragon and phoenix archway. Bas-relief Buddhas and colorful paper lanterns make this Chinese and Korean restaurant a delight. Specialties include boneless tenderloin pork marinated in a spicy Korean bean sauce and barbecued duck with lychee nuts, pineapple and a sweet orange sauce. Closed Monday. ~ 8720 Menaul Boulevard Northeast; 505-292-8788. BUDGET TO MODERATE.

One of the finest restaurants in these parts is the **High Finance**. It's the setting that makes this restaurant so special. At the top of the Sandia Peak Tramway, the restaurant affords an incomparable view of Albuquerque glistening in a vast, empty landscape a mile below. Entrées include prime rib, steaks and lobster. Guests with dinner reservations here receive a discount on their tramway fares. ~ Sandia Crest; 505-243-9742, fax 505-856-6364; www.highfinancerestaurant.com, e-mail info@highfinancerestaurant.com. DELUXE TO ULTRA-DELUXE.

When the King of Spain granted a chunk of land to Domingo de Luna in 1692, he might have been pleased to know that 300 years later it would be the site of **Luna Mansion**, an elegant restaurant. After living here for many generations, the Luna family granted Santa Fe Railroad an easement across their historic property. In return, the railroad agreed to build the family a new mansion. Completed in 1881, this landmark was remodeled over the years into a handsome colonial-style adobe restaurant known for its eclectic menu. Specialties include a delicious red-chile linguine with chicken and portobello mushrooms. Closed Monday. ~ Los Lunas, east of Route 25 at the corner of Routes 6 and 314; 505-865-7333, fax 505-865-3496. MODERATE TO DELUXE.

SHOPPING   Shoppers can buy directly from American Indian craftspersons along San Felipe Street across from the plaza in **Old Town**, which is also Albuquerque's art gallery and boutique district. Almost 100 shops can lure delighted visitors into making Old Town an all-day expedition.

Possibly the only candy store in America to be picketed by anti-pornography forces, **The Candy Lady** is an Old Town institution. This adobe-style candyland tempts sweet tooths with 21 brands of fudge, plus dipped strawberries, bonbons and other sugary yummies. But it's the X-rated section doubling as a human anatomy lesson that has caused all the ruckus. Candy molded into the shape of breasts and cakes with spicy frosting designs—even erotic sculptures—actually prompted the city of Albuquerque to attempt a crackdown. They also offer a huge selection of sugar-free treats. ~ 524 Romero Street Northwest; 505-243-6239, 800-214-7731; www.thecandylady.com, e-mail info@thecandylady.com.

The **Santo Domingo Indian Trading Post,** which specializes in jewelry, is owned and operated by a resident of Santo Domingo Pueblo. ~ 401 San Felipe Street Northwest; 505-764-0129.

At the **Christin Wolf Gallery** you'll see the artist's fine jewelry as well as Southwestern art. Metal sculpture is also sold here. ~ 206½ San Felipe Street Northwest; 505-242-4222; www.christin wolf.com. **Perfumes of the Desert** carries unusual perfumes blended locally using desert-flower scents. ~ 208 San Felipe Street Northwest; 505-243-0859. **The Good Stuff** displays American Indian and Western antiques. ~ 404 San Felipe Street; 505-843-6416.

The **Indian Pueblo Cultural Center** has a series of gift shops surrounding the central dance plaza. All operated by the cultural center, the shops differ by price ranges from curio items to museum-quality collectors' objects. Because the cultural center is owned by a coalition of Indian pueblos, authenticity is assured, making this one of the best places to shop for American Indian pottery, sculpture, sandpaintings, rugs, kachinas and traditional and contemporary jewelry. ~ 2401 12th Street Northwest; 505-843-7270, 866-855-7902; www.indianpueblo.org, e-mail info@indian-pueblo.org.

Martha's Body Bueno Shop carries cards, gifts, lingerie and adult novelty items. Gay-friendly. ~ 3105 Central Avenue Northeast; 505-255-1122; www.marthasbodybueno.com.

Spend some time browsing in **Page One,** the largest independently run bookstore in New Mexico. The friendly staff is always ready to help you find what you need. ~ 11018 Montgomery Boulevard Northeast; 505-294-2026; www.page1book.com.

Known for its broad line of quality boots, **Western Warehouse** offers a variety of popular styles at discount prices. They also

AUTHOR FAVORITE

Inventive, sometimes whimsical modern Southwestern designs make **Tanner Chaney Gallery** a small gem with one of the most intriguing art collections in town. Drop by if you're in the market for Pueblo pottery, loomed rugs or Navajo pictorial weavings—and even if you're not. The gallery also carries folk art from Mexico. ~ 323 Romero Northwest; 505-247-2242, 800-444-2242; www.tannerchaney.com.

carry concho belts, broomstick skirts, bolo ties and a wide array of shirts, Western-style, of course. ~ 6210 San Mateo Northeast; 505-883-7161.

For more practical shopping needs, Albuquerque's major shopping mall is the **Coronado Center**, located at Louisiana Boulevard Northeast and Menaul Boulevard Northeast. ~ 6600 Menaul Northeast; 505-881-4600; www.coronadocenter.com.

If that's not enough, the **Chili Pepper Emporium** has the largest and most complete selection in New Mexico—and the world, probably—of chile items, ranging from spices, sauces and jellies to chile-motif T-shirts and chile-shaped Christmas tree lights. ~ 901 Rio Grande Northwest, Suite A-194; 505-881-9225, 800-288-9648; www.chilipepperemporium.com, e-mail info@chili pepperemporium.com.

> With 712,000 residents in the greater metropolitan area, Albuquerque accounts for more than a third of the state's entire population.

GAY SHOPPING It might not be a San Francisco or New York, but Albuquerque does have a growing gay and lesbian community. While there isn't a strictly gay area, the trendy Nob Hill neighborhood, home to several gay and lesbian bookstores and establishments, is probably where you'll find the closest thing to a "scene."

For information on gay and lesbian resources in Albuquerque and throughout New Mexico, contact the **Sandia Out Professional Alliance of New Mexico**. ~ Albuquerque; www.sopa nm.org, e-mail info@sopanm.org.

Alphaville rents films with gay and lesbian themes in a variety of genres including documentaries and experimental and feature films. Closed Sunday. ~ 3408 Central Avenue Southeast; 505-256-8243; www.alphavillagevideo.com.

NIGHTLIFE A contemporary pianist tickles the ivories Wednesday through Friday evening at **La Posada de Albuquerque Lounge**. On weekends a variety of music can be heard, from *nuevo flamenco* to jazz to Western swing. Closed until 2008. ~ 125 2nd Street Northwest; 505-242-9090, 866-442-4224, fax 505-242-8664.

Laffs Comedy Club features major national standup comedy acts five nights a week and has a full bar. Closed Monday and Tuesday. ~ 6001 San Mateo Boulevard Northeast; 505-296-5653; www.laffscomedy.com.

The dancefloor is always busy at **Caravan East**. Hollywood-style lighting brightens this beam-ceilinged club, which features two country bands nightly. Native New Mexican musicians play on Wednesday. Weekend and Wednesday cover. ~ 7605 Central Avenue Northeast; 505-265-7877.

Sometimes there's nothing more exciting than seeing a big-name performer alongside hordes of rabid fans. With a seating capacity of 12,000, the **Journal Pavilion** fits the bill. The state-of-the-art concert venue hosts top musical performers such as Snoop Dogg, Alan Jackson and the Dave Matthews Band. ~ 5601 University Boulevard Southeast; 505-452-5100; www.jour nalpavilion.com.

OPERA, SYMPHONY AND DANCE There's a lively performing-arts scene in Albuquerque, most of which centers around the University of New Mexico. Productions at the university's **Popejoy Hall** (505-277-4569) include plays by touring Broadway shows, performances of the **Musical Theatre Southwest** (505-262-9119), the **New Mexico Ballet Company** (505-292-4245) and concerts by the **New Mexico Symphony Orchestra** (505-881-9590).

Other theaters on campus include the Department of Theatre and Dance's **Theatre X** in the basement of the Center for the Arts and the **Rodey Theatre for the Arts** next to Popejoy Hall. ~ 505-277-4569.

The New Mexico Jazz Workshop hosts over 30 concerts a year at locations around the city including the Albuquerque Museum and the Hiland Theater. ~ 505-255-9798.

Another important performing-arts venue is the historic **KiMo Theatre**, which hosts performances by groups including the **Opera Southwest** (505-242-5837), the **Ballet Theatre of New Mexico** (505-888-1054) and the unique bilingual **La Compania de Teatro de Albuquerque** (505-242-7929). ~ 423 Central Avenue Northwest; 505-768-3522. The **South Broadway Cultural Center** offers theater, dance and film screenings. ~ 1025 Broadway Southeast; 505-848-1320. The **Albuquerque Children's Theatre** performs for the younger set. ~ 224 San Pasquale Southwest; 505-242-4750.

GAY SCENE If you're looking to dance, head for the high-tech gay hotspot, **Pulse**, located in the Nob Hill district. Designated danceclub nights feature a live deejay playing high-energy and retro music. Their video and cocktail lounge, Blu, and the danceclub itself, Pulse, are open Wednesday through Saturday. Cover on Wednesday. ~ 4100 Central Avenue Southeast; 505-255-3334, fax 505-255-3335; www.pulseandblu.com, e-mail rh@ pulseandblu.com.

The vast **Albuquerque Mining Co.** offers something for everyone, with events most nights of the week. The clientele is both gay and lesbian. Call for cover details. ~ 7209 Central Avenue Northeast; 505-255-4022.

Another place to dance the night away is **Foxes Booze n Cruise**. The gay, lesbian, transgender and straight clientele boogie to deejayed disco music. There are drag shows on the weekend. ~ 8521 Central Avenue Northeast; 505-255-3060.

A leather bar is only one of the attractions that makes **Sidewinders** a hit with the gay community. This Western-style club also features a wide-open dancefloor and a deejay operating out of a chuckwagon. If you're a little rusty on the Tennessee waltz, you can always work on your pool game. ~ 8900 Central Avenue Southeast; 505-275-1616; www.sidewindersranch.com.

PARKS

RIO GRANDE NATURE CENTER STATE PARK 🚶 This urban wildlife refuge is one of several access points to the bosque and riverbank. The visitors center has exhibits on the river's ecology; observation windows on one side of the building overlook a three-acre pond frequented by ducks, geese and herons, especially during migration seasons—November and April. The park is a favorite spot for birdwatching in all seasons. Two nature trails, each a mile-long loop, wind through the bosque, and one of them leads to several peaceful spots along the bank of the Rio Grande. Other facilities here are restrooms and a gift shop. Day-use fee, $3 per vehicle. ~ 2901 Candelaria Road Northwest, where Candelaria ends at the river a few blocks west of Rio Grande Boulevard; 505-344-7240, fax 505-344-4505; www.rgnc.org, e-mail rgnc@nmia.com.

PASEO DEL BOSQUE 🚶🚲🐎 The bosque, or cottonwood forest, lining the banks of the Rio Grande is protected for future park development all the way through the city of Albuquerque. Most of this area remains wild, undeveloped and inaccessible to motor vehicles. A ten-mile paved trail for joggers, cyclists and horseback riders runs along the edge of the bosque, following the river north from the Rio Grande Zoo to Paseo del Norte Boulevard in the North Valley. ~ Trail access from Campbell Road, Mountain Road or Rio Grande Nature Center on Candelaria Road Northwest.

▼ ▼ ▼ ▼ ▼ ▼ ▼ ▼ ▼ ▼ ▼ ▼ ▼
Outside Albuquerque

Exploring the area surrounding Albuquerque proper is well worth any visitor's time. Traveling north of Albuquerque on Route 25, motorists can explore a number of ancient and modern Indian pueblos, including the largest of the Rio Grande Indian pueblos.

SIGHTS

Thirteen miles south of Albuquerque, **Isleta Pueblo** is a labyrinthine mixture of old and new houses comprising one of New Mexico's larger pueblos. Visitors who wander the narrow streets of the town will eventually find their way to the mission church, one of the oldest in the country. The pueblo operates a fishing lake and campground in the Isleta Casino and Resort. Several shops around the plaza sell the local white, red and black pottery. Photographing ceremonies is prohibited. ~ Route 25; 505-869-3111, fax 505-869-4236; www.isletapueblo.com.

The two nearest pueblos to Albuquerque—Sandia Pueblo and Santa Ana Pueblo—are so small that they often go unnoticed. **Sandia Pueblo** has an arts-and-crafts market and a Las Vegas–style casino. They also operate Sandia Lakes Recreation Area (505-897-3971), which is open to the public for fishing. Admission. The Sandia people number about 300 and speak Tiwa, a different language from that spoken at other pueblos in the vicinity. Kuaua was an ancestral home of the Sandia people. Photography and sketching are prohibited. Closed weekends. ~ Route 313, about seven miles north of Albuquerque; 505-867-3317, fax 505-867-9235; www.sandiapueblo.nsn.us.

Just up the road, **Santa Ana Pueblo** has about 700 tribal members; nearly all live here, away from the old pueblo off State Highway 550. The tribe owns a golf course nearby and operates a nursery of native plants and a casino. The old pueblo itself is only open to the public on January 6, July 26 and December 25. ~ 2 Dove Road, off Route 313, ten miles west of Bernalillo; 505-867-3301, fax 505-867-3395; www.santaana.org, e-mail info@santaana.org.

Founded beside the Rio Grande around the year 1300, Kuaua was a thriving pueblo when a Spanish expedition led by Francisco Vasquez de Coronado arrived in 1540. The 1100 explorers spent the winter there and at first found the people of Kuaua

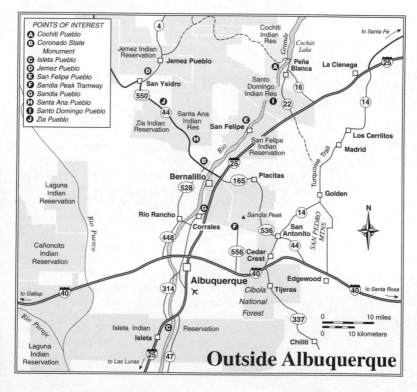

POINTS OF INTEREST
- Ⓐ Cochiti Pueblo
- Ⓑ Coronado State Monument
- Ⓒ Isleta Pueblo
- Ⓓ Jemez Pueblo
- Ⓔ San Felipe Pueblo
- Ⓕ Sandia Peak Tramway
- Ⓖ Sandia Pueblo
- Ⓗ Santa Ana Pueblo
- Ⓘ Santo Domingo Pueblo
- Ⓙ Zia Pueblo

Outside Albuquerque

hospitable, but as supplies ran short and demands on the pueblo increased, the Indians became uncooperative and Coronado destroyed the pueblo.

Today, the ruins of Kuaua are preserved at **Coronado State Monument,** 15 miles north of Albuquerque. The unique feature of this ruin is a ceremonial kiva (an underground chamber) that, when excavated, was found to have murals around its interior—the only pre-Columbian pueblo kiva paintings known to have survived the centuries. Archaeologists carefully removed and mounted the painted layers, and the original murals are now displayed in a room adjoining the visitors center along with diagrams that explain their meanings. The kiva itself has been fully restored and ornamented with replicas of the paintings, and visitors are welcome to climb down into it. The visitors center also contains exhibits about both the pueblo people and the Spanish conquistadors. Closed Tuesday. Admission. ~ Route 550/44, one mile west of Route 25 from the town of Bernalillo; 505-867-5351, fax 505-867-1733.

Tradition is strong at **San Felipe Pueblo,** ten miles from Bernalillo north on Route 25. The pueblo is known for spectacular dances (the bowl-like central plaza has actually been worn down three feet below ground level by centuries of ceremonies) and beadwork. The pueblo's artisans specialize in *heishi* (disklike beads used for necklaces).The tribe's main source of income, though, is its flashy casino just off the interstate. Photographs and sketching are strictly prohibited. ~ One and a half miles west of Route 25 at Exit 252; 505-867-3381, fax 505-867-3383; e-mail erika@ sanfelipe-pueblo.com.

Santo Domingo is the largest of the Rio Grande Indian pueblos and one of the most conservative. After admiring the horses and other ornate designs painted on the church facade, visitors may wish to stroll through the narrow, old streets and hear the residents speaking in the native Keresan language. Pueblo artists sell fine silver jewelry and other crafts from their homes. ~ Five miles west of Route 25, Exit 259; 505-465-2214, fax 505-465-2688.

HIDDEN ►

The mission church at **Cochiti Pueblo** dates back to 1628 and is among the oldest on the Rio Grande. Cochiti artisans originated the pottery storyteller figures that now are popular collectibles. At Cochiti Lake there is a campground and other lake services, and fishing is permitted in the Rio Grande at the bottom of the dam and also on the lake with a fishing license. Cochiti Pueblo is farther removed from the interstate than any of the other pueblos between Albuquerque and Santa Fe. No photography. ~ To get there, travel north on Route 25, then take Route 22 for about 15 miles; 505-465-2244, fax 505-465-1135.

American Indians have lived in **Zia Pueblo** since the middle of the 13th century, though diseases introduced by European settlers caused their population to dwindle from 15,000 to less than 100 by the end of the 19th century. But today this reservation, located 35 miles northwest of Albuquerque off State Highway 550, is thriving once more, with about 850 American Indians making their home here. Spread across 150,000 acres of piñon-juniper and ponderosa pine woodlands, the Zia reservation features a small cultural center that showcases arts and crafts. No photography or sketching. Closed weekends. ~ Route 44, Zia Pueblo; 505-867-3304, fax 505-867-3308.

In the vicinity, **Jemez Pueblo** is also open to tourists on a very limited basis; call ahead. No photography. ~ On Route 4 just north of State Highway 550. However, guests are welcome at the Walatowa Visitors Center, where there is Jemez pottery and sculpture for sale. It is located six miles north of San Ysidro on Route 4. ~ Off Route 4, three miles north of Jemez Pueblo; 505-834-7235, fax 505-834-2221; www.jemezpueblo.org, e-mail tourism@jemezpueblo.org.

LODGING

Corrales, a rural North Valley community located near Bernalillo and Coronado State Monument, is home to some of the Albuquerque area's best small bed and breakfasts. **The Nora Dixon Place** epitomizes New Mexico's unique Territorial-era architecture: the home is adobe brick with pine trim and has divided-light windows. Set on an acre and a half of wooded area by the Rio Grande, the property is filled with cottonwood, native plants, vegetable gardens and fruit and olive trees. Its three guest rooms come with a private bath, a fridge and a microwave. All open to an enclosed courtyard. A full breakfast is served. ~ 312 Dixon Road, Corrales; 505-898-3662, 888-667-2349, fax 505-898-6430; www.noradixon.com, e-mail noradixon@aol.com. MODERATE TO DELUXE.

The **Chocolate Turtle Bed and Breakfast**, besides having a name that immediately evokes trust, is a lovely B&B on a one-

LOOK WHAT'S COOKIN'

As every visitor discovers immediately, New Mexico boasts a distinctive culinary style. The two regional specialties that set it apart from Mexican food familiar in other regions are blue corn, grown by the Pueblo Indians and considered sacred in their traditions, and green chile. New Mexico produces virtually all the chile peppers grown in the United States, and while most chiles are exported to the rest of the country in the form of red chile powder, the local preference is to pick the chiles while green, then roast, peel and eat them as a vegetable—chopped as a stew, breaded and fried as *rellenos* or poured as a sauce over just about any entrée.

and-a-half-acre spread in Corrales. The Territorial-style digs are cheerfully outfitted with Southwestern art, and each of the four rooms has a private bath. Full breakfast is included (if you're lucky, you'll get mangos and blue-corn pancakes). ~ 1098 West Meadowlark Lane, Corrales; 505-898-1800, 877-298-1800, fax 505-898-6491; www.chocolateturtlebb.com, e-mail innkeeper@ chocolateturtlebb.com. MODERATE TO DELUXE.

Four lovely suites make up **Casa de Koshare Bed & Breakfast**. Each is decorated in Southwestern style and offers a cool retreat from the New Mexican sun. Coffee, tea and snacks are offered throughout the day, while a full, hot breakfast is served. No children under 12. ~ 122 Ashley Lane, Corrales; 505-898-4500, 877-729-8100; www.casadekoshare.com, e-mail info@casadekoshare.com. MODERATE TO DELUXE.

DINING

Even when in the middle of the Southwestern desert, sometimes all you want is a good ol' slice of pizza. **Village Pizza** serves up an amazing array of pies, from those with whole-wheat crusts and smoked oyster toppings to no-sauce options. All this comes in an airy adobe-style restaurant with a lovely outdoor patio perfect for enjoying a mild New Mexican evening and a slice of dee-lish pizza. ~ 4266 Corrales Road, Corrales; 505-898-0045. MODERATE TO DELUXE.

The **Range Cafe** is a favorite spot among locals, so much so that they've opened two additional cafés in Albuquerque. Menu items include salads, Mexican-style entrées and gourmet vegetarian selections, including a grilled portobello mushroom "burger" with poblano chile aioli. If you're here for breakfast, try the oatmeal with cinnamon ice cream, walnuts and strawberries. Breakfast, lunch and dinner are served. ~ 925 Camino del Pueblo, Bernalillo; 505-867-1700; www.rangecafe.com, e-mail mail@rangecafe.com. MODERATE TO DELUXE.

HIDDEN ►

The elegant **Prairie Star** is 15 minutes north of the city off Route 25 in a sprawling, mission-style adobe house. The menu changes seasonally, but typical entrées may be seared house-smoked North Atlantic salmon served with gooseberry salsa and Chama Valley lamb chops accompanied by sun-dried-tomato polenta. They also offer over 2000 varietals of wine. Dinner only. Closed Monday. ~ 288 Prairie Star Road off Tamaya Boulevard, Santa Ana Pueblo; 505-867-3327; www.santaanagolf.com, e-mail pstar@santaanagolf.com. DELUXE TO ULTRA-DELUXE.

NIGHTLIFE

Live music comes to Bernalillo on weekend evenings at the **Range Cafe**. ~ 925 Camino del Pueblo, Bernalillo; 505-867-1700.

PARKS

COCHITI LAKE   At the confluence of the Santa Fe and Rio Grande rivers lies Albuquerque's flood-control reservoir and also its local water recreation area. Windsurfing on the lake is popular, and some people paddle kayaks. Power boating is permitted but is restricted to no-wake speed. Fishing is good for largemouth and smallmouth bass, catfish and walleye. It's also a good place to swim. Facilities here include a picnic area, restrooms and showers. ~ Located 46 miles north of Albuquerque on Route 25 and then 15 miles northwest on Route 22; 505-465-0307, fax 505-465-0316.

▲ There are two campgrounds overlooking the lake, operated by the Army Corps of Engineers. Cochiti has 57 sites (38 with RV hookups) and Tetilla Peak has 46 sites (35 with RV hookups); $8 per night for standard sites, $12 per night for hookups. Tetilla Peak is closed November through March.

Turquoise Trail

There are places worth visiting along Route 25 between Albuquerque and Santa Fe—particularly San Felipe and Santo Domingo Indian pueblos. But if you want to take your time, avoid big truck traffic, and experience a taste of old-fashioned, undeveloped New Mexico, take the two-lane route known as the Turquoise Trail (see Driving Tour) around the back of Sandia Crest and over the Ortiz Mountains, and discover some hidden little towns that are short on water but long on personality.

SIGHTS

About a mile down the Turquoise Trail, a mile west of Route 14 on Route 536, is a small wonder for those traveling with children—the **Tinkertown Museum**, which exhibits a miniature Western town and a three-ring circus entirely hand-carved from wood with mechanical people and moving vehicles. The museum is easily recognized by its fence made of glass bottles. Closed November through March. Admission. ~ Route 536; 505-281-5233; www.tinkertown.com, e-mail tinker4u@tinkertown.com.

When Madrid was a thriving mining town, water was brought in by train; today the train no longer runs and residents buy bottled drinking water.

You won't have trouble discovering Madrid's roots if you go to the **Old Coal Mine Museum**. This block-long memorial pays tribute to an industry that peaked here in 1928. Your self-guided tour includes a visit to a coal mine shaft, a wide array of mining machinery, vintage railroad equipment and antique trucks—look in the parts storage building for a Model T pickup truck. Admission. ~ Route 14, Madrid; phone/fax 505-438-3780; e-mail coalminemuseum@earthlink.net.

Featuring a collection of gems, cattle skulls and pottery, the **Casa Grande Trading Post** is a good place to learn about the region's geologic history. The offbeat, sometimes whimsical collection of artifacts is highlighted by guides who are more than happy to fill you in on local lore. The collection in the **Turquoise Museum**

DRIVING TOUR
Turquoise Trail

A number of historical sights make the Turquoise Trail a rewarding route from Albuquerque to Santa Fe—and it takes just 30 minutes more driving time than the interstate. To find the Turquoise Trail (Route 14), take Route 40 eastbound from Albuquerque to the Tijeras/Cedar Crest exit, a distance of about ten miles from the city center, and turn north.

SANDIA PEAK   At Cedar Crest, a few miles from the interstate exit, a well-marked paved road, steep in places, forks off from the Turquoise Trail and leads up the eastern slope of the Sandias to Sandia Peak summit, with its spectacular views of central New Mexico.

GOLDEN   Midway between Albuquerque and Santa Fe, the Turquoise Trail crosses the San Pedro Mountains, a small but rugged range that was the site of major gold-mining operations from the 1880s to the 1920s. Once the area's residential hub, Golden is now practically a ghost town. Beside the highway, the ruins of an old stone schoolhouse and other collapsing buildings can still be seen. There is also a beautifully restored mission church dating back to 1830.

ranges from prehistoric pieces to locally mined Cerrillos turquoise. Take your children next door to the **Petting Zoo**, where they can feed the llamas, peacocks and goats. Admission. ~ 17 Waldo Street, Los Cerrillos; 505-438-3008.

The Turquoise Trail intersects Route 25 at the western edge of Santa Fe, where it becomes Cerrillos Road, a busy main street.

LODGING

HIDDEN ▶

For those seeking a remote setting, still within easy commuting distance of Albuquerque's attractions, **Elaine's** is the ideal choice. This bed and breakfast, nestled among ponderosa pines, adjoins Cibola National Forest near Cedar Crest. Outdoor enthusiasts have ample opportunities for hiking, biking, skiing, horseback riding and birding. There's even a resident dog to accompany guests on walks through the foliage. The three-story log house has five guest rooms, big balconies, a grand country fireplace and European antiques everywhere you look. Some rooms have jacuzzi tubs. A full breakfast is included. ~ 72 Snowline Estates, Cedar Crest; 505-281-2467, 800-821-3092, fax 505-281-1384; www.elaines bnb.com, e-mail elaine@elainesbnb.com. MODERATE TO DELUXE.

Located on the Turquoise Trail, **Madrid Lodging** is a quaint, two-suite bed and breakfast that was once a 1930s boardinghouse.

MADRID   Eleven miles away, on the other side of the pass, the town of Madrid (pronounced "MAD-rid") owes its existence to coal mining. The all-wood buildings, atypical of New Mexico architecture, give the community a look reminiscent of Appalachian coal towns. Abandoned after World War II, Madrid has since been partly repopulated by artists and historic-district entrepreneurs, but growth is limited due to a lack of water. (Water used to be brought in by a train that no longer runs.) Attractions in Madrid include a mining museum, a summertime melo-drama and a baseball field where concerts are presented regularly.

LOS CERRILLOS   A third old mining town along the Turquoise Trail, Los Cerrillos (shortened to "Cerrillos" by locals) still retains the appearance of an old Spanish village. While silver, gold, copper, zinc and lead have all been mined in the hills north of town—and Thomas Edison once built a $2 million laboratory here in an unsuccessful attempt to develop a method for refining gold without water—Los Cerrillos is best known for turquoise. American Indians mined turquoise here as early as A.D. 500. Later, the people of Chaco and other Anasazi pueblos traveled from hundreds of miles away to dig pit mines for the stone, which was their most precious trade commodity. Others, from Spanish colonists to modern-day prospectors, have likewise wandered the maze of the Cerrillos hills in search of turquoise.

As one would expect, the atmosphere is casual and relaxed. The units are splashed with muted colors and accented with antiques and Asian and Southwestern touches. A large, outdoor hot tub will soothe away any remnants of stress. Breakfast is included. ~ 14 Opera House Road, Madrid; 505-471-3450; www.madridlodging.com, e-mail info@madridlodging.com. MODERATE.

DINING

The oak floor and tables, New Mexican murals and beam ceiling add to the charm of the historic **Mine Shaft Tavern**, home of the state's longest standup bar, 50 feet total. Mingle with the locals at the lodgepole pine slab or take a table and order a chef's salad, enchiladas, hamburgers or ribeye steak; wash it down with a local beer. For dessert, try the homemade pie. Lunch is served daily; dinner served Wednesday (special theme night), Friday, Saturday and Sunday. ~ 2846 Route 14, Madrid; 505-473-0743; www.mineshafttavern.com, e-mail mineshafttavern@earthlink.net. BUDGET TO MODERATE.

At **Mamma Lisa's Ghost Town Kitchen**, everything from the soups and stews to the breads and desserts is homemade. The menu changes daily, and some of its most popular offerings are the New Mexican entrées and main-dish salads. Be sure to try the red chili chocolate cake. Lunch only. Call for hours. ~ 2859 Route 14, Madrid; 505-471-5769. BUDGET.

SHOPPING   Al Leedom Studio specializes in hand-blown glass and *really* expensive, high-quality jewelry. Call ahead for a schedule of glass-blowing demonstrations. ~ Route 14, Madrid; 505-473-2054, 888-388-6608; www.alleedom.com.

Gifted Hands has myriad pottery, sculpture and jewelry all created by local artists. ~ 2851 Route 14, Madrid; 505-471-5943. For wraps and other hand-woven wearables, stop by Tapestry Gallery. ~ 2863 Route 14, Madrid; 505-471-0194.

NIGHTLIFE   Madrid Melodrama offers memorable classic Victorian melodramas at the Engine House Theater in the Old Coal Mine Museum next to the Mine Shaft Tavern. Shows are on weekend afternoons and Saturday evenings from late May to mid-October. ~ Route 14, Madrid; 505-438-3780; www.madridmelodrama.com.

There's live music on Friday or Saturday evenings at the Mine Shaft Tavern. ~ 2846 Route 14, Madrid; 505-473-0743; www.mineshafttavern.com.

▼▼▼▼▼▼▼▼▼▼▼

Santa Rosa Area

Drivers crossing eastern New Mexico on Route 40 may find the experience brain-numbing in its monotony—flat and featureless with an endless flow of speeding semi trucks. Those who venture a short detour from the main route, however, will discover a little bit of the special character of Santa Rosa, Fort Sumner and the other communities that dot the boundless prairie. This area is of particular interest to history buffs, for this is where the legend of Billy the Kid is rooted and, indeed, this is where the young outlaw is buried.

SIGHTS   Located along the Pecos River, the town of Santa Rosa (population 2700) lies 110 miles east of Albuquerque at the junction of Routes 40 and 54. It was settled by Spanish farmers during the 1860s, but its historic roots extend back to 1541, when Spanish explorer Vasquez de Coronado built a bridge across the Pecos River at Puerto de Luna, ten miles south of present-day Santa Rosa—or so the story goes. In the 1880s, Puerto de Luna was the largest community in the southeastern quarter of New Mexico Territory; today it is virtually a ghost town. But even though the bridge no longer exists and the stone county courthouse is beginning to crumble (along with a rock-faced church and a saloon where Billy the Kid hung out from time to time), Puerto de Luna still makes for an interesting short excursion off the interstate.

Santa Rosa's main vacation attractions are lakes, to the point that it calls itself "The City of Natural Lakes." Those who find the claim improbable for a town in the arid high plains of New

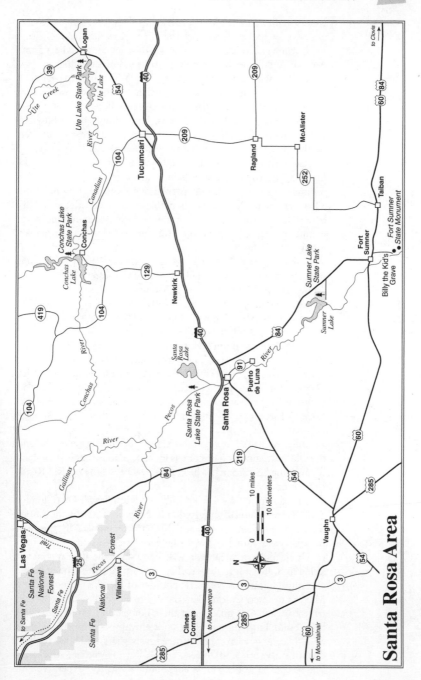

Santa Rosa Area

Mexico will be even more surprised to learn that Santa Rosa is a mecca for scuba divers. (See the "Parks" section below.)

If you want to Kid around, drive 46 miles south to **Fort Sumner,** where Billy the Kid happened to be hiding out when the law caught up with him for the last time. You might expect that "Billymania" would be more prevalent in the outlaw's hometown of Lincoln, 100 miles to the south, where most of his escapades took place. But the fact is, Fort Sumner is the Billy the Kid capital of the Southwest. It was here (or at least at a ranch on the outskirts of town) that he was shot to death in 1881.

Two privately owned museums pay tribute to Billy the Kid's life and legend. Each is interesting enough to occupy the curious for an hour or two and spur speculations about whether Billy was a frontier Robin Hood, a psychopathic killer or a product of media hype. There is some duplication between the two museums, since a number of the documents on exhibit are photocopies of originals in the state archives.

The **Billy the Kid Museum,** which showcases a large collection of Billy memorabilia and a jail cell, is near the eastern edge of town on the way to Fort Sumner State Monument. Closed the first two weeks of January. Admission. ~ 1601 East Sumner Avenue, Fort Sumner; 505-355-2380; www.billythekidmuseumfortsumner.com, e-mail contact@billythekidmuseumfortsumner.com.

The **Old Fort Sumner Museum** displays letters written by Billy to the governor to negotiate a pardon, letters from Sheriff Pat Garrett to his wife describing his search for the outlaw, a history of impostors who have claimed to be the real Billy the Kid and a chronology of more than a dozen motion pictures about his brief, violent career. Admission. ~ Billy the Kid Road, Fort Sumner; 505-355-2942.

Billy the Kid's Grave, in the Maxwell family cemetery behind the Old Fort Sumner Museum, is locked securely behind iron bars because the headstone has been stolen twice. ~ Billy the Kid Road, Fort Sumner.

Just down the road from Billy the Kid's grave, **Fort Sumner State Monument–Bosque Redondo Memorial** marks the site of the Army outpost for which the town was named. By the time Billy the Kid came to town, the fort had been converted to a ranch headquarters, and it was here that Sheriff Pat Garrett killed him. Just a few years earlier, the fort was the scene of larger and more infamous events. The leader of the U.S. Army in New Mexico ordered Colonel Kit Carson to force the entire Navajo tribe to walk 450 miles from their homeland to this place and help build Fort Sumner as a concentration camp. More than 8500 Navajo lived in captivity here for six years, and 3000 of them died of starvation and disease. Finally the government concluded that keeping the Navajo at Fort Sumner was too expensive and that their homeland was without value to the white man. Then the surviving Navajo people were allowed to walk back home. No trace remains of the original fort, but you can explore some of the subterranean ruins of the main fort buildings. The most moving part of the monument is a simple shrine of stones brought from all over the path of the Long Walk from the Navajo homeland and left here by American Indians in loving memory of those who lived and died here. Closed Tuesday from November through April. Admission. ~ Billy the Kid Road; 505-355-2573, fax 505-355-2573; e-mail hweeldi@plateaupel.net.

From Fort Sumner, it's about an hour-and-a-half drive to the border town of Tucumcari. Drive 11 miles east on Route 60/84 to Taiban. From here, Route 252 climbs the corner of Llano Estacado, a high mesa that covers much of eastern New Mexico, and heads northeast until the town of Ragland. At Ragland, the road drops off from the Llano Estacado into the Canadian River Basin and merges with Route 209. The view of the bluffs as you descend the mesa is quite dramatic and unusual for this characteristically flat area. Take Route 209 north until you reach Tucumcari.

The town of Tucumcari was named for a Comanche lookout.

Tucumcari, created by the Rock Island Railroad at the turn of the 20th century, is actually best visited during the day when the **Tucumcari Historical Museum** throws open its doors. What you'll see at this Richardsonian Romanesque complex is a compilation of American Indian artifacts, gems, a still from Prohibition days and other odd items donated by locals. Pioneer wagons and a pre-1900 windmill highlight the outdoor displays. Closed Sunday year-round; also closed Saturday in winter. Admission. ~ 416 South Adams Street, Tucumcari; 505-461-4201; e-mail museum@city oftucumcari.com.

Santa Rosa has more than a dozen budget-priced motels—most of them locally owned and operated. The exception is the **Best Western Adobe Inn**, which straddles the budget and moderate price ranges for its spacious, modern rooms. ~ 1501 Historic Route 66 (Will Rogers Drive) at Route 40 Exit 275, Santa Rosa; 505-472-3446, 800-528-1234, fax 505-472-5759; www.bestwestern.com. BUDGET TO MODERATE.

LODGING

A cruise down the main street, Will Rogers Drive, reveals that close to half the commercial buildings in Santa Rosa are motels. A good bet is the **Travelodge**, which has double-room units for families. ~ 1819 Historic Route 66 (Will Rogers Drive), Santa Rosa; 505-472-3494, 800-578-7878. BUDGET.

Billy the Kid fans might consider spending the night in Fort Sumner at one of the two motels, both budget-priced. The **Billy the Kid Country Inn** is a roadside motel with kitchenettes and cable TV; continental breakfast is included. ~ 1700 East Sumner Avenue, Fort Sumner; 505-355-7414, fax 505-355-7478. BUDGET. The **Coronado Motel** has all the basic amenities of motels everywhere. ~ 309 West Sumner Avenue, Fort Sumner; 505-355-2466. BUDGET.

Motels have been an important industry in Tucumcari since the 1940s, when the town was a natural stop along Old Route 66 because it was the only place for many miles. Today, billboards along Route 40 for hundreds of miles in each direction tout the fact that Tucumcari has 2000 beds for rent. A number of motels in town still offer the authentic flavor of roadside America half a century ago. Even their names—Buckaroo, Lasso, Palomino, Apache—evoke a notion of the West in an earlier era.

> Contrary to many visitors' misconceptions, green chile is *not* milder than red chile.

Lovely gardens, a big pool and generous patios make the **Historic Pow Wow Inn** an ideal choice. Sixty-two modern rooms and suites appointed with American Indian prints and kachina-style lamps offer king- and queen-size beds as well as large vanity areas. ~ 801 Route 66, Tucumcari; 505-461-0500, 800-527-6996, fax 505-461-0135; www.powwowinn.net, e-mail office@powwowinn.net. MODERATE.

DINING

Settle into a booth at the **Comet II Drive-In Restaurant**, one of the last original Route 66 restaurants in town. The Comet is a '50s classic, well-known for its Chimayo–style New Mexican specialties, particularly the blue-corn chicken and smothered *chiles rellenos*. Gringos may want to stick with burgers and the like, but everyone can enjoy the homemade pies. Closed Monday. ~ 217 Parker Avenue, Santa Rosa; 505-472-3663. BUDGET.

Santa Rosa also has a dozen other restaurants of more recent vintage, most of them either nationwide franchises or motel restaurants but all of them in the budget range. For Mexican food, we recommend **Mateo's Family Restaurant**. If you haven't had a Mexican breakfast, try it here. ~ 500 Historic Route 66, Santa Rosa; 505-472-5720. BUDGET TO MODERATE.

Steaks, seafood and New Mexican food are found at **Joseph's Bar and Grill**. Breakfast, lunch and dinner are served. ~ 865 Historic Route 66, Santa Rosa; 505-472-3361. BUDGET.

One of the most attractive dining rooms on this side of the state, the **Pow Wow Restaurant** features a Navajo storm design motif. Hand-painted lamps and American Indian blankets add a handsome touch to this cheery restaurant. Choose from New Mexican specialties like *carne adovada* or stick with the more standard rib-eye steak and rainbow trout. Breakfast, lunch and dinner are served. ~ Historic Pow Wow Inn, 801 Route 66, Tucumcari; 505-461-0500, fax 505-461-0135. MODERATE.

If you've maxed out on New Mexican fare, why not head over to the **Golden Dragon** for a bowl of wonton soup and a generous serving of Mongolian beef. This Chinese restaurant overflows with shrines and Buddhas. ~ 1006 Route 66, Tucumcari; 505-461-2853. BUDGET TO MODERATE.

SHOPPING

We were so put off by the billboards advertising **Clines Corners** that we almost took a pass. Talk about a blight on the landscape! But like just about everyone else whistling along the interstate, we hit the brakes and drove on in to New Mexico's largest souvenir shop. The operating definition of kitsch, this tourist mecca warehouses thousands of moccasins, silkscreen lamps and baja jackets. It just might be the ultimate tourist trap. On the other hand, the prices aren't bad and there's plenty of selection. ~ Route 40 at Route 285, 1 Yacht Club Drive, Clines Corners; 505-472-5488, fax 505-472-5487.

The last of the original Route 66 curio shops in eastern New Mexico, **Tee Pee Curios**, a stucco tepee built in the '40s, offers a great photo opportunity for students of this region's recent past. Whether you're shopping for worrystones, twig baskets or authentic Navajo designs, this gift shop is a fun place to browse. If nothing else, buy a wooden postcard to send to your colleagues back at the office. Closed Sunday in winter. ~ 924 Route 66, Tucumcari; 505-461-3773.

NIGHTLIFE

Joseph's Bar and Grill has a deejay on Friday and Saturday nights. On weeknights, sports fans gather around the big-screen television to cheer on their favorite teams. ~ 865 Historic Route 66, Santa Rosa; 505-472-3361.

The kachina-style **Lizard Lounge** at the Historic Pow Wow Inn lounge has occasional live music on the weekends. ~ 801 Route 66, Tucumcari; 505-461-0500.

PARKS

BLUE HOLE The amazingly clear water at this spot attracts dive-club caravans from Texas, Oklahoma and Colorado on most weekends. Formed by a collapsed cave and fed by a subterranean river, the lake is deeper (81 feet) than it is wide. Carp live in the dark reaches far below the surface. Swimming is popular, and on hot summer days teenagers can often be seen cannonballing into Blue Hole from the cliffs above even though the year-round water temperature is a very chilly 64°. Facilities include restrooms, a picnic area and a dive shop. ~ Blue Hole Road, at the southeast edge of Santa Rosa. Follow the signs from Historic Route 66. For information and diving permits, call the Santa Rosa Information Center (505-472-3763, 505-472-3404, fax 505-472-3848; www.santarosanm.org).

Text continued on page 486.

Be a Road
Warrior

Albuquerque residents know it as the "Big I"—the congested freeway interchange in the middle of the city where two famous routes of bygone eras meet. Interstate Route 25 follows the path of the oldest highway still in use in the United States. Originally known as El Camino Real de Tierra Adentro ("the Royal Road to the Inner Land"), it was established in 1598 to link Mexico City with New Mexico, the northernmost province of the Spanish empire in America. El Camino Real spanned a distance of 1700 miles, crossing brutal expanses of desert and venturing through lands guarded by hostile Apache warriors. Spanish soldiers in armor traveled its length, as did hooded monks on foot. Horses, cows and *vaqueros* (cowboys) first came to the American West via the old Royal Road.

Interstate Route 40 traces Old Route 66, the first paved highway connecting the eastern United States and the West Coast. Route 66 was the kind of highway dreams are made of. It ran across vast, sunbaked, brightly colored desert inhabited by cowboys and Indians all the way to Hollywood, capturing America's imagination as it went. John Steinbeck wrote about it. Glenn Miller immortalized it in song. The television series *Route 66* was one of the most popular programs of the 1960s. Old Route 66 became practically synonymous with the mystique of the open road.

Before the two-lane, blacktop road was replaced by today's high-speed, limited-access highway, travelers had no alternative to driving down the main street of each small town along the route—places like Tucumcari, Santa Rosa, Laguna and Gallup. Today, chambers of commerce in these towns enthusiastically promote Route 66 nostalgia, and what used to be cheap roadside diners and tourist traps are now preserved as historic sites.

While both El Camino Real and Old Route 66 have been paved and straightened into modern interstate highways, travelers willing to take the extra time can still experience much of what it must have felt like to travel either of these roads in times past.

Alternate highways, usually traffic-free and often out of sight of the busy interstate, parallel Route 25 almost all the way from the Indian pueblos north of Albuquerque to El Paso and the Mexican border. These secondary highways trace El Camino Real more exactly than the interstate does, and the New Mexico state government has put up historical markers along them to identify important landmarks from Spanish colonial days such as the stark landscape of the Jornada del Muerto ("Journey of Death").

Good Camino Real alternatives to the interstate include Route 313 from Albuquerque north to San Felipe Pueblo; Routes 47 and 304 south of Albuquerque on the opposite side of the Rio Grande from the interstate, serving old rural communities such as Bosque Farms, Valencia and Belen; Route 1 from San Antonio through Bosque del Apache Wildlife Refuge to Elephant Butte Reservoir; Route 187 from Truth or Consequences to Las Cruces; and Route 28 from La Mesilla, just west of Las Cruces, to El Paso and the border.

Most of Old Route 66 has been obscured by interstate Route 40. Only a few sections of frontage roads and old secondary highways—notably Route 124 from Mesita through the villages of the Laguna Indian Reservation to Acoma—give any hint of the road that used to carry travelers across the desert. The place to look for remnants of Old Route 66 is along the main streets of towns that the interstate has bypassed. Deco-style diners, quaint ma-and-pa motels and old-fashioned curio shops with concrete Indian tepees out front and signs like "Last Chance Before the Desert!" and "See the Baby Rattlers!" can still be found on Route 40 business loops all across New Mexico, from Tucumcari to Albuquerque's Central Avenue to Gallup, where the main street was renamed Historic Route 66.

Traveling any of these alternate routes takes twice as long as driving the interstate. The rewards are several—avoiding busy truck routes, discovering the offbeat charm of small-town New Mexico and sampling what cross-country travel used to be like in the American Southwest.

SANTA ROSA LAKE STATE PARK A flood-control reservoir along the Pecos River, Santa Rosa Lake provides so much irrigation water to the surrounding farmlands that some years it can practically disappear in late summer. (Phone ahead to make sure the lake has water in it.) In wet years, the extensive shallows make for some of the best fishing in the state. Especially known for walleye, the lake is also stocked with crappie, catfish and bass. Most fishing here is done from boats. Waterskiing is also popular. A short "scenic trail" starts from the state park's Rocky Point Campground. The park has picnic tables, restrooms, showers and a visitors center. Day-use fee, $5. ~ From Santa Rosa, take Exit 277 from Route 40. Turn left on 2nd Street; continue to Eddy Avenue and turn right; continue north for seven miles; 505-472-3110, fax 505-472-5956.

▲ Rocky Point has 50 sites (23 with RV hookups), Juniper has 25 and Los Tanos has 15 (no hookups); $10 for standard sites, $14 per night for hookups. Reservations: 877-664-7787; some sites are first-come, first-served.

SUMNER LAKE STATE PARK On the Pecos River between Santa Rosa and Fort Sumner, this irrigation reservoir is one of New Mexico's most underused fishing lakes, with the added bonus of several quiet side canyons and a little village of summer cabins. The Y-shaped lake offers good spots for fishing from the shore in shallow, medium or deep water. Crappie, catfish, bluegill, northern pike and walleye are the common catches. State park areas below the dam provide access to both banks of the river. Swimming is permitted. There are picnic tables, restrooms and showers. Day-use fee, $5. ~ Located six miles off Route 84. The marked turnoff is 35 miles south of Santa Rosa and ten miles north of Fort Sumner; 505-355-2541, fax 505-355-2542.

▲ There are 32 developed sites (18 with RV hookups); primitive camping is available. Fees per night are $8 for primitive sites, $10 for developed sites, $14 per night for hookups.

AUTHOR FAVORITE

Janes-Wallace Memorial Park is really no more than a local fishing hole. But don't be put off. It's a great place to drop a line and is stocked with what may just be your dinner. Expect to catch bass, catfish and rainbow trout. There are no facilities. ~ Follow 3rd Street, which becomes Route 91, south from Historic Route 66. For information about the park, call the Santa Rosa Information Center; 505-472-3763, 505-472-3404, fax 505-472-3848; www.santarosanm.org.

BOSQUE REDONDO This Fort Sumner city park consists of a series of small lakes on 15 acres. The grassy shore, shaded by cottonwood trees, is a nice picnic spot. It's also a good place to fish. Ducks live on the lakes year-round. The park has outhouses. ~ Located two miles south of Fort Sumner on a marked road from the east edge of town.

CONCHAS LAKE STATE PARK Conchas Lake, on the Canadian River north of Tucumcari, is one of the most popular recreation lakes in New Mexico. Most of the 50-mile shoreline is privately owned, so the only easy public access to the lake is the state park, which includes developed areas on both sides of the dam. It's a good spot to fish and swimming and scuba diving are also permitted. There are picnic tables, restrooms, showers, marinas, bait and tackle, and groceries. Day-use fee, $5. ~ Located 25 miles north of Route 40 from the Newkirk/Route 129 exit, which is 27 miles east of Santa Rosa, or 34 miles northwest of Tucumcari on Route 104; 505-868-2270, 888-667-2757, fax 505-868-9641.

▲ There are 104 sites (40 are full RV hookups). Primitive camping available. Fees per night are $8 for primitive sites, $10 for developed sites and $14 for hookups.

GORDON WILDLIFE AREA Tucumcari has a municipal wildlife refuge on the edge of town where a number of lucky bird-watchers have actually seen eagles. The 770 acres of wetlands provide a rest stop for migrating ducks and geese. There are hiking trails as well as an auto road. ~ Located just east of town, marked by a sign on Tucumcari Boulevard (Route 40 Business Loop).

UTE LAKE STATE PARK This reservoir was created in 1963 specifically for recreational purposes to bring tourism to the Tucumcari area. Records have been set here for the largest smallmouth bass ever caught in New Mexico. The park has picnic tables, restrooms, showers, a marina and hiking trails. Day-use fee, $5. ~ Located 25 miles northeast of Tucumcari on Route 54, or three miles west of Logan via Route 540; 505-487-2284, fax 505-487-2497.

▲ There are 110 standard sites (77 with electric and water hookups) and three primitive camping areas. Fees per night are $8 for primitive sites, $10 for developed sites and $14 for hookups.

Mountainair Area

For centuries, the Mountainair area was one of New Mexico's most populous regions. Three large Anasazi pueblos, dating back to the 1200s, flourished here. Salt from nearby dry lakebeds was gathered and traded to other pueblos and to the Plains Indians as well. The communities still flourished in 1598, when the first Spanish soldiers and priests arrived and began building their missions. The

Spanish colonial presence lasted less than 80 years before famine, drought, disease and Apache raids forced priests and Indians alike to abandon all the pueblos in the area, moving to Isleta and other Rio Grande pueblos. Today, the Mountainair area is sparsely populated but serves as the backdrop for exploring the ruins of these ancient peoples.

SIGHTS

East of Route 25, 39 miles from Belen via Routes 47 and 60, **Mountainair** serves the local ranching community and provides travelers a base for exploring the widely separated units of **Salinas Pueblo Missions National Monument**. The national monument preserves the ruins of three sizable ancient pueblos that date back to the 1200s. Massive, crumbling walls of Franciscan churches adjoin each pueblo site. The **park headquarters** in town is a good starting point for your exploration of the national monument's three units. ~ On the corner of Broadway (Route 60) and Ripley Street, Mountainair; 505-847-2585, fax 505-847-2441; www. nps.gov/sapu.

The **Abo unit** of the national monument is just off Route 60. Unexcavated pueblo ruins and the remains of the Mission of San Gregorio de Abo fill the small park area sandwiched between private farms. A ceremonial kiva built within the church *convento* at Abo puzzles archaeologists, since elsewhere in the Salinas pueblos priests destroyed kivas to halt native religious practices. ~ Off Route 60, nine miles west of Mountainair; 505-847-2400, fax 505-847-2441.

The red-walled Franciscan mission at **Quarai** was in operation from 1630 to the late 1670s. Today, in its tranquil setting alongside big cottonwoods at the foot of the Manzano Mountains, Quarai is perhaps the most photogenic of the three Salinas mission ruins. The adjoining pueblo remains are thoroughly buried and difficult to see. A small museum displays relics found at the site as well as replicas. ~ Route 55, eight miles north of Mountainair; 505-847-2290, fax 505-847-2441.

HIDDEN ▶

Gran Quivira presents the national monument's most extensively excavated ruins. One of the largest pueblos in New Mexico, the limestone complex was home to about 2000 people at its height. Facilities include a visitors center with interpretive displays and a picnic area. There is no camping at any of the Salinas Pueblo Missions National Monument sites. ~ Route 55, 25 miles south of Mountainair; 505-847-2770, fax 505-847-2441.

LODGING

Because this area is sparsely populated and doesn't have much in the way of accommodations, people usually visit it as a daytrip from Santa Fe or Albuquerque.

However, if you need to rest your head while traveling through Mountainair, **Turner Inn & RV Park** will do. There are ten rooms (five singles and five doubles) and each comes with a microwave, refrigerator and coffeemaker. Eighteen RV sites are available for those who bring their lodging with them. ~ 303-East Route 60, Mountainair; 505-847-0248, 888-847-0170, fax 505-847-0202; www.turnerinnandrvpark.com, e-mail turner inn@uphi.net. BUDGET.

DINING

For sandwiches and burgers as well as fresh-baked pies and cakes, try **Granny's Sweet Shop**. Closed weekends. ~ Route 60, Mountainair; 505-847-1850. BUDGET.

SHOPPING

Cibola Arts is a great place to pick up a gift and see what Mountainair's local artisans are up to. A co-op gallery, it sells a broad range of paintings, jewelry, tin works, handmade dolls, weavings, batik silks, greeting cards and hand-dipped wax candles. Closed Monday. ~ 327 West Broadway, Mountainair; 505-847-0324; www.cibolaarts.com, e-mail marysbeads@yahoo.com.

PARKS

MANZANO MOUNTAINS STATE PARK 🏃 Located in the foothills near the village of Manzano and the Quarai Unit of the monument, this small state park provides the most convenient camping for visitors to the Salinas Pueblo Missions National Mon-

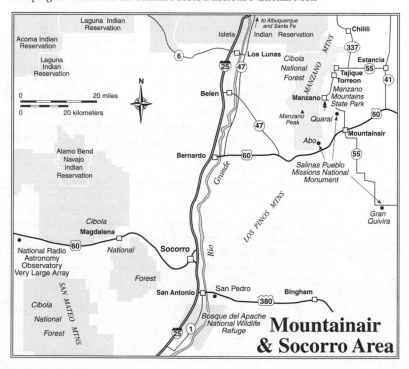

Mountainair & Socorro Area

ument. The forest road that continues past the state park turnoff leads to the Red Canyon trailhead at the Manzano Mountains Wilderness boundary. There are picnic tables, restrooms and nature trails. Closed November through March. Day-use fee, $5. ~ Off Route 55, 13 miles northwest of Mountainair, follow the highway signs; phone/fax 505-847-2820, 888-667-2757.

▲ There are 37 sites, one is handicapped reserved with a concrete ramp (8 with electric RV hookups). There are water hydrants in the park; primitive camping is also available. Fees for camping are $8 for primitive sites, $10 for standard sites, $14 per night for hookups.

▼▼▼▼▼▼▼▼▼▼
Socorro Area

Seventy-five miles south of Albuquerque just off Route 25 is Socorro, a town so small that the strip of motels and gas stations along the interstate business loop overshadow its distinctive character. But take the time to look around; it will be worth it. This sleepy municipality of 8000 souls is actually one of the oldest towns in the state, dating back to 1615 when Franciscan priests began building a mission. A couple of detours off the interstate will pique the interest of birders and history buffs.

SIGHTS

Socorro's plaza is surrounded by a small, attractive historic district a short distance west of California Street on Manzaneras Avenue. Noteworthy are the restored **San Miguel Mission** (505-835-2891, fax 505-835-1620; e-mail smiguel@sdc.org) at 403 El Camino Real, built in 1820 on the site of the church that was destroyed during the Pueblo Revolt of 1680; the old **Val Verde Hotel** at 203 Manzaneras Avenue East, built in 1919 and now used as apartments; and the **Garcia Opera House**, one of two opera houses in town during the 1880s. The **Hilton Block**, near the opera house, is named for a relative of hotel tycoon Conrad Hilton, who operated a drugstore there in the 1930s. Hilton was born and raised in San Antonio, a town about nine miles south of Socorro that is so tiny it has no hotel or motel.

Northwest of Socorro's downtown area is the **Mineral Museum** at the New Mexico Institute of Mining and Technology. The museum's possessions have been combined with specimens donated by prominent mining speculator C. T. Brown to form one of the better rock collections in the Southwest. The more than 10,000 pieces include gems and mining artifacts. ~ Corner of Olive Lane and Canyon Road, Socorro; 505-835-5140, fax 505-835-6333; www.geoinfo.nmt.edu.

An 18-mile drive south of Socorro, **Bosque del Apache National Wildlife Refuge** is especially worth visiting between November and March when it presents one of the most spectacular birdwatching opportunities around. The refuge was established during the 1930s to protect the sandhill crane, which had nearly vanished along the Rio Grande. Local farmers grow corn for the birds on refuge land during the summer months. The refuge also provides a winter home for about 40,000 snow geese. The white geese often rise en masse from the manmade wetlands to fill the sky in a noisy, dazzling display. Admission. ~ Off Route 25 Exit 139; 505-835-1828, fax 505-835-0314; www.southwest.fws.gov.

Of several ghost towns in the Socorro area, perhaps the most interesting is old **San Pedro**, across the river from San Antonio where visitors exit the interstate to go to Bosque del Apache. An abandoned mission church and ruins of several adobe houses in Mexican and early Territorial styles are about all that remain of San Pedro, a town where people once grew grapes and produced champagne. Tamarisks have grown up through the floors of the houses to conceal much of the village. ~ To get to San Pedro, drive east from San Antonio for 1.4 miles on Route 380 and turn south on an unpaved road.

New Mexico was a province of Mexico from 1821 until the 1848 treaty that ended the Mexican War with the United States.

Forty-six miles west of Socorro is the unusually named **National Radio Astronomy Observatory Very Large Array**. These 27 giant parabolic dish antennas, each weighing 235 tons, are used to search deep space for faint radio waves emitted by celestial objects. Together, the antennas can "see" as well as a telescope with a lens 20 miles in diameter and are used in combination with other radio observatories around the world to explore the far limits of the universe. A visitors center at the site explains how it works, and a one-hour, self-guided walking tour lets visitors see the antennas up close. ~ Route 60; 505-835-7000; www.nrao.edu, e-mail info@nrao.edu.

LODGING

Every motel in Socorro falls within the budget range. Accommodations are found in two clusters along California Street, the business loop from Route 25. The best in town is the **Days Inn**, about a block from San Miguel Mission. ~ 507 North California Street, Socorro; 505-835-0230, fax 505-835-1993. BUDGET.

Representative of the good, clean independent motels found in Socorro is the **Socorro Inn**. ~ 1009 North California Street, Socorro; 505-835-0276, fax 505-835-4142. BUDGET.

DINING

Don Juan's Cocina serves New Mexican fare. Closed Sunday. ~ 118 Manzaneras Avenue, Socorro; 505-835-9967. BUDGET.

In tiny San Antonio, nine miles south of Socorro, the **Owl Bar & Cafe** offers everything from inexpensive sandwiches to moderately priced steak dinners. Their claim to serve the best greenchile cheeseburgers in the world may well be accurate. Breakfast, lunch and dinner are served. Closed Sunday. ~ Route 380, Main Street, San Antonio; 505-835-9946. BUDGET TO MODERATE.

▼▼▼▼▼▼▼▼▼▼▼▼▼
Outdoor Adventures

FISHING

Although there aren't many options for skiing in the area, the easy access and reliable snowpack offered by the primary resort makes up for the lack of choices. You'll find both cross-country and downhill skiing right next to Albuquerque in the Sandia Mountains, and equipment rentals are readily available in town.

ALBUQUERQUE An average annual snowfall of 183 inches makes Sandia Peak one of the most popular ski slopes in New Mexico. Proximity to Albuquerque makes it the most crowded. **Sandia Peak Ski Area,** a short steep slope with an 1800-foot vertical drop, can be reached either by car or by the Sandia Peak Aerial Tramway. Snowboarding is allowed. The ski slope has six lifts serving trails rated 35 percent beginner, 55 percent intermediate and 10 percent expert. The ski season, which is unpredictable because there is little artificial snowmaking equipment, typically runs from mid-December to mid-March.

Sandia Peak also offers great cross-country skiing, especially on the Crest and 10-K trails, which begin near the Sandia Crest House at the top of the auto road. Alpine ski equipment and snowboards are available for rent. Adult and children's ski lessons are also offered. ~ 505-242-9133; www.sandiapeak.com.

Ski Rentals In Albuquerque, **The Bike Coop Ltd.** rents cross-country skis. ~ 3407 Central Avenue Northeast; 505-265-5170.

WIND-SURFING

New Mexico may not conjure up thoughts of windsurfing, but sailboards do shred the water at many of the state's lakes. Grab your board—or rent one—and hoist your sail. The sport is most popular at Cochiti Lake. Windsurfing is also permitted on Santa Rosa Lake, Conchas Lake and Ute Lake in the eastern part of the state.

BALLOON RIDES

Home of the annual balloon festival, Albuquerque has practically become synonymous with ballooning—at least, the sport is one of the city's major tourist attractions. If you rise early enough on a clear day (and most of them are), you'll see the multicolored creatures making their graceful ascent. Those who want to see what it's like to float above the city on the breeze can do so by contacting a local company like the **World Balloon.** They take to the air over Albuquerque with early-morning flights followed by champagne. ~ 1103 La Polana, Road Northwest, Albuquerque; 505-293-6800, 800-351-9588; www.worldballoon.com, e-mail info@worldballoon.com.

GOLF

Central New Mexico is an excellent place to spend a day on the greens—whether you stay in Albuquerque or head to the outlying areas, you'll find a nice spot to swing your clubs. Most facilities have club and/or cart rentals, as well as golf pros who offer lessons. For information on golf courses statewide, contact the **Sun**

In the Land
of Hot Air

On any weekend morning you can see as many as 50 hot-air balloons soaring gracefully across the sky above Albuquerque—or sometimes, when the air temperature is wrong, bouncing off suburban rooftops—with their gas burners roaring like dragons. Indeed, hot-air balloons are so much a symbol of Albuquerque that they appear as a motif decorating everything from fast-food restaurants to New Mexico's license plates.

Balloon fever, of course, is the result of the **Albuquerque International Balloon Fiesta**, the world's largest balloon event, which now lasts for nine days in early October. The fiesta's most spectacular events are dawn mass ascensions, in which more than 700 hot-air balloons, tethered to the ground, are illuminated from the inside in a colorful display. In between are many other events, from "splash-and-dashes," in which contestants try to touch the bottoms of their baskets in the Rio Grande without crashing, to a gas balloon distance race in which contestants start from Albuquerque and see who can fly farthest, sometimes landing as far away as the East Coast.

A victim of its own popularity, the Balloon Fiesta now requires advance planning and more than a little endurance of its audience. Part of the problem is that balloons fly best just after dawn, when the air temperature is cool and rising. To be at the Albuquerque Balloon Park before dawn means getting on the road by 3 a.m. so that you can get in line for the parking lots in time. Worse yet, in recent years the number of vehicles attending the Balloon Fiesta has exceeded the capacity of the parking lots, causing traffic jams that paralyzed Route 25 for hours. Then, too, there are not nearly enough hotel and motel rooms in Albuquerque to accommodate all the Balloon Fiesta spectators. Santa Fe's hotels are also packed, and many visitors end up searching for vacancies as far afield as Grants and Socorro.

While the city of Albuquerque experiments with solutions such as shuttles from other parts of the city, the best strategy—one that few people try—may be to spend the night in a campground on the back side of Sandia Crest, drive to the top ridge of the mountain before dawn, and view the mass ascension from above. ~ 4401 Alameda Northeast, Albuquerque, NM 87113; 505-821-1000, 888-422-7277, fax 505-828-2887; www.balloonfiesta.com, e-mail balloons@balloonfiesta.com.

Country Amateur Golf Association. ~ 1440 Rio Rancho Boulevard, Rio Rancho, NM 87124; 505-897-0864, 800-346-5319; www.newmexicogolf.org, e-mail scaga@prodigy.net.

ALBUQUERQUE   Tee off in Albuquerque at the 18-hole **University of New Mexico South Course.** ~ 3601 University Boulevard Southeast; 505-277-4546. The public **Arroyo del Oso Golf Course** is also popular and has both a 9-hole course and an 18-hole course, plus a driving range and putting greens. ~ 7001 Osuna Road Northeast; 505-884-7505.

OUTSIDE ALBUQUERQUE   Many Albuquerque golfers travel 40 miles north to play in a lovely setting below the rugged volcanic canyons of the Jemez Mountains at the Indian-owned **Pueblo de Cochiti Golf Course,** an 18-hole course in a beautiful lakeside setting surrounded by the multicolored foothills of the Jemez Mountains. ~ 505-465-2239.

SANTA ROSA AREA   Work on your line drives at the **Santa Rosa Golf Course,** with nine holes. There are carts available to rent, but no clubs. ~ 535 Chuck-n-Dale Lane; 505-472-4653. The nine-hole **Tucumcari Municipal Golf Course** is also open for public golfing. Closed Monday. ~ 4465-C Route 66; 505-461-1849.

SOCORRO AREA   Tee off at the 18-hole **New Mexico Institute of Mining and Technology Golf Course.** ~ 1 Canyon Road; 505-835-5335.

TENNIS   Tennis courts are very rare outside Albuquerque in central New Mexico. If you want to keep up your backstroke while on vacation, sign up for a court in Albuquerque at **Arroyo del Oso Park.** There are six unlit courts. ~ Wyoming Boulevard and Osuna Road Northeast. You can also serve and volley at the six lit courts at **Los Altos Park.** ~ 10300 Lomas Boulevard Northeast. You can also play a couple of matches on one of the 18 hardtop, unlit public courts at the **Albuquerque Tennis Complex.** Reservations recommended. Fee. ~ 1903 Avenida Cesar Chavez Southeast; 505-848-1381. **Sierra Vista West** has full facilities and ten courts: eight hard and two omni. ~ 5001 Montano Road Northwest; 505-897-8819.

BIKING   Central New Mexico is a popular place to pedal, with both on-road and off-road riders. Hit the trails to explore petroglyphs on an extinct volcano, or simply use your wheels to explore the urban outback of Albuquerque.

ALBUQUERQUE   A well-developed system of bike trails runs throughout Albuquerque. **Paseo del Bosque** is a paved bike and horse trail running for over 20 miles along the Rio Grande from south of Rio Bravo Boulevard to the northern edge of town, passing through the Rio Grande Nature Center. The **Paseo del**

Norte/North Channel Trail (7 miles) connects the Paseo del Bosque with the **Paseo del Noreste,** a six-mile trail, allowing residents of the fashionable Northeast Heights area to commute downtown by bicycle. **Paseo de las Montañas,** a 4.2-mile biking and jogging trail between Tramway Boulevard Northeast and the Winrock Shopping Center on the northeast side of the city, offers grand views of Albuquerque. For more information about bike trails and bike routes, contact the **Outdoor Recreation Division of Parks and Recreation.** ~ P.O. Box 1293, Albuquerque, NM 87103; 505-768-5300; e-mail jhart@cabq.gov.

MOUNTAINAIR AREA The roads in the vicinity of **Fourth of July Campground** in the Manzano Mountains are popular with mountain bikers.

SOCORRO AREA Outside Albuquerque, popular cycling trips include the level, unpaved 15-mile tour loop at **Bosque del Apache National Wildlife Refuge** near Socorro. ~ 505-835-1828.

Bike Rentals & Tours Northeast Cyclery Inc. rents mountain bikes and does repairs. ~ 8305 Menaul Boulevard Northeast, Albuquerque; 505-299-1210. For information on bike routes, call or pass by **Two Wheel Drive,** a good shop although they don't rent bikes. Closed Sunday. ~ 1706 Central Avenue Southeast, Albuquerque; 505-243-8443; www.twowheeldrive.com/bicycles.

HIKING

The trails of Central New Mexico, with their varied elevations, let you explore a variety of terrain—and your hike can be as convenient to Albuquerque or as remote as you wish. Hike in a lush north-facing valley or on a barren western slope, in a forest of Douglas fir, maple or quaking aspen—or in no forest at all. Climb 10,000-foot peaks or do a bit of spelunking underground, the choice is yours. Just be prepared for changeable weather . . . and breathtaking views. All distances are one way unless otherwise noted.

ALBUQUERQUE **Sandia Peak,** the 10,378-foot mountain that fills Albuquerque's eastern skyline, offers hiking trails for every preference, from gentle strolls to ambitious ascents.

The easiest way to hike Sandia is to either drive or take the aerial tramway to the crest of the mountain and walk the well-worn trail between the restaurant at the top of the tramway and

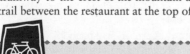

AUTHOR FAVORITE

My favorite mountain-biking area in Albuquerque is the series of five extinct volcanoes that make up a city-owned open space on **West Mesa,** the western skyline of the city. Dirt roads ramble all around the volcanoes and lead to petroglyphs at the edge of the West Mesa Escarpment.

the gift shop at the end of the auto road, a distance of about a mile with continuous views of the city below. The **Crest Trail** continues along the top ridge through the Sandia Wilderness Area all the way down to Canyon Estates, 10.5 miles to the south near Route 40, and Placitas, almost 16 miles to the north.

The **10-K Trail** (4.8 miles) starts at a trailhead two miles down the road from the crest and reaches the top ridge at the broadcast towers north of the gift shop. The hike to the summit leads through shady forests of Douglas fir, aspen and spruce with a 1000-foot elevation gain. A continuation of the trail follows the road back down to the trailhead to close the loop.

> Temperatures on the crest of Sandia Peak run about 20° cooler than on Albuquerque's downtown streets.

A trailhead midway up the Sandia Peak road marks the **Tree Spring Trail** (2 miles), which climbs to the top ridge, joining the Crest Trail a mile and a half south of the tram station. It is a 1400-foot climb from the trailhead to the crest.

One of the most challenging trails on Sandia Peak is **La Luz Trail** (5.8 miles), which takes expert hikers up the seemingly sheer west face of the mountain from Juan Tabo Picnic Ground to the tram station on the crest. It's a climb from 7060 feet elevation at the foot of the mountain to 10,378 at the summit. You can ride the tram to the top and hike back down the trail. The **Pino Canyon Trail** (4.7 miles) is newer—and even more difficult, some hikers say—rising 2800 feet from Elena Gallegos Picnic Ground to the summit. The hike is quite scenic and shadier than La Luz Trail.

On the north side of Sandia Peak, lush **Las Huertas Canyon** is accessible by the road that leads from Route 25 through the village of Placitas or by a steep, narrow road that descends from the Sandia Crest Highway. Near the upper end of the canyon, an easy .75-mile trail takes hikers along the canyon wall to **Sandia Man Cave**, where University of New Mexico archaeologists found artifacts left by Paleo Indians at the end of the last Ice Age. A flashlight and safety gear are needed to reach the inner recesses of the cave—plan on getting dirty. For more information on trails in the Sandia area, call 505-281-3304, fax 505-281-1176; www.fs.fed.us/r3/cibola.

MOUNTAINAIR AREA   A profusion of bigtooth maple trees makes Fourth of July Campground near Tajique, located about 30 miles south of the Tijeras exit from Route 40, a favorite for fall hiking. The moderate **Fourth of July Trail** (1.3 miles) leaves from the campground and climbs northwest to the **Manzano Crest Trail** (22 miles), which affords great views of the Rio Grande and Estancia valleys. The moderate **Albuquerque Trail** (3.4 miles roundtrip) begins at the end of Forest Road 55C, a half mile northeast of the Fourth of July Campground, and runs north to the Isleta Indian Reservation boundary.

The southern Manzano Mountains offer excellent hiking opportunities. Two of the best trails here start from the unpaved road past Manzano Mountains State Park near the town of Manzano, just north of the Quarai unit of Salinas Pueblo Missions National Monument.

The difficult **Red Canyon Trail** (2.4 miles) follows a creek with small waterfalls into the Manzano Mountain Wilderness until it's within scrambling distance of the summit of Gallo Peak, elevation 10,003 feet. It is a strenuous climb with a 2000-foot altitude gain.

The **Kayser Mill Trail** (3.3 miles) climbs 1794 feet to intersect the **Manzano Crest Trail**, which runs along the top ridge of the Manzanos. To reach the summit of Manzano Peak, elevation 10,098 feet, follow the Crest Trail for about a mile south of the intersection. For more information, contact the Mountainair Ranger District of Cibola National Forest. ~ 505-847-2990, fax 505-847-2238.

SOCORRO AREA From the upper ridges of the Magdalena Mountains, you can see Sandia Peak in the distance. Notice the difference. While hiking any of the Sandia trails on a summer day can be a very social experience, few people visit the Magdalenas. **North Baldy Trail** (6 miles), the best hiking access, is a challenge to reach. Beyond Water Canyon Campground, off Route 60 about 16 miles west of Socorro, eight miles of unpaved, narrow, rocky road lead to the trailhead. The trail starts near the summit, where the state operates a laboratory to study thunderstorms. After a short, steep climb, the main trail runs along a ridgeline of high mountain meadows to the North Baldy summit (elevation 9858 feet).

Transportation

CAR

Two major interstate highways, **Route 25** and **Route 40**, cross near the center of Albuquerque, an intersection known locally as the "Big I." Santa Rosa is on Route 40, two hours east of Albuquerque, and Tucumcari is another hour east of Santa Rosa.

The most direct way to reach Mountainair from Albuquerque is by exiting Route 25 at Belen and taking **Route 47**, which merges into **Route 60** and runs through Mountainair. Route 60 parallels Route 40 across eastern New Mexico and runs through Fort Sumner. A straight and very empty two-lane highway through pronghorn antelope country, **Route 41** is the most direct route between Santa Fe and the Mountainair area. Driving south of Albuquerque on Route 25 will bring you to Socorro. For New Mexico road conditions, call 800-432-4269.

AIR

Albuquerque International Sunport is the only major commercial passenger terminal in the state. Carriers include American Airlines, Continental Airlines, Delta Air Lines, Frontier Airlines, Great Plains Airlines, Mesa Airlines, Northwest Airlines, Skywest Airlines, Southwest Airlines, United Airlines and US Airways. ~ 505-842-4366; www.cabq.gov/airport.

Taxis and hotel courtesy vans wait for passengers in front of the airport terminal. **Santa Fe Shuttle** (505-243-2300, 888-833-2300) and **Sandia Shuttle** (505-243-3244, 888-775-5696; www.sandiashuttle.com) provide transportation to and from Albuquerque and Santa Fe. **Twin Hearts Express** (505-751-1201, 800-654-9456) and **Faust's Transportation** (505-758-3410, 888-830-3410) provide transportation between Albuquerque and Taos. **Sun Tran**, Albuquerque's public bus system, also serves the airport. ~ 505-243-7433.

BUS

Greyhound Bus Lines (800-231-2222; www.greyhound.com) and **TNM&O Coaches** provide service to Albuquerque, Tucumcari, Clovis and Portales. ~ Albuquerque Bus Transportation Center: 320 1st Street Southwest; 505-243-4435. Tucumcari: 2618 South 1st Street; 505-461-1350. Portales: 820 West 2nd Street; 505-356-6914.

TRAIN

Amtrak's "Southwest Chief," which chugs between Chicago and Los Angeles, stops daily at the Albuquerque passenger station. ~ 214 1st Street Southwest; 505-842-9650, 800-872-7245; www.amtrak.com.

CAR RENTALS

Agencies at Albuquerque International Sunport include **Advantage Rent A Car** (800-777-5500), **Avis Rent A Car** (800-331-1212), **Budget Rent A Car** (800-527-0700), **Dollar Rent A Car** (800-800-4000), **Enterprise Rent A Car** (800-736-8222), **Hertz Rent A Car** (800-654-3131), **National Car Rental** (800-227-7368) and **Thrifty Car Rental** (800-847-4389). Located just outside the airport, **Alamo Rent A Car** (800-462-5266) offers free shuttle service to and from the terminal. ~ 2200 Sunport Boulevard Southeast.

Any of the agencies listed in the Albuquerque Yellow Pages can arrange car pickups and drop-offs at the airport or a hotel.

PUBLIC TRANSIT

Sun Tran, Albuquerque's metropolitan bus system, has routes covering most parts of the city, including the airport, the bus depot, Old Town, the University of New Mexico and all major shopping malls. ~ 100 1st Street Southwest; 505-243-7433.

TAXIS

Taxi services in Albuquerque include **Albuquerque Cab Co.** (505-883-4888) and **Yellow Cab Co.** (505-247-8888).

THIRTEEN

Southern New Mexico

Southern New Mexico has little in common with the northern part of the state. In pre-Columbian times, when the Ancestral Pueblo people were building cities in the Four Corners area, the Mogollon occupied the southern region, living in small cliff-dwelling communities. Their pottery has long been famed for the imaginative artistry of its animal motifs, but scientists are only now realizing what a sophisticated knowledge of astronomy the Mogollon people possessed. It is believed that they merged with the Ancestral Pueblo and Sinagua cultures of the Mogollon Rim, just to the north, centuries before nomadic Apaches moved into the region and the first European settlers arrived in New Mexico.

The Spanish colonists who settled Santa Fe avoided the south, where the land was parched and arid, and Apache Indians terrorized any outsider who set foot in their territory. Most of the development in southern New Mexico has come in the 20th century, from air force bases to ski resorts and huge boating reservoirs. Today descendants of the Apaches operate exclusive recreation facilities at the edge of the Mescalero Apache Indian Reservation near Ruidoso.

With the exception of Carlsbad Caverns National Park, southern New Mexico is less visited by vacationers than other parts of the state. That's surprising, and somewhat disappointing, for this region boasts enough outdoor sports and road-side sightseeing to fill a two-week vacation easily. Cool islands of high mountain forest offer relief from the scorching summers of the Chihuahuan Desert. On top of this, they're great for winter skiing. The lowlands enjoy a much longer warm season for spring and fall outdoor activities than Albuquerque, Santa Fe or Taos, making the entire region an attractive year-round destination.

Southern New Mexico is divided into several geographic regions. The area east of the mountains is, for all practical purposes, indistinguishable from west Texas. Carlsbad Caverns is closer to the Texas state line than to any New Mexico town. Ruidoso, the horse racing and skiing town in the mountains west of Roswell, caters almost exclusively to visitors from Texas. South of Ruidoso, memories of the Wild West live on in Lincoln, once among the most lawless towns on the frontier, now a low-key historic district.

Driving on Route 25 or the older highway that parallels it, motorists find an empty landscape flanking a series of large recreational lakes. Taking Route 54 through the Tularosa Basin, the sights are more unusual—a giant lava field, many ancient Indian petroglyphs, and miles of pure white sand dunes. In the mountains just west of Alamogordo, charming little Cloudcroft is a bustling ski town in the winter and a cool, quiet haven the rest of the year.

The southwestern part of the state is filled with national forest. Driving to the boundary of the roadless Gila Wilderness, the largest wilderness area in the lower 48 states, you won't find any gas stations or grocery stores along the route, but you will discover many scenic lookouts, mountain lakes and hiking trails. Travel within the Gila Wilderness is restricted to horseback riders and hikers. A driving trip from Gila Cliff Dwellings National Monument in the canyonlands at the heart of the wilderness to the Catwalk on the western perimeter and then north through the ghost town of Mogollon to Snow Lake on the high mountain slopes can take several scenic, pleasurable and adventurous days.

▼ ▼ ▼ ▼ ▼ ▼ ▼ ▼ ▼ ▼ ▼ ▼ ▼ ▼ ▼ ▼

Southeastern New Mexico

Travelers to Southeastern New Mexico won't be disappointed. Carlsbad Caverns National Park, one of New Mexico's top vacation destinations, offers a vast, silent world of gemlike crystals and massive stalactites deep below the earth's surface. Those who venture to this region can also discover Carlsbad's peaceful river park and desert museum and Roswell's unique "bottomless" lakes. The Lincoln historic district recalls the bloody days when six-guns ruled the land, while the Mescalero Apache operate a five-star ski resort in Ruidoso. Technicolor sunsets, secluded mountain lakes and great mountain biking are just the extra attractions.

SIGHTS   **Carlsbad Caverns National Park** takes you 750 feet underground inside a limestone reef in the foothills of the Guadalupe Mountains, where sulfuric acid from oil pockets trapped in Permian Basin shales hollowed out a spectacular honeycomb of caves. Eons of dripping dampness decorated the cave with an amazing display of natural mineral spires, curtains, crystals and lace. Bottomless pits, fairy temples and alien landscapes challenge your imagination. There are more than a hundred known limestone caves in the park, nine of which are open to cavers with permits; only three are open to the public. Admission. ~ The entrance to Carlsbad Caverns is either off Route 285 or off Route 62/180. It is 23 miles northeast of the town of Carlsbad and only 17 miles from the Texas state line; 505-785-2232, 800-967-2283, fax 505-785-2133; www.nps.gov/cave, e-mail cave_interpretation@nps.gov.

Carlsbad Cavern is the cave most people visit, the big one with the visitors center on the surface and an elevator that runs to the cave's Big Room 750 feet below. Visitors can choose from two self-guided tours or a ranger-led tour. On the easy Big Room Tour,

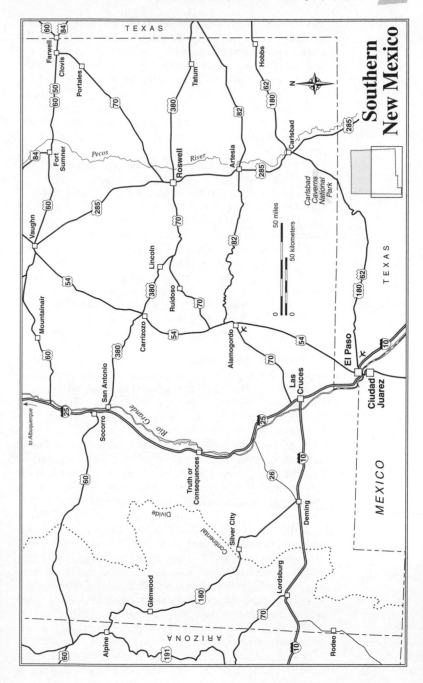

Southern New Mexico

they ride both ways on the elevator to see only the Big Room on a mostly level one-mile paved loop trail. Those who pick the much more strenuous—and more rewarding—1.5-mile Natural Entrance Tour walk a switchback trail from the mouth of the cave down to a depth of 750 feet at the deepest point, climb back to the Big Room and ride the elevator back up to the ground level. However you reach it, the Big Room inspires awe with its eight acres of floor area, 200-foot-high ceiling and massive, looming stalactites and towering stalagmites and columns. The ranger-led King's Palace Tour takes visitors to four different rooms: King's Palace, Queen's Chamber, Papoose Room and Green Lake Room. Be sure to bring a flashlight.

HIDDEN ▶   Another cave open to the public is **Slaughter Canyon Cave,** in an isolated part of the park backcountry reached via a county road that is gravel part of the way. Though it has been open for tours since 1974, Slaughter Canyon Cave is undeveloped and can only be toured with a ranger. Tours must be booked in advance at the main visitors center (all tours require reservations: 800-967-2283), and children under age six are not allowed. The hardest part of the tour is the climb to the cave entrance 500 feet above

HIDDEN ▶   the parking lot. **Spider Cave** is a primitive cave also in the backcountry. The small ranger-led tour (Sunday only) takes about four hours and involves lots of crawling and climbing; children under 12 are not allowed.

The **Million Dollar Museum,** just outside the park entrance, is the largest historical museum in southeastern New Mexico, with 11 rooms of exhibits including dolls, guns, music boxes, ranch antiques and mummified Indians. Admission. ~ 30 Carlsbad Caverns Highway, Whites City; 505-785-2291 ext. 204, fax 505-785-2283.

In the town of **Carlsbad,** a marked auto tour route runs along the Pecos River, which is partially dammed to form long, narrow Carlsbad Lake through town. At **Port Jefferson** you can take a 40-minute scenic tour aboard the vintage paddlewheeler, *George Washington.* Open Memorial Day through Labor Day. ~ Park Drive, Carlsbad; 505-887-8343.

Living Desert Zoo and Gardens State Park offers a close-up look at the animal and plant life of the Chihuahuan Desert. Inhabitants include a mountain lion, a bobcat, "Maggie" the painting black bear, rare Mexican wolves, bison, elk and javelinas, to name a few. There is a mineral exhibit in the visitors center and an indoor exhibit that contains giant tropical cactus species from around the world. Admission. ~ Just off Route 285; 505-887-5516, fax 505-885-4478; www.livingdesertfriends.org, e-mail livingdesertzoo@zignet.com.

The largest town in southeastern New Mexico, with a population of nearly 50,000, **Roswell** is the shipping and commercial center for thousands of square miles of ranchlands in the region. At first glance, Roswell does not look like the kind of place that would have much to offer vacationers. But explore a bit and you'll discover some little-known sightseeing treasures. Bottomless Lakes State Park and Bitter Lake National Wildlife Refuge are described in the "Parks" section below.

The **Roswell Museum and Art Center** is one of the best in the Southwest, with collections ranging from Western art and Indian artifacts to early rockets. The museum highlights a collection of paintings by famed landscape painter and portraitist Peter Hurd, who was born in Roswell and spent most of his life on his ranch nearby. Another exhibit is the Rogers and Mary Ellen Aston Collection, which features 2000 pieces from the American West. Other artists represented here include Georgia O'Keeffe and Marsden Hartley. The museum also boasts the **Robert H. Goddard Planetarium** (admission), which presents educational programs and laser lightshows. It is not open on a regular basis so call ahead. ~ 100 West 11th Street, Roswell; 505-624-6744,

Southeastern
New Mexico

fax 505-624-6765; www.roswellmuseum.org, e-mail rmac@ roswellmuseum.org.

Roswell is perhaps most famous as the site where UFO buffs believe an extraterrestrial spacecraft crashed in 1947. At the time, the "flying saucer" was officially dismissed as a stray weather balloon. In the decades since, with the general fading of the federal government's credibility, the Roswell myth has been enhanced through movies and television.

At the **International UFO Museum and Research Center**, founders include retired military personnel on duty at the time of the 1947 retrieval of alleged space aliens. There's an Area 51 exhibit, a gift shop and a research library where you can learn about mysterious abduction reports and unusual personal experiences. ~ 114 North Main Street, Roswell; 505-625-9495, fax 505-625-1907; www.iufomrc.com, e-mail iufomrc@iufomrc.com.

> Satellites use south central New Mexico as a landmark to calibrate their cameras—the jet black lava flows of the Valley of Fires and the dazzling dunes of White Sands form the highest-contrast terrain feature on the entire surface of the earth.

What do football great Roger Staubach and New Mexico artist Peter Hurd have in common, other than that they're good with their hands? Both were students at New Mexico Military Institute, an institution that has sent more than 2800 graduates into combat duty since the Spanish American War. The proud heritage of NMMI is captured at the **General Douglas L. McBride Museum**. Grouped by war, the exhibit areas showcase many little-known treasures, including a machine-gun-toting Harley Davidson used by one of General Pershing's squadrons in the assault on Pancho Villa in 1916. Closed Saturday through Monday and when school is not in session. ~ 101 West College Boulevard, Roswell; 505-622-6250, fax 505-624-8258; www.nmmi.cc.nm.us, e-mail hardman@email.nmmi.edu.

Experience turn-of-the-20th-century New Mexican life at the **Historical Center for Southeast New Mexico, Inc.**, a museum that spans the period from 1865 to 1940. It's located in a grand 1910 prairie-style structure and is decorated with pioneer antiques and Victorian furniture. The collection of artifacts is drawn from local Chaves County residents. Children will be fascinated by the display of vintage toys. ~ 200 North Lea Avenue, Roswell; 505-622-8333, fax 505-623-8746; www.hssnm.net, e-mail history@hssnm.net.

About 70 miles west of Roswell, and a world apart, is **Ruidoso**. Set among soaring pines and secluded valleys, Ruidoso is a year-round resort offering skiing, sledding, hiking, fishing and, its biggest summer draw, horse racing.

The racetrack, **Ruidoso Downs Racetrack and Casino**, is located five miles east of town. Quarter horses and thoroughbreds run here Thursday through Sunday afternoons during the summer season, climaxing with the All-American Futurity, the world's richest quarter horse race with a $2 million purse. At the end of the racing season, high-priced horse auctions are a last burst of excitement. The Ruidoso Downs Casino offers pari-mutuel betting on simulcast races year-round. The racetrack is closed from September to Memorial Day, but the casino is open daily. ~ Route 70 East, Ruidoso; 505-378-4431, fax 505-378-4631; www.rdracing.com.

Adjacent to the racetrack is a noteworthy collection of horse memorabilia at the **Hubbard Museum of the American West**. An upstairs gallery traces 30,000 years of equine history and offers some surprising insights on the development of the West. Exhibits change quarterly. Admission. ~ 841 Route 70 West, Ruidoso; 505-378-4142, fax 505-378-4166; www.hubbardmuseum.org, e-mail info@hubbardmuseum.org.

A 45-minute drive from Ruidoso is the historic town of **Lincoln**. The village of Lincoln would have faded from the map generations ago had it not been the scene of an infamous "war" between two competing groups of storekeepers and ranchers in 1878. After the leader of one faction was assassinated, one of his employees, a professional gunman known as Billy the Kid, avenged him by killing all the participants in the ambush and their bosses. The Lincoln County War ultimately brought down the territorial government of New Mexico and made Billy the Kid a legend.

The whole village and its surrounding area is now a historic district, giving Lincoln the authentic feel of a late-19th-century town. The focal points of a walking tour of Lincoln are several units of **Lincoln State Monument** as well as other structures. The Old Courthouse contains exhibits explaining the Lincoln County War and an actual bullethole made by Billy the Kid during a jailbreak. The restored Montaño Store Museum represents the Hispanic culture of the area with exhibits about the Montaños, who lived here during the Lincoln County War. Admission. ~ Off Route 380, Lincoln; phone/fax 505-653-4372; www.nmmonuments.com.

A few miles west of Lincoln, the sightseeing highlight in the small town of Capitan is **Smokey Bear Historical State Park**. A must for kids and anyone interested in the history of advertising, this small museum traces the career of America's best-known bear from early artist's sketches through more than 60 years of forest service propaganda, children's comics and commercial kitsch. A film tells the story of the "real" Smokey the Bear (1950–1976), who was rescued by rangers from a fire in Lincoln National Forest and sent to live in a Washington, D.C., zoo. The live bear was named after the imaginary character, not vice versa as legend suggests. Admission. ~ 118 Smokey Bear Boulevard, Cap-

Text continued on page 508.

In the Land of Outlaws

No other character in New Mexico's history captures the imagination like Billy the Kid. He was the west's enigmatic "live fast, die young" character, a sort of 19th-century James Dean who has lived on in novels and movies. More than a century after his violent death at the age of 21, Billy the Kid's legend seems stronger than ever. Travelers can explore throughout southern New Mexico, from Lincoln to Mesilla to Silver City and beyond, following historical markers that recall the outlaw's exploits.

Lincoln is where the foundation was laid for Billy the Kid's immortality. There, visitors learn about the 1878 Lincoln County War, a violent conflict between a naive newcomer and a ruthless cattle baron that spread to involve the whole county in gunfights and arson for months and finally toppled the government of territorial New Mexico. Billy the Kid was on the side of the "good guys," legally deputized to capture the gunmen who had murdered his employer. Instead of arresting them, however, he shot them to death, causing modern scholars to believe that he was a violent sociopath.

After ridding Lincoln County of its nest of cattle rustlers, robber barons and corrupt politicians, Billy was granted amnesty by the new governor of New Mexico, Lew Wallace. Many people throughout the county reputedly saw him as a Robin Hood character. Yet he became the region's leading cattle rustler himself before he was hunted down for the murders of two sheriffs and a deputy and shot to death by the newly appointed Lincoln County sheriff, his old friend Pat Garrett.

One of the things Billy the Kid did best was escape. Two of his most daring escapes—one from a burning house under siege by a local posse and federal troops, the other from a makeshift jail cell in the old courthouse that houses the Lincoln State Monument headquarters today—took place in Lincoln.

South of Lincoln, in Ruidoso, visitors can see the water wheel of Dowlin's Mill, where gunmen cornered Billy the Kid seeking revenge for a friend he had shot. Billy escaped by hiding in a flour barrel. Located south of Ruidoso, Blazer's Mill near Mescalero was the site of a furious shootout during which the leader of the band of gunmen known as the Regulators was killed, after which Billy, the youngest and wildest member of the gang, took command.

Billy the Kid enthusiasts—and southern New Mexico sees its fair share of them—can find traces of the outlaw and his legend all across the state. On the outskirts of Fort Sumner (see Chapter Five for more information) is the site of Billy the Kid's grave near the ranch where Pat Garrett caught up with him. Fort Sumner also has the two biggest Billy the Kid museums in the state.

On Route 70 east of Las Cruces, a state sign marks the spot where Garrett himself was later killed in a dispute over goat grazing. In old Mesilla, just outside of Las Cruces, visitors can see the courthouse where Billy was convicted and sentenced to hang for murdering a lawman. (He escaped.)

North of Carrizozo on the way to Corona, a marker tells of yet another siege in which Billy and his gang were trapped by a posse inside a burning stagecoach station but escaped in the confusion after a deputy sheriff was killed in the crossfire while trying to negotiate a surrender.

Before the Lincoln County War began, Billy the Kid worked in a general store at Seven Rivers. The townsite is lost beneath the waters of Brantley Dam, but details can be found in the small historical museum in Artesia. Earlier, Billy spent part of his boyhood and attended school briefly in Silver City. His childhood cabin and his mother's grave are there, along with the first jail he ever escaped from—at the age of 15 while in custody for robbing a Chinese laundry.

Populist hero or psychopathic killer? Historians and Hollywood scriptwriters are still guessing. But one thing's for sure: Billy the Kid wandered far and wide across some of the prettiest country anywhere.

itan; 505-354-2748, fax 505-354-6012; www.smokeybearpark.
com, e-mail smokeybear@state.nm.us.

LODGING   Visitors to Carlsbad Caverns may choose to stay at Whites City
by the national park entrance or in the town of Carlsbad, a 20-
minute drive away.

In Whites City, the **Whites City Resort** includes the **Best Western Cavern Inn** and the **Walnut Canyon Inn**, both of which offer
fairly standard motel accommodations. ~ 17 Carlsbad Canyon
Highway, Whites City; 505-785-2291, 800-228-3767, fax 505-
785-2283; www.whitescity.com, e-mail whitescity@whitescity.
com for both inns. MODERATE.

In the town of Carlsbad, the **Ocotillo Inn** offers spacious
guest rooms surrounding a courtyard patio and pool. A deluxe
continental breakfast is included. ~ 3706 National Parks Highway, Carlsbad; 505-887-2861, 800-321-2861, fax 505-887-2861
ext. 310; www.ocotilloinn.com. BUDGET TO MODERATE.

Roswell's lodging scene is unexceptional. The top of the line
is the **Best Western Sally Port Inn**, with its tropical atrium, spa facilities and guest rooms with tall picture windows and some with
refrigerators and microwaves. ~ 2000 North Main Street, Roswell;
505-622-6430, 800-528-1234, fax 505-623-7631; www.bestwest
ern.com. BUDGET TO MODERATE.

One of the better low-priced motels is the **Frontier Motel**. ~
3010 North Main Street, Roswell; 505-622-1400, 800-678-1401,
fax 505-622-1405. BUDGET.

HIDDEN ►   For more than half a century **Dan Dee Cabins** has been the
quintessential cottage resort, a tradition among families who
know this mountain region well. Thirteen cabins—with one to
three bedrooms each—spread across five nicely landscaped acres
with picnic and barbecue areas. Equipped with full kitchens and
fireplaces, these units are a short walk from a fishing stream and
convenient to year-round resort activities. Dan Dee Cabins is one
of the friendliest places we found in New Mexico. ~ 310 Main
Road, Ruidoso; 505-257-2165, 800-345-4848; www.dandee
cabins.com. MODERATE.

Several complexes near the Ruidoso River rent 30 cabins,
from one-room to six-bedroom in the pines with kitchens and
fireplaces, including **Story Book Cabins**. ~ 410 Main Road, Ruidoso; 505-257-2115, 888-257-2115, fax 505-257-7512; www.
storybookcabins.com, e-mail cabins@ruidoso.net. **Whispering
Pines Cabins** is another such establishment, renting 22 cabins,
most with fireplaces and many with kitchens. ~ 422 Main Road,
Ruidoso; 505-257-4311. MODERATE TO DELUXE.

Lower-priced motels in the Ruidoso area cluster east of town
on Route 70 near the Ruidoso Downs racetrack. For low-cost
lodging, try the comfortable, 17-room **Economy Inn**. It's clean and

simple and has color televisions. ~ 2019 Route 70, Ruidoso; 505-378-4706, fax 505-378-8698. BUDGET TO MODERATE.

Lincoln has a small selection of memorable places to stay, and advance reservations are essential at all of them.

Located in the oldest building in Lincoln County, **Ellis Store Country Inn,** a Territorial-period adobe, offers eight rooms with private and shared baths. A full breakfast is included; a six-course gourmet dinner is available by reservation. ~ Mile Marker 98, Route 380, Lincoln; 505-653-4609, 800-653-6460, fax 505-653-4610; www.ellisstore.com, e-mail ellistore@pvtn.net. DELUXE.

Art lovers should seek out the **Hurd Ranch Guest Homes,** where artist Michael Hurd has renovated four adobe *casitas* (one to three bedrooms) with a blend of traditional Southwestern and contemporary furniture. Located on the 2300-acre Sentinel Ranch, all units feature saltillo tile, wood-burning fireplaces, complete kitchens and patios. The main house (the Henrietta Wyeth House) has two bedrooms. Also available is the more expensive contemporary suite in the Hurd–La Rinconada Gallery. This two-story unit, which features a private balcony, is decorated with original paintings by members of the famous Hurd family. ~ Mile Marker 281, Route 70, San Patricio; 505-653-4331, 800-658-6912, fax 505-653-4218; www.wyethartists.com, e-mail hlrg@pvtnetworks.net. DELUXE TO ULTRA-DELUXE.

Cavern Coffee Shop serves inexpensive fare in the national park visitors center. It is often crowded enough to make hungry sightseers wish they'd brought a picnic lunch. Inside the cave, near the elevators that carry visitors back to the surface at the end of the tour, the restaurant serves lunch specials with sandwiches and burgers. ~ Carlsbad Caverns National Park; 505-785-2281, fax 505-785-2302; www.nps.gov/cave. BUDGET.

DINING

Cortez has been a popular place with locals for more than 50 years with its affordably priced Mexican dishes. Seasonal hours,

AUTHOR FAVORITE

Whenever I need to pamper myself, I check into the **Apple Tree Inn & Retreat Center,** which has five full-kitchen suites and five suites with bedrooms and living rooms, as well as a two-bedroom stone house. Most rooms have fireplaces and individual in-room jacuzzis; all have private baths and entrances. All open onto the spa pavilion with its hot tubs, steam room, and massage and exercise area. Lodging is limited in April and early November. ~ 100 Lower Terrace, Ruidoso; 505-257-1717, 877-277-5322, fax 505-257-1718; www.stayinruidoso.com, e-mail questions@stayinruidoso.com. MODERATE TO DELUXE.

call ahead. ~ 506 South Canal Street, Carlsbad; 505-885-4747. BUDGET.

Yes, **A Taste of Europe** can be found in Roswell. Granted, their most popular dishes are Italian, but they still offer a smorgasbord of samplings from Poland, Hungary, France, Germany and more. So be adventurous and order knödel (dumplings) instead of veal parmesan. Breakfast on weekends. Closed Monday. ~ 1300 North Main Street, Roswell; 505-632-0313. BUDGET TO MODERATE.

For some good old-fashioned American fare, try **Mountain Annies**. Steaks, barbecue and hearty sandwiches round out the menu, while a hearty salad bar offers vegetarians an option. Annies serves up casual elegance at affordable prices. Call for winter hours. ~ 2710 Sudderth Drive, Ruidoso; 505-257-7982. BUDGET TO MODERATE.

Ruidoso has the **Flying J Ranch** featuring the summer evening combination of an authentic chuckwagon dinner of chicken or beef served on a tin plate, and singing cowboys. Reservations recommended. Closed Sunday from Memorial Day to Labor Day; open Saturday only from September to mid-October. Closed mid-October to Memorial Day. ~ Route 48, Ruidoso; 505-336-4330, 888-458-3595; www.flyingjranch.com, e-mail info@flyingjranch.com. DELUXE.

The plant-filled **Greenhouse Restaurant**, in the former art gallery of Hotel Chongo, is across the street from the excellent Smokey Bear Historical State Park in tiny Capitan. Restaurateurs Tom and Gail Histen grow vegetables hydroponically in their own nearby greenhouse (hence the name), and use them to great effect. Tom cooks with enormous flair. Try the light chicken stroganoff served in puff pastry or the tilapia on baby spinach and grilled polenta with fresh dill. Only brunch is served Sunday. Closed Monday and Tuesday. ~ 103 South Lincoln Avenue, Capitan; 505-354-0373. BUDGET TO MODERATE.

For true New Mexican cuisine, you might venture out to **El Paisano Restaurant** in Capitan. Chef and cook Esther Flanagan

---

AUTHOR FAVORITE

An elegant dining possibility in Ruidoso is **Sundance Steak and Seafood**. Located in an adobe building with green canopies, the chandeliered dining room has upholstered chairs, fine silver, white linen and a good collection of regional art. Entrées include rack of lamb, châteaubriand and roast duck. Lunch is served Wednesday through Saturday. Dinner is served Monday through Saturday. Closed Monday from November through May; closed Sunday. ~ 2523 Sudderth Drive, Ruidoso; 505-257-2954, fax 505-258-9060. DELUXE TO ULTRA-DELUXE.

keeps alive a restaurant started in the late 1940s by her grandmother. Everything at this quaint stop is homemade, including the wonderfully tasty *chiles rellenos*. Art, jewelry and pottery fashioned by locals and Pueblo Indians on display may be purchased. Closed Sunday. ~ 442 Smokey Bear Boulevard, Capitan; 505-354-2206. BUDGET.

SHOPPING

In Carlsbad, the **Horticultural Gift Shop** at Living Desert Zoo and Gardens State Park sells an assortment of cacti that make good souvenirs. ~ 505-885-9988.

Ruidoso has a number of art galleries that seem to keep a lot of racetrack winnings from leaving town. More than a dozen of them can be found along Mechem and Sudderth drives.

Mitchell's, devotes an entire store to hand-made silver and turquoise jewelry. They also offer American Indian crafts like kachinas and gourds. ~ 2622 Sudderth Drive, Ruidoso; 505-257-6924; www.mitchellssilver.com.

Ceremonial weapons of war along with peace pipes share the shelves at **White Dove**. However, the shop's real specialty is authentic American Indian art and jewelry, especially Hopi, Navajo and sterling silver designs. ~ 2501 Sudderth Drive, Ruidoso; 505-257-6609.

"We Cheat You Right" is the whimsical slogan at **Rio Trading Company**. It's a barnlike store, well stocked with everything from donkey carts to miniature windmills and American Indian dreamcatchers. ~ 2200 Sudderth Drive, Ruidoso; 505-257-9274.

The museum shop located at **Historic Lincoln,** a division of the Hubbard Museum of the American West, sells a remarkable array of Billy the Kid books, posters and motion picture videos. How the outlaw's legend has endured! ~ East Route 380, Lincoln; 505-653-4025.

Peter Hurd, his wife Henrietta Wyeth and their son, Michael Hurd—three of the best-known painters in the Southwest—show originals of their work at the **Hurd–La Rinconada Gallery,** one of the most important art collections in New Mexico. Also on display in this adobe gallery are the works of Henrietta's distinguished father, N. C. Wyeth and her brother, Andrew Wyeth. Paintings, lithographs and signed reproductions are all available. Closed Sunday. ~ Mile Marker 281, Route 70, San Patricio; 505-653-4331, 800-658-6912, fax 505-653-4218; www.wyethartists.com, e-mail hlrg@pvtnetworks.net.

Ranked among the best galleries in southern New Mexico, **Benson Fine Art** exhibits an outstanding array of works by period and contemporary Southwestern artists along with museum-quality American Indian and ethnographic art and artifacts. It is located in a late 1800s adobe hacienda in the San Patricio historic district south of Ruidoso. ~ On the east end of Peter Hurd Loop (White Cat Road) off Route 70, San Patricio; 505-653-4081; www.bensonfineart.biz, e-mail benson@pvtn.net.

NIGHTLIFE For evening entertainment, nothing can compete with the sunset flight of more than 300,000 Brazilian (Mexican) freetail bats from the entrance of **Carlsbad Caverns/Bat Flight Program**. The bats put on their show nightly from May to October. They migrate to Mexico for the winter. Call ahead for information. ~ 505-785-3012 (program times), 505-785-3137 (general information); www.nps.gov/cave.

Alto's **Spencer Theater for the Performing Arts** is as spectacular as the performances it presents. The 514-seat hall's futuristic architecture features 430 tons of mica-flecked Spanish limestone facing, a gleaming lobby faceted with 300 panes of glass—none of them the same size—and an exterior waterfall. The year-round calendar of events includes everything from dance and classical music to Broadway shows and children's theater. Tours of the theater are conducted on Tuesday and Friday at 10 a.m. ~ Airport Road (Route 220), Alto; 505-336-4800, 888-818-7872, fax 505-336-0055; www.spencertheater.com, e-mail boxoffice@spencertheater.com.

The **Flying J Ranch** near Ruidoso represents a traditional Western genre of tourist entertainment. After a barbecue-beef dinner served "chuckwagon style" (that is, in a chow line), singing cowboys take the stage to perform classics like "Red River Valley" and "Git Along, Little Dogie." It's corny, but lots of fun. Closed Sunday from Memorial Day to Labor Day; open Saturday only from September to mid-October. Closed mid-October to Memorial Day. Reservations highly recommended. ~ Route 48, Ruidoso; 505-336-4330, 888-458-3595; www.flyingjranch.com.

Ruidoso is the liveliest town after dark in this part of the state. Blues bands play on Sunday while classic rock outfits entertain Wednesday through Saturday night at **The Quarters**. There is karaoke on Monday. There's a dancefloor, a big bar and com-

BEAUTY'S IN THE EYE OF THE BEHOLDER

One painting you won't see on display at the Hurd–La Rinconada Gallery is Peter Hurd's famous "official" portrait of President Lyndon Baines Johnson, completed in 1967. Hurd's fellow Southwesterner was less than taken with the likeness, describing it as "the ugliest thing I ever saw." (This portrait can now be seen at the National Portrait Gallery in Washington, D.C.)

fortable table seating at this lounge. ~ 2535 Sudderth Drive, Ruidoso; 505-257-9535.

You'll find live country-and-western music every night at **Win Place & Show Lounge.** ~ 2516 Sudderth Drive, Ruidoso; 505-257-9982.

PARKS

CARLSBAD MUNICIPAL PARK This large park runs through town for more than a mile along the west bank of Lake Carlsbad, a portion of the Pecos River that has been dammed to make it wider and deeper. It is used for waterskiing, swimming, fishing and sailing. A playground, a golf course and tennis and handball courts are also located in the park. On the shore, the park has broad lawns and shade trees. There are restrooms and picnic areas. Paddlewheel boats are available to rent. ~ Take Greene Street east several blocks from Route 285 to the river; 505-887-6516.

SITTING BULL FALLS Although it is a long drive through uninhabited backcountry, Sitting Bull Falls is a locally popular spot, likely to be crowded on summer weekends. It's one of the largest falls in New Mexico—130 feet high—and practically the only running water in the arid foothills southwest of Carlsbad. Swimming is permitted in the pool at the bottom of the falls. There are hiking trails, including a wheelchair-accessible trail to the falls, a picnic area and restrooms. Day-use fee, $5. ~ From Route 285 about 12 miles north of Carlsbad, take Route 137 southwest for 25 miles and watch for a sign to Sitting Bull Falls. The falls are at the end of an eight-mile paved road off Route 137; 505-885-4181, fax 505-887-3690.

BRANTLEY LAKE STATE PARK This irrigation reservoir on the Pecos River north of Carlsbad offers several opportunities for water recreation from boating and fishing to scuba diving and waterskiing. The park features a picnic area, restrooms, showers, volleyball, horseshoe pits, a nature trail and two children's playgrounds. There is also a fishing dock. Day-use fee, $5. ~ County Road 30, just off Route 285, 12 miles north of Carlsbad; 505-457-2384, 888-667-2757, 877-664-7787 (reservations), fax 505-457-2385.

▲ There are 51 sites with RV hookups; $14 to $18 per night. Primitive camping is allowed; $8 per night.

BOTTOMLESS LAKES STATE PARK One of New Mexico's oldest state parks, Bottomless Lakes, consists of seven natural lakes, small in surface area but as much as 90 feet deep, formed by collapsed underground salt and gypsum deposits. The largest, Lea Lake, is the only one where swimming is allowed. It also has a public beach and pedalboat and paddleboard rentals (Memorial Day to Labor Day only) and is a popular site for scuba diving. There's a visitors center near Cotton-wood Lake. Trails lead to beautiful Mirror Lake, surrounded by red cliffs. Ducks, geese and other waterfowl abound on the lakes during spring and fall migration seasons. The park has a picnic area, restrooms and showers. Day-use fee, $5. ~ From Roswell, take Route 380 for 12 miles east, then turn south on Route 409 for 13 miles to the park entrance; 505-624-6058, fax 505-624-6029; e-mail botlakes@roswell.net.

▲ There are 69 sites, 32 with RV hookups; $10 to $18 per night.

BITTER LAKE NATIONAL WILDLIFE REFUGE 🚶 🚲 🐎 This 25,000-acre wildlife area straddling the Pecos River annually attracts thousands of migratory geese, ducks and sandhill cranes, and boasts a large number and diversity of colorful dragonflies in the summer. Horseback riding is allowed on portions of the refuge. The wilderness area is open for hiking. There's also an auto-tour route. ~ From Route 285 go east on Pine Lodge Road and follow the signs to the refuge headquarters; 505-622-6755, fax 505-623-9039.

▼▼▼▼▼▼▼▼▼▼▼▼▼▼▼▼▼▼

South Central New Mexico

Birthplace of the atomic age, a favorite resting place of Apache revolutionary Geronimo and a bonanza for petroglyph buffs, south central New Mexico is famous for its gypsum dunes and lava fields. Juxtaposing desert and mountains, this Rio Grande region offers a number of popular dammed lakes ideal for outdoor enthusiasts. It is also a must for ghost-town buffs.

SIGHTS

The northern part of the Tularosa Basin, which begins north of Carrizozo and extends 80 miles to the south, is a jagged wasteland of black lava. At **Valley of Fires Recreation Area,** a self-guided nature trail, the first half of which is fully wheelchair-accessible, leads across a portion of the 2000-year-old lava field for a closeup look at this strange and forbidding landscape. There is also a visitors center and a bookstore. Admission. ~ Off Route 380 just west of Carrizozo; phone/fax 505-648-2241.

From Carrizozo to Alamogordo, Route 54 runs along the eastern edge of **White Sands Missile Range,** a vast area used by the military to test weapons; turn west on Route 70 at Alamogordo to enter the site. It's been off-limits to the public since World War II, when it was the site of the first atomic bomb test. Open year-round, however, are the museum and missile park, where you can see examples of tested missiles. Trinity Site, where the original bomb was exploded, is open to the public twice a year, on the first Saturday in October and April. Everyone who enters must have picture ID. ~ Route 70; 505-678-1134, fax 505-678-7174; www.wsmr.army.mil.

Halfway between Carrizozo and Alamogordo, the **Three Rivers** **◄ HIDDEN**
Petroglyph Site contains thousands of pictures chipped into the
dark patina of boulders by artists of the Mimbres people, an
American Indian culture centuries older than the Anasazi of the
Four Corners area. An often-steep three-quarter-mile trail follows the crest of a high hill to let you see the mysterious pictures
of animals, humans and magical beings as well as abstract symbols whose meanings can only be guessed at. A pleasant picnic
area lies at the foot of the trail. Admission. ~ Five miles off Route
54; 505-525-4300 or 505-585-3457, fax 505-525-4412.

In Alamogordo, the **New Mexico Museum of Space History**
houses one of the world's largest collections of space exploration
artifacts. The gleaming five-story gold cube on the hillside contains antique rockets, space suits, Apollo and Gemini capsules,
moon rocks, satellites and lots more. An outdoor park displays
larger rockets and the Sonic Wind Rocket Sled, which was used

South Central
New Mexico

to test the effects of rocket acceleration on humans. Adjoining the museum is the **Clyde W. Tombaugh IMAX Dome Theater**, a planetarium that presents IMAX movies as well as educational astronomy programs. It is named after the man who discovered Pluto. Admission. ~ At the top of Route 2001, Alamogordo; 505-437-2840, 877-333-6589, fax 505-437-7722; www.nmspace museum.org, e-mail cathy.harper@state.nm.us.

To learn more about the exploration of space, drive up to the National Solar Observatory–Sacramento Peak on the crest of the mountains to the east. First, take the 16-mile drive on Route 82 from Alamogordo to the village of **Cloudcroft**. Nestled in the pines near the crest of the Sacramento Mountains, Cloudcroft has seen little of the rampant resort development evident at Ruidoso on the other side of the Mescalero Apache Indian Reservation, and it retains the weathered charm of a little Rocky Mountain logging town.

Explore a pioneer barn, granary and hand-hewn log house chinked with mud at the **Sacramento Mountains Historical Museum**. Of special interest is an exhibit about the Cloudcroft Baby Sanatorium, a high-country facility that saved the lives of hundreds of children suffering from summer heat sickness in the nearby lowlands between 1912 and 1932. There is also a pioneer village and a farm and ranch exhibit. The collection of artifacts includes an Edison cylinder talking machine and a rifle once owned by explorer Zebulon Pike. Closed Wednesday and Thursday. Admission. ~ Route 82, across from the chamber of commerce, Cloudcroft; 505-682-2932, fax 505-682-3638.

From the museum, take Scenic Byway 6563 for 16 miles, following the signs to "Sunspot." Maintained by the National Science Foundation for the use of various universities, the **National Solar Observatory–Sacramento Peak** has several solar telescopes. The Dunn solar telescope extends from 20 stories below ground level to 13 stories above. Visitors on self-guided tours of the facility can view solar activity on a video screen in the visitors center or observe work inside the Dunn solar telescope. Open daily from April through October; call for hours from November through March. Admission. ~ Scenic Byway 6563; 505-434-7000, fax 505-434-7079; www.nsosp.nso.edu, e-mail sunspot@nso.edu.

A trip to this area would not be complete without a stop at the world's largest gypsum dunefield, **White Sands National Monument**. The monument protects the southern part of the 275-square-mile White Sands dune field, open for public use. A 16-mile roundtrip scenic drive takes you into the heart of the white-as-snow gypsum dunes, where you can park and step out into this strange landscape. The juxtaposition of pristine white sand and bright blue sky can make you feel like you're walking on clouds.

Several readers recommend the sunset ranger stroll. Admission. ~ Off Route 70 between Alamogordo and Las Cruces; 505-479-6124, fax 505-479-4333; www.nps.gov/whsa.

As beautiful as it is unusual, the landscape is ever-changing: Desert winds constantly reshape the dunes, creating pure white sculptures that disappear with each fresh gust. Surrounded by a spectacular wasteland, with an occasional yucca plant the only sign of life, it's difficult to decide whether this is heaven, hell or simply the end of the earth. Hiking is allowed without limitation, but camping is only permitted at a backcountry campground (for back-packers only) with ten sites, available first come, first served. Camping fee is $3 per person. Rangers conduct evening nature walks.

Most of the population of southern New Mexico is centered in and around **Las Cruces** (population 75,000). The name Las Cruces, Spanish for "The Crosses," pays tribute to the grave-markers of settlers killed here in the 1800s by Apache Indians. A busy, spirited college town, home to New Mexico State University, Las Cruces is situated in an otherwise quiet landscape—an agricultural zone along the Rio Grande where farmers specialize in chili peppers and pecans. This county seat—one of the fastest growing cities in the nation—recently surpassed Santa Fe to become the second-largest city in New Mexico. Las Cruces is noteworthy for the Organ Mountains that loom east of the city. Vaulting 5000 feet above the valley, these peaks derive their name from the spires and minarets that resemble the pipes of a church organ cast in stone.

At the handsome adobe-walled **Cultural Complex** are two museums. The **Branigan Cultural Center/Historical Museum** (500 North Water Street) tells of local and regional history. The **Las Cruces Museum of Fine Art & Culture** (490 North Water Street) exhibits a variety of contemporary paintings, sculpture and arts and crafts. Closed Sunday. ~ Las Cruces; 505-541-2155, fax 505-541-2152; www.las-cruces.org.

A short distance southwest of Las Cruces on Route 10, the village of **Mesilla** is one of the state's prettiest and best-preserved historic districts, dating back to 1598. Mesilla achieved further

---

BOMBS AWAY

Even as recently as 1945, southern New Mexico was considered so godforsaken that the U.S. Army picked it as the perfect place to test the first atomic bomb. There was hardly anyone to evacuate from the area. Today the population of this region lives along two main north–south routes separated from each other by the huge White Sands Missile Range, which is off-limits to all nonmilitary persons.

El Camino Real

Route 25 follows the path of the oldest highway still in use in the United States. Originally known as El Camino Real de Tierra Adentro ("the Royal Road to the Inner Land"), it was established in 1598 to link Mexico City with New Mexico, the northernmost province of the Spanish empire in America. Today, Route 25 has taken the place of the old Camino Real, but it keeps its distance from the Rio Grande. For most of the distance from Albuquerque to Las Cruces, slower, traffic-free, two-lane highways follow the original Camino Real, usually out of sight of the interstate. The New Mexico state government has put up historical markers along them to identify important landmarks from colonial times such as the stark landscape of the Jornada del Muerto ("Journey of Death"). There are three separate segments of this parallel highway; taking them all requires about twice the time the interstate would.

historical significance by serving as the Confederate capital of the Arizona Territory for a short period during the Civil War. The downtown plaza and several of its surrounding Territorial-style buildings have been designated as **La Mesilla State Monument.** Points of interest around the plaza include the **San Albino Church,** the oldest in the area, built in 1853.

Fifteen miles north of Las Cruces, **Fort Selden State Monument** includes the ruins of an adobe fort used by the Army from 1865 to 1891. It was a base for troops guarding the Mesilla Valley and providing protection for wagon trains and later the railroad. A small museum recalls what life was like at the fort during the Territorial era. Admission. ~ Off Route 25 Exit 19; 505-526-8911; www.nmmonuments.org.

Farther north along Route 25 is **Truth or Consequences**—that's "T or C" to most New Mexicans. The sprawling retirement community of Truth or Consequences merits a look-see, and maybe even a soak in its bubbling hot springs. Long before it was founded, the site was an American Indian place of healing and a hideout for Geronimo, the renegade Apache leader. Truth or Consequences now serves as the food and lodging center for visitors to nearby Elephant Butte Reservoir, the largest lake in New Mexico at 38,000 acres.

The main point of interest in town is the geothermally heated **Geronimo Springs Museum.** It is a fairly large museum with 14 exhibit rooms full of prehistoric Mimbres-Mogollon pottery, farming and ranching antiques, Hispanic and military artifacts,

ISLETA PUEBLO   Route 47 leaves Route 25 at Exit 215 to Isleta Pueblo (page 470) just south of Albuquerque. It passes through 40 miles of farmlands and small towns like Bosque Farms and Los Lunas before rejoining the interstate north of Socorro, where the old highway reaches the boundary of Sevilleta National Wildlife Refuge, which is closed to the public.

BOSQUE DEL APACHE NATIONAL WILDLIFE REFUGE   Twenty-eight miles farther south, at Exit 147 in Socorro, the old highway resumes as Route 1. It skirts the edge of Bosque del Apache National Wildlife Refuge (page 490), continuing for 58 miles before merging with the interstate again near **Elephant Butte Lake State Park** (page 525).

CHILE COUNTRY   Another 25 miles south on Route 25, the old highway splits away again at the lower end of **Caballo Lake State Park** (page 524) to become Route 187. From here, it takes you another 56 miles through the green chile farmlands around **Hatch** (page 523) before arriving in historic **Mesilla** (page 517) on the west side of Las Cruces.

mammoth and mastodon skulls, petrified wood, works by local artists, awards for wool production and other curiosities from all over Sierra County. A highlight of the museum is the Ralph Edwards Room, commemorating the television show that inspired Hot Springs, New Mexico, to change its name to Truth or Consequences in 1950. Admission. ~ 211 Main Street, Truth or Consequences; 505-894-6600, fax 505-894-2888.

Truth or Consequences' popularity as a spa resort has long since faded, but the hot springs themselves remain intact. Next to the Geronimo Springs Museum is a 105° natural spring where Apache leader Geronimo himself is said to have relaxed. One spring open to the public for bathing is **Sierra Grande Lodge and Health Spa**. Admission. ~ 501 McAdoo Street, Truth or Consequences; 505-894-6976, fax 505-894-6999; www.sierra grandelodge.com, e-mail sglodge@riolink.com.

The most interesting of the several ghost towns in the Truth or Consequences vicinity is **Chloride**, 29 miles off the interstate on Route 52 and then just over two miles on a marked, unpaved forest road. This is one of the few New Mexico ghost towns that looks the way you expect a Western ghost town to look, with about a dozen falsefront buildings still standing along a deserted main street. In its heyday during the late 19th century, Chloride was a center for silver mining and had a population of about 500.

◄ HIDDEN

Virtually all Alamogordo accommodations are standard highway motels and with few exceptions their rates are in the budget

LODGING

range. Representative of the type is the **Satellite Inn**, which has phones, cable TV, an outdoor pool and 40 rooms (two with kitchenettes). A continental breakfast is included. ~ 2224 North White Sands Boulevard, Alamogordo; 505-437-8454, 800-221-7690, fax 505-434-6015; www.satelliteinn.com, e-mail info@satelliteinn.com. BUDGET.

A more interesting option is to spend the night in Cloudcroft, high in the mountains and just 16 miles from Alamogordo. The most elegant hotel in town is the **Lodge at Cloudcroft**, with rooms, suites and a day spa. The three-story lodge has been in operation since the turn of the century and has been completely refurbished and modernized. Rooms have high ceilings and some antique furnishings. ~ 1 Corona Place, Cloudcroft; 505-682-2566, 800-395-6343, fax 505-682-2715; www.thelodgeresort.com, e-mail info@thelodge-nm.com. MODERATE TO ULTRA-DELUXE.

The lodge also operates the **Lodge Pavilion Bed & Breakfast**, offering accommodations in one of the town's oldest buildings. Both the Lodge and the Pavilion are listed on the New Mexico State Historic Register. ~ 1 Corona Place, Cloudcroft; 505-682-2566, 800-395-6343, fax 505-682-2715; www.thelodgeresort.com, e-mail lodgereservations@thelodgeresort. DELUXE.

For more modest, quiet and cozy lodgings, Cloudcroft has numerous cabins for rent. For example, **Buckhorn Cabins**, located in the center of town, has rustic-style cabins ranging from single rooms with kitchenettes to two-bedroom cabins with living rooms and fireplaces. ~ Route 82, Cloudcroft; 505-682-2421; e-mail buckhorncabins@aol.com. BUDGET TO MODERATE.

Equipped with fireplaces and tucked amid the pines, **Tall Timber Cabins** is a prime choice for a family holiday. All nine cottage and duplex units offer picnic tables and grills that allow guests to take advantage of the setting—a quiet residential area—as well as full kitchens. After a day behind the wheel, you'll be happy to fall into the comfy king- or queen-size beds. ~ 1102 Chatauqua Canyon Boulevard, Cloudcroft; phone/fax 505-682-2301, 888-682-2301; e-mail talltimbercabins@earthlink.net. MODERATE.

In Las Cruces, the most luxurious hotel is the **Hotel Encanto de Las Cruces**, situated in the foothills on the east edge of town off Route 25 and across the street from Mesilla Valley Mall. The exquisitely renovated hotel features bright, attractive guest rooms, and the swimming pool is surrounded by palm trees. ~ 705 South Telshor Boulevard, Las Cruces; 505-522-4300, 866-383-0443, fax 505-522-4707; www.hhandr.com/encanto, e-mail confirmation-helc@hhandr.com. MODERATE.

Budget motels cluster along West Picacho Avenue. Try the **Keyfort Inn**, which offers all standard amenities including an outdoor pool, phones and cable television. ~ 2160 West Picacho Avenue, Las Cruces; 505-524-8627, fax 505-523-2606. BUDGET.

More unusual lodging can be found at the **Lundeen Inn of the Arts**, where each of the seven units, including a second-floor two-bedroom suite with kitchenettes, are named after well-known New Mexican and American Indian artists. The Georgia O'Keeffe room is done up in Santa Fe style, the Olef Wieghorst has a clawfoot tub and the Fritz Shoulder boasts a bidet. There is also an observation tower where guests can admire the view of Las Cruces. ~ 618 South Alameda Boulevard, Las Cruces; 505-526-3327, 888-526-3326, fax 505-647-1334; www.innofthe arts.com, e-mail lundeen@innofthearts.com. MODERATE.

Nearby in historic Mesilla is the **Meson de Mesilla**, an elegant boutique hotel. All 15 rooms in this modern adobe inn have private baths and are appointed in Southwestern decor. Guests may stroll the flagstone pathway through a courtyard filled with yuccas, cacti and desert blooms or enjoy the sweeping views of the Organ Mountains from the inn's lawn. There is a swimming pool. Full complimentary breakfast served in the dining room atrium. ~ 1803 Avenida de Mesilla, Mesilla; 505-525-9212, 800-732-6025, fax 505-527-4196. MODERATE TO DELUXE.

Accommodations in Truth or Consequences range from a scattering of very low-priced older independent motels to quality contemporary motor inns.

With a hot-springs mineral bath setting it apart from other hostels (guests soak for free), **Riverbend Hot Springs** provides clean, air-conditioned dorm-style accommodations; private rooms and kitchenettes are available, as are outdoor accommodations (tents, tepees). There's a common kitchen and a barbecue, and if you're game, you can join in the organized activities. Reservations recommended. ~ 100 Austin Street, Truth or Consequences; 505-894-7625; www.riverbendhotsprings.com, e-mail river bendsprings@gmail.com. BUDGET.

South central New Mexico is home to the only city in America renamed for a game show—Truth or Consequences.

The relaxing **Sierra Grande Lodge**, built on a natural hot spring, has 16 clean and comfortable rooms tastefully decorated with Mission-style furniture. The best part of staying here: Guests enjoy a free mineral bath (by appointment). A wonderful continental breakfast is also complimentary. In addition, you can arrange a number of spa treats such as massages, Reiki, reflexology and facials. ~ 501 McAdoo Street, Truth or Consequences; 505-894-6976, fax 505-894-6999; www.sierra grandelodge.com, e-mail sglodge@riolink.com. DELUXE.

The **Elephant Butte Inn** belongs in the latter group and boasts 47 rooms with Southwestern furnishings, all with coffeemakers and free wi-fi. There is also a seasonally heated pool. ~ Route 195, off of Route 25 Exit 83, Elephant Butte; 505-744-5431; www.elephantbutteinn.com, e-mail guestservices@elephantbutte inn.com. MODERATE.

DINING   In Alamogordo, fast-food places are the norm, with the exception of a few family-style restaurants such as **Memories Restaurant**, serving American fare (chicken fried steak, ribeye) plus some Americanized entrées (lasagna, chicken cordon bleu). ~ 1223 New York Avenue, Alamogordo; 505-437-0077. BUDGET TO MODERATE.

Cloudcroft has a number of good restaurants, many featuring Texas-style cuisine. In the middle of town is the cafeteria-style **Texas Pit Barbecue**, a real find for pecan-smoked beef. ~ Route 82, Cloudcroft; phone/fax 505-682-1101. BUDGET TO MODERATE.

For fine dining, consider **Rebecca's**, the dining room at the Lodge at Cloudcroft, where steaks, seafood and Continental selections are served in an atmosphere of Victorian elegance with a view of the pine forest. White linen, wicker furniture, historic portraits and a pianist make this a romantic spot. Breakfast, lunch and dinner are served. ~ 1 Corona Place, Cloudcroft; 505-682-2566, fax 505-682-2715; www.thelodge-nm.com. DELUXE TO ULTRA-DELUXE.

Fine restaurants surround the plaza in Mesilla. The most elegant of them is the **Double Eagle**, where the turquoise margaritas arrive garnished with genuine turquoise stones. With museum-quality period decor in a restored Territorial adobe, it is listed on the National Register of Historic Places. The Sunday champagne brunch features a three-foot chocolate fountain. ~ 2355 Calle de Guadalupe, Mesilla; 505-523-6700, fax 505-523-0051; www.double-eagle.com. ULTRA-DELUXE.

A favorite with locals, the historic **La Posta de Mesilla** compound is a series of dining areas, many named for their past significance: The Winery, The Blacksmith Room, The Bunkhouse. An extensive menu of New Mexican specialties includes *chile con queso*, folded tacos, chimichangas and beef tenderloin with green chile. Closed Monday except in summer. ~ 2410 Calle de San Albino, South Plaza, Mesilla; 505-524-3524; www.laposta-de-mesilla.com, e-mail laposta@zianet.com. BUDGET TO MODERATE.

Most Truth or Consequences restaurants present standard interstate highway exit fare. One exception is the **Damsite Restaurant**, located five miles east of town on the dam road. In an

AUTHOR FAVORITE

In Las Cruces, I like to check out the scene at **Nellie's Cafe**. This long-time local favorite serves New Mexican and Old Mexican dishes like *carne adovada*, *chiles rellenos* and *sopaipilla compuesta* (which is like a Mexican pizza). Breakfast and lunch served all day; dinner also served on Thursday and Friday. Closed Sunday and Monday. ~ 1226 West Hadley Avenue, Las Cruces; 505-524-9982. BUDGET.

old adobe overlooking Elephant Butte Lake, the restaurant serves steaks and other American fare. Seasonal hours; call ahead. ~ Englestar Route, Truth or Consequences; 505-894-2073. MOD-ERATE TO ULTRA-DELUXE.

Moore's Trading Post is one of the few places we know that has live rattlesnakes. But if you'd just as soon not drive home with a fanged pet, Moore's carries plenty of reptilian "accessories," everything from skins and heads to snake-bite kits. If slinky critters give you nothing but the jitters, choose instead from the thousands of secondhand items: combat boots, military fatigues—you name it. ~ 215 Route 82 East, Alamogordo; phone/fax 505-437-7116.

SHOPPING

Local artists and craftspeople display their works at galleries around the small plaza in the old Spanish village of **La Luz**. ~ Located eight miles northeast of Alamogordo via Route 70 and Route 545.

Pick up a thriller for the trip home at **Coas: My Bookstore**. This is one of the largest bookstores in southern New Mexico, with more than 100,000 titles—new, used and rare. (Coas also carries games as well as used CDs, videos and DVDs.) ~ 317 North Main Street, Las Cruces; 505-524-8471.

A five-block collection of shops dubbed "Nostalgia City" can be found in Las Cruces lining West Picacho Avenue from Valley Drive to Alameda Street. If poking through antique stores searching for that perfect treasure is your activity of choice, this is where to go. Shops range from **Refound Antiques** to the **Things for Sale**. Keep poking, you'll find it.

Every Wednesday and Saturday morning 50 to 120 exhibitors head for the **Las Cruces Farmers and Crafts Market** on the downtown mall. These vendors generally offer the top pick in local produce, nuts and flowers, though they plug everything from honey and salsa to Southwestern furniture. The toys and dolls make first-class gifts. ~ North of Las Cruces Avenue on the downtown mall, Las Cruces; 505-541-2288.

Hatch, located midway between Las Cruces and Truth or Consequences off Route 25, has a reputation for producing the best-tasting chile in New Mexico, and most of the stores in the little town are **chile shops**. In September, they sell fresh-roasted green chiles. The rest of the year, they stock it dried, canned, powdered, shaped as Christmas tree lights and as a T-shirt motif.

Up in the mountains, the **Lodge at Cloudcroft** has a piano player most evenings in the dining room. ~ 1 Corona Place, Cloudcroft; 505-682-2566; www.thelodge-nm.com.

NIGHTLIFE

El Patio is the place for live music Wednesday through Saturday nights. It's mostly jazz and blues, but rock-and-roll bands take the stage on weekend evenings. Cover. ~ 2171 Calle de Parian Southwest, Mesilla; 505-526-9943.

New Mexico State University provides a steady flow of cultural activities. Stop by the Corbett Center Student Union during the school year or check out their website. ~ Locust Street, Las Cruces; 505-646-3235; www.nmsu.edu/~upc.

PARKS

Several dams on the lower Rio Grande form lakes used for recreation, ranging from little Leasburg Lake (hardly more than a wide spot in the river) to huge Elephant Butte Lake (one of New Mexico's largest bodies of water). From south to north, these lakes are:

LEASBURG DAM STATE PARK This park is located near a small dam on the Rio Grande, set in a desert of creosote bushes and cholla cacti near Fort Selden State Monument. It is a popular area for swimming and boating (canoes and rafts). Fishing is also permitted. The park also features a nature trail, picnic areas, restrooms, showers and a playground. Gates close at sunset. Day-use fee, $5. ~ Off Route 25 at Radium Springs, 15 miles north of Las Cruces; 505-524-4068, fax 505-526-5420.

The Gadsden Purchase, signed in Mesilla in 1854, fixed the current international boundaries of New Mexico and Arizona.

▲ There are 50 sites (18 with RV hookups); primitive camping is allowed. Fees are $8 for primitive sites, $10 for standard sites and $14 for hookups.

PERCHA DAM STATE PARK Another small dam widens the river at this park, which is primarily a campground and a riverbank fishing area. Unlike Leasburg Lake, Percha Dam has tall old cottonwoods to provide shade on hot summer afternoons. Fishing is permitted. Facilities at the park include a picnic area, restrooms, showers and a playground. Day-use fee, $5. ~ Off Route 25 near the village of Arrey, 53 miles north of Las Cruces (21 miles south of Truth or Consequences); 505-743-3942, 888-667-2757, fax 505-743-0031; e-mail mcclelland@state.nm.us.

▲ There are 30 sites with RV hookups; $10 per night for standard sites, $14 to $18 for hookups. The camping area features green lawns—a rarity in southern New Mexico. Reservations: 877-664-7787.

CABALLO LAKE STATE PARK The name, Spanish for "horse," comes from the days when wild horses used to live in Caballo Canyon before it was dammed in the 1930s to form Caballo Lake. The lake is more than a mile wide and 12 miles long, with more than 70 miles of shoreline. It is popular, especially in the spring, with anglers fishing for channel catfish, bass and walleye pike. The visitors center, main campground and picnic area are on the west side of the lake (one mile north from Exit 59 off Route 25). From there, Route 187 follows the shore all the way to the upper end of the lake. Below the dam is a river fishing area with drinking water and campsites shaded by cottonwood trees. The park has restrooms and showers. Day-use fee, $5. ~ Off Route 25, 60 miles north of Las Cruces (20 miles south of Truth or Consequences); 505-743-3942, 888-667-2757, fax 505-743-0031; e-mail mcclelland@state.nm.us.

▲ There are 135 sites (63 with RV hookups) and primitive camping along the shoreline. Fees are $8 for primitive sites, $10 for standard sites and $14 to $18 for hookups. Reservations: 877-664-7787.

ELEPHANT BUTTE LAKE STATE PARK The dam creating this 40-mile-long reservoir, the second-largest lake in New Mexico, was originally built in 1916 to impound irrigation water for the whole Rio Grande Valley downriver. Today, it is New Mexico's most popular state park. Recreational activities include fishing, boating (there are marinas and boat rentals), waterskiing, windsurfing, sailing and even houseboating. The lake also has miles of sand beaches and several protected swimming areas. On display at the visitors center are dinosaur and early mammal fossils found in the area, including a tyrannosaurus rex jawbone. A network of unpaved roads provides access to a series of remote points along the lake's west shore, but all of the east shore can only be reached by boat. In addition to nature trails and a playground, there are picnic areas, restrooms and showers. Day-use fee, $5. ~ The main entrance to the park can be reached from Route 25 by taking either Exit 79 or Exit 83 and following the signs; 505-744-5421, fax 505-744-9144.

▲ There are 127 sites (104 with RV hookups) and an area for primitive camping. Fees are $8 for primitive sites, $10 for developed sites and $14 for hookups.

Southwestern New Mexico

Geronimo's base, southwestern New Mexico is home to Mogollon, one of the state's finest ghost towns, as well as the Gila (pronounced "hee-lah") Wilderness, cliff dwellings and the frontier boomtown of Silver City. If you like to pack in to high-country lakes, cycle through national forests or explore cliff dwellings, this remote area is your kind of place. While here you can learn about the legend of Pancho Villa, who made the mistake of invading this area in 1916.

SIGHTS

Gila Cliff Dwellings National Monument, 44 slow miles north of Silver City, preserves five natural caves that were inhabited by peoples of the Mogollon culture about 700 years ago. Visitors who have seen the Southwest's great Indian ruins, such as those at Chaco Canyon, Mesa Verde or the Jemez Mountains, sometimes find Gila Cliff Dwellings a disappointment because they consist of only 40 rooms, which housed a total of 10 to 15 families. But the small scale of these ruins and nearby pit houses, representative of the many communities scattered throughout the Gila country, is marvelous in the context of the vast surrounding canyonlands. Admission to the dwellings. ~ Route 15; 505-536-9461, fax 505-536-9344; www.nps.gov/gicl.

The real reason a national monument exists at Gila Cliff Dwellings is to administer the central trailheads for one of the nation's most important wilderness areas. Encompassing much of the 3.3 million-acre Gila National Forest, the rugged mountain and canyon country of the **Gila Wilderness** and adjoining **Aldo Leopold Wilderness** comprise the largest roadless area in the United States outside of Alaska. The Gila was the nation's first designated wilderness area, established by an act of Congress in 1924. Aldo Leopold, a New Mexico forest ranger, originated the idea of wilderness protection.

An **overlook** on Route 15 just before the descent to Gila Cliff Dwellings gives a good idea of the Gila's extent and complexity. Three forks of the Gila River join near the cliff dwellings. One of the three main hiking and horse trails into the Gila Wilderness follows each fork through a river and high mesa canyon that meanders between mountains for many miles. A treacherous tangle of side canyons off the main ones defied all pioneer efforts at settlement and provided a stronghold for renegade Apache leaders, including Geronimo.

Today mounted rangers take a full week to cross the wilderness as they patrol, and hiking from boundary to boundary is practically impossible without a horse, mule or llama to carry your food supply. The rugged mountains visible from the overlook—the Black, Diablo, Mogollon, San Francisco and Tularoso—are also part of the wilderness area. Of the many natural hot springs in the vicinity of the Gila Wilderness, the most popular is a series located a short hike up the Middle Fork from the Forest Service visitors center.

While the main roads are paved, visitors should not underestimate the trip to Gila Cliff Dwellings. The 44-mile drive from Silver City on Route 15 will take at least two hours; for the 99-mile trip via Routes 152 and 35 from Exit 63 on Route 25 south of Truth or Consequences, allow about three hours. There are no gas stations or other travelers' services along the way, with the exception of a small store with a gasoline pump less than four miles from the cliff dwellings on Route 15. Even if you're not planning to hike into the wilderness, it is wise to allow a full day for any trip to the Gila.

Also rewarding is a drive around the western perimeter of the Gila Wilderness, taking Route 180 west from Silver City, 63 miles to the little town of **Glenwood**. Just outside of Glenwood, to divert water for a small hydroelectric generator in the 1890s, a mining company suspended a water pipeline from the sheer rock walls of **Whitewater Canyon**. To maintain the pipeline, workers had to balance on it 20 feet above the river. Today the mining company and its pipeline are gone, but the forest service has installed a steel mesh walkway, known as **The Catwalk**, along the old pipeline route, affording visitors a unique look at this wild canyon. The upper end of Whitewater Canyon is a wilderness trailhead.

Seven miles north of Glenwood, Route 159 turns off to the east and takes you four miles to **Mogollon** (pronounced "moh-gi-YONE"), one of New Mexico's most intriguing and beautifully located ghost towns. A silver and gold mining boomtown in the 1890s, Mogollon had a population of more than 2000—larger

◀ HIDDEN

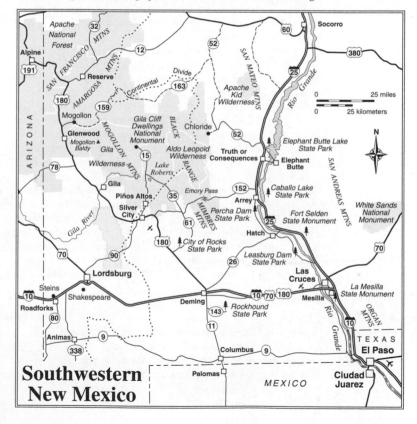

Southwestern New Mexico

than in any town in the area today. It boasted a theater, several stores and saloons, two churches and two separate red light districts (one Anglo, the other Spanish). Many of Mogollon's historic wood and stone buildings still stand in various states of disrepair. One portion of the street was spruced up for use as a motion picture location in the 1970s, and since then a few people have taken up residence here during the summer months to restore old buildings, create artwork and engage in low-key tourist enterprises. However, fewer than a dozen people live here year-round.

Past Mogollon, the road turns to dirt, passable by regular automobiles but not by long motor homes or vehicles with trailers. It winds along the northern wilderness boundary through the **Mogollon Mountains**, the highest in the Gila with four peaks more than 10,000 feet high, giving access to several hiking trails, forest service campgrounds and fishing streams and lakes.

Seven miles north of Silver City on the way to Gila Cliff Dwellings via Route 15, the historic town of **Piños Altos** also offers a look at life in southwestern New Mexico a century ago. While this "ghost town" has never been completely abandoned, it is a mere shadow of its glory days.

Among the points of interest in Piños Altos are a replica of **Santa Rita del Cobre** (also referred to as Fort Webster)—the original was built to protect residents from marauding Apaches who lived in the Gila Wilderness—and a turn-of-the-20th-century opera house. Also here are a gift shop built where Judge Roy "Law West of the Pecos" Bean's store was located before he moved to Texas, and the Hearst Art Gallery, dedicated to the memory of William Randolph Hearst's father, who struck it rich mining in Piños Altos. Admission. ~ Main Street, Piños Altos.

Silver City is a pretty hillside town of 10,500 people, a quarter of them college students. Located in the Piños Altos foothills, the city's Victorian commercial district turns back the clock to frontier days. Bisected by a steep canyon, this town could easily be a set for a Hollywood Western. It's also the jump-off point for one of the state's most picturesque mountain ranges, the Mogollon.

The best sightseeing highlight in Silver City is the **Western New Mexico University Museum**. The museum has the world's

A STREET NO MORE

Big Ditch Park, a tree-lined 50-foot-deep arroyo with a small promenade, runs right through the center of Silver City. In fact, it was originally Silver City's main street, but floods washed it away to its present depth, which explains why some of the original storefronts face the ditch instead of the street.

largest collection of 200- to 1150-year-old Mimbres pottery, painted with the distinctive animal designs that have been revived as a popular decorative motif throughout southern New Mexico in recent years. Not easy for visitors to find, the museum is in a four-story white building with light-brown trim in the center of campus, which is on the hillside on the west side of town. Closed during university holidays. ~ Top of 10th Street, near the library bell tower, Western New Mexico University, Silver City; 505-538-6386, fax 505-538-6178; www.wnmu.edu/univ/museum.htm.

Silver City also has an interesting downtown historic district. While a few of the old buildings stand vacant, others provide space for art galleries and student-oriented stores.

In the downtown area, the **Silver City Museum** is devoted to the history of southwestern New Mexico. Collections include ranch and business relics as well as pottery and artifacts from the Mimbres and Mogollon peoples. There is also an extensive photo archive, a research library and a gift shop. Closed Monday. ~ 312 West Broadway, Silver City; 505-538-5921, 877-777-7947, fax 505-388-1096; www.silvercitymuseum.org, e-mail info@silvercitymuseum.org.

Silver City was home for a time to young **Billy the Kid**, as several minor historical sites attest. His mother's grave is located on the east side of town on Memory Lane. For information and tour maps contact the **Silver City/Grant County Chamber of Commerce** (closed Saturday and Sunday), which also operates the visitors center (closed Sunday from late October to mid-April). ~ 201 North Hudson Street, Silver City; 505-538-3785, 800-548-9378; www.silvercity.org, e-mail scgcchamber@cybermesa.com.

One of the West's premier ghost towns, **Shakespeare** flourished in an 1870s silver boom, when some 3000 miners came here seeking their fortunes. After a second boom played out in 1935, the town was purchased by the Hill family, which has done its best to preserve local history, going so far as to stage dramatic re-enactments of 19th-century Shakespeare murders and hangings. Guided tours (held the second Sunday and preceding Saturday of each month) take you to the old Butterfield stagecoach stop, a saloon, the Stratford Hotel, the mail station, a blacksmith shop, an assay office and a gunpowder magazine. (Call ahead or check their website for a schedule of the re-enactments, staged on the fourth weekend of the month in April, June, August and October.) Admission. ~ Take Exit 22 off Route 10 at Lordsburg and follow the signs south two and a half miles; 505-542-9034; www.shakespeareghostown.com, e-mail visit@shakespeareghostown.com.

Cooperation between the United States and Mexico is commemorated by a monument at **Pancho Villa State Park**, a desert botanical garden where cholla, *ocatillo*, large prickly pears, century plants, tall yuccas and other plants of the Chihuahuan Desert grow in profusion on the slopes of the only hill around. Visitors may wish to drive the three miles to the border and walk across to the Mexican village of Palomas. Admission. ~ Corner of Routes 9 and 11, Columbus; 505-531-2711, fax 505-531-2115; e-mail sylvia.brenner@state.nm.us.

LODGING   The sign for the 90-acre **Casitas de Gila Guesthouses** warns wanderers: "Entering a stress-free zone." The signage is not hyperbole: You can wander the semi-isolated grounds, doze in a hammock, watch the sunset while you barbecue your dinner, peer through the telescope or just sit in the hot tub gazing at the evening constellations and congratulating yourself on your luck. There are five individually decorated *casitas*, each with its own bath, kiva fireplace and fully stocked kitchen. ~ 50 Casita Flats Road, Gila; 505-535-4455, 877-923-4827, fax 505-535-4456; www.casitasdegila.com, e-mail info@casitasdegila.com. DELUXE.

General John Pershing and his troops—who thwarted Pancho Villa's 1916 invasion of the U.S.— were the first to use cars and airplanes in combat.

Besides conventional motels, Silver City has a couple of special, surprisingly affordable places to stay. The **Palace Hotel** is in a former bank building (circa 1882) located on the main street of the downtown historic district. The guest accommodations, which range from five small rooms with showers only to spacious three-room suites (with full bath), feature quaint Territorial-period furnishings and open onto a central sitting room where a continental breakfast is served. ~ 106 West Broadway Street, Silver City; phone/fax 505-388-1811; www.zianet.com/palacehotel. BUDGET.

Deming, an agricultural and mining community on an interstate highway, holds no surprises where lodging is concerned. Every motel in town is budget-priced. The town's top-of-the-line hotel is **Grand Motor Inn**. ~ 1721 Pine Street, Deming; 505-546-2631, fax 505-546-4446. BUDGET. An older independent motel with rock-bottom rates is the **Mirador Motel**. ~ 501 East Pine Street, Deming; phone/fax 505-546-2795; e-mail sweet3pari@yahoo.com. BUDGET.

Columbus, a little town about as far off in the middle of nowhere as any place that can be reached by highway, has a few unexpected touches of sophistication. One is **Martha's Place**, a bed and breakfast. The five elegant second-floor guest rooms have balconies overlooking the rooftops of this one-story town. Full breakfast included. ~ Main and Lima streets, Columbus; 505-531-2467, fax 505-531-7177. BUDGET TO MODERATE.

HIDDEN ►

DINING   The fanciest dining in the area is at the **Buckhorn Saloon** in the historic town of Piños Altos, seven miles north of Silver City on Route 15. The restaurant and saloon are in a beautifully restored adobe building from the 1860s with big stone fireplaces and elegant place settings. Steaks are the specialty. Dinner only. Closed Sunday. ~ 32 Main Street, Piños Altos; 505-538-9911. MODERATE TO ULTRA-DELUXE.

Homestyle food made very well is **Diane's Restaurant and Bakery**'s hallmark. At lunch, there are tasty salads (grilled tuna over mixed greens) and sandwiches (grilled chicken with cheddar cheese, chile and chipotle aioli). Dinner is more elegant; entrées include crispy duck breast with a cranberry-ginger sauce and Thai coconut curry with assorted seafood and Asian vegetables. Weekend brunch is served, but no dinner on Sunday. Closed Monday. ~ 510 North Bullard Street, Silver City; 505-538-8722, fax 505-388-1255; www.dianesrestaurant.com. DELUXE TO ULTRA-DELUXE.

In between the chain fast-food places, Deming has a number of local restaurants that feature Mexican and American food. **La Fonda Restaurant** serves fajitas and has a good salad bar. Breakfast, lunch and dinner are served. ~ 601 East Pine Street, Deming; 505-546-0465. BUDGET TO MODERATE.

Sí Señor has stuffed *sopaipillas* and red or green *huevos rancheros*. ~ 200 East Pine Street, Deming; 505-546-3938. BUDGET TO MODERATE.

The **Grand Restaurant** features a comprehensive menu of steak, seafood and Mexican food. Breakfast, lunch and dinner are served. ~ 1721 East Pine Street, Deming; 505-546-2632, fax 505-546-4446. BUDGET TO MODERATE.

Even more authentic is the Mexican food at any of the hole-in-the-wall *taquerías* across the border in **Palomas, Mexico**—nothing fancy, but certainly foreign.

SHOPPING

The gift shop at the **Western New Mexico University Museum** has a good selection of T-shirts, jewelry, local artworks, Mimbres ceramic reproductions, coffee cups, tote bags, stationery and anything else they determined could brandish the unique Mimbres animal motifs from ancient pottery. ~ Top of 10th Street, near the library bell tower, Western New Mexico University, Silver City; 505-538-6386.

A number of local artists have studios in Silver City's downtown historic district. Many of them are well-hidden in the residential blocks north of Broadway. You can pick up a gallery guide at the Chamber of Commerce or the Yankee Creek Gallery. The latter is home to the **San Vicente Artists of Silver City**. ~ 300 North Bullard Street, Silver City; 505-534-4401; www.silvercity artists.org.

NIGHTLIFE

Near Silver City, the historic **Buckhorn Saloon** in Piños Altos is as authentic as Old West saloons come, complete with a collection of paintings of nude women, a buffalo head on the wall and a pot-belly stove to warm the saloon in winter. Live bands perform Wednesday through Saturday. Closed Sunday. ~ 32 Main Street, Piños Altos; 505-538-9911.

Down in the town of Columbus, the favorite nighttime entertainment is to cross the border to Palomas, where **mariachi bands** perform on the plaza on weekend evenings.

PARKS

LAKE ROBERTS 🚶 🚴 🛥 🚤 ⛵ Gila National Forest has a number of pretty little mountain lakes, of which Lake Roberts is the best known and most accessible. Boating and rainbow trout and catfish fishing (seasonally good) are popular on the 69-acre lake. The southeast shoreline is only accessible by foot trail or by boat (electric motors only). One of the two campgrounds is on a mesa overlooking the lake and the other is at the upper end of the lake. About a quarter-mile from the shoreline are privately operated summer cabins and a convenience store. The park has a picnic area and restrooms. ~ Just off Route 35, about three miles east of the intersection with Route 15 (a narrow mountain road), which is 25 miles north of Silver City on the way to Gila Cliff Dwellings; phone/fax 505-536-2250.

▲ Mesa Campground has 24 sites; $7 per night. There are 12 additional sites at the upper end of the lake; $7 per night. Closed mid-October to mid-May.

SNOW LAKE 🚶 🚤 🛥 🚤 ⛵ This beautiful 100-acre mountain lake is at the north boundary of the Gila Wilderness at the foot of the Mogollon Mountains. Anglers consider it a great trout lake, especially in the springtime. Some people also catch, boil and eat the abundant crawfish. Use is limited to canoes, rowboats and other small boats without gas motors. There is a picnic area and restrooms. ~ Follow unpaved Route 159 from Mogollon for about 30 miles. This is a slow, sometimes narrow, winding and quite scenic unpaved mountain road. The road is passable by passenger cars when dry, but tight curves pose serious problems for long motor homes and towed vehicles. An alternate route is the 50-mile Forest Road 141 from Reserve, the last half of which is

JORNADA DEL MUERTO

Jornada del Muerto ("Journey of Death") is the name Spanish colonists gave to the bone-dry, barren sands of the Chihuahuan Desert, which extends up from Texas and Northern Mexico into the Carlsbad and Alamogordo regions of Southern New Mexico. These pioneers dreaded crossing that sun-crackled expanse on their way from El Paso to Santa Fe and Taos.

gravel; 505-533-6231, 505-533-6232, fax 505-533-6605; e-mail shutchinson@fs.fed.us.

▲ Dipping Vat Campground has 40 tent/RV sites (no hookups) overlooking the lake; $5 per night. Primitive camping is allowed at the north end of the lake outside the recreational boundaries; no fee.

CITY OF ROCKS STATE PARK 🏃 🚴 South of Silver City on the way to Deming, this park makes an extraordinary spot for a picnic stop. At first sight, it appears to be a no-big-deal rockpile in an otherwise featureless desert marred by open-pit copper mines. As you approach, the strangeness of this little geological park becomes apparent. Picnic sites surround a rock dome that has been fractured and eroded into a fantastic maze of oddly shaped stone monoliths and passages that form a natural playground that children and the young at heart can explore for hours. It is impossible to get lost in the maze, since the park road surrounds it on all sides. The park has a star observatory, a visitors center, restrooms and showers. Day-use fee, $5. ~ Route 61, three miles off of Route 180, 28 miles east of Silver City, or 23 miles west of Deming on Route 180; 505-536-2800, 888-667-2757, fax 505-536-2801.

▲ There are 52 sites, 10 with hookups; $10 per night for tent sites; $14 per night with hookups.

ROCKHOUND STATE PARK 🏃 Mainly of interest to rock collectors in search of the garnets and other semiprecious stones found here, the park has the best public campground in the Deming-Columbus area and offers a close-up look at the arid, rocky slopes of the Florida Mountains. The park features trails, a visitors center, a picnic area, a playground, restrooms and showers. Day-use fee, $5. ~ Off Route 143, 14 miles southeast of Deming; 505-546-6182.

▲ There are 29 sites, 24 with hookups; $10 per night for tent sites, $14 per night for hookups.

Outdoor Adventures

SKIING

Even though you're pretty far south, the high elevations here translate into good skiing. You can swoosh down a 12,000-foot mountain at an Indian-owned resort, or explore the backcountry on skinny skis. So strap the boards on your feet and take to the hills!

SOUTHEASTERN NEW MEXICO Ski Apache, 16 miles northwest of Ruidoso on the slopes of 12,003-foot Sierra Blanca, is one of New Mexico's most popular downhill ski areas. Owned and operated by the Mescalero Apache Indians, Ski Apache has 11 lifts and 55 groomed runs and trails (20 percent beginner, 35 percent intermediate and 45 percent advanced), with vertical drops of up to 1900 feet. There are no restrictions on snow-boarding. Ski lessons are available for adults and children. Ski and snowboard rentals are available. ~ 505-464-3600, fax 505-336-8340; www.skiapache.com, e-mail info@skiapache.com.

Some trails and primitive roads in **Lincoln National Forest** outside Ruidoso are used for cross-country skiing in the winter. For current trail information and snow conditions, contact the **Smokey Bear Ranger Station.** ~ Ruidoso; 505-257-4095.

RIDING STABLES

Although this region is full of horse-breeding ranches, southern New Mexico offers surprisingly little in the way of public horse rentals or tours.

SOUTHEASTERN NEW MEXICO   Near Ruidoso, the **Inn of the Mountain Gods** offers guided one-hour trail rides, as well as half-day and full-day trips in the mountains west of the hotel complex; reservations are required for the half-day and full-day rides. ~ 505-464-7777; www.innofthemountaingods.com. Also in the Ruidoso area, **Cowboy Stables** leads rides of one hour or longer for up to 20 people to mountain overlooks above town. ~ 1027 North Lane, Ruidoso Downs; 505-378-8217; www.ruidosotoday.com.

Elite Outfitters explores the Sacramento Mountains on their guided trail rides. ~ P.O. Box 2573, Alto, NM 88312; 505-354-1299; www.eliteoutfitters.com.

GOLF

Despite the arid climate, golf enthusiasts manage to keep Southern New Mexico green. Grab your caddy and head to one of several private or municipal courses. Most courses offer cart and equipment rentals.

SOUTHEASTERN NEW MEXICO   The **Lake Carlsbad Municipal Golf Course** has both a 9-hole and an 18-hole course open to the public. ~ 901 Muscatel Avenue, Carlsbad; 505-885-5444. In Roswell, check out the 18-hole **Spring River Golf Course.** ~ 1612 West 8th Street; 505-622-9506. Closed during winter but open the rest of the year is the course at the tribally owned 18-hole **Inn of the Mountain Gods** near Ruidoso. ~ Carrizo Canyon Road, Mescalero; 505-464-7777; www.innofthemountaingods.com. **The Links at Sierra Blanca** is another winning 18-hole semipublic Scottish-style links course in Ruidoso. ~ 105 Sierra Blanca Drive, Ruidoso; 505-258-5330.

SOUTH CENTRAL NEW MEXICO   Visitors to the Alamogordo area can work on their swing at the driving range of the 18-hole **Desert Lakes Golf Course.** ~ 2351 Hamilton Road, Alamogordo; 505-437-0290; www.desertlakesgolf.com. Play an 18-hole round at **The Lodge Golf Course.** ~ 1 Corona Place, Cloudcroft; 505-682-2098; www.thelodgeresort.com. Nearby is the public, nine-hole **Ponderosa Pines Golf Course**. Located in the middle of Lincoln National Forest, it has an elevation of 8000 feet. Closed in winter. ~ 878 Cox Canyon, Cloudcroft; 505-682-2995; www. ponderosapinesatvianet.com.

SOUTHWESTERN NEW MEXICO In Silver City is the **Silver Fairways Golf Course**, an 18-hole public green. ~ South of Silver City off of Ridge Road on Fairway Drive; 505-538-5041. Hopefully your concentration won't put your game in jeopardy at the public, nine-hole **Truth or Consequences Golf Course**. ~ 685 Marie Street, Truth or Consequences; 505-894-2603.

Tennis is pretty scarce in this neck of the woods, but there are some courts to be found.

TENNIS

SOUTHEASTERN NEW MEXICO Nine lighted courts are available at **Carlsbad Municipal Park**. A tennis pro is available for lessons. ~ 700 Park Drive, Carlsbad; 505-887-1980. There are six lighted courts at **Cahoon Park**. ~ 1101 West 4th Street, Roswell; 505-624-6720. For a fee, nonguests can use the six lighted courts at **Inn of the Mountain Gods** near Ruidoso. Pros are available for lessons. ~ 505-464-7777; www.innofthemountaingods.com.

Of the many natural hot springs in the vicinity of the Gila Wilderness, the most popular is a series located a short hike up the Middle Fork from the Forest Service visitors center.

SOUTH CENTRAL NEW MEXICO In Las Cruces, public courts are at **Apodaca Park** (two courts; Madrid Road at Solano Drive), **Lions Park** (twelve courts; Picacho and Melendres streets), **Young Park** (two courts; Nevada and Walnut streets) and **Frenger Park** (two courts; Parkview Drive). All the courts are hard-surfaced, lighted for night play and open to the public except during scheduled group lessons. Call the Las Cruces Recreation Department for a current lesson schedule. ~ 505-541-2563.

Low-elevation summers can be sweltering, and high-elevation winters can be frigid, but aside from climactical concerns, cyclists will find good places to pedal in Southern New Mexico. You'll even find a few shops offering rentals, cycling equipment and ride recommendations.

BIKING

SOUTHEASTERN NEW MEXICO The nine-and-a-half-mile unpaved scenic drive that begins near the visitors center in **Carlsbad Caverns National Park** makes for a good mountain-bike ride during the spring or autumn. (In summer months, the drive is too hot and often has too much car traffic for enjoyable biking.)

In the Roswell area, cyclists ride the back roads in the ranchlands east of town, particularly the paved roads through **Bitter Lake National Wildlife Refuge** and **Bottomless Lakes State Park**.

Mountain bikers around Ruidoso use the six-mile unpaved forest road from the Ski Apache Road up to Monjeau Campground or any of several jeep roads going into the national forest around Bonito Lake.

SOUTHWESTERN NEW MEXICO Mountain bikes are prohibited within the Gila Wilderness, but several jeep roads in the **Piños Altos** area lead into other parts of the national forest. Ambitious cyclists may wish to tackle unpaved Route 159, which skirts the northern boundary of the wilderness beyond Mogollon.

Bike Rentals Rent mountain bikes in Ruidoso at **High Altitude**, a full-service bike shop. Closed Tuesday from September to late May. ~ 2316½ Sudderth Drive; 505-682-1229; www.highaltitude.org.

In Silver City, the place for mountain-bike rentals and repairs is **Gila Hike & Bike**, which offers free information sheets on day hikes, road rides and mountain-bike rides in Gila National Forest. ~ 103 East College Street; 505-388-3222.

HIKING Whether your interests lean toward history, geology, panoramic views or just plain exercise, you'll find the hiking options in this area tempting. Explore a quarter-mile-long cave on your own; scale the steep sides of Sierra Blanca; seek out the grave of the notorious Apache Kid; or examine ancient petroglyphs and cliff dwellings. All distances are one way unless otherwise noted. Happy trails!

SOUTHEASTERN NEW MEXICO About three-fourths of **Carlsbad Caverns National Park** is a wilderness area restricted to horse and foot travel, with a system of seven trails ranging in difficulty from easy to strenuous. Backcountry trails are primitive and not well marked; take water, a compass and a topographical map. Overnight camping is allowed with a free backcountry permit. Some of the trails are accessed from the scenic drive that starts near the visitors center, while others start from inconspicuous dirt roads off of Route 62/180.

One of the more interesting hikes is **Yucca Canyon** (2 miles), which leads through piñon and oak forest and past old cabins to cool Longview Spring, with a magnificent view of the Carlsbad Caverns Wilderness. This is part of the longer **Yucca Ridge Trail** (11-mile loop), which climbs 1520 feet from the canyon floor to the top of the ridge.

The **Slaughter Canyon Trail** (6 miles) winds through the cobble-filled, lower portion of Slaughter Canyon and up a prominent limestone ridge, gaining 1850 feet before it connects with the Guadalupe Ridge Trail. Persons wishing to enter any cave must first obtain a special permit (a process that can take a month) from the **Cave Resource Office** (505-785-3137) at the Carlsbad Caverns visitors center, which is also the place to ask for up-to-date information on these and numerous other hikes in the national park.

Lincoln National Forest has a network of more than 50 miles of trails throughout the **White Mountain Wilderness** northwest of Ruidoso.

From the Ski Apache ski area, a three-mile trail leads to the summit of **Lookout Mountain**. This is a strenuous hike with an elevation gain of 2100 feet. In summer and fall, people hike to the summit to enjoy the spectacular view.

Another great hike is up **Argentina Canyon** (2.5 miles) with its lush ancient forest and streams fed by mountain springs. To get there, take Route 48 north out of Ruidoso to County Road 37. Follow the signs west to Bonito Lake and Argentina/Bonita trailhead.

SOUTH CENTRAL NEW MEXICO   One of the main features of **Oliver Lee Memorial State Park** (505-437-8284, fax 505-439-1290), 12 miles south of Alamogordo, is Dog Canyon, a hidden oasis in the barren-looking foothills of the Sacramento Mountains.

Dog Canyon National Recreation Trail is long and steep (5.5 miles) and reaches a high spring. The trail continues, climbing out of the canyon to a high ridgeline. Note that this trail rises more than 3000 feet in elevation, making it a very challenging hike.

In the Organ Mountains just east of Las Cruces, the easy **Dripping Springs Trail** (1.5 miles) leads up a steep-walled canyon to Dripping Springs, the former site of a stage stop, a major turn-of-the-20th-century resort and a tuberculosis sanitarium.

The **San Mateo Mountains** west of Truth or Consequences are probably the least-visited mountains in New Mexico. This is a beautiful area characterized by rugged, narrow canyons. It is hot for summer hiking but far enough south to be relatively snow-free in the early spring.

AUTHOR FAVORITE

My favorite hiking trail in south central New Mexico is the difficult **Three Rivers Trail** (6.5 miles) in the White Mountain Wilderness. It starts at the Three Rivers Campground at the end of the unpaved road beyond Three Rivers Petroglyph Site, midway between Carrizozo and Alamogordo. Eventually the trail climbs up to Elk Point on the north side of Sierra Blanca, where it intersects several other major trails leading to all parts of the wilderness area. Many more hikers enter the wilderness from the other side, near Ruidoso, than from Three Rivers.

The heart of the San Mateos is the 45,000-acre Apache Kid Wilderness, named for a renegade who hid out here in the late 19th century. The main route through the wilderness is the **Apache Kid Trail** (a total of 21.1 miles, 12.9 of which are located within the Apache Kid Wilderness), an ambitious hike that follows Nogal Canyon for about a mile from the trailhead at Cibola National Forest's Springtime Campground and then climbs steeply to the upper ridge of the mountains. Hiking the whole trail takes three days and two nights.

Several side trails off the Apache Kid Trail lead to hidden canyons and midway along the trail is the Apache Kid's gravesite, where he was shot down by local ranchers.

SOUTHWESTERN NEW MEXICO The **Gila Wilderness** is restricted to just foot and horse travel, and more than 400 miles of trails extend to all areas of the wilderness. Several guidebooks devoted to hiking trails in the Gila Wilderness are locally available in Silver City. A few of the top hiking options in the Gila include:

The **West Fork Trail** (15.5 miles) is, for the first five miles, the most used trail in the Gila Wilderness. For an adventurous day hike, follow the moderate trail upriver about three miles to a narrow, deep section of canyon where caves containing ancient cliff dwellings can be seen high on the sheer rock faces. The trail fords the cold river 32 times in the six-mile roundtrip. The trail begins at the Gila Wilderness National Monument parking lot.

Those planning longer backpacking trips should note that the trails following the river forks from the Gila Cliff Dwellings area all eventually climb several thousand feet from canyon floors to mountain slopes. A less strenuous approach to the Gila high country is to hike one of the numerous trails that cross the unpaved forest route from Mogollon to Snow Lake on the north boundary of the wilderness. The trails there start at higher altitudes, so less climbing is involved.

Nine major side trails branch off the moderate **Crest Trail** (11 miles), which starts at the marked Sandy Point trailhead, 14 miles up the road from the ghost town of Mogollon. Through lush ancient forest, the main trail climbs to the crest of the mountain range and follows it to the 10,770-foot summit of Mogollon Baldy, where an old fire-lookout station affords a panoramic view of boundless wilderness. It is a moderate two- to three-day backpacking expedition. For a one-day hike, take the first four miles of the trail to Hummingbird Spring.

Another major Gila hiking area, the **Aldo Leopold Wilderness**, is accessible from the top of 8100-foot Emory Pass on Route 152, the most direct way from interstate Route 25 to the Gila Cliff Dwellings. The main trail runs north from the pass through stately ponderosa and Douglas fir forest up 10,011-foot **Hillsboro Peak** (5 miles). On the way up the mountain, it intersects six other major trails that go to all corners of the wilderness.

Carlsbad and Roswell are on **Route 285**, a two-lane highway that crosses unpopulated plains from Santa Fe all the way to Del Rio, Texas. The distance from either Santa Fe or Albuquerque is about 200 miles to Roswell and another 100 miles to Carlsbad Caverns National Park. From El Paso, it is a 150-mile drive to Carlsbad Caverns via **Route 62/180**.

Transportation

CAR

Ruidoso and Lincoln are both about 65 miles west of Roswell via **Route 70/380**. The highway forks 47 miles west of Roswell at Hondo, with Route 70 going to Ruidoso and Route 380 going to Lincoln.

Two highway corridors run north and south through south central New Mexico: interstate **Route 25** along the Rio Grande through Truth or Consequences and Las Cruces, and the more interesting and isolated **Route 54** down the Tularosa Valley through Carrizozo and Alamogordo. Both highways lead to El Paso, Texas. Four-lane **Route 70/82** links Alamogordo with Las Cruces, making a loop tour of the south central area an enjoyable possibility.

Southwestern New Mexico is the most remote, undeveloped part of the state. The most convenient hub for exploring this area is Silver City, 52 miles north of **Route 10**. An apparent shortcut, **Route 152** from Route 25 south of Truth or Consequences over the Mimbres Mountains to Silver City, saves mileage but not much time compared to driving south to Deming and then north again.

Mesa Airlines (800-637-2247) provides passenger service to Carlsbad's **Cavern City Air Terminal, Silver City–Grant County Airport** and **Roswell Industrial Air Center** from Albuquerque.

AIR

Many visitors to Carlsbad Caverns fly into the airport at El Paso, Texas, and rent cars for the trip to the caverns. Aerolitoral, America West, American Airlines, Continental Airlines, Delta Air Lines, Frontier, Northwest Airlines, Southwest Airlines and United Airlines service **El Paso International Airport**. ~ 915-780-4749.

Silver Stage Lines shuttles passengers from Deming to the international airport in El Paso. ~ 800-522-0162. In Alamogordo, airport transportation is available from **Alamo–El Paso Shuttle Service**. ~ 505-437-1472. In Las Cruces, call **Las Cruces Shuttle Service**. ~ 505-525-1784.

In the southeastern part of the state, **TNM&O Coaches** has daily bus service to the terminals in Carlsbad at 1000 South Canyon Street, 505-887-1108; in Roswell at 1100 North Virginia Street, 505-622-2510; in Ruidoso at 138 Service Road, 505-257-2660; in Alamogordo at 601 North White Sands Boulevard, 505-437-3050; in Las Cruces at 490 Valley Drive between Picacho and

BUS

Amador streets, 505-524-8519; and in Truth or Consequences at 8 Date Street, 505-894-3649.

Greyhound Bus Lines (800-231-2222; www.greyhound.com) stops in Las Cruces at 490 North Valley Drive, 505-524-8518; in Truth or Consequences at 8 Date Street, 505-894-3649; in Deming at 332 East Pine Street, 505-546-3881; and in Lordsburg at 112 Wabash Street, 505-542-3412.

CAR RENTALS

Avis Rent A Car (800-331-1212) and **Hertz Rent A Car** (800-654-3131) are your options at the Roswell airport.

Taylor Car Rental, for a fee, offers pickup and delivery from the Silver City–Grant County Airport, which is 30 miles outside of Silver City. You may also rent cars from their location in Silver City. Closed Sunday. ~ 808 North Hudson Street; 505-388-1800.

At the El Paso airport try **Advantage Rent A Car** (800-574-6000), **Avis Rent A Car** (800-331-1212), **Budget Rent A Car** (800-527-0700), **Dollar Rent A Car** (800-800-4000), **Enterprise Rent A Car** (800-736-8222), **Hertz Rent A Car** (800-654-3131) or **National Car Rental** (800-227-7368).

PUBLIC TRANSIT

Pecos Trails operates a fixed route through Roswell. ~ 515 North Main Street; 505-624-6766. **Roadrunner Transit** offers bus service in Las Cruces. No service on Sunday. ~ 1501-A East Hadley Street; 505-541-2544.

TAXIS

In Alamogordo, taxi service is provided by **Dollar Cab Company**. ~ 505-434-8294. In Las Cruces, **Yellow Cab of Las Cruces** supplies citywide service. ~ 505-524-1711.

FOURTEEN

Southwestern Utah

A child's jumbo-size crayon box couldn't contain all the pastels, reds, violets, greens and blues found in the unspoiled lands of southwestern Utah. What's most striking about this country is not only that it has managed to avoid the grasp of developers but also that it's been seemingly skipped by the hands of time. This region puts the letter "p" in pristine.

For starters, consider national parks like Zion, established in 1919, and Bryce, officially designated a park in 1928. Ever popular, these preserves draw hoards of visitors. Added to these treasures, not more than a few hours away, are national monuments like Cedar Breaks and Grand Staircase–Escalante, and state parks like Goblin Valley, Kodachrome Basin State Park, Snow Canyon and Coral Pink Sand Dunes.

The area we call southwestern Utah is bordered roughly by the Henry Mountains to the east, Vermilion Cliffs and Beaver Dam Mountains to the south and the arid Great Basin to the west. A unique topographic variety is contained within these lands, as high mountain lakes and forests overlook the twisted rock found in Goblin Valley. Ever-evolving sculptured rock pinnacles in Bryce coexist adjacent to bristlecone pines, thought to be the oldest living things on earth.

Generally low humidity and rainfall in the lower elevations provide a favorable growing climate for the rare Joshua trees, sagebrush and yucca, while up high aspen and pine trees, oaks and juniper flourish.

Until recently, the powers in charge appeared to be in no hurry to sell this land. That is really no surprise. Despite being a primary connector, scenic Route 12 between Escalante and Torrey was paved only in the late 1980s. The rugged Henry Mountains were the last range in this country to be charted, and herds of buffalo still roam freely as do bighorn sheep, antelope and bear. The little town of Boulder, northeastern gateway to the Grand Staircase–Escalante National Monument, was the very last place in the 45th state to switch over to modern carriers after having its mail delivered by mule team for half a century.

Promotional efforts have begun to expand the possibilities for "Color Country," yet even the construction of skyscrapers couldn't detract from the rainbow-hued rocks, endless forests, lush gardens and those many, many waterways.

Southwestern Utah offers lakes and creeks like Panguitch, Gunlock and Quail brimming with fish not fishermen, hiking trails crying out for someone to traipse over them, ski areas with volumes of snow and biking areas that aren't akin to freeways. Ghost towns have probably stayed that way for a reason.

Working ranches have not yet disappeared, and some towns appear to have more horses than people. The area has managed to remain true to its Western heritage as rodeos are a popular diversion in the summertime. The rugged terrain is well suited to these sturdy equines. Probably the most famous quote about the area was made by 19th-century pioneer Ebenezer Bryce, who, upon seeing the peculiar landscape that today carries his name as a national park, is said to have remarked, "It's a hell of a place to lose a cow."

Among the landowners there's still a certain genuine country courtesy that can be traced to their Mormon traditions and culture rooted in a strong work ethic and family values. The accommodations and eateries reflect this same simplicity in which clean air and water, a good church community and schools are reason enough to celebrate life. But don't be concerned that everything here is rustic. In the resorts and larger cities such as St. George and Cedar City, there are plenty of comfortable places to stay as well as a range of decent places to eat.

Mind you, in the outlying areas, at times you're better off sleeping under the stars and using the local grocery for meals. But isn't there a certain beauty in this contrast?

Nor should you fear that this is a cultural wasteland. The Utah Shakespearean Festival, based in Cedar City, draws more than 150,000 theater-lovers to the region each summer. And the internationally acclaimed American Folk Ballet calls Cedar City home as well. Concerts, plays, dance companies and more are booked into large convention complexes and tiny high school auditoriums alike. Both Dixie State College in St. George and Cedar City's Southern Utah University are known for their academic excellence.

Still, it's the church that remains the heart of the area. The Iron Mission at Cedar City was founded in 1851, shortly after the settlement of Parowan, the first in southern Utah. St. George was founded in 1861 as the Cotton Misson, which is known as Utah's Dixie because of the balmy weather prime for growing cotton. Despite some of the misgivings of the settlers, structures such as the towering St. George Temple or more modest Mormon Tabernacle serve as testament to the hard-working and dedicated pioneers who tamed the land with their new-found-irrigation techniques and made the desert bloom.

American Indians once claimed title to this land, beginning with the Desert Archaic culture, who were thought to inhabit southwestern Utah about the time of Jesus. These American Indians used gardening skills and built small settlements and crafted pottery. A later medieval culture, the Ancestral Pueblo, were agriculturalists who built homes into the rock.

Historians believe the Indians of the desert evolved into the Fremont culture, which disappeared from the area during the 1200s. The modern-day Paiutes now live in small reservations, having relinquished their territory to early white settlers.

Text continued on page 546.

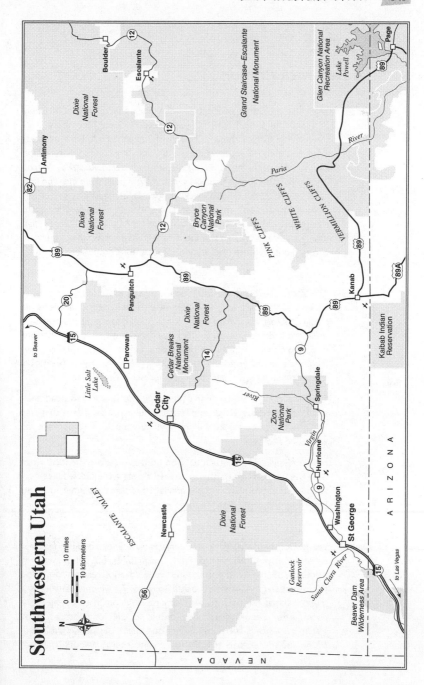

Southwestern Utah

A Red-rock Primer

The close proximity of Zion National Park, Bryce Canyon National Park and the Grand Staircase–Escalante National Monument begs travelers to visit all three in one swing, as each portrays a uniquely different aspect of southwestern Utah. Standing on the floor of Zion Canyon, the rocky ramparts of the state's oldest national park soar ever upward. At Bryce Canyon, most visitors peer *down* into the colorful bowls studded with rocky hoodoos and goblins masterfully created by erosion's many faces. The undeveloped Grand Staircase monument offers a more primitive look into the Southwest's high desert, revealing only to the most determined visitors its serpentine slot canyons, delicate arches, and 19th-century homesteads.

Day 1   The **Zion Lodge** (page 561), although not in the rich heritage of stately national park lodges, is a well-centered base of operations for a stay at **Zion National Park** (page 556). Board a shuttle outside the lodge and head north to the end of the canyon and the **Temple of Sinawava**, an impressive red-rock amphitheater. Stroll down the **Riverside Walk** and into the mouth of **Zion Canyon Narrows** for a glimpse into the park's most impressive slot canyon.

After returning from the narrows, board the shuttle and head back south to **Weeping Rock** and its beautiful hanging gardens that stay lush and colorful even at the height of summer. It's a great place for you to cool off, too.

From Weeping Rock return to Zion Lodge and cross the footbridge over the Virgin River to the **Emerald Pools** trailhead. It takes only about an hour to hike to the waterfalls and three shimmering pools that make this a parkie's favorite.

Day 2   Leave Zion National Park through the east entrance and head for **Bryce Canyon National Park** (page 574), 86 miles away via Routes 9, 89 and 12. If you haven't made advance reservations for a room in **Bryce Canyon Lodge** (page 577), which normally is a must, check at the desk to see if any cancellations have opened up a room. After securing a room, either in the lodge or at **Best Western Ruby's Inn** (page 577) just outside the park, drive south to the end of the road at **Rainbow Point**. There's a short trail here that winds through a small bristlecone grove, and from the lip of the overlook you can gaze into the Grand Staircase monument.

On your way back to the lodge, stop at **Sunset Point** for some beautiful pictures.

Day 3 Rise early and, after a hearty breakfast, take the park shuttle bus to **Bryce Point** (page 576). After admiring the view, hike a short way down the **Under the Rim Trail** to gain some perspective of the towering hoodoos and goblins.

After lunch, leave Bryce Canyon and head east on Route 12. At Cannonville, 13 miles from the park, veer south onto **Cottonwood Canyon Road** (page 584). Over the course of the next 46 miles you'll pass **Kodachrome Basin State Park**, **Grosvenor Arch**, **the Cockscomb** and **Cottonwood Narrows**, each worthy of at least a short stop.

At the end of Cottonwood Canyon Road, turn right (west) onto Route 89 and head toward Kanab. In almost 16 miles you'll come to a dirt road on your right that heads north to the **Old Paria Movie Set** (page 560). After a stop here, continue on to Kanab and a night at the **Parry Lodge** (page 562). The next morning you can either head south to the Grand Canyon, or work your way back north to Salt Lake City.

Lately, snowbirds and retirees have latched onto Utah's Dixie (so called because the area first served as a cotton mission for the Mormon Church, and the warm, dry, almost subtropical climate reminds many of the South). Their varied backgrounds and interests have infused the region with new life and a desire to grow.

Local city leaders, realizing the region's natural beauty is its greatest resource, work to attract small industry to the area to create jobs that will keep the younger generation here as well. They even *boast* of the "golden arches" along main thoroughfares. Until the 1980s, few national franchises thought enough of southwestern Utah to try their luck. But in less than a decade, cities like St. George have doubled in size.

But no matter how much growth you find, it only takes a few moments to step back in history. The old courthouses located in Panguitch, Kanab and St. George reflect the best of pioneer architecture. Historic Hurricane Valley Pioneer Park captures the essence of the region's unique history, and hamlets such as Santa Clara, Pine Valley and Leeds are filled with pioneer homes and churches, arranged in traditional grid patterns with the church as the epicenter.

St. George Area

St. George (pop. 64,000) is not only a winter resort for snowbirds and retirees but also a key gateway to Zion National Park, Dixie National Forest and Snow Canyon State Park. The area is also a historical gold mine, full of restored homes, buildings from the 1800s and fascinating ghost towns.

The city began when, in 1861, Brigham Young sent some 300 families from the comparatively lush land of northern Utah to the southern Utah desert. Young envisioned a huge cotton mission that could supplement the West's supply during the Civil War, which had cut off shipments from the South.

Though initially successful, the cotton mission (and others to grow wine grapes and silkworms as well) ultimately failed because of an inability to compete in the marketplace after the Civil War. However, a warm climate and bevy of recreational activities eventually made St. George the fastest-growing city in the state.

SIGHTS

Any tour of the city should begin at the **St. George Chamber of Commerce**, located in the Old Washington County Courthouse. The brick-and-mortar building, completed in 1876, and originally used as a schoolroom and courtroom, today serves as a museum and information center with original wall paintings of Zion and Grand canyons in the upper assembly room, an old security vault and much more. Closed Sunday. ~ 97 East St. George Boulevard, St. George; 435-628-1658, fax 435-673-1587; www.stgeorgechamber.com, e-mail hotspot@stgeorgechamber.com.

The courthouse serves as first stop on the **St. George Walking Tour**. The six-square-block trek points out 27 sights including some of the city's finest pioneer buildings. Pick up a map at the Chamber of Commerce.

The best way to see St. George, if you're visiting between June and August, is with a one-and-a-half to two-hour tour called **Historic St. George: Live.** You'll travel by bus as a guide in 19th-century costume escorts you to various old buildings, including the Opera House and jail, to meet actors impersonating such legendary former residents as Brigham Young. Tours begin at 9 a.m. and 10:30 a.m., Tuesday through Saturday. Fee. ~ Departs from the Pioneer Center for the Arts, 200 North and Main Street, near the post office; 435-634-5942.

Next door to the courthouse is the **Daughters of Utah Pioneer Museum,** where you'll see a vast collection of community artifacts, including a dress made entirely of locally produced silk, as well as spinning wheels, quilts and Brigham Young's bed. Closed Sunday. ~ 145 North 100 East, St. George; 435-628-7274.

The **Pioneer Center for the Arts,** located next to the restored 1875 St. George Opera House, exhibits permanent and rotating collections of paintings, vintage photographs, local artworks, pottery and sculpture. Closed Sunday. ~ 47 East 200 North, St. George; 435-634-5942; www.sgcity.org/arts.

At the **Brigham Young Winter Home,** a guided tour showcases beautiful furnishings and memorabilia owned by the second president of the Mormon Church from 1869 until his death in 1877.

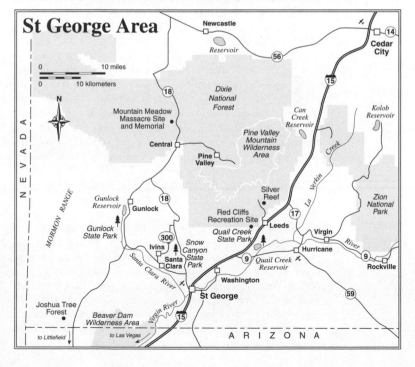

St George Area

Fruit, nut and mulberry trees (fodder for those silkworms) still cover the grounds. ~ 89 West 100 North, St. George; 435-673-2517, 435-673-5181 (temple visitors center).

Stop 16 on the St. George walking tour is **Judd's Store**, a turn-of-the-20th-century mercantile, dishes up old-fashioned soda fountain treats on those hot Utah days. Closed Sunday. ~ 76 West Tabernacle Street, St. George; 435-628-2596.

It took 13 years to complete the **Mormon Tabernacle** in St. George. Tour guides show off the building with pride, telling how the limestone for three-foot-thick basement walls was hand quarried and the red sandstone blocks were hand cut stone by stone from a nearby site. Take special note of the intricate, plaster-of-Paris ceiling and cornice work. Glass for the windows was shipped to California by boat and then hauled by wagon team to St. George. ~ 18 South Main Street, St. George; 435-628-4072.

> Pine Valley's picturesque, satin-white chapel, believed to be the oldest Mormon chapel, is still in continuous use.

Only card-carrying members of the Mormon Church may tread through the sparkling-white **St. George Temple**, built in 1877, but an on-site visitors center provides a pictorial history of the temple's construction and other background on the Church of Jesus Christ of Latter-day Saints. ~ 300 East 490 South, St. George; 435-673-5181, fax 435-656-5975.

Also in St. George is the **St. George Area Convention & Visitors Bureau**, which can provide information on the entire region. ~ 1835 Convention Center Drive, St. George; 435-634-5747, 800-869-6635, fax 435-628-1619; www.utahstgeorge.com.

If you're a real history buff, you might want to venture out to **Old Fort Pierce**, east of St. George. The adobe fort was built in 1866 to protect settlers. Only a few remnants and partial walls remain at the site, but there is a nice monument explaining the history of the fort. While there, you can also explore a series of **dinosaur tracks** (three-toed impressions left in the mud millions of years ago). ~ Getting to Old Fort Pierce and the tracks requires a high-clearance vehicle and dry roads. Follow 700 South to the east until it becomes River Road and take another left on Stake Farm Road (1450 South) through Washington Fields. Then follow the signs.

HIDDEN ▶

Elsewhere, a short (200-yard) walk takes adventurous souls to more **dinosaur tracks**. Drive to the heart of **Washington**, a few miles east of St. George, and turn north on Main until you pass under Route 15. Follow the dirt road north and turn right at the road that goes up the hill to the pink water tank. Park here, then walk up the road to a chained cable gate. Turn right and walk northeast to a deep wash. Go down into the wash and follow it downstream until you find a flat, greenish slab of rock. Here you'll find the foot-long tracks from another age.

Three miles west of St. George sits the rural community of **Santa Clara**. Settled by Swiss immigrants, Santa Clara lays claim to the house built by noted missionary, Indian agent and colonizer Jacob Hamblin. Built in 1862, the rough-hewn, red sandstone **Jacob Hamblin Home** clearly demonstrates the sturdiness of frontier construction designed to withstand Indian attack and showcases a number of furnishings and tools from that period including old no-springs beds, Indian rugs and a wagon. ~ Old Santa Clara Road, Santa Clara; 435-673-2161.

Heading north from St. George on Route 18, you'll approach **Snow Canyon State Park**. A small park, the canyon itself is a white-and-red mix of Navajo sandstone covered with black lava beds. Elevations range from 3100 to 4875 feet atop the volcanic cinder cones. Grasses, willows, cacti and other shrubbery peer through cracks. Admission. ~ Snow Canyon Road, off Route 18; 435-628-2255, fax 435-628-9321; www.stateparks.utah.gov.

Twenty-five miles north of St. George on Route 18 is the town of Central and the turnoff to the mountain hamlet of **Pine Valley**. Along the way are numerous extinct volcanic cones and lava fields, many beckoning to be explored. Nestled in the Dixie National Forest, surrounded by 10,000-foot peaks and ponderosa pine, is the Pine Valley Mountain Wilderness Area and reservoir with numerous picnicking areas. ~ Forest Road 035.

Just north of the Pine Valley turnoff is a stone marker and memorial for the **Mountain Meadow Massacre Site and Memorial**. Here, in 1857, a group of emigrants—120 men, women and children—en route to California was slaughtered by Mormons and Indians. The event is considered a dark period in Mormon history and one the church has tried to live down ever since. ~ Route 18.

LODGING

Located midway between Salt Lake City and Los Angeles, St. George is awash in hotels, motels and bed and breakfasts. Virtually every major chain is represented, making it simple to find one that meets your requirements and pocketbook.

◄ HIDDEN

No one walks away unsatisfied from the **Seven Wives Inn**, perhaps one of the nicest accommodations in St. George. Deluxe in every way except price, the 13-room bed and breakfast is graciously decorated in Victorian antiques. Some rooms boast fireplaces, woodburning stoves, or jacuzzi tubs, and most have outside doors to porches or balconies. All have private baths. Rates include a huge gourmet breakfast in the elegant dining room and use of the swimming pool. ~ 217 North 100 West, St. George; 435-628-3737, 800-600-3737, fax 435-628-5646; www.seven wivesinn.com. MODERATE TO ULTRA-DELUXE.

There's a lot of bang for the buck at **Howard Johnson Express Inn & Suites**. More than half the 52 units are classified "kitchenette suites," meaning they house a microwave oven, refrigerator, conversation-and-dining area, plus fully tiled bath with mirrored vanity. An outdoor jacuzzi, guest laundry and heated pool round out the amenities. Continental breakfast is included. ~ 1040 South Main Street, St. George; 435-628-8000, 800-332-0400, fax 435-656-3983; www.igohojo.com. BUDGET TO MODERATE.

Holiday Inn Resort Hotel likes to think of itself as a complete recreational facility. Besides the 164 well-appointed rooms, restaurant and atrium-style lobby, guests are treated to a large indoor/outdoor heated swimming pool (you can actually swim in and out of the hotel), whirlpool spa, lighted tennis court and game room. ~ 850 South Bluff Street, St. George; 435-628-4235, 800-457-9800, fax 435-628-8157; www.histgeorgeutah.com, e-mail hotelinfo@histgeorgeutah.com. MODERATE.

Due to the number of settlers originally from the South, St. George was—and still is—known as Utah's "Dixie."

The Bluffs Inn & Suites has 61 accommodations (24 of them apartments with full kitchens), exceptionally well decorated in soft tones with large bathrooms and a living-room area. There's also an outdoor heated pool and jacuzzi. Complimentary continental breakfast is offered in the sunny lobby. ~ 1140 South Bluff Street, St. George; 435-628-6699, 800-832-5833, fax 435-673-8705; www.bluffsinnsuites.com. BUDGET TO MODERATE.

A collection of nine restored pioneer homes makes up **Green Gate Village Historic Inn,** a unique bed-and-breakfast complex designed to intrigue and delight. Surrounded by a flower-laden courtyard, manicured lawns, swimming pool and garden hot tub, the village has elegant decor—wallpapered rooms, duvets, antique furnishings, plump pillows—and a conscientious staff. Six rooms have large whirlpool tubs. A delicious country breakfast completes the picture. ~ 76 West Tabernacle Street, St. George; 435-628-6989, 800-350-6999, fax 435-628-6989; www.greengatevillageinn.com, e-mail stay@greengatevillageinn.com. MODERATE TO ULTRA-DELUXE.

Situated off the main drag, **Ramada Inn** offers quiet refuge. An expansive lobby provides portal to 136 rooms, each with desk and upholstered chairs. The hotel also has one of the prettiest swimming-pool settings with palm trees surrounding the site. Breakfast is included. ~ 1440 East St. George Boulevard, St. George; 435-628-2828, 888-704-8476, fax 435-628-0505; www.ramadainn.net, e-mail ramadasales@ramadainn.net. MODERATE TO DELUXE.

The streamlined architecture of **Best Western Coral Hills Motel** is reminiscent of *The Jetsons,* but the 98 rooms are more down-to-earth with carpeting, upholstered chairs and dark woods. Indoor and outdoor swimming pools, a children's wading pool, spas, putting green and exercise room are bonuses. An expanded continental breakfast is included. ~ 125 East St. George Boulevard, St. George; 435-673-4844, 800-528-1234, fax 435-673-5352; www.coralhills.com, e-mail bwcoral@infowest.com. MODERATE.

DINING

St. George has no lack of choices when it comes to places to eat. Besides the requisite chains (and none, it seems, are missing), there are plenty more eateries that offer a hearty meal at a reasonable cost.

The Painted Pony is an elegant affair serving contemporary American cuisine. The chef borrows from Asia, Europe and North Africa for such dishes as sesame-crusted escolar with sweet potato–green onion hash, Moroccan-spiced chicken with a pomegranate molasses sauce, and grilled tenderloin with a shiitake demiglace. No lunch on Sunday. ~ 2 West St. George Boulevard, St. George; 435-634-1700; www.painted-pony.com, e-mail info@painted-pony.com. DELUXE.

Feast on fondue at the European-style bistro **La Soirée**. There's classic Swiss fondue, as well as a Southwest version (cheddar and jack with jalapeños). Meat and seafood entrées are simmered in a choice of four broths, while the dessert concoctions include chocolate caramel and coconut almond. Lunch features sweet and savory crepes. Live music Friday evenings adds to the romantic atmosphere. No lunch on Sunday. Closed Monday. ~ Main Street Plaza, 20 North Main Street, St. George; 435-674-9994; www.lasoiree.net. MODERATE.

Breakfast and lunch are the specialties at the **Bear Paw Coffee Company**. ~ 75 North Main Street, St. George; 435-634-0126. BUDGET.

Fajitas are tops at **Pancho & Lefty's**, a busy, fun Mexican restaurant with colorful wall murals. The menu also features tostadas, burritos and tacos. ~ 1050 South Bluff Street, St. George; 435-628-4772. BUDGET TO MODERATE.

Service is erratic, but **The Palms Restaurant** can be a good option for family dining in a pleasant setting. Besides an extensive salad bar with homemade soups and breads, dinner fare range from fish and chips to shrimp scampi to chicken teriyaki. Sandwiches, hamburgers and salads comprise the lunch menu, while breakfast includes omelettes and griddle items. The Palms also offers Sunday brunches. ~ Holiday Inn, 850 South Bluff Street, St. George; 435-628-4235, fax 435-628-8157. MODERATE TO DELUXE.

SHOPPING

Shopping in this region is evolving as local retailers become more conscious of tourists' buying power. Malls, however, remain the primary outlet for shoppers.

Text continued on page 554.

Ghost Towns of Color Country

While much of Utah's history is neatly preserved in museums and restored homes, a more fascinating (and sometimes poignant) look can be found in the ruins eroded by time, nature and man. One of the most popular and representative ghost towns of southwestern Utah is **Silver Reef**, which took its name from a sandstone formation that resembles an ocean reef, 18 miles north of St. George and only three miles off the freeway.

"Silver!" was the cry that brought more than 1000 fortune-hunters to Silver Reef more than a century ago. According to newspaper accounts, Silver Reef was the only spot in the Utah States where silver was discovered in sandstone. John Kemple is credited with the 1866 find, and the town boomed into a notorious camp of 1500 non-Mormon miners. Citizens of nearby Mormon communities were warned not to mix with the rowdy populace rumored to participate in brawls, shootings and lynchings. With 29 mines scattered over two square miles, Silver Reef proved bountiful, yielding $9 million in silver from 1877 to 1903.

Today, separate cemeteries for Protestants and Catholics remain, along with abandoned mine sites. Area historians are slowly working to restore community. Fittingly, the **Wells Fargo & Co. Express Building**, constructed in 1877 of sandstone blocks and metal doors, survived the ravages of time. It now houses the **Silver Reef Museum**. Authentic mining tools, maps, clothing and other historical paraphernalia fill shelves and glass cases. Old newspapers recount Silver Reef's heyday, and town plats show how vast the boomtown spread. Visitors can even walk into the original Wells Fargo bank vault.

Half the Wells Fargo building is used by Western bronze sculptor Jerry Anderson as a **studio and gallery**. Both his work and that of other prominent local artists are displayed and sold, along with a good assortment of books recounting Utah's ghost towns. Closed Sunday. ~ 2002 Wells Fargo Drive; 435-879-2359.

Nearby is a small structure that once served as the Powder House. Today, the building houses the **Silver Reef information center** with models of the original township and more original plats.

It only takes a few minutes to drive around and look at the nearby store ruins scattered among a new neighborhood development. At the site of the **Barbee and Walker Mill** all that remains are rock walls. The same is true of the drugstore and the Chinese laundry.

In the virtual ghost town of Silver Reef, there's a surprisingly popular restaurant. **The Cosmopolitan Restaurant** serves Chilean seabass with tomato and ginger ragout, along with a variety of European-inspired entrées. Dinner only. Closed Sunday. ~ 1915 Wells Fargo Drive, Silver Reef; 435-879-6826; www.cosmodining.com. MODERATE TO DELUXE.

While most Utah ghost towns lie in a stark desert environment, **Grafton** is an exception. Amid vast fields, mulberry trees and rambling cattle, the abandoned settlement sits beside the Virgin River near the red-rock cliffs of Zion National Park. Today work is under way by the Grafton Heritage Partnership Project to preserve the few historic log and adobe buildings that remain from the settlement that got its start in the 1850s as part of the region's "Cotton Mission."

Five Mormon families settled Grafton in 1859, naming the town after a Massachusetts community. Assisted by then-friendly Paiute Indians, the families dammed the Virgin River for irrigation, hoping to plant cotton. In 1861, a flood ravaged the entire area and swept away homes, barns and fields. Survivors moved their settlement to higher and safer ground, digging a system of canals and ditches. Besides cotton, they planted corn, wheat and tobacco. By 1865, 200 acres were cultivated.

Later, Indian attacks disrupted community life. Settlers were killed in alarming numbers, and Grafton residents were forced to work the fields in armed bands. Occasionally, the entire town was evacuated. After the Indian threat eased in the 1870s, the settlers obtained Brigham Young's permission to plant mulberry trees and grow silkworms.

Grafton headed toward ghost town status after 1907, as persistent problems became too much for the settlers to face. But the quaint village charmed Hollywood, and since 1950 many films, including scenes from *Butch Cassidy and the Sundance Kid*, have been filmed here. Several of the buildings still stand, including a few woodframe homes and the one-room, brick schoolhouse with small belltower. All are open for exploring.

To get to Silver Reef, go northeast from St. George on Route 15 for 18 miles to the Leeds exit. Head east one mile through town to a sign marked "Silver Reef." Turn north under the freeway and drive about two miles.

For Grafton, take Route 9 (the road to Zion National Park) to the town of Rockville. Turn south on Bridge Lane, which crosses the Virgin River. After crossing the bridge, head west and backtrack along a rutted, dirt-and-gravel road for several miles. Note that in some sections you are crossing or bordering private land so don't abuse the privilege.

Ancestor Square, located in the St. George Historic District, offers art galleries and other shops. ~ Main Street and St. George Boulevard, St. George.

NIGHTLIFE   World-class entertainers are spotlighted through the **Celebrity Concert Series.**

The **Southwest Symphony**, a community orchestra, and the **Southwest Symphonic Chorale** perform throughout the year in the M. C. Cox Auditorium. ~ Dixie State College, Avenna Center, 225 South 700 East, St. George; 435-652-7800.

Dixie State College Theater offers plays and musicals during the school year. ~ 225 South 700 East, St. George; 435-652-7800.

The **One and Only** is a beer bar serving a lively crowd. There's karaoke on Tuesday and Wednesday and live music on Friday. Cover for men on Friday. ~ 64 North 800 East, St. George; 435-673-9191.

PARKS   **SNOW CANYON STATE PARK** 🏃 🚲 🐎   Black lava rock crusted over red Navajo sandstone make for a striking visual effect in this colorful canyon. Several volcanic cones welcome visitors to the northern end of the 6853-acre park, considered a treat for photographers. The park features a covered group-use pavilion, picnic areas, restrooms and hot showers. Day-use fee, $5. ~ Off Route 18: take Snow Canyon Parkway six miles and make a right on Snow Canyon Road. Snow Canyon Road leads directly into the park; 435-628-2255.

▲ There are 33 sites (including 14 with partial hookups); $15 to $18 per night; reservations recommended in spring and fall. There's a sewage disposal station. Reservations: 800-322-3770.

GUNLOCK STATE PARK 🎣 ⛺ 🚤 🛥 🚣   Twenty-five miles northwest of St. George, the heart of this state park is a 240-acre reservoir that lies in the rugged ravine of the Santa Clara River.

◆◆◆

ON THE BORDER

Heading south on Route 91 over the summit to the Beaver Dam Slope, you'll be driving toward the Arizona border. Along the way you'll pass the 1040-acre, desert-like **Joshua Tree Natural Area**, claimed to be the farthest north these picturesque trees grow. Route 91 connects with Route 15 at Beaver Dam, Arizona. Head north back toward St. George and drive through the **Virgin River Gorge**, a giant gash in the rocky earth where the Virgin River heads out of Utah through Arizona and into Nevada. It took 12 years to build this 23-mile stretch of spectacular highway.

Surrounding the shimmering waters are red-rock hills dotted with green shrubbery. Superb year-round boating, waterskiing and bass fishing abound. There are toilets. ~ Old Route 91, 25 miles northwest of St. George; 435-680-0715.

▲ Primitive camping allowed within the park; $9 per night. Note: Bring your own drinking water.

QUAIL CREEK STATE PARK ⚓ 🚣 🎣 ⛴ ⛴ 🛥 ⛵ Stark rock escarpments surround a 600-acre reservoir with a state park set on its west shore. Quail Creek attracts anglers eager to reel in bass, trout, crappie and bluegill. Besides being an ideal site for camping and picnicking, Quail Creek Reservoir is noted for its waterskiing, boating and windsurfing. There are picnic areas and restrooms. Day-use fee, $7. ~ Just off Route 9, 14 miles north of St. George; 435-879-2378.

▲ There are 23 sites; $12 per night.

RED CLIFFS RECREATION SITE 🚶 🚲 Maintained by the Bureau of Land Management, this camping area is a red-rock paradise at the foot of the Pine Valley Mountains. Desert trees and plants crowd every campsite. Facilities include picnic tables, pit toilets and drinking water. Day-use fee, $2. ~ From St. George go north on Route 15 about 17 miles to the Leeds exit. From there, drive south two and one half miles and west two miles; 435-688-3200.

▲ There are ten sites; $8 per night.

If you've got rocks in your head, you've come to the right place. This is not to question your sanity but rather to underline the spectacular rock formations found here. From canyon walls to monuments to cliffs, the Zion area has it all. Coupled with this are some neat historic buildings and movie-set towns that have been featured in hundreds of films.

▼▼▼▼▼▼▼▼▼▼
Zion Area

Halfway between St. George and Zion National Park on Route 9 lies the town of **Hurricane** (pronounced hur-i-kun), a rural community that often attracts the overflow from Zion into its motels and restaurants. In the center of town lies **Hurricane Valley Heritage Park**. The museum and information center stands amid a grassy lawn filled with pioneer-era wagons and farm machinery. The museum depicts the history of the town and displays pioneer items including an authentic kitchen. Closed Sunday. ~ 35 West State Street, Hurricane; 435-635-3245.

SIGHTS

Nearby, the historic Bradshaw Hotel is now the **Heritage House Museum**, whose collection includes a pioneer schoolroom and doctor's office and a fine doll exhibit. Closed Sunday. ~ 95 South Main Street, Hurricane; 435-635-7153.

A relaxing break from the rigors of the road may be found at **Pah Tempe Mineral Hot Springs**, a large grouping of five soaking- and swimming-pool areas. Rustic but congenial, Pah Tempe resembles a '60s commune with a tiny bed and breakfast, lodge and campsites. Bathing suits are required. Massage therapy programs, facial packs and other services can be arranged. Admission. Note: A conflict with the local water district has diverted Pah Tempe's water flows; the hot springs are closed until that is resolved. Only day groups of ten or more are allowed, reservations required. ~ 825 North 800 East, Hurricane; 435-635-2879; www.infowest. com/pahtempe.

ZION NATIONAL PARK   Carved almost singlehandedly by the Virgin River for over 13 millions years, **Zion National Park**, grandfather of Utah's national parks, is a breathtaking, 147,551-acre natural gallery of vividly colored cliffs, sheer-rock walls, massive stone monoliths and unique formations. Cottonwoods, willows and velvet ash trees line the river, which flows along the canyon floor, providing an ever-changing kaleidoscope of colors as one season follows another. Skittering, flitting and ambling throughout the park are mountain lions, mule deer and more than 289 species of birds, including golden eagles and rarer peregrine falcons and Mexican spotted owls.

Featuring towering cliffs, narrow slot canyons, and a wide variety of hiking trails geared to all abilities, this "heavenly city of God" is a park for all people—and lots of them. To really avoid the crowds and traffic, gear your visit to November through April, although this season can see a lot of snow in the park's upper reaches. Cars have been prohibited in Zion Canyon from April through October because of the world-class traffic jams. Only those with reservations at Zion Lodge are allowed to drive up the canyon; others must take a free, continuously running shuttle system that conveniently and quickly hauls visitors back and forth between the town of Springdale and eight stops along Zion Canyon Scenic Drive. Outside of the canyon floor, the rest of the park is open to vehicle traffic.

Depending on time and specific interest, you can take the shuttle, bicycle or walk through Zion Canyon. But don't miss out on the fabulous sights that await just off the roads. Zion is best appreciated close-up, and you'll miss the true majesty of the park if you don't wander around and stare up, or down, at this awesome geology.

Be sure to stop at the **Visitor Center** (435-772-7616), where park rangers are happy to provide maps, brochures and backcountry permits. Specific dates and times for naturalist guided walks, evening programs and patio talks are posted at the center. Oversized vehicles must be escorted through the Zion tunnel (fee). Admission. ~ Main entrance: Route 9, Springdale; 435-772-3256; www.nps.gov/zion.

Youngsters ages six through twelve can get down and dirty with nature at the **Zion Nature Center** through the Junior Ranger Program. From June through Labor Day, park rangers and the Zion Natural History Association conduct a variety of outdoor-adventure and environmental-science programs that acquaint the younger set with everything from the flight pattern of a golden eagle to the difference between a Utah beavertail cactus and a maidenhair fern.

Among the first things you'll encounter is **The Watchman**, a 2555-foot monolith of sandstone and shale that stands guard over the park entrance.

Zion Canyon Scenic Drive takes visitors about six and a half miles into the heart of Zion Canyon and its 2000- to 3000-foot-high walls carved inch-by-inch by the North Fork of the Virgin River cutting through the Markagunt Plateau. Just past the entrance you're likely to spot **West Temple**, the highest peak in Zion's southern section. Notice the delineated strata of rock as it rises 4100 feet from base to peak.

One of the first places you might want to pause at is **Court of the Patriarchs** viewpoint. From here you can see reverently named monuments like the Streaked Wall, the Sentinel, the Patriarchs (a series of three peaks called Abraham, Isaac and Jacob), Mt. Moroni, the Spearhead and the sheer-walled sandstone monolith Angels Landing, perched 1500 feet above the canyon bed. To the east and above are two other monuments, Mountain of the Sun and the Twin Brothers.

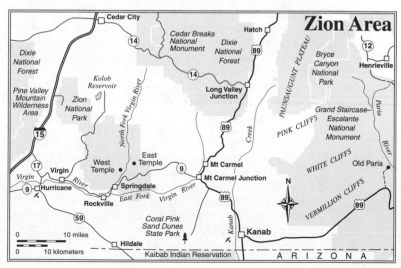

Emerald Pools parking area, two and a half miles up the Scenic Drive, offers access to a trail network serving both the Upper and Lower pools. A creek from Heaps Canyon sends water cascading down waterfalls into pools below. Yucca, cacti and scrub oak line the trail to the upper pool, and the path affords views of shaded, north-facing slopes rich with ponderosa pine and Douglas fir. Since the creek is fed primarily by runoff, the pools are fullest in spring and early summer, and dwindle as summer wears on, barring a torrential downpour. This creates spectacular waterfalls shooting off the steep walls of the canyon. If you happen to visit Zion between mid-October and late November, this is a prime spot to see the changing colors.

A little over a half mile away to the northeast, paralleling the Scenic Drive, **The Grotto Picnic Area** is the perfect spot to take a break from exploring the park. In the cool shade of broadleaf trees and gambel oak you'll find fire grates, picnic tables, water and restrooms. Directly across the road from the Grotto is the trailhead for the West Rim Trail, which leads to Angel's Landing.

A quarter of a mile later along the same road you'll spot **The Great White Throne** on the east side. Notice how this 2400-foot monolith ranges in color from a deep red at the base to pink to gray to white at the top. The color variations arise because the Navajo sandstone has less iron oxide at the top than the bottom.

A bit farther is a short, paved walk that leads to **Weeping Rock**, where continuous springs "weep" across a grotto. Even on a hot day, the spot remains cool. Like other parts of Zion, you should see lush, hanging cliff gardens thick with columbine, shooting-stars and scarlet monkeyflower.

The end of the road, so to speak, comes at **Temple of Sinawava**, perhaps the easiest area in the park to access. Named after the Paiute wolf spirit, the huge natural amphitheater is formed by sheer, red cliffs that soar to the sky and two stone pillars—the Altar and the Pulpit—in the center.

Route 9 branches off of Zion Canyon Drive and heads east from Zion National Park on what is called the **Zion–Mount Carmel Highway**. Considered an engineering marvel of its day (1930), the 13-mile road snakes up high precipices and around sharp, narrow turns before reaching the high, arid plateaus of the east. And, if you've ever ridden Disneyland's Matterhorn, you'll love the mile-long, narrow, unlit **tunnel**. Rangers control traffic through the darkened tube, stopping drivers when an oversized truck or recreational vehicle is passing through. Even with delays, the tunnel is a treat—huge, window-like openings allow sunlight to stream in every so often, affording unparalleled views of the vermilion cliffsides.

On the east side of the tunnel lies the park's "slickrock" territory. It's almost like a time warp from one country to another.

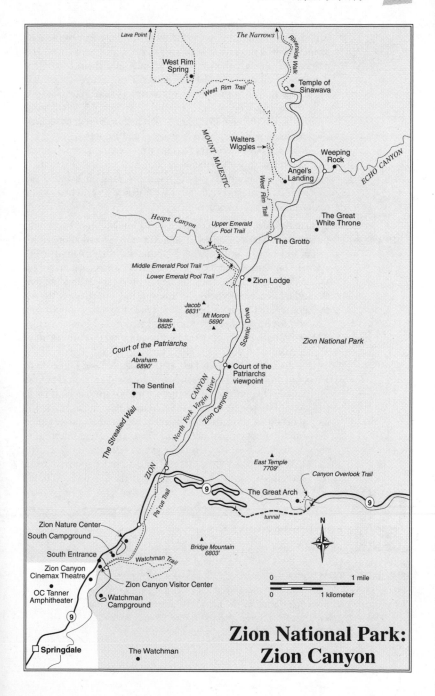

Lava Point

The Narrows

Riverside Walk

West Rim Spring

West Rim Trail

Temple of Sinawava

MOUNT MAJESTIC

Walters Wiggles

Weeping Rock

ECHO CANYON

Angel's Landing

West Rim Trail

Heaps Canyon

Upper Emerald Pool Trail

The Great White Throne

The Grotto

Middle Emerald Pool Trail

Lower Emerald Pool Trail

Zion Lodge

Jacob 6831'

Mt Moroni 5690'

Isaac 6825'

Scenic Drive

Zion National Park

Court of the Patriarchs

Abraham 6890'

Court of the Patriarchs viewpoint

The Sentinel

ZION CANYON

North Fork Virgin River

Zion Canyon

The Streaked Wall

East Temple 7709'

Canyon Overlook Trail

ZION

The Great Arch

9

9

Pa rus Trail

tunnel

Zion Nature Center

South Campground

N

South Entrance

Watchman Trail

Bridge Mountain 6803'

Zion Canyon Cinemax Theatre

Zion Canyon Visitor Center

OC Tanner Amphitheater

0   1 mile

Watchman Campground

0   1 kilometer

9

Springdale

The Watchman

Zion National Park:
Zion Canyon

Canyon Overlook is a moderately easy, half-mile self-guided walk on the Zion–Mount Carmel Highway just east of the long tunnel. Unlike the lush Zion Canyon floor, this area showcases plants and animals that make rock and sand their home. The overlook itself provides views of lower Zion Canyon, including the Streaked Wall with its long, black marks sharply contrasting with the red canyon walls; West and East Temples, giant stone monoliths with temple-like edifices perched on top; and the massive, multicolored cliff called Towers of the Virgin.

Don't miss **Checkerboard Mesa**, a prime example of sandstone etched over time with horizontal lines and vertical fractures to resemble a mountainous playing board. ~ Stay on Route 9 out of Zion National Park to connect with Route 89 and head south toward the Arizona border.

EAST OF ZION Thirteen miles east of Zion National Park in the tiny town of Mount Carmel lies the **Maynard Dixon Home**, a log cabin and nearby studio where Dixon, an early to mid-1900s Western landscape painter who enjoyed national acclaim for his sweeping vistas and American Indian profiles, spent his summers. Walk the hillside trails behind the home and you're likely to pass the spot where Dixon's ashes were spread. Tours by appointment. Closed November through April. Admission. ~ Mount Carmel; 435-648-2653; www.maynarddixon.com, e-mail heather@maynarddixon.com.

HIDDEN ►

All that's missing is the surf at **Coral Pink Sand Dunes State Park**, but those who prefer sand to water will revel in the inviting dunes. This is Mother Nature's sandbox just aching to be frolicked in by young and old alike. Some of the dunes reach 100 feet in height. A resident park ranger is on hand to answer questions about this unusual area, and there are a few interpretive signs as well. A boardwalk trail leads to a vista point of the main dunes. Admission. ~ Yellow Jacket Road, 12 miles south of Route 89 between Mt. Carmel Junction and Kanab; 435-648-2800, fax 435-648-2801.

AUTHOR FAVORITE

Although I can't act, I can envision the action through the actor's eyes when I visit the **Old Paria Movie Set** (now part of Grand Staircase–Escalante National Monument), 30 miles east along Route 89. Here, fans will find the West of their imaginations come alive on a false-front movie-set town that's open to the public and was once used for the *Gunsmoke* television series. Some also use Route 89 as a backdoor entrance to Lake Powell, with the highway continuing into Page, Arizona.

Continuing on Route 89, you'll pass what looks like an Ancestral Pueblo cliff dwelling. That's **Moqui Cave**, which claims the largest collection of dinosaur tracks in the Kanab area. Other displays include Indian artifacts, foreign money and fluorescent minerals. Closed Sunday. Admission. ~ Route 89, five miles north of Kanab; 435-644-8525; www.moquicave.com, e-mail sevenseas@xpressweb.com.

Farther south, Route 89 heads toward the base of the colorful Vermillion Cliffs and **Kanab**, the gateway to the Grand Staircase–Escalante National Monument and a town known as "Little Hollywood" for the more than 200 movies, most of them B-grade Westerns, filmed in the area in the mid-1900s. Today, Kanab is a crossroads for travelers headed to Lake Powell, the Grand Canyon or Bryce and has numerous motels and restaurants.

Some movie-set towns are still evident throughout the area. Because some sit on private property, check with the **Kane County Travel Information Center** to see which are open to the public. Closed Sunday during the off-season. ~ 78 South 100 East, Kanab; 435-644-5033, fax 435-644-5923; www.kaneutah.com.

In Kanab, a bit like the Universal Studios tour is **Frontier Movie Town**, a replica of a Wild West movie set that caters to groups but lets individuals tag along. Here, marshals in white hats battle black-hatted villains during mock gunfights. You can walk along the boardwalk and peer into the false storefronts. Shops, a snack bar and historic exhibits are also on-site. ~ 297 West Center Street, Kanab; 435-644-5337, 800-551-1714; e-mail frontier@xpressweb.com.

Heritage House is an 1893 restored pioneer mansion built of brick and red rock and one of seven homes making up the Kanab walking tour. You can find brochures at the house or at Kane County Travel Information Center. Closed during the winter; call ahead. ~ 100 South Main Street, Kanab; 435-644-3966.

One of the neatest hidden attractions in Kanab is **Best Friends Animal Sanctuary** in Angel Canyon, just north of town off Route 89. This no-kill animal sanctuary is set among the red rocks and Ancestral Pueblo ruins in a peaceful setting and features a changing menagerie of dogs, cats, donkeys and other animals. Guided tours are available. ~ 5001 Angel Canyon Road, Kanab; 435-644-2001; www.bestfriends.org, e-mail visiting@bestfriends.org.

◀ **HIDDEN**

Massive vermilion cliffs surround **Zion Lodge**, set in the heart of the park. A huge lawn and shade trees welcome guests to the property, which is actually a replica of the original property. That Zion Lodge burned down in 1966 and was quickly (within 100 days) replaced by the current facility, which includes motel-style rooms, suites and cabins. While standard furnishings are the norm, location is everything. Cabins afford more privacy and

LODGING

feature fireplaces and private porches. A dining room, snack bar and gift shop are on-site. ~ Zion National Park; 435-772-7700, 888-297-2757, fax 435-772-7792; www.zionlodge.com. DELUXE.

Flanigan's Inn evokes a rustic park lodge atmosphere with decks and patios, ponds and gardens against the backdrop of scenic Zion Canyon. All of its 34 rooms and suites feature plush sofas and bedding. Amenities here include a pool, hot tubs, nature trail, labyrinth, spa, restaurant and bistro. ~ 450 Zion Park Boulevard, Springdale; 435-772-3244, 800-765-7787, fax 435-772-3396; www.discoverzion.com, e-mail info@flanigans.com. MODERATE TO DELUXE.

American and English antiques fill **Under the Eaves Bed & Breakfast**. Constructed of sandstone blocks from nearby canyon walls, the 1929 home resembles a cheery English cottage. All six rooms have private baths. There's also a large suite upstairs with vaulted ceilings, a wood-burning stove, and a sitting room. Full breakfast is served each morning. ~ 980 Zion Park Boulevard, Springdale; 435-772-3457, 866-261-2655; www.under-the-eaves.com. MODERATE.

HIDDEN ▶

Located in a quiet neighborhood, **Harvest House Bed & Breakfast** is sure to please even the most demanding. All four rooms are exquisitely decorated; all have private baths. Expect bright, airy spaces full of wicker furniture and plush carpeting; balconies offer an unparalleled view of Zion National Park. Stargazing from the backyard hot tub is a great way to end the day. A gourmet breakfast is included. ~ 29 Canyon View Drive, Springdale; 435-772-3880, fax 435-772-3327; www.harvesthouse. net, e-mail harvesthouse_utah@yahoo.com. MODERATE.

Tree-shaded lawns and gardens mark the **Driftwood Lodge**. Forty-two oversized rooms bring the outdoors inside with oak furniture and Southwestern artwork. An art gallery, a restaurant, a heated outdoor swimming pool and a hot tub are nice pluses. ~ 1515 Zion Park Boulevard, Springdale; 435-772-3262, 888-801-8811, fax 435-772-3702; www.driftwoodlodge.net, e-mail driftwoodlodge@qwest.net. MODERATE.

Some of the rooms are on the small side, but you can't beat the history when you stay at the **Parry Lodge** in Kanab. Built in 1931 to accommodate the film industry when it came to southern Utah for its red-rock backdrop, the lodge served as the hangout for such film stars as John Wayne, Glen Ford, Charlton Heston, Barbara Stanwyck and Ava Gardner. Small plaques over various rooms point out which actor/actress slept where. The lodge also has a small pool to ward off the desert heat, and a restaurant. ~ 89 East Center Street, Kanab; 435-644-2601, 800-748-4104, fax 435-644-2605; www.parrylodge.com, e-mail parrylodge@kanab.net. BUDGET TO MODERATE.

Pay close attention and you might spot the tiny Zion snail, a creature found in Zion National Park and nowhere else.

Located right in the heart of Zion National Park, **Zion Lodge Restaurant** satisfies every appetite with bountiful breakfasts, hearty lunches and tasty dinners that revolve around Southwestern fare and beef. Hamburgers, salads, seafood, chipotle barbecued chicken and steak are pleasantly presented amid the beauty of Zion. Dinner reservations are recommended. ~ Zion National Park; 435-772-3213, fax 435-772-7790. MODERATE TO DELUXE.

DINING

The rustic cantina appearance of **Bit and Spur Saloon and Mexican Restaurant** belies what many consider Utah's best Mexican restaurant. The dinner menu focuses on traditional cuisine like *flautas*, tostadas, *rellenos* and burritos. You'll also find chili stews and creative Southwestern chicken dishes. From spring until early fall, reservations are a must. There's also a small bar with a pool table if you're just looking for a place to escape from the heat. Dinner only. Closed December. ~ 1212 Zion Park Boulevard, Springdale; 435-772-3498; www.bitandspur.com, e-mail bitandspur@infowest.com. MODERATE.

◀ HIDDEN

You'll get outstanding Italian-style fare along with Utah microbrews at the **Zion Pizza & Noodle Co.** Housed in a former church building in the heart of Springdale, the restaurant has indoor and patio seating and an adjacent gift shop and outdoor gear store. The menu is "eclectic Italian": traditional pizza with cheese and tomato sauce, Thai chicken pizza with peanut sauce. Dinner only Thursday through Sunday in December. Closed in January and February. ~ 868 Zion Park Boulevard at Paradise Road, Springdale; 435-772-3815; www.zionpizzanoodle.com, e-mail info@zionpizzanoodle.com. BUDGET TO MODERATE.

For three healthy meals a day, **Oscar's Cafe** is the place to go. Breakfast burritos, mesquite-smoked chicken salad and pork enchiladas are served in this casual eatery. Be forewarned, though: this is not the place to go if you're in a hurry, as the kitchen can be painfully slow. ~ 948 Zion Park Boulevard, Springdale; 435-772-3232. MODERATE.

You can't miss at **Flanigan's Spotted Dog Café & Pub.** The bright, airy establishment serves creative Southwestern cuisine. Entrées might range from halibut with chipotle chili aioli to tournado of beef tenderloin with smoked tomato chutney. With a 2000-bottle wine cellar, pairing a bottle with your dinner should be easy. The menu changes seasonally. Breakfast and dinner only.; dinner reservations are recommended. ~ 428 Zion Park Boulevard, Springdale; 435-772-3244, 800-765-7787, fax 435-772-3396; www.flanigans.com, e-mail info@flanigans.com. MODERATE TO DELUXE.

Although short in stature, downtown Springdale boasts an eclectic shopping scene, one that offers crafts and paintings from regional artists, antiques, and the expected national park mementoes.

SHOPPING

Heavy, intricately carved wooden doors that date to the mid-1800s can be found along with cowboy and American Indian antiques at **Frontier Plunder**. Throughout the adobe building's rooms cowboy boots, saddles and spurs are joined by wooden snowshoes, antique American Indian beadwork baskets and pottery, and books detailing the West. Closed Wednesday and from November through March. ~ 1200 Zion Park Boulevard, Springdale; 435-772-3045, fax 435-772-2485; e-mail plunder@infowest.com.

NIGHTLIFE From May through September "Saturday Night Live" means live music at the **O. C. Tanner Amphitheater** near the south entrance of Zion National Park. Depending on which Saturday you head to the arena you might encounter a symphony, bluegrass, jazz or maybe even a modern dance exhibition. Picnics are encouraged. Admission. ~ 300 West Lion Boulevard, Springdale; 435-652-7994, fax 435-656-4080; www.dixie.edu/tanner, e-mail gbunker@dixie.edu.

Across Zion Park Boulevard, the **Zion Canyon Giant Screen Theatre** presents movies daily on a six-story-high giant screen. *Zion Canyon Treasure of the Gods* offers an interpretive look at the legends of Zion Canyon. Admission. ~ 145 Zion Park Boulevard, Springdale; 435-772-2400, 888-256-3456; www.zioncanyontheatre.com, e-mail ziontheatre@infowest.com.

HIDDEN ► The local hangout for drinks and occasional live music on weekends is the **Bit and Spur Saloon**. Cover for live music. ~ 1212 Zion Park Boulevard, Springdale; 435-772-3498; www.bitandspur.com.

PARKS **ZION NATIONAL PARK** 🏃 🚲 🐎 🏊 🛶 A true gem. Sheer, towering cliffs surround the verdant floor of Zion Canyon as lush hanging gardens and waterfalls stand in marked contrast to the desertlike terrain of stark rock formations and etched red-rock walls. There are guided walks, and a hiker shuttle service can be arranged through the on-site visitors center. Facilities here include picnic areas, a restaurant, a snack bar, a gift shop and restrooms. No driving in the park allowed between April and October unless you're staying at Zion Lodge; the shuttle bus system is handy, reliable and relaxing. The $20 vehicle fee is good for a week (oversized vehicles pay a higher fee). ~ The main entrance is one mile north of Springdale via Route 9. The east entrance is 13 miles west of Mount Carmel Junction along Route 9. A one-mile tunnel connects Zion Canyon with plateaus on the east. Buses and many recreational vehicles are too large to navigate the tunnel in two-way traffic, so traffic may be temporarily halted; 435-772-3256, fax 435-772-3426; www.nps.gov/zion.

▲ There are 288 sites in the Watchman and South campgrounds near the visitors center. Watchman has hookups at about half of the sites, and reservations are required from April through October. South is a first-come, first-served campground open from March through October. Both are $16 to $20 per night. Primitive camping is allowed in the six-site Lava Point Campground and in the backcountry with a $25 permit (for one to two people) available from the visitors center; no water; no fee. Reservations: 800-365-2267; reservations.nps.gov.

CORAL PINK SAND DUNES STATE PARK 🏃 The beach (without water) comes to Utah at this expansive site of coral-pink sand dunes. Visitors here are encouraged to play in the six square miles of sand, ride off-road vehicles or build a sand castle or two. There are restrooms and showers. Day-use fee, $5. ~ Sand Dunes Road, 12 miles south of Route 89 and about 25 miles northwest of Kanab; 435-648-2800.

▲ There are 22 sites; $15 per night. Reservations: 800-322-3770.

▼▼▼▼▼▼▼▼▼▼

Cedar City Area

Though now called "Festival City" because of its ties to the Utah Shakespearean Festival, it was iron that initially brought Mormon pioneers to Cedar City. Early Utah settlers worried about the lack of iron ore, and when deposits were discovered in the mountain 15 miles west of what is now Cedar City, an iron mission was established in 1851. Despite initial success, the foundry closed a mere seven years later,

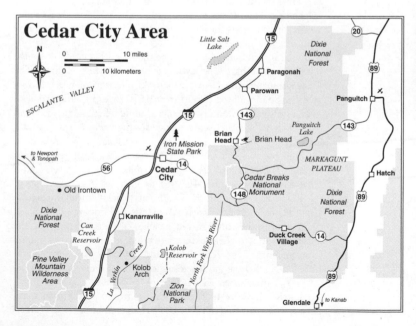

Cedar City Area

but Cedar City managed to survive and today hosts numerous cultural and sporting events.

SIGHTS   Young people know Cedar City as the location of 104-acre **Southern Utah University**, a 6000-student liberal-arts school that celebrated its centennial in 1997. Many leading cultural events, including the Utah Shakespearean Festival and American Folk Ballet (see "Nightlife" below), are presentations of this four-year school, as are the Utah Summer Games (435-865-8421; www.utah summergames.org), an Olympic-style sporting event that draws 7500 athletes from the state of Utah to compete in 44 events every June. SUU's **Braithwaite Fine Arts Gallery** (435-586-5432) presents a variety of visual-art exhibits throughout the year. It's on the east side of campus, just south of Old Main. Closed weekends. ~ 351 West Center Street, Cedar City; 435-586-7700.

John Wayne, Sammy Davis, Jr., Glen Ford, Dean Martin, Charlton Heston, Barbara Stanwyck, Ava Gardner and many more stayed at the Parry Lodge when they were working on films.

One of the best ways to explore Cedar City is via a self-guided **Historical Tour**, as presented in a brochure distributed by the **Cedar City/Brian Head Tourism and Convention Bureau**. The tour features 19 sites—14 of them markers and monuments—spread throughout the town. The chamber also offers advice on what to do in the area. Closed Friday. ~ 581 North Main Street, Cedar City; 435-586-4484, 800-354-4849, fax 435-586-4022; www.scenicsouthernutah.com.

The highlight of the historical tour is **Iron Mission State Park**, whose museum tells the story of early Cedar City with a diorama of its original foundry. There are also three pioneer cabins (one of them dating from 1851, said to be the oldest log cabin in southern Utah) and a half acre devoted to antique farm machinery. The show stopper is the Gronway Parry Collection of horse-drawn vehicles. Spanning the period from 1870 to 1930, it contains all manner of coaches and wagons, including buggies, surreys, mail carts, sleighs, a bullet-scarred stagecoach, a white hearse and a water-sprinkling wagon. All are in tiptop shape; some have been featured in Western movies. Closed Sunday from November through February. Admission. ~ 635 North Main Street, Cedar City; 435-586-9290, fax 435-865-6830.

Town residents built the Cedar City **Rock Church** during the Great Depression with native materials and donated labor. Red cedar adorns the interior and benches of the chapel, while the colorful stones on the exterior—including various ores mined from such areas as Cedar Breaks and Bryce Canyon—were carefully matched. Free guided tours are offered daily in summer. ~ 75 East Center Street, Cedar City; 435-586-8475.

Sixteen miles north of Cedar City on Route 15, the small community of **Parowan** (southern Utah's oldest town) evokes a Western atmosphere with a strong heritage. Gateway to Brian Head Ski Area and Cedar Breaks National Monument, Parowan has a few motels and restaurants among many examples of original pioneer architecture.

Old Irontown, 25 miles west of Cedar City on Route 56, still displays remnants of open-pit mining operations of the late 1800s. A beehived-shaped coke oven, foundry and blast furnace are on-site.

In sharp contrast to the manic crowds at the main section of Zion National Park, the **Kolob Canyons** entrance is virtually deserted. Arches, cliffs and mountains point like fingers to the sky in this part of the park, which claims one of the world's largest free-standing arches. A small visitors center offers backcountry permits and information including an invaluable interpretive autodrive pamphlet that guides you to ten stops along the five-and-a-half-mile road into the Finger Canyons of the Kolob. Deeply colored cliffs of vermilion and goldenrod mark Kolob Canyon, a markedly different section of Zion. A huge rock scar just left of Shuntavi Butte is the result of a cataclysmic break of the cliff from the rock face in 1983. Admission. ~ Just off Route 15 at Exit 40, 17 miles south of Cedar City; 435-586-9548, fax 435-772-3426; www.nps.gov/zion.

Kolob Canyons Viewpoint provides the ideal spot from which to view the canyon walls of massive Navajo sandstone laid down as windblown dunes 150 million years ago that now extend as fingers into the edge of the high terrace. ~ Located at the end of Kolob Canyons Road.

Though a product of the same natural forces that shaped Zion and Bryce, **Cedar Breaks National Monument** clearly holds its own. You head east from Cedar City along Route 14 then turn north on Route 148. The drive through huge glades of evergreen forest doesn't adequately prepare the viewer for the grandeur of the brilliant rock amphitheater. The jaded may surmise they've driven to 10,350 feet for nothing until they look out the huge glass windows of the visitors center. Closed mid-October through May. Admission. ~ Route 148; 435-586-0847, fax 435-586-3781; www.nps.gov/cebr.

Like the coliseum of ancient Rome, Cedar Breaks is expansive and wide. Only here, visitors gaze upon a natural gallery of stone spires, columns and arches instead of warring gladiators. The sheer cliffs reveal a candy store of colors—lavenders, saffrons and crimsons—all melted together and washed across the rocks.

In marked contrast to the flowers are the bristlecone pines, called the "Methuselah" of trees. Small stands grow on the relatively poor limestone soil that is within and along the rim of the amphitheater. One gnarled and weatherbeaten pine that can be seen from the Wasatch Ramparts Trail near Spectra Point on the breaks' rim is estimated to be more than 1600 years old.

A five-mile road accesses the park's main attractions. Four scenic overlooks, trailheads and all visitor services are on or near the road.

Returning to Route 14 and continuing east past the Cedar Breaks entrance, you'll come to **Navajo Lake** and **Duck Creek Pond,** splendid spots both known for their trout fishing. Formed by lava flows that left no drainages, Navajo Lake drains through sinkholes that sit beneath the surface and feed water into Duck Creek.

Grassy meadows and groves of aspen also surround **Duck Creek Village,** a hamlet best known as the film location for *My Friend Flicka* and *How the West Was Won.* Duck Creek is often frequented by cross-country skiers and snowmobilers eager to lay tracks on the extensive trails. ~ Route 14; www.duckcreek village.com.

HIDDEN ► Worth a visit is **Mammoth Cave,** a network of lava tubes that includes a two-tiered section of tunnel. Be sure to bring flashlights to explore the cave. Closed Labor Day to Memorial Day. ~ To get there from Duck Creek Village, take Route 14 one mile west to Mammoth Creek Road. Follow Mammoth Creek Road north about five miles. A sign to the caves will mark a dirt road on the right, which will take you three miles to the caves. The Duck Creek visitors center, one and a half miles west of Duck Creek Village, has information on the caves.

LODGING The **Bard's B&B** offers an Elizabethan setting just a short walk away from the center of the Shakespearean Festival. Each of the seven rooms is furnished with antiques and has its own private bath, while throughout the home are Shakespearean touches. The full breakfasts revolve around homemade pastries, soufflés, egg dishes and fresh fruits. Wi-fi is available. ~ 150 South 100 West,

HISTORICAL GRAFFITI

If you venture 12 miles northwest from Parowan on an all-season gravel road, you'll discover the **Parowan Gap Petroglyphs**. More than 1000 years of American Indian cultures—Fremont peoples, Anasazi, southern Paiute and others—inscribed such designs as snakes, lizards, bear claws and obscure geometric patterns on the smooth-surfaced walls of this 600-foot notch in the Red Hills. The site is protected by the Bureau of Land Management. ~ Head north on Main Street in Parowan, turn left at 400 North and drive for ten and a half miles; 435-586-5124; www.ut.blm.gov/cedar_city.

Cedar City; 435-586-6612; www.bardsbandb.com, e-mail bards bandb@sisna.com. MODERATE.

The **Stratford Court Hotel**, a three-story, brick building, has 50 guest rooms furnished in typical hotel fashion. A large swimming pool and hot tub (summer only) and complimentary breakfast are nice touches. The staff is extremely cordial. ~ 18 South Main Street, Cedar City; 435-586-2433, 877-688-8884, fax 435-586-4425; www.stratfordcourthotel.com, e-mail stratfordcourt@ netutah.com. BUDGET TO DELUXE.

At the **Abbey Inn** you'll find 81 rooms and suites, some with kitchenettes, all with dataports, microwaves, coffee makers and refrigerators. There's an indoor pool and spa. A complimentary breakfast is served. ~ 940 West 200 North, Cedar City; 435-586-9966, 800-325-5411; www.abbeyinncedar.com, e-mail res@abbey inncedar.com. BUDGET TO MODERATE.

Cedar City's largest hotel is the **Best Western Town & Country Inn**, split into two parts: the main motor inn and a newer annex across the street. Rooms are outfitted with typical Best Western aplomb, and guests can use either of the two swimming pools (one enclosed during the winter), and spas. ~ 189 North Main Street, Cedar City; 435-586-9900, 800-493-0062, fax 435-586-1664; www.bwtowncountry.com, e-mail info@bwtown country.com. MODERATE.

French provincial meets nouveau Southwest at the **Cedar Breaks Lodge and Spa**, Brian Head ski resort's premier property. Forty minutes from Cedar City, the lodge offers large, well-appointed rooms that range from studio units to two-bedroom suites. Jacuzzi baths help work out the après-ski kinks. Or visit the indoor pool or exercise room. A ski and bike check are available. ~ 223 Hunter Ridge Road, Brian Head; 435-677-3000, 888-282-3327, fax 435-677-2211; www.cedarbreakslodge.com. MODERATE TO ULTRA-DELUXE.

Brian Head, like most ski resorts, has many condominiums of all shapes and sizes for rent. Contact **Brian Head Condominium Reservations** for information. ~ P.O. Box 190217, Brian Head, UT 84719; 435-677-2045, 800-722-4742, fax 435-677-3881; www.brianheadcondoreservations.com.

DINING

You wouldn't expect quality grub inside a livestock market, but the **Market Grill** delivers just that. From hearty country breakfasts to rib-eye steaks and chicken fried steak, the grill is a taste of the West. Closed Sunday. ~ 2290 West 400 North, Cedar City; 435-586-9325. BUDGET TO MODERATE.

An extensive menu geared to family dining has made **Sullivan's Café** a popular choice for more than 50 years. Sandwiches, soups, salads, steaks, egg dishes and pancakes are among the bountiful selections. BUDGET TO MODERATE. The adjacent **Sulli's Steak House** (dinner only) offers steak, seafood and Italian dishes in a more intimate, upscale atmosphere. ~ 301 South Main Street, Cedar City; 435-586-6761. MODERATE TO ULTRA-DELUXE.

HIDDEN ▶ **Milt's Stage Stop** is just a short, five miles up Route 14 in Cedar Canyon, and the locals head there regularly for the juicy steaks, lobster and crab. A roaring fire heightens the atmosphere during the winters, when the surrounding mountains are cloaked in white. Dinner only. ~ Five miles up Route 14, Cedar City; 435-586-9344. MODERATE TO ULTRA-DELUXE.

At the Brian Head ski area, Cedar Breaks Lodge's **Double Black Diamond Steak House** offers an intriguing menu that ranges from the expected steak and chicken to unusual wild game and seafood in a business-casual atmosphere. Dinner only. Open Friday and Saturday only; closed mid-October to mid-November and mid-April to mid-May. ~ 223 Hunter Ridge Road, Brian Head; 435-677-3000, fax 435-677-2211. DELUXE.

Also at the Cedar Breaks Lodge, the less-formal **Cedar Breaks Cafe** serves breakfast standards as well as steaks, chicken, seafood, burgers, quesadillas and pastas for dinner. ~ 223 Hunter Ridge Road, Brian Head; 435-677-3000, fax 435-667-2211. MODERATE.

SHOPPING Spring 2000 saw Cedar City embark on an ambitious, downtown restoration project intended to create a quaint **Towne Square** area that would recall the city's historic ambience with retro-architecture while establishing a natural gathering place in town. Efforts to give the two-block area from Center Street to 200 North along Main Street a unified "feel" led to a mixture of restoring old facades and building new ones to mirror the old. A main cog of the restoration project is the 1000-seat Heritage Center, a performing-arts theater. There's also a small outdoor amphitheater with a fountain that delights kids when it's hot.

AUTHOR FAVORITE

Those visiting Cedar City between late June and late August should take in a performance at the renowned **Utah Shakespearean Festival**. Nine plays rotate afternoons and evenings at both the Adams Theatre, an authentic open-air re-creation of London's Globe Theatre, and the modern indoor Randall L. Jones Theatre on the campus of **Southern Utah University**. Even if you can't attend a performance, an authentic re-creation of the Tiring House Theater of Shakespeare's era has production and literary seminars during the festival season. The festival returns for a fall season in late September and October. ~ 351 West Center Street, Cedar City; 435-586-7880; www.bard.org.

Among the shops involved in the community project is **Mountain West Books**, which is worth a look for maps and literature. Closed Sunday. ~ 77 North Main Street, Cedar City; 435-586-3828.

Bulloch Drug and Main Street Soda Fountain reaches out to the past with its soda fountain, where kids can enjoy a malt or banana split while you search for sundries. There's also a well-stocked candy counter. Closed Sunday. ~ 91 North Main Street, Cedar City; 435-586-9651.

The acclaimed **Utah Shakespearean Festival** stages their season on the Southern Utah University campus beginning in late June and continuing into the fall. ~ 351 West Center Street, Cedar City; 435-586-7878 (box office), 800-752-9849; www.bard.org.

NIGHTLIFE

Southern Utah University plays host to a variety of cultural attractions year-round. The **University Theater Arts Department** schedules plays in the fall and spring. ~ 435-586-7746.

A college crowd likes to hang out at **Sportsmen's Lounge**, where there is live music or a deejay kicking out the jams. Cover Wednesday, Friday and Saturday. ~ 900 South Main Street, Cedar City; 435-586-6552.

Music is country or rock-and-roll at **The Playhouse**, which features live music on Friday night. The rest of the week, go for pool tournaments. Cover on Friday when there is live music. ~ 1027 North Main Street, Cedar City; 435-586-9010.

Quality bands come from near and far to play at the **Cedar Breaks Club** in the Cedar Breaks Lodge during the ski season. ~ 223 Hunter Ridge Road, Brian Head; 435-677-3000.

ZION NATIONAL PARK–KOLOB CANYONS 🚶 🐎 Less widely known than Zion Canyon, 49,150-acre Kolob remains relatively untrodden yet provides as much colorful scenery as its more famous counterpart. Jackrabbits, snakes, lizards, cougars and mule deer are commonly seen; piñon, juniper and cottonwood trees abound. You will find a visitors center, a picnic area and restrooms; water is only available at the visitors center so it's a good idea to bring your own. The $25 entrance fee is good for a week. ~ Off Route 15 at Exit 40, 17 miles south of Cedar City; 435-586-9548; www.nps.gov/zion.

PARKS

▲ Backpack camping permitted with a $10 permit (good for more than two people) available from the visitors center.

CEDAR BREAKS NATIONAL MONUMENT 🚶 🚴 ⛺ Millennia of erosion and uplift have carved one of the world's greatest natural amphitheaters, filled with stone pinnacles, columns, arches and canyons of soft limestone three miles from rim to rim and 2500 feet deep. Some call it a Bryce Canyon in miniature. Surrounding Cedar Breaks is a sub-alpine environment with evergreen forest of bristlecone pine, spruce and fir trees, flower-laden meadows and tall grasses. Sorry, no cedars. The Mormon settlers confused them with the gnarled juniper trees found throughout. The monument features a visitors center, a picnic area and restrooms. Services and roads are usually closed from mid-November to mid-May due to heavy snows, though snowshoeing, cross-country skiing and snowmobiling are allowed on the unpaved roads only. Day-use fee (summer only), $4 per person. ~ Located 23 miles east of Cedar City via Route 14 (turn north on Route 143 for the last three miles) or take Route 143 south two miles from Brian Head; 435-586-9451, fax 435-586-3781; www.nps.gov/cebr.

▲ There are 28 sites (no hookups), first-come, first-served; $14 per night.

▼▼▼▼▼▼▼▼▼▼
Bryce Area

A couple of wonderful parks (surprise) await you here along with historic towns and one of the prettiest byways in the West. And for a bonus you can see the log cabin of Ebenezer Bryce, namesake of the region's stunning national park.

SIGHTS

The handsome architecture in the historic town of **Panguitch**, settled in 1864, is evidence of its early pioneering spirit. Around the turn of the 20th century, a communal brick kiln was supervised by an English potter who was sent here by Brigham Young to be the company's craftsman. Part of the workers' weekly salaries was paid in bricks! That accounts for the great number of stately, brick homes still found in Panguitch. English and Dutch influences are also evident in the buildings' Dixie dormers, delicate filigree and Queen Anne windows.

A short walking tour through the center of town gives you a chance to see the best of what's left. Begin the tour at the **Garfield County Courthouse**, built for just over $11,000 in 1906. ~ 55 South Main Street, Panguitch; 435-676-8826 ext. 100.

Cross to the **Houston home**, which was constructed in 1906 of extra-large brick fired in a Panguitch kiln. The home's lumber and shingles came from a local sawmill. ~ 72 South Main Street, Panguitch.

The building called **Southern Utah Equitable** at 47 North Main Street is a classic bit of architecture. It has housed just about every kind of business you can think of, from general merchandise to furniture, groceries and, most recently, a gift shop and restaurant. You can't go in, but the outside is worth looking at.

Prominent on Center Street is the **Panguitch Social Hall Corporation**, which was first built in 1908 but burned shortly thereafter. On the same spot, using some original materials, another social hall was built. ~ 35 East Center Street, Panguitch.

Next door is a former library (now an antique shop) that was built in 1908 thanks to a generous donation from philanthropist Andrew Carnegie. ~ 75 East Center Street, Panguitch.

Finally, the city's **Daughters of Utah Pioneer Museum** is a lovely, brick monolith on the site of the old bishop's storehouse. Back in the mid-19th century, members of the Mormon Church paid their tithes with cattle and produce that were kept on this lot. Now, visitors trace the region's history here. Closed November through April. Closed Sunday. ~ Center Street and 1st East, Panguitch; 435-676-2289.

Driving south from Panguitch on Route 89 takes you to the start of one of the most scenic byways in the West. After passing a few souvenir shops and cafés near the highway junction, Route 12 starts to wind through rock tunnels. That's when you know you're in **Red Canyon**. A Dixie National Forest **visitors center** (435-676-2676; closed in winter) on the road's north side offers information about the small recreation area that's usually bypassed by people hurrying toward Bryce Canyon. Pink and red rocks stand amid huge pines in this compact and user-friendly park.

Be sure to stop by the **Paunsagaunt Wildlife Museum** during your drive along Route 12. Located in a newly built 14,000-foot facility, the museum features more than 600 animals from North America in their natural habitats. Other displays include exotic game from Africa, India and Europe, a large butterfly collection, rare birds of prey and American Indian artifacts, tools, pottery and weapons. Visit the gift store on your way out. Closed mid-November through April. Admission. ~ Route 12, Bryce; 435-

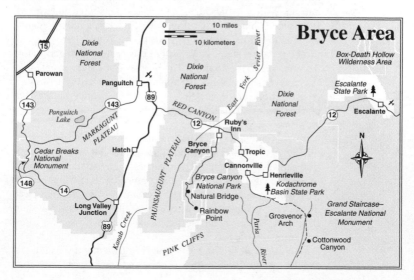

834-5555; www.brycecanyonwildlifemuseum.com, e-mail robert@brycecanyonwildlifemuseum.com.

BRYCE CANYON NATIONAL PARK   It's another ten miles on Route 12 to the Bryce Canyon National Park turnoff. Bryce is a national park on the jagged edge of the Paunsaugunt Plateau that really does defy superlatives. Even the large summertime crowds can't distract from the natural amphitheaters carved into the Pink Cliffs of southern Utah. Who would have ever thought there were this many shades of red or shapes of rock? The limestones and sandstones of Bryce, some softer than others, have been sculpted by eons of erosional forces. These rock forms come in countless profiles, which have been named "hoodoos"; they are ever-changing because of rain and snow seeping into the cracks of the rock, freezing and thawing to wear away the layers. For a quick primer on the park, stop at the visitors center, which houses a wealth of geologic information on this rugged gem of the park system as well as a nice museum that chronicles the region's human and wild life. Admission. ~ Bryce Canyon Scenic Drive, Route 63; 435-834-5322, fax 435-834-4102; www.nps.gov/brca.

Bryce offers 14 huge bowls of Creamsicle-colored spires and pinnacles. Located between 7500 and 9100 feet above sea level, the 35,000-plus acres of Bryce receive more than their fair share of snow during the wintertime. Some say that the rocks covered with dollops of snow are at their most beautiful in winter.

Fifty to sixty million years ago the area was covered by an inland lake. Rivers and streams carried silt and sediments from throughout the region to the lake, and the sediments settled at the bottom. With climatic changes, the lake disappeared and the sediments left behind slowly turned to rock. Later, a major regional uplift exposed the old lake deposits to the forces of erosion; colorful layers took shape as a result of this process. Red and yellow hues are due to iron oxides. The purples come from manganese. White reveals an absence of minerals in that part of the rock.

At sections of the park like Silent City and other natural amphitheaters, the rock figures resemble chess pieces, a preacher, a woman playing the organ or faces that belong on Easter Island.

Bryce Canyon's nooks and crannies are best explored on foot. For those who want to sit back and enjoy the views, a shuttle system that debuted in mid-2000 carries visitors to the mid-section of the park. The shuttle, which operates from mid-May through September, travels from Fairyland Point to Bryce Point, as well as from the northern visitors center. Unlike the Zion Park shuttle, this one is not mandatory, but why not give your car a rest and enjoy the ride?

For those who want to drive on their own and if time is a factor, it's wise to drive to the overlooks on the 18-mile park road

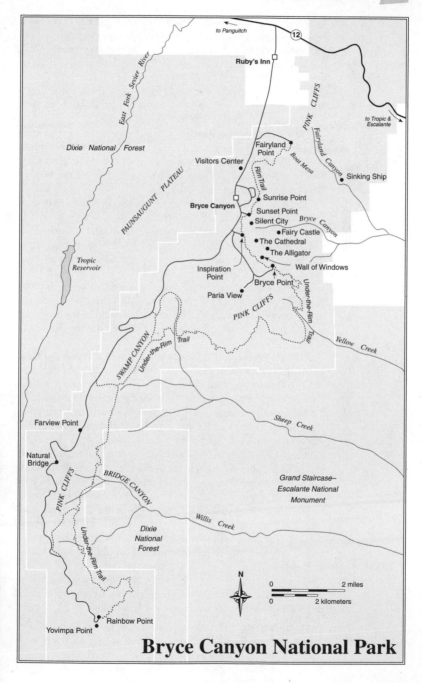

Bryce Canyon National Park

for a sweeping look at the big picture. Start at the **Fairyland Point** lookout about two miles north of the visitors center to see the imaginary creatures, the looming **Boat Mesa** and mysterious **Sinking Ship** in Fairyland Canyon. The rather strenuous Fairyland Loop Trail also begins here.

For a concentrated collection of formations, travel to the park's nucleus and either the **Sunrise** or **Sunset Point** lookouts to view the chess set–like people in **Queen's Garden**.

Walking along the Rim Trail, which skirts the canyon edge for a roundtrip distance of 11 miles, takes you to **Inspiration Point** and the eerie army of stone "people" called the **Silent City**. From the Rim Trail at this point it's possible to see the **Wall of Windows** and the majestic **Cathedral**.

The Rim Trail continues south for another one and a half miles to **Bryce Point**, which allows breathtaking views of the whole Bryce Amphitheater. Three hiking trails, the Rim, Under-the-Rim and Peekaboo Loop, may be accessed from here. Horses share the Peekaboo Loop and take riders past profiles such as the **Alligator** and **Fairy Castle**.

From the main park road continue south for seven miles to **Farview Point** to gaze at the natural wonders stretching hundreds of miles outside Bryce. The flat-topped landform to the northeast is the **Aquarius Plateau**. Southeast of the park are the distinctive **White Cliffs**.

Natural Bridge, with a huge opening in a rock, stands distinctly about two miles south of the Farview lookout. It's another four miles to **Ponderosa View Point**, where you can pick up the Agua Canyon connecting foot trail while seeing the lovely pink cliffs.

Drive the final two miles to **Rainbow Point** and **Yovimpa Point** and end up at the park's highest points, towering at over 9000 feet above sea level. A little more barren and rugged than other sections of Bryce, these two overlooks serve as trailheads for several hiking paths. It's worth the short jaunt on the **Bristlecone Loop Trail** to see the rare, gnarled trees up close and personal.

To fully explore the multimillion-year-old wonders of Bryce, begin the at-times arduous 22-mile **Under-the-Rim Trail** from here and travel north on a two- or three-day backpacking excursion. Camping in the park's backcountry is especially rewarding, as the stars tend to put on quite a show in this rarefied, high altitude air. However, in late summer and fall water can be very scarce in the backcountry, requiring you to carry your own. The added weight is worth it, though, as the beauty and solitude of this seldom-visited side of the park is spectacular.

EAST OF BRYCE The closest real town to Bryce Canyon is Tropic—where Ebenezer Bryce, a native Scotsman, lived for a couple of years. Bryce was a Mormon pioneer who helped settle the valley below the park. Neighbors called the beautiful canyon west of his ranch "Bryce's Canyon." There is a back route to Bryce from Tropic for foot travelers only. This trail connects with the Peekaboo Loop and Navajo Loop trails of the main Bryce Amphitheater. The easier way to go is by returning to Route 12 and traversing the ten miles or so through lovely **Tropic Canyon**. You need a sharp eye to spot the natural bridge on the east side of the highway about three-tenths mile north of the Water Canyon Bridge.

Once in Tropic, stop for a snack or to stretch your legs in this special village that remains true to its name. Flowers seem to dance in the gardens, and old trees stretch their limbs languorously. At the south end of town is **Ebenezer Bryce's old log cabin**, which houses American Indian artifacts.

LODGING

Cheap, clean and very basic describes the **Color Country Motel** with its flowered bedspreads and scenic vistas on the walls. There are 26 rooms; facilities include a seasonal swimming pool and spa. ~ 526 North Main Street, Panguitch; 435-676-2386, 800-225-6518, fax 435-676-8484; e-mail bobbie@color-country.net. BUDGET.

A step up in quality—and price—is the 55-room **Best Western New Western Motel**. The housekeeping is spotless and there is a cool pool and (warm) jacuzzi for those toasty summer days. ~ 180 East Center Street, Panguitch; 435-676-8876, 800-528-1234. MODERATE.

There's nothing like a full-service resort when you really feel like getting away from it all. **Best Western Ruby's Inn** operates as a world of its own, with a general store, restaurants, a liquor store, a campground complete with tepees, mountain bike rentals and shuttles, a laundromat, an auto repair shop and gas station, a helicopter pad, riding stables—even its own post office on site!

AUTHOR FAVORITE

The **Bryce Canyon Lodge**, listed on the National Register of Historic Places, is the only survivor of the original lodges built by the Union Pacific Railroad at Bryce, Zion and the North Rim of the Grand Canyon. Its four types of rooms—suites, cabins, doubles and studios—fit most budgets and tastes. Quaint log cabins have gas fireplaces, porches and dressing areas. Standard rooms are furnished in Southwest style. Book your reservations early; the lodge tends to book well in advance. If you arrive in the area without a reservation, check for a cancellation. Closed November through March. ~ Bryce Canyon National Park; 435-834-5361, 888-297-2757, fax 435-834-5464; www.brycecanyonlodge.com. MODERATE TO DELUXE.

Cross the street and you'll find Ruby's summer rodeo grounds, trail rides, and a replica of an Old West town. An international clientele can be found anytime. Rooms are decorated in Southwestern decor, and the staff remains friendly even after a long tourist season. ~ Route 63, Bryce Canyon; 435-834-5341, 800-468-8660, fax 435-834-5265; www.rubysinn.com, e-mail info@rubysinn.com. MODERATE TO DELUXE.

Kodachrome Basin State Park is chock full of petrified geyser holes (65 at last official count) believed to be freaks of nature and unique to this area.

Cottages, motel rooms and mini-suites with kitchens and fireplaces are available for guests at **Bryce Canyon Pines Resort**. Set in a grove of ponderosa pines, the motel complex also offers an RV park, restaurant, indoor pool and spa, and horseback rides. ~ Route 12, six miles northwest of the Bryce Canyon entrance; 435-834-5441, 800-892-7923, fax 435-834-5330; www.brycecanyonmotel.com, e-mail bcpines@color-country.net. BUDGET TO MODERATE.

Another very comfortable residence is the **Bryce Point Bed and Breakfast**, found about eight miles east of Bryce in the perpetually flowering little town of Tropic. Guests enjoy a private entrance and private baths. Each of the five rooms features handmade oak cabinets and picture windows that look out on Bryce Point. Out back there's a cabin. The wraparound porches are perfect for enjoying the sunsets, and there's a hot tub for erasing any kinks that arise on the trail. A sit-down breakfast is included. Closed November through March. ~ 61 North 400 West, Tropic; 435-679-8629, 888-200-4211, fax 435-679-8629; www.brycepointbb.com. MODERATE.

DINING

If the aroma of the mesquite grill doesn't lure you into **Cowboy's Smoke House**, the quaint rustic decor and continual strains of country-and-western music surely will. Barbecued ribs and other meats, homemade bread and Utah's best peach cobbler highlight the menu. Closed Sunday and from mid-March to mid-October. ~ 95 North Main Street, Panguitch; 435-676-8030, fax 435-676-8451. MODERATE TO DELUXE.

When it comes time to settle down and have a semi-fancy meal, there's little doubt that the top choice in this area is the beautiful old log restaurant in the **Bryce Canyon Lodge**. Service is quick and attentive though hardly fussy, the cuisine Continental but not generic. Delicious breads and Levi-busting desserts complement the generously portioned entrées. Breakfast, lunch and dinner. Dinner reservations are required. Closed November through March. ~ Bryce Canyon National Park; 435-834-5361; www.brycecanyonlodge.com. MODERATE TO DELUXE.

Equipped to serve large groups, the **Cowboy's Buffet & Steak Room** presents satisfying meals, though surely not imaginative fare, in its spacious dining room. The Continental cuisine features steaks and chops for dinner. The dining room can be a little noisy when large groups converge. ~ Best Western Ruby's Inn, Route 63, Bryce Canyon; 435-834-5341. BUDGET TO DELUXE.

During the busy summer months, the **Canyon Diner**, adjacent to the Cowboy's Buffet & Steak Room, is a convenient spot for quick and tasty on-the-go meals. Closed November through March. ~ Best Western Ruby's Inn, Route 63, Bryce Canyon; 435-834-5341. BUDGET.

The booths are inviting, the coffee steaming and the pies and soups fresh and delicious at **Bryce Canyon Restaurant**, which also offers specials every evening. Closed November through February. ~ Route 12, six miles northwest of Bryce Canyon entrance; 435-834-5441. BUDGET TO MODERATE.

Had a local not made the recommendation, we'd have never stumbled onto the very modest **Pizza Place**. A wisecracking chef kept the starving wolves at bay, appeasing our ravenous hunger with an order of wonderfully gooey mozzarella cheese sticks, before the main event—a hefty, generously topped, sweet-crusted pizza that could be the tastiest pie this side of Chicago. No breakfast on Sunday. Closed Sunday through Wednesday from November through February. ~ 21 North Main Street, Tropic; 435-679-8888. BUDGET.

◄ HIDDEN

It may seem corny, but you gotta love the **Old Bryce Town**, filled with shops and services. Among them, the **Canyon Rock Shop** has a huge selection of polished stones, fossils and petrified wood, plus a place to pan for gold! Stop in the **Christmas Store** to stock up on ornaments and decorations. The **Western Store** has a great selection of pseudo-Stetsons so you can set out on the range and not feel like a total city slicker. Old Bryce Town is open roughly from mid-May through September. ~ Route 63, across from Ruby's Inn, Bryce Canyon; 435-834-5484.

SHOPPING

Chile *ristras* line the front porch, while Navajo rugs and baskets are omnipresent inside the **Bryce Canyon Trading Post**, a good place to pick up the requisite postcard, T-shirt or turquoise stones. You can even find jewelry made by local American Indian craftsmen, film and a free cup of coffee. Closed December through March. ~ Routes 12 and 89; 435-676-2688; www.color-country.net/~brycetp, e-mail brycetp@color-country.net.

Rodeos featuring local talent are held nightly except Sunday through the summer at the **Rodeo Grounds** across from Ruby's Inn in Bryce Canyon. Barrel racing, bull wrasslin', roping and riding make for a full evening. Closed Labor Day to Memorial Day. ~ Route 63, Bryce Canyon; 435-834-5341.

NIGHTLIFE

PARKS

PANGUITCH LAKE 🏃 🚴 🛶 ⛷ 🚤 🛥 ⛵ One of the top fishing spots in the area, 1250-acre Panguitch Lake in Dixie National Forest offers fishing along its ten-mile shoreline and in boats for rainbow, cutthroat and brown trout. There are boat rentals as well as tourist cabins, a general store and a snack shop. ~ Route 143, about 17 miles southwest of Panguitch; 435-865-3200.

▲ Three national forest campgrounds are nearby. Panguitch Lake North has 50 sites starting at $12 per night. Panguitch Lake South has 19 primitive sites ($10 per night). Whitebridge campground offers 28 sites ($12 per night). There are also several privately owned campgrounds in the area. Closed October to Memorial Day. A few sites remain open through hunting season.

TROPIC RESERVOIR AND KING'S CREEK CAMPGROUND 🏃 🛶 ⛵ Also in the 1.9-million-acre Dixie National Forest, this recreation site is a nice place for a picnic or just a place to fish for stocked trout and relax in the shade of ponderosa pines. Above the south side of the reservoir is the east fork of Sevier River. The only amenities here are restrooms and drinking water. ~ Turn south off Route 12, down the east fork of the Sevier River on Forest Road 087, about ten miles west of Bryce Canyon junction; 435-676-8815.

▲ There are 37 sites; $10 per night.

RED CANYON 🏃 🚴 A lovely collection of sculptured pink, red and scarlet rocks sit in the shadow of Bryce Canyon. Because its neighbor is so well known and considerably larger, Red Canyon tends to be overlooked by visitors. Take advantage and explore the trails of this scenic but compact U.S. Forest Service property, dotted with towering ponderosa pines and red and white juniper. If you scan the skies during the winter, you may glimpse golden and bald eagles. Pay more attention to the ground and you might spy seven plant species unique to the Claron geologic formation that runs through the area. A visitors center, showers, dump stations and restrooms are located about a half-mile down the road. ~ Route 12, about four miles east of Route 89; 435-676-8815.

▲ There are 37 sites; $11 per night.

BRYCE CANYON NATIONAL PARK 🏃 🚴 🐎 🏕 Famous for its stupendous rock formations that seem to change color within the blink of an eye, Bryce contains a maze of trails that wind in and around its many wonders. Areas are named according to prominent "inhabitants" and structures: Fairyland, Cathedral, Queen's Garden. The 35,000-plus-acre park features its own lodge, a restaurant, a visitors center, nature walks, campfire programs, a general store, laundry, restrooms and showers. (Facilities are mainly seasonal; the visitors center is open year-round.) The $25 vehicle fee is good for a week. ~ The entrance is located three miles south of Route 12 on Route 63, eleven miles northwest of Tropic; 435-834-5322, fax 435-834-4102; www.nps.gov/brca.

▲ Permitted at North Campground (year-round) and Sunset Campground (summer only). More than 200 campsites are open during the summer; $12 per night. There are also several back-packing campsites ($5 permit required) for those looking to escape the crowds and see the park from a different perspective.

KODACHROME BASIN STATE PARK 🏃🏇 Vividly colored sand-stone chimneys, towering rock spires and arches fill this untouched, 2240-acre park that the National Geographic Society named for its photographic value. Facilities include picnic area, a general store, restrooms and hot showers. Day-use fee, $6. ~ Located nine miles south of Cannonville off Cottonwood Canyon Road; 435-679-8562, fax 435-679-8543.

▲ There are 24 sites; $15 per night.

Escalante Area

Nature's beauty, wildlife, prehistoric reminders and a region rich in the Indian and Mormon heritage await you in the Escalante area along scenic Route 12. Here you'll find a petrified forest, intriguing rock formations, orchards, dinosaur fossils and, for a wonderful surprise, buffalo. While the arrival of the Grand Staircase–Escalante National Monument in 1996 drew increased attention to Escalante and Route 12, the area didn't need the monument to convince adventurous travelers in search of intriguing, off-the-beaten-path destinations to find it.

SIGHTS

Route 12 climbs from red rock to lush forest and back again to a semi-arid setting. Begin just southwest of the town of Escalante, which was settled in 1876 by Mormon ranchers, in the **Escalante State Park**. It's a showcase for petrified wood, and the visitors center holds fossilized dinosaur bones and remnants from the Fre-

CRACKS IN THE EARTH

Slot canyons are gorgeously fluted channels through the red-rock landscape. Cut by streaming flood waters that bore through sandstone, "slots" vary in size. Some might be 20 feet across and only 50 feet deep, others 100 to 200 feet high and only a few feet wide. Some might meander for a quarter mile, others for many miles. All can be deadly when thunderstorms spawn flash floods. Before heading out for a day of exploring these canyons, be sure to check the regional forecast, as storms ten miles away can create floods.

mont Indian Village thought to be 1000 years old. This small park has moderate to strenuous trails. Admission. ~ 435-826-4466.

Huge petrified logs in a spectrum of colors, dinosaur bones and nature trails help to explain the evolution of the 160-million-year-old wood and bones turned to stone that became rainbow-colored by the earth's minerals. It is thought that ancient trees were buried in the sand, causing the logs to become petrified. Millions of years later the natural weathering process exposed the wood from its rough outer shell.

Hole in the Rock Road, a Mormon pioneer passage, zigs and zags its way to Lake Powell from its starting point just southeast of Escalante. Along the historic, 62-mile road you'll see landmarks such as Chimney Rock, Dancehall Rock and the Broken Bow Arch. An annual pilgrimage retraces the steps of the first settlers.

Route 12, the high-altitude road linking Bryce to Capitol Reef through Escalante, Boulder and Torrey, has been called one of the most **scenic drives** in America as it weaves past deep canyons, fossilized sand dunes and over aspen- and conifer-studded Boulder Mountain. So scenic and dramatic is the landscape along the highway that the U.S. Department of Transportation in 2002 designated Route 12 an "all-American road." There are several campgrounds and dirt roads leading to mountain lakes along the way, plus opportunities to view vistas of the Henry Mountains, San Rafael Reef and distant shale deserts.

In tiny **Boulder**, the last town in the United States to receive its mail by mule team, is **Anasazi State Park**. It's located on the site of a former Anasazi community said to have been nearby between A.D. 1050 and 1200. Here you'll find over 100 excavated village structures, a self-guided trail through the site and a museum showing an informative movie. Admission. ~ Route 12; 435-335-7308; e-mail anasazi@utah.gov.

When Route 12 meets Route 24, it's less than a dozen miles east to the entrance of **Capitol Reef National Park**. Domed cliffs reminiscent of the rotunda in Washington, D.C., prompted early explorers to give Capitol Reef its unusual name. Another explanation for the moniker's origin is that maritime men were reminded of barrier reefs. Long before white men arrived, American Indians were said to have grown corn, beans and squash along the Fremont River. Admission. ~ Route 24; 435-425-3791, fax 435-425-3026; www.nps.gov/care.

Wrinkled earth that was formed by the forces of nature, Capitol Reef is a mélange of domes and cliffs, spires and other amazing rock formations tossed together in a beautiful jumble. Elevations range from 4000 feet to 8200 feet, and summers can be quite warm. The cliffs of Waterpocket Fold, a 100-mile bulge in the earth's crust, slice through the park's epicenter. The **visitors center**, adjacent to Route 24 on Scenic Drive, offers a slideshow exploring the formation of Capitol Reef. ~ Located on Scenic Drive, right off Route 24.

Capitol Reef has several aspects. To the south, white sandstone dominates the scene. Near the center is lush Fruita with its orchards. At Capitol Reef's north end is the grandeur and peacefulness of Cathedral Valley.

When the Mormons came a century ago they planted beautiful orchards on the banks of the Fremont and Sulphur Creek in a settlement first called Junction, later renamed the more fragrant Fruita. Apples, pears, peaches, cherries and apricots are still harvested in **Fruita** orchards, which are administered by the National Park Service. Fruita is also home to several reminders of the past, including a one-room log schoolhouse built in 1896, a pioneer homestead—**Gifford Farm**—dating from 1908 and an early-20th-century blacksmith shop. The Gifford home, which added electricity in 1948, was lived in until 1969.

Capitol Reef's wild beauty continues along the park's 25-mile roundtrip scenic drive south of Fruita where there are numerous opportunities for excursions in the rock. Branch off onto either the dry Grand Wash or Cassidy Arch hiking trails, located east

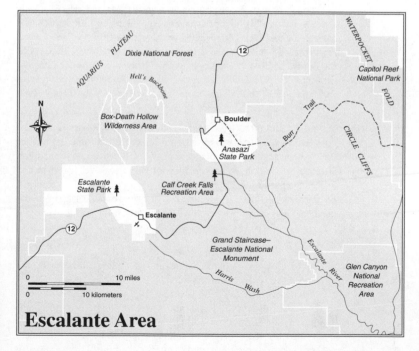

Escalante Area

SCENIC DRIVE

Cottonwood Canyon Road

GRAND STAIRCASE–ESCALANTE NATIONAL MONUMENT   In the 1930s, conservationists petitioned the U.S. Congress to create Escalante National Park in southern Utah. It would have been the largest park in the United States—but the plan was rejected. Portions of the proposed park were set aside as Capitol Reef National Park, Glen Canyon National Recreation Area and several protected wilderness areas, while other parts were flooded by Lake Powell, but it was not until 1996 that then President Bill Clinton exercised his power under the Antiquities Act to protect all remaining land in the would-be national park as Grand Staircase–Escalante National Monument.

COTTONWOOD CANYON ROAD   Although most of the 1.7-million-acre monument is virtually inaccessible, a few unpaved roads cross it. The most scenic of these is the 50-mile Cottonwood Canyon Road, which runs between Route 12 (the road from Capitol Reef to Bryce Canyon) in the north and Route 89 (between Page and Kanab) in the south. This rough gravel road crosses the Kanab Fault several times and offers unusual scenery and fossils plus opportunities to explore on foot. It is usually passable by passenger car in good weather, though four-wheel-drive is recommended at some times. Before attempting this trip, check with the Bureau of Land Management at the National Interagency Office in Escalante (435-826-5499) or ask the rangers at Kodachrome Basin State Park, and be sure to read the "Desert Survival" section in Chapter One. No services are available along the route.

KODACHROME BASIN STATE PARK   Turn south off Route 12 at Cannonville. The road is paved for seven miles to Kodachrome Basin State Park, which adjoins the north boundary of the national monument. Studded with multihued rock formations in red, pink, yellow, white and brown, the park's most distinctive feature is an array of 65 "chimneys," or spirelike petrified geyser holes. Is it any wonder that when the National Geographic Society asked Kodak for permission to name the

of the road. Stay on the route until its conclusion and access **Capitol Gorge**, a sinuous canyon, and the yellow sandstone monoliths of the Golden Throne Trail.

Backtrack at day's end to a few miles west of the visitors center and cruise by Sunset Point where the light is kind to the mummylike formations and landmark Castle Rock.

Not far from here you can walk up the short **Goosenecks Trail** (.1 mile) overlooking the gurgling Sulphur Creek below or basin after its patented color film process, Kodak jumped at the chance? Admission. ~ 435-679-8562.

GROSVENOR ARCH   Nine miles southeast of Kodachrome Basin, Grosvenor Arch—a double arch that is the largest of several white-and-gold natural arches in the area—is one of the largest arches in Utah. It was named after a past president of the National Geographic Society, which sponsored the first official exploration of the area. Petrified wood throughout the area attests to the fact that this was once a primeval forest on the shore of a vast sea.

THE COXCOMBS AND GILGAL   Continuing south from Grosvenor Arch, the road parallels The Coxcombs, a series of colorful sandstone cliffs, and eventually reaches the site of two manmade circles of alabaster stones named Gilgal. Vaguely reminiscent of Stonehenge, the concept for Gilgal is biblically rooted, and modern-day pilgrims make an annual trek here to celebrate the summer solstice.

PARIA MOVIE SET   The road grows rougher as it enters Cottonwood Canyon, where relatively lush riparian vegetation along the Paria River contrasts dramatically with the arid rock landscape. Many travelers turn around at the mouth of the canyon, but persistence and a sturdy vehicle will eventually bring you out on Route 89. Five miles before you reach the highway, a side road goes to the Paria Movie Set. Although there was once a real town of Paria nearby, no trace of it remains, and the movie version now looks much like a ghost town in an advanced stage of decay. It was built in 1963 for the filming of *Sergeants Three*, starring Dean Martin. The town and surrounding landscape have since been used as a location for Clint Eastwood's *The Outlaw Josey Wales* and a dozen other Westerns, including some starring John Wayne and Gregory Peck, as well as the biblical epic *The Greatest Story Ever Told*.

BUCKSKIN GULCH SLOT CANYON   Upon emerging onto Route 89, travelers with plenty of time and a yen for hiking may wish to stop at the nearby trailhead around mile marker 26 and explore Buckskin Gulch Slot Canyon. The longest and deepest slot canyon in the Southwest, Buckskin Gulch is 12 miles long, up to 500 feet deep, and in places as narrow as four feet wide.

sit and gaze at Boulder Mountain and the Aquarius Plateau. At day's end, a tiny trek from the car to **Sunset Point** (.2 mile) yields a view of the amazing Waterpocket Fold that reaches southward toward Lake Powell. With the Henry Mountains to the east, this is when Capitol's wild beauty bursts in all its splendor.

Petroglyph panels have never been so easy to find as at a pull-out on Route 24 about a mile east of the visitors center located near the campground.

Farther along this highway, you can step back in time at the **Behunin Cabin**, a one-room, dirt-floored, sandstone structure that was home to a family of ten when it was built in 1882.

It's a rather bleak landscape between Capitol Reef and Hanksville, but before turning north on Route 24 to Goblin Valley, stop at the historic **Wolverton Mill** in Hanksville, a log structure once used to cut wood and crush ore. ~ 380 South 100 West, Hanksville; 435-542-3461.

Looking south from Hanksville, the lush Henry Mountains come into view. Home to the only free-roaming buffalo herd in the country, towering **Mt. Ellen** rises from the barren rock.

Heading north on Route 24 toward Route 70 and Green River, there are few roads and diversions. But on the western part of the road halfway between Hanksville and Green River is the entrance to **Goblin Valley State Park**. On the road leading to the park, you'll be stunned by the rock sculptures of Wild Horse Butte and Molley's Castle. It's an enchanting land of countless standing rocks and troll-like figures. Gravel roads lead to beautiful Little Wild Horse Canyon, where there are two and a half miles of narrows to explore. Admission. ~ Route 303 (Goblin Valley Road) west of Route 24; 435-564-3633.

The effects of wind, rain and sand on rock play tricks on the imagination to where it appears there are goblin-like faces staring from every corner of this small—just four miles by seven miles—wonderland. Remote, yet not inaccessible, Goblin Valley would make a great setting for an episode of the *Twilight Zone*. Photographers find many models in the Valley of Goblins.

LODGING

Linoleum-floored bathrooms, a credenza and a desk contribute to the comforts of the **Padre Motel**. Small but tidy. Closed December to early April. ~ 20 East Main Street, Escalante; 435-826-4276; www.padremotel.com. BUDGET TO MODERATE.

A 12-acre wetland bird sanctuary provides a backdrop for **Boulder Mountain Lodge**, a beautiful multibuilding complex at the foot of the Aquarius Plateau. Some of the 20 very spacious rooms have high vaulted ceilings with exposed timber beams. In the main building, the Boulder House, you'll find a warming fireplace, a hot tub and a nice library. The lodge's restaurant (closed November to March) should be your first stop in the morning and last at night. ~ Route 12, Boulder; 435-335-7460, 800-556-3446, fax 435-335-7461; www.boulder-utah.com, e-mail info@boulder-utah.com. MODERATE TO DELUXE.

Capitol Reef Inn & Café provides more than its simple facade would suggest. Ten spacious guest rooms with two double beds and a working area are welcome to those toting a lot of high-country gear. There's a communal hot tub and, as the name implies, a restaurant. But the walls can seem a little thin, depending on who your neighbors are. Closed November through March. ~ 360 West Main Street, Torrey; 435-425-3271; www.capitolreef inn.com, e-mail cri@capitolreefinn.com. BUDGET.

Cheerful local art dresses up the 50 rooms at **Wonderland Inn**, atop a hill at the edge of Torrey. All rooms have views; artificial-wood furniture is the only detractor. Guests can enjoy an indoor/outdoor pool and jacuzzi. There's also a three-meals-a-day restaurant and free wi-fi. ~ Route 12 and 24, Torrey; 435-425-3775, 800-458-0216, fax 435-425-3212; www.capitolreefwonderland.com, e-mail info@capitolreefwonderland.com. BUDGET TO MODERATE.

SkyRidge is more than a hilltop B&B inn near the entrance to Capitol Reef National Park. It's also a gallery of locally produced art, most of it Southwestern in motif. Without question, this is one of the finest lodgings in all of southern Utah. All six nonsmoking rooms are comfortable affairs boasting Southwestern decor, large beds, and plenty of windows from which to savor the surrounding rockscape. All have private baths; two have their own hot tubs, and there is also a large outdoor hot tub. The library is well stocked with books, videos and compact discs. In addition to breakfast, hors d'oeuvres and drinks are served nightly near the big living-room fireplace. Wonderful views extend across Rabbit Valley. ~ 950 East Route 24, Torrey; phone/fax 435-425-3222, 800-448-6990; www.skyridgeinn.com; e-mail info@sky ridgeinn.com. MODERATE TO DELUXE.

◄ HIDDEN

American standards are served all day at the **Golden Loop Café**. ~ 39 West Main Street, Escalante; 435-826-4433. BUDGET.

For decent sandwiches, try the seasonal **Escalante Frosty Shop**. Closed Sunday and from October through March. ~ 40 East Main Street, Escalante; 435-826-4488. BUDGET.

DINING

AUTHOR FAVORITE

In 1995, former Utah "chef of the year" Gary Pankow opened **Café Diablo** at the west end of Torrey; its innovative Southwestern cuisine seems startlingly out of place in this rural location. House specialties include rattlesnake cakes with ancho-rosemary aioli, pumpkin seed–crusted trout with cilantro lime sauce, and pork ribs in chipotle sauce with sweet potatoes. On the walls, intermingled with Mexican-style masks, are original paintings for sale by local artists. There's also a children's menu. Dinner only. Closed mid-October to mid-April. ~ 599 West Main Street, Torrey; 435-425-3070; www.cafediablo.net, e-mail gary@cafediablo.net. DELUXE.

Blake Spalding, a Buddhist and gourmet cook, and his business partner Jen Castle, an award-winning dessert maker and restaurateur, moved to tiny Boulder with a dream of building community and pursuing "right livelihood." They took over the **Hell's Backbone Grill** on the grounds of Boulder Mountain Lodge and things haven't been the same since. If food can feed the soul, this is the place. Everyone—from local Mormons to *Oprah* magazine—has embraced this backcountry gem. The small seasonal menu is inspired by Pueblo, Southwest, Ranch and Mormon dutch-oven cooking traditions and showcases local organic beef, buffalo, chicken and trout raised in nearby Loa. All the produce and herbs are grown organically onsite. Save room for Jen's famous lemon chiffon cake. Closed November to late March. ~ 20 North Route 12, Boulder; 435-335-7464; www.hellsback bonegrill.com, e-mail hellsbackbonegrill@color-country.net. MODERATE TO DELUXE.

One word of warning: Don't pick any pieces of petrified wood as souvenirs because legend has it that bad things come to those who do. Instead, buy a piece of wood at one of the rock shops located in Escalante.

Specializing in locally raised foods, the **Capitol Reef Café** likewise surprises with its fresh approach to cooking. Utah rainbow trout, vegetarian dishes, homemade soups and heaping gardens of salad are the order of the day, along with hearty breakfasts. Espresso and café au lait are nice touches. The café is often busy, so be prepared to wait for a table. Closed November through May. ~ 360 West Main Street, Torrey; 435-425-3271; www.capitolreefinn.com, e-mail cri@capitolreefinn.com. BUDGET TO MODERATE.

For a quick snack, try **Brink's Burgers**. In addition to cheeseburgers, they serve good fries and thick, old-fashioned milkshakes. Closed November to mid-February. ~ 165 East Main Street, Torrey; 435-425-3710 (in season). BUDGET.

You will want to try the steaks and Mexican dishes, but pies are the specialty of the house at **Sunglow Family Restaurant**, which is located in Bicknell eight miles west of Torrey. Pinto-bean pie, fruit pies and a renowned pickle pie outclass other standard diner fare at this friendly eatery. Closed Sunday. ~ 91 East Main Street, Bicknell; 435-425-3701; www.sunglowpies.com, e-mail info@sunglowpies.com. BUDGET TO MODERATE.

SHOPPING   For jeans and T-shirts, but more important, to stock up on backpacking and camping supplies and maps before meeting the wilderness, stop at **Escalante Outfitters**. Open seasonally; call ahead. ~ 310 West Main Street, Escalante; 435-826-4266; www.esca lanteoutfitters.com, e-mail info@escalanteoutfitters.com.

The store at the **Capitol Reef Inn** has plenty of good guidebooks, maps and trinkets of the area. Closed November through

May. ~ 360 West Main Street, Torrey; 435-425-3271; www.capi
tolreefinn.com, e-mail cri@capitolreefinn.com.

Robber's Roost Bookstore and Café is the headquarters of
the Entrada Institute, a nonprofit educational group that helps
preserve the Capitol Reef area by putting on workshops, author
readings, one-person shows and talks during the summer. They
have a good book selection, as well as coffee and pastries. ~ 185
West Main, Torrey; 435-425-3265; www.robbersroostbooks.
com, e-mail info@robbersroostbooks.com.

Undoubtedly the region's best place to shop for authentic
handmade items is the **Gifford Homestead & Gift Shop** in Capitol
Reef National Park. Local artisans reproduce the same utensils
and household tools used by early Mormon pioneers, demonstrating and selling them at this historic site. Look for boot jacks,
butter churns and hand-dipped candles. Hours vary; call ahead.
Closed Columbus Day through May. ~ Scenic Drive, Fruita; 435-
425-3791.

ESCALANTE STATE PARK 🚶 🦫 🎣 🏊 🏕️ 🛶 🚤 ⛵ Trails in
this well-known though tiny (it's two square miles) park lead to
outcroppings of petrified wood that date back 140 million years.
Wide Hollow Reservoir, which is included within the park boundaries, is a good picnicking spot; anglers try for largemouth bass,
bluegill, and rainbow and cutthroat trout. There's also an interpretive trail here as well as a visitors center and restrooms. Day-
use fee, $6 per vehicle. ~ Located one mile west of Escalante
north of Route 12; 435-826-4466.

▲ There are 22 sites; $15 per night. Reservations: 800-322-
3770.

PARKS

GRAND STAIRCASE–ESCALANTE NATIONAL MONUMENT 🚶
🚲 🐎 🛶 ⛵ As yet undeveloped, the nation's largest national
monument, established in 1996, comprises 1.9 million acres
(more than 2600 square miles) of unsullied desert lands between
Route 12 and Glen Canyon National Recreation Area. It is
named for the colorful and geologically intriguing series of plateaus and precipices that descend like steps from central Utah to
the Colorado River, through the Pink, Gray, White, Vermilion
and Chocolate cliffs. Those who explore via four-wheel-drive vehicle, horseback or even foot will find awesome vistas everywhere, as well as slot canyons, natural bridges and arches, cliff
dwellings and petroglyphs, even prehistoric fossils. No services
are available inside the monument, which is administered by the
Bureau of Land Management. Information on road and trail
conditions, as well as topographical maps of the region, can be
obtained from the Escalante Interagency Office. ~ 755 West
Main Street, Escalante; 435-826-5499; www.ut.blm.gov/monu
ment, e-mail escalante_interagency@blm.gov.

▲ Primitive campsites (435-826-5499) are located throughout the national monument; overnight permits are required for camping, but there is no charge. You must supply your own water.

CALF CREEK FALLS RECREATION AREA 🏊 ↲ Gorgeous canyons and a waterfall that rushes down 126 feet over sandstone cliffs are reached after a six-mile walk. The lush setting of cottonwood trees makes Calf Creek a cool place to dine outdoors. There are restrooms. Day-use fee, $2 per vehicle. ~ Route 12, about 15 miles east of Escalante; 435-826-5499.

▲ There are 13 sites; $7 per night.

CAPITOL REEF NATIONAL PARK 🏊 🚲 🏇 🛶 ↲ Covering 378 square miles of contorted desert, this national treasure is veined by roads and hiking trails that lead past the region's sculptured rock layers to vista points, deep canyons and remote waterfalls. The park features a visitors center, evening programs, a paved scenic road and restrooms. Swimming in the Fremont River is inadvisable due to a deceiving undertow. Day-use fee for vehicles, $5, payable at station south of Fruita on Scenic Drive. ~ Route 24, 11 miles east of Torrey; 435-425-3791, fax 435-425-3026; www.nps.gov/care.

> Sevier River is the only river in the U.S. that runs *entirely* south to north.

▲ There are 71 sites at Fruita and 10 sites in two primitive Cathedral Valley and Cedar Mesa campgrounds; $10 per night at the Fruita campground, no charge at Cathedral Valley and Cedar Mesa.

HIDDEN ►

GOBLIN VALLEY STATE PARK 🏊 Curious rock formations created by erosion are the hallmark of this remote state park located off Route 24 and 26 miles south of Route 70. The effects of wind, rain and sand on rock play tricks on the imagination—goblin-like faces appear to stare from every corner of this small (just two miles by three miles) wonderland. Remote, yet not inaccessible, Goblin Valley would make a great setting for an episode of *The Twilight Zone*. Gravel roads lead to beautiful Little Wild Horse Canyon, where there are two and a half miles of narrows to explore. A few short trails wind through rock hoodoos, goblins, mushrooms and other odd configurations. Day-use fee, $6. ~ Temple Mountain Road west of Route 24, halfway between Hanksville and Green River; 435-564-3633.

▲ There is one scantily shaded campground with 21 sites; $15 per night; 14-day maximum stay. Reservations: 800-322-3770.

Outdoor Adventures

FISHING

Rainbow, brook, cutthroat and German brown trout are plentiful, while bass, crappie, catfish and bluegill can be found in a few bodies of water. More than a dozen reservoirs, as well as natural lakes, creeks and rivers in southwestern Utah, are stocked for fishing. Remember to get a state fishing license; nonresidents 14 and over pay $32 for seven days, $70 for a full year, while residents pay $16 for a week, $26 for a year. These can be purchased online at www.wildlife.utah.gov.

ST. GEORGE AREA   The two most popular lakes among anglers are in state parks. **Gunlock Reservoir**, 16 miles northwest on the Santa Clara River, has year-round fishing for bass and crappie. **Quail Creek Reservoir**, 11 miles northeast near the Hurricane exit from Route 15, is good for rainbow trout, bass and bluegill. For more information, licenses and tackle, try the **Hurst Sports Center**. Closed Sunday. ~ 160 North 500 West, St. George; 435-673-6141; www.hurststores.com.

ZION AREA   The Virgin River running through the park is stocked with trout, but anglers report a distinct lack of success. Better to try **Kolob Reservoir**, 21 miles north of Virgin via North Creek and Kolob Terrace Road.

CEDAR CITY AREA   **Parowan Creek**, flowing northward from Brian Head, and **Yankee Meadow Lake**, on Bowery Creek southeast of Parowan, are likely trout locations. **Ron's Sporting Goods** has information on where to catch fish and get a license. Closed Sunday. ~ 138 South Main Street, Cedar City; 435-586-9901.

BRYCE AREA   Trout-rich **Panguitch Lake** is nearly as popular in the winter for ice fishing as it is as a summer resort. Boats, bait and tackle can be secured on Panguitch Lake through the venerable **Aspen Cove Resort**. Call ahead for seasonal closures. ~ 225 North Shore Road, Panguitch Lake; 435-676-8988, 866-497-5581; www.aspencoveresort.com.

Just west of Bryce Canyon, south of Route 12, **Tropic Reservoir** offers excellent trout fishing. Northeast of the national park, **Pine Lake** is another fine angling destination.

ESCALANTE   The Boulder Mountain lakes north and west of Escalante and Boulder contain a world-class brook trout fishery, as well as rainbow, cutthroat and German brown trout. Many of them, however, are inaccessible except by four-wheel-drive vehicle, foot or horseback. Among the most accessible are **Barker Reservoir**, **Posey Lake** and **Lower Bowns Reservoir**.

Virtually in the town of Escalante itself is 30-acre **Wide Hollow Reservoir**, at Escalante Petrified Forest State Park. The lake has fine rainbow trout, bluegill and bass fishing: ice fishing is popular in winter. **Alpine Angler Fly Shop** operates fishing and hunting camps and a knowledgeable guide service throughout the Escalante Area. Call ahead as guides are frequently in and out of the shops. ~ 310 West Main Street, Torrey; 435-425-3660; www.fly-fishing-utah.net.

WATER SPORTS   There is a modest degree of boating at New Castle and Upper Enterprise reservoirs, west of Cedar City; at Gunlock and Quail Creek reservoirs, north of St. George; at Panguitch and Navajo lakes, on either side of Cedar Breaks National Monument; at Tropic Reservoir and Pine Lake, in the Bryce Canyon area; and at Wide Hollow Reservoir in Escalante. Gunlock, Quail Creek and Wide Hollow are especially popular among waterskiers and windsurfers.

CLIMBING   Zion National Park's rock faces are a favorite destination of technical climbers. Backcountry permits are required for overnight climbs, but are available at no cost from the visitors center. Some areas may be closed for reasons of safety or resource management, so climbers are advised to consult park rangers before beginning a trip. Climbing at Bryce Canyon and Cedar Breaks, while they may be inviting, is not permitted. The sandstone in these amphitheaters is too soft to be safe for climbing.

WINTER SPORTS   While primarily a summer destination, more and more people are discovering how beautiful southwestern Utah is once the snow falls.

ZION AREA   Sledding and tubing are popular at **Coral Pink Sand Dunes State Park**. ~ Twelve miles south of Route 89 between Mount Carmel Junction and Kanab; 435-648-2800.

CEDAR CITY AREA   **Brian Head Ski Resort**, 12 miles southeast of Parowan, is renowned for the volumes of light, dry snow it receives: well over 30 feet a year. Catering to both alpine skiers and snowboarders, Brian Head's six chairlifts serve mostly intermediate terrain on two separate mountains. There's a 1300-foot vertical drop from the mountain's summit at 10,920 feet. Full equipment rentals and ski-school instruction are available. Cross-country skiers like to glide to colorful Cedar Breaks and beyond. About 25 miles of trails extend from the resort center; lessons and rentals are available, but there is no trail-use charge. ~ 329 South Route 143, Brian Head; 435-677-2035, fax 435-677-3883; www.brianhead.com.

Snow Canyon has served as movie location for several films including *Butch Cassidy and the Sundance Kid.*

Catch ski fever just by walking into **George's Ski Shop & Bikes**, where you've probably never seen so much merchandise crammed into a single chalet. Past season's gear is discounted for those who really don't care about this year's colors. A variety of skis plus knowledgeable advice make this the ski shop of choice at Brian Head. ~ 612 South 143, Brian Head; 435-677-2013.

BRYCE AREA   Nordic trails are groomed on the rim of Bryce Canyon. But within the park, skiers can break trail and wander through literally thousands of acres of wilderness, beyond the red-tipped fantasyland of rock spires and figures. Rentals and maps may be secured through **Best Western Ruby's Inn.** ~ Route 63, Bryce Canyon; 435-834-5341.

Sledding and tubing fans head toward Red Canyon, just west of Bryce Canyon on Route 12.

Since many of Utah's most beautiful roads are unpaved, venturing out on a jeep tour is an excellent idea. Geological wonders, stunning scenery and historical points of interest await.

JEEP TOURS

ZION AREA If you'd like to venture out on a solo backcountry adventure, you might tour **Kolob Terrace Road,** a two-lane, paved path along the fringes of Zion National Park's west side that turns to dirt beyond the park's border. The route provides overviews of the Left and Right Forks of North Creek, climbing through dense evergreen forests past Tabernacle Dome and Firepit Knoll. North Creek canyons, Pine Valley Peak, North Gate Peak and the Guardian Angels are just a few of the other scenic sights. Kolob Terrace Road starts at the town of Virgin, 14 miles west of Zion's south entrance on Route 9.

ESCALANTE AREA Hondoo Rivers & Trails offers guided tours of the area, including the trips described below, as well as guided horseback, hiking and custom trips. ~ 90 East Main Street, Torrey; 435-425-3519, 800-332-2696; www.hondoo.com.

Burr Trail from Boulder to the Circle Cliffs of Capitol Reef is a gorgeous, 30-mile scenic drive on a chip-and-seal road across Deer Creek, Steep Creek and into the breathtaking Long Canyon. At the junction of Notom Road in Capitol Reef, travelers have the option of driving another 25 miles southeast to Bullfrog Marina at Lake Powell or going north to Route 24 into the heart of Capitol Reef National Park.

Hell's Backbone Road from Boulder to Escalante straddles the mountain ridge with the daunting drop of Death Hollow keeping drivers alert. The road winds around Slickrock Saddle Bench, Sand Creek canyons, creeks, hills and vistas.

The 9200-foot Boulder Mountain, located south of Route 24, has excellent four-wheel-drive roads. North of Route 24, over the back of **Thousand Lake Mountain** from Loa is the scenic, 25-mile ride to Capitol Reef's Cathedral Valley. Travelers can either backtrack 25 miles to Loa or complete the 125-mile trip to Route 24.

Leave the masses behind and play the golf courses of southwestern Utah; scenic and uncrowded best describe the greens out here. Most golfing activity centers around St. George, but you can also find courses farther afield.

GOLF

ST. GEORGE AREA Temperate weather, even in winter, means year-round play. In fact, many believe it's golf that has put St. George on the map. There are eight public golf courses in the immediate city area, including the 18-hole **St. George Golf Club**, noted for its long fairways. ~ 2190 South 1400 East; 435-634-5854; www.sgcity.org. **Entrada at Snow Canyon** is a pricey, rolling course designed by professional golfer Johnny Miller. ~ 2537 West Entrada Trail; 435-674-7500; www.golfentrada.com. Pine Valley Mountain provides a backdrop for **Green Spring Golf Course**. ~ 588 North Green Spring Drive; 435-673-7888; www.greenspring. com. **Southgate Golf Course** borders the Santa Clara River. ~ 1975 South Tonaquint Drive; 435-628-0000. *Golf Digest* has ranked **Sunbrook Golf Course** as one of Utah's best. ~ 2366 West Sunbrook Drive; 435-634-5866; www.sg.org. The first golf course built in St. George, the nine-hole **Dixie Red Hills Golf Course** is surrounded by sandstone cliffs. ~ 645 West 1250 North; 435-634-5852.

ZION AREA Thunderbird Golf Course is a challenging nine-hole links where golfers must tee off over cliffs and ponds. ~ Route 89, Mount Carmel Junction; 435-648-2188. **Coral Cliff Golf Course** is another nine-hole course, wedged in the Red Canyon on the road toward Lake Powell. ~ 755 Fairway Drive, Kanab; 435-644-5005.

CEDAR CITY AREA Cedar Ridge Golf Course is an 18-hole course open year-round, weather permitting. ~ 200 East 900 North; 435-586-2970.

RIDING STABLES

Riding through the sometimes-rugged Color Country on leisurely horseback trips is one of the best ways to explore steep canyons. The horses are likely to be as sure-footed as mules at the Bryce and Zion National Park concessions, the only horse rides allowed into these parks—the others are relegated to their peripheries.

ZION AND BRYCE AREAS The main place to hitch up is with **Canyon Trail Rides**, the concessionaire in both of these national parks as well as the North Rim of the Grand Canyon. Inquire at the park lodges between April and October (Zion: 435-772-3810), or reserve ahead. ~ P.O. Box 128, Tropic, UT 84776; 435-679-8665; www.canyonrides.com. Several Bryce trails are specifically set aside for riding.

Adjacent to Bryce Canyon, **Ruby's Red Canyon Horseback Rides** offers a variety of trips ranging in length from one-and-a-half hours to all day. ~ Best Western Ruby's Inn, Route 12; 866-782-0002; www.horserides.net. Day trips are also offered by **Red Canyon Trail Rides** from May through October, depending on weather. Call for a reservation. ~ Bryce Canyon Pines Motel, Route 12, six miles northwest of the Bryce Canyon entrance; 435-834-5441, 800-892-7923. At Panguitch Lake, try **Black Mountain ATV & Horse Rentals**. ~ 435-676-2664.

ESCALANTE AREA Boulder Mountain Ranch has trips that climb to the Aquarius Plateau. ~ Boulder; 435-335-7480, www. boulderutah.com/bmr. **Hondoo Rivers & Trails** offers guided horseback tours of the area. ~ 90 East Main Street, Torrey; 435-425-3519, 800-332-2696; www.hondoo.com.

PACK TRIPS & LLAMA TREKS

Southwestern Utah's canyon country begs you to get out of your car and explore. While there's a lot you can do on your own, if you feel a bit timid about striking off cross-country, there are a few groups ready to help out.

ZION AREA Check with **Colorland Outfitters** for pack trips. ~ St. George; 435-628-8388; www.colorlandoutfitters.com.

BRYCE AREA Adjacent to the national park, you can take one-hour, two-hour, half-day, full-day, or overnight rides along the canyon rim with **Ruby's Scenic Rim Trail Rides**. ~ Best Western Ruby's Inn, Route 12; 435-679-8761, 800-679-5859; www.bryce canyonhorseback.com. Or you can hit the backcountry with **Red Rock Ride**. Week long trips are only offered a few times in May and September; call ahead. ~ P.O. Box 128, Tropic, UT 84776; 435-679-8665; www.redrockride.com.

ESCALANTE AREA **Red Rock 'n Llamas** will get a beast of burden to carry your load into Escalante Canyon or Glen Canyon for a variety of adventures. ~ Boulder; 877-955-2627; www.red rocknllamas.com.

BIKING

Cyclists are starting to discover this region for its sights, interesting topography and varied terrain. While mountain bikers overrun Moab at certain times of the year, these trails are just being discovered.

AUTHOR FAVORITE

Hole in the Rock Road from Escalante to Lake Powell is a drive/bike ride that's not to be missed. First forged by Mormon pioneers looking for a " shortcut" to southeast Utah to establish new settlements, the famous and now vastly improved dirt road (54 miles) skirts along the Straight Cliffs and sandstone markers to landmark Dance Hall Rock, a natural amphitheater where the pioneers were said to have held a party and dance. Just past this point are the Sooner Tanks, potholes that often fill with water. Beyond the holes is a set of natural bridges. But this is where the route really deteriorates; just imagine how tough the trail would have been 100 years ago when you were riding in a covered wagon! From the end of the road there is a steep foot trail down to the lake.

ST. GEORGE AREA An intermediate loop ride is **Pine Valley Pinto**, a 35-mile trek across dirt road and pavement. Best ridden between April and October, the route is mostly gentle, although hills sneak in on occasion. Give yourself three to five hours. Take Route 18 north from St. George 25 miles to the town of Central. Turn right (east) toward Pine Valley recreation area. The loop begins on Forest Road 011, six miles from the Route 18 junction.

Snow Canyon Loop takes riders about 24 miles, passing through the towns of Santa Clara and Ivins before climbing through Snow Canyon State Park. (The part of the loop through the state park is on the highway and can be dangerous.) Start the loop at the northwest end of St. George along Bluff Street. Go west at the Bluff Street and Sunset Boulevard intersection. Route 91 takes you to Santa Clara, veer north to Ivins, then climb six miles to the park. After one climb, Route 18 is downhill all the way home.

ZION AREA An easy ride is Route 9 from **Springdale through Zion National Park** (11 miles), but there are steep switchbacks and a one-mile tunnel through which bicycles are not permitted to pass. You should arrange for a car to transport you and your bicycle through the tunnel. A bicycle is one of the best ways to tour Zion Canyon Scenic Drive from the south visitors center to the Temple of Sinawava, a massive rock canyon. Another good bike route in Zion is the two-mile **Pa'rus Trail**, which follows the Virgin River from the south entrance of the park to Scenic Drive.

Mount Carmel Junction to Coral Pink Sand Dunes is also a favored road ride. Take Route 89 toward Kanab, and after three uphill miles you'll spot a turnoff sign to the park ten miles away.

CEDAR CITY AREA Both beginners and advanced riders will enjoy **New Harmony Trail** (3.6 miles), one of southern Utah's finest single-track rides. The trail offers a view point of Kolob Canyons, then a gradual uphill climb to Commanche Springs. Take Route 15 to Exit 42, then follow a westbound road four miles to the town of New Harmony and park your car at the far outskirts of town.

MISTAKEN IDENTITY

Paiutes referred to the amphitheater we know today as Cedar Breaks National Monument as "un-cap-i-un-ump," which means "circle of painted cliffs." Nineteenth-century settlers, however, referred to areas that were too steep for wagons as "breaks," and thought most of the trees growing in the area were cedars (they're actually junipers) and so coined the name "Cedar Breaks."

Fir and aspen forests enshroud Route 14, a scenic byway from **Cedar City to Cedar Breaks National Monument.** While the paved road is a delight, you'll need stamina and good lung capacity to make the more-than-4000-foot climb (25 miles).

When the snow melts, bike lovers hold forth on the trails around Brian Head. Mountain biking season at Brian Head usually begins in mid- to late June and runs into October, when cold weather and snow signals that ski season isn't too far off. Experts enjoy the single-track rides, while those less inclined to tight spaces go for the dirt roads and double-track trails. A moderate ten-mile loop in the Brian Head vicinity is the **Scout Camp Loop Trail.** Begin from the Brian Head Town Hall on Route 143 and ride to Bear Flat Road and Steam Engine Meadow. There's a cabin and, you guessed it, an engine on the trail. The trail continues toward Hendrickson Lake and the namesake scout camp.

Another popular ride that's relatively easy is **Pioneer Cabin,** about a six-mile journey on a wide, dirt road and single track that begins from Burt's Road. The 1800s-era cabin has aspen trees growing out of its roof!

BRYCE AREA Dave's Hollow Trail (4 miles) near Bryce Canyon National Park is a pleasant ride through meadows and pine forests that's recommended for all abilities. At the boundary line to the park, about one mile south of Ruby's Inn, is a dirt road that heads west. Follow the road about one-half mile, then turn right about three-fourths mile along the trail. This begins a ride along a mellow, double-track trail that ends at the Forest Service station.

ESCALANTE AREA Atop the Aquarius Plateau, highest plateau in the United States, via the true-to-its name Hell's Backbone Road from Escalante, mountain bikers have a party on the spur roads near **Posy Lake** and the **Blue Spruce Campground.**

Bike Rentals For gear and equipment rentals in Cedar City, call **Bike Route.** Closed Sunday. ~ 70 West Center Street; 435-586-4242.

Some of the most spectacular hiking in the country can be found in this corner of Utah. Take your pick of national parks and monuments, fill your water bottle and head for the trails. All distances listed for hiking trails are one way unless otherwise noted.

HIKING

ST. GEORGE AREA Short on time and even shorter on endurance? We have just the place for you. Drive north on Main Street until it deadends, take a hard right and wind to the top of Red Hill. Park at the base of **Sugar Loaf,** the red sandstone slab with the white DIXIE letters, and start walking for a few yards. The view of St. George is nothing short of spectacular.

Snow Canyon offers several excellent hikes. One of the most popular is **Hidden Pinyon** (.75 mile), which takes you past a wide variety of plant life and geological formations. See if you can find the hidden piñon pine tree at the end of the trail.

Another popular Snow Canyon hike is to the **Lava Caves** (.75 mile) near the north end of the canyon. If you plan on exploring the rugged caves, take along a flashlight and good judgment. Watch for the sign along the road north of the campgrounds.

ZION AREA   Zion National Park is considered one of the best hiking parks in the nation with a variety of well-known trails. A comprehensive list is included in the Zion National Park brochure. Regardless of which trail you choose, expect the unexpected—a swamp, waterfall, petrified forest or bouquets of wildflowers.

Also expect company, and lots of it, on **Riverside Walk** (1 mile), which traces the Virgin River upstream to Zion Canyon Narrows, just one of the tight stretches where 20-foot-wide canyons loom 2000 feet overhead. The concrete path winds among high cliffs and cool pools of water where many visitors stop to soak their tootsies. This easy trail begins at the Temple of Sinawava.

In the Paiute language, *Panguitch* means "big fish," *Paunsaugunt* is "place of the beavers," and *Paria* translates into "muddy water" or "elk water."

Angels Landing (2.4 miles) is a strenuous hike that begins at The Grotto Picnic Area and offers incredible views over the sheer drops of Zion Canyon. Believe it or not, the trail is built into solid rock, including 21 short switchbacks called "Walters Wiggles." The last half-mile follows a steep, narrow ridge with a 1500-foot dropoff. While a support-chain railing is of some help, the trail isn't recommended for the faint of heart or anyone with "high" anxiety.

Another heavily visited trail system is at **Emerald Pools**. The easy, paved trail (.6 mile) to Lower Emerald Pool is shaded by cottonwood, box elder and Gambel oak. Trail's end finds a waterfall with pool below. The more stout-of-heart can venture to the Upper Pool (1.3 miles), a rough and rocky trail. The trailhead is at Zion Lodge.

Views of the West Temple, Towers of the Virgin and the town of Springdale are the reward at the end of the **Watchman Trail** (1 mile). Considered moderately difficult, the trailhead is located at the visitors center.

Considered one of the most strenuous hikes within Zion, **West Rim Trail** (13.3 miles) takes two days, culminating at Lava Point. Hikers are blessed with scenic vistas including Horse Pasture Plateau, a "peninsula" extending south from Lava Point, surrounded by thousand-foot cliffs. Lightning strikes are frequent on the plateau, and uncontrolled wildfires have left some areas robbed of vegetation. Other views along the way include Wildcat Canyon, the Left and Right Forks of North Creek and Mt. Majestic. The trailhead starts at the Grotto Picnic Area.

CEDAR CITY AREA   There are two developed trails within Kolob Canyons. **Taylor Creek Trail** (2.7 miles) follows a small creek in the shadow of Tucupit and Paria Points, two giant redrock cliffs. The creek forks in three directions, but the path straight down the middle goes past two of the three homesteading cabins that still exist in Kolob Canyons and ends at Double Arch Alcove, a large, colorful grotto with a high arch above. The trail starts from the Taylor Creek parking area two miles into Kolob Canyons Road.

The only way to see one of the world's largest freestanding arch involves a two-day trek along **Kolob Arch Trail** (7 miles), a strenuous descent following Timber and La Verkin creeks. After reaching the magnificent arch, which spans 310 feet from end to end, you might continue on to Beartrap Canyon, a narrow, lush side canyon with a small waterfall.

Two highcountry trails are within **Cedar Breaks National Monument**. Both explore the rim but don't descend into the breaks itself. **Alpine Pond Trail** (2 miles) is a loop that passes through a picturesque forest glade and alpine pond fed by melting snow and small springs. The trailhead begins at the Chessmen Meadow parking area.

Wasatch Ramparts Trail (2 miles) starts just outside the visitors center and ends at a 9952-foot overlook of the Cedar Breaks amphitheater. Along the way, pause at Spectra Point, a 10,285-foot viewpoint.

BRYCE AREA   Two hours worth of hiking time in **Red Canyon** can bring big rewards. The **Buckhorn Trail** (1 mile) begins at the campground and ascends high above the canyon past handsome rocks. **Pink Ledges Trail** (.5 mile) is a simple, short jaunt through brilliant-red formations. The trailhead starts near the visitors center. If you don't mind sharing your turf with a horse, try the **Cassidy Trail** (9 miles), named for that famous outlaw, that traverses ponderosa pine and more of those ragged rocks.

Bryce Canyon is hiking central because it's so darn beautiful. Uneasy around hordes of people? Either set out extra early or later in the day—the light shines deliciously on the rocks at both sunrise and sunset—or plan on spending a few days in the backcountry to wander into castles and cathedrals, temples, palaces and bridges. There are more than 60 miles worth of trails on which to wander.

The outstanding **Under-the-Rim Trail** (23 miles) connecting Bryce Point with Rainbow Point could be turned into a multiday trip if side canyons, springs and buttes are explored to their full potential.

Riggs Spring Loop Trail (8.8 miles) starts at Yovimpa Point and takes best advantage of the Pink Cliffs. More moderate is the **Bristlecone Loop Trail** (1 mile) that begins atop the plateau and leads to sweeping views of spruce forests, cliffs and bristlecone pines.

One of the most famous, and rightly so, trails within the Bryce boundaries is **Queen's Garden** (1.5 miles). Start from Sunrise Point and dive right into this amazing amphitheater. Taking a spur to the **Navajo Loop Trail** (an additional mile) brings you within view of the Silent City, a hauntingly peaceful yet ominous army of hoodoos. The trail ends at Sunset Point.

In the park's northern section is the **Fairyland Loop Trail** (8 miles). Moderately strenuous, the loop provides views of Boat Mesa and the fantasy features of the fairy area. Near the splitting point for the horse trail is the monolith known as Gulliver's Castle. An easier route is **Rim Trail** (up to 11 miles) along the edge of the Bryce Amphitheater that can be taken in small or large doses.

At **Kodachrome Basin State Park** the trails are short and sweet, offering plenty of satisfaction with little effort. From the **Panorama Trail** (3 miles) you get to see the Ballerina Slipper formation. At **Arch Trail** (.2 mile) there is—surprise, surprise—a natural arch. The most arduous of Kodachrome's trails is **Eagle View Overlook** (.5 mile), but the valley views make it all worthwhile.

Driving or hiking south of Kodachrome on the dirt road for about 15 miles brings you to **Cottonwood** and **Hackberry Canyons** which merit exploration for their fossils, springs, homesteaders' cabins and hidden wonders. Because the area is such virgin country, a good topographic map is imperative before setting out, and good route-finding skills are helpful in the backcountry.

ESCALANTE AREA Because of high temperatures during the height of summer, the best hiking weather on the Grand Staircase–Escalante National Monument are April 1 to June 1 and September 1 to October 31. There are several access points to the awesome and somewhat mysterious **Escalante Canyons**. A main point of departure is east of town one mile on Route 12. Turn left on the dirt road near the cemetery and left again after the cattle guard. Follow to the fence line and begin at the hiker maze. The trail leads into the upper Escalante Canyon portion of Death Hollow, an outstanding recreation area. For an overnight or three-night trip continue on to where the trails come out 15 miles down the river.

Quite popular here is the **Lower Calf Creek Falls Trail** (2.8 miles), about a mile up the highway from the lower Escalante Canyon entrance. The sandy trail passes towering cliffs on a gradual incline. You are rewarded with a beautiful waterfall.

Plenty of terrain awaits your exploration in **Capitol Reef National Park**, twice the size of nearby Bryce. Trails range from easy to steep, offering enough unexplored back country that you might not see people for days. Rock cairns mark some trails, while other routes are found with careful study of topographic maps.

Near Route 24 is **Hickman Bridge Trail** (1 mile), a self-guided, family-oriented nature hike to a 133-foot rock rainbow with a gentle elevation gain (400 feet). Skirt past the Capitol Dome with its white mounds of Navajo sandstone capping the rock. Continuing up the rim takes you past triple-decker ice cream cone–colored rocks to the overlook (2.3 miles).

From the **Chimney Rock Trail** (1.75 miles), three miles west of the visitors center on a trail with petrified wood, this path winds past the sandstone up switchbacks. (Remember, no specimens may be collected in national parks.)

The **Lower Spring Canyon Route** (9 miles), which skirts chocolate-brown canyons, begins at Chimney Rock Trail; it negotiates two 10-foot dry falls and crosses a river. Some of the path is on a river bed that is a flash-flood risk in threatening weather.

South of Route 24 on Scenic Drive, the splendid Waterpocket Fold ridge seems to go on forever. A logical first stop is the flat **Grand Wash** (2.3 miles), which cuts through towering thrones en route through the fold. The trail leads into narrow canyons and past pockmarked rocks.

A short, steep detour off Grand Wash to **Cassidy Arch** (1.75 miles) traverses canyon depths to cliffs. Late-19th-century outlaw Butch Cassidy is said to have hidden out in these honeycombs.

From Burr Trail (see "Earning Your Views"), a rugged road shaves over two miles off the **Upper Muley Twist** (5.5 miles) hike, which offers drama in the form of Saddle Arch and narrows within Waterpocket Fold. Access is one mile west of the Burr Trail switchbacks.

Lower Muley Twist (12 miles) boasts areas that are steep and narrow enough to "twist a mule pulling a wagon." The colorful route traverses Waterpocket Fold. Start from Burr Trail west of Notom Road. Much easier but still spectacular hiking amid sheer walls and similar scenery is **Surprise Canyon** (1 mile), north of The Post turnoff.

There are only two "trails" in Goblin Valley but plenty of room to wander. **Carmel Canyon** (1.5 miles) is an erosion trail to the Molly's Castle formation. It's located on the edge of the Valley of Goblins, a land of funny, little shapes, forms and hideaways in the rock.

Across the park's only road is a trail to the **Curtis Formation** (1 mile). In this parched soil, wild daisies and mule ear seem to miraculously bloom in the spring as does greencantian, an unusual plant that changes shape depending on the season.

Outfitters **Wild Hare Expeditions** provide expert guides for backcountry hiking and backpacking. ~ 116 West Main Street, Torrey; 435-425-3999, 888-304-4273.

Escalante Canyon Outfitters reach some of the more forsaken corners of Grand Staircase–Escalante National Monument. ~

Route 12, Boulder; 435-335-7311, 888-326-4453; www.eco hike.com.

Transportation

CAR

Route 70 almost slices Utah in two as it runs east–west from the Colorado border. It ends at **Route 15**, Utah's main north–south artery that passes through Cedar City and St. George.

Route 14 branches east off Route 15 at Cedar City toward Cedar Breaks, while **Route 9** heads east from Route 15 to Springdale and the entrance of Zion National Park.

Route 89, a scenic byway, heads south from Route 70 through parts of Dixie National Forest before crossing Kanab, intersecting Routes 9, 12 and 14 en route. **Route 12** provides a pretty path to Bryce Canyon National Park and Grand Staircase–Escalante National Monument.

AIR

Skywest/Delta Connection serves **St. George Municipal Airport** (435-634-3480) and US Airways flies to **Cedar City Regional Airport** (435-586-2950). **Quality Cab** provides taxi service for the St. George airport. ~ 435-656-5222.

BUS

Greyhound Bus Lines (800-231-2222; www.greyhound.com) can bring you to southwestern Utah from around the country. The bus stops in St. George at a McDonald's restaurant. ~ 1235 South Bluff Street; 435-673-2933.

CAR RENTALS

Rental agencies at St. George Municipal Airport include **Avis Rent A Car** (800-331-1212), **Budget Rent A Car** (435-673-6825) and **Hertz Rent A Car** (435-652-9941, 435-674-4789).

At the Cedar City Municipal Airport, cars can be rented from **Avis Rent A Car** (800-331-1212) and **Enterprise Rent A Car** (435-865-7636).

TAXIS

In Cedar City, cab service is provided by **Iron County Shuttle**. ~ 435-865-7076.

FIFTEEN

Southeastern Utah

How best to describe southeastern Utah? For starters, Teddy Roosevelt, America's quintessential outdoorsman, once traveled here. Then consider the fact that amusement-park thrills and manmade attractions have nothing on this place. Forget the Coney Island roller coaster. Plummet down a 30-degree incline at Moki Dugway or the Moab Slickrock Bike Trail. The rickety bridge on Tom Sawyer Island in Disneyland? You can sway and swing across a genuine suspension bridge over the San Juan River outside Bluff. And Gateway Arch in St. Louis becomes a mere modern toy after you see Mother Nature's natural design at Arches National Park.

This truly is a magic kingdom for the outdoors enthusiast, the naturalist, the archaeologist. Leave those luxury resorts, white-sand beaches and gleaming steel museums behind. In this region, the land reigns.

What's really ironic is that Mormon exiles thought they were entering America's wasteland when they fled to Utah in 1847—this land is anything but barren. Take all the earth's geologic wonders, toss them into a blender and you have southeastern Utah. An array of mesas abuts dense forests adjacent to broad deserts with red-rock canyons and slender spires thrusting out of semiarid valleys. In this portion of the Colorado Plateau lie the spectacular Arches and Canyonlands national parks, Glen Canyon National Recreation Area (Lake Powell), a national forest, two national monuments and a host of state parks.

Because southeastern Utah is so vast and diverse we have divided it into four geographic areas—Moab, Northern San Juan County, Southern San Juan County and Lake Powell. At the heart of the entire region sits Canyonlands National Park. Canyonlands divides into three sections, which though contiguous are not directly connected by roads. Therefore you will find The Maze section of the park described in the Lake Powell section, the Needles district in the Northern San Juan County listings and the park's Island in the Sky section within the Moab area listings.

Erosion is the architect of southeastern Utah. Over the millennia, land masses pushed through the earth's crust, rivers and streams carved deep canyons, wind and water etched mountainsides. On some of the rock walls are pictures and stories left behind by early man that seem to transcend the ages.

The first known people in southeastern Utah were here long before the Europeans even knew about America. They were the ancestors of today's Pueblo Indians. Evidence of these early builders and farmers is abundant in the sites of their homes found among the cliffs, on the mesa tops and in the canyons.

When the tribes disappeared from southeastern Utah and the Four Corners region around the 13th century, they left dwellings, tools and plenty of personal possessions behind. Theories abound as to what prompted their hasty departure. Some look to about A.D. 1276 when a long drought ruined the harvest and depleted the food supply. There were dangers from marauding bands of fierce nomadic tribes. Others theorize that inexplicable fears caused by religious beliefs may have contributed. Still others—*The X-Files* generation—insist that they zapped back to their point of origin via flying saucers. Regardless of influences, the Pueblo peoples abandoned the region, and their living spaces and remnant continue to fascinate generations of archaeologists and amateur sleuths.

By the 14th century, the Navajo had become part of the landscape. Today, their reservation sprawls across 16 million acres of Utah, Arizona and New Mexico.

The first known contact by Europeans came in 1765 when Juan María de Rivera led a trading expedition north from New Mexico, hoping to establish a new supply route with California. That route, which became known as the Old Spanish Trail, opened portions of southeastern Utah near what is now Moab.

In July 1776, a small band led by Franciscan friars, Fathers Francisco Dominguez and Silvestre Vélez de Escalante, ventured from Santa Fe, New Mexico, intent on an overland journey to Monterey, California. They never made it, but their adventurous trek took them in a great loop through unexplored portions of the region including what is known today as Wahweap Marina at Lake Powell.

When traders finally realized that the crossing of the Colorado River near Moab bypassed more hazardous terrain in Colorado, the 1200-mile Old Spanish Trail opened great portions of Utah to commercial wagon trains. By 1830 the trail began to serve as a major trade route for European expansion into the West.

Nearly a century after the adventurous Spanish priests, a one-armed veteran of the Civil War, John Wesley Powell, led an expedition party on a thrilling and sometimes dangerous 1400-mile rowboat trip from Green River in Wyoming to the lower Grand Canyon, charting the Colorado River and a deep southern Utah canyon that almost a century later would be inundated with a manmade lake that would bear his name.

To extend its boundaries and promote its principles throughout Utah, the Mormon Church decided to settle the area. Brigham Young sent 42 men down the Old Spanish Trail to Moab. But after an attack by Ute Indians, the settlers departed. Twenty-two years later, however, another group of hearty souls tried again, this time establishing the town of Moab in 1877.

In April 1879, an exploration party scouted the San Juan country and reported that the area could be colonized. A group of 250 pioneers, 83 wagons and 1000 head of cattle left the relative safety of Cedar City in southwestern Utah for a 325-mile journey to what is now Bluff. Originally estimated as a trip of six weeks, their arduous journey took six months as they chiseled and chopped their way through sand and rock and at one point lowered wagons down the western wall of Glen Canyon through what is now the legendary Hole-in-the-Rock.

Settlers here discovered that Mother Nature rewarded southeastern Utah with more than scenic beauty. Rich with tremendous natural resources, the land bursts with coal, crude oil, oil shale, natural gas and more. In the 1950s uranium mining formed the heart of this area until the boom turned bust, but beds of potash and magnesium salts found deep within the soil continue to be mined.

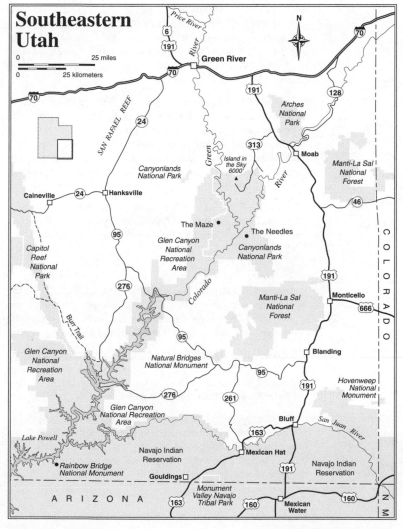

Southeastern Utah

0 ————— 25 miles

0 ————— 25 kilometers

N

Price River

River

Green River

6
191

70

70

191

128

Arches National Park

70

SAN RAFAEL REEF

24

313

Green

Island in the Sky 6000'

Moab

Manti-La Sal National Forest

Canyonlands National Park

Caineville

24 **Hanksville**

46

The Maze

The Needles

95

Glen Canyon National Recreation Area

Canyonlands National Park

Capitol Reef National Park

Colorado

276

191

Manti-La Sal National Forest

Monticello

666

95

Burr Trail

Glen Canyon National Recreation Area

Natural Bridges National Monument

Blanding

Hovenweep National Monument

95

276

261

191

Glen Canyon National Recreation Area

Bluff

San Juan River

163

Lake Powell

Mexican Hat

Rainbow Bridge National Monument

Navajo Indian Reservation

191

Navajo Indian Reservation

Gouldings

ARIZONA

163

Monument Valley Navajo Tribal Park

160

Mexican Water

160

C O L O R A D O

N M

Text continued on page 608.

Rock of Ages

Day 1 • After a hearty breakfast at the **Sorrel River Ranch Resort** (page 634), your base camp for the next three days, return to Moab via River Road and then head north on Route 191 and then west on Route 313 to the **Island in the Sky** district (page 628) of Canyonlands National Park. Spend some time in the visitors center to gain an appreciation for this canyon-riddled landscape, then head into the district to get an up-close look at it. **Mesa Arch**, six miles south of the center, is an open window that tightly frames Buck Canyon.

• From Mesa Arch, drive five miles west to **Whale Rock**, a portly rock outcropping that invites scampering across. Jutting above the desert landscape, the rock provides great views in all directions. Nearby is a trail leading to **Upheaval Dome**, which is really a 1500-foot-deep hole in the ground, not a dome. Geologists are divided over what created the crater—a meteorite or the shifting of underground salt beds?

• From Whale Rock, backtrack towards Mesa Arch and then head south to **Grand View Point Overlook**, which provides spectacular views of the White Rim, the Colorado and Green rivers.

Day 2 • After loading your cooler with a picnic lunch and plenty of cold drinks, head into **Arches National Park** (page 629). A stop at the visitors center helps orient you and allows you to top off any water bottles. From there, head toward **Balanced Rock**, stopping at the **Park Avenue Viewpoint** and **Petrified Dunes Viewpoint**.

• From Balanced Rock, drive to the **Devils Garden Trailhead** and a hike towards Devils Garden, passing **Pine Tree Arch**, **Tunnel Arch** and **Landscape Arch** along the way. Hardy hikers will enjoy the **Primitive Trail** that gets little traffic.

• In late afternoon, backtrack to the **Delicate Arch** trailhead. The hike to the arch is not undertaken at mid-day, both because of the heat in summer and the high sun. By late afternoon things have started to cool a bit and the setting sun creates great light conditions for photography.

- After your hike to Delicate Arch, sate your hunger at **Center Café and Market Bistro** (page 637) or back at Sorrel River Ranch Resort.

Day 3
- The entire day could be spend exploring the **Slickrock Trail**, Moab's renowned mountain bike circuit that skitters across the desert's slickrock. Those not inclined for such an undertaking can tour **Castle Creek Winery** (page 632) or ride to the top of the **Moab Rim** via the **Moab Skyway** for a panoramic view of the area.

IF YOU ONLY HAVE ONE DAY

If you only have one day, spend it in **Arches National Park**.

Whether a pioneer Mormon or a modern-day adventurer, people have always found the weather to be a blessing. It gets hot here (summers average in the 90s), but during the other seasons the climate by and large is mild. Winter ranges in the 30s to low 40s, and precipitation is extremely low except in October, when there might be all of an inch of rainfall. Yet within the La Sal and Abajo mountains, skiers and snowshoers find abundant powder in wintertime.

To this day, southeastern Utah remains sparsely populated. Towns here are small (the largest, Moab, boasts just over 4000 residents) and exude a "pioneer" atmosphere. Tightly clustered buildings set up in traditional Mormon pattern along wide streets, these are sensible towns with a strong backbone. Youngsters still ride their bicycles at sunset or walk hand-in-hand to Sunday services. Going out for a drink is more likely to mean a soda pop than a beer.

Moab now supports a diverse and growing population based on tourism, mining, agriculture and retirement. It is considered one of the most cosmopolitan small communities in Utah and is one of its fastest growing.

South of Moab, present-day San Juan County has a population of more than 14,000 scattered among farms, hamlets and communities like Monticello, Blanding and Bluff. Most growth can be attributed to natural resource–based industries. The Navajo and Ute Indian reservations comprise a large portion of the southern end of the county, with American Indians making up about 54 percent of the San Juan population.

In southeastern Utah, history and geology combine to draw the curious and the hearty. Though man has always explored the region by foot or automobile, the advent of mountain bikes opened up entirely new portals into the backcountry areas. John Wesley Powell's historic trip down the Green and Colorado rivers can now be easily run by whitewater enthusiasts. And onetime rugged cattle-drive routes are covered up with asphalt for the less-intrepid explorers.

Prized nooks and crannies are being "discovered" every day. This glorious land remains ever changing, continually revealing surprises long after any new wonders were thought to remain.

▼ ▼ ▼ ▼ ▼ ▼ ▼ ▼ ▼ ▼ ▼
Lake Powell Area

Like life, Lake Powell is grand, awesome and filled with contradictions. Conservationists considered it a disaster when Glen Canyon Dam was built in Page, Arizona, flooding beautiful Glen Canyon and creating a 186-mile-long reservoir that extended deep into the heart of Utah.

Today the environmental "tragedy" is Utah's second-most popular tourist destination. Part of the Glen Canyon National Recreation Area that covers one and a quarter *million* acres, the lake boasts nearly 2000 miles of meandering shoreline. Not only is that more shoreline than along the entire West Coast of the United States, much of it is in the form of spires, domes, minarets and multi-hued mesas.

SIGHTS   The depth of **Lake Powell's** turquoise waters varies from year to year depending on mountain runoff and releases from Glen Canyon Dam. An interesting cave discovered on one trip may well be under water the next season. The same holds true for favorite sandy beaches, coves and waterfalls. But part of the fun of exploring this multi-armed body of water is finding new hidden treasures and hideaways around the next curve.

Lake Powell's waters usually warm to a comfortable temperature for swimming by May or early June. During the summer months, when the majority of the three-million-plus annual visitors come, the surrounding temperatures can exceed a sizzling 100 degrees. Vacationers seek cool relief and a relaxing getaway

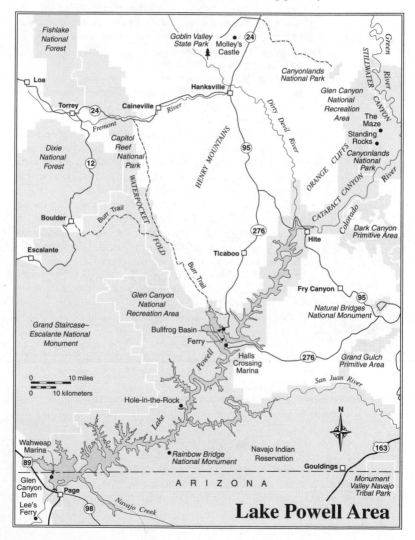

Lake Powell Area

in this stark desert ocean. Even at peak periods like July 4th and Labor Day weekends, when all the rental boats are checked out and hotel rooms booked, Lake Powell still manages to provide ample shoreline for docking and camping and, as always, clear, blue-green water for aquatic pursuits. But aficionados claim the best season to visit is early fall, when rates and temperatures drop to comfortable levels.

The lake can be entered from three marinas accessible by car. **Halls Crossing** (435-684-7000, 800-528-6154, fax 435-684-2319) is connected to neighboring **Bullfrog** (435-684-3000, 800-528-6154, fax 435-684-2355) marina by convenient car and passenger ferry service. The 20-minute ferry crossing, offered morning to evening at two-hour intervals, eliminates 130 road miles. ~ Route 276; www.lakepowell.com.

Wahweap Marina in Arizona offers the most services to boaters, sightseers and overnight visitors. ~ Route 89 near the Glen Canyon Dam; 928-645-2433, 800-528-6154, fax 602-331-5258; www.lakepowell.com.

Dangling Rope Marina, about seven miles southwest of the entrance to Rainbow Bridge Canyon, is a floating repair/refueling stop and supply store accessed only by boat. Enjoy a seasonal soft-serve ice cream cone while pumping gas. Closed late November through February. ~ Phone/fax 928-645-2969.

You can become acquainted with Powell from atop its sky-high buttes and adjacent byways, but those truly interested in getting to know its complex personality, curves and quirks must travel by vessel to the quiet box canyons and deep, gleaming pools for an experience akin to spiritual cleansing.

Speedboats and houseboats are most popular for exploring, but a smaller water vehicle like a skiff or canoe will give access

sights

AUTHOR FAVORITE

The best way to see Lake Powell is from the stern of a boat with the breeze passing through your hair and water sprays cooling the temperature. **Lake Powell Resorts & Marinas** offers plenty for rent at the Wahweap, Bullfrog, Halls Crossing and Hite marinas, including flat-topped houseboats (they only average two miles a gallon, so many groups also rent a powerboat or jet skis for exploring the shoreline). Waterskis, tubes, bobsleds, kneeboards and water weenie-like "wavecutters" are also available. A word to the wise: Don't be in a hurry to check out boats. Lake employees seem to operate on a "desert clock" and the time-conscious visitor only adds stress to a vacation by trying to hurry the process. ~ 800-528-6154; www.lakepowell.com.

to outlying areas where you can just pitch a tent or throw down a sleeping bag on the shore.

Groups of friends and family typically rent a fuel-inefficient houseboat, fully equipped with bunks, bathroom and kitchen, as their mobile base and pull along a smaller boat for exploring nooks not easily charted with the lumbering mother ship. Sole concessionaire for Lake Powell is **Lake Powell Resorts & Marinas,** which rents boats at all marinas except Dangling Rope. The marina has houseboats equipped for travelers with disabilities. ~ 100 Lakeshore Drive off Route 89, near Glen Canyon Dam; 800-528-6154, fax 602-331-5258; www.visitlakepowell.com.

Before setting out, the logical place to become acquainted with the second-largest manmade lake in the country is the **Carl Hayden Visitors Center** at the Glen Canyon Dam in Page, Arizona. The visitors center has a relief map and exhibits. ~ Route 89, Page, AZ; 928-608-6404; www.nps.gov/glca.

For more information on Glen Canyon Dam and Page, Arizona, see the "Arizona Strip" section in Chapter Two.

Another way to explore Lake Powell is to take a **boat tour.** A tour to Rainbow Bridge lasts seven hours and includes a box lunch. Dinner cruises also available. The boat tours and paddle-wheel cruises depart Wahweap Lodge & Marina. ~ 100 Lakeshore Drive; 928-645-2433, 800-528-6154, fax 602-331-5258; www. lakepowell.com.

The highlight of the Lake Powell boat tours is **Rainbow Bridge National Monument,** the world's largest natural bridge located about 50 miles from Wahweap. "Nonnezoshi"—or rainbow turned to stone, as it's called by the Navajos—spans 275 feet and rises 290 feet above the canyon floor. Declared a national monument in 1910, it wasn't until Glen Canyon Dam was completed 53 years later, and the lake started to fill, that the site became a favorite destination. Well touristed and commercialized on countless posters and cards, the stone arch with its awesome girth and prisms of color never ceases to amaze. Rainbow Bridge is reached only by boat, foot or horseback.

South of the awesome bridge, between Warm Creek and Wahweap bays, is **Antelope Island,** site of the first known expedition of whites to the area. Franciscan priests Francisco Dominguez and Silvestre Vélez de Escalante trekked across a low point in the river (before it became a lake) and established camp on the island. Nearby **Padre Bay** was also named for the priests. Within these waters is the rock fortress called **Cookie Jar Butte.**

A landmark visible from the Wahweap section of the lake is the hump-backed, 10,388-foot **Navajo Mountain** and the striking **Tower Butte,** both located on the Navajo Indian Reservation. They are good landmarks to keep in mind when your directional sense gets churned in the water.

A primitive Indian "art gallery" is located approximately ten miles east of the Rainbow Bridge Canyon up the San Juan River arm in **Cha Canyon**. You must motor past what are termed the Bob Hope Rock (check out the profile) and Music Temple Canyon to reach Cha.

When the heat is on, you'll be spending a lot of time in the refreshing, crystal-clear water. Five miles upstream (while some landmarks and obstacles are marked with buoys, a map is still essential) from Dangling Rope Marina is a water cave in Cascade Canyon that invites exploring. If you're more interested in things that swim than swimming, throw in a line and wait for the bass, crappie, pike and trout to bite.

Highly recommended for fishing is the **Escalante River Arm**, located about 25 miles north and east of Dangling Rope. Bridges, arches and ravines also abound in the Escalante's coves. Keep an eye peeled for prehistoric dwellings and drawings on a ledge above the mouth to **Willow Creek**, nine and a half miles from the confluence with the main channel.

Continuing farther into the Escalante arm, at approximately the 20-mile mark, you'll come to **Coyote Gulch** and its natural bridge and pair of arches.

From the main channel, the steep sandstone ridges of the Straight Cliffs and the 100-mile-long rock uplift called the **Waterpocket Fold** loom to the north. Respect must be given to those who were unintimidated by these fortresses. Just imagine being among the 230 or so Mormons who reached the towering canyons above the river in 1880 en route to establishing a new settlement —and not turning back.

Men blasted in solid rock for more than a month to create the **Hole-in-the-Rock**, permitting passage through the earth's mantle. The steep slope and landmark near the mouth of the Escalante River is still worth scaling, although erosion has partially closed the original notch.

TREAT WITH RESPECT

Rainbow Bridge is considered sacred by many American Indians, and the site has religious significance. To the Navajo, Rainbow represents guardians of the Universe. Boat tour passengers approach the bridge on a quarter-mile walkway that's part pontoon. The bridge may be photographed from a viewing area, but visitors are not permitted to walk under the bridge. Although signs that advise of the site's sacred status are clearly posted, many visitors tend to ignore the request to remain in the viewing area and must be called back by tour guides or boat crew members.

North and east of the Hole-in-the-Rock is a little ol' swimming hole called **Annie's Canyon** about 12 miles from Bullfrog Marina. Boaters may notice more traffic and wake when nearing Halls Creek Bay, Bullfrog Bay and the busy marinas. Those on multiday excursions may want to stock up on ice and other necessary items at this point.

About five miles north of Halls Crossing is **Moki Canyon**. With its archaeological sites and petroglyphs, the area holds many secrets of the Pueblo peoples. Supposedly the canyon was a miniature city back in prehistoric times. From Moki Canyon upstream about five miles are the odd and eerie **Moki steps**, thought to be hand and foot holds of this same tribe of ancient climbers.

Turn right and follow the next water pocket to Forgotten Canyon. At the end is the **Defiance House Site**, believed to have been occupied during the Pueblo's peak years from A.D. 1050 to A.D. 1250. Defiance House represents the lake's finest restored sites and petroglyphs and includes unusual animal/man anthropomorphs.

You'll pass by Tapestry Wall on the left side of the channel before coming to the long stretch of water in handsome **Good Hope Bay**, below the mesa of the same name, that's usually a haven for flatwater—a waterskier's dream. The lake twists and turns past a handful of other canyons in the remaining 15 miles to Hite Marina, the start (or end, depending on how you look at it) of Lake Powell.

CANYONLANDS NATIONAL PARK—THE MAZE Natural boundaries of rock and water divide the park into three distinct districts—Island in the Sky (see "Moab Area"), Needles (see "San Juan County Area") and the Maze—and make travel between the sections almost impossible. Island could be considered the park's overlook, Needles leads visitors into the heart of rock country, while the remote Maze fulfills the promise of solitude and renewal that some seek.

North of Lake Powell via Route 95/24, Henry David Thoreau would have liked the uncharted territory of Canyonlands' Maze District because it demands self-reliance. Services to this section, considered by some to be a "mini-Grand Canyon," are almost nonexistent save for the emergency water available at the Hans Flat Ranger Station. The ranger will probably check your vehicle for road-worthiness before allowing you to proceed. Extra gas, and of course plenty of water, must be on hand before proceeding because you may not see another car for days. The Maze remains some of the wildest land in the West and is accessible only by foot or high-clearance four-wheel-drive vehicle. ~ Ranger Station: 46 miles from the Route 24 turnoff via rough dirt road; 435-259-2652, fax 435-259-4533; www.nps.gov/cany.

Puzzle-like chasms twist and turn through no-man's land where the junipers, piñon pine, sagebrush, yucca and spring wildflowers seem surprising given the desert dryness. From Hans Flat it's 34 miles to the Maze Overlook, a good starting point for hikes or for a bird's-eye view of the rock **Chocolate Drops**, which resembles candy bars left too long in the sun.

Hikers who drop into the steep canyon below the lookout are rewarded with eight-foot-tall pictographs at **Harvest Scene**. As with any remnants of ancient art, it is important not to touch these stunning works because human body oils can cause damage over time.

Traversing from one section to another in the Maze can be difficult and confusing because of the puzzle of canyons. Using Hans Flat as your starting point again, drive 45 miles past Bagpipe Butte Overlook and Orange Cliffs to the Land of Standing Rocks. There you'll have the option for further foot exploration of the **Doll House**'s red-rock spires and massive fins in Ernie's Country. You may actually see more people here than in other sections of the Maze because some backcountry outfitters and rafting companies access the canyons from the edge of the Colorado River. Still, it's far from a thoroughfare.

More ice cream is consumed per capita in Utah than in any other state in the nation.

Horseshoe Canyon, on the northwestern edge of the Maze about 32 miles from the Route 24 turnoff, contains the prehistoric rock-art collection of the **Great Gallery**. Considered some of this country's best-preserved pictographs and painted art, the gallery is full of haunting, life-size drawings of people and animals. There is evidence that a prehistoric Indian culture, as well as the later Anasazi and Fremont tribes, dabbled on these walls.

LODGING

At the **Defiance House Lodge**, cool desert room colors mimic the canyon hues outside. Coffeemakers and mini-refrigerators are standard in all 48 rooms, many of which have lakeside views. Closed October through March. ~ Bullfrog Marina; 435-684-3000; www.lakepowell.com/lodging-rates.php. MODERATE TO DELUXE.

Three-bedroom housekeeping units with linens, kitchens and utensils are a viable option for families. They're available at **Bullfrog** (435-684-3000) and **Halls Crossing** (435-684-7000) marinas. **Hite** (435-684-2278) marina has mobile homes. ~ 800-528-6154; www.lakepowell.com, e-mail emaillakepowell@aramark.com. DELUXE.

Even those who don't enjoy roughing it in a tent and sleeping bag will take to the great outdoors experience on a **houseboat**. Under Lake Powell's silent, starry skies, waves gently rock the boat, providing the perfect tonic for deep sleep. During the day, is there a more relaxing pastime than reclining on the boat's flat-topped roof with book or drink in hand? The mobile floating homes come equipped with all-weather cabins, bunk beds, showers, toilets and kitchens. Six classes of boats sleep up to 12 people and are equipped for travelers with disabilities. **Lake Powell Resorts & Marinas** rents houseboats at Wahweap and Bullfrog. Prices vary depending on the season and the class of houseboat, but are not cheap by any stretch of the imagination. ~ Lake Powell Resorts & Marinas, 800-528-6154; www.lakepowell.com. ULTRA-DELUXE.

See Chapter Two for accommodations on the Arizona side of Lake Powell.

DINING

Restaurants are few around Lake Powell as most visitors opt to eat on their houseboats or at their campsites. But realizing that people need a break, Lake Powell Resorts & Marinas, which operates as the sole concessionaire for the National Park Service in Lake Powell, has a better-than-average restaurant at the Bullfrog end of the lake. The **Anasazi Restaurant** sits perched above the marina and serves Continental cuisine. Steaks, burgers, fish-and-chips and Southwestern specialties please most palates, especially those who've eaten houseboat food for a week. Closed October through March. ~ Defiance House Lodge, Bullfrog Marina; 435-684-3037. MODERATE.

PARKS

GLEN CANYON NATIONAL RECREATION AREA 🏃 🚴 🛶 🚣 🚤 🏊 Glen Canyon Dam confines the waters of the Colorado River forming Lake Powell, the second-largest man-made reservoir in the country. Sheltering Pueblo Indian sites, the 186-mile-long lake harbors countless inlets, caves and coves that are ever-changing because of the water level. Marinas are found at four separate locations on the lake: Bullfrog, Halls Crossing and Dangling Rope in Utah, and Wahweap and Antelope Point in Arizona. All kinds of water sports, from skiing to windsurfing, kayaking to inner tubing, have their place at Powell. Largemouth and smallmouth bass, striped bass and catfish are common catches. You'll also find hotels, restaurants, boat rentals (except at Dangling Rope), groceries, visitors centers, picnic areas and restrooms. Entrance fee, $15 per vehicle or boat, good for up to a week. ~ Routes 95, 276 and 89 lead to Lake Powell, where Routes 95 and 276 lead to Utah marinas; 928-608-6404, fax 928-608-6283; www.nps.gov/glca, e-mail glca_info@nps.gov.

▲ There are sites at four campgrounds: Bullfrog, Halls Crossing, Lees Ferry and Wahweap; $12 to $18 per night. Primitive sites are available at Bullfrog ($6) and Hite ($10). RV hookups are available ($30) through a private concessionaire (800-528-6154) at Wahweap, Bullfrog and Halls Crossing only. Backcountry camping is free. Camping is not allowed within one mile of marinas or at Rainbow Bridge National Monument.

RAINBOW BRIDGE NATIONAL MONUMENT 🚶 🐎 🚤 Greatest of the world's known natural bridges, this symmetrical salmon-pink sandstone span rises 290 feet above the floor of Bridge Canyon. Rainbow Bridge sits in Glen Canyon National Recreation Area, adjacent to the Navajo Nation. Tours of the monument leave regularly in the summer season from Wahweap marina; during the rest of the year service is sporadic. Water levels vary and affect hiking distances. Facilities are limited to restrooms. ~ Accessible by boat, on foot or by your own horse. To go the land route means traversing 13 miles of rugged trails through Navajo Indian Reservation land and requires a permit (928-698-2801); the number for the monument is 928-608-6404; www.nps. gov/rabr, e-mail glca_info@nps.gov. For information on boat trips call 800-528-6154 or visit www.lakepowell.com.

CANYONLANDS NATIONAL PARK—THE MAZE 🚶 🚲 🐎 The Colorado and Green rivers naturally divide this 337,570-acre, unspoiled park into three distinct and separate districts: Island in the Sky, Needles and the Maze. Uncharted and untamed, wild formations of the Maze are enjoyed only after negotiating a labyrinth of canyons and jumbled rock. Another option for reaching the Maze is from the Colorado River's edge. The seemingly other-worldly formations and Indian artifacts in this 30-mile-wide jigsaw puzzle are found west of the Colorado and Green rivers. There are no facilities here. ~ Located via Route 24 south 46 miles to the dirt road turnoff to the east; 435-259-2652 or National Park Office (Moab), 435-719-2313.

▲ Primitive camping for backpackers and mountain bikers is allowed in several areas in the Maze at Land of Standing Rocks and Maze Overlook with a permit ($15 to $30); no water available. Reservations are highly recommended: 435-259-4351. People planning to camp with a vehicle must provide their own portable toilet system, which can be rented or purchased in Moab. No fires or pets allowed.

▼▼▼▼▼▼▼▼▼▼▼▼▼▼

San Juan County Area

Most people come to San Juan County to visit either Canyonlands National Park— Needles district or to drive the Trail of the Ancients. Time permitting, the two combined reveal more about the geology and history of southeastern Utah than almost any other tour. Route 211 to the Needles first sidles along Indian Creek, named for the area's first residents. As you approach the steep canyon curves leading to Newspaper Rock, sparse desert landscape turns lush and green: Is it any wonder numerous tribes settled here? When you're ready to retreat from the red rock, you can head to Monticello or Blanding, two towns that got their start as agricultural outposts but are now warming to tourism.

Newspaper Rock Recreation Site is a tiny park usually on the "hit and run" list of most visitors. Though somewhat tarnished by graffiti, the huge sandstone panel is etched with fascinating Indian petroglyphs. This "rock that tells a story" is a compendium of American Indian history over a 2000-year span. The petroglyphs span three distinct periods, making this giant mural an archaeological find. Some of the figures, such as the horseman with a bow and arrow, were not made by the Pueblo peoples but were done

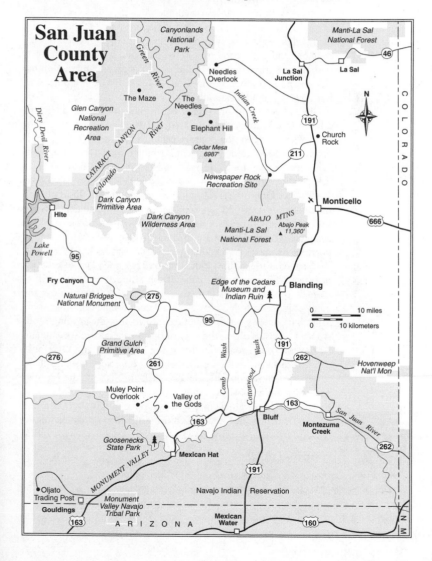

San Juan County Area

by later Indians (probably the Ute and Navajo), indicating that the sacred nature of the shrine was abandoned. A quarter-mile interpretive loop around the monument offers a chance to check out native flora and fauna, and some opt to set up camp here rather than amid the starker Canyonlands. ~ Route 211, 11 miles west of Route 191; 435-587-1500, fax 435-578-1518.

CANYONLANDS NATIONAL PARK—NEEDLES In the Needles section of Canyonlands National Park you tend to feel a part of the scenery rather than a casual and detached observer. With its myriad roads and trails, Needles is the most user-friendly of the Canyonlands sections. It also features the finest collection of petroglyphs and prehistoric sites in the park and is positively packed with natural stone sculptures in the form of arches and monoliths. Admission. ~ Route 211; 435-259-4711, fax 435-259-4266; www. nps.gov/cany, e-mail canyinfo@nps.gov.

The **Needles Visitors Center** can provide maps and advice to adventurers. From here a paved road leads six and a half miles into the park. Just past the visitors center a quarter-mile loop trail passes **Roadside Ruin**, an ancient Pueblo granary. Down the road, **Cave Spring Trail** loops three-fifths of a mile past a cave and former cowboy camp.

Needles Outpost Store is a necessary stop before heading into the backcountry. Ice, food, propane, firewood and guidebooks are sold at non-ripoff prices. Camping supplies and groceries are also available. Closed December through March. ~ Located .6 mile north of Route 211, outside the Needles district; 435-979-4007.

Farther along, **Squaw Flat Rest Area** is a fine place to get your bearings and absorb the magic of the orange-, rust- and white-striped stone fortresses ("the needles") ahead. Then follow the main road to **Pothole Point Nature Trail** (.6 mile), another short loop that passes a series of potholes formed in the eroding sandstone. The vistas along the way of distant mesas are spectacular. At the end of the road you'll find **Big Spring Canyon Overlook**, gateway to a view of the Colorado and Green rivers' meeting place.

The Pueblo peoples left their mark throughout the Needles with Canyonlands sites dating from A.D. 900 to A.D. 1200. A four-wheel-drive vehicle or a well-equipped mountain bike and a good pair of legs are key to exploring the **jeep roads** leading to

AUTHOR FAVORITE

Otherworldly is an apt description of **Canyonlands National Park—Needles**. This jumble of multicolored geology made me think the gods must have been playing with Play-Doh when they designed this corner of the park. See above for more information.

backcountry arches, canyons and the Pueblos' ancient drawings. A dirt road around the park's circumference is a fine way to view the Needles' unique topographic features. But beware: This route is not for the inexperienced driver.

For a grand view of the Needles section of Canyonlands, be sure to take in the **Needles Overlook** in the BLM-administered Canyon Rims Recreation Area. You'll be rewarded with a mesa-top vista that scans the Abajo and Henry mountains and the Colorado River and extends all the way to the park's Maze district. ~ Getting there means driving back on Route 211, heading north a few miles on Route 191, then turning west on a dead-end road.

MONTICELLO–BLANDING AREA Fourteen miles south of the Needles turnoff on Route 191, civilization reappears. Named for Thomas Jefferson's Virginia home, **Monticello** is the San Juan County seat. Complete information on the nearby national parks and monuments, state parks and local attractions can be obtained at the **Southeast Utah Welcome Center**. Call for winter hours. ~ 216 South Main Street, Monticello; 435-587-3401, 800-574-4386; www.utahscanyoncountry.com, e-mail info@utahscanyon country.com.

Early area history is revealed at the **Frontier Museum**. Besides Pueblo artifacts, the museum contains articles from pioneer life— an old stove, a wagon keg, a sewing machine, a vanity case, picture albums and flat irons. ~ 232 South Main Street, Monticello; 435-587-3401.

Another 20 miles south of Monticello on Route 191 is **Blanding**, once a trading center for nearby ranches. The log building a few miles farther along is home to **Huck's Artifact Hall of Fame**. Owner Huck Acton has assembled a stellar display of pottery and American Indian artifacts dating back to ancient times. The private collection of arrowheads, beads, pendants, effigy bowls, cooking pots and tools is sure to impress. Admission. ~ 387 South Main Street, Blanding; 435-678-2329.

A gem of the Utah state park system is **Edge of the Cedars Museum and Indian Ruin**. Site of an Anasazi Indian ruin, Edge of the Cedars allows visitors to explore the small village inhabited from A.D. 750 to A.D. 1200, even climbing down a wooden ladder into a kiva. The modern museum details the many cultures— Anasazi, Navajo, Ute and Anglo—that have played a role in regional development. The exhibits include pottery, artifacts and tools as well as video presentations. The museum walls showcase reproductions of ancient Indian pictographs. Day-use fee, $3 per person. ~ 660 West 400 North, Blanding; 435-678-2238, fax 435-678-3348; e-mail edgeofcedars@utah.gov.

◄ HIDDEN

Two other attractions are helping to make Blanding an important regional center for tourism. The **Nations of the Four Corners Cultural Center** resides on a low, sagebrush-covered hill at the edge of town. On the property you'll find several trails, including one half-mile-long path that winds past a central watchtower and replica dwellings of early Anglo, Spanish, Navajo and Ute cultures. It's a nice idea, and a free one, although most structures are kept under lock and key. Closed weekends. ~ 707 West 500 South, Blanding; 435-678-4035.

Nearby, in a big, red warehouse, is the **Dinosaur Museum**. Well organized and nicely presented, this collection includes a wide variety of fossils, from skin and footprints to full skeletal replicas of some of the largest beasts ever to walk the earth. Film fans won't want to miss the history hall of Hollywood dinosaur movies! Closed mid-October to mid-April; closed Sunday. Admission. ~ 754 South 200 West, Blanding; 435-678-3454, fax 435-587-2054; www.dinosaur-museum.org, e-mail dinos@dinosaur-museum.org.

West of Blanding, **Natural Bridges National Monument**, is home to three of the largest known natural bridges in the world: Sipachu, Kachina Bridge and Owachomo. The monument, the first in Utah, was established in 1908 by President Theodore Roosevelt. The monument maintains a visitors center, hiking trails, a campground and a paved, nine-mile loop road. Each mammoth stone bridge can be viewed by walking a short distance to an overlook. Archaeological sites can be seen from perches along the rim. Hiking to the base of the bridges is a popular attraction. Admission. ~ Route 95; 435-692-1234, fax 435-692-1111; www.nps.gov/nabr.

The monument area is mostly desert-like with a smattering of piñon-juniper trees, shrubs and grasses among the white sandstone. While ancient Indian tribes lived in the area, the canyons were apparently too small to sustain the farming activities of many families. Nonetheless, **Horsecollar Site**, the cliff dwelling remains of one community, can be viewed.

The three bridges, which resemble arches but are formed solely by flowing water, are known as Sipapu, Kachina and Owachomo.

AN OVERLOOK WITH A VIEW

Southwest of Moab off Route 191 is the **Anticline overlook**, a 2000-foot-high mesa overlooking archlike rocks, the mighty Colorado, Dead Horse Point and Arches National Park to the north. Here Canyonlands travelers can see where they've been and where they're going. ~ Keep an eye out for Anticline and Needles overlook signs when heading south of Moab on Route 191.

Sipapu, a flat-topped spur of rimrock, is the largest bridge in both height (220 feet) and span (268 feet). Its name means "the place of emergence." The "younger" **Kachina Bridge** was found to have prehistoric pictographs resembling kachinas (dancers). White Canyon floodwaters, frosts and thaws are still enlarging Kachina Bridge. **Owachomo**—"rock mounds" in the Hopi language—is so named for the large, rounded rock mass found nearby and is the oldest of the three bridges with only a narrow strip of nine-foot-thick rock remaining in the center of the bridge. Interestingly, it is tall enough to fit Washington's Capitol building underneath.

South of Blanding, at the intersection of Routes 163 and 191 is the tiny town of **Bluff.** While the Mormons first settled Bluff in 1880, some archaeologists believe Paleo Indian hunters may have stalked bison herds through the area 11,000 years ago. Kiva and cliff dwellings confirm the presence of ancient Pueblo tribes. Visitors to the town (the oldest community in San Juan County) may view sandstone Victorian-style homes left by early settlers, some of whom are buried in the historic **Pioneer Cemetery** overlooking the town. ~ The cemetery is easy to get to: Follow the Bluff Historic Loop past Rim Rock Drive to the end of the road.

On your way to Pioneer Cemetery you will pass the **Old County Jail,** a hand-hewn sandstone structure in the center of town. It was originally erected as an elementary school in 1896. ~ Bluff Historic Loop.

St. Christopher's Episcopal Mission, two miles east of Bluff, is a house of worship built of native sandstone. The Navajo Madonna and Child stand on the site of the original church, which was destroyed by fire. ~ Route 163.

About three miles east of Bluff, across a swinging footbridge that spans the San Juan River, is the **Fourteen Window Ruin** cliff dwelling (also known as the Apartment House Ruin). Take the dirt road on the south side of Route 163 to the bottom of the hill. After crossing the rickety bridge and coming to the clearing, the site can be spotted straight ahead in the rock. For closer inspection of these honeycombed dwellings, walk the additional mile on the dusty trail. Please be respectful—this site is on Navajo tribal land, and access can be denied at any time.

About 20 miles southwest of Bluff along Route 191/163, **Mexican Hat** is a tiny community separated from the Navajo Indian Reservation by the San Juan River. Its name comes from a stone formation resembling an upside-down sombrero just north of town. There are a few trading posts, motels, cafés, service stations and an RV park. ~ Two miles west of the Route 163 intersection with Route 261.

Text continued on page 624.

Trail of the Ancients

A scenic, historical and archaeological tour of San Juan County begins at Edge of the Cedars, just northwest of Blanding, and follows a counterclockwise, 125-mile loop that includes more than a dozen sites of interest such as Natural Bridges National Monument and the towns of Mexican Hat and Bluff. The trail derives its name from Anasazi, "the ancient ones," and much of the tour passes ancient sites of this now-extinct people. Detailed maps are available at the Edge of the Cedars Museum and Indian Ruin.

WESTWATER CLIFF DWELLINGS Just west of Blanding a paved access road from Route 191 leads across a swinging natural bridge to the Westwater cliff dwellings, which include five kivas (circular, underground structures used for gathering of kin groups) and open work areas. The dwelling was occupied from around A.D. 1150 to A.D. 1275 Unfortunately, much of the site has been destroyed by vandals searching for ancient relics.

COTTON, WASH, COMB From Route 191, the trail turns west onto Route 95, passing Cottonwood Falls, Butler Wash and Comb Ridge. Only a large depression, almost 80 feet in diameter, marks the great kiva at **Cottonwood Falls**. Looking south from the eastern end of the hole, a prehistoric road may be spotted. Farther on, **Butler Wash** houses the highly developed stonework remains of a 20-room dwelling area plus several smaller Anasazi structures. The cliff houses can be viewed from an observation area at the end of a mile-long hiking trail. Beyond Butler Wash, **Comb Ridge** is an eroded monocline, or bending of the earth's crust in a single direction, and extends some 80 miles south into Arizona.

ARCH AND MULE CANYONS The highway continues to cut through the red walls of Arch Canyon, where centuries of erosion have chiseled and sculpted massive sandstone formations. Seven ancient towers, thought to have been built more than 900 years ago, are clustered high atop the rim of Mule Canyon. Three of the seven are visible at the site and considered a rare find because only a few such tower-like ruins are still standing. At the **Mule Canyon Ruin and Rest Stop** is an excavated 12-room pueblo with a pair of kivas and a tower, all extremely well preserved and stabilized. The Bureau of Land Management has even constructed a sheltering ramada over the kiva, affording extra protection and interpretive signs offering clues to its history.

SALVATION KNOLL Later explorers of the region included an 1879 scouting party that lost its way while looking for the Hole-in-the-Rock Trail.

The scouts climbed to the top of Salvation Knoll, from where they were able to regain their bearings and continue their search for a passable route to the east. What the scouting party didn't spot was **Natural Bridges National Monument** (page 620), which wasn't discovered by white men until 1883. You'll find the entrance to the park off Route 95 just past the junction with Route 261.

GRAND GULCH   From Natural Bridges, backtrack to the highway junction. and turn south on Route 261. This 34-mile segment of the trail first brings you to Grand Gulch, where Anasazi habitation was omnipresent. Found within the 50-mile-long canyon system (managed as an outdoor museum) are six representative sites from both Basketmaker and Pueblo periods. Extensive remains of Anasazi dwellings, tools and artwork may be seen. Travel is limited to horseback riders and hikers.

MULEY POINT OVERLOOK   Like stepping into a new world, Muley Point Overlook abruptly jolts travelers from cedar forests to austere desert scenes. In the distance, keen observers can spot the monolith-filled Monument Valley. Be warned: Route 261 leading to Muley Point travels over the **Moki Dugway**, a graveled, three-mile series of tight (and we mean tight!) switchbacks ascending to the lookout.

VALLEY OF THE GODS   Descending from the overlook, the road leads into the Valley of the Gods which, with its unique rock formations jutting hundreds of feet into the air, is considered a mini-Monument Valley.

GOOSENECKS STATE PARK   From the canyon rim of Goosenecks State Park (page 627), you can view the San Juan River 1000 feet below forming a series of "gooseneck" switchbacks as it winds its way toward Lake Powell. ~ Route 261; 435-678-2238, fax 435-678-3348; e-mail edgeofthe cedars@utah.gov.

ROUTE 163   Just north of the tiny Navajo border town of **Mexican Hat** (page 621), turn east on Route 163. This highway passes **Sand Island**, a primary boat launch for the San Juan River. Petroglyph panels here showcase five Kokopelli flute players—mythological Indian figures.

END OF THE TRAIL   Route 163 rejoins Route 191 at the little town of **Bluff** (page 621). Turn north and continue for 26 miles across the Ute Reservation to return to Blanding. Those with ample time may want to detour into **Hovenweep National Monument** (page 662), located in both Colorado and Utah.

LODGING   As tourism generates most of this area's summer economy, hotels are numerous. Yet with few exceptions, most are of the motel variety, designed to provide a clean bed and bath but little else.

Though nothing to write home about, the red-brick **Best Western Wayside Inn** is nevertheless a good place to hang your hat for a night or two. Rooms are large, with oak furniture and computer jacks. The on-site swimming pool and hot tub are pluses, as are the tastefully landscaped grounds. ~ 197 East Central Street, Monticello; 435-587-2261, 800-633-9700, fax 435-587-2920. BUDGET TO MODERATE.

Budget-minded travelers will appreciate **Navajo Trail National 9 Inn**. Immaculate rooms have typical hotel decor with queen beds. For a few extra dollars, a kitchen can be yours complete with stove, refrigerator and microwave. They also have free wireless internet and a computer station. ~ 248 North Main Street, Monticello; 435-587-2251, 888-449-6463; www.84535.com, e-mail national9@84535.com. BUDGET.

For those wanting a safe bet, **Days Inn Monticello** won't disappoint. The two-story complex is decorated in maroon and forest green. Rooms are large with ample drawer space. Adding to the hotel's popularity are complimentary continental breakfast and a huge indoor swimming pool with a whirlpool spa. ~ 549 North Main Street, Monticello; 435-587-2458, 800-329-7466, fax 435-587-2191. BUDGET TO MODERATE.

One of the better properties in the area, the **Best Western Gateway Inn** boasts nicely appointed rooms and a congenial staff. Contemporary appointments in blues and earth-tones are used in both the large lobby area and 60 spacious units. The swimming pool and free continental breakfast are nice extras. ~ 88 East Center Street, Blanding; 435-678-2278, fax 435-678-2240. MODERATE.

In Bluff is the **Desert Rose Inn**. Backing up to the San Juan River, the lodge looks north to rugged sandstone desert. Along

◆◆

REST AND RECAPTURE

There's something very inviting about the **Recapture Lodge**. An oasis of shade trees populates the site, shielding guests from the hot Utah sun. There are 26 homey rooms, nothing fancy, but quiet and comfortable. Lawn chairs, ideal for lounging, line the upper deck. A nice-sized swimming pool provides another way to beat the heat. Adventuresome souls can arrange geologist-guided tours of the nearby canyons, cliff dwellings and American Indian sites—or even multiday llama treks—the lodge has information on all these activities. ~ Route 191 West, Bluff; phone/fax 435-672-2281; e-mail recapturelodge@hubwest.com. BUDGET.

with the 30-room lodge, which is highlighted by massive timbers, the Desert Rose offers a bit more privacy via six guest cabins, each with two full beds, television, microwave, coffee maker and small refrigerator. Almost every room in the lodge looks out over the red-rock bluffs. ~ 701 West Main Street, Bluff; 435-672-2303, 888-475-7673, fax 435-672-2217; www.desertroseinn.com, e-mail reservations@desertroseinn.com. BUDGET TO MODERATE.

Tucked away in a corner of the desert at the foot of the Moki Dugway is one of the unlikeliest outposts of civilization you'll find in the Southwest. **The Valley of the Gods Bed & Breakfast** offers four charming guest rooms (all with private baths) in a 1933 stone ranch house and separate lodging in a two-story root cellar. The B&B's architecture alone is worth a visit: two-foot-thick walls of native rock, thick ceiling beams, and a wonderful living room with comfy log furniture, a fireplace and great views through the picture window. There is not another home within miles . . . and this one is solar powered! From the rocking chairs on the 75-foot-long covered front porch you have great views into the Valley of the Gods. ~ One-half mile east of Route 261 on Valley of the Gods Road, Mexican Hat; 970-749-1164 (cellular); www.valleyofthegods.cjb.net. DELUXE.

◀ HIDDEN

Don't expect to watch your cholesterol in San Juan County. Basic country cooking is standard fare, with a real salad bar about as rare as a rosebush in the desert.

DINING

A quick pizza fix may be had at long-standing **Wagon Wheel Pizza**. Fresh deli sandwiches, calzones and pizzas are prepared in a flash. Take out or hunker down in a blue-leather booth under mock Pepsi-Cola Tiffany lamps. Closed Sunday. ~ 164 South Main Street, Monticello; 435-587-2766. BUDGET.

A solid choice is the **Old Tymer Restaurant**, adjacent to the Comfort Inn at Blanding's south end. The exterior of this big gray building belies a rustic interior adorned with historic photographs. The three-meals-a-day menu is traditional American (steaks, prime rib, fish) with a sprinkling of Mexican items. ~ 722 South Main Street, Blanding; 435-678-2122. MODERATE.

Surprisingly, it's in the tiny town of Bluff where you'll discover some of the best dining. **Cow Canyon Restaurant** changes its entrées weekly and features traditional Navajo dishes as well as an eclectic array of international dishes. One week the choices might be spinach lasagna, Greek salad or stuffed butternut squash. Desserts range from an apple dumpling to ice cream splashed with Kahlua and baked almonds. Housed in an old stone trading post, Cow Canyon's ambience more than matches the food. Dinner only. Closed Tuesday and Wednesday and from November through March. ~ Routes 191 and 163, Bluff; 435-672-2208; e-mail cowcanyn@sanjuan.net. BUDGET TO MODERATE.

◀ HIDDEN

There's also the **Cottonwood Steakhouse**. Many patrons enjoy dining outdoors, under a huge cottonwood tree and near a campfire; others enjoy the rustic decor inside. Barbecued ribs and chicken, as well as steak, are the house specials; they're served with salad, grilled potatoes and baked beans. Dinner only. Closed November through February. ~ Route 191 West, Bluff; 435-672-2282; e-mail cwsteak@frontiernet.net. MODERATE TO DELUXE.

SHOPPING   After perusing the wares for sale at **Cedar Mesa Pottery** take a behind-the-scenes tour of the pottery factory. Here, you can watch American Indian artisans create and decorate their hand-painted pottery. Closed weekends in winter. ~ 333 South Main Street, Blanding; 435-678-2241, 800-235-7687; www.cmpottery.net.

Trading posts selling sandstone folk art, pottery, baskets, silver jewelry, pipes, papooses and rugs are **Thin Bear Indian Arts** (1944 South Route 191, Blanding; 435-678-2940) and **Hunt's Trading Post** (146 East Center Street, Blanding; 435-678-2314).

Offering a variety of pottery, jewelry, pipes and rugs, other trading posts to choose from are **San Juan Inn Trading Post** (Route 163, Mexican Hat; 435-683-2220, fax 435-683-2210) and **Twin Rocks Trading Post** (913 East Navajo Twins Drive, Bluff; 435-672-2341, 800-526-3448, fax 435-672-2370; www.twinrocks.com).

As gateway to Navajo tribal lands, San Juan County is blanketed with trading posts. Best of the lot is **Cow Canyon Trading Post**, a log-and-stone structure dating from the 1940s. Jewelry, pottery, rugs and ethnographic artifacts of the Navajo and Zuni are well displayed and honestly priced. There is also a photographic gallery. ~ Routes 191 and 163, Bluff; 435-672-2208.

NIGHTLIFE   The **Olde Bridge Grille** is open for over-the-bar beer sales. ~ San Juan Inn, San Juan Drive at Route 163, Mexican Hat; 435-683-2220.

PARKS   **NEWSPAPER ROCK RECREATION SITE** 🕴 Camping within this 50-acre park is encouraged, and the lush, evergreen area provides a sharp contrast to nearby Canyonlands. A short trail here leads to the base of the Newspaper Rock Petroglyph Panel. The only facilities available here are toilets. ~ From Monticello take Route 191 north for 15 miles, then Route 211 southwest for 11 miles; 435-587-1500, fax 435-587-1518.

CANYONLANDS NATIONAL PARK—NEEDLES 🕴 🚲 🐎 Sculptured rock spires, arches, canyons and potholes dominate the landscape. Grassy meadows like Chesler Park offer striking contrasts to the mostly bare rock. Traces of the ancient Pueblo Indians can be found throughout the area in well-preserved pictographs and petroglyphs. The meeting place of the Colorado and

Green rivers, before they join forces and rumble down to Lake Powell, can be seen from Confluence Overlook. If Island in the Sky is the observation deck for Canyonlands, then the Needles could be considered the main stage—you start out right at ground level and become immediately immersed in its unfolding tale. The park has a visitors center, picnic areas and restrooms. The $10 vehicle fee is good for seven days in all Canyonlands districts. ~ Proceed south from Moab on Route 191 for 40 miles (or north from Monticello 15 miles), then 35 miles southwest on Route 211; 435-259-4351, fax 435-259-4285, or National Park Office (Moab), 435-259-7164; www.nps.gov/cany, e-mail canyinfo@nps.gov.

> Natural Bridges National Monument is home to the world's second and third largest natural bridges.

▲ There are 26 sites in Squaw Flat Campground; $15 per night. Permits are required for backcountry camping. Nearby, there is also camping at Needles Outpost Store (435-979-4007) from March to October.

NATURAL BRIDGES NATIONAL MONUMENT 🚶 🚲 Three natural bridges are found within this 7500-acre, canyon-like park first discovered by white pioneers in 1883. You'll find a visitors center and restrooms, as well as picnic areas. Entrance fee, $6 per vehicle. ~ Off Route 95, about 40 miles west of Blanding; 435-692-1234, fax 435-692-1111.

▲ There are 13 primitive sites; $10 per night. Water is available at the visitors center.

GOOSENECKS STATE PARK 🚶 An impressive example of "entrenched meander," Goosenecks is a 1000-foot-deep chasm carved by the San Juan River as it winds and turns back on itself for more than six miles while advancing only one and a half miles west toward Lake Powell. A picnic area and restrooms are the park's only facilities. ~ Off Route 261, nine miles northwest of Mexican Hat; 435-678-2238, fax 435-678-3348.

▲ Primitive camping is allowed within the park; four sites; free. No water is available.

Movies made Moab famous, but the area has a lot more going for it. Used as a home base for many who explore southeastern Utah, the city has a well-preserved, colorful history. Add to this two wonderful national parks in the region, a neat loop drive, even a winery. What more could you want?

Moab Area

Moab serves as gateway to both Arches National Park and Canyonlands National Park—Island in the Sky. On your way to Island in the Sky, be sure and stop at **Dead Horse Point State Park**. An isolated, 5250-acre island mesa, 5900 feet above sea level and surrounded by steep cliffs, Dead Horse Point State Park showcases

SIGHTS

◀ *HIDDEN*

150 million years of canyon erosion, buttes, pinnacles, bluffs and towering spires plus the Colorado River 2000 feet below. Views from the park overlook 5000 square miles of the Colorado Plateau including the La Sal and Abajo mountain ranges. Admission. ~ Route 313; 435-259-2614.

CANYONLANDS NATIONAL PARK—ISLAND IN THE SKY Route 191 connects with Route 313, a road leading into the northern portion of Canyonlands National Park. If ever you doubted Utah scenery could steal your breath away, this promontory will change your mind. Depending on weather and time of day, the Colorado River Gorge below is an artist's palate of ever-changing hues. The **Visitors Center** has a bookstore as well as information and maps. Nearby paths also offer an interpretive guide to regional flora. But don't make the center your only stop. From there drive another mile and a half to the park's majestic overlook. It won't disappoint. ~ 435-259-4712.

Wilder and less trodden than Arches National Park is Canyonlands National Park—Island in the Sky district. It's a broad, level mesa serving as observation deck for the park's 527 square miles of canyons, mesas, arches and cliffs. From this vantage point the visitor can enjoy views of the two powerful rivers (the Colorado and Green) that constitute the park's boundaries and the three mountain ranges (the La Sals, Abajos and Henrys).

Just past the Island in the Sky Visitors Center on the left side is the **Shafer Canyon Overlook** and the winding Shafer Trail Road, which swoops down the canyon to connect to the **White Rim Road,** so named for the layer of white sandstone that forms its line of demarcation. The White Rim parallels the Colorado and later the Green River, forming a belt around Island in the Sky's circumference. Permits are required for campsites along the relatively level trail (reservations recommended; there is a $30 charge), which can be comfortably covered by bike or sturdy four-wheel-drive vehicle in two to four days.

Back on top of the mesa that is the Island, enjoy a bird's-eye view of **Lathrop Canyon** and the Colorado River via the **Mesa Arch** path. Short and sweet, this trail provides a vantage point for distant arches like Washer Woman, menacing Monster Tower and Airport Tower.

Just a quarter mile west, near the intersection of the park's only two roads, are the Willow Flat campground and the true-to-its-name **Green River Overlook,** a fine contrast to the muddy Colorado. On the road's north side is the short trail to **Aztec Butte,** where you'll find Indian archaeological sites.

At the end of this side road, see the bulbous **Whale Rock** jutting out of its parched home near the geologic paradox of **Upheaval Dome,** a 1500-foot-deep crater with a questionable origin. Theories are divided whether this was a natural occurrence or meteor-created. Weird, moonlike craters with peaks spring from its center.

At the most southerly end of the main road is the **Grand View Point Overlook**. From this vantage point at 6000 feet above sea level, Utah's geologic contrasts become crystal clear. There are totem pole-like spires and the rounded La Sal and Abajo mountains in the distance. The Colorado River cuts so deeply in the canyon below that it's invisible from the overview. Columns and fins and other contorted rocks comprise a gang of soft sandstone structures called **Monument Basin**. By crossing the White Rim trail it's possible to get a closer look at these monuments.

ARCHES NATIONAL PARK　Traversing the width and breadth of Arches National Park on the paved road that author Edward Abbey deplored in his book *Desert Solitaire* (a must-read for any visitor) is easy—maybe too easy. To truly experience the greatest

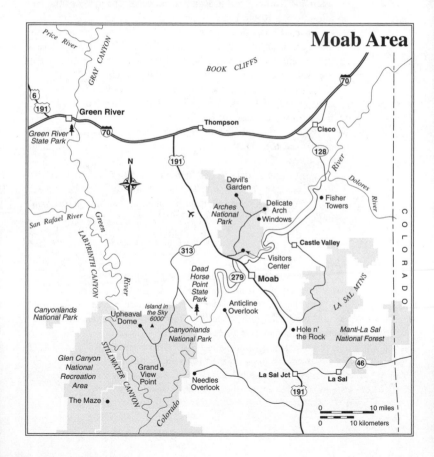

number of natural arches in the country, get out of your car and wander. You won't want to miss the sensation of sandstone beneath shoe, the delicious scent of juniper and sage, even the hauntingly lonely sound of whistling desert wind on the short hiking trails. Admission. ~ Route 191, five miles north of Moab; 435-259-8161.

The world's largest concentration of natural stone arches, extraordinary products of erosion, makes this 76,519-acre park one of the most spectacular in red-rock country. Sandstone panoramas formed by weathering, movement of the earth's crust and erosion range in size from three to 306 feet. Natural monoliths in this semiarid land resemble everything from city skyscrapers to a whale's orb: The interpretation is all in the eye of the beholder.

Make your first stop the **Visitors Center** for a bevy of maps and other publications as well as a slide-show orientation, geology museum and history exhibit. Rangers can point out many of the best attractions. ~ Route 191 at the entrance to the park; 435-719-2299.

From the visitors center the main park road climbs into the heart of the arches region. **Moab Canyon**, a multi-hued example of geological slippage, opens to view about a mile from the center. About six million years ago activity along the Moab fault caused one section of the canyon to shift, resulting in rock formations on the bottom of one side that are identical in age with those on the far side of the canyon.

Farther along at the **South Park Avenue Overlook** you'll see giant sandstone rockfaces that rise sheer on either side of a dry creek bed.

Appearing to defy gravity is **Balanced Rock**, a formation that looks like it might fall from its pedestal at any moment. A short but strenuous trail (.3 mile) can be taken to examine all the boulder's vantage points.

HOLLYWOOD'S BACKLOT

Director John Ford put the area on the map when he filmed the 1949 classic *Wagonmaster* here. Ford returned to film *Rio Grande* the following year, and Hollywood has favored it ever since. A detailed guide to area movie locations—including *The Greatest Story Ever Told*, *Cheyenne Autumn*, *Indiana Jones and the Last Crusade* and *Thelma and Louise*—is available at the visitors center. And you can pursue your own film career as an "extra" by filling out an application with the **Moab to Monument Valley Film Commission**, whose offices are lined with publicity stills and posters from movies shot in the area. ~ 89 East Center Street, Moab; 435-259-1346; www.filmmoab.com, e-mail info@filmmoab.com.

One of the easiest areas to visit is **Windows**. Four large arches that provide natural picture frames for distant panoramas can be effortlessly viewed. The North and South Windows are a short walk in one direction from the parking lot. Take a jaunt the other way and see the Turret Arch. Splendid Double Arch is just across the road. Preludes to the panoramic windows via the Windows road are Garden of Eden viewpoint, providing sweeping views to the north, and Elephant Butte. ~ About 12 miles from the visitors center via the main park road and Windows turnoff.

Balanced Rock marks the start of a rough, four-wheel-drive road into the more secluded Willow Flats and **Herdina Park** sections. Herdina Park's claim to fame is that it's the home to five mini-canyons and the unusual **Eye of the Whale Arch**. With a little imagination, you can see the beast's orb.

Those with heavy-duty vehicles may want to venture another ten miles to the vast and scenic Klondike Bluffs, home to the **Tower Arch**, a hole in a wall of solid rock, and minarets that form the **Marching Men**. Check with the ranger for conditions before traveling this road.

The park's northern section, where the main park road ends, has the largest grouping of spires and openings-in-the-rock. No less than seven arches can be viewed in **Devil's Garden**, the park's longest maintained trail. The most distant of these arches is the Double O, which is about a two-mile trek from the trailhead that feels longer under the hot desert sun. If stamina allows, hike an extra quarter-mile on a more primitive trail to the ominous **Dark Angel** formation.

Halfway to the trail end is **Landscape Arch**. At 306 feet long (and at one spot only six feet thick) it's one of the world's longest natural stone spans. **Navajo Arch**—did it protect Indians at some juncture?—is one and a half miles from the trailhead. Piñon plants, junipers—the most common tree in the park—the Mormon tea plant, the obnoxious prickly pear and evening primrose and Indian paintbrush flowers dot the area. Pick up an interpretive brochure at the visitors center before setting out to enhance your understanding of the desert garden.

From Devil's Garden it's about one mile south on the main road to the fins (yes, they do look like fish fins) of up to 100 feet high in **Fiery Furnace**, which does not live up to its threatening name on hot days. (Instead, the pinnacles provide a degree of relief when temperatures scorch.) The ranger-guided tour of the Furnace is recommended, since winter erosion and labyrinthine trails make this an easy place in which to get injured or lost.

Traveling back toward the park entrance, take the first turnoff to the left and drive two miles to the **Delicate Arch** trailhead. Set aside several hours to really enjoy this graceful monument (some early explorers interpreted it as being a bowlegged cowboy!) that stands 65 feet high with a 35-foot opening. Arguably Utah's most beautiful natural wonder, the sensuous bit of slickrock stands boldly against the desert and the distant La Sal Mountains. The one-and-a-half-mile trail skirts historic **Wolfe Ranch**, sole remains of a 19th-century cattle operation that somehow survived more than a generation in this harsh land. Those unable or uninterested in hiking to Delicate Arch can drive an additional mile from the trailhead to the **Delicate Arch Viewpoint** and gaze from there.

HIDDEN ►

MOAB Moab truly is an oasis in the wilderness. Red-rock cliffs really do meet verdant valleys, all in the shadow of the towering La Sal Mountains. First settled in 1855 by missionaries, Moab is laid out in typical Mormon fashion with large, square blocks, wide streets and huge poplar trees. The city takes its name from a remote biblical kingdom east of the River Jordan. Present-day Moab is "sporting central" for the lean-and-mean Lycra-wearing crowd. Spring is high season in Moab, as thousands of ski bums and heat-seekers flock here for desert warmth.

For area information, stop at the **Moab Information Center**. Hours vary, call ahead.~ Center and Main streets, Moab; 435-259-8825, 800-635-6622, fax 435-259-1376; www.discovermoab.com.

Moab's rich history is preserved in the **Dan O'Laurie Museum**. Though the collection is small, it is comprehensive, examining the geology and paleontology of Moab's beginnings. Dozens of photographs recount the development of mining, ranching, early transportation and the Old Spanish Trail. There's even the old switchboard that served all of Moab until 1951. Closed Sunday. ~ 118 East Center Street, Moab; 435-259-7985.

Star Hall, just northeast of the museum, is the start of the **Moab Historic Walking Tour** of 23 homes and commercial structures. Pick up a map at the visitors center.

It was young geologist Charles Steen who first discovered uranium deposits in the region, touching off the rush of miners. The "uranium king" built a **million-dollar home** overlooking the Moab Valley and rivers. The house is now the Sunset Grill (see "Dining"). ~ 900 North Route 191, Moab; 435-259-7146, fax 435-259-7626; www.moab-utah.com/sunsetgrill, e-mail sunsetgrillmoab@moab.com.

Utah's first commercial winery, Arches Vineyard, was renamed **Castle Creek Winery** in 2002 and produces cabernet sauvignon, merlot, pinot noir, chardonnay, chenin blanc and gewürztraminer. Located along with the Red Cliffs Lodge on a working ranch along the Colorado River northeast of Moab, the winery has a tasting room that's open from mid-March through November. ~ Milepost 14, Route 128, Moab; 435-259-3332, 866-812-2002, fax 435-259-5397; www.castlecreekwinery.com, e-mail info@castlecreekwinery.com.

Twelve miles south of Moab is **Hole n' the Rock**. You can't miss the gargantuan white letters painted onto the cliffside announcing the place. Attractions like this you either love or hate, and those intrigued by a 5000-square-foot home and gift shop inside solid sandstone will love it. Check out the sculpture of Franklin D. Roosevelt on the rock face above the entrance. Admission. ~ 11037 South Route 191; phone/fax 435-686-2250; www.moab-utah.com/holeintherock.

La Sal Mountains meet red rock along the **La Sal Mountain Loop Drive**. The roundtrip ride from Moab is about 60 miles from start to finish and can be driven in either direction. Plan on a minimum of three to four hours to fully enjoy the views and side trips in the evergreen-laden forests that rise 4000 feet above the red rock. ~ Look for the road marker about eight miles south of downtown Moab off Route 191. Turn left and head into the hills.   ◀ *HIDDEN*

The land seems to change almost immediately as sandstone gives way to forests and foothills. A popular fishing hole and windsurfing spot, **Ken's Lake** is off to the left via a dirt road. Continuing on the La Sal Mountain Loop Drive brings you to a turnoff on the right called Geyser Pass. This road accesses a popular area for cross-country skiing.

Back on the loop road another few miles are turnoffs on the right to scenic lakes Oowah and Warner and a U.S. Forest Service campground. At this point the scenery may make it difficult to remain focused on driving.

Three miles farther on the left is the back entrance to Moab via Sand Flats Road. It's a 20-mile bumpy ride back into town. If you choose to continue on the loop road to the summit, you'll be rewarded with sweeping views of the Castle Valley below.

Nearby on the left side is a turnoff to the **Pinhook Battlefield Monument** and burial grounds. Here, eight members of a posse were laid to rest after battling Indians.

Across the loop on the right is the rough road to the site of an 1890s gold camp called **Miner's Basin**. This ghost town is reported

CREATURE COMFORTS

Aching for a little respite from the frenetic tourist scene? The **Scott M. Matheson Wetlands Preserve**, jointly owned and managed by The Nature Conservancy and the Utah Division of Wildlife Resources, offers just such an escape. Encompassing nearly 900 acres where Mill Creek flows into the Colorado River west of Moab, the preserve is home to nearly 200 species of waterfowl, songbirds and raptors, as well as numerous amphibians and such riverine mammals as otters and beavers. ~ Kane Creek Road, two miles west of Main Street, Moab; 435-259-4629.

to have produced gold ore valued in excess of $1000 per ton. Note: A four-wheel-drive vehicle is often needed to get to the 10,000-foot-elevation spot.

Beginning your descent into the Castle Valley brings you to Gateway Road on the right side—it's the rear entrance to Gateway, Colorado—and the abandoned mining town of **Castleton**, which boomed in the early 1900s with a hotel, two grocery stores, a school and two saloons.

The desert returns past Castleton as you ease into the truly stunning **Castle Valley**. At left is the volcanic remnant **Round Mountain**. There are the **Priest and Nuns** rock formations (yes, they do resemble a padre and his faithful sisters) jutting heavenward to your right, as well as the landmark **Castle Rock** that's been featured in more commercials than Michael Jordan.

In another four miles the loop road merges with Route 128 and the scenic river route back to Moab. A worthwhile stop before returning to the city is at the Big Bend picnic area for swimming, camping and picnicking.

LODGING

HIDDEN ►

One of the most picturesque, and nurturing, stays can be found 17 miles northeast of Moab at the **Sorrel River Ranch Resort**. Cupped by a bend in the Colorado River, the ranch is backed by towering red-rock buttes that inspired the name of the Castle Valley. Offering a variety of suites that front the river (and some standard rooms that don't), some of the accommodations include fireplaces. The ranch also contains a restaurant, as well as a swimming pool and spa. There is a barn for your horses, too. ~ Route 128, 17 miles northeast of Moab; 435-259-4642, 877-359-2715, fax 435-259-3016; www.sorrelriver.com, e-mail stay@sorrelriver.com. ULTRA-DELUXE.

Don't be put off by the plastic and neon located along the Route 191 strip through Moab. While generic, two-story motels dominate, a few blocks off the main drag are some charming inns that welcome weary travelers with a personal touch.

Entering town from the north via Route 191, you can't miss the **Aarchway Inn**. This sprawling complex offers everything from simple rooms to executive suites and ultra-deluxe-priced two-room apartments. Set in the motel's courtyard is a pool and grassy common areas equipped with barbecue grills. There's also a hot tub and exercise room; the rooms are equipped with small refrigerators, microwaves, TVs and phones. A continental breakfast is complimentary. ~ 1551 North Route 191, Moab; 435-259-2599, 800-341-9359 or 800-341-9359, fax 435-259-2270; www.aarchwayinn.com, e-mail reservations@aarchwayinn.com. MODERATE TO DELUXE.

The pink-adobe exterior with hanging dried chiles makes the **Kokopelli Lodge** easy to spot. Though small, the eight rooms are clean, and the service is friendly. The eco-conscious owners provide on-site recycling and earth-friendly products in the rooms. Cyclists appreciate a secured area set aside for bikes, and there's also a hot tub in which you can soothe what aches. ~ 72 South 100 East, Moab; 435-259-7615, 888-530-3134, fax 435-259-8498; www.kokopellilodge.com, e-mail info@kokopellilodge.com. BUDGET.

Best of the "strip" motels is the **Best Western Greenwell Inn**. Seventy-two rooms are conventionally furnished in pinks, mauves and blues with queen-sized beds, flat-screen TVs and wi-fi. Bonuses include the on-site restaurant, an outdoor swimming pool, hot tub, laundry facilities, exercise room and bike storage. ~ 105 South Main Street, Moab; 435-259-6151, 800-528-1234, fax 435-259-4397; www.bestwesternmoab.com, e-mail bwgreenwell@quin star.com. BUDGET TO DELUXE.

The charming **Cali Cochitta Bed & Breakfast** is a lovingly restored adobe brick house that dates to the 1870s. There are three rooms and a suite; each offers its own bathroom and queen-sized bed. Out back you'll find a cottage that offers a little more privacy. ~ 110 South 200 East, Moab; 435-259-4961, 888-429-8112, fax 435-259-4964; www.moabdreaminn.com, e-mail calicochitta@ moabdreaminn.com. MODERATE TO DELUXE.

A Colonial-style brick exterior houses the **Landmark Inn**. Thirty-five units feature tile baths, individual air conditioning and handpainted panoramic murals above the beds. Offering a pool, hot tub, guest laundry and continental breakfast, the motel is popular among families, especially large ones who appreciate the rooms with three queen beds and extra-thick walls. ~ 168 North Main Street, Moab; 435-259-6147, 800-441-6147, fax 435-259-

AUTHOR FAVORITE

There are more than a dozen bed-and-breakfast establishments in the immediate Moab area, but none nicer than the **Sunflower Hill Bed & Breakfast Inn**. Though located just a few blocks from downtown, it is like a country estate with two separate homes sharing spacious central grounds. The Garden Cottage has six guest rooms with European-style antique furnishings and a Great Room with a fireplace and library, while the Farm House boasts six additional units with country-style decor. All rooms are air-conditioned and have private baths. Family suites are available. A full breakfast is served indoors or out, and there's a big hot tub in the garden. Laundry facilities are available. ~ 185 North 300 East, Moab; 435-259-2974, 800-662-2786, fax 435-259-3065l; www.sunflowerhill.com, e-mail innkeeper@sun flowerhill.com. DELUXE TO ULTRA-DELUXE.

5556; www.landmarkinnmoab.com, e-mail landmark@aol.com.
BUDGET TO DELUXE.

A complete make-your-own breakfast is the best reason to
spend the night at **Cedar Breaks Condos**. The half-dozen two-bedroom condominiums have full baths, kitchens and living rooms
with high-speed internet. Upstairs units feature private balconies
while downstairs units have patios. There's a hot tub on the premises. ~ Center Street and 400 East, Moab; 435-259-5125, 800-
748-4386, fax 435-259-6079; www.moabutahlodging.com, e-mail
info@moabutahlodging.com. MODERATE.

Bright is one word for the paint used in the 43 rooms and
suites at **The Gonzo Inn**. But if you play hard during the day in
the surrounding national parks, you shouldn't have any trouble
falling asleep at night. If money's not too much of a problem,
splurge for the Gecko Suite with its gas fireplace, jetted tub, kitchenette, stereo and wet bar. ~ 100 West 200 South, Moab; 435-259-
2515, 800-791-4044, fax 435-259-6992; www.gonzoinn.com,
e-mail gonzoinn@gonzoinn.com. DELUXE TO ULTRA-DELUXE.

The Redstone Inn is conveniently located in south central
Moab, just about five miles south of Arches National Park.
These folks offer not only rooms that might include an indoor
hot tub and high-speed internet, but packages that cover white-
water rafting, four-wheeling, and equestrian trips. ~ 535 South
Main Street, Moab; 435-259-3500, 800-772-1972, fax 435-259-
2717; www.moabredstone.com, e-mail office@moabredstone.com.
BUDGET.

Certainly off the beaten track, hidden behind a storage center,
is the **Lazy Lizard International Hostel**. You can't go wrong at the
cheapest sleep in Moab. Both the dormitory and the private rooms
are clean, and bedding and towels are provided (there is a small
extra charge for them if you're staying in the dorm). Log cabins
are available for a few dollars more than the private rooms. There
is also a common kitchen, a TV room, a hot tub and a laundry. It's
popular with a European clientele. ~ 1213 South Route 191,
Moab; 435-259-6057; www.lazylizardhostel.com, e-mail reserva
tions@lazylizardhostel.com. BUDGET.

DINING

Locals say Moab restaurants have improved greatly of late to meet
demands of a more sophisticated, traveling public. As the town
is a center for so many outdoor activities, burning calories have
created a demand for decent fueling spots.

It's appropriate, perhaps, that the million-dollar 1952 home of
uranium miner, Charles Steen, is now the finest dining option in
Moab. The spacious **Sunset Grill**, perched on a bluff top at the
north end of town, serves such classic American and Continental
dishes as escargot, *vol au vent*, Provimi veal rib and Cajun shrimp
fettuccine. The restaurant is reached via a steep, winding third-of-

a-mile drive above the highway. But don't feel you have to dress up: Diners in T-shirts and shorts are welcomed, and there's a separate children's menu. Dinner only. Closed Sunday. ~ 900 North Route 191, Moab; 435-259-7146, fax 435-259-7626; e-mail lisa@emoab.com. MODERATE TO DELUXE.

What looks like a log fort from the outside is actually a haven for American cuisine. **Buck's Grill House** boasts grilled steaks, fresh fish and game and luscious homemade desserts, served in an understated Western atmosphere. House specialties include buffalo meatloaf, duck tamales and, for vegetarians, a polenta-zucchini lasagna. Dinner only. ~ 1393 North Route 191, Moab; 435-259-5201, fax 435-259-6092; e-mail grilling@lasal.net. MODERATE TO DELUXE.

Pizza reigns supreme at **Eddie McStiff's**, Moab's oldest legal brewery. Pastas, salads, sandwiches and steaks are offered, but the best bets are the special combination pizzas such as the Dosie Doe topped with roasted garlic, sundried tomatoes, parsley, scallions, and gorgonzola and parmesan cheeses. Beverages, including a selection of 12 house-microbrewed beers and homemade root beer, are served in mini-pitchers—a nice touch for desert thirsts. Dinner only. ~ 57 South Main Street, Moab; 435-259-2337, fax 435-259-3022; www.eddiemc stiffs.com, e-mail eddie@eddiemcstiffs.com. BUDGET TO MODERATE.

> Once the home of the world's richest uranium miner, the Sunset Grill is now Moab's most upscale restaurant.

The **Center Café and Market Bistro** is year-in and year-out one of Utah's finest restaurants. The eclectic menu offers dishes ranging from seafood specials to beef, poultry and vegetarian entrées, such as roasted eggplant lasagna. The café's deli allows you to build a budget-friendly picnic lunch with a nice array of imported cheeses and meats. Closed December and January. ~ 60 North 100 West, Moab; 435-259-4295; www.centercafemoab. com, e-mail chefmcc2@frontiernet.net. DELUXE.

Breakfasts, and only breakfasts, are doled out at **The Jailhouse Café**. Housed in the town's historic jail, the restaurant churns out thick stacks of pancakes, french toast, a rich variety of omelets, as well as lower-calorie granolas. Get there early to avoid the long lines that often form in summer. Closed November to early March. ~ 101 North Main Street, Moab; 435-259-3900. BUDGET.

SHOPPING

At first glance, Moab doesn't appear to be a mecca for shoppers. But take some time to look around town and you'll find not only the requisite souvenir and T-shirt shops but also a surprising number of noteworthy exceptions, ranging from art galleries to rock vendors.

The best rock shop in Moab also happens to be the best rock shop in southeastern Utah. The **Moab Rock Shop** not only has a large collection of fossils, crystals and minerals, but you also can find maps and guidebooks here. Limited winter hours. ~ 600 North Main Street, Moab; 435-259-7312.

Hogan Trading Co. carries an impressive variety of Indian art such as kachina dolls, pottery and alabaster sculptures. The store also carries Navajo rugs as well as Southwestern prints, baskets and sand paintings. ~ 100 South Main Street, Moab; 435-259-8118, fax 435-259-2618; www.hogantrading.com.

What must be one of the most comprehensive collections of books on the Southwest can be found at **Back of Beyond Bookstore**. Edward Abbey, Tony Hillerman and others with local ties take up the most shelf space, and there is a plethora of works on the outdoors, natural and Western history, American Indian studies and the environment. Popular novels are stocked, along with hiking, biking and river guides. ~ 83 North Main Street, Moab; 435-259-5154, 800-700-2859, fax 435-259-8883; www.backofbeyondbooks.com, e-mail backobey@citilink.net.

The hub for sports of all sorts, **Rim Cyclery** sells practical outdoor gear, footgear, regional guides and tools of the trade. Wise-cracking mechanics proffer knowing advice about destinations if you seem credible. "Cool central" for serious sporting athletes, or at least those who look the part. Closed Tuesday in January. ~ 94 West 100 North, Moab; 435-259-5333, 888-304-8219; www.rimcyclery.com.

NIGHTLIFE Utah's strict liquor laws mean an abbreviated bar scene. Moab fares better than most with a few nightspots.

One of the oldest nightly entertainments in the Moab area is **Canyonlands By Night**, a boat trip at sunset up the Colorado River. Complete with light and sound show, the voyage offers a unique perspective on river landmarks. Canyonlands also offers a nightly Dutch-oven dinner, cooked and eaten on the banks of the Colorado. April to October only. ~ 1861 North Route 191, Moab; 435-259-2028, 800-394-9978, fax 435-259-2788; www. canyonlandsbynight.com, e-mail info@canyonlandsbynight.com.

Live music and/or dancing on weekends keep **Rio Colorado Restaurant and Bar** hopping. This is a private club with cover on weekends. ~ Center Street and 100 West, Moab; 435-259-6666.

Two brewpubs are popular haunts for telling tales of slick-rock biking and four-wheel excursions. **Eddie McStiff's** is in the heart of downtown. ~ 57 South Main Street, Moab; 435-259-2337. One-half mile south is the **Moab Brewery**. ~ 686 South Main Street, Moab; 435-259-6333.

PARKS

HIDDEN ►

DEAD HORSE POINT STATE PARK 🏃 This 5250-acre mesa 2000 feet above the Colorado River has been preserved as a park that offers innumerable possibilities for hikers, campers and other outdoor enthusiasts. Park facilities include a wheelchair-accessible visitors center, picnic areas and restrooms. Day-use fee, $7 per vehicle. ~ From Moab go north on Route 191 nine miles, then south on Route 313 for 22 miles; 435-259-2614, fax 435-259-2615.

▲ There are 21 sites with electric hookups (no water hookups for RVs); $14 per night. Reservations are recommended ($7 reservation fee): 800-322-3770.

ARCHES NATIONAL PARK 🏃 🚲 Popular with plenty of easily accessible geologic wonders, Arches National Park is a magnet for the recreational-vehicle crowd and back-country enthusiasts alike. Guided walks (some for a fee) are offered March through October and may be arranged through the visitors center. The park features picnic areas, a visitors center and restrooms. The vehicle entrance fee is $10, good for seven days. ~ Route 191, five miles north of Moab; 435-719-2299, fax 435-719-2305; www.nps.gov/arch, e-mail archinfo@nps.gov.

Dead Horse Point got its name, legend claims, when cowboys corralled wild horses here, selected the best of the herd, and left the rest to die.

▲ There are 52 sites at Devil's Garden; $15 per night. Reservations: 877-444-6777.

CANYONLANDS NATIONAL PARK—ISLAND IN THE SKY 🏃 🚲 This "island" mesa, 6000 feet in elevation, features rugged and beautiful terrain veined with hiking trails. The sparse vegetation and rain on the Island does not keep wildlife like foxes, coyotes and bighorn sheep from calling this land their home. The facilities at this park include picnic areas, a visitors center and vault toilets. Bring all you will need; the visitors center sells limited amounts of bottled water. The vehicle entrance fee is $10, good for seven days in all Canyonlands districts. ~ From Moab go north on Route 191 nine miles, then Route 313 for 26 miles; 435-719-2313, fax 435-719-2300; www.nps.gov/cany, e-mail canyinfo@nps.gov.

▲ There are 12 primitive sites at Willow Flat; $10 per night. No water available.

Outdoor Adventures

FISHING

Lake Powell is the most popular place in the region to go fishing; the expansive reservoir is rich in catfish, bass, crappie and rainbow trout. Elsewhere in the area, the Colorado, Green and San Juan rivers are hard to access because of the steep canyon walls that contain them. But several small lakes in the Manti–La Sal National Forest, west of Monticello and east of Moab, are stocked with trout.

For licenses, equipment and advice, visit **Canyonlands Outdoor Sports**. ~ 446 South Main Street, Moab; 435-259-5699.

RIVER RUNNING & BOAT TOURS

The mighty Colorado River weaves its way through the desert rock of southeastern Utah en route to its final destination in the Gulf of Mexico. Burnt sienna–colored water rushes boldly in some sections, slowing to a near crawl in others. Kayaking, canoeing, whitewater rafting and jetboat tours are abundant throughout the region. For information on the river runs, see "Up the River" in this chapter.

LAKE POWELL AREA   At Lake Powell, you can "see Rainbow Bridge and leave the driving to someone else." Guided full-day tours of the monument are available from **Bullfrog Marina**, which also leads an early-evening cruise past archaeological sites. ~ 800-528-6154. **Wahweap Marina** also leads tours of Rainbow Bridge and has shorter sightseeing tours to Antelope and Navajo canyons. ~ 800-528-6154.

SAN JUAN COUNTY AREA   In the San Juan area, try **Wild Rivers Expeditions**. ~ 101 Main Street, Bluff; 435-672-2244, 800-422-7654; www.riversandruins.com.

MOAB AREA   To explore canyons such as Westwater (northeast of Moab via Route 70) by kayak or raft contact **Tag-A-Long River Expeditions**. ~ 452 North Main Street, Moab; 435-259-8946, 800-453-3292; www.tagalong.com. **Western River Expeditions** leads kayak and rafting tours as well. ~ 225 South Main Street, Moab; 435-259-7019, 866-904-1163; www.westernriver.com.

Like ducks in a shooting gallery, you can't miss finding a professional river-running company along the Moab highway. All enjoy good reputations and can verse travelers in the water's idiosyncracies. Alphabetically first is **Adrift Adventures**. ~ 378 North Main Street; 435-259-8594, 800-874-4483; www.adrift.net. **Canyonlands by Night** is another reliable operator. ~ 1861 North Route 191; 435-259-5261, 800-394-9978; www.canyonlandsbynight.com. Or take to the whitewater with **Sheri Griffith River Expeditions**. ~ 2231 South Route 191; 435-259-8229, 800-332-2439; www.griffithexp.com.

SWIMMING

Desert summers heat up like a microwave oven. When temperatures soar into the 90s and above, any body of water looks good. Many people opt for a dip in the Colorado or Green rivers and, of course, in Lake Powell.

SAN JUAN COUNTY AREA   For swimming, fishing, picnicking and nonmotorized boating in the Monticello area try **Lloyd's Lake** on the road to Abajo Peak, about three miles west of town. Another good swimming hole is the multipurpose **Recapture Reservoir** about five miles north of Blanding. Turn west off Route 191 and follow the signs.

CLIMBING

Experienced climbers can test their mettle on the precipices near Fisher Towers, Arches National Park and in the Potash region

"Up the River"

Running the rivers in Utah allows a pure view of the land from deep within the canyons. It's a different world, thousands of feet away from manmade distractions. Sometimes the only sounds are the whoop of a crane, the river's gurgle or a paddle dipping into the water. Novices shouldn't be deterred by the challenging Class V rapids of sections in Cataract Canyon; tours are offered in all degrees of difficulty. Those seeking rushing rapids must be willing to put up with frigid mountain runoff in early spring. By mid-summer, the rivers are warmer and mellower. Because of the rivers' idiosyncracies, it's wise to verse yourself in their courses before taking the plunge.

Along the Colorado River northeast of Moab via Route 70 is **Westwater**, which packs a real punch in a relatively short jaunt. Pre-Cambrian, black-granite walls line the deep canyons and stand in contrast to the red-sandstone spires above. Westwater, with 11 telling sections sporting names like Skull Rapid, is a favorite destination for whitewater junkies.

The most heavily used section of the Colorado River is below **Dewey Bridge** off Route 128. When runoff peaks, there are a few mild rapids between here and Moab. But for most of the year expect to kick back and enjoy a scenic float. **Fisher Towers**, **The Priest and Nuns** rock formations and **Castle Valley**—backdrop of many favorite Westerns—can be lazily viewed from a raft, kayak or canoe, or in low water on an air mattress or inner tube.

Floating along the sinuous Green River and in the rapidless **Labyrinth and Stillwater canyons** is a first choice for families and river neophytes more interested in drifting past prehistoric rocks than paddling through a wild ride.

When the Colorado meets the Green River in the heart of Canyonlands National Park, crazy things happen. Below the confluence is the infamous **Cataract Canyon**, where no fewer than 26 rapids await river runners. During the period of highwater (usually May and June), Cataract can serve up some of the country's toughest rapids, aptly named Little Niagara and Satan's Gut. When the river finally spills into Lake Powell at Hite Crossing, 112 miles downriver from Moab, boaters breathe a sigh of relief.

Unique to the **San Juan River**, another tributary of Lake Powell, are sand waves. These rollercoaster-like dips and drops are caused by shifting sands on the river bottom. Below the town of Mexican Hat, the San Juan meanders among deep goosenecks through the scenic Cedar Mesa Anticline and charges through reasonable rapids before spilling into Lake Powell.

For information on outfitters, see "River Running & Boat Tours" in Outdoor Adventures.

near Moab and Indian Creek east of the Canyonlands Needles entrance. Sunbaked walls make summer climbing a drag, but temperatures are generally pleasant during the rest of the year. Deep, sunless canyons are also prime ice-climbing spots in the winter and perfect for canyoneering the rest of the year.

Rentals, gear, pointers and directions to climbs can be found at **Pagan Mountaineering**. ~ 59 South Main Street #2, Moab; 435-259-1117; www.paganmountaineering.com.

CROSS-COUNTRY SKIING

The only commercial ski area in the region, Blue Mountain in the Abajo range near Monticello is now defunct. But Nordic aficionados still crisscross the slopes, ski the trees and camp out in snow caves.

MOAB AREA The La Sal Mountains are the second-highest range in the state, so adequate white stuff is rarely a problem. There is continuing, but as yet unfulfilled, talk about developing an alpine resort here. Snow-filled meadows beckon cross-country skiers. **Rim Cyclery** rents cross-country ski equipment and snowshoes in Moab. Closed Tuesday in January. ~ 94 West 100 North; 435-259-5333, 888-304-8219; www.rimcyclery.com.

JEEP TOURS

Much of Southeastern Utah's rugged, undeveloped wilderness remains inaccessible to regular vehicles. For that reason, many visitors opt for a jeep tour.

MOAB AREA With **Adrift Adventures** discover the stunning beauty of the natural Gemini Bridges located northwest of Moab; from an overlook here, you'll see La Sal Mountain and the surrounding layers of red sculpted rock. ~ 378 North Main Street, Moab; 435-259-8594, 800-874-4483; www.adrift.net.

For more extensive history and sightseeing tips on Lake Powell, Stan Jones' *Boating and Exploring Map* is essential to your enjoyment and is available at almost any Lake Powell shop.

Dan Mick's Guided Tours will take you to the spectacular Onion Creek. You'll pass fluted red cliffs and drive through the creek with water splashing at your wheels. A one-man operation with a wealth of knowledge of the outback in this corner of Utah, Dan will take you out in your Jeep, a rented Jeep, or his own Jeep. ~ 600 Mill Creek Drive, Moab; 435-259-4567; www.danmick.com, e-mail tours@danmick.com.

For a journey deep into the Needles, Maze or Island in the Sky districts of Canyonlands National Park, or if you have a specific itinerary in mind, contact **Tag-A-Long Expeditions**. Tag-A-Long offers packages ranging from half-day tours to week-long customized trips. ~ 452 North Main Street, Moab; 435-259-8946, 800-453-3292; www.tagalong.com.

GOLF

The desert heat seems to keep golf courses from springing up in southeastern Utah, but the few available ones are well-maintained, albeit not championship in caliber.

MOAB AREA In Moab, there's the 18-hole **Moab Golf Course**. ~ 2705 South East Bench Road; 435-259-6488.

Clippity-clopping leisurely on horseback is one of the best ways to explore the red-rock landscape and river bottomlands around Moab.

RIDING STABLES

MOAB AREA Horseback rides for guests can be arranged through **Sorrel River Ranch**. ~ Route 128, 17 miles northeast of Moab; 435-259-4642, 877-359-2715; www.sorrelriver.com. A steed can also be found at **Red Cliffs Lodge**. ~ Milepost 14, Route 128, Moab; 435-259-2002, 866-812-2002; www.redcliffs lodge.com.

The Moab area has become mountain-biking central for gearheads throughout the West. Miles and miles of dirt, sandstone and paved trails within a 40-mile radius offer options for fat-tire enthusiasts of all abilities.

BIKING

LAKE POWELL AREA Outfitters are an absolute necessity if you are planning to tour the remote **Canyonlands Maze District**. You can zigzag on the slickrock trails in Teapot Canyon en route to the rock fins of the Doll House. The inaccessibility of the Maze ensures that few others will traverse your cycling tracks.

Canyonlands is spectacular from any vantage point, but to really enjoy its splendor from the ground up, take the 100-mile roundtrip **White Rim Trail**. The trip typically takes about four days and meanders through rainbow-colored canyons and basins, skirting the Colorado and Green rivers. Since it's almost impossible to carry enough water and supplies in your panniers, a supported trip from an outfitter is recommended. The trail starts 40 miles from Moab via Routes 191 and 313 and Shafer Trail Road.

SAN JUAN COUNTY AREA **Gold Queen Basin** in the Abajo range near Monticello winds through nine miles of fragrant aspen and pine stands to the Blue Mountain skiing area. Mountain greens provide stark contrast to the red-rock country in the north. Take the ski area road due west of Monticello and follow the signs.

MOAB AREA By far the most popular ride is the **Slickrock Bike Trail**, a technically demanding grunt. Slickrock has become so well known that in spring cyclists line up wheel to wheel at the trailhead. Super steep to the point of being nearly vertical in some sections, Slickrock's 9.6-mile trail can take up to six hours to complete. But canyon, river and rock views, coupled with thrilling descents are dividends to those willing to work. Not for the faint of heart, leg or lung.

Kane Creek Road begins as a flat, paved, two-lane road that hugs the Colorado River. It's the gateway to numerous biking trails. Access Kane Creek from Route 191, just south of downtown Moab.

The **Moab Rim Trail**, about 2.5 miles from the intersection, is a short route for experienced cyclists that climbs steadily from the trailhead. Views of the La Sal Mountains and Arches vie for your attention; don't forget to look for ancient petroglyphs on rock walls.

Several miles down Kane Creek Road the pavement turns to dirt as it climbs through the canyon. You can head toward the **Hurrah Pass Trail** (17 miles) at this point. Another fun ride is **Behind the Rocks** (25 miles), which ends on Kane Creek Road. Pick up the trailhead 13 miles south of town via Route 191. The trailhead will be on the right side of the road marked Pritchett Arch. As its name suggests, ride behind the rocks and through Pritchett Canyon. Consult a detailed topographic or bike map before embarking on these journeys, as it is easy to get lost amid the sandstone.

There may be other traffic on the famous **Kokopelli's Trail**, but you're likely to share space with animals as humans on this trail that links Moab with Grand Junction, Colorado. Single-track trails, four-wheel-drive roads, dirt-and-sand paths for traversing mesas, peaks and meadows—you'll find them all along the 128 miles. Detailed maps showing access points are available at bike shops and the Moab Visitors Center.

American Indians considered the humpbacked Kokopelli to be a magic being, and Kokopelli's Trail more than lives up to its namesake.

Follow your nose to **Onion Creek** four-wheel-drive trail. The colorful, easy-to-moderate, 19-mile trail, with views of rock, river and mountains, saves its toughest hill until the end. Take Route 128 north 20 miles from Moab; watch for the turnoff between mileposts 20 and 21, near the road to Fisher Towers.

Hidden Canyon Rim is also called "The Gymnasium." The eight-mile trip can be completed in three hours by almost anyone. About 25 minutes from Moab via Route 191 to Blue Hills Road, the trailhead is approximately three and a half miles from the road.

When the desert turns furnace hot, cyclists pedal for the hills. In the La Sal Mountains near Moab, try **Fisher Mesa Trail**. The 18-mile roundtrip passage appeals to less-experienced riders. Drive 15 miles north of Moab on Route 128 to the Castle Valley turnoff. Take the road about 13 miles to where the pavement ends. Look for Castleton/Gateway Road. The trail begins on the left side off this road about four miles from the turnoff.

Bike Rentals For friendly advice, bike rentals or to arrange private guides or fully supported tours, try **Escape Adventures and Moab Cyclery**. ~ 391 South Main Street, Moab; 435-259-7423, 800-596-2953; www.escapeadventures.com. **Western Spirit Cycling** also does the White Rim, as well as longer Telluride-to-Moab and Bryce-to-Zion trips. ~ 478 Mill Creek Drive, Moab; 435-259-8732, 800-845-2453; www.westernspirit.com. Also try

Rim Cyclery for bikes and equipment. Closed Tuesday in January. ~ 94 West 100 North, Moab; 435-259-5333, 888-304-8219; www.rimcyclery.com. **Poison Spider Bicycles** also has mountain, road and kids' bikes for rent. ~ 497 North Main Street, Moab; 435-259-7882, 800-635-1792; www.poisonspiderbicycles.com. Don't forget **Slick Rack Cycles**, which rents and sells bikes and gear. ~ 415 North Main Street, Moab; 435-259-1134, 800-825-9791; www.slickrack.com.

Coyote Shuttle offers drop-offs for cyclists who want to do one-way rides. The firm also arranges trips through local bike shops. ~ 435-259-8656; www.coyoteshuttle.com.

Expect the unexpected when hiking in the Utah desert. For around the next bend there could be Indian petroglyphs, a stunning rock bridge or, be prepared—a rattlesnake. All distances listed for hiking trails are one way unless otherwise noted.

HIKING

LAKE POWELL AREA If you can tear yourself away from the water, Lake Powell has plenty of petroglyphs, arches and archaeological sites waiting to be explored.

Up the Escalante River arm, about 25 miles from Halls Crossing marina is **Davis Gulch Trail** (1.5 miles). Climb through the lovely "cathedral in the desert" and the Bement Natural Arch to what some consider one of the lake's prettiest sections.

John Wayne, Zane Grey and Teddy Roosevelt all visited the Rainbow Lodge. It's now the **Rainbow Lodge Ruins**. The trail (7 miles) begins about a mile past Rainbow Bridge National Monument and skirts painted rocks, cliffs and Horse Canyon en route to its destination in the shadow of Navajo Mountain.

Take the left-hand spur from the monument and head toward Elephant Rock and Owl Arch via the **North Rainbow Trail** (6 miles).

SAN JUAN COUNTY AREA Like spires reaching for the sky, the striped rock formations of **Canyonlands National Park—Needles** beckon visitors to explore their secrets. A trail starting at Elephant Hill trailhead meanders through Elephant Canyon with optional side trips to Devil's Pocket, Cyclone Canyon and Druid Arch. Depending on your chosen route, the trip can be as long or as short as you choose.

Chesler Park (3 miles), one of the park's most popular routes, is a desert meadow amid the rock needles. Accessible from the Elephant Hill trailhead.

Lower Red Lake Canyon Trail (8.5 miles) leads to the gnarly Cataract Canyon section of the Colorado River. Start this steep and demanding multiday hike at Elephant Hill trailhead.

A spur of the Trail of the Ancients, the **Butler Wash** (.5 mile) interpretive trail is exceedingly well marked with cairns and trail symbols. After crossing slickrock, cacti, juniper and piñon, the hiker is rewarded with an Anasazi cliff-dwelling overlook. Take Route 95 west from Blanding. Turn right between mile markers 111 and 112.

Several scenic hikes are found within **Natural Bridges National Monument.** Paths to each bridge are moderate to strenuous in difficulty, and you may encounter some steep slickrock. But the National Park Service has installed handrails and stairs at the most difficult sections.

Owachomo Bridge Trail (.2 mile) is the shortest of three hikes at Natural Bridges National Monument; it provides an up-close and personal view of the oldest of the bridges.

MOAB AREA Canyonlands National Park—Island in the Sky, provides both short walks and long hikes for exploring some of its most outstanding features. **Upheaval Dome Crater View Trail** (.5 mile) is a short hike to the overlook of dramatic Upheaval Dome; viewing its different stratified layers provides a glimpse into its millions of years of geologic history.

You can also traverse the entire dome via the **Syncline Loop Trail** (8 miles), an arduous route with a 1300-foot elevation change.

Neck Spring Trail (5 miles) also leads through the diverse landscape of the Canyonlands—Island in the Sky district. From the trail, hikers can view seasonal wildflowers and the sandstone cliffs of the Navajo Formation. The trail follows paths that were originally established by animals using the springs, so don't be surprised if a mule deer or chipmunk crosses your path.

Arches National Park teems with miles of trails among the monoliths, arches, spires and sandstone walls.

HIDDEN ► **Delicate Arch Trail** (1.5 miles) sports a 480-foot elevation change over sand and sandstone to Delicate Arch. Along the way, you'll cross a swinging bridge and climb over slickrock. The most photographed of all the famous arches, Delicate Arch invites long, luxurious looks and several snaps of the Instamatic.

Another Arches favorite, **Windows** (.5 mile or less) culminates with an opportunity to peer through the rounded North and South Windows, truly one of nature's greater performances. This easy

AUTHOR FAVORITE

From the Glen Canyon Dam, there is a short hike to a lovely arch in a recently charted area called **Wiregrass Canyon** (1.5 miles). Drive about eight miles north of the dam on Route 89 to Big Water. Turn east on Route 277 to Route 12 and continue four and a half miles south on Warm Creek Road to the start of Wiregrass Canyon. Bring a picnic—and a camera.

and accessible trail starts just past Balanced Rock at the Windows turnoff.

A stream will be at your side for the length of the **Negro Bill Canyon Trail** (2 miles), a favorite Moab stomping ground. Negro Bill ends up at Morning Glory Bridge, the sixth-longest rock span in the U.S. At canyon's end is a spring and small pool. From Moab, take Route 128 three miles east of the junction with Route 191.

The **Canyonlands Field Institute** sponsors seminars, workshops, field trips and naturalist hiking for groups of eight or more. Contact them for the schedule. ~ P.O. Box 68, Moab, UT 84532; 435-259-7750, 800-860-5262; www.canyonlandsfieldinst.org.

Transportation

▼ ▼ ▼ ▼ ▼ ▼ ▼ ▼ ▼ ▼

CAR

From the Colorado border, **Route 70** heads due west forming the northern boundary of the region. **Route 191** travels north–south, passing through Moab, Monticello, Blanding and Bluff and intersecting the entrance roads to Arches and Canyonlands National Parks. Those traveling west from the Colorado border near Grand Junction should opt for **Route 128**, a scenic byway that connects Route 70 with Route 191 at Moab.

Route 95 branches off Route 191 west from Blanding toward Natural Bridges, while both Route 95 and **Route 276** lead to Glen Canyon National Recreation Area and Lake Powell.

AIR

Few visitors to southeastern Utah choose to come by commercial air. Perhaps one reason they don't is that commercial carriers are continually changing at Moab's **Canyonlands Field**. Several flightseeing charters operate from this airport. Shuttle service into Moab is provided by **Roadrunner Shuttle** (435-259-9402; www.roadrunnershuttle.com).

Visitors to Lake Powell fly into Arizona's **Page Municipal Airport**. Page is served daily by Great Lakes Airlines. In Utah, airstrips help connect vast desert distances divided by mountains, canyons and rivers. There are public landing fields at Blanding and near the Bullfrog and Halls Crossing marinas.

TRAIN

The **Amtrak** station nearest to the Moab and San Juan County areas is in Green River, about 50 miles north of Moab. The "Zephyr" hits points west to California. ~ 800-872-7245; www.amtrak.com.

FERRY

Lake Powell ferry service, on Route 276 between Halls Crossing and Bullfrog marinas, runs six times a day westbound (at two-hour intervals from 8 a.m. to 6 p.m.) and six times eastbound (9 a.m. to 7 p.m.) from mid-May through September. There are four crossings a day (8 a.m. to 3:30 p.m.) from November to mid-April, five transits daily during shoulder seasons. The 3.2-mile crossing aboard the 150-foot *John Atlantic Burr* saves 130 road miles. The charge is $16 per standard passenger vehicle. ~ Halls Crossing Marina; 435-684-3000.

CAR RENTALS   The main auto-rental firm in Moab is **Thrifty Car Rental** (435-259-7317, 800-847-4389) at the Moab Valley Inn lobby (711 South Main Street). In addition to conventional vehicles, it offers four-wheel-drive vehicles, a must for exploring the backcountry roads and byways.

Other rental agencies strictly renting four-wheel-drive vehicles in Moab include **Farabee Jeep Rentals** (435-259-7494).

TAXIS   Shuttle services take the place of taxis in Moab. For bike and raft shuttle service, or trips to or from the airport or Amtrak station, contact **Roadrunner Shuttle**. ~ 435-259-9402.

SIXTEEN

Southwestern Colorado

From the Ancestral Puebloan, who built their remarkable cliff dwellings here 700 years ago and then mysteriously disappeared, to the 19th-century miners who made millions in the silver and gold fields, southwestern Colorado has always been synonymous with adventure. Today, myth and dreams surround this region that is home to American Indians, cowboys who work cattle in the high country and tourists who flock to its mountain meadows and peaks.

Arguably the most picturesque mountain range in the Americas, the local San Juans compare favorably with the Swiss Alps.

Three hundred yearly days of sunshine and reliable water supplies cascading out of snow-capped mountains were probably two big reasons the Ancestral Puebloan became the first known settlers of the area—the same reason for today's thousands of yearly visitors. Originally nomadic, the Ancestral Puebloan eventually settled the fertile mesas, raising beans, corn and squash in the lush river valleys flowing out of the San Juan Mountains.

They first lived in caves or pit houses dug out of the ground, weaving baskets of yucca and hemp that earned their nickname—Basketmakers. They had no written language—historical records consist of paintings and carvings on cave walls that can still be seen today. Combined with other archaeological artifacts, including the architecturally unique dwellings made of rock dating back to A.D. 550, visitors now find only mute evidence of these early inhabitants.

The later Ancestral Pueblo people built the multistory cliff-side and mesa-top dwellings that are best preserved in Mesa Verde National Park's 52,000 acres, the first national park to be dedicated to preserving manmade artifacts. Other Ancestral Puebloan sites are more remote and less well known, such as the Sand Canyon Pueblo—possibly the largest ruin in the Southwest. The Ute Mountain Tribal Park surrounds Mesa Verde on three sides and contains stabilized but unrestored cliff dwellings.

These ancient Indians dispersed around A.D. 1200, gradually drifting away from Mesa Verde and nearby locations. Today, their descendants live along the Rio

Grande, on the Hopi mesas and at Zuni and Acoma. Later tribes—the Ute, Pawnee and Navajo—passed through, claiming the land by the 1600s. Around the same time, Spanish explorers stopped long enough to leave their mark.

The town of Silverton was founded in 1874, Cortez, now a small ranching community and access point to ancient and modern Indian lands, was first settled in 1889. Dolores, favored today by anglers, hikers and river runners, sprang to life when the railroad came to town in 1891, prospering for 60 years until the trains pulled out for good in the mid-20th century.

The railroad company built bridges over raging rivers and blasted through vertical rock cliffs to provide lucrative service to the mines, which were churning out millions of dollars in gold and silver ore. As the boom continued and money flowed out of the mountains, the region grew to include gunfighters, prostitution, gambling and rowdy saloons. Today, many of the towns created by the mining and agriculture boom have found a new life catering to tourists eager to explore this rugged corner of the world.

The physical geography of southwestern Colorado cuts through two distinct landscapes. The jagged peaks of the San Juan Mountains attain heights above 14,000 feet near Silverton. Then the western edge of the Rockies drops off and the peaks merge with the Colorado plateau—characterized by dramatic mesas, buttes and graceful sandstone configurations carved over eons by wind and water.

Today's visitor to the southwestern corner of Colorado can experience the best of the region's scenic beauty and history. The largest city in this mountain region is Durango, population 14,000. Second is Cortez, with 8000, trailed by the smaller communities of Dolores, Mancos, Hesperus and Silverton. Far from interstate highways, each of these communities showcases the region's rich and varied history.

The towns are separated by vast reaches of trails to hike or ski, rivers to run or fish, forests to camp in or hunt, deserts spotted with ruins and canyons to ride in or explore. An outdoor-lover's mecca, Durango hosts several mountain-biking competitions—there are hundreds of miles of world-class bike trails on and off the roads of the entire region. Equestrians, hikers and backpackers trek the hundreds of pristine wilderness trails preserved from development. River rafters, canoeists and kayakers ply the waters of the Animas and Dolores rivers, claiming some of the most challenging whitewater in the world. Controlled hunting for deer and elk still attracts aficionados from far and wide, and the fishing is good. Add top-class skiing, world-class archaeological digs and warm hospitality served up with a historic Western flare and you have an idea of how the heirs of cowboys and Indians are doing things today.

Durango–Silverton Area

Steam trains sending up billowing clouds as they wind along river canyons. Brick office blocks, saloons with mirrored back bars, newspapers with handset type and grand hotels where the furniture is museum quality. Remote trails leading up through alpine forests to remote mountain lakes. Resorts accessible only by rail or helicopter. Chuckwagons and American Indian galleries. Is there any reason not to visit Durango and Silverton?

Each of these mountain towns has a distinctive spirit that will immediately transport you back in time. The largest community in these parts, **Durango** is a shady Animas River town with historic boulevards, one of the West's most popular tourist railroads and classic Victorian architecture. More placid, Silverton comes to life in the summer when the frontier-style hotels, restaurants and shops cater to the tourist trade. A well-preserved mining town, this community is an ideal base for jeep and fishing trips, hiking, mountain biking and tracking down ghost towns. Unspoiled and well preserved, here's your chance to slip back into the 19th century.

First laid out in 1881 to haul an estimated $300 million in gold and silver out of what is now the San Juan National Forest, the **Durango & Silverton Narrow Gauge Railroad**—a National Historic Landmark and a National Civil Engineering Landmark—is the biggest attraction in these two towns. Closed the first three weeks of November. Admission. ~ 479 Main Avenue, Durango; 970-247-2733, fax 970-259-3570; www.durangotrain.com, e-mail info@durangotrain.com.

This train out of yesteryear belches black, billowing gusts of smoke and cinders, exactly as it did in 1891. It still carries more than 200,000 passengers each year over the 45 miles of track between Durango and Silverton, one of the most stunning rail trips anywhere. In keeping with the historic responsibility of one of the

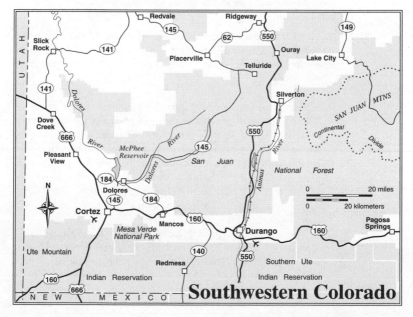

Southwestern Colorado

San Juan Skyway

This paved 227-mile loop trip from Durango was one of the first routes selected under a 1988 federal law directing the National Forest Service to designate the most picturesque roads in national forests as "scenic byways." While it is clearly marked, you don't really need special signs to tell you that you're on one of America's most scenic drives. Drivers unaccustomed to edgy mountain roads should take the route in the clockwise direction described here because the road segment south of Ouray is much easier to drive uphill than downhill.

MESA VERDE NATIONAL PARK   From Durango, take Route 160 for 27 fast miles to Mancos, the small town near the turnoff to Mesa Verde National Park (pages 663, 666). From there, go 20 miles northwest (right) on Route 184 to Dolores, where you may wish to visit the **Anasazi Heritage Center** (page 662).

LIZARD HEAD PASS   Turn northeast (right) onto Route 145 and follow the Dolores River for 40 miles as the highway grows steeper and climbs to the summit of 10,222-foot Lizard Head Pass, named for the nearby mountain with the 400-foot spire of granite on top. Rock climbers rate the towering monolith as one of the most difficult technical climbs on earth.

TELLURIDE   From Lizard Head Pass, Route 145 descends nine miles to the turnoff for the ski town of Telluride. If you're passing by early in the week, when the road into town is not jammed with traffic for the Bluegrass

longest remaining narrow-gauge routes, authentic gold-and-black 1880s Victorian-style coaches and open gondola cars are pulled by coal-fired, steam-powered locomotives originally made for the Denver & Rio Grande Railroad between 1902 and 1925. All equipment is kept in top condition at the station roundhouse in Durango. The **Roundhouse Museum** traces the history of the Denver & Rio Grande line with paintings, photographs and memorabilia. Admission is included with the train ticket price. ~ 479 Main Avenue; 970-247-2733.

The train chugs through remote areas of the national forest, crossing the Animas River several times, running parallel to the river for much of the route. These areas are accessible only by the train, on horseback or on foot. There are no roads through these steep-sided narrow gorges, pine forests and undisturbed lands that look much the same as they did in the 1880s.

Festival, the Jazz Festival, the Film Festival, or one of the dozen other festivals that cram the town's whole summer schedule, take a short detour into this spectacular little hideaway surrounded by 13,000-foot peaks and ride the free gondola that runs 'round-the-clock (except in October and April) to Coonskin Ridge, 2000 feet above town, for a great view.

RIDGEWAY AND OURAY   Route 145 continues for 12 more miles before intersecting Route 62 at Placerville. Turn northeast (right) here and drive 23 miles to Ridgeway, a ranching town in a pretty valley setting where residents include retired general Norman Schwartzkopf, actor Dennis Weaver and designer Ralph Lauren, whose logo decorates miles of fence on the way into town. Turn south (right) on Route 550 and drive 11 miles toward the seemingly impassable wall of jagged mountains surrounding Ouray, a quiet Victorian-style town known for its artist studios, hot springs and ice climbing.

RED MOUNTAIN PASS AND SILVERTON   South of Ouray, Route 550 climbs steep cliffs in a sweeping series of switchbacks and finally reaches the summit of 11,008-foot Red Mountain Pass, the highest point on the San Juan Skyway, and then descends to the turnoff for Silverton (page 650), a total distance of 23 miles.

DURANGO & SILVERTON NARROW GAUGE RAILROAD   The road then crests two more passes with magnificent views as it parallels the Durango & Silverton Narrow Gauge Railroad (page 651) along a different but no less spectacular route before descending along the Animas River to Durango, a distance of 47 miles, to complete an all-day journey you'll never forget.

The trip takes three and a half hours each way, with a two-hour layover in Silverton, covering an elevation gain of nearly 3000 feet from Durango. The train currently makes the run to Silverton from early May through October; during the winter months, it only travels halfway to Silverton and back. Starting in September, fall color is an exceptional time on the tracks when the forest colors envelop the swaying train cars. Hop aboard anytime for the lonesome train whistle, clattering metals and clouds of coal smoke that harken back to times when fortunes and accompanying romance rode the rails.

Housed in a 1904 Animas city school, Durango's **Animas Museum** offers both permanent and changing exhibits on the history and culture of the San Juan Basin. Permanent exhibits featured in the 1904 schoolhouse include Navajo and Ute artifacts, a restored classroom and the pioneer "Joy Cabin." The museum also features a research library, a photo archive, a gift shop and on-site gardens. Closed Sunday in summer, and Sunday and Monday from November through April. Admission. ~ 31st Street and West 2nd Avenue, Durango; 970-259-2402, fax 970-259-4749; www.animasmuseum.org, e-mail animasmuseum@frontier.net.

The **Center of Southwest Studies** is part of the Fort Lewis College Museum and Archive. Displays include Southwestern and American Indian artifacts, as well as books, photographs, documents and maps pertaining to the historic background of the entire Four Corners region. Closed weekends. ~ Fort Lewis College, College Heights, Durango; 970-247-7456; www.fortlewis.edu.

For a soothing dose of history updated in a modern context, **Trimble Hot Springs** offers refreshing access to an ancient mineral hot springs favored by Chief Ouray and his Ute warriors. The property includes an Olympic-size lap pool and two therapy pools; massages are available. This spot is a particular favorite with weary bike riders, hikers and skiers. Admission. ~ 6475 County Road 203, Durango; 970-247-0111; www.trimblehotsprings.com, e-mail ruedi@trimblehotsprings.com.

Molas Pass, 40 miles north of Durango on Route 550 at 10,910 feet, is the highest point on the road between Durango and Silverton. The views make you feel as if the world is at your feet. Maybe it is.

Silverton, "the mining town that never quit," is a historic testament to the boom years of the mining industry, with virtually every building on Greene Street dating to the early 20th century. The entire town is a registered National Historic Landmark. Among the most informative of these Victorian-era structures is the County Jail, built in 1902 and now home to the **San Juan County Historical Museum**. Exhibits detail early-day Silverton life and mining history. The museum is open from Memorial Day to mid-October, but the archive and research facility, in an adjacent building, is open year-round on Monday and Wednesday afternoons and by appointment. Admission. ~ Courthouse Square, 1567 Greene Street, Silverton; 970-387-5838, 970-387-5309.

Next door to the old jail, the **San Juan County Court House** is capped by an ornate gold-painted dome and clocktower. It was built in 1907 and is still in use today. ~ 1557 Greene Street, Silverton; 970-387-5790.

The **Silverton Standard and Miner** is the oldest continuous newspaper and business in western Colorado. ~ 1139 Greene Street, Silverton; 970-387-5477; e-mail editor@silvertonstandard.com.

Completed in 1901, the **American Legion Hall** was the original home of the Western Federation of Miners. The brick structure contains a former dance hall on the second floor, now used for local theatrical productions. Legionnaires use the downstairs for a bar and a meeting room. ~ 1069 Greene Street, Silverton; 970-387-9885.

The **United Church of Silverton** was constructed in 1880 to house Silverton's Congregational Church at a time when the first call to worship was achieved by pounding on a saw blade. Constructed of stone, it is the oldest Congregational Church structure in the state still offering services, though the denomination has changed. The church is one of the rare wooden frame churches still standing, and is the subject of an Ansel Adams photograph of a white church with a steeple in the background. ~ 1060 Reese Street, Silverton.

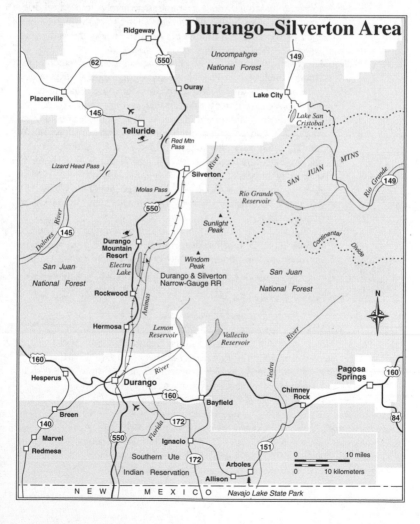

The town's public library, **Silverton Public Library** was erected in 1906. The interior furnishings are largely original period antiques, and the lower level has been restored through a mammoth local effort to provide library services. The library replaced a series of free reading rooms that had been scattered throughout the community since the 1880s. Closed Sunday and Monday. ~ 1111 Reese Street, Silverton; 970-387-5770, fax 970-387-0217; e-mail jleithau@frontier.net.

Thirteen miles northeast of Silverton, accessed by following Greene Street East, is **Animas Forks**, a ghost town where gold and silver ore were mined in the 1880s. Abandoned structures include houses, foundations and basic mine structures. A four-wheel-drive vehicle is recommended for the ride that passes through several shallow river beds as it follows the Animas River to its headwaters.

LODGING

The best-known historic hotel among many in the region is the **Strater Hotel**. Built in 1887, it is a repository of the world's largest collection of antique Victorian walnut furniture. Each of its 93 guest rooms is different; comfortable and impeccably cared for, they are furnished with antiques, and all have modern tiled bathrooms. A restaurant, a martini bar and a jacuzzi are added amenities. The building is a Durango landmark, located two blocks from the Durango & Silverton Narrow Gauge Train Station. Reservations may be scarce at times during the summer. ~ 699 Main Avenue, Durango; 970-247-4431, 800-247-4431, fax 970-259-2208; www.strater.com, e-mail sales@strater.com. MODERATE TO ULTRA-DELUXE.

Located a block closer to the train station, the 1898 **General Palmer Hotel** is another Victorian-era structure, furnished with antiques and reproductions. The 39 guest rooms are individually

AUTHOR FAVORITE

In Durango I'm partial to the **Rochester Hotel**, one of the town's oldest hotels. The Rochester has been in operation since 1892, when—under the name Peeple's Hotel—it rivaled the Strater and the General Palmer in prestige. It continued to thrive until the 1950s, then became a boardinghouse, a residential hotel and finally a flophouse. New owners rescued the hotel in 1993, converting its 33 old rooms to 15 spacious ones individually renovated in the spirit of movies filmed in the Durango area, including *How the West Was Won* and *City Slickers*. The hotel lobby is like a cowboy movie museum, its walls festooned with vintage posters and publicity stills. A full breakfast is included in the rates. ~ 721 East 2nd Avenue, Durango; 970-385-1920, 800-664-1920, fax 970-385-1967; www.rochesterhotel.com, e-mail stay@rochesterhotel.com. DELUXE TO ULTRA-DELUXE.

decorated with four-poster beds, pewter and brass lamps, etched glass and hand-crocheted bedspreads. Most are on the small side and some "inside rooms" have no windows, though all are well maintained. Continental breakfast included. ~ 567 Main Avenue, Durango; 970-247-4747, 800-523-3358, fax 970-247-1332; www. generalpalmerhotel.com, e-mail gphdurango@yahoo.com. MODERATE TO ULTRA-DELUXE.

The **Leland House Bed and Breakfast** offers six suites and four studios in a restored 1927 brick building. Each room is named after a historic figure associated with the home. A complimentary breakfast is served directly across the street at the 15-room Rochester Hotel, which is under the same management. ~ 721 East 2nd Avenue, Durango; 970-385-1920, 800-664-1920, fax 970-385-1967; www.leland-house.com, e-mail stay@ rochesterhotel.com. DELUXE TO ULTRA-DELUXE.

The 1892 **Gable House Bed & Breakfast** is housed in a large brick Queen Anne Victorian listed on the National Register of Historic Places. Each antique-filled room features hardwood floors, wallpaper and its own private entrance. Guests can relax on the first-floor wraparound porch or on one of two second-story balconies. A full gourmet breakfast is served in the dining room or outside in nice weather. ~ 805 East 5th Avenue, Durango; 970-247-4982; www.durangobedandbreakfast.com, e-mail ghbb@frontier.net. MODERATE TO DELUXE.

The guest rooms at the **Iron Horse Inn** are spacious bi-level suites, and all come with fireplaces and small refrigerators. Amenities include an indoor pool, a spa and a sauna. ~ 5800 North Main Avenue, Durango; 970-259-1010, 800-748-2990, fax 970-385-4791; www.ironhorseinndurango.com, e-mail information@ironhorseinndurango.com. MODERATE.

Jarvis Suite Hotel features studios as well as one- and two-bedroom suites decorated in a Southwest style. Suites are small but compensated by cozy living rooms and full kitchens. Rates represent an especially good deal for families who use the sleeper sofa in the living room. ~ 125 West 10th Street, Durango; phone/fax 970-259-6190, 800-824-1024; e-mail jarvis@frontier.net. DELUXE.

Tall Timber is among the most highly regarded properties in the United States. Accessible by the narrow-gauge train or helicopter only, it is situated in the heart of the San Juan National Forest in a pristine and peaceful valley, six miles from the nearest road. For privacy seekers who relish comforts, there are ten luxurious modern units with fireplaces and decks. Guests may use an indoor-outdoor pool, a sauna, a whirlpool, three hot tubs, a nine-hole golf course, a basketball court, ski and hiking trails and an exercise room. Horseback riding, fishing, flyfishing instruction, whitewater rafting, high-peak trekking and massage therapy are also available. Rates include meals and transportation to the resort.

◄ *HIDDEN*

Three-day minimum stay. Closed November and from January to mid-May. ~ 1 Silverton Star, Durango, CO 81301; 970-259-4813; www.talltimberresort.com. ULTRA-DELUXE.

Located 20 miles northeast of Durango, **Durango Resort on Vallecito Lake** is situated right on the lake. With 23 cabins to choose from, there's one to fit everyone's budget. Smaller cabins sleep two people and are priced in the budget to moderate range, while larger cabins can sleep 12 to 16 people and carry a deluxe-to-ultra-deluxe tab. Fishing, boating and horseback riding are some of the activities offered. Closed mid-October through April. ~ 14452 County Road 501, Bayfield; 970-884-2517, 866-280-5253, fax 970-884-7712; www.durangoresortonlake.com, e-mail rab@durangoresortonlake.com. BUDGET TO ULTRA-DELUXE.

Silverton's **Inn of the Rockies at the Historic Alma House** was built in 1898 and has been restored in keeping with that era. The small rooms are simply appointed with modern amenities, including queen- or king-size beds, as well as antique dressers and period wallpaper. Some rooms share a bath. Full breakfast is included. ~ 220 East 10th Street, Silverton; 970-387-5336, 800-267-5336, fax 970-387-5974; www.innoftherockies.com. MODERATE TO DELUXE.

The Grand Imperial Victorian Hotel offers 40 rooms with private baths, some with oak pull-chain toilets. Rooms feature antique decor such as brass beds, brocade settees and crystal chandeliers converted from candles to electricity. There are a restaurant and a saloon, complete with bullet holes in the back bar. The hotel is closed in November and April. ~ 1219 Greene Street, Silverton; phone/fax 970-387-5529, 800-341-3340; www.grandimperialhotel.com, e-mail info@grandimperialhotel.com. BUDGET TO MODERATE.

The nicest bed and breakfast in the entire region is **Blue Lake Ranch**, about 15 minutes southwest of Durango. The 200-acre property includes a main house with four antique and flower-bedecked rooms, two suites in the old barn, a three-story log cabin set in the woods, a homestead set on the river and eight outlying *casitas*. There are flower and herb gardens and a European-Southwestern breakfast including wheels of cheese, fruits, meats, cereal and juice every morning. Deer are frequent visitors. Breakfast is included. ~ 16000 County Road 140, Durango; 970-385-4537, 888-258-3525, fax 970-385-4088; www.bluelakeranch.com, e-mail bluelake@frontier.net. DELUXE TO ULTRA-DELUXE.

DINING

The Palace Restaurant wins recognition year after year as one of Durango's most popular restaurants in local opinion polls. A location adjacent to the narrow-gauge train station and its 200,000 yearly visitors does not hurt business; outdoor patio dining and pleasant Victorian decor are bonuses. Specialties include honey duck, chicken and dumplings and Colorado beef; vegetarian dishes can be made to order. Closed Sunday from November through May. ~ 505 Main Avenue, Durango; 970-247-2018, fax 970-247-0231; www.palacedurango.com, e-mail info@palacedurango.com. DELUXE TO ULTRA-DELUXE.

Seasons Rotisserie & Grill serves terrific New American comfort food in a warm and inviting atmosphere. Starters are familiar favorites with a twist, such as hoisin-glazed baby back ribs or fried calamari with grilled tomato salsa and lemon aioli. Satisfying entrées include butternut squash cannelloni with sage brown butter and braised Colorado lamb shank with creamy polenta. There's an excellent wine list as well. No lunch on Saturday and Sunday. ~ 764 Main Avenue, Durango; 970-382-9790, fax 970-382-0452; www.seasonsofdurango.com. DELUXE TO ULTRA-DELUXE.

A local favorite in the budget range is the **Durango Diner**. Nothing fancy here, just plain formica counters and tables, fast service and huge servings of standard breakfast and lunch selections such as bacon and eggs, pancakes, homemade hash browns, *huevos rancheros*, sandwiches and homemade desserts—all spiced with local gossip, making this a good place to find out what is going on around town. Breakfast and lunch are served. ~ 957 Main Avenue, Durango; 970-247-9889; www.durangodiner.com, e-mail thedurangodiner@hotmail.com. BUDGET.

At **Carver Brewing Co.** you can dine casually on fresh salads, eggs Benedict, sandwiches and locally brewed beer. Bread and pastries are baked in-house. Breakfast, lunch and dinner are served. No dinner on Sunday. ~ 1022 Main Avenue, Durango; 970-259-2545, fax 970-385-7268; www.carverbrewing.com, e-mail carvers@carverbrewing.com. BUDGET TO MODERATE.

The best Italian food in the area is found at another affordably priced restaurant, **Mama's Boy**. Ambience is zilch, with small,

AUTHOR FAVORITE

For a refreshing change of culinary pace in a region where "seafood" generally means rainbow trout, I head for **Red Snapper**. Although far from any ocean, the restaurant nevertheless manages to offer remarkably fresh seafood. Cajun shrimp and Colorado trout are among selections that vary daily. All this is served in a stylish contemporary setting highlighted by 200 gallons of aquariums filled with tropical fish. The 40-item salad bar is the best in town, and for dessert, Death by Chocolate should not be missed. Dinner only. ~ 144 East 9th Street, Durango; 970-259-3417, fax 970-259-3441; www.frontier.net/~thered snapper, e-mail theredsnapper@frontier.net. MODERATE TO ULTRA-DELUXE.

crowded tables, but the pizza is primo. Also check out the egg-plant parmesan and calzones, not to mention the Philly cheese steak sandwiches. Closed Sunday. ~ 32223 Route 550 North, Hermosa; 970-247-9053. BUDGET TO MODERATE.

Silverton is justifiably un-renowned for dining. Most restaurants cater to the narrow-gauge train passengers who have an hour or two layover at lunch time.

SHOPPING   Durango's Main Avenue and side streets are filled with gift shops and galleries. The best one in town, featuring fine art, jewelry and contemporary Western and American Indian crafts, is **Toh-Atin Gallery**. ~ 145 West 9th Street, Durango; 800-525-0384; www.toh-atin.com.

Termar Gallery offers an array of Indian, Spanish and Anglo fine arts, jewelry and pottery, as well as works by many of the best-known Southwestern artists. ~ 780 Main Avenue, Durango; 970-247-3728; www.termargallery.com.

If you're looking for the perfect vacation read, the knowledgable staff at **Maria's Bookshop** will gladly make a suggestion. Or you can leisurely browse the thousands of books lining the custom-made shelves. ~ 960 Main Avenue, Durango; 970-247-1488; www.mariasbookshop.com.

For an interesting assortment of antiques, collectibles, railroad memorabilia, and used and rare books, try **Southwest Book Trader**. ~ 175 East 5th Street, Durango; 970-247-8479.

Silverton contains a plethora of take-your-pick gift shops clustered mainly along Greene Street between 11th and 14th streets. None stand out. All seem to offer souvenir rocks, T-shirts, jewelry, cowboy hats, leather goods and train whistles, as well as practical area guidebooks, maps and camping gear.

NIGHTLIFE   Many of the area's evening offerings are seasonal. The **Bar D Chuckwagon** has a chuckwagon supper and Western show, which runs Memorial Day weekend through Labor Day. ~ 8080 County Road 250, Durango; 970-247-5753; www.bardchuckwagon.com.

The **Diamond Circle Theatre** features vaudeville and 19th-century melodramas. Closed Tuesday and in winter. Cover. ~ Strater Hotel, 699 Main Avenue, Durango; 970-247-3400, 877-325-3400; www.diamondcirclemelodrama.com.

The **Durango Pro Rodeo** presents professional rodeo events on Tuesday and Wednesday evenings in July. Cover. ~ La Plata County Fairgrounds, 25th Street and Main Avenue, Durango; 970-247-2308.

Aside from these activities, nightlife is pretty much limited to restaurants, bars and a few movie theaters. The **Diamond Belle Sa-**

loon features an antique gold-leaf filigree back bar, a honky-tonk piano player, live bluegrass music on Sunday, waitresses dressed in 1880s saloon-girl finery and bartenders with garters on their sleeves. ~ Strater Hotel, 699 Main Avenue, Durango; 800-247-4431; www.strater.com.

Silverton's nightlife makes Durango seems like Manhattan by comparison. Try the **Gold King,** a Victorian-appointed bar located in the Grand Imperial Victorian Hotel. Closed November to early May. ~ 1219 Greene Street, Silverton; 970-387-5834.

SAN JUAN NATIONAL FOREST   PARKS

The site is huge. The national forest covers about two million acres of southwestern Colorado, offering hundreds of miles of trails and the San Juan Skyway, a scenic byway connecting Durango, Silverton, Telluride and Cortez. Vallecito Reservoir and Lemon Reservoir, among other sites, satisfy anglers with trout, kokanee salmon, bluegill and crappie. Also here are rivers and boating, hunting grounds and some of the most spectacular scenery of alpine lakes, cataracts and waterfalls you'll ever see. Unusual geologic formations and historic mines add to the splendor. Deer, elk and eagles live in the pine and aspen forests that are a special treat during fall when bright colors are abundant. There are picnic areas and restrooms. ~ The national forest extends from Telluride to the New Mexico border, from McPhee Reservoir to Wolf Creek Pass, 30 miles east of Pagosa Springs. The main access is via Routes 160 and 550; 970-247-4874, fax 970-385-1243; www.fs.fed.us/r2/sanjuan.

With the towering elevations found in San Juan National Forest (peaking at 14,000 feet), snow is usually on the ground in the high country until July and may fall again as early as September.

▲ There are 48 campgrounds; less-developed sites are free while standard ones are $10 to $14 per night plus $2 to $4 for hookups. Reservations: 877-444-6777.

WEMINUCHE WILDERNESS   One of the nation's largest wilderness areas, Weminuche consists of 487,000 acres set aside by the federal government to retain its primeval character. The average elevation of the area is 10,000 feet and there are 400 miles of hiking trails. Hiking and horseback riding are allowed through this very rugged slice of the scenic West. Fishing is permitted while bicycles and motorized vehicles are not. There are no facilities here. ~ Located 26 miles northeast of Durango, main access is via hiking trails at Vallecito Reservoir, from trails outside of Silverton or Pagosa Springs, or via the Durango & Silverton Narrow Gauge Railroad; 970-247-4874, fax 970-375-2319.

▲ Backpack camping is allowed for groups of 15 or fewer.

▼▼▼▼▼▼▼▼▼▼▼▼▼▼▼
Cortez–Dolores Area

Many of southwestern Colorado's most fascinating destinations are a short drive from popular Mesa Verde. One of the finest Indian preserves in the Americas, the Ute Mountain Tribal Park offers a American Indian–led look at Anasazi country. You can also see another side of this region's special heritage at Lowry Ruins and Hovenweep National Monument, straddling the Colorado–Utah border. Because each is slightly off the beaten track, you'll be able to enjoy a leisurely uncrowded visit to this magical region.

SIGHTS

The scrubland desert north of the San Juan River is broken by mesas and isolated canyons where pre-Columbian Pueblo Indians lived until around 1300. Established on the Colorado–Utah border in 1923, **Hovenweep National Monument** contains 785 acres and five groups of ruins. These ruins are most noted for the substantial size of the community they once housed, as well as their square, oval, circular and D-shaped towers, indicating sophisticated masonry skills. Some of the walls stand 20 feet high despite the total deterioration of ancient mortar over the centuries. Admission. ~ 40 miles west of Cortez off Route 666; 970-562-4282; www.nps.gov/hove, e-mail hoveinfo@nps.gov.

Square Tower Ruins (just over the Utah border) are the best preserved. The visitors center (970-562-4282) at Square Tower is a good place to stop for information. All sites are essentially accessible by car, although hikes of varying lengths are necessary for close examination of the ruins. Noteworthy ruins include the two pueblos of **Cajon Ruins**, also located in Utah, which are the least well preserved, having been heavily vandalized before the monument was established, and **Holly, Hackberry Canyon, Horseshoe, Cutthroat Castle** and **Goodman Point Ruins**, located in Colorado.

Considered one of the world's largest collections of ancient Ancestral Pueblo artifacts, the **Anasazi Heritage Center** is adjacent to the 12th-century Dominguez and Escalante pueblos. The museum is operated by the Bureau of Land Management. There are ancient pottery exhibits, interactive displays, 12th-century archaeological sites and changing exhibits. Many of the museum items here were rescued prior to the flooding of an area now underwater at Dolores' McPhee Reservoir. Admission. ~ 27501 Route 184, Dolores; 970-882-5600, fax 970-882-7035; www.co.blm.gov/ahc.

The densest concentration of archaeological sites in the nation, the **Canyons of the Ancients National Monument** contains hundreds of archaeological sites, including many dwellings, petroglyphs, hunting camps and shrines that hold evidence of cultures spanning thousands of years. Located in a backcountry area with no water and minimal facilities, visitors are asked to go to the Anasazi Heritage Center to obtain information on how to get to this remote area. ~ 27501 Route 184, Dolores; 970-882-5600, fax 970-882-7035; www.co.blm.gov/canm.

The **Crow Canyon Archaeological Center** is a school and research center developed to create a greater understanding of the prehistoric Ancestral Puebloan who populated the Four Corners area. Visitors who have made advance reservations may take seasonal day tours of the laboratory research facilities and a working archaeological site, or sign up for cultural exploration programs led by Pueblo scholars from March through November. Fee for programs. ~ 23390 County Road K, Cortez; 970-565-8975, 800-422-8975, fax 970-565-4859; www.crowcanyon.org.

A tiny museum off Main Street in downtown Cortez, the **Cortez Cultural Center** displays exhibits of the Basketmaker and Pueblo periods of Ancestral Puebloan culture, as well as informative videos on various aspects of Ancestral Puebloan life. There is also a gift shop. Closed Sunday. ~ 25 North Market Street, Cortez; 970-565-1151, fax 970-565-4075; www.cortezculturalcenter.org, e-mail cultural@fone.net.

South of Cortez and surrounding nearby Mesa Verde on three sides, the **Ute Mountain Tribal Park** has long been considered sacred ground by the Ute Mountain tribe, whose reservation encompasses the park. Following the Mancos River valley, the site contains hundreds of surface ruins, cliff dwellings, petroglyphs and paintings. Maintained as a primitive area and administered by American Indians, this is one of the most evocative Ancestral Puebloan sites in all of southwestern Colorado.

Visitors must make reservations for a daily guided tour with a tribe member. The tours cover 82 miles in six to eight hours

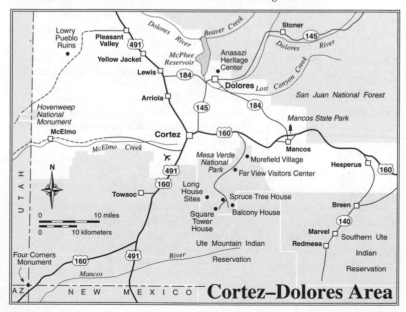

Cortez–Dolores Area

(half-day tours are also available)—stopping numerous times to walk through fields littered with thousands of distinctive pottery shards, to stand beside pit houses and burial mounds, to hike to petroglyphs, rock paintings and sentinel posts, or to scale ladders as high as 30 feet to reach excavated but unrestored Ancestral Puebloan ruins, left intact much the way they were 800 years ago. Bring water, food and a full tank of gas. A day here can be physically exerting and only primitive facilities are available. Closed November through March, depending on weather conditions. Admission. ~ Towaoc; 970-565-9653, 800-847-5485, fax 970-564-5317; www.utemountainute.com, e-mail utepark@fone.net.

Sleeping Ute Mountain west of the tribal park is a landmark you cannot and should not miss. From its head to the north, to its feet to the south, this mountain with an elevation of more than 9800 feet appears to be an American Indian lying on his back with his arms folded across his chest.

LODGING

Strip motels and chains predominate, but there's at least one unusual choice.

HIDDEN ►

A real get-away-from-it-all bed and breakfast is located between Cortez and Hovenweep National Monument. **Kelly Place** is situated on a secluded dirt road, miles from anywhere. Set in the midst of fruit orchards, vineyards and sandstone canyons, the two-bedroom suite, three adobe cabins and seven guest rooms in the main lodge are large and comfortably furnished in contemporary Western style. There are Indian ruins on the 38-acre property. Pottery and weaving instruction in the traditional Navajo style, as well as horseback riding and tours of the area, can be arranged before arrival. Breakfast included. ~ 14663 Road G, Cortez; 970-565-3125, 800-745-4885, fax 970-564-9440; www.kellyplace.com, e-mail kelly@kellyplace.com. MODERATE TO DELUXE.

DINING

Here we truly begin to stretch in seeking the best restaurants. Chains are well-represented along with a number of small cafés serving undistinguished food. However . . .

sights

AUTHOR FAVORITE

Of the many ancient Ancestral Pueblo ruins in the Four Corners area, some of my favorites are at **Hovenweep National Monument**, whose remote location, along with the hikes required to explore the unique square towers, keep tourist hordes away. For more information, see page 662.

Ponderosa Restaurant and Lounge serves hamburgers, sandwiches, Mexican dishes, home-baked pies, cinnamon rolls, cookies and muffins in a setting of nouveau K-Mart decor. This restaurant and lounge, convenient to McPhee Reservoir, is open for breakfast, lunch and dinner. ~ Railroad Drive and 8th Street, Dolores; 970-882-7910. BUDGET TO MODERATE.

Old Germany Restaurant, located in a historic Victorian building, serves shrimp, German-style sausage and Bavarian specialties, imported beers and German wines. Closed Sunday and Monday, and from November through January. ~ Route 145 and 8th Street, Dolores; 970-882-7549, fax 970-882-2170. MODERATE.

Genuine New Mexican food is served at plant-bedecked **Francisca's**. Entrées include *chiles rellenos*, chimichangas, stacked enchiladas and vegetarian dishes. Also popular are the Blue Curaçao margaritas. No lunch on Tuesday and Saturday. Closed Sunday and Monday. ~ 125 East Main Street, Cortez; 970-565-4093. BUDGET TO MODERATE.

The closest place to a tea room in Cortez is the delightfully chintzy **Earth Song Haven**, a low-key, friendly place. It occupies part of the eclectic Quality Bookstore, and there's something very restful about dining surrounded by books. You'll find tasty egg breakfasts, soups, salads and sandwiches at lunch, as well as tea, coffee and baked goods anytime. ~ 34 Main Street, Cortez; 970-565-9125. BUDGET.

Stop at the **Main Street Brewery** in a historic building in downtown Cortez and you'll find German-style brewskis as well as the usual pub grub, from pizza, burgers and fish and chips to bratwurst and sandwiches. The restaurant also serves Rocky Mountain trout and dry-aged Angus beef from its own herd. ~ 21 East Main Street, Cortez; 970-564-9112. BUDGET TO MODERATE.

SHOPPING

The gift shop at the **Anasazi Heritage Center** offers more than 400 titles on American Indian culture among its books on the Southwest, archaeology and children's topics, plus a variety of Ancestral Pueblo art items such as replica pottery. ~ 27501 Route 184, three miles west of Dolores; 970-882-5600, fax 970-882-7035.

Mesa Indian Trading/Mesa Verde Pottery has a selection of American Indian pottery crafted on the premises, as well as drums, sand paintings, collectible Ancestral Puebloan pottery, kachina dolls, weavings, fine jewelry and sculptures. Closed Sunday in winter. ~ 27601 East Route 160, Cortez; 970-565-4492, 800-441-9908, fax 970-565-3433; www.mesaverdepottery.com.

NIGHTLIFE

In Cortez, from Memorial Day through August, there are American Indian storytellers and dance performances at the **Cortez Cultural Center**. ~ 25 North Market Street, Cortez; 970-565-1151.

The **Ponderosa Restaurant and Lounge** may offer a semblance of nightlife at times, although it does close at 8 p.m. ~ Railroad Road and 8th Street, Dolores; 970-882-7910.

PARKS   **HOVENWEEP NATIONAL MONUMENT** 🚶 🚴 This 785-acre park straddles the Colorado–Utah border. Here you will find six major groups of Ancestral Pueblo ruins on the mythic Colorado plateau country. Camping, hiking and bike riding are allowed in the slickrock canyon country characterized by sweeping unobstructed vistas of the pastel high desert. The monument's facilities are limited to picnic sites and restrooms; restaurants, food, gas and supplies are available in Cortez (42 miles east), Blanding, UT (43 miles northeast) and Bluff, UT (38 miles southwest). Vehicle fee, $6. ~ Located 42 miles west of Cortez, access is via paved McElmo Canyon Road (recommended by rangers) three miles south of Cortez, or by the newly paved Pleasant View Road, 20 miles north of Cortez; 970-562-4282, fax 970-562-4283; e-mail hoveinfo@nps.gov.

▲ There are 25 tent sites and 5 RV sites; $10 per night. Bring your own firewood; campfires are permitted in fire grates, but wood gathering is prohibited.

MCPHEE RESERVOIR 🚶 🏇 ⛵ 🚤 🛥️ 🚣 This 4470-acre manmade lake is located northwest of Dolores and offers a full range of recreational opportunities, including fishing and boating. Most activities are centered around the developed areas at Lone Dome, House Creek and the McPhee Recreation Area. Open since the late 1980s, the lake is snuggled in between mountains to the west and the desert to the east. You'll find water, picnic sites, hiking trails and restrooms. ~ Located northwest of Dolores, main access is via Route 145; 970-882-7296.

▲ McPhee Recreation Complex has 76 sites (16 with hookups); $12 to $15 per night. House Creek Camp has 60 sites (17 with hookups); $12 per night plus $3 for electricity. Reservations: 877-444-6777; www.reserveusa.com.

AUTHOR FAVORITE

In Cortez, the gift shop at **Cortez Cultural Center** has some of the best prices in the region on a small selection of contemporary American Indian pottery, weavings and other crafts. You'll also find a museum, an art gallery, American Indian Games and a one-woman play held on the premises. Closed Sunday. ~ 25 North Market Street, Cortez; 970-565-1151, fax 970-565-4075; www.cortezcultural center.org, e-mail cultural@fone.net.

UTE MOUNTAIN TRIBAL PARK 🏃🚲🐎 This is a primitive area surrounding Mesa Verde on three sides. There are limited facilities, and access is restricted to group tours or those who reserve an Indian guide for backpacking, biking or horseback trips through the 125,000 acres of rugged canyon country and prehistoric Indian ruins. Surrounding the once-lush Mancos River Valley, the arid parklands sprawl through cactus and sage-studded habitats for elk, deer and mountain lions. Facilities include picnic tables and restrooms; the Ute Mountain Casino and Ute Mountain Travel Center have on-site lodging and dining. Other restaurants are available in Cortez. ~ Located 20 miles south of Cortez in Towaoc, access is via Route 160/491; 970-565-9653, 800-847-5485, fax 970-564-5317; www.utemountainute.com, e-mail utepark@fone.net.

▲ There are 12 primitive campsites; $12 per night per car. Reservations required.

Mesa Verde Area

Travel east from Cortez on Route 160 to reach the turnoff to Mesa Verde National Park. Ascending the highway to this legendary plateau, you'll enjoy panoramic views of the Four Corners region. The turnoff will take you south into the park; if you continue on Route 160, you'll head into Mancos, the town closest to Mesa Verde. The park has some food and lodging facilities in the high season; Mancos handles the overflow and off-season travelers. As you travel through this magical region, keep an eye out for the great Kachinas, the gods of the tribal lands. If you don't spot a real one, you'll have plenty of opportunity to purchase carved renditions of them in the Mesa Verde gift shop.

SIGHTS

Mesa Verde National Park is the number-one tourist attraction in southwestern Colorado, drawing 700,000 visitors yearly to its deserted canyons, outstanding views and preserved archaeological sites. Easily reached by a convenient loop drive, each of the cliff dwellings, pit houses and other Pueblo sites tucked inside sandstone cliffs is an authentic Southwestern treasure. A visit makes it clear that the builders of these structures were among the leading architects of their day. The park celebrated its hundredth birthday in 2006. Mid-June to mid-September is the busiest season; the best times to go are spring and fall. Admission. ~ Route 160; 970-529-4465, fax 970-529-4637; www.nps.gov/meve.

Although major cliff dwellings and mesa-top sites may be seen from overlooks on roadways, visits to other sites are strenuous, requiring hikes varying in altitude from 7000 feet to 8400 feet, aided by steps and ladders.

Traveling up the steep entrance road for four miles, **More-field Village** is the site of the park's only campground and the starting point for three hiking trails most popular for panoramic views. The shortest trail (1 mile) leads to **Point Lookout** at the tip of the mesa.

Nine miles farther along the road is the **Far View Visitors Center** (970-529-5036), the commercial hub of the park and location of most visitor services, where tickets can be purchased for guided tours of Cliff Palace, Balcony House and Long House. The visitors center displays contemporary American Indian arts and crafts. Closed mid-October to mid-April.

> Winter is the least crowded and most haunting time to visit Mesa Verde National Park.

In summer only, **Wetherill Mesa** may be accessed from a turnoff at Far View. It is a short walk to the **Step House**, where you can catch a mini-train (they operate every half-hour) to **Long House Sites**, containing subterranean pit houses from the Basketmaker period and structures from the Classic Pueblo period, around A.D. 1200.

The main park sites and a fascinating archaeological museum (970-529-4631) are clustered around Chapin Mesa, 20 miles from the park entrance, a minimum 45-minute drive. The museum contains exhibits and artifacts detailing the history of the Ancestral Puebloan peoples as well as the development of the national park. From here you can take a short hike to **Spruce Tree House**, one of the major park sites (which can also be viewed from an overlook).

Other significant sites and isolated cliff dwellings, carved improbably out of sheer rock faces, are accessible via the Mesa Top Loop Road. The westerly loop, a paved road well marked with signs, leads over its two-mile length past several interesting sites, including **Square Tower House**, pit houses and Pueblo ruins, **Sun Point** overlook at the edge of **Fewkes Canyon** and **Cliff Canyon** and the **Sun Temple**. The easterly loop is approximately the same length, also paved. It leads through similar pine, scrub brush and sage hillsides along the mesa top to numerous view sites as well as the **Cliff Palace** and **Balcony House**.

Guided interpretive tours led by rangers are conducted at all major cliff dwellings in the summer. In winter, guided tours are offered to Spruce Tree House only, weather permitting. A minimal fee is charged for the tours. Although the park is open year-round, roads may be closed due to weather conditions in winter months.

LODGING   The only motel within the national park is the **Far View Lodge**. It is actually a fairly modest place in a spectacular setting. Each of the 150 nonsmoking rooms is standard motel style, with American Indian print bedspreads and a balcony offering 100-mile views across the mesa country. There's a restaurant; two cafeterias are nearby. Open from the first week in May to the first week in November. ~ P.O. Box 277, Mancos, CO 81328; 970-529-4422, 800-449-2288; www.visitmesaverde.com. MODERATE TO DELUXE.

For a truly *hidden* lodging experience deep in the San Juan National Forest, travel 14 miles north of Mancos along Forest Road 561, a gravel road. Prices are budget rate at the **Jersey Jim Lookout Tower,** and you won't be troubled by noisy neighbors. However, you'll have to climb several flights of zigzag stairs en route to your room, a glass-lined facility measuring 15 feet square. But once you arrive the views are extraordinary. Jersey Jim, it seems, is a fire lookout tower that has been converted into a wilderness version of an efficiency apartment. Sleeping up to four people (bring your own sleeping bags), it contains a stove, refrigerator and lanterns. Water is available at a campground four miles away, and can be hauled up to the tower by a pulley system. Reservations are required. Closed mid-October to late May. ~ Call the Jersey Jim Foundation at 970-533-7060. BUDGET.

◄ HIDDEN

For dudes and dudettes, **Lake Mancos Ranch** offers 17 units accommodating 55 guests in private cabins or ranch-house rooms. The decor is plain—Western wood-paneled rooms with wooden furniture—but guests do not come here to stay inside. They come to enjoy horseback riding, fishing, jeeping, mountain biking and the great outdoors. There are a pool and supervised children's programs. Meals and activities are included in the rates. There are different rates for riders and nonriders. Minimum stay is one week, although it's a three-day minimum stay during the adults-only season from late August to October. Closed October through May. ~ 42688 County Road N, Mancos; 970-533-1190, 800-325-9462, fax 970-533-7858; www.lakemancosranch.com, e-mail ranchlml@fone.net. ULTRA-DELUXE.

The best restaurant in this area is seven miles east of the national park entrance. **Millwood Junction** serves budget-priced specials nightly, moderately priced dinners and a memorable Friday night seafood buffet in a comfortable rough-hewn, wood-paneled dining room. Regular menu items include steaks, fresh fish, pasta and baby back ribs. The salad bar is a meal in itself, but save room for homemade ice cream, cheesecake, black-bottom pie or a raspberry torte. Closed Monday and Tuesday. ~ Route 160 and Main Street, Mancos; 970-533-7338; www.millwoodjunction.com. MODERATE TO DELUXE.

DINING

Within the national park you will find four restaurants operated by the concessionaire. The **Far View Terrace Marketplace** (970-529-4444) and **Spruce Tree Terrace** (970-529-4521) are cafeterias offering Navajo tacos, burgers, sandwiches and salads. The **Knife Edge Café,** located in the Morefield Campground Village, offers pancake breakfasts and fast-food bites. BUDGET TO MODER-

ATE. The **Metate Room** (970-529-4423), at Far View Lodge, serves tasty Pueblo-inspired cuisine as well as New York strip steak, fried shrimp and other American dishes. The food is a cut above the usual park fare and well-priced, considering the great views. MOD-ERATE TO ULTRA-DELUXE. Far View Terrace, The Knife Edge Café, and the Metate Room are closed from November to May.

SHOPPING   Mesa Verde National Park has a gift shop (970-529-4481) located at the park headquarters on Chapin Mesa, as well as a gift shop at the Far View Visitors Center. Closed mid-October to mid-April.

NIGHTLIFE   Nightlife in this neck of the woods consists largely of looking at expanses of stars in a clear sky. **Millwood Junction** has occasional live music and open-mike nights. Cover. ~ 101 Railroad Avenue, Mancos; 970-533-7338.

PARKS   **MESA VERDE NATIONAL PARK** 🚶 🚲 🏛 In the high-canyon country between Cortez and Mancos, the park offers scenic roads leading to short trails to American Indian ruins and stunning mesa-top views of the desert and the mountains.

Biking is limited to paved roads (although it is discouraged because it is dangerous). There are restrooms, groceries, gas, showers and a laundromat; a lodge and restaurants are in the park; the ranger station, visitors centers and services operate mid-April to October only, though the park and museum are open year-round. Day-use fee, $10 per vehicle for a seven-day pass. ~ The park entrance is on Route 160, nine miles east of Cortez; 970-529-4465; www.nps.gov/meve.

> Maintained by the National Park Service, the Mesa Verde area contains the most accessible concentration of prehistoric cliff dwellings in the United States.

▲ Morefield Campground has 435 sites including 15 with hookups; starting at $20 per night. Closed mid-October to late April.

MANCOS STATE PARK 🚶 🚲 🐎 🏛 ⚓ 🛶 🚤 🎣 Jackson Lake (also known as Lake Mancos) is situated at 7800 feet and surrounded by 338 acres of mature ponderosa pine forest laced with hiking and horseback trails. Nonmotorized boats are permitted. The park has picnic sites, volleyball and horseshoes, restrooms and showers. ~ Located ten miles northeast of Mesa Verde, the park is north on Route 184 in Mancos to County Road 42, then four miles farther to County Road N; 970-533-7065; e-mail mancospark@state.co.us.

▲ There are 32 campsites; $12 per night.

Outdoor Adventures

FISHING   Anyone with a license can fish for rainbow, cutthroat and brown trout. A number of outfitters make their livings by knowing where these babies may be found.

DURANGO–SILVERTON AREA The best fishing is found north of Durango at Haviland Lake, Lemon Lake or Vallecito Reservoir. For fishing trips and flyfishing instructions, call **Duranglers**. They offer half- and full-day guided trout-fishing adventures as well as three-day trips on the Gunnison River. ~ 923 Main Avenue, Durango; 970-385-4081, 888-347-4346, fax 970-385-1998; www.duranglers.com, e-mail durnglrs@frontier.net.

CORTEZ–DOLORES AREA Flyfishing is good on the Dolores River. McPhee Reservoir is stocked with trout, kokanee salmon, large- and smallmouth bass, perch, bluegill and catfish. **Circle K Ranch** offers fishing trips in the summer. ~ 27758 Route 145, Dolores; 970-562-3808; www.ckranch.com, e-mail vacation@ckranch.com.

RIVER RUNNING

Whether the rivers are raging during spring runoff, or relatively calm, waterborne sports are always a good way to explore desert canyons or mountain streams. The upper stretch of the Animas River from Silverton to Rockwood offers the only two-day Class V whitewater trip in the West and is suitable for expert kayakers or experienced rafters only. The Class I, II and III whitewater of the river's lower reaches in the Durango area may be rafted by one and all. The Dolores River is considered tops for whitewater in late May.

DURANGO–SILVERTON AREA **Four Corners River Sports**, one of the area's leading outfitters, rents canoes and rafts; they lead guided raft trips on the Animas River from mid-May through August. ~ 360 South Camino del Rio, Durango; 970-259-3893, 800-426-7637; www.riversports.com. **Durango Rivertrippers** are whitewater specialists, offering trips on the Animas River ranging from two hours to a half-day in length, and trips on the Dolores River ranging from two to ten days. Closed October to April. ~ 720 Main Avenue, Durango; 970-259-0289, 800-292-2885; www.durangorivertrippers.com. **Peregrine River Outfitters** specializes in guided kayak and raft trips from early April through October. ~ 64 Ptarmigan Lane; 970-385-7600, 800-598-7600; www.peregrineriver.com.

JEEP TOURS

Traveling the four-wheel-drive roads between Silverton and Lake City is the best way to get close to the stunning Fourteeners, the group of mountains in this area that top 14,000 feet. These roads are among the highest in the country; careful on the curves as you cruise past Handies, Sunshine and Redcloud peaks. For guided jeep tours in this area, call **San Juan Backcountry** in Silverton. They take visitors on two-hour, four-hour, all-day and overnight excursions into the hundreds of miles of old wagon roads that lead to area ghost towns and old mines. Closed November to mid-May.

Text continued on page 674.

Skiing the Best—
The Southwestern Rockies

Many experts think some the best skiing in the world is found in the southwestern Rockies of Colorado. The snow is deep, averaging more than 300 inches a year of feather-soft powder; temperatures average ten degrees higher than more northerly resorts. Telluride and Purgatory offer unparalleled vertical terrain amid crowning mountain beauty. It's only because the areas are harder to reach than better-known ski resorts that they tend to stay less crowded.

Telluride Ski Area—It's the mountain! Top elevation is an ethereal 11,975 feet, with a vertical drop of 3522 feet, offering distinct ski terrain for all levels of skiers. Experts enjoy controlled out-of-bounds skiing, but must be willing to hike half an hour or more—to an elevation of 12,247 feet—to reach the sites. Twelve lifts, including four high-speed quads and a gondola, carry you up to the designated runs.

Telluride's growing popularity and powerful reputation has been helped by scheduled airline service into Telluride Regional Airport—the highest commercial airport in the United States at an elevation of 9086 feet. Skiers can also fly into the Montrose airport, 65 miles from Telluride.

Telluride opens in late November. Some special programs offered include "Ski week," emphasizing a daily two-hour class focusing on physical, mental and social aspects of skiing. ~ Route 145, Telluride; 888-605-2578; www.visittelluride.com.

The entire old mining town of Telluride is a National Historic Landmark. Victorian structures predominate. The **New Sheridan Hotel**, where William Jennings Bryan delivered his famous "Cross of Gold" speech in 1904, is a gem. Closed mid-April to mid-May and mid-October to mid-November. ~ 231 West Colorado Avenue; 970-728-4351, 800-200-1891; www.newsheridan.com, e-mail info@newsheridan.com.

Ski-in, ski-out lodging, lift-ticket sales, equipment rentals, ski school, restaurant and nursery services are located at **Telluride Ski and Golf**. ~ 565 Mountain Village Boulevard; 970-728-6900, 800-801-4832; www.tellurideskiresort.com. The **Wyndham Peaks Resort** offers ski-in, ski-out access, as well as winter activities including snowmobiling, ice skating and dinner sleigh rides. ~ 136 Country Club Drive; 970-728-6800, 866-282-4557; www.thepeaksresort.com.

Purgatory at Durango MountAir Resort is north of Durango and around 100 road miles from Telluride, though actually just over the hill—the hill being ridges of the San Juan Mountains, roughly 14,000 feet high.

The area covers 2500 acres with good snow and mild weather, all adding up to record-breaking ski days year after year. The difference here, for some, is in the vertical terrain. Purgatory has long been considered an intermediate skier's nirvana. Now, however, an area called The Legends has boosted the overall ski field by 25 percent and added nine advanced trails with a vertical drop of 2000 feet. Nevertheless, a good portion of the resort's business comes from a low-key, fun-loving trade, compared with Telluride's trendier skiers.

Half of Purgatory is considered mid-level terrain, and there is a separate Columbine Station area for beginners. It is serviced by its own triple chairlift, providing novices with a private, pristine spot for learning the basics. A justified claim to fame here is that there is rarely a lift line, even during peak season. Purgatory serves 300,000 skiers yearly, the most of any southwestern Colorado area. Four triple chairs, four doubles and a high-speed quad help.

Purgatory–Durango is open all year, with mountain biking and music festivals in summer. Excellent instructional programs include group lessons, as well as individualized classes. They also have cross-country ski trails. ~ Route 550 North, Durango; 970-247-9000, 800-982-6103; www.durangomountainresort.com, e-mail dmrr@durangomountain.com.

Condominiums line the base of Purgatory's slopes. Durango is 25 miles south, offering various lodging/ski/transportation packages through hotels such as the **Strater Hotel** (see "Lodging" in the Durango–Silverton Area section).

Southwestern Colorado also boasts some fantastic cross-country skiing. In the winter, **Hillcrest Golf Club** has about three miles of groomed trails. ~ 2300 Rim Drive, Durango; 970-247-1499. Though the majority of trails in **San Juan National Forest** is not maintained, a few trails are groomed; either way, the forest provides some great cross-country spots. ~ 15 Burnett Court, Durango; 970-247-4874.

See you on the slopes!

~ P.O. Box 707, Silverton, CO 81433; 800-494-8687; www.san juanbackcountry.com.

If you want to drive on your own, you can rent jeeps at **Triangle Service Station** from mid-May through September. ~ 864 Greene Street, Silverton; 970-387-9990.

GOLF

Out here, golf usually takes a back seat to the rugged high desert and mountain terrain, but if you're bent on being a duffer, there are a few places to swing and putt.

DURANGO–SILVERTON AREA   To tee off, visit the 18-hole **Hillcrest Golf Club.** ~ 2300 Rim Drive, Durango; 970-247-1499. Located six miles north of Durango in the Animas Valley is the 18-hole **Dalton Ranch Golf Course.** Closed November through March. ~ 589 County Road 252, Durango; 970-247-8774.

CORTEZ–DOLORES AREA   The public, 18-hole **Conquistador Golf Course** is the main course in this area. Closed seasonally. ~ 2018 North Dolores Road, Cortez; 970-565-9208.

TENNIS

The courts around here are all public, pardner, so don't worry about donning fancy duds; throw on your old sweats, grab your racquet and head to one of these school or park tennis courts.

DURANGO–SILVERTON AREA   The eight lighted courts at **Durango High School** are open to the public when not being used by students. ~ 2390 Main Avenue, Durango; 970-259-1630. You'll also find public courts in Durango at **Fort Lewis College.** ~ College Heights; 970-247-7010. In Silverton there are courts in **Memorial Park** at the northeast end of town.

CORTEZ–DOLORES AREA   Cortez has six lighted tennis courts in **Centennial Park,** adjacent to the Cortez Public Library. ~ 830 East Montezuma Avenue; 970-565-3402; www.cityofcortez.com/ parks.shtml.

RIDING STABLES, PACK TRIPS & LLAMA TREKS

There are still plenty of horses in this part of the West, and you can ride gentle or spirited steeds for an hour, a day or as long as you can take it, pal. In addition, you can hike with a llama that carries your gear over terrain ranging from high desert to forested alpine trails.

AUTHOR FAVORITE

I find few experiences as breathtaking as a **jeep tour** on old mining roads in the San Juans during fall when the aspens turn gold. On the most exciting of these roads, I'm happy to leave the driving to an experienced guide. See "Jeep Tours" on page 671 for specific tour companies.

DURANGO–SILVERTON AREA   To arrange a guided horseback, hiking or pack trip ranging from two hours to seven days or longer in the San Juan National Forest near Durango, call **Over the Hill Outfitters.** ~ 4140 County Road 234, Durango; 970-385-7656, 970-247-1694; www.overthehilloutfitters.com. **San Juan Outfitting** offers spring pack trips to study Anasazi ruins, and summer pack trips into the Weminuche Wilderness. ~ 186 County Road 228, Durango; 970-259-6259; www.sanjuanoutfitting.com. **Ron-D-View Ranch** also offers overnight horse and mule pack trips into the Weminuche Wilderness. ~ 1151 Anna Road, Ignacio; 970-563-9270; www.rondviewoutfitting.com. **Circle K Ranch** offers horseback riding from May through August. ~ 27758 Route 145, Dolores; 970-562-3808; www.ckranch.com.

Day hikes with llamas are available seasonally from Durango's **Buckhorn Llama Co., Inc.** Advance reservations are required. You can rent llamas with or without a guide, and they'll meet you at any of several major wilderness trailheads in western Colorado. Closed October through April. ~ P.O. Box 64, Masonville, CO 80541; 970-667-7411, 800-318-9454; www.llamapack.com, e-mail buckhorn@llamapack.com.

MESA VERDE AREA   In Mancos you can take a trail ride from **Echo Basin Ranch**, where guides lead groups of up to 20 riders through a 600-acre natural area on the ranch. Closed October through May. ~ 43747 County Road M, Mancos; 970-533-7000, 800-426-1890; www.echobasin.com.

Fast becoming one of the most popular sports in the region, mountain biking has taken off in a big way, due in part to the popularity of two events. The Iron Horse Bicycle Classic, held yearly over Memorial Day weekend, pits riders against the narrow-gauge train in a 50-mile race over two 10,000-foot mountain passes from Durango to Silverton. The best bike riders always beat the train. The championship course at Purgatory is open to riders in the summer. The terrain for biking is challenging and scenic. The variety of roads and trails on public lands is immense.

BIKING

DURANGO–SILVERTON AREA   The Animas Valley Loop is considered easy by locals who always ride at 6500 feet; it is mostly flat—the flattest road ride in Durango—rising only 280 feet, and can be ridden in 15- or 30-mile versions. The long route follows County Road 250 north out of Durango and up the east side of the Animas Valley, crossing the main Route 550 at Baker's Bridge and heading back to Durango via County Road 203, on the west side of the valley.

A beautiful intermediate ride is **Old Lime Creek Road**, between Silverton and Cascade Creek, north of Purgatory. It starts 11 miles south of Silverton, off Route 550, and follows the old highway for 12 miles past beaver ponds and a brick retaining span called the

"Chinese Wall," which once separated stage coaches from a sheer drop down the steep mountainside.

The **Animas City Mountain Loop** follows an advanced, five-and-a-half-mile trail that gains 1500 feet in elevation. The trail starts off of 4th Avenue, north of 32nd Street, in Durango, and offers stunning views of Falls Creek, the Animas Valley and the West Needle Mountains from the top of a tilted mesa.

The first unified World Mountain Biking Championship was held in Durango in 1990.

CORTEZ–DOLORES AREA The **Horseshoe Ruins Trail** starts 23 miles south of Pleasant View off the road to Hovenweep. It is an easy ten-mile loop through the rolling mesa country that predominates in this area. It takes you to Horseshoe, Holly and Hackberry ruins within the national monument. The **Cutthroat Castle Trail** starts in the same place, circling north over similar terrain into Hovenweep Canyon and past the Cutthroat Castle ruin. The 17-mile loop is for intermediate riders.

MESA VERDE AREA Several easy-to-intermediate rides may be found on roads through **Mesa Verde National Park**, particularly in the spring and fall when the air is cooler and there are fewer cars on the roads. Please take note that the roads are narrow and must be shared with motorized vehicles. Be cautious.

Bike Rentals **Mountain Bike Specialists** rents bikes from May through October. Sales and repairs are available year-round. Closed Sunday from October to late May. ~ 949 Main Avenue, Durango; 970-247-4066; www.mountainbikespecialists.com. The largest bike shop in Durango is **Hassle Free Sports**; besides rentals from mid-April through October, it does sales and repairs year-round, as well as ski rentals in the winter. ~ 2615 Main Avenue, Durango; 970-259-3874, 800-835-3800; www.hassle freesports.com.

HIKING Looking for that Rocky Mountain High? Southwestern Colorado may not be the heart of the Rockies that John Denver was crooning about, but the scenery and altitudes make it pretty darn close. Trails in this region will lead you up to the Continental Divide, or over 12,000 feet on the Colorado Trail. If you're bent on bagging Fourteeners, you can ride a narrow-gauge railroad to a high-country trailhead and take your choice of three peaks over 14,000 feet. Or opt for the desert terrain and explore ancient settlements at Hovenweep and Mesa Verde. All distances listed for hiking trails are one way unless otherwise noted.

DURANGO–SILVERTON AREA Numerous hiking trails are found in the San Juan National Forest and Weminuche Wilderness Area. Backpacking trips of several hours to several days are possible. Forest service maps and information are available from the San Juan

Public Lands Center, 15 Burnett Court, Durango; 970-247-4874; www.fs.fed.us/r2/sanjuan.

The southwest portion of the 471-mile **Colorado Trail**, connecting Durango and Denver, begins in the La Plata Mountains, west of Durango atop Kennebec Pass. Access is at the end of County Road 124, in Hesperus or via Junction Creek from downtown Durango. This trail offers rugged hiking through alpine wilderness ranging from 7000 to 12,680 feet in altitude.

Needle Creek Trail (14 miles) is accessed via the narrow-gauge railroad that will drop off passengers in Needleton for rugged hiking in the Weminuche Wilderness. Hikers spend at least one night, then flag the train down for the return trip to Durango or Silverton. The challenging trail, which climbs 4000 feet in eight miles, leads to Chicago Basin, Mount Eolus (14,084 feet), Sunlight Peak (14,059 feet) and Windom Peak (14,082 feet).

Elk Creek Trail (8 miles), also accessed via the train at Elk Park, leads hikers to Hunchback Pass on the Continental Divide, 4000 feet above Elk Creek Valley.

Purgatory Flats Trail (4 miles) begins 26 miles north of Durango on the east side of Route 550. It leads to the Animas River. Eight miles farther on the **Animas River Trail** you will end up in Needleton and the Weminuche.

CORTEZ–DOLORES AREA   The big attraction to hikers in this part of Colorado is the abundance of Ancestral Pueblo sites in the slickrock and canyon country. Hikes along mesa tops afford 100-mile views on clear days.

Navajo Lake Trail (5 miles) begins one mile past Burro Bridge campground off West Fork Road, 12.5 miles east of Dolores and then 24 miles up Forest Road 535. The trail leads to Navajo Lake, at 11,154 feet, which sits at the foot of 14,000-foot El Diente Peak.

Hovenweep Trails are accessed via short marked trails within the national monument leading to the Cajon Ruins in Utah, or in Colorado, to Holly Ruins, Hackberry Canyon Ruins, Cutthroat Castle Ruins and Goodman Point Ruins. The trails wind through arid mesa country, mostly treeless scrublands that see few visitors. Since there are no roads for vehicles, hiking is the only way to see these sites.

Ute Mountain Tribal Park contains numerous hiking trails leading to excavated and unexcavated Ancestral Puebloan sites along a 25-mile stretch of the Mancos River. You must have an Indian guide with you at all times. The most popular hiking trail covers 13 miles from the park entrance following the river and affording views of wildlife as well as sites of archaeological interest.

MESA VERDE AREA   Hikes in this region of Indian country pass through piñon and juniper forests, canyons, mesas and archaeological sites, including cliff dwellings. Hiking within the national park is limited to five well-marked trails, and hikers must register at the ranger's office or at trailheads. It is very hot in the summer. Bring water.

Petroglyph Point Trail (3-mile roundtrip) begins on the Spruce Tree House Trail adjacent to the park office and museum. It travels along the mesa top leading to ancient rock art at Petroglyph Point.

Spruce Canyon Trail (2-mile loop) also begins on the Spruce Tree House Trail and leads into forested Spruce Canyon at the base of the mesa.

Transportation

CAR

Southwestern Colorado is a large, sparsely populated area with few major roads along the vast stretches of desert and forest lands and dispersed communities. The main north–south highway connecting Durango and Silverton is **Route 550**. From Durango to Cortez the main road is **Route 160**, which is also the access road to Mesa Verde National Park. It veers south in Cortez and shares a designation with **Route 666** for 20 miles. At that point Route 160 heads west to the Four Corners Monument and Arizona, while Route 666 continues south into New Mexico.

Southwestern Colorado is a holy place known to the Utes as "the rim of the little world."

Cortez and Dolores are connected by **Route 145**. Dolores and Mancos are connected by **Route 184**, which meets Route 160 in Mancos.

To reach Hovenweep National Monument the main access is south of Cortez on Route 160 to **McElmo Canyon Road**, only partially paved, or north of Cortez, via Route 666 to the **Colorado turnoff** at Pleasant View, which also passes Lowry Ruins.

AIR

The main airport with scheduled service for the entire region is the **Durango–La Plata County Airport**. Much smaller, and with far fewer flights daily, is the **Cortez Municipal Airport**. For ski buffs, there's **Telluride Regional Airport**.

Durango is served by America West Airlines, American Airlines, Continental Airlines, Rio Grande Air and United Express. Cortez is served by Great Lakes Aviation while both America West Express and Great Lakes Aviation fly into Telluride.

BUS

Greyhound Bus Lines (800-231-2222; www.greyhound.com) and **TNM&O Coaches** offer scheduled service through Durango. ~ 275 East 8th Avenue; 970-259-2755.

CAR RENTALS

In Durango, contact **Avis Rent A Car** (800-331-1212), **Budget Rent A Car** (800-527-0700), **Dollar Rent A Car** (800-800-4000), **Hertz Rent A Car** (800-654-3131) or **National** (800-227-7368).

The only scheduled public transportation in Durango is the **PUBLIC**
Durango Transit, which operates within the city limits year- **TRANSIT**
round. No Sunday service in winter. ~ 970-259-5438.

In Durango try **Durango Transportation**. ~ 970-259-4818. **TAXIS**

A true bird's-eye view of Durango, the Animas Valley and the **AERIAL**
majestic San Juans from the plexiglass cockpit of a quiet glider **TOURS**
is offered by **Durango Soaring Club, Inc.** ~ Val-Air Glider Port,
27290 Route 550 North; 970-247-9037; www.soardurango.com.
For airplane charters or scenic flights contact **Gregg Flying Service.**
~ Animas Air Park, Durango; 970-247-4632.

Index

Lodging Index

Dining Index

ABOUT THE AUTHORS

NICKY LEACH, the update author for this edition, is a Santa Fe–based author specializing in writing books on the natural and cultural history of the American West. She has written over 40 guidebooks, including several award-winning visitor guides to national parks. Nicky lives in a historic artist's home off the Santa Fe Trail with her tabby cat Molly.

RICHARD HARRIS, the author of the introductory, Northwestern Arizona, Central New Mexico and Southern New Mexico chapters, has written or co-written 31 other guidebooks including Ulysses' *Hidden Colorado*. He has also served as contributing editor on guides to Mexico, New Mexico, and other ports of call for John Muir Publications, Fodor's, Birnbaum and Access guides. He is a past president of PEN New Mexico and currently president of the New Mexico Book Association. When not traveling, Richard writes and lives in Santa Fe, New Mexico.

STEVE COHEN is a travel writer, photographer and author of more than a dozen travel books on the Caribbean and the Southwest. His writing and photography appear in *National Geographic Adventure*, *Outside* and *Travel Holiday*. Author of the Southwestern Colorado chapter, he is the travel editor for iUniverse.com. Residing in southwest Colorado, he is a member of the Society of American Travel Writers.

LAURA DAILY is a freelance journalist living in Snowmass Village, Colorado. A member of the Society of American Travel Writers, she regularly contributes to *National Geographic World*, *Active Times*, *Physicians Financial News* and *Restaurant Business*. Together with Madeleine Osberger she co-authored the Utah and Northern New Mexico chapters.

MADELEINE OSBERGER is editor of the *Snowmass Village Sun* and a freelance writer for regional and national publications. She also covers the Aspen/Snowmass area for the Associated Press. Author of *Country Roads of Colorado*, Osberger is also co-author of *Adventure Guide to Utah*.

ABOUT THE ILLUSTRATOR

GLENN KIM is a freelance illustrator residing in San Francisco. His work appears in many Ulysses Press titles, including *Hidden Belize* and *Hidden Walt Disney World, Orlando and Beyond*. He has also done illustrations for a variety of magazines, book covers and greeting cards. He is now working with computer graphics and having lots of fun.